CHURCH, STATE AND NATION IN IRELAND
1898–1921

CHURCH, STATE AND NATION IN IRELAND
1898-1921

David W. Miller

University of Pittsburgh Press

First published in 1973

Gill and Macmillan Limited
2 Belvedere Place
Dublin 1
and internationally, except in the United States,
its possessions, and the Philippines,
through association with the
Macmillan Publishers Group

Published in the United States by the University of Pittsburgh Press

Jacket designed by Graham Shepherd

Library of Congress Cataloging in Publication Data

Miller, David W   date

  Church, state and nation in Ireland, 1898-1921.

  Bibliography: p. 561

    1. Catholic Church in Ireland.   2. Ireland—

  Politics and government—1901–1910.   3. Ireland—

  Politics and government—1910–1921.   I. Title.

  BX1505.M54   1973   261.7'09415   72–95453

  ISBN 0–8229–1108–6

Printed and bound in the Republic of
Ireland by The Richview Press, Dublin

To Margaret

ROMAN CATHOLIC DIOCESES OF IRELAND

Contents

Preface

TODAY, when an Irishman of any religious persuasion speaks of 'the Church', he almost certainly means the Roman Catholic Church. It was not always so: before disestablishment in 1869 the terms 'the Church' and 'the Irish Church' were often used to refer to the established Church of Ireland. In the period covered by this book there was still some ambiguity in the use of these terms in common speech, but I have used them consistently to refer to the Roman Catholic Church, confident that this would cause no confusion for the contemporary reader. I hope also that it will cause no offence. I have, moreover, used the term 'Catholic' as a synonym of 'Roman Catholic', for which I ask the indulgence of Anglican and other readers who understand that term in a more catholic sense. I have left the term 'nationalist' in lower case when it refers to the general ideal that Ireland should enjoy some degree of self-determination, but I have capitalised it when it refers to the Irish Parliamentary Party, its allied organisations and splinter groups.

This book originated in a doctoral dissertation for the Committee on the History of Culture at the University of Chicago. Professor Martin E. Marty, more than anyone else, pointed me in the direction which led to this study. During my research in Dublin in 1965–66 the late Mrs Maureen Wall of University College, Dublin, and Dr John Whyte, now of Queen's University, Belfast, were generous with their time and became continuing sources of advice and encouragement. My greatest debt is to my stern mentor and valued friend, Professor Emmet Larkin.

For access to historical sources I record my thanks as follows: to His Eminence William Cardinal Conway for a

calendar of materials not yet open to public inspection in the
Armagh archdiocesan archives, to His Eminence John Cardinal Heenan for the Bourne Papers, to the Taoiseach for
materials in the State Paper Office, to Mr Mark Bonham
Carter for the Asquith Papers, to Mrs Eibhlín MacNeill
Tierney for the Mac Néill Papers, to Miss Margaret Digby
for the Plunkett Papers, to Mr A. J. P. Taylor, Hon. Director
of the Beaverbrook Library, for the Lloyd George Papers, to
the Archbishop of Canterbury for the Davidson Papers, and
to Mr C. P. Hyland for a letter of the Rev. Michael Curran.
I want also to thank the staffs of the University of Chicago
Library, the Hunt Library of Carnegie-Mellon University,
and the various repositories listed in section I of my bibliography. Like so many students of Irish history, I am especially
indebted to Mr Alf MacLochlainn of the National Library
of Ireland.

For summer grants to turn the dissertation into the present
work I am grateful to the Sarah Mellon Scaife Foundation
and the Falk Foundation. Many of my colleagues in the
Carnegie-Mellon history department have been both pro-
fessionally and personally supportive. Finally, my wife has
contributed a great deal more than the index.

D.W.M.
Sweetwater, Texas
Christmas, 1972

Introduction

'No one can visit Ireland', wrote Louis Paul-Dubois in 1907, 'without being impressed by the intensity of Catholic belief there, and by the fervour of its outward manifestations.'[1] Few, if any, would dispute Paul-Dubois' assertion today, and fewer still would have disputed it at the time it was made. Religion was the central fact of Irish life. In the north-eastern corner of the country, where the Protestant descendants of English and Scottish settlers formed a substantial proportion of the population, religious differences had for centuries been a source of bitter animosities. In the Southern rural village, where all the inhabitants were Catholics, except perhaps the families of the local landlord and the Anglican parson, the Church was the focus of the entire social life of the community. In the Southern towns and cities a man's religion was the primary fact about him which had to be discovered before comfortable relations with him could be established. Above all, religion was a badge of nationality. The Catholics, who comprised three-quarters of the population of the country, were the 'mere Irish', the natives, whose ancestors had been only nominally under English suzerainty at the time when the English Reformation was nominally and artificially extended to Ireland. To be a Protestant implied that one's forebears had immigrated from Great Britain, or that they had yielded to the temptations of self-interest and forsworn the faith of their fathers.

The persecutions of the seventeenth and eighteenth centuries, which drove many members of the native Catholic gentry into exile and persuaded others to alienate themselves from their countrymen by becoming converts, had left the Catholic clergy as the only natural leaders in the rural communities. With the growth of democracy in the nineteenth century, the local leadership of the clergy took on an important political dimension. In 1907 Sir Horace Plunkett noted in his diary a conversation with Sir W. Hart Dyke: 'He remembered 50 years ago staying . . . with Sir Richard Savage. He wanted to get in for Westmeath; he had simply to arrange it with the Bishop.'[2] If matters were no longer quite so simple —which is presumably why Plunkett thought the anecdote worth recording—the Church did still play a crucial role in what I have chosen to describe as the Irish political system.

We are accustomed to thinking of modern western history as dominated by the State, whose ideal type was classically defined by Max Weber as 'a human community that (successfully) claims the monopoly of the legitimate use of physical force within a given territory'.[3] To the extent that a particular country conforms to the ideal type of the State, we expect other political institutions, for example the ecclesiastical or feudal courts, to lose successful claims upon legitimate use of coercion. Students of revolutions, however, are familiar with the case in which, for a brief period, a parallel institution is established alongside the State and exerts, with varying effectiveness, claims upon the allegiance of the citizens in proportion to its prospects for *future* success in monopolising the legitimate use of physical force—i.e. its prospects of supplanting the existing State. Nineteenth-century Ireland presents a similar case which, however, was not limited to a brief period of revolutionary upheaval. Probably as early as Daniel O'Connell's movement for repeal of the Act of Union in the 1840s, it is meaningful to speak of a parallel political institution: the Nation. Whereas the human community which comprised the State was the peoples of the entire British Isles, that which comprised the Nation was the people of Ireland. Just as the legitimacy of the State's monopoly of physical force in Ireland was denied, in varying degrees, by a majority of the Irish people, the Nation's similar claims were denied by a majority of the Protestant population of the north-eastern corner of Ireland. Indeed, as will become clear in this study, there was grave ambivalence in the Nation as to whether or not the Protestant minority was properly part of the community which comprised the Nation. Put slightly differently, although the 'given territory' claimed by the Nation consisted of the whole island of Ireland, it was never 'successful' in its assertions of legitimacy beyond the territory in which there was a Catholic majority. Of the 103 Irish seats in the Commons under the 1884 Franchise Act, some eighty were absolutely safe Nationalist seats and some twenty were equally safe Unionist seats except, in a few cases, when the majority camp was itself divided.

The fact that two institutions, the State and the Nation, laid claim to the prerogatives which, in modern Europe, are normally reserved to the State alone, together with the intensity of popular devotion to the Church noted by Paul-Dubois, gave the Church a political role which she did not enjoy in most of Europe at this time. The modern State's claims to legitimacy generally rest upon purely secular foundations: the divine right of kings has carried very little weight since the French Revolution. Allegiance, i.e. the individual's assent to a political institution's claims to legitimacy, remains, however, a profound ethical question. When a church effectively retains the power of moral arbiter for the overwhelming majority of a people, it can have a significant voice in the settlement of that question. In the late nineteenth century, therefore, the Church assumed a crucial role in the Irish political system alongside the State and the Nation, both of which needed the Church to reinforce their claims to legitimacy.

The fact that the Irish Church had not enjoyed a privileged position under the State in the centuries prior to the appearance of the Nation as a meaningful political force both strengthened her positive moral influence over the people and partially shielded her from the kind of attacks which several continental States were making upon the Church at this time. In countries like France and Italy, where the Church had given uncompromising sanction to an anachronistic *ancien régime,* she now found herself practically defenceless against attacks upon her vital interests in such areas as education from those who held the monopoly of physical force. Though individual churchmen might lean heavily toward endorsing the claims of the State or of the Nation, the Irish Church, on the whole, was sparing in her use of the power to confer legitimacy, and she prudently exploited such gestures to win protection for her own interests and the advancement of her ideals.

This study attempts to describe the interaction of the Church with the State and the Nation within patterns of institutional behaviour which I have chosen to call 'conventions'. I use the term 'convention' in something like the sense in which it was employed by noted constitutional lawyers and constitutional historians who flourished during the period of this study; A. V. Dicey, in particular, pointed out that the English constitution embodies not only laws, both written and unwritten, but also practices so well established that their violation would be regarded as 'unconstitutional'.[4] There were obviously different degrees of acceptance attached to such conventions. The convention that the monarch did not veto a bill passed by both Houses of Parliament—the last exception being in the reign of Queen Anne—was very firmly established. The convention 'that the House of Lords ought not persistently to resist the will of the House of Commons about matters of first-rate importance'[5] was much less firmly established (until it was removed from the category of *convention* and made a written *law* of the constitution in the Parliament Act of 1911). The most important conventions of the Irish political system had originated comparatively recently, so that they were not so firmly established as the fact that the royal veto was moribund. They nevertheless existed and exerted an influence on the behaviour of men and institutions.

The most important of the conventions governing relations between Church and State in the mid-nineteenth century, when the Nation still lacked unity, strength and effective leadership, were that the State would respect the Church's vested interests, especially in the area of publicly financed education, and that the Church would use her very considerable influence to curb direct challenges to the State's monoply of physical force. These conventions operated in their most unadulterated form during the generation following the Great Famine of the 1840s. Under the direction of Paul Cardinal Cullen, the Church achieved, for example, the conversion of the primary education system from its original

nondenominational design to an effectively segregated operation—an arrangement which was formalised in a nonstatutory
convention in 1860 to the effect that the seats on the National
Education Board would be divided evenly between Catholics
and Protestants. Cullen, who had spent his early career in
Rome, saw a Mazzini behind every bush, and carried most
of his episcopal colleagues with him in a policy of denying
the sacraments to the Fenian revolutionaries of this period.
When Cullen died in 1878, public attention was focusing on
Charles Stewart Parnell, a Protestant landlord from Co.
Wicklow who was coming into prominence as a dissident
member of the Irish Home Rule Party of Isaac Butt. Under
Butt's leadership, the Home Rule Party had been a loose
and undisciplined group of M.P.s committed only to act
together on behalf of some readjustment of Anglo-Irish relations in the direction of 'federalism'. Butt, under attack
from those of his parliamentary followers who favoured a
more aggressive posture, died in 1879, at a time of great
unrest in the country over the system of land tenure. Parnell,
who had been advocating a 'New Departure' in Irish politics
which would harness the land-hunger of the peasantry to a
disciplined parliamentary Nationalist Party, easily captured
the party leadership in 1880. The hierarchy was, to say the
least, lukewarm toward the new leader, whose associations
with the 'physical force' nationalists seemed to threaten the
principles of Church-State relationships on which they had
operated under Cullen's leadership. Parnell, however, moved
from strength to strength, and in the 1885 general election
his party captured eighty-six seats, exactly enough, as it happened, to hold the balance between the Liberal and Conservative Parties in the Commons. The leader of the Liberal
Party, William Ewart Gladstone, declared his conversion to
the policy of Home Rule; and the hope that the Nation
would eventually make good its claim to 'the monopoly of the
legitimate use of physical force within a given territory'
suddenly became a virtually unquestioned assumption in
nationalist politics. In this assumption Irish opinion was
altogether correct, although many Irishmen deceived themselves over the extent of the Nation's 'given territory' and
many others did not live to see the attainment of self-

government. The Church, however, would live for ever, and those mortals who guided her generally shared the popular assumption that eventually there would be a new secular order. It was therefore essential that the Church secure her interests by establishing a relationship with the Nation analogous to her relationship with the State.

Accordingly, shortly after Gladstone's conversion, the hierarchy formally endorsed the Home Rule demand as representing 'the *legitimate* aspirations of the Irish people'.[6] Significantly, a year and a half earlier the hierarchy had publicly called upon the party to advocate Catholic claims 'in all branches of the education question'.[7] In the interim between these two actions, the Church had established the right of clergy to a major voice in the selection of parliamentary candidates[8] and in general satisfied herself that Parnell's movement was essentially 'constitutional' rather than 'revolutionary' in its methods. In other words, a new set of conventions was established between the Church and the Nation. Stated simply, they were that the Nation's representatives would defend and work to enlarge the Church's vital interests in education and the Church would sanction the Nation's aspirations to supplant the State so long as those aspirations were pursued along 'constitutional' lines. These conventions were easily reconciled with those which governed relations between Church and State, for one of the two principal parties in the State, the Liberals, now recognised the legitimacy of 'constitutional' action on the Nation's part to achieve the 'monopoly of the legitimate use of physical force'.

The internal political structure of the Nation in 1898, when this study begins, had its origins in the great crisis which befell Parnell in 1890, when he seemed about to deliver Home Rule as soon as the existing Conservative government should be defeated. Just at this moment, his political fortunes collapsed in a divorce scandal involving the wife of another politician. The party split into Parnellite and Anti-Parnellite factions, the Church, after some initial hesitancy, assuming a prominent role in the Anti-Parnellite assault upon the discredited leader.[9] William J. Walsh, the Archbishop of Dublin, was active in the formation of Anti-Parnellite strategy, and throughout most of the country bishops and clergy used every atom of influence they possessed to defeat Parnellite candidates on the hustings. After Parnell's sudden death in 1891, the Parnellite faction, under the leadership of John Redmond, retained only nine seats at the 1892 general election. The Church had seemingly won a great victory which reduced most of the Nation's representation to something like a political arm of the Church—a situation approximating that which obtained before the rise of Parnell. Though the Anti-Parnellites were dubbed the 'clerical' party by English commentators, they nevertheless included important individuals who were by no means anxious to submit to clerical control. Within a few years the Anti-Parnellites themselves had split into two factions under the leadership of John Dillon and T. M. Healy respectively, the 'Healyite' group inheriting the role of 'clerical' party. This study begins with a series of events which reconfirmed the integrity of the Nation as a distinct element in the Irish political system rather than a mere appendage of the Church.

The powers of the State in eighteenth-century Ireland had been divided between the Anglican landlord minority, who dominated both the Irish parliament and the apparatus of local administration, and the British government of the day, which controlled the central administration in Dublin Castle through the Crown's official representative, the Lord Lieutenant, and his Chief Secretary. In the aftermath of the American Revolution, the Protestant gentry were able to strengthen their power in the State vis-à-vis that of the British cabinet. In the face of revolutionary France's expansion, however, the British government, by a combination of alarmism, patronage and bribery, persuaded the Protestant gentry to abolish their separate parliament in 1800 and create a legislative Union of Great Britain and Ireland. During the eighteenth century, the British government of the day was usually a collection of ministers whose primary mission was to get the monarch's necessary business conducted in the British parliament. This ministry's interest in Ireland was always peripheral and subordinate to its primary task. Parties existed, but it was not until well into the nineteenth century that they became well-articulated combinations regularly appealing to the electorate with a programme which they could, with some certainty, act upon as the Crown's ministry if they won a majority of seats in the Commons.

The development of such well-defined parties, and especially of the Liberal Party, in the middle decades of the nineteenth century, together with the rapid adaptation of the Irish Nation to the politics of a democratising social order, made Irish affairs a central preoccupation of the State. The threat of widespread disorder in Ireland in 1828, when the electors of Co. Clare returned Daniel O'Connell to parliament in defiance of the law against Catholics sitting in that body, had persuaded a Tory government to remove the most galling civil disabilities of Catholics. Moreover, the anomalies of the Irish Protestant Church establishment and of Irish land tenure practices became likely targets for the reforming zeal of Liberal ideologues. Modest inroads upon the vested interests of the Protestant Church of Ireland in the 1830s and its complete disestablishment in 1869, revisions in the landlord-tenant relationship to the advantage of the latter in 1870 and 1881 : these demonstrated that, at least during those inevitable swings of the pendulum when the Liberals were in power, the State's authority might be turned against the privileges of the Protestant landlord minority in Ireland. The Home Rule crisis of the mid-1880s so reinforced the polarisation of English parties over Ireland that one of them, the Conservatives plus a number of defectors from the Liberals, came to be known as the Unionist Party—acknowledging that maintenance of the Act of Union with Ireland was its guiding principle. From 1886—when Gladstone split the Liberal Party in the Commons by trying to enact Home Rule—until 1905, the Unionists under Lord Salisbury and then under his nephew, Arthur James Balfour, held power in the State continuously except for a Liberal interlude in 1892–95. During that interlude the ageing Gladstone attempted again to carry Home Rule but was frustrated by an overwhelming Unionist majority in the House of Lords. His successor in the Liberal leadership, Lord Rosebery, seemed to be relegating Home Rule to oblivion when he declared that it could only be taken up again by the Liberals when the 'predominant partner' in the United Kingdom should itself agree. In other words, a majority of the English M.P.s alone, not counting the approximately eighty Irish Nationalists, would have to favour such a measure.

At the close of the nineteenth century, therefore, the party in power in the State was implacably hostile to Irish national aspirations and the opposition party was reluctant to champion them again. The Church, therefore, had to take the State quite seriously for the immediate future. Despite the fact that the Unionists frequently played upon anti-Catholic feeling to win support in Great Britain and in the North of Ireland, however, the Church knew quite well that Conservative politicians could be very friendly to her claims so long as they did not directly attack the bases of Unionist support among the Irish Protestant community. In particular, the Conservatives had never been committed to the secularist, Nonconformist opposition to denominationalism in education which informed much Liberal thinking on that subject. Furthermore, now that Liberal governments had done such violence to the privileges of landowners, Unionist ministers were themselves thinking creatively about ways to improve the lot of the mainly Catholic tenant-farmers. Notably, the Congested Districts Board, founded by Balfour as Chief Secretary in 1892, was taking steps to rejuvenate rural life in the West of Ireland; this, as will become clear, accorded well with the social ideals of many churchmen. To understand the delicate position of the Church, poised between the Nation and the State, it is now appropriate to look closely at the structure of that institution at the end of the nineteenth century.

To bigoted Protestants the Irish Catholic Church's political activities were merely the local manifestations of machinations in Rome. It is, of course, hardly necessary to observe that the Irish Church was thoroughly loyal to the Holy See. It is true that in the Middle Ages the Irish Church had strongly resisted Roman jurisdiction and discipline, but it should be remembered that Roman discipline might mean subjection to the See of Canterbury or, later, acceptance of the Anglo-Norman conquest. After Protestantism came to be the religion of the English, national feeling worked in favour of loyalty to Rome. Of course, there were recurrent instances of friction between Rome and the Irish Church, but in the late nineteenth and early twentieth centuries such friction could generally be traced to fears that Rome might betray that Irish national separatism which had cemented the ties between the Irish Church and the Holy See. For example, though the Irish hierarchy was quite distinct from the Catholic hierarchy of England, the Irish bishops were occasionally fearful that their juridical independence might be undermined by English Catholic forces and that the Irish hierarchy might be subordinated to the Catholic Archbishop of Westminster. Even more dangerous to the Irish Church's independence were the repeated efforts of British governments to influence the appointments of Irish bishops and especially the efforts of Unionist governments to persuade Rome to take a Unionist view of Irish affairs. On two occasions in the 1880s Rome had dramatically intervened in opposition to the national movement. In 1883 a letter from the Congregation for the Propagation of the Faith (which had jurisdiction over Ireland) had forbidden clerical participation in the National League, Parnell's nationwide organisation. In 1888, after considerable prompting from government envoys, the Pope issued a rescript against boycotting and the so-called 'Plan of Campaign' agitation by which tenants were attempting to force landlords to reduce rents.[10] The 1888 rescript was particularly disconcerting to Irish churchmen, many of whom had become prominently involved in the agitation. At the end of the century, therefore, Irish ecclesiastics were very conscious that the 'Roman flank' must be covered. Nevertheless, though Rome's favour might strengthen the position of certain individual bishops, the essential decision-making machinery remained within the national hierarchy.

The Catholic Church in Ireland is governed by a hierarchy of twenty-seven[11] prelates whose dioceses are grouped into four ecclesiastical provinces with metropolitan sees at Armagh, Dublin, Cashel and Tuam. These provinces correspond roughly to the civil provinces of Ulster, Leinster, Munster and Connacht. The Archbishop of Armagh enjoys the title 'Primate of All Ireland' and the Archbishop of Dublin holds the lesser dignity 'Primate of Ireland', but these distinctions are purely honorific, and the actual distribution of power within the hierarchy is determined by more subtle considerations than the tenure of such medieval honours. By all odds the most capable man in the hierarchy in 1898 was William Joseph Walsh, Archbishop of Dublin.[12] In addition to professional expertise in such varied fields as law, economics, theology, history and music, Walsh possessed administrative and diplomatic skills which would have served him as well in some very demanding secular calling as they did in his ecclesiastical office. His advocacy of the claims of the tenants during his presidency of St Patrick's College, Maynooth, the national seminary, had earned him a reputation which prompted strenuous, and almost successful, government efforts at Rome to prevent his appointment in 1885 to the vacant archbishopric of Dublin. Combining nationalist sympathies with a canon lawyer's respect for constitutional procedures, Walsh was admirably suited to guide the hierarchy through the treacherous waters of Irish politics in the late 1880s and early 1890s. The course which he steered enabled the Church to develop a working relationship with the national movement at a time when the Church had seemed in danger of losing a significant measure of her political influence. When the divorce scandal broke, the Church was able, under Walsh's leadership, to play a decisive role in the organising of a rival Nationalist Party to defeat the forces of Parnellism.

The personality of the Archbishop of Armagh, Michael Logue, was the very antithesis of that of Walsh. Walsh's senior by only a few months, Logue, the son of a Donegal innkeeper, also joined the Maynooth faculty, but in the same year that Walsh advanced to the vice-presidency of that institution (1878) Logue was just achieving a chair in theology. In the following year, however, he became Bishop of Raphoe, and in 1887 he was elevated to the archbishopric of Armagh. In contrast to the Archbishop of Dublin's extensive writings on quite varied topics, Logue's entire bibliography is limited to a few pastorals and an article in *Le Monde* in 1870 refuting, characteristically, the view of Bishop Dupanloup that a declaration of papal infallibility was inopportune. Logue had sufficient acumen to realise that the Home Rule cause should not be opposed, but Sir Shane Leslie's description of Logue's politics as 'national rather than nationalist'[13] succinctly conveys the degree of the archbishop's enthusiasm for the cause. He enjoyed waiting upon royalty, delighted in entertaining visiting British dignitaries with champagne and oysters,[14] and, in short, possessed none of that political sensitivity which enabled Walsh to lead the hierarchy in such a creative fashion. Nevertheless, it was the prosaic Archbishop of Armagh, and not the imaginative Archbishop of Dublin, upon whom Leo XIII chose to confer the cardinal's hat in 1893. Walsh's Roman flank had been turned.[15]

The other two archbishoprics were held, in 1898, by men two decades older than the primates. Both had entered the Irish hierarchy during Cullen's largely successful efforts to reform and regularise the chaotic structure of Irish ecclesiastical administration. John McEvilly, Bishop of Galway from 1857 to 1878, had fought for Cullen's programme in Connacht against the Cardinal's most determined opponent, Archbishop John MacHale of Tuam, and had, after several years as MacHale's coadjutor, succeeded to the archbishopric in 1881. Though a comparatively colourless figure, McEvilly deserves credit for bringing discipline and order to the ecclesiastical administration of the most backward province of Ireland. 'Colourless' is hardly the word, however, to describe his archepiscopal colleague at Cashel, Thomas William Croke. Though the story that Croke had fought at the barricades in Paris in 1848 may be apocryphal,[16] it is indicative of the reputation this prelate enjoyed. After holding a bishopric in New Zealand during the early 1870s, he was appointed Archbishop of Cashel in 1875 and soon became known for his 'advanced' views on the land and national questions. Several times in the late 1880s the government contemplated prosecuting Croke under the special Crimes Act then in force, though even when he took a cavalier attitude toward the papal rescript of 1888 the cabinet decided not to brave the public outcry that would inevitably follow the arraignment of an archbishop.[17] Croke, who shared Walsh's capacity to take a broad, unparochial view of the great issues of the day, held political opinions very similar to those of Walsh and worked closely with the Archbishop of Dublin in his efforts to formulate episcopal policy. The fact that Croke's see was not at the centre of national life, however, enabled him to enter more unreservedly into popular agitation than would have suited either Walsh's task or his temperament. By 1898, however, he had 'put the shutters up' on his political life, and rarely intervened in public affairs.

The leadership of Walsh and Croke was weakened not only by Rome's decision to give the cardinalate to Logue, but by the hostile activities of two suffragans. Bishops Edward Thomas O'Dwyer of Limerick and John Healy of Clonfert (coadjutor until 1896, translated to Tuam, 1903) were known as 'Castle bishops' because of their outspoken opposition to the agitation of the late 1880s.[18] Both had deliberately embarrassed Walsh in 1890 by refusing to sign the initial episcopal pronouncement against Parnell upon which the Archbishop of Dublin hoped to build a unified ecclesiastical policy.[19] Though O'Dwyer and Healy spoke for only a minority within the hierarchy, and though neither yet held the rank of archbishop (Healy was to become Archbishop of Tuam in 1903), they constituted a seriously disruptive influence. Their power probably derived in part from the sympathetic hearing which their views received at Rome. They also profited, however, from the fact that formal unanimity was much more important to the hierarchy than it would be to a secular deliberative body. The hierarchy's special claim to speak with authority was gravely compromised by any public dissent within its ranks. An individual prelate who, like O'Dwyer, was prepared to take an independent line could exercise an influence over ecclesiastical policy out of proportion to the popularity of his views among his colleagues.

Among the remainder of the bishops were several who, like Patrick O'Donnell of Raphoe (i.e. most of County Donegal), possessed considerable competence but had not made their mark on political affairs and others who, like Henry Henry of Down and Connor (i.e. Belfast and vicinity), had extensive political involvements though they lacked outstanding abilities. The average bishop, however, though he might adopt a deliberate line of action in his own diocese, probably looked to a few able and/or influential prelates, such as those who have been mentioned, to give central direction to the Church's relations with the Nation and the State. This very natural situation was, in a sense, formalised in an arrangement by which the hierarchy ordinarily met only twice a year and much of its business was handled in more frequent meetings of a Standing Committee of the four archbishops and about five or six of the more prominent suffragans. In the closing years of the century, as has been indicated, the most prominent prelates were not in sufficient accord to permit the kind of vigour and dispatch in policy-formation which Walsh and Croke had exercised in the late 1880s and early 1890s. To be sure, the divisions within the hierarchy were not so sharp as those within the Irish Parliamentary Party. Indeed, the hierarchy's internal problems had little political significance so long as the party was badly fragmented and the country remained relatively free of social protest activity. The pangs of land hunger, however, would inevitably recur, and the Nation's representatives would not indefinitely be content with the political impotence to which their divisions condemned them.

This study commences at the point when the national movement began to recover from the doldrums into which it had fallen after the crisis of 1890–92. Parts One and Two describe the Church's role in the political system in a period, 1898–1908, in which the Nation's displacement of the State was more a hope than an imminent possibility. In these years the Church functioned within the delicate system of conventions by which she safeguarded her position with respect to both the State and the Nation. Throughout most of the period covered by Parts Three and Four, 1909–1921, the situation is changed, and the great transfer of power from the State to the Nation seemed just around the corner. Though the Church's task was simplified by the fact that she could concentrate on her relations with the Nation, it was seriously complicated by the fact that the Nation itself was, for much of the period, divided. It is a remarkable story in which the Church protected, and indeed augmented, her interests—the fervent devotion of her people and the institutional conditions which, she believed, fostered that devotion—up to the last hours of the old order and yet entered the new order with those interests intact for the future as well.

PART ONE

Equipoise, 1898-1904

CHAPTER I

Two Leagues

IN 1897 the potato crop failed in the West of Ireland. Maud Gonne believed that widespread starvation was a very real possibility in the so-called 'congested districts' of the Atlantic seaboard. With the assistance of the young labour leader, James Connolly, Miss Gonne prepared and distributed a pamphlet citing eminent ecclesiastics from Clement I to Cardinal Manning in defence of socialist ideals, and, despite episcopal disfavour, she was able to rally some of the clergy of the Belmullet district to lead a successful protest against the way in which relief work was being administered locally.[1] Citations, even from Aquinas, on the right to steal on plea of necessity, however, were hardly the way to win enthusiastic clerical support, and the Belmullet Poor Law Union was scarcely a body from which to seek sweeping social reforms. The fact that the leadership of such an agitation fell to such a person as Miss Gonne was a symptom of the weakness of the fundamental organ of the Irish Nation—the Irish Parliamentary Party. Just as the party was divided into warring factions at Westminster, the social protest movement which Parnell had fashioned into a constituency political organisation had become fragmented into separate networks of local organisation—the Irish National League (Parnellite), the Irish National Federation (Dillonite) and the People's Rights Association (Healyite). The Nation's political leadership seemed as incapable of mounting a protest against the crying social evils of the West as they were of pursuing a concerted policy in the House of Commons.

The problem of the West was not exactly the same problem which the country had faced in the 1840s. People were hungry, ill-clothed and wretchedly housed, but they were not dying in large numbers. The Great Famine had taught Irishmen that as an alternative to starvation they might leave the country for the industrial cities of Great Britain, the United States or the colonies. In consequence of the great tide of emigration which began in the 1840s, together with the growing practice of late marriages, the Irish population had declined from 8,175,124 in 1841 to 4,458,775 by 1901. Along the western seaboard even those who did not emigrate permanently were often obliged to supplement their incomes by seasonal labour in England or Scotland. Though emigration was, from a strictly economic point of view, a blessing which relieved population pressure on the land and enabled both emigrants and the remaining population to achieve a higher standard of living, it had become, in Irish eyes, a curse. Politicians cited official figures on depopulation as evidence of the continued misgovernment of Ireland, and the close-knit rural society felt the departure of each emigrant as something like a death in the family. The Church, while sharing these feelings, had more definite grounds upon which to deplore emigration, for churchmen were deeply disturbed by reports from abroad that Irish emigrants had lapsed from their faith, and they associated grave moral danger with life in cities— where most emigrants settled.

The decline in population had been accompanied by the conversion of previously cultivated land into large grazing ranches, so that in many areas most of the local population was still crowded on tiny, uneconomic holdings within sight of open, untilled fields. In such districts, so long as land reform was conceived primarily as a revision of the landlord-tenant relationship on existing holdings, it could not create an economically viable society free from emigration. It was the realisation of this fact which had prompted the establishment of the Congested Districts Board in 1891. In its early years the C.D.B. had undertaken a few schemes of economic development in the limited western districts where its powers extended, but financial and legal limitations had prevented it from undertaking major redistribution and resettlement schemes by which alone agriculture could be made viable along the Atlantic seaboard. Gradually, however, the powers of the Board were enlarged, and it was enabled to purchase large tracts of land and divide them into holdings large enough to support families.[2] One of the first such projects was the creation of economic holdings for ninety-five families on Clare Island, just west of Westport, Co. Mayo. To encourage the scheme, William O'Brien, one of the Anti-Parnellite leaders, and Archbishop McEvilly of Tuam had, during 1894–95, jointly guaranteed the tenants' obligations for the first seven years of repayment.[3] The action was significant not only because it gave a new turn to O'Brien's energies for social reform, but because it demonstrated that the leading ecclesiastic of Connacht shared his ideal of redistribution of the grazing lands. The Archbishop made it plain, however, that he intended that this ideal should be realised only through legal means such as had been employed on Clare Island. When several clergymen in the area just north of Westport organised a local agitation during 1895–96 to force tenants of several large grazing farms to surrender the land for distribution among tenants of small neighbouring holdings, McEvilly denounced the boycotting and outrage connected with the agitation and transferred one of the priests to another parish.[4]

O'Brien, who had retired from parliament in 1895 in disgust over the party's internal wranglings and was living in seclusion near Westport, saw in the issue of the grazing farms a possible means of rejuvenating the national movement. In the winter following the crop failure which had prompted Maud Gonne's little venture he decided to undertake a new agitation, which he launched at a public meeting in Westport on 23 January 1898 under the name of the United Irish League—a name intended, no doubt, to call up memories of the United Irishmen of 1798 whose centenary was about to be celebrated throughout Ireland. The meeting was chaired by a local clergyman, and Canon Greally of Newport, one of the participants in the 1895–96 agitation, spoke in favour of 'the boycotting of grabbers and ranch-holders, and of their supporters'.[5] According to police reports, the clergy of the district 'threw themselves with energy into the movement', and 'upon Sunday after Sunday' exhorted their congregations to support it.[6] The Archbishop moved quickly to establish an ecclesiastical position with respect to the new movement. In his Lenten pastoral, read in churches on 20 February, he spoke of the distress which—as the police noted, with their customary regard for the rules of evidence—he 'alleged' to exist in the region, and suggested that a remedy lay in the division of relatively unproductive grazing land. He was careful to stress that the change must be brought about 'under legal sanction' and 'without trenching on the just or equitable rights of any class of the community'.[7]

In the district around Westport and Newport the clergy promoted the League with considerable zeal. The Parish Priest in Louisburgh called for a U.I.L. branch 'to hunt the grabbers and Scotch graziers out of the country'.[8] Father Coen, P.P., Islandeady, instigated a boycott of certain local graziers (one of whom had reportedly angered him by opposing clerical wishes in the Board of Guardians), even declining himself to accept dues (i.e. the regular annual contribution to support the clergy) from a herdsman employed by one of the graziers.[9] Even in this disturbed area, however, clergymen used their relationship with the League to set limits on its action, for example by condemning a specific illegal action and disclaiming League responsibility for it.[10] In other parts of the archdiocese, clergymen were in no hurry to give any sanction to the new League. During its first eight months, there was clerical opposition to the U.I.L. in at least eight communities outside the Westport-Newport area, and of the two reported instances of clerical support, one involved a priest with a direct personal grudge against a 'land-grabber'.[11]

A police official who called upon Archbishop McEvilly in March left with the impression that the Archbishop would bring one particularly inflammatory priest, Father Coen, to account and would try to prevent the League's expansion. McEvilly stressed, however, his sympathy with the goals of the agitation.[12] The police noted little change in Father Coen's behaviour, and late in September learned 'from several sources' that the Archbishop had directed several clerical opponents of the League to drop their opposition, giving as his reasons, 'that the people had taken up the matter so warmly as to have gone beyond the control of the clergy, and that clerical opposition to the League would only lead to friction between clergy and people'.[13] In several parishes there were abrupt shifts from firm clerical opposition to clerical acquiescence, even involvement in the League.[14] During the autumn the League spread rapidly through the archdiocese with frequent clerical participation in its meetings.[15] Moreover, when the League began to develop a level of organisation above the parish by holding a convention for the South Mayo parliamentary division on 16 November, ten of the delegates were priests and Archdeacon Kilkenny of Claremorris, who 'had hitherto strenuously opposed the League', presided.[16] Indeed, the only places in the archdiocese where clerical resistance to the League apparently persisted late in 1898 were two parishes where the agitation had encroached upon the specifically religious sphere. In Breaffy, where the League carried a boycott of a landlord's steward to the point of walking out of church when the steward entered, the archbishop and local clergy threatened excommunication.[17] In Ballinrobe, where League organisers blamed the Parish Priest for the government's proclamation (i.e. formal prohibition) of a proposed meeting, the clergy were boycotted when they went to hold Mass in outlying villages. The locality was placed under an interdict.[18]

Carefully distinguishing between the agitation's aims and its attendant excesses, McEvilly was coping skilfully with a potentially explosive situation. Early in the year he had apparently hoped to confine the movement to the Westport-Newport area, but while allowing clerical opposition to it outside that area he was careful not to alienate the movement from the Church by any severe curbs on clerical participation in the area where it had clearly taken hold. When it was evident that the League was spreading, he moved quickly to reach an accommodation throughout his archdiocese, excepting only those areas where the movement had turned against the Church itself. The Archbishop's flexible response paid generous dividends in clerical influence upon League activity. When the civil authorities learned of a conference between Michael Davitt and McEvilly and several of his clergy, they cancelled plans to proclaim a forthcoming meeting near Claremorris which was to be addressed by Davitt. They concluded, correctly, that the clergy were co-operating in plans for the meeting.[19] On the Sunday of the proposed meeting, the local Parish Priest announced it to his congregation, stating candidly

that he had not sought the meeting, but as it had come he would take part in it, believing that he could thus do more good than by staying away. The meeting would be a constitutional one, otherwise he would not take part in it.[20]

The priest's stipulation was fulfilled, for, it was reported, the 'distinctly constitutional tone' which he imparted in his opening address was strictly followed by Davitt and the other speakers, who included two other parish priests as well as several U.I.L. organisers.

By early 1899, however, the League was spreading beyond the bounds of McEvilly's archdiocese and into the five suffragan dioceses which encircled the archdiocese. In Irish ecclesiastical polity, a metropolitan's precedence over his suffragans is essentially honorific, and any dominance he may exercise in the formation of policy for his province depends solely upon such factors as his personal capacity for leadership, his influence at Rome and his standing within the Irish hierarchy as a whole. Although McEvilly was certainly stronger in this respect than some archbishops who figure in this study, the force of his example was only one factor in the determination of his suffragans' response to the League. Probably a more decisive factor was the political leanings of the bishops and influential clergy. Though O'Brien was not currently sitting in parliament, he was prominently identified with Dillon, who, despite private reservations over the value of his colleague's new departure, had publicly associated himself with the League. The U.I.L. was therefore inevitably regarded as a Dillonite organisation. The diocese of Achonry was represented in parliament entirely by Dillonites, including Dillon himself, who lived in Ballaghaderreen, the see of the diocese, and sat for East Mayo. The League seems to have had a favourable reception from clergymen in almost every part of the diocese except Swinford.[21] The Rev. Denis O'Hara, P.P., Kiltimagh, a close friend of Dillon's and a member of the Congested Districts Board, told a U.I.L. meeting at Charlestown that the only remedy for the agrarian problem was 'to clear out, bag and baggage, every mother's son of the landlords of Ireland', though he made it clear that such a solution should embody full compensation to the landlords.[22] Personal friendship with Dillon may also have shaped the attitude of Bishop MacCormack of Galway. Though reports of clerical activity in his diocese are too sparse and conflicting for generalisation, MacCormack associated himself with the new movement early in 1899 by sending a letter 'in approval of the League' to a provincial congress of the organisation in Claremorris (which was addressed by Dillon and attended by 1,200 delegates, including sixty priests).[23]

In contrast, the diocese of Killala contained very few clerical friends of Dillon and O'Brien. In a hotly contested by-election in North Sligo during 1891 it had become evident that there was substantial Parnellite sentiment among the Killala clergy.[24] More significant, in 1898 the sitting member for North Mayo, which encompassed most of the diocese, was a staunch Healyite named Dan Crilly, whom the Dillonite forces had failed to dislodge in 1895 in a sharp encounter with the local clergy.[25] The League had even less chance for gaining clerical support from Healyite clergy than from Parnellite priests, and it is therefore not surprising that in only two Killala communities was any clerical sanction of the movement reported, while in at least eight other places it was noted that the priests either opposed the League or abstained from participation in it.[26]

Something of a unified policy for the entire province emerged from an episcopal meeting at Tuam late in September 1899 in the form of a series of resolutions adopted unanimously by all six Connacht bishops, published and forwarded to Gerald Balfour, the Chief Secretary for Ireland, in his capacity as Chairman of the Congested Districts Board. The bishops expressed their approval of the C.D.B.'s attempts 'to create a peasant proprietary with enlarged holdings in the most impoverished districts of the west of Ireland'[27] and urged the extension of the policy of purchasing and subdividing the grazing lands as a means of stemming the seasonal migration to Great Britain. In particular, they hoped that the Board 'with your powerful help' would seek extended powers from parliament to enable them to apply this policy to the entire province, for only the poorest districts were within the C.D.B.'s jurisdiction. The bishops assured the Chief Secretary that they would greatly regret any unjust or illegitimate methods which might be employed in the interests of the tenants. 'A just cause can only be weakened and a holy cause can only be sullied, by the commission of any crime,' they observed, and for their part, they promised that 'If necessary, we shall not fail to take steps to warn our clergy and our flocks to abstain from any course of action that could be rightly regarded as unjust or immoral.' The bishops were undoubtedly quite sincere in this disavowal of unlawful methods. The need for making such an explicit declaration on this point, however, arose not so much from their own scruples as from their realisation that their policy must be defensible at the Holy See. One of the lessons impressed upon the hierarchy in the 1880s was that British overtures at Rome might at any time undermine episcopal policy in Ireland.

There were two distinct ways in which distribution of the grazing land might be achieved: (1) the tenants of each grazing ranch might be intimidated into giving it up, and other persons intimidated into refusing to take the land for grazing, thereby forcing the landlord to accede to the popular desire and subdivide the ranch into tillage plots, or (2) pressure might be applied to the government to adopt a policy of compulsory redistribution over a widespread area, presumably through the Congested Districts Board, but not under the restrictions which currently governed that body. The two methods could, of course, be synthesised. Father Brett, C.C., president of the Errismore branch of the U.I.L. advised members of the branch

to leave all grazing farms lying idle for a year, when the tenants could memorialise the Congested Districts Board to buy the farms, and he would get Canon O'Hara (of the Congested Districts Board) influenced in the matter. He promised that if the farms were surrendered he would see that no one should put cattle on them. He, however, advised that no outrage should be committed.[28]

Although in specific instances the agitation was ordinarily directed more against individuals than against the government, most of the bishops, as indicated in the letter to Gerald Balfour, no doubt hoped to redirect it toward pressing for legislative and administrative changes and in the process to moderate its excesses.

The Bishop of Elphin, John Clancy, gave expression to these hopes when he advised the South Roscommon U.I.L. executive, through their president, Mgr McLaughlin, that the local League branches 'could not do better in the immediate future than, by tongue and pen and determined constitutional action, advocate the extension of existing legislation to the extent of having the whole of Connaught included within the purview of the Congested Districts Board'.[29] In this policy, the Bishop was confident, the League would have the 'earnest support and united co-operation' of the Connacht bishops, and he himself had already made representations to the Board and certain of its members which had brought 'very substantial favours' to certain districts of Sligo and Roscommon. Clancy was a very energetic man who entered enthusiastically into movements for the economic regeneration of Ireland and who does not seem to have been prominently identified with any political faction. In his diocese the ecclesiastical policy clearly was for priests to become intimately involved in the League for the purpose of guiding it along acceptable lines.[30] Although Clancy had to intervene occasionally to restrain the zeal of an individual priest,[31] he was inclined to allow the movement considerable latitude so long as his clergy were involved in it. In the Newbridge district, when a meeting announced for 29 April 1900 was proclaimed, the police had to chase two priests and an M.P. to three different sites in their efforts to enforce the proclamation.[32] Speaking in Newbridge about three weeks later, Clancy stated that if the meeting's purpose was the encouragment of boycotting and intimidation, the proclamation was justified, but he softened his remarks by insisting on his own support of freedom of speech and legal agitation. Moreover, he demonstrated his continued confidence in clerical participation as a means of moderating the agitation by asking 'the clergy and others who had influence to use their best endeavours to put down boycotting and intimidation'.[33]

Although Bishop Conmy of Killala had signed the letter

to Gerald Balfour in September 1899, he does not seem to have shared his colleagues' strategy of attempting to direct the agitation toward the attainment of the stated episcopal goals. There was no perceptible change in the Killala diocesan policy of clerical abstention from and opposition to the League.[34] One other western bishop might have been expected to follow the example of Killala rather than that of Tuam, Achonry and Elphin. The Bishop of Clonfert, John Healy, was a conservative churchman whose feelings were seldom in harmony with popular sentiment, though he was very capable and was to succeed McEvilly as Archbishop of Tuam in 1903. He had been regarded as a 'Castle bishop' during the land agitation of the late 1880s, and he had joined only with great reluctance in the general episcopal offensive against Parnell in 1890–91. Realising, no doubt, that his own 'Tory' views would not serve him well in a public contest, he tended to restrict his political activities to high-level dealings with government officials and to eschew actions which might draw him into the public arena. Nevertheless, he was genuinely anxious for a settlement of agrarian problems, and perhaps his aloofness from party politics made him better able than the Killala authorities to come to terms with the League. Reports from his small diocese are sparse, but it appears that there was very little clerical involvement in the League in Clonfert before the provincial hierarchy's meeting of September 1899.[35] Though Bishop Healy himself seems to have continued to avoid direct involvement in the League after the bishops' action, several of his clergy did become active in the League or at least express approval of its general objects while condemning its excesses.[36]

By early 1900 the ecclesiastical authorities of Connacht—outside Killala diocese—had developed a very useful relationship with the League. Though not so closely bound to the new organisation as to be implicated in questionable actions which it might undertake, the bishops had shown it sufficient sympathy and gained sufficient influence in its counsels through their own clergy to be able to direct its course with some success and to avert unpleasant consequences to the Church's own interests. During the summer of 1900 a dispute over a farm near Ballaghaderreen owned by Bishop

Lyster of Achonry and some of his clergy led to a sermon in which the Bishop strongly denounced recent outrages and boycotting. When the U.I.L. was founded in the district, Lyster stated, it was a constitutional movement, but, because of the accession of certain men to the League, 'all decent men' had withdrawn from it. 'There is, therefore,' the Bishop reasoned, 'no League here at present.' This ploy worked beautifully. At a public meeting in the town a resolution of sympathy with the clergy was passed, and the U.I.L. branch itself followed suit. A party of men marched to the farm in question and mowed the hay which otherwise would have been lost through the boycott of the farm, and the clergy organised a new League branch to replace the discredited one.[37] At about the same time Bishop Clancy of the neighbouring diocese of Elphin preached a strong sermon against boycotting. Noting that boycotting was being promoted by an organisation which he had hitherto supported 'because he looked upon it as a means of helping to keep our poor people at home and enabling them to earn a living in their own country', he threatened to 'wash his hands clean of it' if it 'descended to the glorification of injustice, and to an atrocious system of boycotting for ignoble ends'. Shortly after this sermon one of his priests wrote to a local branch that he would only support the League if the principles enunciated by Clancy were observed, and another priest threatened to resign his presidency of a branch if it resorted to boycotting in a pending case.[38] Both Lyster and Clancy were able to exert pressure upon the League because they had come to terms with it from the beginning, and the League had an interest in retaining their favour. Underlying the attitude of five-sixths of the hierarchy of Tuam province was their acute realisation of the peculiar economic misery of the Connacht peasantry. Not only did these bishops sincerely sympathise with the aims of the agitation, which seemed to offer an alternative to emigration, but they recognised that the popular sense of grievance against the grazing system was so strong in their province that the movement could not be destroyed.

The response of ecclesiastics to any public issue was governed by a combination of their ideals and the interests of their institution. The Tuam provincial hierarchy's accommodation of the United Irish League up to 1900 had reflected predominantly the genuine congruence of their social ideals with the stated aims of the new movement, tempered by an equally genuine abhorrence of violence and ill-feeling. Churchmen were also keenly aware, however, of the difficulties of the Catholic Church in various continental countries, where substantial segments of the working classes were abstaining from their religious duties and where the State, in several cases, was depriving the Church of more and more of her privileges. The Irish Church's position for or against such a popular movement as the U.I.L. might call forth either renewed devotion or anticlerical hostility. Such considerations were given urgency by the fact that the new movement was becoming an outwork of the (Dillonite) Irish Parliamentary Party and, as such, an agency of the Nation. As the Nation was the State *in posse,* it was vital to the Church's interests that good relations with the Nation be safeguarded. The most prominent of these interests was the protection and enlargement of the Church's role in publicly supported educational systems.

Nearly every Irish child received his elementary education in a school under the nominal jurisdiction of the National Education Board, which had been established in 1831. In its original conception, the system of 'National Schools' was to be basically nondenominational. Children of all religious denominations were to receive instruction together in all secular subjects and to be taught religion in separate classes. The Board was charged with excluding any textbooks of a sectarian or controversial nature. Grants of up to two-thirds of the cost of construction were made by the Board to local individuals or bodies willing to erect schoolhouses, and the Board maintained a staff of inspectors who regularly visited the schools and reported on the instruction conducted in them. In actual fact, however, the administration of the schools was virtually controlled by local 'managers', who were nearly always clergymen. The manager had the right to appoint and dismiss the teacher, and though good cause was supposed to be shown for a dismissal, the Board rarely interfered with a manager who was dissatisfied with his teacher.[39]

During the early decades of the system there was considerable controversy over the principles on which it would operate. Some Irish Protestants wanted to turn the system to their own purposes, and some English statesmen hoped as far as possible to exclude the Churches from its affairs. It is not, therefore, surprising that a number of Catholic ecclesiastics were wary of the system or that, under the leadership of John MacHale, Archbishop of Tuam, they tried to prevent its acceptance by the Church. Daniel Murray, Archbishop of Dublin, had accepted one of the places on the Board and, during 1838–41, engaged in a heated public controversy with MacHale.[40] Rome, however, refused to take MacHale's side, and the Church gradually acquiesced in the system with misgivings and worked to adapt it to Catholic concepts of education. In 1860 the Board was reconstructed, and a convention was established by which exactly half of the seats were reserved for Catholic appointees and half for Protestants. Though the system continued to be described officially as 'nondenominational', Bishop O'Dwyer of Limerick could observe with obvious satisfaction in 1900 that in three-fourths of Ireland secular education was denominationally segregated just as thoroughly as religious education.[41] O'Dwyer proudly noted that in Limerick they had two distinct sets of schools in one of which 'the priest was the manager; every teacher was a Catholic; every pupil was a Catholic; and side by side with that they had a Protestant school in which the parson was the manager, and the teachers and children were all Protestants'. To emphasise his point O'Dwyer cited the fact that although originally the National Board had a rule prohibiting the foundation of one school within a certain distance of another, the rule had now been repealed, and a Protestant and a Catholic school might be built side by side. The Board had ceased to make any serious efforts to promote 'mixed' instruction and was in practice allowing each denomination to create its own, *de facto* segregated, system within the National system. A few minor features of the situation remained aggravating to Catholic ecclesiastics. Several 'Model Schools' under the direct management of the Board had been established, mainly in the 1850s, for the purposes of exhibiting improved teaching methods to the surounding schools and training young persons to become teachers. Because these schools were 'mixed' and because they were entirely outside clerical control, they were the object of special attack from the Church. Nevertheless, they were merely a relic from the period when the Board had taken nondenominationalism seriously, and there was, after about 1860, no danger that they would make inroads upon the denominational system. The Board also maintained a nondenominational training college for teachers in Marlborough Street, Dublin—another relic from before 1860—and though separate denominational colleges received government grants after 1883, the maintenance of the Marlborough Street College continued to irritate the Catholic clergy. Nevertheless, the system as a whole was basically satisfactory to the Church by the beginning of the twentieth century.

So clear had it become by 1878 that nonsectarianism had failed in the National system, that the Intermediate Education Act of that year made no attempt to repeat the experiment in the secondary schools. Denominationalism was recognised as a fact, and State support of secondary education took the form of prizes to students who scored high on nationwide examinations and results fees to the masters of the schools they had attended. The Intermediate Board was given even less cognizance than the National Board over the conduct of instruction in the system it administered. The Intermediate system affected only a very small segment of the population, for State aid was far from sufficient to provide free instruction at secondary level. Because only a few middle-class Catholics could afford to send their children to secondary schools, and because secondary education therefore remained essentially a private endeavour, the Intermediate system generally provoked less controversy than the National system. A third system, technical schools, was being established under the Department of Agriculture and Technical Instruction which was founded in 1899. This system did not contain the same sort of safeguards for denominationalism as did the two Boards. The Department was a government agency staffed and directed by paid officials rather than a semi-autonomous body of unpaid commissioners selected to foster denominational balance. Nevertheless, under the leadership of the energetic Irish Protestant, Sir Horace Plunkett, founder of the co-operative movement in Ireland, the technical instruction programme was able to maintain the support of many ecclesiastics, so long as it did not encroach upon the responsibilities of the National Schools. No doubt, clerical desires for any means of stemming emigration and preserving a rural society—desires which Plunkett shared—helped to smooth the way for the Department's work.

By the end of the nineteenth century, therefore, the Church had won from the State an educational structure up to the university level, which was essentially satisfactory. She had, moreover, made it plain to the accredited representatives of the Nation that her support for the national claim as put forward by them was conditional upon their respect for and defence of her position in that structure and their advocacy of its completion by the establishment of a State-endowed Catholic university (or university college). Parnell himself had deferred to ecclesiastical wishes in this matter, and the continued deference of his successors in the national leadership was one of the conventions of Irish politics. Like the convention by which the State appointed equal numbers of Catholics and Protestants to the education boards, this convention governing relations between the Church and the Nation was nowhere written down, but it was comparably sacrosanct.

Nevertheless, almost everyone who devoted any attention to the condition of Irish education—ecclesiastics not excluded —recognised that some basic changes were sorely needed. The method of payment by results, upon which the Intermediate system had been founded in 1878, had in the same decade been introduced into the National (primary) system.[42] What had been hailed in the 1870s as the enlightened application of scientific principles to education was by 1900 widely denounced as productive only of senseless cramming on the part of students, needless rigidity in the curriculum and the stifling of originality and creativity in teachers. Moreover, even by most diligently preparing his students for the all-important examinations, a teacher could only hope to raise his income to the barest subsistence level. In 1902 the average annual salary of Irish male headteachers was £99 9s. 3d. compared with £147 10s. 2d. for male head-teachers in England and Wales and £174 6s. 11d. in Scotland. Incredible as it may seem, the Irish teacher sometimes found it necessary to pay from his own pocket the expense of essential supplies for his classroom and even to contribute to the cost of heating the building in the winter.[43]

Most galling of all to the teacher was the fact that under the Board's rules the manager could dismiss him without notice or compensation for misconduct or other sufficient reason and could, for no stated reason, dismiss him at any time on three months' notice or for three months' salary. In the 'Maynooth Resolution' of 1894 the hierarchy did provide some protection for teachers dismissed without stated cause by requiring prior consent of the manager's bishop in such cases and granting the teacher the right to be heard in his own defence. This protection was not extended, however, to teachers dismissed summarily for alleged misconduct.[44] In 1897 a young curate, Father Flood, who had recently taken up his first mission at Leixlip, just outside Dublin, became dissatisfied with the musical ability and behaviour of the girls in the church choir. Father Flood seems to have held the schoolteacher of thirty-two years' standing, Mrs O'Sullivan, accountable for the conduct of the choir girls, one of whom was a monitress in the school. On one of several visits to the school to complain of the girls' behaviour, Father Flood, accompanied by Canon Hunt, P.P., who was officially the school manager, got into an argument with Mrs O'Sullivan. Although there were conflicting accounts of what was actually said, village gossip soon portrayed Father Flood as attacking the character of the pupils. On 30 October Mrs O'Sullivan was summarily dismissed. When she appealed to Archbishop Walsh, the latter, with scrupulous regard for the letter of the Maynooth Resolution, declined to interfere, thereby throwing upon Canon Hunt the burden of defending in the civil courts his allegation of misconduct. In a widely publicised trial, in which the Catholic judge (Lord Chief Baron Palles) helped to ease any misgivings the jury might have had toward finding against a priest, Mrs O'Sullivan was exonerated and awarded three months' salary and £200 damages.[45] Clearly the Church was not well served by a policy which allowed such a trivial episode to become a *cause célèbre*. Walsh immediately saw to it that Mrs O'Sullivan was reinstated.[46] At their first opportunity the hierarchy extended the protection of the Maynooth Resolution to teachers dismissed summarily.[47]

Before the hierarchy had a chance to plug the loophole in its appeal procedure, however, the central executive committee of the Irish National Teachers' Organisation had dispatched a memorial to the National Board calling attention to the O'Sullivan case as 'only an illustration of what has been going on and what in the nature of things must go on as long as irresponsible managers are clothed with the power of dismissing state paid servants at their own whim without assigning any cause'.[48] Walsh, in a public letter, made it plain that the hierarchy expected their amended Maynooth Resolution to be a final settlement of the security of tenure question. Realising no doubt that Walsh was one of their few friends in the hierarchy and that their own membership was aghast at their audacity, the authors of the memorial resolved in August 1898 to thank the hierarchy 'on behalf of the teachers under Catholic clerical management for their recent enactment on the managerial question and to accept it as a satisfactory settlement of the claims of *all teachers affected by it* ' (my italics).[49] One might think that this action would have ended the matter. Clerical opposition to the teachers' leadership continued, however, and at its 1899 Annual Congress the Organisation solidly voted out the President (a Protestant) and Vice-President and the proposer and seconder of the original memorial. The election changed the religious composition of the executive committee from five Protestants and eight Catholics to three Protestants and ten Catholics. The delegates rejected the report of the outgoing executive committee, expressed confidence in the Maynooth Resolution, extended thanks to the hierarchy, and changed the Organisation's rules to provide for election of future executive committees by ballot of the entire membership rather than by the Congress. Neverthless, clerical wrath was not assuaged, for a few days later a conference of representative Catholic clerical managers in Armagh province agreed to refuse appointments to any teacher belonging to the I.N.T.O. 'as at present constituted'. This ban was also adopted by the managers in Tuam province. Though it was never formally promulgated in the two southern provinces, and though its enforcement was uneven—Bishop O'Donnell is said to have declared that it would never run in Raphoe diocese—it stood for several years as a symbol of the disgrace of the I.N.T.O. in clerical eyes.[50]

The crux of the matter seems to have been that the I.N.T.O. was nondenominational. Although its Protestant members were willing to abjure any interest in the tenure question as far as it affected Catholics, they were understandably unwilling to renounce an interest in their own tenure. Any change in the law to protect the tenure of Protestant teachers, however, would inevitably affect the Catholic manager-teacher relationship as well. The Church would not tolerate the involvement, even passive, of Catholic teachers in such a cause, and in consequence the Protestant teachers were driven in the autumn of 1899 to form their own union.[51] A further effort at the 1900 Annual Congress to repudiate the memorial 'as far as the Roman Catholics are concerned' was rebuffed by leading prelates.[52] The Organisation was made virtually to grovel as well as to divest itself of any significant Protestant voice in its policy before it could regain the indulgence, if not the confidence, of the Church.

The Church thus put down with a very heavy hand the teachers' threat to her position in education. A simultaneous challenge from another quarter, however, was handled in a very different way. For generations the decline of the Irish language had been a subject of mild concern in polite circles, while the mass of the population had quite sensibly welcomed the spread of English as a means of economic betterment. By the 1880s there were only a few hundred thousands of Irish speakers remaining in rapidly shrinking areas on the western seaboard. Though Irish had been made an optional subject in the curricula of the National and Intermediate school systems in 1878, there was no widespread enthusiasm for its preservation until the 1890s. In 1892 Douglas Hyde, the son of a Co. Roscommon Church of Ireland clergyman, called upon his countrymen to 'arrest the decay of the language'[53] in a lecture before the National Literary Society provocatively entitled 'The Necessity for De-Anglicizing the Irish Nation'. At the instigation of Eóin Mac Néill, a young Catholic scholar from the Glens of Antrim, Hyde's exhortation was given practical effect through the establishment in the following year of the Gaelic League, which carried the movement to revive the language out of the drawing-rooms and into the hundreds of villages of Ireland, where classes in Irish were established and Irish arts, crafts and music encouraged.

In the progress of a movement which affected virtually every parish in Ireland, it was inevitable that friction with clergymen would occur. For example, rumour reached a priest on one of the Aran Islands, where young Gaelic Leaguers went to practise their language skills, that one of the Leaguers had suggested that his parishioners should walk out of the chapel when he preached in English. If he had known this while the offender was still on the island, he told his congregation, 'I would have banded the men of the island together and we would have got him into a boat & packed him off from the island.'[54] Humourous little episodes of this sort, a recurring feature of the Gaelic League's activities, tended to attract more attention than they perhaps deserved as indicators of relations between the clergy and the League. League organisers did frequently meet instinctive suspicion from old parish priests, especially in remote districts where the priests were unaccustomed to the intrusion of 'outsiders' into their territory. When a Leaguer in Co. Donegal reported to Mac Néill that some of the clergy were 'not taking up the League business as they should and some think they cannot be done without', he added, perceptively, that such clerical complacency was mistaken, for 'the students now in Maynooth are imbued with different ideas from those of twenty years back and will be very useful and active supporters when they come out.'[55] Nevertheless, the League leadership, not wanting to postpone their programme to the distant day when these seminarians would become parish priests, seem to have recognised that it was 'in the power of the priest to kill a branch of the League in his parish in a few months'.[56] The opinion of John Hogan, a prominent member of the League, that 'It should be our aim to rather praise the Clergy for what they are doing than to blame them for what they are leaving undone,'[57] seems to have represented the policy the League leadership tried to follow. Reports in the League's official organ, *An Claidheamh Soluis,* of the activities of their organisers indicate that the first step in organising a branch was ordinarily to seek the assistance of the parish clergy.

The League leadership was also quite aware of the need to cultivate friends in the hierarchy. Indeed, within a few months of the founding of the League, Mac Néill was in active correspondence with Archbishop Walsh, who, characteristically, was developing a timely scholarly interest in fine points of Irish grammar and spelling and in techniques of language instruction. While developing cordial personal relations with Mac Néill, Walsh moved very cautiously toward public endorsement of the League, which he seems to have first extended in 1897 by offering a prize of £20 in an essay competition to be sponsored by the League.[58] Noting that he had withdrawn from one of the earlier Irish language societies because he found himself 'entangled in some unseemly strife between rival associations', he told one of the League's leaders: 'I can now, I think, feel safe in again taking some share in the good work, as it seems to have passed out of the stage of meaningless and demoralising contention.' He authorised him to 'make any use you wish of my name in connection with the League'.[59]

Around 1899 it was becoming clear that, unlike the effete little language societies which had preceded it, the League was a force to be reckoned with in Irish society. During that year a number of Walsh's episcopal colleagues followed his lead and associated themselves with the League's work. In March the first issue of *An Claidheamh Soluis* carried a report that Archbishop McEvilly had given the movement his blessing and an announcement that Bishop Clancy of Elphin and Bishop Owens of Clogher had joined the League's Council.[60] A few months later at a League organising meeting at Roadford, Co. Clare, a priest listed among the supporters of the movement Cardinal Logue, Bishop O'Donnell, Bishop Sheehan of Waterford and Bishop Browne of Cloyne.[61] Although the hierarchy was not acting as a body, enough of the most influential prelates had spoken to preclude any open opposition to the movement from members of the hierarchy. At their June 1900 meeting the hierarchy endorsed the teaching of Irish in the primary schools. An accommodation between the Church and the League, however, would require more than the acquiescence of the hierarchy. Despite the array of prelates under the League's banner, John Hogan was apprehensive that certain articles in *An Claidheamh Soluis* would cause the deanery conferences—whose resolutions were a common outlet for opinion among the lower clergy—to 'drive out the movement as being secretely anti-clerical'.[62] The sensibilities of the parish priests were becoming especially crucial at this point because language enthusiasts were beginning to look beyond little informal evening classes in Irish as the means for propagating and preserving the language. They were coming to see the National Schools as a means of achieving their objective, and, as was clear in the teachers' security of tenure dispute, it was at the parish level that clergy were most prickly over the Church's role in education. Mac Néill had learned as early as 1894 how delicate such matters were when he asked for Walsh's influence on behalf of a particular teacher—presumably one qualified to teach Irish—who was seeking an appointment in one of the National Schools in the archdiocese. Walsh replied by outlining, quite candidly, the practical constraints on episcopal dictation in such matters:

The *appointment* of teachers is a matter that I never like to interfere in. However this is plainly a very exceptional case, and I have written to the Parish Priest. Of course he has not as yet been appointed manager, so there is abundant time to make arrangements.

I ought to say that I could not feel justified in doing more than calling his attention to the matter in a general way, so that if he, as manager, has no special arrangement in view in any other direction, he may be led to take the case into favourable consideration.[63]

At any time Walsh could have ordered a manager to appoint a particular teacher, and it would be a brave priest who would have risked the consequences of refusal. The power to appoint teachers, however, was no doubt a privilege which this new parish priest had coveted throughout the long years which he probably served as a curate. A bishop who circumscribed that power might soon have a serious morale problem among his clergy. Furthermore, bishops had to be extremely careful not to compromise any position they had already taken vis-à-vis the State, as Walsh indicated when he added: 'I assume, of course, that the teacher has not been trained in the "mixed" State College in Marlborough Street. That would be an insuperable obstacle.'

The danger that individual Gaelic Leaguers might antagonise school managers by harassing them to promote the cause of the language was materially reduced by an action of the League Executive early in 1900. School managers in Irish-speaking districts were asked to sign a memorial petitioning the National Board to make provisions which would facilitate prompt introduction of bilingual instruction into these schools.[64] The 183 managers who complied seem to have represented virtually the entire territory which could conceivably fit the description 'Irish-speaking'.[65] It is quite possible that some episcopal influence may have been exercised in favour of signing the memorial,[66] but the procedure had the advantage of allowing priests, at minimal cost, to appear to be in the vanguard of an attack, not upon their own prerogatives, but upon a 'Castle Board'. Moreover, the proposal to allow native Irish speakers to be instructed in their own language was the least controversial of the League's programmes—drawing sympathetic comment, on educational grounds, even from the staunchly Unionist *Daily Express*.[67] Walsh, who as early as 1897 had used his position as a member of the National Board to advocate the League's claims for more favourable treatment of Irish in the National system,[68] took up the cause of bilingual instruction. Though he was plainly annoyed by the intemperate criticism which some Leaguers now directed at the Board,[69] he saw the issue through to a successful conclusion. To be sure, managers' signatures on the memorial did not guarantee that those same managers would take the trouble—if indeed they could find the staff—to introduce bilingual education as soon as the Board authorised it. Father Gerald O'Donovan, an enthusiastic young priest who later left the clergy, was probably correct a year later when he charged that 'not ten per cent of the managers who signed the memorial had made the slightest effort' to implement this reform.[70] Despite such divergence between the ideal and the reality, however, the managers' memorial represented the practical side of a process by which, around 1900, a place was found for the language movement within the existing pattern of relationships among the institutions of Irish society.

The League, it is often said, arose out of the frustrations of nationalists in the aftermath of Parnell's fall. Politics seemed hopeless as an outlet for nationalist energy, and so young Irishmen turned away from politics to cultivate new sources of national consciousness. From its inception, therefore, the League claimed to be nonpolitical and nonsectarian. A few individuals like Dr Kane of Belfast, who 'observed that though he was a Unionist and a Protestant he did not forget that he had sprung from the Clan O'Cahan',[71] were proudly exhibited as proof of the League's neutrality in the politico-religious polarisation of Irish society. Hyde himself was able for a time to maintain this policy without dampening the zeal of his followers. Invited to speak in Irish at one of the ceremonies marking the centenary of the 1798 rebellion, Hyde refused, but advised the League's committee to permit a less prominent Gaelic Leaguer to go in his place, 'providing he kept his name out of the papers'.[72] Similarly, when a priest included sectarian passages in a pamphlet written for the League, Hyde suggested that the League pay for its printing, but not as an official League publication.[73] Some Protestant nationalists undoubtedly hoped that the language would replace the Catholic religion as the primary symbol of Irish nationality. They longed for a means of identifying with the Ireland of the Catholic majority while nurturing the hope of eventually bringing their own coreligionists into the national fold as well. One Derry Protestant, R. Farmer, a minor civil servant who had voted Liberal in England and scandalised his friends by voting Nationalist in Ireland, urged upon Mac Néill the view that

Any man who learns a moderate amount of Gaelic may be classed as a Gael at heart, whatever his blood may be: my blood is in all probability a mixture & my wife is at least ½ a Gael as her mother is a Catholic & an O'Leary. . . .

As to race half the Leinster Catholics have Saxon blood, and as to religion we are all just what we were born—these things are really *accidents*—and the true test is what is a mans attitude to Ireland.[74]

'Gaelic', he maintained, ought to be 'a common bond'. In his opinion, however, certain League spokesmen by their flagrant disregard of the nonpolitical, nonsectarian rule were threatening to make the language 'only another point of difference'. Though Farmer was, for the moment, mollified by assurances of moderation from Mac Néill, his letter was symptomatic of an important change which was overtaking the movement.

At this point in its history the League was facing a crucial choice. It could retain the enthusiasm of a few liberal-minded Protestants by adhering to the ideal of a truly integrative role in Irish society or it could gain the enthusiasm of a much larger proportion of the Catholic majority by allowing its work to be identified with the cause of the Nation. Insofar as that cause appealed to the emotions of the majority it was —however it might be disguised—deeply 'political' and unavoidably 'sectarian'. The matter came to a head in 1899, when a Pan-Celtic alliance of language movements in Scotland, Wales, etc., invited the League to affiliate with it. Ties with movements in the British Celtic countries would accord well with the psychological needs of 'the Belfast people'[75] in the League—emphasising an identity separate from the English but softening the Catholic tinge of that identity with some Scottish Presbyterians and Welsh Methodists. John Hogan saw to the heart of the issue when he urged Mac Néill to limit contact with the other Celtic movements to 'correspondence and festive interchange of greetings'. How could there be closer union, he asked rhetorically.

We do not speak the same national language, we do not belong to the same Church, at no period of History, as far as I know, (Scotland excepted) did we form one nation or speak a common language. There is no such language as 'Celtic' and there is no such country as 'Celtia' but there is an Irish language and a country called Eire.[76]

'Let not the issue of this struggle of ours be confounded,' he advised. 'Irish nationality is the motive power, our people will never rise to a Celtic movement, individuals may, and if we draw the herring of Celticism across the path, our movement will lose the only force that can bring success.'

Though Hyde himself hoped to join the Pan-Celtic General Committee, the party in the League which deprecated what Father Peter O'Leary called 'the Pan-Celtic humbug' was strong enough to dissuade him.[77] Moreover, the anti-Pan-Celts were soon plotting to replace *An Claidheamh Soluis* with a new organ to be edited by D. P. Moran, a Waterford Catholic pursuing a journalistic career in London who had been contributing a series of articles expounding his 'Irish Ireland' philosophy to the *New Ireland Review*.[78] Moran proposed to carry Hyde's philosophy of de-anglicisation to the logical conclusions which Hyde, in hopes of retaining support from his co-religionists, shrank from enunciating, though like Hyde he was relatively disinterested in 'politics'—except as an object of ridicule. Mastery of the language was essential, in his view, but it was only one of a number of ways in which Irishmen should purge themselves of 'West Britonism'. Though the effort to replace *An Claidheamh Soluis* failed, a new weekly paper, *The Leader,* was established in September 1900 under Moran's editorship. Among the symptoms of West Britonism which were attacked in its early issues were 'Gutter Literature' and the 'imported amusements' offered in Dublin's theatres and music halls.[79] Needless to say, such concern with sexual morality coincided with the preoccupations of many Catholic clergymen. The conception of 'the Irish mind' as 'chaste, idealistic, mystical', sullied only by 'the invading tide of English ideas', particularly those ideas embodied in 'trashy' periodicals,[80] was attractive to many clerics.

Hyde himself was adept at using this willingness of the clergy to associate the Irish language with Irish piety in his efforts to promote the language revival. At times he appealed to priests with the claim 'that with the decay of Irish went the Gael's devotion to the rosary'.[81] Moran departed from Hyde, however, in his definition of Irish nationality.

If an English Catholic does not like to live in a Protestant environment [*The Leader* declared], let him emigrate; if a non-Catholic Nationalist Irishman does not like to live in a Catholic atmosphere let him turn Orangeman, become a disciple of Dr. Long, or otherwise give up all pretence to being an Irish Nationalist. . . . We can conceive, and we have full tolerance for a Pagan or non-Catholic Irishman, but he must recognise, and have respect for the potent facts that are bound up with Irish Nationality.[82]

Protestant nationalists attracted little sympathy from Moran for their more inclusive brand of nationalism.[83] In the new climate represented by *The Leader* they generally lost interest in the movement, not seeing 'much use in national-izing Catholic Ireland . . . without nationalizing Protestant Ireland too'.[84] Some years later, A. E. Clery, a frequent con-tributor (under the pseudonym 'Chanel') to *The Leader,* recalled this general withdrawal of 'the Protestant settlers' from the movement without any apparent remorse.[85] The loss was, in his opinion, compensated for by the fact that *The Leader* 'had an immense influence in bringing the Catholic Church in Ireland wholeheartedly into the League, a tremendous accession of strength'. 'It is largely the work of *The Leader*', he maintained in 1919, 'that practically all the Catholic clergy of the twentieth century have been on the side of the Irish Ireland movement.'

Although the League did not formally abandon the non-sectarian, nonpolitical rule until 1915, *The Leader* was so closely identified with the League's cause that the rule had little practical effect except, perhaps, to keep the organisa-tion out of disputes between Catholics themselves over nat-ionalist political strategy. As the language movement of 1898 was transformed into the Irish Ireland movement of 1901, it assumed the character of an accepted organ of the Nation, alongside the Irish Parliamentary Party. This fact differen-tiated it from the teachers' organisation, which also divested itself, though less willingly, of meaningful Protestant par-ticipation in the same period. The teachers made no claim to represent the Nation or the State, and therefore the Church had no need to make terms with them over her vital inter-ests in education. As an organ of the Nation, however, the language movement was not rudely crushed like the teachers' organisation, but, like the Irish Parliamentary Party before it, was gently taught that it could enjoy rewards from the

Church if it tacitly accepted responsibilities. Its primary responsibility over the next few years would be as a popular pressure-group whenever it should suit the Church's purposes to adopt a hostile attitude toward the State in educational matters. Bishop O'Dwyer hinted at such a responsibility in a speech during the height of the League's agitation for National Board acceptance of the managers' memorial on bilingual instruction. Joining with so many of his colleagues in endorsing the language movement, and echoing the widely held belief that the National Board bore 'exceptional responsibilities' for the decline of the language, he observed that

The Board was peculiarly constituted. They were nominees of the Lord Lieutenant, and represented nobody, and the question of religious equality was observed by having an equal number of Catholics and Protestants on the Board; so, while there were 700,000 or 800,000 Catholic children on the register of National schools, and from 200,000 to 300,000 Protestants, it was considered equal and just treatment to have the Board thus composed half of Catholics and half of Protestants. That Board so constituted had done more than any agency in Ireland to kill our language. It should submit to criticism, and its actions should be under the control of public opinion in Ireland.[86]

The *Daily Nation*, no doubt purely for reasons of space, omitted these remarks in its report of the speech, but O'Dwyer probably considered them the most important part, for the next day's issue contained a correction, dutifully restoring the excised passage. Though O'Dwyer himself, one of the hierarchy's most doctrinaire champions of clerical claims in education, may have been spoiling for a fight, the time was not propitious for contesting the composition of the Board. In a few years, however, when such a tactic became advantageous to the Church, the Nation—that is the Gaelic League as well as the Irish Parliamentary Party—would rise to the occasion.

'Two United Irish Parties'

AT the same time that the role of the Irish Ireland movement as an organ of the Nation was being defined, the role of the Nation's dominant organ, the Irish Parliamentary Party, was being redefined. Since Parnell's fall in 1890 many churchmen had cherished hopes of a fundamental retrogression to the lopsided character of Irish politics before Parnell, in which 'national' interests were subordinate to 'Catholic' interests and clerical influence predominated over lay. Such hopes rested mainly upon T. M. Healy. Healy's special claims upon the political affections of many clergymen resulted in part from his active championship of Catholic interests at Westminster. At a time when English Liberalism was hostile to denominational claims in education, Healy was more willing than Dillon to forego friendship with the Liberals, the only party from which Home Rule could conceivably come, and to demand more loudly than Dillon a policy of independence from all English parties. Healy's real strength among clergymen, however, arose from his ideas on the proper structuring of Irish politics. In Parnell's time 'all the reins of power were gathered into the leader's hands'.[1] Parnell, though he consulted influential lieutenants, made the essential strategic decisions. Parnell controlled the party funds out of which members were paid. Parnell ordinarily made known to the constituencies whom he wished to have nominated, and his wishes were almost always respected. After the split Dillon wanted to perpetuate this system of strong central leadership, preferably with himself as leader. Healy argued in favour of much more democratic decision-making machinery within the party, and he proposed that members should be solely responsible to their constituencies,

which should be accorded complete freedom in choosing
their candidates. Churchmen who hoped to maintain a high
degree of clerical influence in political affairs were particularly attracted by the prospect of constituency autonomy, for
it was at the local level that clerical influence could most
effectively be exercised. Of course, the spectacle of the priest
marching his flock to the polls and virtually casting their
votes *en bloc* was now unlikely to occur. Most Irish constituencies, however, were seldom contested, and the really
important decision was made at the divisional convention.
When the 'priests and people' of a rural parish met to select
delegates to a divisional convention, one could rely upon the
priests to have a disproportionate voice in the selection. In
many districts it would be rare for a layman to challenge
openly the spiritual leadership of the parish in such a situation. Moreover, when the convention met, the clergy, though
in a minority, would be the most articulate and best organised group present. Unless the party's central authorities were
strong and willing to back a local lay revolt, the clergy in
many constituencies could feel fairly certain that their united
will would not be defied by the lay members of the convention. It was quite another matter for churchmen to try to
exert their influence directly upon national leaders. Unlike
the laymen who sat in local conventions, national leaders such
as Dillon were often strong-willed and articulate. They had
been to London and perhaps to America and had become
accustomed to patterns of behaviour in which exaggerated
deference to clerical desires played no part. Healy, therefore,
was holding out the prospect of maximum clerical influence
in political affairs.

The prospect could be credible only so long as the country
was quiet. As soon as widespread agrarian agitation recom-
menced in 1898, the clergy—especially the older, more conservative clergy who were attracted by the prospect—inevitably had to follow and if possible restrain, rather than lead.
O'Brien envisaged the U.I.L. fostering a public spirit which
would result in party unity. The League, he told Dillon late
in 1898, was creating 'a public opinion live, real, resolute,
not depending upon the priests on the one hand nor the
toleration of the *Independent* on the other for its existence

or growth'[2]—an allusion to the sources of Healyite and Parnellite opinion respectively. Unity, he maintained, would follow as a matter of course when the League had spread throughout the country. Dillon, not thoroughly convinced, turned his attention to negotiations with the Parnellites. During the ensuing year the various Nationalist factions engaged in a complex game of manoeuvre in the continual negotiations to bring about reunion, each leader trying to engineer the merger in such a fashion as to salvage as much as possible of his own influence. Professor Lyons has traced these manoeuvres in considerable detail.[3] By early 1900 Redmond and Healy were moving rapidly toward a unity arrangement. They shared a suspicion of alliance with the Liberals which provided an ideological link between them which did not exist between either of them and Dillon. Though Redmond and Healy might seem strange bedfellows because of their apparent divergence over a basic issue of internal nationalist politics—the political role of the clergy —Healy had confided to a friend as early as May 1899 that he 'never thought his [Redmond's] anti-clericalism more than skin deep'.[4] (Indeed, one might ask whether Healy's 'clericalism' was more than skin deep.) Healy conceded, however, that if, as was briefly mooted, Redmond were selected Chairman through the arbitration of the ageing Young Irelander, Sir Charles Gavan Duffy, 'the priests would not easily reconcile themselves', though most of his friends would favour Redmond over Dillon. Dillon lost the initiative to Redmond and Healy, and he was faced with the possibility that he would be excluded from influence in the reunited party. At joint meetings of the parties in late January and early February 1900 the details of reunion were worked out. Although it was understood that the new Chairman would be a Parnellite, Dillon hoped to swing the decision to some other Parnellite than Redmond. At the last moment O'Brien, who at this time was not an M.P. and was therefore excluded from direct participation, exerted pressure upon Dillon to support Redmond as a means of undermining Healy. Dillon was dubious of O'Brien's reasoning but acquiesced reluctantly, and on 6 February 1900 John Redmond was unanimously elected Chairman of the united Irish Parliamentary Party.

While the M.P.s were negotiating, O'Brien had continued to organise, and by early 1900 the League had spread well beyond the borders of Connacht. Outside Connacht, the intensity of economic misery dropped off rather sharply, and, concomitantly, the propensity of the clergy in the other three provinces to come to terms with the movement was not so strong, for its economic programme did not seem so compelling or so certain to capture popular sentiment with or without the clergy. In the three dioceses immediately beyond the ecclesiastical province of Tuam—Killaloe to the south and Kilmore and Ardagh and Clonmacnoise to the east—the League encountered serious clerical resistance such as it had hitherto met only in Killala.[5] Bishop Hoare of Ardagh and Clonmacnoise demonstrated his hostility to the League when Edward Blake, former Premier of Ontario who had become the Dillonite M.P. for South Longford, visited his constituency in January 1900, to address a large U.I.L. meeting. On previous visits to Longford, the police noted, Blake had always been entertained by Hoare, but this time the Bishop 'gave a large dinner party . . . to his clerical and lay friends' without inviting Blake and pointedly expressed to his guests his disapproval of certain League actions.[6] In the determination of clerical attitudes outside Connacht, however, there were more important factors than the League's methods for achieving its economic goals. By the end of 1899 a number of Parnellites were associating themselves with the League, and the movement was beginning to look like a coalition of Nationalist forces against T. M. Healy, who, alone among important Nationalist politicians, continued to hold aloof from it. This political colouration which the League was assuming did not prevent two prominent and sincerely nationalist prelates—the ageing Archbishop Croke of Cashel and his younger colleague, Bishop O'Donnell of Raphoe—from publicly endorsing the League during 1899.[7] Indeed, the anti-Healyite character of the League may have been attractive to these two ecclesiastics. They were both astute enough to realise that Healy's promise of easy clerical dominance in politics was illusory and that the League represented authentic aspirations of lay Catholics with which the Church must come to terms.

Cardinal Logue was slower to perceive the realities of the nationalist resurgence. In April 1900 he candidly revealed his thinking on the current political situation in reply to an address from the Belfast Catholic Association, a local political machine created on the Healyite model by Bishop Henry Henry of Down and Connor. The Association, in Logue's view, 'represented the principles on which . . . their country could find the source both of its spiritual and of its temporal welfare'.[8] From time to time the cry 'No Priest in Politics' was heard in Ireland, His Eminence continued, and of late

The priests had been crushed out to a certain extent, but they had not the less interest in the affairs of the country. It suited them sometimes to let young giants try their strength and see what they could do for themselves. He thought there was now less attention to registration and the money was not flowing in so far, and the prospects of the political parties in the country somehow did not appear to be so flourishing since they appeared to endeavour to carry out that great principle of no priest in politics (*applause*).[9]

The Cardinal was absurdly underestimating the power of the reunited party, founded as it was upon the U.I.L. The League organisers worked furiously during the months following the reunion to spread the organisation into the eastern and southern parts of the country. Though a sharp rise during 1900 in the number of branches known to police probably reflected mainly the absorption of old National League and National Federation branches,[10] the new organisation possessed a dynamism which had long been lost by those older bodies. Plans were being laid for a Nationalist Convention to be held in June under U.I.L. auspices. In May T. C. Harrington, one of the former Parnellites, expressed to Redmond his misgivings about the dominant role which the League would play in the convention and his fears not only that their own former supporters would be almost unrepresented, but that clergy hostile to the League would be alienated from the party. 'The Cardinal and his priests are very indignant that they should have their people excluded from the convention,' he wrote, 'and it is quite on the cards that they will probably repudiate the whole proceeding.'[11] Redmond had the difficult task of trying to balance such considerations as this with the obvious fact that the League would be the dominant factor in Nationalist politics for the foreseeable future. Indeed, when the Convention met in June, the League, predictably, was proclaimed the official Nationalist organisation. Redmond accepted the League presidency from the Convention, while Healy practically ignored the entire proceeding and kept his own skeletal organisation, the People's Rights Association, in existence. The stage was thus set for a direct confrontation between Healy and the League, and—though Redmond continued to try to be scrupulously fair to Healy—the Healyites were left to face the League alone in the general election of September and October 1900.

It is not possible to divide the membership of the former Anti-Parnellite party into Dillonites and Healyites with absolute precision. Healy's group consisted of his 'friends', and the strength of individual friendships varied with time and circumstances. The best available indication of just who the Healyites were is provided by Healy's list of the twenty-five M.P.s who voted with him in an 1895 Anti-Parnellite party meeting when he tried to force publication of certain correspondence concerning arrangements to allow the Liberals to contest several northern seats without Nationalist interference.[12] Healy's strength lay primarily in Ulster and Leinster. It would be dangerous, however, to attempt to generalise about the reasons for geographic concentrations of Healyites, for many of them had held their seats without Dillonite opposition since before the split. Because the constant threat of Parnellite opposition had made it unwise for Dillon to challenge Healy at the polls, the geographic distribution of Healyites was probably more fortuitous than indicative of the sentiments of the electorate. Nevertheless, that distribution is important, for the clergy in the divisions held by Healyites tended to put up the strongest resistance to the League.

In the 1900 election Healyism was most resilient in northern Leinster and in the part of Ulster which lay on the ill-defined border between Catholic and Protestant districts. In three seats—Newry, North Monaghan and Mid-Tyrone—where a Nationalist split might have allowed a Unionist victory, Healy's colleagues were left undisturbed. Five other

Healyite seats lay in Cardinal Logue's diocese of Armagh and in the neighbouring diocese of Meath which had a strong tradition of active clerical involvement in politics, exemplified by a famous dictum of the late Bishop Nulty in 1892:

No man can remain a Catholic as long as he elects to cling to Parnellism. The dying Parnellite himself will hardly dare to face the justice of his Maker till he has been prepared and anointed by us for the last awful struggle and the terrible judgment that will immediately follow it.[13]

Neither Nulty's successor, Bishop Gaffney, nor Cardinal Logue left any doubt as to their sentiments in the 1900 contests. When the League Directory dispatched a Protestant Nationalist, E. Haviland Burke, to North Louth to oppose Healy himself, one of Logue's canons declared that Healy's candidature 'had the warm approval of his Eminence Cardinal Logue'.[14] He cited a letter from the Cardinal deploring the opposition to Healy and expressing the hope that the constituency would resent the contest 'if any electoral liberty was left in the country'. Similarly, when the North Westmeath clergy deliberately absented themselves from the divisional League convention, which nominated Laurence Ginnell, and held their own convention, which nominated the Healyite sitting member, P. J. Kennedy, Bishop Gaffney publicly endorsed Kennedy's candidacy, saying: 'It would be a woeful day for Ireland if we had only one newspaper, one ruler, or even a triumvirate—and this is the goal that is sought.'[15] In South Armagh, the clergy did attend the official convention, but when they found that they could not command a majority in favour of the candidate they preferred, they walked out and ran their own candidate in opposition to the convention's nominee.[16] At a convention for South Westmeath, where the U.I.L. was quite weak, League delegates tried to extract a pledge from Donal Sullivan, the Healyite sitting member, that he would join the League. They had to be satisfied, however, with a promise that he would join when the priests of the constituency did so—a rather empty gesture, as the clergy of the diocese were rigidly abstaining from League activities and the clergy present at the convention made it plain that their hostility was unlikely to abate.[17] Sullivan therefore had a walkover, and the 'clerical'

candidates in North Louth, South Armagh and North Westmeath defeated their League rivals by comfortable, if not
overwhelming, margins. In only one division in this region
—North Meath—was a Healyite candidate, enjoying strong
clerical backing, defeated, and his defeat was by a rather
narrow margin.[18] In the area from Tyrone to Westmeath,
therefore, the forces of Healyism managed to retain seven
out of eight seats—three of them by default because of the
danger of triangular contests, but four because of active and
vigorous clerical support.

Outside this region only two Healyites survived the election—J. Hammond in Carlow and P. Ffrench in South Wexford. Both constituencies, significantly, were in the extreme
south-eastern corner of Ireland where the League did not
yet effectively exist. According to Redmond there was not
yet a single branch of the League in Co. Wexford,[19] and the
list of delegates to the Carlow convention contained the
names of only four U.I.L. representatives, all from the same
village.[20] Obviously the League was not in a position to
challenge clerical desires in this area. No opposition was
offered to Hammond who was renominated on the recommendation of Bishop Foley of Kildare and Leighlin. The
opposition of Foley's clergy to the League was common
knowledge,[21] and though he insisted that his priests were
free to join it so long as it did not violate specified ecclesiastical regulations, the Bishop stated that he would not at present
subscribe to League funds and expressed the hope that
eventually Redmond might be able to assure that these funds
would 'be used for more worthy purposes than the support
of . . . [U.I.L.] candidates . . . no matter who they happen
to be'. Only then, Foley maintained, would 'the whole
Nationalist body be prepared to do their part'.[22] Since
Redmond had been the leader of the supposedly anticlerical
party during the previous decade, this expression of hope
that he would prevail against what were now regarded as
anticlerical forces is significant. The hope was not entirely
without foundation, for it was apparently through Redmond's
direct intervention that no opposition was offered to Ffrench,
the Healyite member for South Wexford,[23] though he was
unable to prevent opposition to Healy's own brother, T. J.

Healy, in North Wexford. This latter contest, however, was promoted not by the U.I.L., but by a dissident section of the local clergy. In a curious contest, in which each candidate was backed by a substantial contingent of priests, T. J. Healy lost to Sir Thomas H. Grattan Esmonde by more than two to one.[24] This result demonstrated very clearly how dependent the Healyites were upon united, unequivocal clerical support.

A more significant instance of Healy's dependence upon the clergy was Co. Donegal, where three of the four seats were in the hands of his friends. Bishop O'Donnell, whose diocese of Raphoe covered most of the county, had been an early supporter of the U.I.L., and after the party was re-united he agreed to become one of the trustees of the Parliamentary Fund. O'Donnell seems to have had some difficulty in leading his clergy away from Healyism and toward support for the U.I.L.,[25] and even at the time of the election there was some indication of clerical dissatisfaction with the policy the Bishop was pursuing.[26] Nevertheless, a U.I.L. convention for East Donegal, attended by fifteen priests and furnished with a letter of support from O'Donnell, rejected the sitting member, Arthur O'Connor, one of Healy's ablest associates, in favour of a Mr McFadden.[27] Similarly, in West Donegal, Healy's father-in-law, T. D. Sullivan, author of 'God Save Ireland' (and brother of Donal Sullivan, M.P. for South Westmeath) found that the Bishop and some of the priests of the division opposed his candidacy.[28] Sullivan prudently retired from active politics, but O'Connor tried to seek refuge in the other Healyite seat in the county, North Donegal, which lay mainly outside the diocese of Raphoe. Despite clerical opposition to the League and its candidate in the part of the division which lay in Derry diocese, O'Connor was defeated by 2,562 votes to 1,613.[29]

In several other constituencies scattered throughout the country the clergy vainly fought to restrain the U.I.L. tide. Healy dispatched the wealthy Nationalist William Martin Murphy to North Mayo which had been represented by his friend Dan Crilly in the previous parliament. Murphy launched his campaign against the League nominee, Conor O'Kelly, by dining with the Bishop, Dr Conmy, and the Killala clergy vigorously championed Murphy's cause. Both

sides threw their top leadership into the contest, which was
a straight fight—Healy and the clergy *versus* O'Brien and
the League.[30] The League, as the clergy should have realised,
was absolutely invincible in the West, and it won easily,
2,504 votes to 1,116. The two-member Cork City constituency
experienced a contest between a U.I.L. slate composed of
William O'Brien himself and one of the sitting members,
J. F. X. O'Brien, and a Healyite slate consisting of the other
sitting member, Maurice Healy (T. M. Healy's brother) and
an Alderman J. C. Blake (a former Parnellite). Although the
two O'Briens were accompanied on their campaign rounds
by a handful of curates, the Dean of Cork and other influential clergy were ranged on the Healyite side.[31] O'Brien had
wanted to challenge Maurice Healy in 1895, believing that
his own popularity in the city would offset the danger of
Parnellite opposition,[32] and he may have been correct, for in
the 1900 election he and his colleague defeated the Healyite
slate by more than two to one. In North Kildare the clergy
failed in an attempt to retain the Healyite member, C. J.
Engledow,[33] who lost by 1,461 votes to 1,229, but the most
pathetic clerical effort in the country was in Mid-Tipperary.
If Archbishop Croke had been younger and in fuller command of his faculties, he no doubt would not have allowed
his clergy to walk out of a League convention and put forward
their own candidate only to be defeated by the ridiculous
margin of 2,316 to 587.[34] A similar result might have been
expected in nearly every western and southern constituency
if the clergy had not generally been wiser than the Mid-
Tipperary priests.

The Church was divided not so much over the principle of
retaining a clerical voice in political affairs as over the most
expedient means of achieving that purpose. Cardinal Logue
—who, according to Healy, had 'told a priest who attended
a meeting of the O'Brien League . . . that, as he had been
obliged to "suspend" him once already, he hoped he would
not compel him to repeat the process!'[35]—represented the
view that the Church's political influence could best be
maintained by concerted application of the clergy's power.
The Church should refuse to recognise forces which did not
show due deference to her authority and thereby crush them

out. The contrary view, which most of the western bishops had adopted, and which was most effectively represented by Bishop O'Donnell's active participation in the reunited party's national organisation, was that the popular forces embodied in the League could not be crushed. The fact that these forces were rejecting the clergy's client, Healy, need not entail hostility to the Church, but such hostility might well develop if the Church took the inflexible stand favoured by Logue. The divergence between Logue and O'Donnell apparently resulted in some personal ill-feeling on the Cardinal's part, for Healy confided to his brother on 3 October: 'Cardinal Logue is bitter against Bishop O'Donnell for his conduct towards T. D. Sullivan, and says it is disgraceful.'[36] Logue in fact felt so strongly on the subject that he, along with Bishop Gaffney of Meath, gave active support to a movement to raise a testimonial fund for Sullivan.[37] It should be noted in Logue's favour, however, that his policy of unstinting support for those whom he regarded as the Church's faithful friends did not seem entirely unrealistic within his own diocese and the neighbouring territory. In this region only one Healyite had suffered defeat.

The Healyite M.P.s themselves could see beyond their own constituencies, however, and except for Healy they generally made their peace with the national organisation after the election. Nevertheless, O'Brien and Dillon could not abide Healy's continued presence in the reunited party, and at a Nationalist Convention in December he was solemnly expelled despite the strong opposition of T. C. Harrington, one of the former Parnellites, and the mild opposition of Redmond.[38] The expulsion gave rise to a public letter from the Dean of Armagh, suggesting that 'Now that the great convention has come and gone . . . it is about time that the Irish priesthood should give to the world their opinions on the subject for which it was held.'[39] The Dean expressed the hope that his fellow priests did not have the 'political ingratitude' to sympathise with O'Brien's 'vendetta' against Healy, who had 'fought our fight when O'Brien and Dillon were skulking in Galway gaol to escape the expression of a manly opinion on Parnellism'. He had an interesting suggestion:

Let there be an address of confidence in Tim Healy's political honesty and competency expressive of gratitude for past services to the cause of his country, drafted and submitted for signature to every priest in Ireland. Such an address . . . will remove to a great extent the waspish sting inflicted on him by men who envy him the possession of abilities and brains which have so often thrown in the shade their own puny efforts at statesmanship.[40]

Not a word of the Dean's letter cast aspersion directly upon Redmond, who had, after all, expressed a 'manly opinion' on Parnellism, albeit not the opinion which found favour with the clergy. The ecclesiastical authorities realised that they had more to fear from their unsubmissive friends than from their former openly avowed enemies in the political arena.

Redmond's ability to command clerical confidence was already being tested, for on 1 December 1900 one of Healy's friends, Dan MacAleese, who had been left undisturbed in North Monaghan for fear of a triangular contest, had died. All the principals of Irish politics had begun to manoeuvre for position in the constituency. Bishop Owens of Clogher instructed his administrator, Father Keown, to write to Redmond urging him to 'take the earliest available opportunity of moving for the writ' for the impending by-election, an action which would, in Father Keown's words, 'tend to remove any friction that might possibly arise in the selection by the constituency of a Nationalist Candidate'.[41] The anticipated source of such friction was, of course, the League, which would require some time to dispatch its organisers and promote the cause of some candidate of its choosing. Redmond replied immediately, undertaking to move for the writ 'at the earliest practicable opportunity, probably next week'.[42] On the strength of this assurance, a convention was called by the local U.I.L. executive (which was apparently on good terms with the clergy) for 18 December, 'the only day during the month on which priests and people could conveniently meet'. When this decision was communicated to the central executive of the U.I.L. in Dublin, the local executive was apparently advised that the summoning of conventions rested with the national headquarters. Father Keown appealed to

Redmond to sustain the decision for the early convention, protesting that they were acting according to published League regulations.[43] When, in spite of this appeal and further representations to League headquarters, the national U.I.L. authorities publicly disavowed the call for a convention on 18 December, Father Keown was indignant and fearful that the constituency would be 'forced to spend an indefinite period of time in turmoil and confusion'. He expressed his hope that even yet Redmond would have the convention held as early as possible.[44] On the same day that Father Keown wrote this appeal, Healy turned the tables by moving for the writ in the House of Commons,[45] and the sheriff accommodatingly fixed 21 December—the earliest legal date—for nominations.[46]

O'Brienite plans for delivering another blow to Healyism were thrown into turmoil by Healy's clever manoeuvre—a manoeuvre which the clergy had hoped Redmond would undertake himself. In the next four days Healyites campaigned vigorously for a Mr O'Hare,[47] whom one priest described to Redmond as 'the creature or nominee of no man', adding, however, that O'Hare was 'recommended strongly by the Bishop, Dr Owens'.[48] The League staked its hopes on Daniel O'Donnell, who despite his being the brother of Bishop O'Donnell of Raphoe, 'was severely heckled by the local priests'. League organisers were physically assaulted by O'Hare's partisans, but the unkindest cut came in the form of a telegram from Bishop O'Donnell disapproving his brother's candidature[49] and thus wrecking League strategy. Redmond went personally to Monaghan on 19 December to preside at a convention and 'was met at the railway station by a large crowd of Roman Catholic priests and delegates'.[50] The party leader did his best to patch up the situation. A compromise was worked out by which O'Hare withdrew and a Dr E. C. Thompson was selected by the convention.[51] Thompson was a former Unionist who had switched his political allegiance and had narrowly failed to defeat T. W. Russell, the Liberal Unionist M.P. for South Tyrone, in the general election. After his defeat, one of Redmond's clerical friends in Tyrone had urged the Party Chairman to find a safe seat for Thompson.[52] *The Times* reported that the compromise upon Thompson was 'regarded as a mitigated victory for Mr. Healy',[53] though perhaps almost anything could be construed as a victory for a politician who had just been so rudely deprived of his influence in national affairs. The incident was rather a victory for Mr Redmond—an individual whom commentators were not yet taking into sufficient account as an independent political force.

The task facing the new leader was to create a unified political organisation, effectively grounded in the realities of Irish society. The ill-feeling between the League and many clergymen transcended the political conflict between Healy and O'Brien, both of whom were to drift to the fringes of Irish politics within the next few years and be drawn into a strange alliance based on their common isolation from political power. The dominance of the Church in Irish rural life made almost inevitable a sense of frustration on the part of young men of ambition among the lower classes. A generation earlier such men had gravitated into pathetic secret protest movements. Now they found a place in the United Irish League, and the suspicions they aroused were well illustrated by the remark of a Westmeath parish priest to Donal Sullivan that he would have nothing to do with the League 'until it is manned and managed properly'. At Redmond's request, Sullivan had written to the parish priests of his constituency suggesting the starting of parochial collections for the Parliamentary Fund. As the only member of Healy's family connection who had successfully weathered the U.I.L. storm, Sullivan no doubt took a certain pleasure in passing on to Redmond their disappointing replies. Only one priest expressed an unambiguously favourable response, and the consensus was best voiced by a clergyman who wrote:

Mr. Arthur O'Connor, Mr. Maurice Healy, and Mr. T. D. Sullivan having been driven from Parliament by the U.I.L. to the irreparable loss of all catholics and Irish interests, after this lamentable occurrence I told my parishioners that I shall never touch the U.I.L. as long as it was under the guidance and control of Mr Wm O'Brien, Mr John Dillon and Mr Michael Davitt. Much as I respect yourself and Mr Redmond, I feel I cannot alter my resolution.[54]

Perhaps this last remark—a mild expression of confidence

in the former Parnellite leader—is the most significant feature of the letter. Redmond was particularly fitted for the task of mediating between the divergent strains of clericalism and anticlericalism in Irish politics. Though his leadership of the Parnellites had placed him at the very centre of the conflict, he was personally above it. Drawn from a Catholic gentry family which had become successful in commerce and continental military service after dispossession in the seventeenth century, Redmond had never been caught up in the pattern of exaggerated deference to the clergy against which so many of his colleagues were revolting. He was, moreover, a man of unimpeachable moral character and great personal dignity who commanded the respect of even those who became his bitter enemies. The Monaghan controversy was an early example of his efforts to steer the party out of the self-destructive course into which either Healy or O'Brien would undoubtedly have led it if either had won unchallenged hegemony. On the morning he left Monaghan, Redmond tried to soothe Father Keown's injured feelings with a promise that he 'would suggest to the [U.I.L.] Directory to pass a resolution thanking the people of Monaghan for their action & saying that the trouble arose from a misunderstanding'.[55] When the Directory did not meet for several weeks and Father Keown protested that Redmond had not honoured his pledge,[56] Redmond, perhaps anxious to avoid a showdown in the Directory, tried to satisfy Father Keown by offering to make a personal public statement on behalf of the League and the party.[57] At this point Father Keown not only rejected the suggestion of a public statement from Redmond, but made clear that he would be satisfied with nothing less than some humiliating act of contrition on the part of the Directory or its Standing Committee.[58] This Redmond could not impose consistently with his efforts to mete out even-handed justice between clerical and anticlerical forces, and he put an end to the correspondence with a letter expressing his own sorrow at the continued bitterness in the constituency.[59]

Outside this troublesome border area between Ulster and Leinster, where Healyism had been strongest, Redmond and the united party had better prospects for building strong relations with the Church. Early in the general election campaign Walsh had telegraphed a guarantee of £50—an extraordinary amount, for the usual gesture at this time was £10 or perhaps 10 guineas—to the party's General Election Fund.[60] The Archbishop corresponded very frequently with Redmond at this time about matters before parliament. Dr Sheehan, the Bishop of Redmond's own constituency, Waterford, was often the medium through which the Episcopal Standing Committee, of which he was secretary, communicated their desires to Redmond, but he did not limit correspondence with the Party Chairman to such official matters. He did not hesitate to seek Redmond's assistance on local problems. By far the most important contact between the hierarchy and the party, however, was Bishop O'Donnell. In their capacities as trustees of the Parliamentary Fund, he and Redmond were in very close touch with each other, and the Bishop of Raphoe was to become a very valuable ally and advisor to the party leadership.

The election and its aftermath had produced, in Healy's phrase, 'two united Irish parties—of which I am one'.[61] Excluding Healy (but including T. P. O'Connor, the party's perennial member from the Irish ghetto in Liverpool) the party had eighty-one members. Though the sincerity of the submission of some former Healyites might be questioned, the party was generally able to act as a unit once again. Unity, for the time being, was of little parliamentary consequence, for the Conservatives and their Liberal Unionist allies had been returned to power with 402 seats against only 186 Liberals, so neither English party had any reason to bargain for Irish votes. Of greater significance was the fact that the Church's relations with the Nation had returned to an equilibrium similar to, though not identical with, that which had been upset in 1890–91. The Church tacitly recognised the integrity of the Nation as an institution distinct from herself. Laymen, not clerics, would bear the responsibility for establishing the Nation's strategy and tactics. Their efforts, and their support in the country, would not be undermined by the very considerable power at the Church's command provided that they played by the rules, which were that they should protect and strive to enlarge the Church's role in education and that they should rely solely upon 'constitutional' methods to achieve the Nation's objectives. This latter condition did not, to be sure, have quite the same import as it had two decades earlier. In the 1880s the Church had associated herself with the Parnell movement as a constitutional alternative to the revolutionary nationalism which still claimed the allegiance of a number of Irishmen. By 1901 revolutionary nationalism was moribund, though it was, of course, to undergo a miraculous recovery.

To understand the significance of this fact, we should examine a difference between the State and the Nation. By the late nineteenth century power in the State was held alternately by two political parties, the Conservatives (or Conservative-Liberal-Unionist coalition) and the Liberals. Of course, any satisfactory description of British politics would make reference to the process by which this procedure had emerged from a very different pattern of politics in the eighteenth and early nineteenth centuries. Nevertheless, at the beginning of the present century, the party system was the established mode of politics in the State. Was there an analogous mode of changing leadership in the Nation? Of course, there was not a party system in the sense that two (or more) parties, each having a continuity longer than the normal career of a single politician, vied for the temporary possession of such a prize as the government. There were, however, parties in the Nation throughout the nineteenth century. One might describe the divisions between parties in nationalist Ireland in two ways, neither of which is wholly satisfactory, but which together can give us a fair approximation of the truth. Firstly, there was a dichotomy during the whole history of the Union, between those nationalists who sought Irish self-government through revolutionary violence—or, to use the quaint Irish term, 'physical force'—and those who sought virtually the same goal through non-violent and constitutional agitation. Secondly, there was a recurrent pattern by which the national leaders, especially those of the 'constitutional' variety, were replaced quite suddenly by new leadership a full generation younger. This happened about every thirty to forty years: around 1812 in the emergence of Daniel O'Connell as leader of the Catholic cause, in the mid-1840s with the rise of Young Ireland and the death of O'Connell, in the late 1870s with the rise of Parnell, and during the First World War when Sinn Féin replaced the party Parnell had founded. There is nothing mysterious about this generational mode of succession to the national leadership. As long as a premium was placed on presenting an unbroken front to the real enemy, the English, intra-national differences had to be suppressed. Inevitably, younger potential leadership would emerge but be denied the leadership role. When an opportunity presented itself, as must eventually happen in the due process of time, they would wrest leadership from their seniors. This pattern is least clear during the generation between O'Connell's and Parnell's leadership, when constitutional nationalism was in disarray and the other description of nationalist divisions—revolutionary *versus* constitutional rather than generation *versus* generation—is most germane. During these years the Church had made plain her insistence upon constitutional methods and had thus helped to confirm the generational pattern of political succession in the Nation.

The generational pattern of succession in the Nation's politics was dictated by the Nation's relationships on the one hand with the State—to which its representatives had to appear implacably hostile—and on the other hand with the Church—which insisted that it abjure violence. The conventions which governed the political system of Church, State and Nation also dictated another salient feature of the system which was reconfirmed between 1898 and 1901. If the Nation's representatives must show irreconcilable opposition toward the State and, at the same time, not question the claims of the Church in education, they could only write off (except for rhetorical purposes) any hope of converting the Protestant North to nationalism. In other words, the territory of the Irish political system embraced those areas with a Catholic majority and no more. Since 1885 this fact had been symbolised by the fact that some eighty of Ireland's 103 parliamentary constituencies were safe Nationalist seats which Unionists and Liberals seldom bothered to contest. When the Irish Ireland movement made most of its Protestant members unwelcome around 1900, it was accepting the territorial limitation which went with being an organ of the Nation. Most Gaelic Leaguers seem to have been receptive or indifferent to this reality, but its acceptance was a necessary concomitant of their achieving the Church's sanction as a legitimate organ of the Nation. The teachers' organisation was learning the hard way the impossibility of being an active champion of the Church's educational demands and retaining the sympathy of even liberal-minded Protestants. The Nation's younger generation thus was brought into the political system under the same rules as its predecessor.

The events of 1898–1901 made it clear, moreover, that Parnell's own generation—for Redmond, Dillon and O'Brien were only a few years his juniors—intended to retain leadership for their full term of years. Despite their successes with the Belmullet Poor Law Union, Maud Gonne and James Connolly had been quickly eclipsed by the political adults. Their time had not yet come. At the very time when the generational pattern of succession was thus being reconfirmed and the Church was readjusting her relations with its present beneficiaries, the Church was also making her peace with the next organised generation of the Nation. An entry in the monthly confidential report of the Inspector-General of the Royal Irish Constabulary for September 1903 conveys the situation succinctly, albeit through the distorting medium of police thinking: 'The Gaelic League continues to be generally under clerical control. It is made up for the most part of women and children.'[62] Children eventually become adults.

CHAPTER III

Ideals and Interests

THE Church's readjustment of her relationships with the Nation between 1898 and 1901 was of crucial long-term significance. For the moment, however, the Nation was clearly not going to supplant the State in the foreseeable future. Power in the State had not changed hands in the 1900 general election, and the Unionists, whose sole point of un-qualified agreement was the denial of the Irish Nation's claim, had been returned with a margin over the Liberals much greater than the Irish Parliamentary Party's numbers. The Church, therefore, continued to seek the proximate realisation of her social ideals and to protect and extend her vital interests primarily through her relations with the State, though the course of these relations would inevitably have important consequences for her relations with the Nation as well.

The one concession which the Church was most anxious to obtain from the State was a publicly endowed university for Catholics. In the 1830s the Church had, with initial mis-givings, accepted the State's establishment of a formally non-sectarian system of primary schools and by working within the system during succeeding decades had transformed it into an essentially denominational system fully consonant with her own interests. By the mid-1840s, when the State attempted to repeat the experiment at the level of higher education by establishing three formally nondenominational Queen's Colleges at Belfast, Cork and Galway, more insular men were coming to dominate the hierarchy. By a very nar-row margin in the National Synod of Thurles in 1850, the Church rejected the State's overture by condemning the so-called 'godless colleges'. She thereby forfeited the opportunity to transform the Cork and Galway colleges into essentially Catholic institutions as she so successfully transformed her share of the National education system into essentially Catholic schools. A Catholic university college founded in St Stephen's Green, Dublin, under the rectorship of John Henry Newman struggled along on meagre voluntary support while the bishops agitated for a State endowment and a royal charter which would validate its degrees. These efforts were unsuccessful, though in the course of considering Catholic claims parliament did abolish the last remaining religious tests in Trinity College, Dublin, in 1873—a gesture which in the bishops' view did not detract from the strength of their claims. Finally in 1879 a Conservative government forged a temporary settlement by establishing the Royal University of Ireland, essentially an examining body empowered to confer degrees upon students of the Queen's Colleges, University College, Dublin (the Catholic college in St Stephen's Green), and, in fact, any other institution or no institution at all. As several fellowships connected with the Royal University were regularly assigned to members of the teaching staff of University College, that institution, which the bishops now placed in the care of the Jesuit fathers, did receive a certain underhand State endowment. Because this endowment was quite small compared with the funds enjoyed by Trinity and the Queen's Colleges, the bishops continued to agitate for a settlement in which 'one or more colleges conducted on purely Catholic principles' might fully participate 'in all the privileges and emoluments enjoyed by other colleges, of whatsoever denomination or character'.[1]

For Conservative politicians, raising the Irish university question was a possible way of winning the bishops away from popular agitation. The concession of the Royal University was made at the height of the 'land war' of the late 1870s. Moreover, in the late 1880s the government gave a sympathetic hearing to suggestions from conservative Catholics, including Bishops Healy and O'Dwyer, for an endowed Catholic college as a kind of bribe to draw the Irish Church out of Parnell's camp.[2] After Parnell's fall, however, Conservative politicians saw no need to play this valuable trump card, and Liberal politicians, who held office from 1892 to

1895, basing their Irish policy on a futile second attempt to enact Home Rule, ignored the university question. With the return of the Conservatives to office, the bishops tried with scant success to resurrect the issue. Arthur James Balfour did offer encouragement to a Liberal private member, Richard Haldane, who in 1898 drafted and obtained ecclesiastical sanction for an Irish university scheme to forestall Irish opposition to his own scheme for reform of the University of London.[3] Balfour's cabinet colleagues would not support the Prime Minister's initiative, however, and the government made no further advances on the subject before 1901. By that time the U.I.L. agitation for division of the grazing lands was beginning to attract attention in England, and the Conservatives once again had a sound political reason for raising the university question.

In the summer of 1901 a Royal Commission was appointed, under the chairmanship of Lord Robertson, 'to inquire into the present condition of the higher, general and technical education available in Ireland outside Trinity College, Dublin, and to report as to what reforms, if any, are desirable in order to render that education adequate to the needs of the Irish People'.[4] The phrase 'adequate to the needs of the Irish People' was obviously intended to mean something like 'consistent with the minimum demands of the Irish bishops', and the Commission tacitly construed it in substantially that sense. One other phrase in the terms of reference was more difficult to interpret. Did 'outside Trinity College, Dublin' mean 'outside the University of Dublin' (of which Trinity was the sole constituent college)? The question was not trivial, for as recently as November 1900 Archbishop Walsh had written in a public letter:

I have never concealed my personal preference for the settlement of our University question on the basis (1) of one National University for Ireland, a University, of course, so constructed as to provide the maximum of possible freedom for all its colleges. Failing that, a settlement on the basis (2) of the establishment of a second college in the University of Dublin has always seemed to me a good solution of the problem.[5]

Both these solutions, Walsh stressed, had been considered by the hierarchy and deemed satisfactory, though, of course, the establishment of 'a separate University for Catholics' was preferred. In particular, Walsh made it quite clear that he was definitely opposed to proposals for an endowed Catholic college within 'the so-called Royal "University"'. If 'outside Trinity College, Dublin', meant 'outside the University of Dublin', then the Commission could recommend neither of the two solutions which Walsh preferred, and, since the hierarchy's ideal of a separate Catholic university (or 'University for Catholics' as Walsh carefully phrased it) was generally regarded as unattainable, the Commission would probably be driven to recommend precisely the reform Walsh deprecated.

Not all the prelates shared Walsh's views on the university question. Indeed, in 1873 the hierarchy had spurned an offer by Gladstone which closely resembled Walsh's first alternative, and the desire, reflected in that action, to hold out for a solution involving maximum Catholic autonomy still survived among some of Walsh's opponents within the hierarchy. The episcopal enemies of Walsh's scheme made an effective move on the second day of the Commission's hearings. Bishop O'Dwyer was giving evidence on behalf of the hierarchy, and when he reached the point in his prepared statement at which he proposed to outline alternative solutions which could be made acceptable to Catholics he was interrupted by Bishop Healy, who was a member of the Commission. Referring to an outline of his statement which Bishop O'Dwyer had handed to the Commission, Healy asked: 'Is it necessary to discuss the question here, under Section B, of an endowed Catholic College, which would be on the same lines as Trinity College, under a great national University— is it necessary to discuss that here?' 'That', replied O'Dwyer, 'is for the Chairman to decide.' Lord Robertson at first seemed inclined to let O'Dwyer proceed according to his outline:

330. CHAIRMAN.—As I understand, you are merely adumbrating the possible changes which might be made?—What I want to do is this: I want to bring out as clearly as I can the underlying idea in our mind of getting equality with people who have already institutions in existence, and I am discussing the various ways in which possibly, that equality might be attained.

331. I understand, if I read aright your notes, that you put this scheme forward in order to reject it?—No, no, my lord; I put it forward not to reject it; but I put it forward for consideration, and I point out the *pros* and *cons* of it as they occur to me. I see a good deal in favour of it, and I see a good deal against it.[6]

At this point Robertson asked O'Dwyer to withdraw, and after ten minutes O'Dwyer was recalled and advised that 'The Commission consider that what you proposed to speak upon is not within the terms of their Reference.'

The decision which was made during those ten minutes was the most important one which the Commission reached. They chose to regard Trinity College as indistinguishable from the University of Dublin for the purposes of their investigation, and they never wavered from this determination despite the assurance of Wyndham, the Chief Secretary, to Robertson, in the presence of Dr W. J. M. Starkie, that the terms of reference 'were intended to include the University of Dublin'.[7] Since Walsh clearly preferred a scheme which would associate Catholic and Protestant students in the capital in one university, though not, of course, in one college, and since the hierarchy had considered such schemes and deemed them 'satisfactory', O'Dwyer, as the hierarchy's principal spokesman before the Commission was, no doubt, obligated to present such schemes as acceptable alternatives. These schemes, however, embodied just enough of the ideal of 'mixed' education to arouse the suspicions of prelates like O'Dwyer and Healy, who in the 1880s had looked upon Walsh as a dangerous radical. Clearly Walsh's old enemies within the hierarchy, Healy and O'Dwyer, were deliberately forcing the issue at an early stage in the Commission's deliberations to exclude Walsh's ideal from the purview of the inquiry.

When the first volume of the Commission's evidence was published late in 1901, there was a wave of disappointment. The *Freeman's Journal,* in articles reviewing the volume,[8] deplored the exclusion of Dublin University from consideration and the implication that some solution within the discredited 'Royal' would be recommended. The *Freeman's* attitude, though buttressed by extracts from various episcopal pronouncements, was attacked by the Rev. William Delany,

S.J.,[9] who as President of U.C.D. was spokesman for the Jesuit interest in that institution, and by the *Daily Independent*,[10] which, under the direction of William Martin Murphy, was becoming an exponent of Healyism. Nevertheless, the *Freeman* received indirect support from a very influential quarter in February 1902 when Walsh published in the *Irish Ecclesiastical Record* the first of two articles demonstrating by extensive legal research that Trinity College and the University of Dublin were juridically distinct institutions. In a letter published in the *Freeman* on 10 February the Archbishop made it clear that his researches were prompted not by a disinterested historical curiosity, but by the fear that the Commission would be driven to recommend 'the College-in-the-Royal-University plan of settlement'.[11] Meanwhile, a committee of Catholic laymen circulated a petition in favour of 'the establishment and endowment of a College in Dublin for Catholic students, affiliated to the University of Dublin'. The *Independent* belittled the movement as the effort of 'a small drawingroom meeting',[12] but the petition was forwarded to the Commission with over four hundred signatures.[13] When asked for his opinion on the committee's efforts, O'Dwyer carefully avoided rejecting the Dublin University solution on its merits, but strongly questioned the wisdom of raising the issue and perhaps weakening the Commission's hand in its efforts to propose a solution which would gain acceptance.[14]

The Commission did allow the eminent Catholic jurist, Christopher Palles, Lord Chief Baron of the Exchequer in Ireland, to give evidence in favour of a Catholic college in Dublin University. Presumably because Walsh had caused such a stir by his publications, he was invited to give evidence as well, but he declined, saying tactfully:

It would be impossible for me to add to the force of the evidence given at the opening of the Commission by the Bishop of Limerick, with whose views, in so far as he had an opportunity of expressing them, I am in full concurrence. In saying this it is right for me to add that on one important aspect of the case, upon which the Bishop of Limerick had not an opportunity of expressing his views, and which, as I gather from the published evidence, is not to be taken account of in the Report of the

Commission, the Lord Chief Baron has said everything that I should wish to say.[15]

Walsh had been outmanoeuvred by Bishops O'Dwyer and Healy, who knew perfectly well that the conventions governing relations within the hierarchy would prevent Walsh from moving against them in the context of the Commission's deliberations. Walsh did not have to rely on the Commission as a means of exerting his influence, however, for as Archbishop of Dublin he was normally, Royal Commissions apart, the Church's chief spokesman in relations with the State.

Of course, the very fact that the government had appointed a Royal Commission was evidence that it was in no hurry to legislate. The social and economic demands which were still being pressed so insistently by the United Irish League had first claim on the attention of the State. Perhaps the Chief Secretary, George Wyndham, was specifying his priorities when he wrote to his brother, on Christmas Eve, 1901 : 'I want to smash the agitation, introduce a Land Bill, get money for a Harbour-fishing Policy in the West and float a Catholic University. After that,' he added, characteristically, 'any one may be a Minister who prefers missing all the joys of life.'[16] Wyndham's desire to 'smash the agitation' had led to renewal of the old coercive measures—suspension of *habeas corpus* in disturbed areas, proclamation of meetings, etc.—which had seen relatively little service for a decade. The elements of the situation were arranged rather differently than they had been in earlier crises. The 1900 general election had confirmed that the U.I.L., as the accredited nationwide organisation of the Irish Parliamentary Party, rather than a merely local movement, partook of the same rights and responsibilities vis-à-vis the Church as any other organ of the Nation. In particular, it could generally count on clerical sympathy as long as it avoided violence and respected the interests of religion. Indeed, the conventions were clearly enough understood that a League branch might behave quite uncharitably without calling down episcopal wrath. Meetings would be held close to the farm of a person whose conduct was disapproved, and he would be denounced. There was always the risk of violence, but little violence actually occurred. Even where the clergy had vehemently fought the League in 1900, they now apparently realised that it could not be destroyed and that their policy should be to accept the League as the basic national organisation and try to work within it. In his 1902 Lenten pastoral, Bishop Gaffney of Meath, who had bitterly fought the League in the general election, cast the blame for the unrest not upon the League but upon the government.[17] Moreover, when Wyndham implied in the House of Commons a few months later that Gaffney approved of the government's measures, the Bishop retorted in a public letter: 'If he means . . . that I condemn the United Irish League it is false; if he mean [*sic*] I approve of coercion it is equally false.'[18]

The Church's stance toward the U.I.L. agitation, however, reflected more than the general role she had accepted with respect to the Nation to protect her vital interests. Many clergymen also had very specific ideals concerning Irish society which were almost exactly congruent with the League's programme, if not its methods, for division of the grazing lands. Within the categories of English classical liberalism, the continued movement of population out of Ireland's stagnant rural economy into industrial cities, which happened to be located in Great Britain, the colonies and the United States, was simply the rational action of free individuals within a free labour market. Any financial gain which a Catholic peasant might achieve by thus following the promptings of self-interest, however, was far outweighed, in the words of one Irish priest, Father Joseph Guinan, by the danger of 'a fate far worse than death—a fate compared with which the poverty, hunger and rags of an Irish hovel would be very heaven'.[19] Father Guinan invariably counselled the young people of his parish 'rather than emigrate to accept any kind of a situation at home, even the not very enviable position of a farmer's "servant-boy" or "servant-girl"'. True, the prospect of one shilling per day plus board was

not a very tempting inducement. . . . But, as I used to tell them, if the wages were small in Ireland, there were compensating advantages. At home in 'holy Ireland' there was an atmosphere of faith and piety; a climate 'soft as a mother's smile;' the deep, strong love of the kindly old folks; the consoling sight of familiar faces; and the strangely sweet charm and the weird witchery of childhood's home. All these are things that wealth in a foreign land could never buy.[20]

More to the point, perhaps, than this list of 'compensating advantages' was Father Guinan's reaction when he took up duties in his remote Irish parish after a period of service in Liverpool. On his first Saturday morning in residence he found a large number of his parishioners waiting for confession, and he noted, significantly, that 'a goodly proportion' were men, especially young men—no doubt in contrast to his Liverpool experience. 'No need', he reflected, 'to drive people to their church in this parish, as I used to sometimes in Liverpool. No; this was holy Ireland, the land of Faith, the land where Religion is not merely the peasant's hope, but his chiefest solace and comfort—ay, his romance.'[21]

Father Guinan was candid and straightforward about the economic implications of his advice to potential emigrants. After he had persuaded a newly married couple to ignore the urgings of 'a pushful emigration agent' and to set up housekeeping in the parish, he observed that the young man 'managed to earn about as many shillings a-week at home as he probably might have earned dollars a-week in America'. Nevertheless, he admitted, 'I felt no compunction at all in being the means of bringing about this seemingly unfavourable turn in his fortunes; for I regarded that humble couple in their hut on the wind-swept mountain side as a valuable asset to the country.'[22] At the episcopal level there was a tendency to be slightly less candid and to belittle the material advantages and emphasise the risks of emigration. The Standing Committee of the hierarchy declared in 1902 that they considered it 'utterly reckless on the part of the vast majority of male emigrants to the United States and Canada to quit Ireland in the present condition of the American labour market'. 'Many young Irishmen are wasting their lives in idleness', they continued, 'and are driven to seek help from public charity far away from home and relatives, in American towns and cities. And many female emigrants, too, have learned to regret that they ever abandoned their Irish homes, attracted by some bright vision beyond the Atlantic.'[23] In a similar vein, one bishop told a congregation in Kilmaley, Co. Clare, a few years later:

Don't let anyone deceive you, the average Irishman or woman
is never so happy as in his Catholic Irish home, where the air
is pure, and where there is a feeling of religion and sympathy
around him. Money is not everything, and the same thrift and
industry and self-discipline which the Irish emigrant must exhibit
abroad to hold his own in the hard race of life, if resorted to at
home would give him a competency and a measure of success
in his own Ireland sufficient to gratify the average human heart.[24]

A dominant social ideal of the Irish clergy, then, was to
maximise the capacity of Ireland to sustain population. At
first glance it might appear that the most practical way to
achieve this ideal would be the development of manufacturing industries. Two or three industrial complexes like Belfast,
but not dominated by bigoted Protestants, might easily stem
the flow of young men and women out of the country. However, from the standpoint of fulfilling clerical ideals, the
matter was not that simple. Industrialisation was viewed with
grave disquiet by many clergymen, for, as one priest noted
with alarm, 'In the work-rooms, factories, and other places
of employment, our young men are brought into daily and
hourly association with people, who have either long since
ceased to be even nominal believers, or who profess allegiance
to a Church other than that of Rome.'[25] People thought, said
Bishop Hoare of Ardagh in 1902 when introducing a lecture
on the technical instruction programme, that

if they had big factories like Belfast and Birmingham they would
have plenty of employment and no need for emigration. Well,
there were some drawbacks to that system too. It was a well-
known fact that the taking of people from the rural districts into
the large towns and cities had led to physical decadence. If they
could get honest work and an honest wage for the poor people
in their cottage homes it would, in his opinion, be much better
than those hives of industry, as they were usually called, but
he would call them huge destroyers of the morals of the people
(*hear, hear*).[26]

There was, the Bishop warned, 'a degrading effect' associated
with these 'hives of industry', and he indicated the direction
of clerical thought on industrial development when he offered
the opinion 'that the boy who could have a trade taught him
and who could ply that trade at home in his father's house

would be much better'. The bishops—according to remarks by Bishop McRedmond of Killaloe in reply to a request for his assistance in a movement to establish a local industry at Ennis—were especially sympathetic to any project undertaken 'for the purpose of keeping the people at home and rooting them, if possible, in the soil'.[27]

The Maynooth Union, an association of graduates of the national seminary which was known as the 'informal ecclesiastical Parliament of Ireland',[28] was a forum whose annual meetings in June often provide insight into clerical thinking. 'No lover of Ireland—no genuine Irishman—', the Rev. Thomas F. Macken told the Union in 1903, 'can contemplate without feelings akin to horror, an industrial Ireland with centres of manufacture such as are to be found in Germany, in England, and in America.'[29] Such industrial complexes were destructive of family life as well as the personal dignity of the workingmen. 'The factory according to the Anglo-Saxon standard' might, 'with proper safeguards' and 'due regard to Christian ethics', be reconciled with 'the spirit of the Catholic Church'. 'But', Father Macken stressed, 'it is emphatically not the ideal to be striven after and attained in this country.' 'If we are to look abroad for examples,' he continued, 'it is to be hoped that Ireland will develop after the model of Belgium or Denmark rather than on the lines of those countries where the land is deserted, and where the toiling millions are congregated in large cities and towns, and leading lives of moral and physical degradation.' From the discussion which followed Father Macken's paper it appears that his audience generally shared his views on the industrial question. Although one priest did defend larger factories if 'carried on under proper regulations, so as to avoid those dangers to morality that occurred in other countries',[30] three other clergymen spoke out for small factories, home manufacture, cottage industries.[31]

To a certain extent the State, through the Department of Agriculture and Technical Instruction and the Congested Districts Board, was already encouraging the development of isolated rural industries, and in several dioceses these efforts had the active co-operation of the Church. At the 1902 Maynooth Union meeting, however, when Bishop O'Donnell spoke in favour of 'industries that will bear the mark of a human impress which a machine cannot imitate', he hit upon a fundamental difficulty: 'To be sure, it must be allowed that, for many years to come the profits coming to our people would be mainly the profits of workers, and those coming to the explorer, the employer of labour, the capitalists, and the shareholder, would scarcely be theirs.'[32] The plain fact was that cottage industries and isolated rural factories were not attractive investments to anyone possessing ready capital and entrepreneurial instincts. To develop scattered enterprises over an extended geographic area was simply not an efficient way to make money. The example of Belgium, where a cottage system of textile production had survived from medieval times, may have created the unfortunate illusion that such a system could easily be implanted in Ireland at this point in history. In fact, the Belgian system, which Father Macken had found so attractive, was an anachronism which, after about 1910, was rapidly replaced by centralised factories. The only way in which the scattered pattern of industrialisation might be created in the twentieth century would be by the intervention of the State on a scale far greater than was conceivable within the assumptions of nineteenth-century liberalism and against the vested interests of existing private industries in Great Britain.

If industrial development was, at best, an imperfect means for realising the Church's ideal of maximising Ireland's population, ecclesiastics had necessarily to look to reform of the agricultural system to achieve their end. The successive land acts of the late nineteenth century had attacked the insecurity of land tenure in Ireland—which many regarded as a root cause of emigration—and established a system of judicially determined rents. The fact that emigration continued even though the worst excesses of the old land tenure system had thus been mitigated lent weight to arguments in favour of a nationwide, State-aided, programme for tenants to purchase their own holdings. Even the 'Tory' prelate, Dr Healy of Clonfert, maintained vigorously that the plea of the working man was:

Give us, on fair conditions, free access to the soil. Give us the conviction, when we are wiping the sweat from our sunburned faces, that we are labouring for our wives and children and for our children's children whom we love more than our lives. Give us the conviction that some day or other the burden of rent . . . will be taken away . . . give us the meat to cook—that is to say, the soil to till—for that is the essential condition for the prosperity and happiness of Ireland.[33]

If Ireland was to retain within her shores the natural increase of her population, however, more was required than clear title to the soil for those peasants fortunate enough to occupy farms of economically viable size. The U.I.L. agitation had focused attention on the fact that many families lived on patches of land too small to provide a decent livelihood even without rent. In a joint pastoral letter at the end of their National Synod in 1900, the bishops were expressing their own ideals, as well as accommodating the Church to the realities of current politics, when they promised to support a just, constitutional and orderly movement both to establish peasant proprietorship and to 'restore to the industry of Irish peasants, who now are driven to starvation on miserable holdings, the great grass plains that are at present worthless to their owners, and are economically lost to the country'.[34]

In 1902 Wyndham, while persisting in at least perfunctory efforts to 'smash the agitation', proposed a new piece of legislation to settle the land question. The bill which he brought forward, however, did not contemplate restoring 'the great grass plains' to 'the industry of Irish peasants', but simply proposed a readjustment of landlord-tenant relationships on existing holdings. The judicial process by which rents were being fixed was to be altered so as to apply pressure to both landlord and tenant to reach an agreement for outright sale of the holding to the tenant. The bishops, while welcoming the bill in principle, made it clear at their June meeting that it did not fulfil their ideal. They felt they had

a solemn duty, in face of the unabated exodus of our population, to declare anew our deep conviction that an adequate solution of the Irish land question never can be reached until the half neglected grazing lands of the country are made available on fair terms for the agricultural population that is still forced to emigrate in such appalling numbers to earn a livelihood.[35]

They proposed that 'some really efficient body' similar to the

Congested Districts Board, should be empowered to purchase unoccupied or grass land, subdivide it into moderately sized holdings and resell it to 'promising agriculturalists'. Such a body, unlike the C.D.B., should not be forbidden to multiply households by creating more holdings than previously existed. 'On the contrary,' Bishop O'Donnell explained at the Maynooth Union meeting the next day, 'that, under the limitations that would be natural to the project, should be their very aim.'[36]

This ideal of maximising the country's capacity to retain population had to be weighed, in the formation of ecclesiastical policy, against two sets of ecclesiastical interests. One set of interests was the maintenance and exploitation of such relations with the State as would protect and enlarge the Church's role in education—especially, just at this moment, university education. The other was the creation and maintenance of such relations with the Nation as would prevent damage to the Church's influential position within the Irish social structure for the time being and ensure her continued influence in the political order which would arise if and when the Nation achieved its stated goal of supplanting the State. The events of the twelve months following the hierarchy's proposal for a 'really efficient body' to subdivide the grazing lands illustrate the priorities which the Church assigned to her ideals and her interests.

CHAPTER IV

Land for the People

On 3 September 1902 the Dublin papers carried a letter from Captain John Shawe-Taylor, an unknown younger son of a Galway landlord, inviting representatives of landlords and tenants to meet and work out a solution to the land question. Though the suggestion was hardly taken seriously at first, public opinion gradually began to crystallise in its favour, the hierarchy declaring their earnest sympathy with it at their October meeting.[1] Despite the relative mildness of the government's coercive measures in this particular agrarian crisis, coercion did impose upon the national leadership a role of outwardly implacable hostility to the government of the day. The political risks of appearing ready to compromise with the British, however, might not pertain to possible negotiations with the landlords who, for all their faults, could still be depicted as 'Irish' in some vague sense. While it was therefore possible for the national leadership to move cautiously toward conciliation with the landlords, it was all the more essential to protect their agrarian flank by remaining vehemently antagonistic to the government. Fortunately, the leisurely pace at which the Robertson Commission was still deliberating prevented the university question from posing a threat on the Irish Parliamentary Party's clerical flank. Nevertheless, there was another issue which made hostility to the government at this time a particularly ticklish policy.

The most notable piece of government legislation in the 1902 session was a bill to reform the chaotic educational system of England and Wales. Since 1870 popular education in England had been a dual system of 'provided' or 'Board' schools operated by local school boards and 'voluntary' or denominational schools operated in most cases by either the Church of England or the Roman Catholic Church. In the board schools, by the so-called Cowper-Temple clause of the 1870 Education Act, religious instruction was limited to the simple Bible teaching which suited the Protestant Nonconformists exactly but was unacceptable to Catholics and most Anglican spokesmen. These schools received aid from local rates as well as exchequer grants and were subject to local democratic control. Rising costs had outrun the resources of the voluntary schools, which were denied the local rate support, and, in a bill which rectified other anomalies of the system, Balfour proposed to abolish the local school boards and make the local government authorities responsible for contributing to the support of both categories of schools. The denominational schools which came into the new system would be allowed to continue their distinctive religious teaching and the local authorities would not be allowed a voice in the appointment of their teachers. The Anglican and Catholic churches welcomed the bill. Some Nationalists such as Dillon and especially Michael Davitt (who no longer sat in parliament but was still influential in Irish politics) had misgivings about the bill, which rode roughshod over the democratic principles to which they and their friends in England were committed. Nevertheless, the Irish Party, which included almost all the Catholic members of the Commons, signified in May 1902 that it would support the principle of the bill,[2] though—barring the defection of the government's own Nonconformist Liberal Unionist supporters—their votes were superfluous. By late summer, however, the Liberal Unionists were beginning to feel pressure from their Nonconformist supporters,[3] and it seemed possible that the government might be forced to make concessions in the bill. 'I watch your difficulties over Education & wish I could help,'[4] Wyndham wrote to Balfour on 24 September. He informed the Prime Minister that the Nationalist leaders were planning a trip to America and intended to advise the party to abstain from attendance in the House of Commons in their absence:

I believe that I have check-mated that move. If it is attempted there will be a 'split'. Healy & the Hierarchy will intervene &

'whip up' a number to attend. This, in itself a gain, may possibly lead to all staying & helping to pass the Bill after denouncing me for Coercion.[5]

Was Wyndham, as he seems to suggest, intriguing directly with Healy to precipitate a split? Though he was certainly on very friendly terms with Healy in this period,[6] in another letter to Balfour four days later he appears to be inferring Healy's intentions from the editorial policy of William Martin Murphy's *Daily Independent* rather than from direct consultation.[7] Still, Wyndham was tolerably well informed about the party's situation.

A party meeting was called for 7 October to discuss strategy for the autumn session. On 6 October Cardinal Vaughan, the Roman Catholic Archbishop of Westminster and an unrepentant Tory in politics, published a letter appealing to the Irish Party 'to aid in securing for the Catholic schools of England the advantages offered them by the Government in the Education Bill now before Parliament'.[8] The letter had been sent to Redmond several days earlier but had been erroneously addressed. Its publication was therefore most embarrassing to Redmond and he publicly announced that he had not received it—an incident which made painfully evident how little communication there was between the party and the English Catholic hierarchy.[9] Meanwhile, the Standing Committee of the Irish hierarchy met at Maynooth and directed their secretaries to communicate privately with Redmond 'in reference to certain rumours that have reached us as to the policy of the Irish Parliamentary Party in relation to the Education Bill now before the House of Commons'. They cited Cardinal Vaughan's 'impressive appeal' as fully expressive of their own views, and asked Redmond 'to say to your colleagues that we should wish them to regard his Eminence's letter as if it were addressed to them by our Committee'.[10] When the party met, it decided to attend the opening of the new session to denounce the coercion policy and otherwise annoy the House, after which they would 'return to Ireland for the purpose of carrying on the struggle against Coercion, and . . . take part in no other business of the House of Commons' until Redmond's return from America. Redmond was directed to reply to the Standing Committee's 'courteous communication', 'explaining the views of the Irish Party and the desirability of keeping their deliberations confidential'. In his very guarded letter Redmond assured the bishops of the deep concern of the party for the 'heavy burthens' cast upon the Catholics of England by the board school system, but he stressed the 'still greater burthens' imposed upon the Catholics of Ireland by the Conservative administration. Were the party to abandon its resistance to the government at this critical moment, 'the inevitable result would be to destroy the influence of the representatives of Ireland upon the Government of England and expose them to contempt and powerlessness in every opportunity that may offer for extorting favourable terms for our fellow-countrymen either in England or in Ireland.'[11]

While Redmond was in America, the hierarchy did respect the party's request that this communication be kept confidential, but they were hardly satisfied with it. Within a week Cardinal Logue was telling an audience at Trim:

We Irish Catholics require to be careful in the selection of our political leaders, and careful in deliberating seriously with regard to the course marked out for us. I have no reason in the world to say anything that would reflect upon any of our political leaders, except that lately there is a little reason to apprehend a spirit growing up that might make it very unpleasant for Catholics to follow. I do not mean to say that this is the case of the whole body, but there are individuals singling themselves out and putting forward principles that are not in keeping with Catholic feelings and Catholic teaching, especially in that part of Catholic teaching which directs us to take great care of the young and to use every diligence to have them brought up as Christian children should be brought up. There are principles announced during the past few months, at least, on the matter of education with which I could not agree, and with which I am sure Catholics generally do not agree. These are mere passing things, but still they should put us on our guard.[12]

Irish clergy were on their guard, just at this moment, against a related and more serious threat from another quarter.

On 12 September Dr William Joseph Myles Starkie, the Resident Commissioner of National Education in Ireland, had provoked consternation throughout the Irish Church by an address before the British Association in Belfast entitled

'Recent Reforms in Irish Education (Primary and Secondary), with a View to Their Co-Ordination'. Starkie, a Catholic product of Trinity College and a classical scholar of considerable eminence, had accepted the post of Resident Commissioner (i.e. a member of the Board paid a salary to devote full time to supervision of the Board's office staff) in 1899. With the active assistance of Archbishop Walsh he undertook the difficult tasks of eliminating the system of payment by results without penalising any teachers with unjust salary reductions and of introducing schemes of manual and practical training which had been recommended by a Viceregal Commission in 1897. These reforms, introduced in 1900 and 1901, caused some friction, but, on the whole, resistance was no greater than might be expected when such sweeping changes are introduced into the professional lives of so many persons. Then in the summer of 1901 Archbishop Walsh quite unexpectedly precipitated a great stir over certain letters sent out by Education Office clerks to individual teachers and resigned from the Board.[13] His motives for taking this drastic action over what can only be described as an extremely trivial matter are obscure, though it was very much in character for him to be a stickler for precise execution of established procedures. The most significant effect of the resignation, however, was to dissociate the Archbishop from Starkie, whom he had earlier praised highly in public and private[14] and with whom he was known to have worked closely in effecting the reforms of curriculum and salaries.

In his Belfast speech Starkie turned his attention to more fundamental reforms which no Catholic ecclesiastic would sanction. Read as a whole, the speech is a studied attempt at persuasion, directed as much toward Starkie's fellow Catholics in the South as toward the largely Protestant audience to whom he spoke in the northern metropolis. The author cited the folly of Henry VIII in disendowing the system of Catholic education built up in England before the Reformation and the equal folly of later generations of Protestants in Ireland who gave schools to the country 'to wean it from its language and its religion'. He reviewed the history of the National Education system, with a suitable reference to 'the well-known racial and religious prejudices' of Dr Whately (Pro-

testant Archbishop of Dublin at the inception of the system).
He paid respect to nationalist sentiment by identifying his
sympathies with the Celtic Revival, insofar as it was nonpolitical, and he spoke of his hopes for the future development of the country from the standpoint of 'a Southerner and
a Catholic'. Perhaps he hoped that his carefully wrought
argument would be read with the same care and attention
that he himself was accustomed to devoting to an Aristo-
phanes play. The popular and clerical reaction to the speech
focused not upon the design of the whole, however, but upon
two passages which the *Freeman's Journal* set off in bold-face
capitals in its report:

MANAGERS, WHO CAN FIND MONEY FOR
EVERYTHING EXCEPT EDUCATION,

and

THE MAJORITY OF MANAGERS ARE QUITE
INDIFFERENT TO EDUCATION.[15]

There was, of course, an outcry. Deanery conferences and
similar meetings of clergy all over Ireland passed resolutions
condemning the speech.[16] The bishops, however, generally let
the lower clergy handle the attack on Starkie at this stage.
Dr Clancy, the very able Bishop of Elphin, even had a few
kind words for the Resident Commissioner, calling him
learned and distinguished and characterising his speech as
brilliant before criticising at length his remarks on the
clergy.[17]

The really threatening part of the speech, however, was not
Starkie's criticism of the managers for neglect of responsibilities which he felt they should accept—a judgement which
could be, and was, hotly disputed,[18] since managerial duties
were only vaguely defined by law—but rather his assertion
that the deficiencies in Irish education resulted from an absence of the 'DRIVING FORCE OF PUBLIC OPINION'.[19]
Irish education was (and is to this day) different from the
school systems of most western countries in that virtually all
the funds for the operation of schools came directly from the
central government. With trivial exceptions there were no
contributions to education from the local government author-

ities. Of course, the poverty of many districts in Ireland provided an argument for greater exchequer subsidies than British schools received, but critics of the system maintained that some local contribution was desirable as an incentive for laymen to take an active interest in the quality and conduct of the schools. The fact that attendance in the National Schools was far below that in English and Scottish schools[20] was cited as evidence of the apathy of parents toward an institution regarded as primarily the concern of the priest. Starkie therefore proposed to decentralise the financial burden of the upkeep of school buildings, and it did not escape clerical attention that such a move might well lead to demands by the local authorities, which levied the rates, for a voice in the conduct of the schools. Dean Byrne, speaking to a meeting of Catholic Clerical Managers of National Schools in the Ecclesiastical Province of Armagh, developed an ingenious argument to counter Starkie's recommendation. The funds for teachers' salaries dispensed by the National Board, he observed, came ultimately from the taxpayers. The Dean conceded the Irish Catholic taxpayers' right to appoint and dismiss teachers, but maintained that the taxpayer freely and confidently delegated that right 'to his most cherished and most trusted pastor'.[21] Such a line of reasoning only restated, in another way, Starkie's central theme that 'of local interest in education there is practically nil'.

It was therefore in an atmosphere highly charged with clerical suspicion of secularist designs that the majority of the Irish Party continued to absent themselves from the Commons as debate proceeded on Balfour's English Education Bill. The word leaked out that O'Brien had moved the abstention resolution at the party meeting.[22] Although Redmond was only absent for a few weeks, before he returned there were signs of possible clerical revolt against O'Brien's policy.[23] Bishop O'Donnell tried to persuade O'Brien to change his course, but without success.[24] When, after Redmond's return, the Irish members did not rush immediately to Westminster and the *Independent* censured the party for rejecting the appeals of Logue and Vaughan, Logue took the opportunity to publish the Standing Committee's letter to Redmond of 6 October as evidence that he was not alone among Irish bishops in interesting himself in the English education question.[25] Redmond was thus forced to publish his reply of 7 October[26] which, given the highly charged atmosphere into which the question had been thrust, did not strengthen the party's position.

On the same day that Logue wrote to the press, Walsh also made public the essential features of the transactions of 6 and 7 October, but in a curiously different way. In a letter to the Rev. Mothers of communities of nuns in his diocese asking for prayers for the interests of religion in education, the Archbishop stated the case rather differently than it had hitherto been presented by Catholic ecclesiastics. He maintained that the system of education in England had been *satisfactory* to the present time and that the bill was a *threat* to Catholic interests. Walsh may have had reference to the so-called Kenyon-Slaney amendment, which had been adopted during the Irish Party's abstention. This amendment, which provided for a measure of lay control of religious as well as secular instruction, had not even been resisted by Balfour, and had passed by the overwhelming margin of 211 to 41.[27] Walsh managed, however, to avoid specifying just what features of the bill were objectionable, but stressed the urgency of the Irish members returning to Westminster. The bishops, he implied, had understood that abstention was to be for a limited period, to expire before the close of Commons consideration of the bill, and he argued that Redmond's return had terminated this period, releasing individual members from any obligation to continue absenting themselves.[28] He hammered this point home in another public letter later in the week.[29]

Walsh seems to have been trying to help the party to pull its chestnuts out of the fire. The Kenyon-Slaney amendment had aroused concern among Anglican as well as Catholic authorities, and the bill would soon go to the Lords where redress might be expected. By posing the issue in the way he did, Walsh made it possible for the party to appear to be rushing into the breach just when it was needed. Redmond took the hint. On 29 November 1902, the day after Walsh's second letter appeared, he wrote to party members that 'We never were for an instant indifferent to the interests of Catholic Education or to the views and opinions of the Irish Hierarchy, and always contemplated the possibility of a contingency arising when it would be our duty to return to Westminster.' Without apologising for the party's actions to date, he stated that if the Lords amended the bill and sent it back to the Commons, their presence might be of real importance. Therefore, 'and in deference to the strong views expressed by the Irish Hierarchy on a subject upon which they have a special right to speak with authority', he requested his colleagues to be ready to come at once to London 'should the contingency I have mentioned arise'.[30]

While resolutions of confidence in the party were being adopted by U.I.L. branches and local government bodies throughout Ireland,[31] the House of Lords amended the bill to satisfy the whims of any but the most exacting denominationalist. Upon return of the bill to the Commons in mid-December, Redmond dramatically produced a phalanx of Irish members who had not been seen in the House for two months, and on a few divisions, where Balfour did not demand Unionist unity, the Irish provided the margin for denominationalist victory.[32] Though the occasion, like much of the party's activity at this particular time, was not without a certain element of play-acting, the performance was carried off with sufficient aplomb to relieve the pressure from the party's clerical and Healyite enemies. There was more, however, to the party's safe passage through these treacherous waters than simple adroitness. Clergy were well aware that the same Conservative Party which in England was the champion of denominational and clerical control of education was supported in Ireland by the enemies of that principle. Starkie's Belfast speech posed a threat from the State to the Irish Church's direct interests, whereas the fate of Balfour's bill could have no such implications. Of course, all Irish Catholic clergymen would endorse the 'Catholic' position on the bill, and many would take the party's action on it as an index of their loyalty to Catholic interests. But while the defence of English Catholic interests was expected of the party, the interests upon whose protection the relations between the Church and the Nation were founded were those of the *Irish* Catholic Church. Those interests, just at this moment, were under attack by a representative of the State— the Resident Commissioner of National Education. However much some priests may have disapproved the strategy pursued by the Nation's representatives toward the State, the situation did not call for any fundamental readjustment of the Church's relations with either the Nation or the State.

Moreover, just as the English education drama was playing itself out, the possibility that the Nation's representatives might gain a land settlement consonant with the interests and ideals of the Church was entering the realm of real probability. Captain Shawe-Taylor's proposal had finally been taken up, and on 20 December representatives of landlords and tenants sat down together at the Mansion House, Dublin, to work out a settlement by consent. The landlord delegation, led by Lord Dunraven, included Lord Mayo, Col. W. H. Hutcheson Poë and Col. Nugent T. Everard, while the tenants were represented by Redmond and O'Brien along with T. W. Russell and T. C. Harrington. By 3 January they had reached agreement and in a unanimous report[33] recommended the substitution of an 'occupying proprietary' for the existing system of dual ownership. No longer, the Land Conference urged, should special courts fix the amount of rent to be paid by a peasant. Rather, the entire tenantry were to be encouraged to purchase their holdings with advances from the imperial exchequer. Under previous land legislation nearly 80,000 of the more fortunate tenants had been able to take advantage of such arrangements, but there was, in general, no legal way to compel landlords to sell (or to compel tenants to buy). The U.I.L.—as well as Russell, who spoke for Ulster tenant farmers—had been advocating legislation making sale of agricultural land compulsory. The Land Conference reached a happy solution: sale was to be made not compulsory, but irresistably attractive, to both parties. The landlords were to be paid for their land a sum capable of producing at 3 per cent or $3\frac{1}{4}$ per cent an income[34] equal to their previous income from rents. The tenants would then repay the State in annuities 15 per cent to 25 per cent lower than the judicially fixed rents they had been paying, and there were to be periodical reductions in the amount of the annuities.

Essentially, all these provisions had been incorporated in the purchase schemes of previous land acts. What was new was the suggestion that arrangements for repayment might 'involve some assistance from the State beyond the use of its credit'. The Conference expressed the opinion that the State should supply 'any reasonable difference arising between the sum advanced by the State and ultimately repaid to it'. This State contribution was to be justified by the desirability of giving the occupiers a favourable start on their new career as owners, of compensating landlords for 'sacrifice of sentiment' and for supposed sufferings under previous land acts, of inducing both parties to undertake the transaction, and of ensuring that the landlords would continue to spend their income in Ireland (presumably by offering inducements for them to retain their demesnes and mansion-houses).

Although the result of the Conference was received by the public as something of a miracle, there was nothing inherently miraculous in this agreement between two traditionally hostile parties. They had simply agreed to settle their differences by calling on a third party, the State, to pick up the chit for the amount over which they were haggling. Nearly three months were to elapse before His Majesty's Government would agree publicly to oblige, and during this period the Conference's report was the subject of intense daily discussion in the press. The Episcopal Standing Committee met about two weeks after the publication of the report and issued a statement calling this instance of co-operation between landlords and tenants 'an event of the best augury for the future welfare of both classes'.[35] In the following week, however, Archbishop Walsh rather spoiled the effect of the gesture by stressing, in the first of a long series of letters on the scheme, that this expression of the bishops' sentiment, together with the earnest hope that the unanimity of the Conference might lead to a fair legislative settlement of the question, was *all* that should be inferred from the Standing Committee's action. The bishops, he insisted, had not approved the scheme itself. He challenged the accuracy of certain figures in a *Freeman's Journal* analysis of the Conference scheme, and he called for clarification of an anomaly in the

4

scheme by which, according to his own interpretation, the landlord of a heavily mortgaged estate might actually substantially increase his income by sale of his property.[36]

At this time O'Brien and the *Freeman* were campaigning vigorously to win public acceptance of the scheme. By presenting its loosely drafted provisions in a very favourable light to both tenants and landlords, proponents of the scheme hoped to extend the good feeling of the Conference to the country at large and thereby persuade the government that it would be worthwhile to take the bold step of underwriting the cost of the scheme. By raising embarrassing points, the Archbishop of Dublin was threatening to disrupt the tide of public opinion which the conferees were marshalling by methods which necessarily involved glossing over some of the difficulties. Two weeks later, when rumours of government unwillingness to make the requisite exchequer contribution began to circulate, Walsh again wrote to the press, this time maintaining that the tenants had been cruelly deceived as to the terms they could expect and that they should be prepared to purchase their holdings without any State aid to bridge the gap between their terms and the demands of the landlords.[37]

This time O'Brien retaliated with a public letter of his own. Without mentioning Walsh by name he implied that the Archbishop would be to blame if the government should reject the scheme.[38] Whether that was Walsh's intention or not, he continued his carping criticisms for several more weeks,[39] to the apparent discomfiture of Bishop Foley of Kildare and Leighlin, who wrote to the press in an effort to smooth over the differences between Walsh and O'Brien,[40] and in evident contrast to the views of Bishop O'Donnell, who voiced cautious optimism that the government could carry a fair bill,[41] and in almost direct contradiction of the admonition of Bishop Kelly of Ross that the tenants should hold out for favourable terms.[42]

The difficulties arose not so much from the particular points Archbishop Walsh raised as from the fact that he insisted on raising them. It was absolutely critical that the government and English opinion generally be convinced that Ireland would accept the scheme as a *final* settlement of the tiresome Irish land question, and Walsh—along with a few laymen of whom the most prominent was Michael Davitt, who favoured outright land nationalisation—appeared to be doing his utmost to frustrate that end. On 27 February, after Wyndham had alluded in the House of Commons to the disputations over the meaning of the Land Conference report being carried on in the Irish press,[43] a meeting of the Irish Party pointedly resolved:

That we have observed with concern the reference in Mr. Wyndham's speech to recent newspaper controversies in Ireland and their effect in England, and in view of the fact that these controversies were largely based upon the idea that no Treasury grant would be forthcoming, we earnestly appeal to the patriotism of Nationalist journalists and public men to abstain, as far as possible, from further public controversies pending the introduction of the Government Land Bill.[44]

Walsh was undeterred and continued to publish, in several letters, a long exposition of previous land acts. Whereas the Conference had prudently left details of financial arrangements vague in order to allow flexibility to the government in drafting a bill, Walsh climaxed his historical synopsis of land purchase finance with 'a sort of "ready reckoner"' for 'tenants who desire to see what precisely is the bearing of the "Conference terms," with which the country generally seems to be well contented, on their own individual cases'.

Walsh, one of the keenest minds in the Irish Church, had a sound knowledge of economics, a deep interest in law, and an absolute passion for minute technical details. These were qualities which would have served a debater well, but unfortunately they are also attributes which can be a hindrance in the pursuit of practical goals within the framework of modern democratic politics. Public opinion does not move with the precision and elegance of an intellect like that of Archbishop Walsh. Politicians are obliged to present issues in simplified, often distorted, terms when addressing the public, and one can only hope that they will exercise in private council a measure of intelligence and statesmanship which would serve no purpose on a public platform. Walsh was not prepared to extend this kind of confidence to the leading Irish politicians of this period. He was a believer in democracy, but he envisioned democracy in ideal terms, operating through enlightened popular opinion, not in the realistic terms which the political leaders were forced to recognise. His tiresome series of public statements on the Land Bill, therefore, were in part an early symptom of dissatisfaction with the style of leadership practised by the national leaders. There may have been more to his obstructive tactics, however, than simply such temperamental factors.

Late in 1902 Wyndham had persuaded Sir Antony MacDonnell to become his Under-Secretary. MacDonnell, an Irish Catholic of avowed Home Rule sympathies, had been one of the early graduates of Queen's College, Galway, and had gone on to earn a distinguished reputation in the Indian Civil Service. The energy and tenacity with which he applied his proconsular experience to his native country soon earned him the sobriquet, 'the Bengal Tiger', among his subordinates in Dublin Castle.[45] At the end of February 1903, shortly after MacDonnell's arrival at the Castle, and in the midst of public excitement over the impending introduction of Wyndham's Land Bill, the Robertson Commission, at long last, issued its report. It recommended the reconstitution of the Royal University as a teaching (not just an examining) university with an endowed Catholic college. This was a makeshift solution which one of the twelve commissioners refused to endorse and to which six others expressed reservations. Four commissioners, including Dr Starkie and the English Catholic intellectual, Wilfrid Ward, had doubts about their decision to exclude the University of Dublin, as well as Trinity College, from the scope of their inquiry. Catholic gentry and professional men—like the four hundred laymen who had petitioned for a University of Dublin settlement when the Commission's decision on this point was published a year earlier—were anxious for a solution which, while satisfying the bishops' demands, would contribute to their own and their sons' upward mobility in Anglo-Irish society. In other words, for prestige reasons they preferred an 'Oxbridge' to a 'redbrick' type of university for Catholics. This solution could only be achieved within the University of Dublin.

Within Dublin Castle Starkie was and MacDonnell was about to become a natural spokesman for such interests—which harmonised well with their ideas of reducing religious animosity and promoting independence from clerical dictation. During 1903, as will become clear, MacDonnell and Walsh launched an effort to persuade the State and the Church, respectively, to settle the university question by enlarging the University of Dublin rather than by acting on the recommendations of the Robertson Commission. Whether MacDonnell approached Walsh as early as January cannot be proved with the available evidence, but some such overtures had clearly been made by late March when Wyndham introduced his Land Bill. The altogether plausible assumption that at least inklings of MacDonnell's attitude on the university question reached Walsh shortly after the Under-Secretary's appointment would account for Walsh's behaviour at this time on the land question, which so mystified and dismayed contemporaries. A treasury grant sufficient to effect the 'Conference terms' of land purchase might well preclude for the time being another—albeit smaller—grant to endow a Catholic college. This was no doubt an unhappy prospect for Walsh just at a moment when the Castle might be receptive to his ideas on the proper structure of a university settlement —i.e. the moment at which he could regain the advantage Bishops Healy and O'Dwyer had seized by their manoeuvre in the Robertson Commission's deliberations.

By mid-March, when it was becoming clear that the government had made up its mind to enact the Land Conference proposal, Walsh accepted the situation. In reply to a letter from Redmond, he wrote:

I quite agree with you that a discussion on the Report of the [Robertson] Commission just now would be unprofitable. I am inclined to think indeed that it might do harm. The Government has so much on hands that we could hardly expect a declaration of policy on the University question just now.

You are, I assume, aware that the only policy that finds favour with the present Irish Government is that of an enlargement of the University of Dublin, by the establishment of a second College, as Catholic as Trinity is Protestant. I dont think there is much, if any, secret made about this, but still they would hardly like to commit themselves to it publicly.[46]

Two days later Wyndham introduced the government's Land

Bill. It was essentially an embodiment of the Conference terms and proposed to spend £12,000,000 to make up the difference between what tenants were presumed to be willing to pay and the income demanded by the landlords. In two further public letters the Archbishop, with a view, no doubt, to maintaining the principle that this grant should not detract from Ireland's claim to an endowment for a Catholic college, complained about the tendency of English journalists to regard the £12,000,000 as a gift from England to Ireland. He suggested that certain savings which Wyndham claimed were already being effected in the Irish administration and which would be increased by the effects of the bill, should be ascertained and an equivalent amount placed in a special account earmarked for Irish purposes.[47] Remarks such as these, whatever justice they may have had, were not calculated to help Redmond to let the English 'imagine if they like that they are doing a fine and generous thing', as he described his task to Wilfrid Scawen Blunt on 1 April.[48]

Most churchmen saw, as Walsh did, that the Church's direct interests at the exchequer would have to take second place to the requirements of land purchase for the moment. Along with his Land Bill, Wyndham introduced an Ireland Development Grant Bill which, in accordance with precedent, provided an annual equivalent grant of £185,000 to compensate for the fact that Ireland had been excluded from the treasury grants established under the 1902 English Education Act. Various Irish educational interests, both Catholic and Protestant, were anxious that the equivalent grant be devoted primarily to education,[49] and Wyndham's Bill did authorise the use of part of the grant for education. First priority was given, however, to the needs of the land purchase programme. When it became clear that pressing their claims on the grant might endanger the land settlement, the various educational interests—including the Catholic Headmasters' Association, which had earlier joined with its Protestant counterpart to urge the special claims of secondary education—quietly dropped the matter.[50]

Because the conventions under which the Nation's representatives worked made it very difficult to have direct public dealings with the State through statesmen who repudiated the national claim, Wilfrid Scawen Blunt, Wyndham's cousin, agreed to act as an intermediary between Redmond and the Chief Secretary in the delicate matter of amendments to the Land Bill. At their first interview on 1 April, Redmond told Blunt: 'There is a party in Ireland headed by Davitt and Archbishop Walsh that is determined to go against the Bill. . . . Davitt is a land nationaliser, and is altogether opposed, and so is Archbishop Walsh.'[51] At a Nationalist Convention in mid-April, Davitt seemed about to lead a revolt against the bill, but Redmond was able to ward off the attack. Late in April Redmond on two separate occasions intimated to Blunt his fears of a coalition of forces against the bill in which Davitt and the Archbishop would be joined by Thomas Sexton (editor of the *Freeman's Journal,* which had abandoned its earlier enthusiasm) and Dillon, who had been out of the country during most of the controversy.[52] Redmond may well have exaggerated his difficulties to Blunt in hopes of gaining further concessions; nevertheless, a coalition against the settlement did materialise, though Dillon did not join it openly until after the bill's enactment was assured, and Walsh never became part of it.

The willingness of Walsh and other ecclesiastics to submerge their desires for increased State expenditure for the Church's direct interests in education was paralleled by a willingness to forego the achievement of the Church's ideal of massive land redistribution to stem emigration. To be sure, the bishops of Tuam province (where Dr Healy had just been elevated to the archbishopric) published a resolution in April which, while approving the bill generally, called for certain amendments, including extension of the powers of the Congested Districts Board to the entire province of Connacht.[53] This time, however, no endorsement of this proposal—such as the bishops' suggestion for wholesale redistribution a year earlier—was forthcoming from the entire hierarchy. The amendments which the Irish Party extracted from the government did not include any geographical extension of the C.D.B.'s powers—a reform which was not achieved until 1909. Nevertheless, in impromptu remarks at the Maynooth Union on 25 June, when the measure was almost in its final form, Archbishop Healy indicated that he was generally satisfied and avoided raising the issue of land redistribution.[54]

A year later, when he wrote *John Bull's Other Island,* George Bernard Shaw caricatured the forces to which the party responded in this crisis in an exchange between Matthew Haffigan and Cornelius Doyle concerning their member of parliament.

MATTHEW (*breaking out with surly bitterness*): Weve had enough of his foolish talk agen landlords. . . .

CORNELIUS : We're tired of him. He doesnt know hwere to stop. Every man cant own land; and some men must own it to employ them. It was all very well when solid men like Doran and me and Mat were kep from ownin land. But hwat man in his senses ever wanted to give land to Patsy Farrll and dhe like o him?[55]

Despite the fact that the demands of the Patsy Farrells for division of the grazing lands had been the original impetus of the U.I.L. in 1898, its transformation from a local movement in Connacht to the primary popular organisation of the Nation made the League, like the party, primarily responsive to the demands of the more numerous and articulate Matt Haffigans and Corny Doyles. The Church's social ideal of giving the Patsy Farrells a secure place in the Irish economy thus had to give way to the Church's political interest of being in harmony with the Nation's will as expressed through its accredited representatives. The urgency of this interest was perceptible to churchmen from archbishops, who had to contemplate the eventual prospect of those representatives at the helm of an Irish State, to the local clergy, who had to cope with the misery and frustration generated in their own parishioners by the injustice and insecurity of the old land tenure system.[56] By obtaining a settlement of the tenants' chief grievances, the party undercut some of the urgency behind the interest of priests in accommodation to the party's programme. The Church's interest in good relations with the Nation was undiminished, but the great force of agrarian discontent which confirmed the party as the legitimate political agent of the Nation could no longer be mobilised so effectively as it had been in the past five years. Though the consequences of this fact were not immediately evident, they would become painfully apparent in years to come.

CHAPTER V

High Hopes

In the aftermath of the land settlement of 1903 the Irish
Parliamentary Party underwent an internal crisis which reflected a fundamental choice facing the Nation. O'Brien
had been the main author and champion of the policy which
had achieved the land settlement. Dillon, partially disabled
by poor health and absence from the country at crucial points
in the discussions, had serious misgivings. If the land question were finally settled, the resulting peace would threaten
the basis of the Home Rule movement. For O'Brien the
settlement of the agrarian problem by consent of both parties
was an occasion to hope that the landlords would join with
their former tenants to settle the national question by consent as well. In Dillon's view, such hopes were simply chimeri-
cal, for his vision of Home Rule was quite incompatible with
the prejudices of the landlords as he knew them. For the
moment O'Brien's rather implausible hope seemed to be
gaining confirmation. Some of the same landlords who had
paved the way for the Land Conference began, under Lord
Dunraven's leadership, to advocate through an 'Irish Reform
Association' a policy of gradual devolution of governmental
powers to Ireland. Hints of sympathy from Wyndham and
scarcely veiled support from MacDonnell buoyed up
O'Brien's hopes that Ireland had somehow entered a new
era in which 'conference plus business' could replace agitation and parliamentary manoeuvre as the primary strategy
for achieving nationalist goals. It soon became apparent that
the good will of Lord Dunraven did not extend very far
down into the rank and file of Irish Unionism. Indeed,
Wyndham's mere flirtation with the new policy brought
down the wrath of his party's principal supporters in Ireland

upon his head in 1905. The quixotic O'Brien continued for another decade to promote the idea of a settlement of the Irish question by conference—in the process drifting farther and farther out of the realm of practical influence.

O'Brien's new cause is, in itself, of little interest for this study. Few churchmen responded to his proposals one way or the other. Among the possible reasons for this silence was the fact that O'Brien's ideas of accommodation with Unionists over the national question logically entailed a definition of the Nation embracing the Protestant North. Such a definition would imply a radical readjustment of the conventions by which the Church governed her political behaviour, and neither O'Brien nor anyone else presented her with compelling reasons why she should make such readjustments. Nevertheless, O'Brien's new departure reflected two important facts to which the Church did respond in the aftermath of the land settlement. Firstly, if the Irish Parliamentary Party was to remain the primary organ of the Nation in an era in which the land question was no longer a grievance of national dimensions it would have to find new ways to consolidate active popular support, though the ways chosen might be very different from the course favoured by O'Brien. Secondly, O'Brien was quite correct in detecting a new desire on the part of Castle authorities to extend the spirit of the Land Conference to a wider range of Irish problems.

Although the Irish question presented itself to most observers as the problem of the most rural portion of the United Kingdom in the late nineteenth century, continued depopulation of the countryside was in fact converting Ireland into a relatively more 'urban' country.[1] Until 1903 the demands of the rural population for land reform may have been a sort of 'consensus' grievance which all other Catholics were expected to recognise as somehow inseparable from the national claim. But even before 1903 the interest of many Catholics in the tenant's troubles was marginal. Indeed, one underlying meaning of the Gaelic League's 'nonpolitical' status may have been that many of its most active adherents were from the towns and were bored by the land reform schemes which were the staple of nationalist political discussion.[2] There were two ways in which the Catholics of the towns could conceptualise their grievances at this time: according to class lines or according to religious divisions. The small but growing Irish labour movement which embodied the class consciousness of urban workers was not yet a serious problem for the party in 1903. The prospect that organisations appealing to Catholics of the towns on the basis of religious solidarity might weaken the party was, however, very real at this time.

This kind of threat had existed for some years in Belfast, where Bishop Henry Henry of Down and Connor had founded a local political machine, the Belfast Catholic Association, in 1896. The B.C.A. was engaged in a continual feud with the local representatives of the party, and, in the aftermath of the 1900 party reunion, tried unsuccessfully to get Redmond to sanction it, rather than the local U.I.L., as the legitimate organisation of the Nation in the northern metropolis.[3] Such a role for a clerically controlled, 'Whiggish' body would have been incompatible with the relationship between Church and Nation which had been confirmed by the rout of Healyism in 1900. Even Henry's own clergy were coming to realise that the policy of their vain, conceited prelate could not be successfully maintained, and by 1902 there were signs of rebellion in their ranks.[4] Though this perception by many lower clergy was essentially correct, the fact that the party seemed primarily responsive to agrarian rather than urban Catholic interests at this time did create a situation in which Bishop Henry's organisation and political preoccupations seemed briefly to be the wave of the future.

In Dublin the narrow, specifically Catholic, nationalism expounded in the columns of *The Leader* was complemented by some efforts to promote exclusive dealing by Catholics in retaliation for Protestant discrimination. In a lecture before the Catholic Commercial Club of Dublin in 1900, the Rev. P. Finlay, S.J., asserted: 'Personally, I feel that as between a Catholic and non-Catholic professional or business man, their merits being equal, I should prefer the former.'[5] In 1902 a Dominican publication, the *Irish Rosary*, promoted the idea of a national Catholic Association because 'they had played the game of tolerance until the game was played out'.[6] A movement was organised, reportedly with the help of William Dennehy,[7] editor of the *Irish Catholic* and the *Independent*, two papers controlled by Healy's friend William Martin Murphy and which were frequently critical of the party. The primary initial thrust of the movement was concentrated in protests against alleged discrimination by the Irish railways in their employment practices, and a plan for a nationwide Catholic Association was presented to the hierarchy at their October meeting. The bishops, according to an account by Bishop Foley of Kildare and Leighlin, took a cautious view of the movement, approving only the stated objects of the organisation. Foley and one other prelate were delegated to interview its promoters, and the hierarchy withheld sanction of the organisation itself pending certain modifications in its rules and constitution suggested as a result of the interview.[8] Apparently without acting on the bishops' suggestions, the Association received gestures of support from several individual bishops.[9] At a meeting of its Provisional National Council on 10 December, Edward Martyn, the playwright and Catholic landlord (who later became the first President of Sinn Féin), was elected President.[10]

As organising activity continued, a number of bishops, including even Foley himself, had enough confidence in the good faith of the promoters to sanction its activities without waiting for the hierarchy as a whole to approve it.[11] It is notable that the two influential prelates who worked most closely with the party at this time, Walsh and O'Donnell, made no gestures of support, while the list of those bishops sanctioning the Association included the prelates most suspicious of the party—Logue, O'Dwyer and Healy—though not Henry, for special reasons. Rather than sanction the new Association in his diocese, Henry apparently caused his own Catholic Association to apply for affiliation with it. This move revealed some strains within the new movement, for some young Catholics who had been attracted to it thought of it as nonpolitical in the same rather attenuated sense in which that term was applied to the Gaelic League. The editor of *St Stephens*, a student organ at U.C.D., expressed the hope that the Association would repudiate all political

aspirations. 'In this connection,' he wrote, somewhat pre-
maturely, 'I am glad to hear that already the application for
affiliation from a certain so-called Catholic Association has
been declined.'[12] *The Leader*, which enthusiastically supported the nationwide Association, carefully distinguished this
new body from the Belfast Catholic Association, which was
taken to task for its disregard of national feeling in sponsoring a recent entertainment which featured a comedy routine
by a 'stage Irishman'.[13] Nevertheless, the Catholic Association's National Council at its March 1903 meeting disre-
garded such considerations and decided to affiliate the Belfast
Catholic Association.[14] Though the new body could not hope
to organise in Belfast against the Bishop's opposition, this
decision was a fateful one. Ecclesiastics who hoped for productive relationships with the party could scarcely view with
equanimity a development sure to poison those relationships
throughout the country as they had been poisoned in Belfast.
The Belfast police detective who wrote a report on the
nationwide Catholic Association two weeks later was only
drawing the obvious conclusion when he asserted that 'It
really represents the "Healyite" section of the Nationalist
Party' and that its 'ostensible object' was 'to form a Catholic
Political Party'.[15]

The bishops, however, had more pressing concerns to
occupy their attention than the Catholic Association problem
at their regular June meeting at Maynooth. Walsh was in a
position to report that the authorities in Dublin Castle were
favourably disposed toward a settlement of the university
question despite the huge financial commitment they had
just undertaken to settle the land question. It is not clear
whether he pointed out that at least MacDonnell favoured not
the Robertson Commission scheme but Walsh's own ideal of
the erection of a second college in the University of Dublin.
The hierarchy unanimously adopted a resolution favouring
enactment of the Robertson scheme, though Walsh apparently persuaded his colleagues not to hinder the adoption of
the Dublin University plan by publication of the resolution,
which was communicated privately to the Castle authorities.[16]

The hierarchy's meeting was followed, as usual, by the
annual Maynooth Union meeting, at which the Rev. G.

O'Donovan, an enthusiastic young priest from Loughrea, Co. Galway, presented a paper promoting the new Catholic Association. He envisaged the movement as a means not only of establishing equality in the country's economic life, but also of fostering 'educated Catholic lay opinion', and he asserted, almost in passing, that the Association had 'obtained the warm approval of the bishops'.[17] Bishop Foley, who happened to be presiding, took the opportunity, as soon as Father O'Donovan had sat down, to deny that the bishops had sanctioned the Association, as opposed to its objects, and indicated that the hierarchy was still awaiting action on their suggested modifications of the Association's rules and constitution.[18] Though a Dominican leaped to the defence of the Association, three other priests in the audience expressed misgivings. One voiced the fear that the Association might try 'to set itself up against their political leaders' and another that it might become 'a sort of Catholic Freemasonry'. The third suggested, somewhat obliquely, his apprehensions that it might encourage lay independence of clerical authority: 'and if they first of all got a Clerical Association, the Catholic Association would then do good.'[19] Despite these warning signals, the Association published a *Handbook* in September setting forth its objects in terms similar to those propounded by Father O'Donovan.[20] The *Irish Catholic*, significantly, took exception to certain provisions of its rules and constitution which placed initiative and control largely in lay hands and stressed that 'So far as we know the Rules and Constitution have received no episcopal approval.'[21]

By this time the Irish administration was beginning to take soundings on the university question rather actively. Wyndham, no doubt reasoning correctly that the bishops saw little chance of a settlement from the Liberal Party, which would very likely come to power with the next election, interpreted the signals he was receiving from the hierarchy to mean that they were 'in a mood to take what they can get'. On the other hand, spokesmen for Trinity College, especially Sir Edward Carson, M.P. for Dublin University, were opposed to 'a College inside Dublin University with a Catholic atmosphere', though Carson favoured endowment of a Catholic college within the Royal University. Wyndham

himself favoured the former alternative, which he depicted
to Balfour in the middle of September as the ideal solution,
but he seemed resigned to deference to Carson's wishes.[22] Less
than two weeks later he was considering an attempt to overcome Trinity's opposition to his ideal with a sort of bribe
'to safeguard that institution from cut-throat competition'.[23]
He still, however, held open the 'second best' alternative of
the Robertson scheme. During the first two weeks of October,
something persuaded Wyndham to opt for his ideal. Perhaps
he was nudged in this direction by Redmond's dismay when,
on 30 September, MacDonnell mentioned to him the hierarchy's unpublicised endorsement of the Robertson scheme
in June. Redmond, unable to square this information with
what Walsh had been telling him, dashed off a letter to Dillon
after the interview confessing that he was 'very much mystified' and 'astonished' by Sir Antony's revelation.[24] 'Of
course,' he wrote, 'if the Bishops unite in pressing such a
settlement upon the Gov^t theirs will be the responsibility,'
implying that this was one of those few situations in which
the conventions between Church and Nation obliged the
party to do exactly what the hierarchy wanted. To MacDonnell, however, the party leader was noncommittal and hinted
that he might oppose a bill based on the Robertson scheme.
Redmond's reaction no doubt helped MacDonnell to persuade Wyndham not to be satisfied with the 'second best'
solution.

The autumn meeting of the hierarchy was scheduled for
14 October, and a few days before it MacDonnell drafted a
specific scheme for a single national university encompassing
Trinity, a Catholic college in Dublin and Queen's College,
Belfast, as well.[25] The formulation of an actual government
proposal put Walsh in a much stronger bargaining position
with his colleagues than he had held in June, when he had
only informal intimations of the Castle authorities' sympathy
with his own ideal and the only formal proposal in circulation was the Robertson report. The hierarchy appointed the
four archbishops—Logue, Walsh, Healy and Fennelly—as
a committee to negotiate with the government on the matter.[26] Wyndham was nearly ecstatic as he wrote, on the day
of the hierarchy's meeting, to Mrs Drew, daughter of W. E.

Gladstone, whose first government had been defeated in 1873 partly because of opposition from the hierarchy to a bill almost identical with the scheme he was now putting forward:

The undoubted and growing desire of many interests in Ireland to draw together and treat each other in a more kindly and reasonable spirit; and, though I can scarcely breathe it to you, the resurrection, in all but absolute identity, of the Irish position on Catholic University Education which your father was prevented from turning to account—all these things bring from day to day a memory of you to my mind.[27]

Walsh now began to work in earnest with MacDonnell to effect their common purpose. For the moment he had turned the tables on his principal enemies within the hierarchy— Healy and O'Dwyer—who had rather treacherously gained the upper hand in the Robertson Commission's deliberations two years earlier. He still had to deal with opposition from Unionist and Protestant opinion. Walsh's difficulties were illustrated on the very day of the hierarchy's meeting when Dr O'Dea, who had just been elevated from the vice-presidency of Maynooth to the bishopric of Clonfert, publicly criticised MacDonnell's scheme for its failure to deal with the Cork and Galway colleges, which some western and southern bishops coveted, and for an implication that Maynooth students desiring an arts degree might have to do some work in residence at the new Dublin college.[28] MacDonnell apparently wrote to Walsh expressing concern over O'Dea's pronouncement. In his reply, Walsh explained the working of the committee of the four archbishops in a way which throws some light on the hierarchy's decision-making procedure:

The impossibility of controlling individual utterances must be evident to you. The outcome of what has been done *with unanimity* by the body is that everyone will (and *must*) stand by whatever *we four* do. I mention this, not at all, of course, as standing in the way of individual communications, but in order to show you the practical unimportance of what *any one else* may say if it is not endorsed by the authorised exponents of the mind of the Bishops as a body.[29]

On 'the particular point regarding Maynooth', the Archbishop assured Sir Antony that he and Healy could 'make out for you a *modus vivendi*', and he added the interesting remark that 'You may take it that whatever *we two* say will be said by the four.'

Meanwhile, rumours of the scheme had, on 22 October, taken the tangible form of a two-column article in *The Times,* whose correspondent reported that the Provost and Senior Fellows of Trinity, with one exception, were hostile to the scheme, and though a considerable minority of the Junior Fellows were believed not to share this hostility, the College's constitution gave the Junior Fellows no voice in the matter.[30] Wyndham tried to overcome this obstacle by offering a grant of £10,000 per annum to Trinity as part of the scheme on condition that the College would give its support to the whole scheme.[31] The news of this offer had leaked to the press by the time of Walsh's letter to MacDonnell of 28 October. The Archbishop had clearly been privy to the offer, and predicted there would be 'a row' whose result would be 'hard to conjecture'. 'The bribe is a big one,' he had written candidly, 'but you have to deal with people who attach more importance to the maintenance of Protestant ascendancy in Ireland, as embodied in its last remaining stronghold, than to any of the real advantages that a Protestant College like T.C.D., *if anxious only about its own good,* would look for.'[32]

The 'bribe' was rejected a week later when the Council of Trinity College formally endorsed resolutions adopted by the College's Board several months earlier, opposing the establishment of any denominational college within Dublin University and offering to provide facilities within the College itself for 'the religious instruction and superintendence of Roman Catholic students'. Although there were indications that a strong minority wanted to postpone the matter while the government's intentions were so vague,[33] the diehard view was the one which attracted attention. When O'Dwyer spoke at a meeting of the University College Literary and Historical Society on 11 November, he took the opportunity to endanger Walsh's delicate bargaining position. 'If the Episcopalian body in Ireland and the authorities of Trinity College wrapped themselves up in their wealth and in their privileges, and turned tail at the idea of uniting with a Romanist College,' he asked rhetorically, 'then why not leave them there? Why not do the simple and straight thing and give the people of Ireland what they wanted, what they would rally to, and what would draw their best enthusiasm— a University ACCORDING TO THEIR HEART?'[34]

Walsh himself may have believed that Wyndham would revert to the Robertson scheme if the bribe were rejected, for before Trinity's action he had written to MacDonnell that rejection of the bribe would 'at any rate leave £10,000 a year free to go towards the establishment of equality in point of endowment, if it cannot be made the means of bringing about equality in the matter of University status'.[35] By this time, however, Wyndham had acquired a determination— foolhardy in retrospect—to persist with the Dublin University scheme even in the face of Trinity's opposition. Walsh's acquiescence in this determination meant his acceptance of an enormous task. If the chief affected institution of Irish Protestant Unionism was not to be won to the scheme with ease, then at least some Unionists would have to be persuaded to look upon (1) the scheme, and (2) Catholics generally, with good will. The creation of a favourable image of these two entities during the next three months would tax Walsh's prestige and influence very heavily.

The crucial unsettled point in the scheme was whether the hierarchy would have, as they had always insisted in the past, a certain number of seats *de jure* on the governing body of the new Catholic college. MacDonnell apparently urged Walsh to press for acceptance of an understanding that the hierarchy would have *de facto* representation guaranteed by the same sort of convention which maintained the denominational balance on the education boards. Walsh, anticipating no doubt the reluctance of his colleagues to abandon their claim to *de jure* representation, tried to persuade MacDonnell that the plan for *de facto* nomination would draw Orange criticism as a devious and 'underhand' scheme just as the *de jure* plan would as a form of special treatment.[36] Realising the weakness of his argument, however, he seems not to have pressed the point, and by the end of the year, according to Walsh's biographer, Archbishops Healy and Walsh, in a meeting with Wyndham and MacDonnell, had approved the main principles of a scheme.[37]

The vehicle for presentation of the scheme was a public letter over Lord Dunraven's signature, but almost certainly drafted by MacDonnell, which was published on 4 January 1904.[38] The letter proposed the establishment within Dublin University of two additional colleges, 'the Queen's College, Belfast, and a King's College to be established in Dublin—which Colleges, like Trinity, should be well equipped financially, and should be autonomous and residential, with governing bodies selected exclusively on academical grounds'. A Senate would be set up to maintain standards for the granting of degrees, and a visiting body would be entrusted with excluding any instruction repugnant to the faith and morals of the students. The letter was carefully and persuasively reasoned, and a movement to promote the scheme was immediately organised. At first episcopal reaction was cautious. Archbishop Healy and Bishop O'Dea addressed noncommittal letters to a public meeting held in Galway on 6 January to press for a university settlement, and Bishop MacCormack, who spoke briefly, called Dunraven's letter admirable, but did not go into details.[39]

Another such meeting was planned for 13 January in Limerick, and—remembering, no doubt, Bishop O'Dwyer's remarks in November—Sir Antony apparently wrote to the Bishop to urge him to say nothing which would endanger the scheme. O'Dwyer began his reply with unctuous thanks 'for your great kindness and friendliness to me in writing to me as you have done', and he continued: 'Of course I need not assure you that your very grave words will make me weigh my own very carefully, and avoid any peremptory tone in discussing the point at issue.' With these preliminary courtesies out of the way, the Bishop felt

bound to state that the danger of allowing Catholic opinion to drift without guidance at this stage is so great, and is so likely to put us Bishops ultimately in a cruelly false position, in case we cannot accept the Government's proposals that I think it necessary to indicate clearly what the position is which we have taken up hitherto in relation to the essential conditions of the problem to be solved.[40]

As Sir Antony had been so good as to write to him, the Bishop thought, it 'only fair to be thus frank with you, and to add that speaking entirely for myself, I could not be a party to accepting a college constituted in the way that Lord Dunraven describes; and I am very strongly of opinion that this will be the view of the majority of the Bishops'. They had waited and worked for a long time, and it seemed to O'Dwyer 'a poor result of it all to surrender every shred of denominational principle for which we strove'.

MacDonnell immediately sent O'Dwyer's letter to Walsh who returned it with the comment that he 'quite took it for granted that the view indicated in it would be not only taken, but expressed'. This was, the Archbishop explained, his primary reason for pressing for a general meeting of the bishops. 'Of course,' he conceded, 'if that be the view of the body, it will be, for the moment, a check, and a very serious one. But it may be possible still to find a way of getting round even that awkward obstacle.' Walsh's description of his plans reveals something of the conventions within which episcopal politics were conducted. For the moment, in Walsh's opinion, the important thing was that he had secured a general episcopal meeting, which was to be held on Tuesday, 12 January, 'the day before the threatened danger', i.e. the projected public meeting in Limerick, where O'Dwyer could be expected to air his views. 'So', the Archbishop wrote, 'the danger is off, in case the majority of the Bishops take the favourable view, as I trust they will— though, no doubt, there will be, at best, a strong body of opinion, and of influential opinion, going the other way.' Apparently Sir Antony had suggested the possibility of delaying episcopal action, and Walsh admitted that calling the meeting was 'a venturesome policy'.

But as I view the case [he wrote], it is the only safe policy. If the view taken be the favourable one, the course is clear of all difficulty. And I think you will now see that if we were not to meet next Tuesday, irreparable harm would be done. The mere fact that a hostile declaration had been made, would undoubtedly influence some few to abstain from taking the other side, even though, on the general merits, they might be inclined to do so.[41]

In other words, one bishop could seriously frustrate the will of a majority of the hierarchy if he managed to state a dissenting view before the entire hierarchy could act.

What the Archbishop said in this passage is indicative of a fundamental change from the rough-and-tumble mode of ecclesiastical politics which had prevailed in the middle of the nineteenth century. The kind of disputation which took place in 1838 between Archbishops Murray and MacHale in the columns of the public press[42] was simply unthinkable in 1904. At the time of the Parnell crisis, O'Dwyer, Healy and one other bishop had silently abstained from the general policy of the hierarchy, but in 1890 even this gesture was most extraordinary. In an age of rapid communications and widespread literacy, open disagreement between bishops could seriously damage the aura of authority which surrounded the episcopal office. The hierarchy was under enormous pressure to seek a consensus and to present at least the appearance of unanimity whenever they acted publicly. Indeed, public displays of dissension had been explicitly prohibited by ecclesistical legislation.[43] O'Dwyer represented the last vestige of resistance to the centralised management of this consensus which had begun under Cullen and which Walsh now carried on. In a postscript to his letter to Sir Antony on 7 January, Walsh wrote: 'No personal influence could be used with effect. Besides I have none in the case in question.' O'Dwyer, though he probably could not again risk the isolated public abstention from general episcopal policy which he had tried to maintain in 1891 even after Healy had submitted to the consensus, was quite capable of taking advantage of the conventions which now worked even more strongly for consensus. By following the plan he outlined to MacDonnell, however, Walsh managed to avert wrecking action by O'Dwyer in this instance.

The Bishop of Limerick might, of course, make a statement on his own initiative before the episcopal meeting, without waiting for the public meeting in Limerick, but events were moving too rapidly for him to take such action. Once the meeting of the hierarchy had been called it would have been very unseemly for a bishop to volunteer his opinion to the public without waiting to consult his colleagues, though if he had been asked for his opinion, as in effect he would be at the proposed public meeting in Limerick, he could hardly be faulted for answering honestly. The bishops duly assembled at Maynooth on 12 January, and while it was 'understood that the business before the meeting had reference to the University Question', their Lordships confined their public action to an expression of sympathy at the death of Count Arthur Moore.[44] Privately, however, all the prelates except O'Dwyer[45] agreed to a resolution that Walsh be authorised

to intimate confidentially to Mr. Wyndham that the Bishops, whilst not expressing any preference for the scheme outlined by the Earl of Dunraven, consider that a satisfactory settlement of the University Question can be arrived at on the lines indicated in his Lordship's letter. But if, from the attitude of Trinity College, or any other [cause], the Government are not prepared to give legislative effect to the proposals of Lord Dunraven, we then call upon them to adopt the alternative scheme for the settlement of the question recommended in the Report of the Royal Commission.[46]

Walsh was unable, it seems, to overcome the desire of more conservative prelates to allow Trinity to kill the scheme. He did manage, however, to bring Wyndham one important concession:

With regard to the particular point of giving the Bishops an *ex officio* representation on the Governing Body of the proposed Catholic College . . . the Bishops deem it a matter of the highest importance to secure such representation, and are unable to see any sufficient reason why it should be withheld. But if insistence on this point would imperil the projected measure they then would not insist on this claim in case the measure should prove otherwise satisfactory.[47]

MacDonnell complained two years later: 'I regard the Bishop of Limerick (O'Dwyer) as an irresponsible vituperative politician. He *alone* of all the Irish Bishops held aloof from the agreement to accept an additional College in the Dublin University as a Solution.'[48] Nevertheless, O'Dwyer was on his good behaviour at the Limerick meeting on the day after the hierarchy's meeting. He said he would accept a college in either the Royal University or Dublin University, but he added that he would have to see the latter scheme presented 'in black and white' by 'responsible persons' before committing himself. He counselled his audience not to despair of a solution if Wyndham should fail to persuade his cabinet colleagues, and concluded with a story of the young Abbé de Bernis who was told by the Archbishop of Paris, 'an old man tottering to his grave', that he would never give him a benefice. '"Monseigneur," said de Bernis, "I can wait."'[49] O'Dwyer, too, preferred to wait, in the confidence that the Orangemen and the Trinity power structure would kill Wyndham's idealistic scheme, and he was absolutely correct in his assessment of the situation.

Walsh had delivered to the Castle an episcopal concession more sweeping than MacDonnell and Wyndham had any right to expect, but already the anti-Catholic and undenominational forces were grouping to defeat the proposal. Probably the Castle officials intimated to Walsh their uncertainties of winning Balfour's support when the Archbishop communicated the bishops' resolution to them, for on 13 January, the day after the episcopal meeting, he wrote a very despondent public letter to Redmond. Ostensibly for the purpose of forwarding his annual subscription to the Parliamentary Fund, the letter was primarily a lament over the state of the university question. 'Of late,' Walsh remarked, 'I have found myself almost driven to abandon the little that still remains to me of faith in the efficacy of Parliamentary action as a means of getting redress of our grievances in this country.'[50] He recounted in some detail how since 1885 the university question had been repeatedly postponed from one parliamentary session to the next or to the indefinite future. He stressed the hierarchy's statement in 1896 that they would accept either a Catholic university or college and concluded by saying that when the history of the question came to be written it could not be said 'that the perpetuation of the present lamentable condition of affairs is in the smallest degree to be ascribed to any failure on the part of the Irish Bishops to make good their words'.

Just at this moment, when Walsh had won a crucial concession from his colleagues, he was confronted by a situation which threatened to undermine whatever support there may have been among English and Irish Protestants for the scheme. During the autumn the Catholic Association seems to have become rather aggressive in its efforts to apply pressure to Protestant businessmen. It was, inevitably, calling forth a hostile reaction from the opposite side, as evidenced by the formation of a Society for the Protection of Protestant Interests.[51] Prominent Catholics as well began to protest against the programme of the Catholic Association.[52] The *Independent,* in response to an inquiry from 'A Catholic', raised the question whether or not Archbishop Walsh had appointed a chaplain to the Association. Walsh replied in a letter published on 9 January. Observing that the Association was not confined to his diocese, he declined to express an individual opinion upon 'the charges . . . made against it in so many letters in the public Press', a 'matter to be dealt with either by the general body of the Irish Bishops or by our standing committee at its next meeting'.[53] He then took the opportunity to recount how, in October 1902 he had received from 'a certain clergyman' of a religious order in Dublin a letter and a circular which was apparently being sent to all the bishops. The objects of the Association as set forth in the circular appeared to Walsh to be of a 'most commendable character', but he was alarmed to find his own chaplain named on the circular as the proposed chaplain of the Association. As neither he nor his chaplain had authorised this action, Walsh called for an explanation and was told that no harm had been intended. The 'certain clergyman' had simply wanted to indicate that the Association was 'in touch with his Grace', a plea which elicited from Walsh the observation that 'It is one thing to state the object of such a proceeding, and another thing to attempt to justify it.' At the regular autumn meeting of the hierarchy a few days later, Walsh had 'explained to his colleagues the facts of his supposed connexion with the association'. Alluding to Bishop Foley's remarks at the Maynooth Union, he stated:

The Bishop of Kildare has already explained how, in the absence of further satisfactory information, the projected association—as distinct from its unquestionably praiseworthy objects —then failed to obtain the sanction of the body of the Bishops. As for myself, the question put to the editor of the *Daily Independent* is very easily answered. I have appointed no chaplain to the Catholic Association. Nor am I likely to appoint a chaplain to any association organized in so improper a fashion as the association has been.[54]

Nevertheless, he reiterated his willingness to support an association 'organized in a business-like way' to promote the original objects which had been presented to the bishops in 1902.

Within a few days, the hierarchy did hold the meeting at which they privately gave conditional approval to the Dunraven scheme. Whether Walsh raised the issue of the Catholic Association's conduct as his letter implied that he would is not clear. In any event, on the following Sunday Walsh acted unilaterally by having a pastoral letter read in all his churches concerning 'the proceedings of the association styling itself the "Catholic Association", as worked in this diocese'.[55] Though he referred briefly to 'the Christian law that forbids the needless stirring up of strife', he concentrated upon 'the enormous injury . . . being done to Catholic interests'. 'I could mention case after case,' the Archbishop wrote, 'many of them very painful ones, in which, as a result of what is being done in Dublin, Catholic traders and Catholic *employés,* and some even of the most worthy Catholic charitable and benevolent institutions in this diocese, have suffered substantial loss.' Dublin Catholics, therefore, were admonished of 'their plain duty not to leave it open to any one to suppose that the evil work which is doing such grievous harm to Catholic interests and exposing the Catholic religion itself to unmerited obloquy has either their support or their countenance'.

Walsh's action, which may well have earned the hostility of some of his colleagues, was justified because the stakes—a university settlement according to his fondest hopes—were very high, even though the risk that the scheme would miscarry was also very high. The Unionists' long period in office was obviously coming to an end, and many ecclesiastics no doubt shared the belief of Bishop MacCormack of Galway, that the university question 'could only be settled by Tory Ministers. If the Liberals came into power they would not settle the question.'[56] On the day after Walsh's pastoral was read, Wyndham screwed up his courage to write to Balfour on the subject. 'We are approaching', he bravely asserted, 'to agreement between all parties exclusive only of the more extreme Orangemen.' 'The R.C. Hierarchy', he reported, 'have, at last, waived their demand for *de jure* representation on the governing body of a new college.'[57] This was his trump card, and once he had played it he held a weak hand indeed. The Catholic laity, he asserted, had 'come to life'—which meant only that they had drawn up another petition as they did whenever the issue came to public attention. 'The Unionists—bar extreme Orangemen—are in favour of action,' Wyndham assured the Prime Minister, ignoring the fact that it was the Orangemen, and not the sensible, aristocratic Unionists like Dunraven, who constituted the government's most important electoral support in Ireland. In the course of composing his letter Wyndham seems to have come to recognise how weak his position was, and he ended with an almost pathetic plea, not for government backing, but simply for a day to debate the question, in the belief 'that a free discussion would disabuse many English Unionists of their misapprehensions on the question'. It was all in vain, for on 22 January Lord Londonderry, Lord President of the Council and President of the Board of Education, spoke in Dublin and made it plain that the government had no intention of acting on the question.[58] Dillon accurately summed up the situation in a letter to Redmond on 24 January: 'I had not heard that the Bishops had given up their claim for a de jure representation. . . . I am glad of it. But they will not get their Bill—the Belfastmen have knocked the bottom out of the whole business.'[59]

PART TWO

Tension, 1904-1908

CHAPTER VI

The Flowing Tide

THE disappointment of the hierarchy's hopes for a university settlement affected the entire balance of political forces in Ireland. Since 1886 the Conservatives, who had held office in the State continuously but for a brief interval in 1892–95, had dangled a Catholic university before the bishops' eyes. It was now obvious that the Conservatives' time was running out and that they had failed to produce this one measure which the bishops most wanted. At the same time the Irish Parliamentary Party was adjusting to the effects of the land settlement in a way which strengthened its claim to be the sole legitimate agency of the Nation. Redmond was dissuaded, primarily by Dillon, from following O'Brien into the policy of settling the question of self-government by conference with Lord Dunraven and other moderate Unionists. Although in retrospect one may be attracted to the ideas of O'Brien and Dunraven as a way by which partition might have been avoided, the majority of the party leadership were acting on sound political judgement by keeping the party clearly identified with a national claim—with the understanding that for practical purposes the Nation did not command the allegiance of Lord Dunraven, his fellow landlords or his more numerous co-religionists in the North. Moreover, the prospect of an end to the long Unionist regime raised the possibilty that the Irish Party might actually achieve a position from which they could extract Home Rule from a Liberal government. At the same time, O'Brien, by petulantly vacating his Cork City seat in the Commons late in 1903 (even though he was re-elected without opposition the following year), permanently isolated himself from the party's inner councils. Thus the party was effectively rid of the one leader who most aroused clerical suspicions.

As the Conservatives' stock as credible representatives of the State was falling and that of the Irish Party as spokesmen for the Nation was rising, the Church naturally adjusted her relations with both. On the available evidence, Walsh's condemnation of the Catholic Association can be read in either of two complementary ways. If he tried at the hierarchy's meeting of 12 January 1904 to secure a general condemnation and was rebuffed, then his action would appear to be a last-ditch attempt to protect his efforts to extract his preferred university settlement from the declining Conservative administration. On the other hand, a month later Bishop Foley described the Catholic Association in his Lenten pastoral as an organisation to which the bishops 'had never committed themselves, and from which . . . they had formally and publicly dissociated themselves through one of their members'[1]—suggesting that perhaps the hierarchy agreed that the Association should be killed, but that, to avoid embarrassment to prelates who had earlier endorsed it, they had deputed Walsh to do the 'dirty work'. On this assumption, the condemnation may have more of the character of an attempt by the Church to minimise conflict with the party, whose stock on the futures market was beginning to look very good indeed.

In October 1903 a by-election was occasioned in West Belfast by the elevation of the sitting member, H. O. Arnold-Forster, a Liberal Unionist, to the post of Secretary for War. The party organisation in Belfast, led by Joseph Devlin, M.P. for North Kilkenny, which had not contested the seat since 1892, decided to put up a candidate and tried to secure the assistance of Bishop Henry. They were especially anxious to obtain the Belfast Catholic Association's files of information on voter registration which were vital to a successful contest in a constituency nearly evenly divided between Catholics and Protestants. The Bishop adamantly refused to co-operate except on terms which would amount to party recognition of the B.C.A. as at least its equal in Belfast politics.[2] Despite some evidence of a willingness on the part of clerical and lay leaders of the Association to make terms with the local U.I.L. branch,[3] the Bishop remained obstinate, the register was not provided, and Arnold-Forster was re-elected by 3,912 votes to 3,671.[4] Party leaders charged that Henry had made a deal with local Unionists to abstain from opposing their candidate in return for Arnold-Forster's support for a Catholic university settlement.[5] Although the evidence Nationalists claimed to have of this transaction was never forthcoming, such a deal would at least have been consistent with Henry's ham-handed political style. Ironically, at the very moment when the efforts to effect a university settlement were foundering in January 1904, Henry sent emissaries to make peace with Redmond, and the party leader reportedly spurned the entreaty with the statement that Balfour had told him that a University Bill would not be introduced precisely because Arnold-Forster threatened to resign if it were.[6]

If Henry did think he was improving the prospects of a university settlement by his action, it is instructive to compare his action with that of Walsh. Henry handled the situation in a way that accomplished nothing but the irritation of the increasingly strong and united Irish Party and its organisation. Walsh, by condemning the Catholic Association in Dublin, admittedly did not gain his university settlement, but in the process he did the party a favour just at a moment when the Church was beginning to need the party's services. The party's supporters in Belfast, smarting from defeat by the B.C.A. in the municipal election two days before Walsh's pastoral, prepared handbills suggesting that the Archbishop's strictures applied to the Belfast Catholic Association. When these tracts were distributed outside Belfast churches, Bishop Henry responded with a pastoral which maintained that 'The local Catholic Association is essentially distinct from the organisation bearing that name in Dublin.'[7] Nevertheless, less than three months later the Belfast Catholic Association was appointing delegates to the national Catholic Association's convention, despite the fact that, according to the *Northern Star*, which was undoubtedly keeping a very careful tally, at least five bishops had condemned the 'All-Ireland Catholic Association . . . as a mischievous body'.[8] Early in March Henry produced a letter from Walsh, disclaiming—as the simple courtesies of episcopal relations would demand—any intention of interfering in the affairs of another diocese. No matter what Walsh might say at this stage, however, his pronouncement was having practical, if not theoretical, effect beyond his own diocese.

While the university question was alive, churchmen had been somewhat reluctant to give vent to their suspicions of the government's intentions in primary and secondary education which had been festering since Starkie's famous speech in 1902. F. H. Dale, an English school inspector, had been commissioned to investigate the National School system in Ireland and to recommend reforms. At their October 1903 meeting the bishops took public note of rumours 'that changes are contemplated in the organisation of Primary and Secondary Education in this country which would have the effect of placing the organisation of our educational systems on a footing similar to that of the Agricultural and Technical Department'.[10] By this circumlocution they meant the replacement of the autonomous boards with an education department directed by paid 'experts' and the introduction of local rate support. Their lordships took 'the earliest opportunity of entering a protest against the introduction of any such scheme'. The rumours the bishops had heard were altogether correct: Wyndham was actively contemplating just such a scheme,[11] though he refrained from announcing his plans until after the publication of Dale's Report in March 1904.

Although Dale gave the National School system satisfactory marks in comparison with English schools in certain areas and was particularly pleased with instruction in the convent schools, he made no attempt to hide deficiencies in other areas in which the clergy were particularly sensitive. He traced many of the problems, in significant measure, to the peculiar financial arrangements of the system. The efficiency of instruction, for example, was impaired by the wasteful proliferation of schools, not only to meet demands of Catholics and various sects of Protestants, but to provide segregated facilities for children of different sexes and ages. This multiplication of schools had occurred because the powers of the managers were 'divorced from any adequate financial responsibility', and he recommended greater powers for the Board to eliminate unnecessary schools and 'to control more effectively the character of the organisation and staffing of any School'.[12] In his opinion, however, 'the most vital defect in Irish education when compared with the English' was not the absence of adequate central control, but 'the lack of any local interest in the conduct of the schools'.[13] He chose his steps very carefully in dealing with the question of physical facilities, with which the problem of local interest was most intimately connected. Distinguishing between town and country schools, he criticised severely the structural quality of the town schools and stated unequivocally that this defect could only be remedied by the establishment of 'local bodies with the power of rating and the responsibility for school supply'.[14] The country schools, however, compared rather favourably with English country schools as regards the actual structures, though there were a few 'extremely unsuitable' premises. The primary defects of the country school buildings were 'the want of cleanliness, the neglect of small repairs, and the insufficient heating'.[15] It had been frequently suggested, he noted, that such defects should be remedied by an additional State grant for repairs, heating and cleaning, but, he argued, 'it would be contrary to every principle of sound finance'[16] for the State to accept responsibility for maintaining structures which it did not own and whose use it did not control. Moreover, in England, Scotland, Germany and France these matters had always been regarded as a local charge because 'such services are most expeditiously and cheaply performed by the locality'. He believed that the proposal of State grants for heating, cleaning and repairs indicated a common misconception as to the cause of the defects:

The unsatisfactory nature of the arrangements for heating and cleaning in many Irish Schools when these arrangements are judged by the standard attained in English country schools, stands on a different footing from the failure to provide universally such expensive buildings as are to be seen in England. The latter defect is due in many cases to poverty; the former is one of the signs of the comparative lack of local interest in Primary Education in Ireland.[17]

He suggested that the defects in cleanliness and heating could be remedied 'only by fixing the responsibility for the condition of the Schools in these respects upon the Managers, and

5

by arousing a general local interest in elementary education'.[18] Although he avoided recommending rates for building maintenance in rural areas as a means of fostering this local interest, he made a dangerous suggestion in connection with the State grant for teachers' salaries. As the lack of local interest was 'due in part to the failure of the present system of State-aid to devolve any financial responsibility on the locality or to provide such inducements to persons of position and education to take a part in the work of School management, as exist in England',[19] the schools should be grouped under some responsible authority which would administer the grant for teachers' salaries under the supervision of the central office.

In a speech in the Commons a few days after the publication of Dale's report, Redmond drew freely upon the inspector's description of filth and disrepair in Irish schoolhouses to argue for allocation of funds from the development grant to primary education. Although he carefully avoided endorsement of Dale's specific recommendations, he did, almost as an aside, repeat the common allegation that expenses of school upkeep had to be met out of teachers' own pockets.[20] Because this contention had often been advanced by teachers in criticism of stingy managers, the remark touched a very sensitive clerical nerve. Bishop O'Donnell wrote to Redmond: 'There is a strong feeling that you were imposed on by teachers unfriendly to their managers,'[21] and warned of possible repercussions at a forthcoming meeting of the Catholic Clerical Managers' Association for Armagh province. Redmond provided O'Donnell with a letter designed to soothe ruffled feelings, and the Bishop placed copies of the letter in circulation among the clergy.[22] Apparently this action was successful, for the Association's meeting the following week produced no public attacks on Redmond. In Elphin diocese, which because it is outside Armagh province was probably unaffected by O'Donnell's lobbying on Redmond's behalf, the Catholic clerical managers declared:

That we consider the statement of a prominent member of the Irish Parliamentary Party in the House of Commons in March last that the repairs, up-keep, and heating of the schools are done by the teachers, misleading and untrue; and that we regret that in this, and other parts of the speech referred to, the speaker relied on the report of Mr. Dale, an English Inspector imported by the Government to prop up Dr. Starkie in his false charges against the managers, and his attack on their present influence in the management of the schools.[23]

Such bitter invective as this against Dale, however, was the exception rather than the rule. Both Mgr Byrne, who delivered the principal address at the Armagh meeting, and Archbishop Walsh, who had commented publicly on the report two days earlier, found certain points in the report to agree with before attacking his suggested financial reforms. Mgr Byrne denounced in particular 'one exceedingly dangerous and mischievous idea pervading the entire report', viz. the suggestion that the upkeep of schools would be inadequate 'until some local body with the power of the public purse at its back shall have acquired a certain amount of control over them'.[24] Walsh, still rankling over the university debacle, commented that 'There is no possible mistake in connection with the work of education in Ireland, that I should be disposed to regard as beyond the capacity of our present Irish Administration to commit.'[25] In general, however, criticism of Dale himself was surprisingly muted in anticipation of a declaration of government policy on the issues he raised.

A few days later the House of Commons conducted its first full-dress debate on Irish education since the publication of Dale's report. Before Wyndham had even stated the government's plans, Redmond, in response to a suggestion by an English M.P. for an education department to replace the autonomous boards, placed the party on record as unalterably opposed to such a move, stigmatising it as merely 'the creation of a new Castle board'.[26] Wyndham, deliberately waiting until enough viewpoints had been expressed to make the problems seem intractable, finally rose and outlined three possible courses for dealing with Irish education. The first course—'to pour Irish money into the three separate and unco-ordinated receptacles afforded by the systems of primary, secondary, and technical education'[27]—he rejected, thereby signalling that the government intended to use financial pressure to overcome resistance to reform. The second course—'a very ambitious and comprehensive attempt' at reform, presumably embodying a co-ordinated department and rate-aid—he rejected as well because it might fail and thereby 'delay the course of educational reform for years'. The course he proposed to follow was to begin the gradual introduction of co-ordination, local control and rate-aid at the level of secondary and technical education with the intention of extending such reforms to the primary system 'at not a very late date'.[28]

With the government's intentions—if not its resolve or even its ability to effect them—now on record, the Church, no longer inhibited by any danger of damaging prospects of an imminent university settlement, began an all-out campaign against 'reform' of primary and secondary education. The first step in ecclesiastical strategy was to make peace with the teachers. The murmurs which greeted Redmond's reference to contributions by teachers to school maintenance suggest that many clergy were still emotionally involved in the dismal round of recriminations between teachers and managers which took place five years earlier. One priest even went so far as to declare that 12,500 of the 13,000 teachers were 'leagued with the hereditary foes of Ireland's faith and Ireland's Nationality in their well-planned plot to kick the priests out of the schools, and turn Ireland into a France'.[29] For the most part the teacher-clergy conflict had died down, the teachers having made profuse gestures of repentance, and the ban under which the I.N.T.O. had been placed in Armagh and Tuam provinces had 'gradually ceased to be enforced',[30] though it remained formally in effect. Early in June the clerical managers of Tuam province resolved that their bishops 'be consulted as to whether the time has now come' when the ban should be withdrawn.[31] A few weeks later the Central Council of the Managers' Association declared that they rejoiced at the disappearance of friction between the Catholic National Teachers and their clerical managers.[32] Although the ban was not formally withdrawn in Armagh province until the following year,[33] the Church clearly now wanted and needed an alliance with the teachers against the reformers.

At their June meeting the hierarchy adopted a long, carefully worded statement on education in which they charged

that the reformers were 'attacking ostensibly the present system, but in reality the power of the clergy in the schools'.[34]
The bishops argued that the recent equivalent grant, most
of which Wyndham had in effect diverted from educational
purposes in connection with his land purchase scheme, would
be sufficient to remedy all practical defects in the schools for
which rate support was proposed. Citing voluntary contributions to refute charges of lack of local interest in the schools,
they defended the 'sensible' attitude of parents who refrained
from interfering in matters 'somewhat outside their competence'. While accepting the need for co-ordination among
the branches of education, they maintained that this whole
question must be deferred until the university question was
settled. They specifically denounced the proposal for 'a
Government Department, subject to the British Parliament
and directed by Government officials' and, significantly, con-
gratulated Redmond for his 'prompt and decisive action'
against it.

In the months that followed, public statements by members of the hierarchy confirmed that they were truly alarmed
by the trend of events. O'Dwyer credited Wyndham himself
with responsibility for evils out of which he had tried 'to
make a case for a secularist department'.[35] Bishop Sheehan
of Waterford and Lismore indicated in a speech at Clonmel
on 20 July his apprehension that 'An attempt may be made
under one pretext or another to divorce our system of education from the spirit of religion.'[36] On 28 August, in a speech
at Fermoy, Bishop Browne of Cloyne alluded to many indications in recent years that persons 'high in authority at the
National Board' were determined to alter the system and
'to make it again a source of danger to the faith and best
interests of our Catholic people (*applause*)'.[37] Several members
of the hierarchy were presented with opportunities to express
themselves in reply to resolutions of local councils who protested suggestions of secularising the schools and, by implication, disclaimed any desire to accept responsibilities in education. Bishop Gaffney of Meath, in replying to such a
resolution from the Mullingar Rural District Council, observed that 'Many of the inspectors are going through the
country spreading terror and dominating everybody and

everything. They are clearly preparing for a coup d'etat.'[38] In reply to a similar resolution from the Sligo District Council, Bishop Clancy of Elphin expressed his pleasure that 'The members of our public representative bodies . . . are determined that under the democratic rule of the future religious interests shall not suffer at their hands.'[39] In addition to local councils, some local teachers' associations passed resolutions of protest,[40] and Dillon, at a meeting in Ballaghaderreen presided over by Bishop Lyster of Achonry, took the opportunity to make considerable political capital out of the government's 'DEEP LAID PLOT TO REVOLUTIONISE THE WHOLE SYSTEM OF EDUCATION'.[41] At their October meeting the hierarchy directed that their June statement be read in churches, and expressed to local authorities their 'gratification at the intelligent and keen appreciation so many of them have manifested of the gravity of the issue'.[42] The Church had summoned the Nation to her defence, and she had not been disappointed.

Ecclesiastics recognised, of course, that they could expect the Nation's representatives to give the Church's interests more than, perfunctory advocacy only if they provided a *quid pro quo*. Not since the reunion of 1900, accompanied as it was by the expulsion of Healy, had the Irish Parliamentary Party received a general espiscopal endorsement. Even yet some ecclesiastics had not reconciled themselves to Healy's political eclipse. At festivities connected with the consecration of Armagh Cathedral in July, Cardinal Logue had proposed a toast to Irish laity present. Expressing his sorrow that Redmond had left early, he substituted the name of Sir Thomas Grattan Esmonde, the party's Chief Whip, in the toast, but he could not refrain from coupling the name of T. M. Healy with that of Sir Thomas, demonstrating thereby that he had not ceased to regard Healy as a special guardian of Catholic interests despite the latter's exclusion from the party.[43] In January 1905, however, in a long resolution on the university question to be read in the churches, the hierarchy's Standing Committee inserted the significant admonition:

The whole country should rally round our Parliamentary representatives and give them the whole strength of the nation's support in their endeavour to secure ordinary civic rights for Irish Catholics in educational, and all other matters.[44]

The party apparently took advantage of the Standing Committee's resolution to urge that the bishops make individual gestures of support in the form of contributions to the annual Parliamentary Fund drive. Dillon reported to Redmond on 30 January that he had a 'very satisfactory' interview with Dr Fennelly, who had succeeded Croke as Archbishop of Cashel. The Archbishop agreed to subscribe and to 'use his best influence to get all his suffragans to do likewise'.[45] Cardinal Logue even subscribed, sending his cheque, significantly, to Bishop O'Donnell, one of the trustees of the Fund, with the comment: 'In the present circumstances of the country it is vital to her highest interests, spiritual and temporal, that she should be represented in the House of Commons by a strong party, united, independent, and efficient.'[46]

Two prelates who during the agitation of the 1880s had been vilified as 'Castle bishops' sent subscriptions. One of them, Archbishop Healy, gave a brief and straightforward explanation of his action:

I was long hoping that Mr. Balfour and Mr. Wyndham would make an earnest effort to remedy the crying grievance of Irish Catholics in the matter of university education. In that hope I, like many others, have been grievously disappointed. As the Irish Bishops have now formally appealed to the Irish representatives to put the struggle for educational equality in the front of the National programme, I feel it my duty to lend them such support as I can in my own small way.[47]

Healy made no pretence of having been converted to enthusiastic nationalism, justifying his action solely on the basis of the university question. His colleague, Bishop O'Dwyer, however, whose contribution to the Parliamentary Fund was equally remarkable, was careful to stress his sympathy with nationalist goals. 'The first and supreme purpose of your political action', he wrote to Alderman Joyce, Mayor of Limerick, in a long letter accompanying his subscription, 'is the recovery of Home Rule for this country.'[48] Only after a lengthy disquisition on this theme did the Bishop of Limerick turn to the university question and urge the party to 'turn out the present miserable government', on the grounds that 'They have trifled with us and deceived us on the great question of University education and the very principle of their existence is the denial of Irish self-government.' In general the letter was one at which the party could feel most gratified, but O'Dwyer did work one passage into his remarks which was a portent of future difficulties. Referring to the Nonconformist agitation in England against the 1902 Education Act, he expressed his confidence that the Irish members would not 'subordinate the interests of their religion to the political intrigues of these people'. 'I have no doubt', he wrote, 'that men such as our Parliamentary representatives will never be deceived into a line of action that will give the actual gains and profits to the English Nonconformists and far-off hopes and unrealised assurances to us.'

In forwarding his subscription to Alderman Joyce, O'Dwyer commented: 'The obstacle which, as I explained to you recently, hitherto stood in the way of my co-operating with the Irish Party seems to have been happily removed.'[49] This obstacle, Joyce told Redmond privately, was the 'differences' between Bishop Henry and 'our friends in Belfast'.[50] O'Dwyer apparently believed that peace had finally come to the Belfast Catholic community because of a decision by the Belfast Catholic Association to respond to the party's annual appeal for funds by itself organising a collection to be forwarded directly to the trustees of the Parliamentary Fund. At the same time that O'Dwyer wrote, however, a great storm was brewing over this latest initiative by the Association. The officers of the local U.I.L., infuriated by this attempt to by-pass their organisation, formally requested that the subscription be declined by the trustees.[51] Other reports reaching Redmond indicated that this feeling was widely shared by nationalists in districts near Belfast.[52] More significant were indications of clerical feeling in favour of rejecting the subscription. At the time of the preceding year's fund drive, Henry had specifically prohibited his clergy from contributing through the local U.I.L., though he had left them free to send subscriptions directly to the national headquarters. Father Crolly, P.P., Newtownards, just outside Belfast, wrote to Redmond on 12 February: 'I have been speaking to Maguire, Rooney [Belfast U.I.L.

officials] Fathers M'Carhin (D & M) M'Cartan, M'Ilvenny & had communications from O'Donnell, P.P., Antrim & Falloona P.P. Ballycastle & the firm conviction of all of them that the acceptance of contribution being raised by B.C.A. would be fatal to the League in Belfast & *a staggering blow to it throughout the Province.*'[53] Another parish priest, Father John Nolan, deliberately sent his personal subscription to the local U.I.L. instead of sending it to Redmond as he had done the previous year in deference to the Bishop's orders. When the defiant letter accompanying his subscription was published,[54] the Bishop wrote a circular letter to his clergy reiterating his prohibition, under pain of suspension, of clerical contributions, even anonymously, through the local U.I.L.[55]

Redmond wrote to Bishop O'Donnell, who as one of the trustees of the Parliamentary Fund would share responsibility for whatever action might be taken. Though Redmond apparently did not preserve his own side of the correspondence, its essential features can be inferred from O'Donnell's replies. On 17 February he wrote:

The situation is certainly serious. But I should greatly hope that with a little patience there will be nothing that would in any way stop the flowing tide that has been with us. . . . I have . . . written correspondents on both sides urging a good understanding in view of what is happening all over the country. What you say of the feeling in the Party I can well understand. Yet, suppose the organization said that in view of the Bishops' pronouncement and its reception by the Party, it was going to adopt a new and loyal attitude toward the Party; it seems to have an exceedingly strong position for the reception of its money. To be sure if we Trustees have to decide we must squarely go into what the thing means in all its bearings.[56]

It would, nevertheless, be 'a sad business if Belfast were not healed in the general healing'. O'Donnell referred to suggestions he had made in a letter to Dillon and advised Redmond: 'I think a strong move on your part to make unity in Belfast could be undertaken without compromising yourself the Party or any side in Belfast, would be very likely to succeed, and would do good to the Party even if it didn't.' Alluding to certain resolutions which Redmond had apparently suggested publishing, the Bishop said he would 'prefer publishing rejected terms of peace first, if reasonable ones were rejected'.

Redmond did not take the kind of initiative for which Bishop O'Donnell hoped. On 21 February the party met and decided unanimously to reject the contribution.[57] Bishop O'Donnell acknowledged on the 23rd that 'Apart from its authority of course the feeling of the Party in regard to any contribution is a primary consideration,' and he told Redmond that 'While most anxious for and still hopeful about a settlement of the Belfast split, it would not be fair to ask you to intervene against your judgement or where your advisers might reasonably fear you might burn your fingers.' In hopes, however, of diverting the party's course, the Bishop listed three further considerations: (1) a suspicion in the country that the U.I.L. branches wanted a monopoly on the raising of party contributions, (2) the probability that a conflict in Belfast would discourage moves towards unity elsewhere, and (3) the prospect that many would be 'in doubt or misinformed as to who are reasonable and who are unreasonable in Belfast'. He expressed confidence that Redmond and his colleagues would do everything possible to alleviate the Belfast split and added, cryptically, that he was going further that very day than he had ever gone before to see if anything could be done 'to bring about a better feeling'. Anticipating no doubt, that the Association would try to involve him personally in the problem, O'Donnell stated that he would send to Dublin the money and letters that reached him.[58] This expectation was quite correct, for before O'Donnell had even written this letter, Bishop Henry had dispatched to him the 'first instalment of the collection which is being taken up with my approval in Belfast in aid of the Parliamentary Fund, in response to the recommendation contained in the resolutions of the Standing Committee of the Bishops'.[59] O'Donnell sent the cheque for £100 to Alfred Webb, Secretary of the Parliamentary Fund, who was formally advised by Redmond on 27 February that he should return any B.C.A. contribution.[60]

Redmond and his colleagues were following sound instincts when they rejected the Belfast contribution. Henry's own clergy were in revolt. Twenty-five of them, of whom sixteen gave their names, sent contributions to party officials on 2 March, stating that they would have sent them through the Belfast branch of the U.I.L. but for the ecclesiastical prohibtion.[61] More important, Henry was isolated from most of his fellow bishops. The *Northern Star* noted with more than satisfaction, two months after the return of the subscription, that not a single prelate had publicly protested the action and that several bishops had sent in contributions after it was taken.[62] That 'the flowing tide' was with the party was most dramatically evidenced on 27 April when Redmond was cordially received by the Pope, who spent nearly two hours talking with the Irish leader.[63]

Conditions were now favourable for a peace settlement in Belfast. In May a conference of representatives from both sides agreed, after only three sittings, upon a compromise settlement of their differences, with certain outstanding matters to be referred to arbitration.[64] In a letter published on 6 June, Henry, whose absence from the city during the conference may have contributed to its success, noted with pleasure the changed tone of the speeches of U.I.L. leaders. He maintained, however, that

The arrangement by the Peace Conference, agreed upon during my absence, to give power to arbitrators to decide practically whether or not the Catholic Association, after a certain period, should cease to exist, constitutes a serious danger to the hope of harmony amongst the Catholic people of the city, who would most likely refuse to acknowledge the right of their representatives to empower an outside tribunal to determine the existence of an Association established by me to protect and safeguard local Catholic interests.[65]

All this blustering rhetoric was but a face-saving preface to the announcement that 'to prevent . . . the possibility of unpleasantness, . . . in the interest of peace, uninfluenced by any superior authority' the Bishop had decided not to convoke Belfast Catholic householders the following March, as he had done in the past, to continue the Association's work. This, the almost pathetic surrender concluded, would not 'prevent the calling of the organisation into active existence in any future years'.

The dismantling of Bishop Henry's political machine was the consummation of a process which began over a year earlier with the disappointment of the hierarchy's hopes for a university settlement. This process had brought the Church and the Nation, as represented by the Irish Parliamentary Party, into a working alliance against forces in the State opposed to what the Church regarded as her vital interests in education. The party was, of course, not the only organ of the Nation, whose younger generation had identified itself with the Irish Ireland movement around 1900. During 1905 this younger generation was also mobilised for the struggle against secularisation. The occasion for their mobilisation was provided by a change in the role of the National Education Board itself in the reform controversy. The annual revision of the rules for the operation of the National system published early in 1905 contained, as Rule 127(b), the provision that 'Boys under eight years of age are ineligible for enrolment in a boys' school where there is not an assistant mistress, unless there is no suitable school under a mistress available in the locality.'[66] A 'suitable school' was the Board's euphemism for one of the same religious denomination as the pupils concerned. There was no threat to the existing system of religious segregation. Rather the rule was an attack on such frequent practices as the maintenance of two separate Catholic schools, side by side, for boys and girls respectively, in districts where neither school could expect an average attendance large enough to justify more than one teacher. Both teachers were required—perhaps with the assistance of older pupils—to instruct children of three years of age and upwards. Despite the obvious inefficiency of the proliferation of small schools which Dale had criticised so strongly, an amalgamation policy ran counter to the interests of the teachers—some of whose jobs might be abolished if amalgamation went very far—and the sentiments of the managers. Perhaps the clergy feared that larger schools might facilitate encroachment by bureaucratic central authorities upon managerial prerogatives, but they also sincerely opposed co-education.

In January 1905 Bishop Foley had accepted the seat on the National Board which had been vacant since Walsh's resignation in 1901.[67] He soon found himself caught between an almost frenzied clerical agitation against the new rule and the difficulty of rationally defending the clerical position to his fellow Board members. While he tried to extract concessions from the Board concerning application of the amalgamation policy,[68] he also tried to calm public fears of its consequences.[69] Late in April the Bishop did succeed in forging a compromise which would (1) lower the age limit from eight to seven and (2) protect a boys' school whose attendance was reduced to less than the minimum for a separate school by the operation of Rule 127(b) from immediate transfer of the older boys to the neighbouring girls' school as well. His part of the bargain was a promise to use his influence to get the hierarchy and clerical managers to drop their opposition to Rule 127(b).[70] It was too late, however, to reverse the agitation against the rule. It had now spread to nearly every diocese, and even bishops (such as O'Donnell) who had previously held aloof from the movement were associating themselves with it. A few ecclesiastics seem to have shared Foley's view that they ought to accept a gradual and moderate programme of amalgamation to forestall 'a scheme of wholesale amalgamation'.[71] Nevertheless, when Foley took the matter before the hierarchy's Standing Committee, he was instructed to tell the Board that though the bishops welcomed the concession which he had gained they would continue to oppose Rule 127(b) as part of an amalgamation programme 'to which they (the Bishops) had insuperable objections on moral grounds'.[72] 'Insuperable' was perhaps too strong a word to apply to the bishops' moral objections. Despite widespread clerical sentiment against coeducation, which probably struck a responsive chord in many laymen, the system already included 2,247 mixed Catholic schools.[73] The real issue was that the Board itself was now aggressively pursuing 'reform' without even having been replaced by the feared 'department'.

In recent years some Catholic spokesmen had become restive over the convention which dictated an inviolable denominational balance on the National Board. When it began in the 1860s this practice represented a kind of equality for Catholics, and in succeeding years it became a key factor in protecting clerical interests in the system. Precisely because the Board was unrepresentative and evenly divided between Catholics and Protestants, it tended not to initiate basic changes in the system. By a sort of tacit understanding its members regarded themselves not as innovators, but as custodians of a system whose principles were fixed. Their task was to accede, within their regulations, conventions and financial resources, to the desires of each religious denomination with respect to its own schools. Now, partly because of the feeling of language enthusiasts that the Board was unresponsive to their demands, many Catholics were beginning to view the denominational balance not as a guarantee of their rights but, in the light of their predominance in the population, as a symbol of their continued subjection. In 1903 the Central Council of the Catholic Clerical Managers' Association had adopted a resolution denouncing the National Board 'as at present constituted' and calling for 'the substitution in its stead of a board that will direct . . . education . . . with due consideration of Catholic interests'.[74] Since the overwhelming majority of the pupils were Catholic, the managers maintained, 'a proportionate majority' of the members of the reconstituted Board should be Catholics. The hierarchy had, however, refrained from attacking the Board's composition, and perhaps Foley's decision to accept a seat on it represented a desire to shore it up in the face of suggestions of replacing it with a department. As one very candid priest expressed it, the Board was 'the main prop by which the managerial system is sustained'.[75]

Now, however, just when the Board seemed to be taking up 'reform', Walter Long, who had succeeded Wyndham as Chief Secretary, announced an economy move which would cut off £12,000 in grants for the teaching of Irish in the National Schools.[76] Though the appropriate target for the ensuing protest would have been the treasury, the Gaelic League focused its wrath on its old enemy, the National Board. At its annual Árd-Fheis in August the League demanded 'That, instead of the present National Education Board, a Board be established in the election of which the people of Ireland would have a voice.'[77] Of course, such a word as 'election', with its connotations of popular control, was unlikely to gain clerical approval, but the young men and women who led the League were astute enough to find out how to gain such approval. Early in September the executive committee of the League asked Eóin Mac Néill to sound the bishops on the attitude they would take toward a 'vigorous agitation for the reformation of the National Board'.[78] It is not clear just what soundings were taken, but such an agitation was launched two weeks later with a large protest meeting in the Rotunda which had at least the degree of ecclesiastical sanction represented by a letter to the meeting from Bishop O'Donnell asserting 'that the managers, the teachers, the parents, and the Gaelic League . . . should between them have on the Board a large proportion of members distinctly representative of their views'.[79] Douglas Hyde presided at the meeting and John Dillon signified the Irish Party's support by his participation. The resolutions adopted by the meeting omitted the earlier allusion to popular election and called instead for the retirement of the existing Board and 'the substitution of a representative Board which shall have the confidence and support of the school managers and teachers and of the Irish public'. During the following two months at least thirty-three local government bodies endorsed the resolutions which the meeting had adopted.[80]

During the summer of 1905 a little episode occurred in Portarlington, in Kildare and Leighlin diocese, which threatened to upset the delicate relations between the Gaelic League and parish clergy which the bishops had attempted to forge around 1900. The local League branch, reinforced by an organiser from the League headquarters, had attempted to set up an evening class in Irish. The Parish Priest and his curate objected to the fact that the class was co-educational, and over the protests of Leaguers that there might not be enough students to sustain two classes, tried to organise a separate class for girls. The dispute soon degenerated into great bitterness, the clergy denouncing the League leaders from the pulpit and the League branch expelling the clergy from membership. In the minds of some laymen, the remark of the Parish Priest that a new Irish class during the daytime, for girls only, would obviate the necessity of their attending the mixed evening classes 'if it be nothing but Gaelic they want' became a slander against their daughters.[81] An appeal to the Bishop, Dr Foley, led to his finding no grounds for disciplining the clergy for their conduct in the affair, which he accurately described as a 'storm in a teacup'. Despite the episode's farcical character, accentuated by the local Leaguers' publication of a crude but lengthy pamphlet, decked out with photographs of the victims of clerical wrath, it could not but be worrying to churchmen anxious to avoid friction with the Nation's younger generation.

As they had done in 1900, the bishops again made a strong gesture of sympathy with the League's cause at their October meeting. Citing the difficulties of encouraging the teaching of Irish in Maynooth and their diocesan seminaries if it was not taught in the National Schools, the bishops 'earnestly exhorted' the managers to see that their teachers could and did teach Irish in their schools. Moreover, they joined with the Gaelic Leaguers in deploring the decision to withdraw fees for the teaching of Irish. In addition, they stated their belief

that certain recent proceedings of the National Board afford evidence of the absolute necessity, in the interests of Irish education, of the appointment of Commissioners, of whom the majority, and not, as at present, a small minority, will understand the educational needs of the country, and be in sympathy with the principles and sentiments of the mass of the population.[82]

By these actions the Church made room for the Gaelic League's special grievances against the National Board within her more general agitation against educational reform. The decision to endorse the attack on the Board itself probably reflected both ecclesiastical alarm at the Board's own drift toward reform activities as represented by Rule 127(b) and a realisation that such a decision would help capture the younger generation's enthusiasm for clerical interests just at a moment when that enthusiasm threatened to take an ugly anticlerical turn. In the struggle against reform forces connected with the State, the decision constituted fighting fire with fire—opposing reform by dramatising the unreformed character of one of the reforming agencies.

Fighting fire with fire is always a risky business, and there is evidence that some of the bishops had misgivings about the

decision. Archbishop Walsh, while cordially co-operating with
the Dublin Gaelic League leaders in the delicate matter of
founding a special training college to prepare teachers of
Irish and thereby deprive managers of an excuse to ignore
the bishops' recent admonition to them, made it clear that
he could not 'take a prominent part in any proceedings
animadverting on the National Board'.[83] The bishops, Foley
pointed out, had carefully avoided calling for abolition or
election of the Board.[84] What they no doubt had in mind
was, in the words of Bishop Henry's 1906 Lenten pastoral,
the assignment of 'an adequate share of representation on
the National Board . . . to the Catholic majority of the
people, in proportion to their numbers'.[85] In other words,
the bishops were asking that the Board be made representative without being made democratic—a most unlikely reform
for any government to adopt, as perceptive bishops probably
realised.[86] The purpose of the bishops' October resolutions
was not so much to achieve a specific reform as to strengthen
relations between the Church and the Nation's younger
generation, and this purpose seems to have been at least
partially achieved. One Gaelic League enthusiast expressed
disappointment when Walsh discouraged a campaign to prod
the Dublin managers to hire only teachers qualified to teach
Irish, thereby implementing the hierarchy's gentle admonition to the managers. He recalled that 'Many little *symptoms*
—scarcely entitled to be called *acts*—of hostility have been
experienced from many managers.' 'On the other hand,' he
admitted, 'there have been recent incidents showing a desire
to manifest friendship.'[87]

In part the good relations between the Church and the
League resulted from the skilful diplomacy of Hyde and,
especially, Mac Néill, who had achieved an extraordinary
rapport with a number of ecclesiastics. When Bishop O'Dea
of Clonfert wrote to Mac Néill for advice on the appointment of an Irish teacher at his diocesan college, he addressed
him as 'My dear John'[88]—a form of salutation which no
bishop ever used, for example, when writing to Redmond.
Late in 1905 some Gaelic League branches protested at the
action of the Swinford Board of Guardians in choosing as
dispensary medical officer a doctor educated at the Catholic

university over another candidate who had been educated at Queen's College, Galway, and was the author of an Irish play. The Guardians' action was in accord with a long-standing resolution to appoint no Queen's College graduates, and the Bishop, Dr Lyster, was outraged at the protests. At the suggestion of Cardinal Logue,[89] he communicated with Mac Néill on the subject in terms suggesting no doubts that Mac Néill would approve the kind of exclusive dealing the Church was promoting in this instance. Indeed, he scarcely bothered to conceal his delight that the Board had dismissed the previous dispensary medical officer, a Queen's College product as well, without a pension after thirty-seven years' service.[90] Mac Néill, characteristically, seems to have smoothed the situation over, for while Lyster's first letter ominously alluded to a possible 'break' between the League and the bishops, his response to Mac Néill's reply evidences a willingness to let the matter drop.

Even as the Church was fitting the Nation's younger generation into a suitable niche in the Irish political system, a few young nationalists were taking action which might complicate these arangements. On 28 November 1905 a little coterie styling itself the 'National Council', which had been formed two years earlier to discourage expressions of loyalty on the occasion of a royal visit to Ireland, sponsored a meeting in the Rotunda at which a 'Sinn Féin' political party was organised.[91] Sinn Féin (literally 'we ourselves') was the name which had become attached to the ideas of Arthur Griffith, a Dublin journalist who had connections with the remnants of revolutionary republican nationalism. Since 1899 Griffith had been editing a little weekly paper, *The United Irishman*, in which he tried to reconcile his extreme separatism with the reality that physical-force nationalism was moribund—though he deceived himself into believing that he might reconcile Protestant and Catholic as well.[92] The formula he devised was modelled on the 'dual monarchy' of Austria-Hungary after 1867, and the precedent he cited was the Renunciation Act of 1783, the basis of the brief, Protestant-dominated legislative independence which preceded the Act of Union. The restoration of an Irish parliament and government under the British monarch was to be achieved not by revolution but by passive resistance. A 'Council of Three Hundred' was to be established in Dublin in association with all those Irish M.P.s who would refuse to take their seats at Westminster, and by the voluntary obedience which its decrees would command it should become the *de facto* Irish parliament. Faced with the unanimous nonco-operation of the Irish people, the administration in the Castle would quietly wither away and the British would accept Irish independence subject only to the symbolic sovereignty of the Crown. Although Sinn Féin attracted only a relatively few partisans—*The United Irishman* never had the wide circulation of *The Leader*[93]—it did provide a kind of mock-political focus for a few young nationalists who were growing restive with the leadership of their seniors in the Irish Party.

On 4 December 1905 Arthur James Balfour tendered his resignation to the King. At that moment the Church enjoyed the most satisfactory relations with the Nation which obtained at any point in the period of this study. Both generations of the Nation had been brought into an active working alliance with the Church in defence of her most vital interests. If the Liberal government which now assumed office in the State had been willing and able to honour the Nation's claim, the Church would no doubt have entered the era of Irish self-government under auspicious circumstances. In the event, however, the Liberals were to possess neither the will, the incentive, nor indeed the power to enact the Home Rule programme of Gladstone for the next four years. The political realities of those years were to create new difficulties for the Nation's older generation and increased frustrations for their aspiring juniors.

The year 1905 had been a kind of era of good feeling between the Church and the Nation. This fact can be explained by the coincidence of three conditions. Firstly, the Church had become disillusioned with the prospects of a Conservative university settlement and fearful that Unionists would tinker with the status quo in primary and secondary education. Secondly, enough time had passed since 1900 for Healyite churchmen to reconcile themselves to the fact that the Nation was to be a distinct element in the Irish political system, not an arm of the Church. And finally, not quite enough time had passed since the succession of Parnell's generation to power in the Nation (in 1880) for the next generation to emerge as a self-consciously political force. Before 1905 the younger generation had acquired a sense of identity, of common purpose, in the Gaelic League and allied phenomena. As early as 1900 they had been brought into the political system to the extent of being apprised of the rules of the game from the Church's point of view. For the most part, however, Gaelic Leaguers who took an interest in politics tended to support the Irish Party. The establishment of Sinn Féin as a political party in 1905 was an event comparable to the parliamentary obstruction campaign of Parnell and Biggar in 1877 and the founding of *The Nation* by Young Ireland in 1842. It marked the emergence within the Nation's current younger generation of potential leadership possessing an alternative political programme and strategy. In the case of Sinn Féin there was a much longer lapse of time before the younger generation supplanted the older—a fact resulting primarily from the historical accident that in 1910 the older generation suddenly found themselves the beneficiaries of a peculiarly advantageous election result in Great Britain. During the decade after 1905 the political energies of the younger generation assumed various forms, not all of which were labelled 'Sinn Féin' but nearly all of which were intended to distinguish them from the Irish Party. There would not be another era of good feeling between the Church and the Nation's two generations together.

CHAPTER VII

The State under New Management

Now that a legislative settlement of the land question, but for some minor subsequent tinkering with financial details, had been achieved, the task of the Nation's representatives was clear: they were to obtain Home Rule. Moreover, it was perfectly obvious (though the *Irish Catholic* disingenuously tried to maintain the contrary)[1] that Home Rule could now come only at the hands of a Liberal government. Although the Liberals had been bitterly divided over the issue since Gladstone's retirement, their new leader, Sir Henry Campbell-Bannerman, himself a Home Ruler, managed to carry his colleagues with him in an ambiguous policy which he discussed with Redmond and T. P. O'Connor at breakfast on 14 November 1905. He would not introduce Home Rule in the next parliament, but he hoped to pass some lesser measure consistent with and leading toward that ultimate goal. Moreover, he would say nothing 'to withdraw the larger measure from the electors',[2] as some prominent Liberals, tired of the unpopular Home Rule albatross, were urging him to do.

In Ireland the prospect of a general election did not portend widespread contests, but it did raise again the issue of the position of Healy, who still sat for North Louth, and of O'Brien. After the passing of the 1903 Land Act, Dillon had embarked on a campaign of criticism of its provisions, on the theory that a lively sense of grievance must be maintained to sustain the national movement.[3] O'Brien took Dillon's action as a personal affront, retired from parliament, and began to advocate a programme of conciliation between moderate Unionists and Nationalists along lines suggested by Lord Dunraven and his Irish Reform Association. Though

O'Brien was returned again for his Cork City constituency during the summer of 1904, he never regained his position of influence within the Irish Party. Redmond, despite initial sympathy with the overtures of Dunraven, decided to side with Dillon and hold out for a Liberal settlement of the Irish question. Though one might feel, in retrospect, that it is unfortunate that the party leadership did not take the opportunity to form a coalition with moderate landlords for the gradual devolution of powers of self-government upon Ireland, Dillon was following a sound strategy in acting as he did. In the first place, Dunraven and his friends were conservatives, whose only political influence was within the Conservative Party. The weakness of that influence became evident when Dunraven's initiative precipitated the fall of his friend Wyndham in 1905. Furthermore, any alliance with landlords, who had been vilified by generations of nationalist politicians, would have automatically raised the very real possibility of a rival nationalist party appealing to the electorate on the claim that it was unsullied by dealings with Ireland's hereditary enemies.

O'Brien caused difficulty not because he differed with Dillon, but because he insisted upon provoking open, public controversy over party policy *outside* the party itself. From the founding of the U.I.L., O'Brien had cherished the notion that Ireland's troubles were caused by the manoeuvrings of politicians who were not effectively responsible to public opinion. In his view, under the new dispensation after 1900, the party should be subordinate to the League, which supposedly was truly representative of feeling in the country. In fact, party members soon came to dominate the highest councils of the League and its administrative machinery. As with the Labour Party during the succeeding generation in Great Britain,[4] pious declarations that the party was responsible to its extra-parliamentary organisation had little effect on the fundamental reality that basic strategic decisions must be made by the M.P.s—indeed by the party leadership—in order for any effective policy to be pursued. Public opinion had, of course, to be taken into account, but to encourage its independent formulation would inevitably undermine the party's position. Public opinion was simply too fickle and changeable to become the sole basis of party tactics. Redmond did not attempt to hide the necessity for parliamentary party dominance in policy-making. Late in 1905, when the Waterford County Council, following O'Brien's lead, called for a national conference on self-government analogous to the Land Conference, Redmond asked rhetorically: 'How could the national movement be conducted at all if proposals of that kind could be publicly made outside the party without consultation with any single man from the leader of the party down?'[5] The party leader told his audience in Wexford that he objected to the conference proposal, 'and, unless he was mistaken his objection would be upheld when the great National Convention met next month in Dublin'.

O'Brien charged that the forthcoming Convention had been rigged against him and indicated before it met that he would ignore it as an unrepresentative gathering.[6] There was probably more than a grain of truth behind O'Brien's allegations. Once he began open campaigning against party policy, he was treated as a 'factionist', and no doubt little was done to facilitate attendance by delegates known to be friendly to his views. There was nothing new in this. Healy had been treated in the same way in 1900, when O'Brien dominated the national movement. Nevertheless, the party's style of operating was provoking reaction in a very important quarter. When Redmond wrote to Walsh asking for a message of encouragement to the Convention, the Archbishop replied that he could not see his way to comply with the request. He had hitherto felt that a Convention might be most useful, 'as it would give poor Wm O'Brien the only conceivable way of extricating himself from his present deplorable position, and in case he is not anxious to mend his ways it would put him in a practical necessity of mending them'.[7] O'Brien, the Archbishop argued, had been appealing for a Convention to decide upon his views, 'and even the most influential of his followers would see that a refusal to abide by the decision of that authority would mean political extinction'. Walsh assured Redmond that he abhorred O'Brien's conduct, but he then admitted that he thought O'Brien had 'a good case' in protesting against the make-up of the Convention. He hastened to add that by a good case he meant one 'plausible enough to satisfy' O'Brien and his friends. O'Brien was contending that a clause of the U.I.L. constitution had been deliberately altered to exclude his friends from the Convention. The Archbishop felt that steps should have been taken to remove O'Brien's 'grievance, or fancied grievance', by inserting the clause which had allegedly been removed. 'The change would have made the Convention a thoroughly representative one, even according to his own exacting standard. He could not but have gone to the Convention. The result would have been decisive. He might, and probably would, have grumbled a good deal. But the mischief would have been at an end.' Thus far the Archbishop was speaking in political terms, but the legalistic side of his mind then took over, and he complained that he had never understood the U.I.L. constitution. He began to speculate as to whether O'Brien might not 'have a good case even in a higher sense than that which [*sic*] I am supposing him to have a "good" one'. After a short reflection on one of O'Brien's points which 'may or may not be a *really* good one', Walsh concluded by saying that, unless the Convention's authority were beyond dispute, it would almost be better to hold no Convention.

The Archbishop's legalistic remarks missed the main point entirely—and perhaps intentionally. The central purpose of League constitutions and other similar expedients was to provide democratic window-dressing for the political dominance of the current party leadership. In 1900 that leadership had consisted primarily of O'Brien and Dillon. In 1905 it consisted of Redmond, Dillon, and to a lesser extent Joseph Devlin and T. P. O'Connor. O'Brien, by refusing to play the game according to the unwritten rules, had forfeited his place in the leadership, though he probably could still have regained it by conforming to the rules once more. So long as he refused to do so, the existing leadership was at liberty to alter the written rules or to interpret them in peculiar fashions for the purpose of preventing him from becoming an independent political threat. Redmond, understandably, did not answer the Archbishop in these terms, but rather replied to Walsh's more practical, political argument. He had, he told the Archbishop, been away in England when O'Brien raised his point about the constitution. 'It might no doubt have been better to have taken even this excuse away from him,' he conceded, 'but he would not have attended in any case.'[8] Though Redmond was probably correct, Walsh was apparently unconvinced. This exchange seems to have been the last direct communication between Walsh and Redmond except for a fruitless attempt by Redmond to obtain a subscription from the Archbishop in 1912.

Although the Convention condemned O'Brien's policy in his absence, the party did not attempt to contest his seat in the general election one month later in January 1906. In two constituencies, however, the party hoped to unseat aggravating incumbents. In Newry borough, P. G. H. Carvill, a Healyite, had been left undisturbed in 1900, presumably for fear of a triangular contest with a Unionist. In spite of the protest of the Bishop, Dr O'Neill, 'that the late member has undoubted claims on the people of Newry, and ought to be allowed to represent the borough again without the turmoil of a contest',[9] the party went ahead with plans to run J. J. Mooney against Carvill. Mooney was returned by 802 votes to 736. The police reported that Mooney 'received the support of the I.R.B. [Irish Republican Brotherhood] party in Newry as against Mr Carvil [sic] the nominee of the clerical party'.[10] While this analysis may have been slightly distorted, the contest was uncomfortably reminiscent of the clerical-anticlerical controversies of 1900, and the passions aroused by this election did not subside for several years.[11]

A more important contest seemed imminent in North Louth, where on 1 January the local U.I.L. executive resolved to oppose T. M. Healy.[12] Healy began intensive campaigning with the support of most of the local clergy,[13] though one priest, Father Lawless, did support the party.[14] Cardinal Logue, whose diocese included North Louth, wrote privately to Redmond asking him not to contest Healy's seat. When the Works Committee of the Dundalk Urban Council passed a resolution on 5 January calling upon the Cardinal to mediate between Healy and the party, citing the 'arrangement' with O'Brien as a precedent,[15] Logue replied by publicly stating that he had already appealed, without effect, to Redmond, and that he deplored the contest.[16] Moreover, Walsh telegraphed to Healy expressing his support, saying:

'If I considered that any of my contribution to the general election fund of the Irish party was being expended on the maintenance of the present deplorable contest in North Louth, I should deeply regret having contributed to it at all.'[17] Redmond might have resisted the private urgings of Logue, but he decided not to go against the public opposition of both primates and wrote to the convention which met in Dundalk on 8 January instructing them in what the *Irish Catholic* accurately described as 'grudging terms' that 'in deference to his Eminence's views' they should not nominate an opponent to Healy.[18] According to rumour, Dillon had favoured 'fighting to a finish' in North Louth.[19] After the election he urged Redmond to 'deal with the Healy question' by having a resolution passed at a party meeting, presumably rejecting any pretensions by Healy to party membership. Dillon predicted that, barring such a resolution, Healy would 'be on his good behaviour for a few weeks' and that then Logue and Walsh would demand his admission to the party.[20]

The elections in British constituencies also had repercussions upon the Irish Party's relations with the Church. Since 1902 English and Welsh Nonconformists had been up in arms over the support from local rates granted to denominational schools under the terms of Balfour's Education Act. Though the Church of England schools were the prime object of this attack, shrill cries of 'Rome on the rates' had occasionally punctuated the public debate. The Nonconformist cause with its implied attack upon the social dominance of the Tory oligarchy in rural England but without any of those awkward implications of attack upon wealth *per se* which marred so many reform proposals of the day, had attracted the support of leading Liberals. As the Catholic Church in England was dominated by its upper-class minority who were descended from sixteenth-century recusants rather than by its working-class Irish immigrant majority, it was inevitable that clerical influence would be exercised in favour of the Conservatives. In October 1905 T. P. O'Connor, the Irish Party's liaison officer with the Liberal leadership and chief organiser of the Irish in Great Britain, had written to Redmond: 'The English priests are Hopeless,' and had predicted, correctly: 'They will fight us bitterly everywhere on the Education question.'[21] Shortly after the Liberal government took office, James Bryce, the new Chief Secretary, reported to the Prime Minister Redmond's intimation that he would 'be placed in the greatest difficulties over the Education Bill, in which he desires to oppose us as little as he can'.[22] Redmond's difficulties were especially manifest when, during the polling in January, Bishop O'Dwyer wrote a public letter denouncing the party's policy, enunciated by O'Connor, of urging Irish voters in Great Britain to support Liberal candidates. If the Liberals gained too great a majority, he argued plausibly enough, they could afford to disregard Home Rule. Moreover, Liberal plans to amend the 1902 English Education Act would cause 'the faith of thousands upon thousands of poor Catholic children' to be 'lost in Protestant and infidel schools'. 'If our Catholic schools are wrecked,' the Bishop maintained, 'if the Catholic Church in England gets the most ruinous blow that has been inflicted on it since the Reformation, great and terrible will be the responsibility of the Irishmen by whose machinations it was brought about.'[23]

Thus, less than a year after their joining in a chorus of episcopal endorsement of the Irish Party, Logue and O'Dwyer had publicly attacked the party leadership. More surprisingly, Walsh had expressed disenchantment with the Nation's representatives. These three churchmen reflected, in varying measure, two distinct sources of clerical dissatisfaction with the party: (1) distaste for various aspects of the party's style of political organisation and action and (2) fear that the party's Liberal allies would attack Catholic interests in education. O'Dwyer was primarily moved by the latter concern. Walsh, though he of course opposed secularisation, did not exhibit the kind of knee-jerk reaction that O'Dwyer had against any threat, however remote, to clerically controlled schools. It was his concern over presumed irregularities in the party's treatment of nationalist dissidents which moved the Archbishop of Dublin to withdraw support from the party. Logue, characteristically, shared both anxieties. His protection of Healy represented his deep unease at sanctioning a lay-dominated national movement, but he was also quite disturbed by the secularist statements of leading Liberals. Shortly before the Liberal government took office an

office-seeker asked both Logue and Walsh for letters of recommendation. Both, predictably, declined on the ground that
they never wrote such recommendations, but they amplified
their refusals in significantly different ways. 'Judging by
all the forecasts,' Logue wrote, 'the Government will contain
members who will be likely to raise very serious religious
questions; and, if such be the case, I must keep myself quite
free to speak out when the need arises.'[24] Walsh, on the other
hand, explained that 'if there were degrees in impossibility',
it would be less possible for him to depart from his rule of
not supporting candidates for political appointments 'in the
case of a friendly than in the case of an unfriendly Government'.[25] Walsh, in other words, was judging the government
primarily by its stance on national, rather than Catholic,
issues. The Liberals, after all, were attacking denominationalism only in *English* (and Welsh) education, and though
Walsh no doubt sympathised with the plight of Catholics in
England, the issue did not touch the vital interests of his own
institution, the *Irish* Catholic Church. Indeed, the main
enemies of the Church's interests in Irish education at this
moment appeared to be the outgoing Conservative administration, which had shelved the university question and begun
a financial squeeze on the National School system to force
acceptance of reform.

The hierarchy had rallied round the party early in 1905
precisely to exploit the party's friendship with the Liberals.
The suspicions of Logue and O'Dwyer did not deter the
Episcopal Standing Committee from calling for a return on
their investment of their prestige in the party's cause. On
25 January 1906 the Committee communicated a more or
less formal request to Redmond over the signatures of their
secretaries, Bishop Henry and Bishop Sheehan of Waterford
and Lismore:

The January Meeting of the Episcopal Standing Committee
takes place this year at a juncture in public affairs when any
pronouncement by the Bishops on the University question might,
from more than one point of view, be inopportune. But it is
with a feeling of no ordinary satisfaction the Bishops are sensible
that the time has come when the Representatives of our people
may ask with confidence that some beginning should be made

and duly developed, on a sound basis, of the government of Ireland according to Irish ideas; and they are profoundly concerned that, in any administrative or legislative or constitutional reforms that are taken in hand, the vital need of Irish Catholics for a suitable system of University Education should hold from the start the place that its essential importance demands.

That is our reason for sending you the present letter. In the way that seems best and most effective we ask you and the Irish Members to put it strongly to the new Government that the Liberal principles enunciated at the Election in regard to Ireland [*sic*] if not the general maxim of Government by consent of the governed, at least must imply, in the domain of Education, such a system as will accord with the wishes and convictions which the great bulk of the Irish people entertain in common with their Bishops and Clergy. In Ireland it should not be too much to expect from Liberal statesmen, so long as they remain responsible for purely Irish affairs, that they would try to forecast the lines that would be followed by a good native administration. Well, it is reasonable to assume that an Irish Parliament would provide a system of University Education suitable to the people, and that, quite independently of the direct merits, they would not be in a hurry to put into the management of education, in any grade, any element which those interested did not desire to introduce.

The Bishops rely with confidence on you and the Irish Party to see that in any changes made in our educational systems Irish ideas and Irish wishes, and not English fads, will be followed. But, as bearing on the immediate subject of this letter, the Bishops, while they do not desire to express a preference for any one solution of the University question, and while they should willingly join in the disposition to be over-generous to the minority, if the minority, in the old spirit of ascendancy and in jealousy of any rights accorded to Catholics did not frustrate every effort to provide the University education our people so urgently require, do earnestly hope that the anomalous position of Trinity College will be considered by the Government without undue delay and with the determination to have justice done once for all. We have had quite enough Commissions; and no further enquiry is needed to establish the fact that Trinity College holds for a small minority of the population the funds that constitute the Irish national endowment for higher education.

There is no need to add that the anxiety of the Bishops for a settlement of the University question on lines that will have the cordial approval of the laity as well as the clergy in no way takes from their anxiety for the other reforms, whether constitutional or social, which our country so greatly needs and so justly demands.

The Bishops do not wish to conclude this letter without expressing the satisfaction with which they have notices [*sic*] the pledges given by the Irish Party to shield the religious education of Irish Catholic children in the schools of England.[26]

The letter contains evidence of two important realities. Firstly, by relegating the English education question to a very brief concluding paragraph, the Committee was indicating that this concern ranked rather below their specifically Irish concerns. The spiritual welfare of Catholics—even those of Irish origin—in England or any other place outside Ireland was an ideal which would move different Irish ecclesiastics in varying degrees, but it was not a vital interest which the institution would systematically mobilise its forces to defend. Secondly, the bishops' well-timed suggestion that their university grievance might be settled through a levelling-down of Trinity's endowments was an unabashed attempt to take advantage of the very same reforming instincts in the Liberal Party which informed the latter's plans to deprive the denominational primary schools of England of their privileged position.

Redmond forwarded a copy of the bishops' letter to Bryce with a plea for the government's immediate consideration of the university question[27] and replied to the bishops, assuring them of the Irish Party's intention to resist 'any changes in the present educational systems which are not in accordance with Irish ideas and wishes' as well as their resolve to press the government for a university settlement. In acknowledging 'with great satisfaction' the bishops' expression of confidence that the party would defend Catholic interests in the English education system, Redmond added, significantly, that he was sure the party could 'count upon the generous consideration of the Bishops in matters of Parliamentary tactics adopted for that end'.[28] Of course, he was not the least bit sure of any such thing. During the succeeding few months, while Bryce toyed with various Irish reform proposals—including that suggested in the bishops' letter, Redmond prudently busied himself with the English education question. T. P. O'Connor advised the party leader that the new President of the Board of Education, Augustine Birrell, would listen sympathetically to specifically Catholic objections to points in the bill he was drafting.

We shall have to consent to full popular control [O'Connor admitted]. I have always regarded that as inevitable and have told the priests so. But I believe that if we assent to that we may get excellent terms on other points. As you know there is no real hostility to our schools; it is the ascendancy of the Anglicans that is assailed; and we have no interest in defending that.[29]

O'Connor, though nominally a Catholic, wore his Catholicism rather lightly, and he candidly admitted that he would not be a good envoy to the new Archbishop of Westminster, Francis Bourne.

Bourne, however, made matters easier than party leaders expected after the clerical-nationalist recrimination that had marked contests in some English constituencies by communicating to Redmond his desire to see him.[30] It is significant that he did not summon the party leader to an interview, but tactfully allowed Redmond to name the time and place. Two days later, when Redmond, accompanied by Dillon, conferred with Bourne at the Archbishop's residence, they found him very different from Cardinal Vaughan, his high-Tory predecessor. Recognising that popular control could not be resisted, he told the Irish leaders that he 'did not favour a frontal attack'.[31] He hoped, however, that the Irish Party 'might by *finesse* get some advantages for Catholics such as where a great majority of the children in a school are of a particular religion that the parents might *demand* from the local authority that the teachers shd. be of that religion'. The Archbishop indicated the fruits of his own communications with cabinet ministers by stating that the government was willing to allow local authorities the right to grant such a demand, but he wanted to have the concession made mandatory upon the local authorities. He demonstrated that he did not take the position which the party had met so often among the English clergy by assuring Redmond that he 'did not ask or expect the Irish Party to adopt an irreconcilable attitude', and added, according to Redmond's memorandum of the conversation, that 'the only hope was that by persuasion & finesse we might accomplish something'. He even called the party's support of the Liberals in the election 'providential', for, he reasoned, if they had acted otherwise they would now be powerless. Finally, Redmond noted in his memorandum: 'He promised to consult us on everything.'

The Irish Party leaders had plenty of time to concern themselves with the English education question partly because the new government had not decided on an Irish policy. Sir Antony MacDonnell, having bided his time since Wyndham's fall some months earlier, now expected a sympathetic hearing for his ideas from an administration less dependent upon the bigoted Irish Protestant opponents of anything which might please the Catholic majority. The Under-Secretary, who had during January been tutoring the new Chief Secretary on the intricacies of Irish politics, began presenting Bryce with his proposals for an Irish policy early in February. The two most urgent issues in Ireland, in his opinion, were improvement of the governmental system and university education for Catholics—i.e. the very projects in which he had been frustrated under the Conservatives. He argued that 'The former of these two is more pressing than the latter; for the former, if solved, will help the solution of the latter.'[32] Bryce did eventually adopt MacDonnell's two projects as government policy, but he reversed the priorities. Perhaps he noted that, in MacDonnell's own words, the Devolution scheme aimed 'to co ordinate and bring under a reasonable measure of popular control, all the Dep^{ts} of Government now working in Ireland—without radically changing the constitution of any (*except the Education Dep^t*)' (my italics),[33] and compared this intention with the expressed desire of the bishops, which he had just received from Redmond, that he 'not be in a hurry to put into the management of education, in any grade, any element which those interested did not desire to introduce'. In any event, a further letter from MacDonnell to Bryce a few days later, enclosing a revised version of his Devolution scheme, seems particularly defensive on the question of how the bishops would react to its educational provisions.[34]

By early March Bryce hit upon the idea of a Royal Commission to enquire into the affairs of Trinity College, Dublin, a proceeding which might accord with the bishops' claim for a levelling-down of Trinity's endowments, if not with their argument that no further enquiry was needed. MacDonnell was willing to go along with such an enquiry, though he still expressed the hope that actual legislation on university reform would be preceded by 'the scheme of Administrative Reform'.[35] MacDonnell, a bright Catholic boy from Co. Mayo who had risen to the highest, and normally Protestant-dominated, councils of the Irish government, probably conceived of his scheme as a means of eventually ending the political disaffection of his co-religionists and sharing with them the kind of benefits which he enjoyed. The cabinet, for all its faults, however, could take a more detached view than Sir Antony. Bryce and his colleagues no doubt realised that the political system of Ireland—in which the Nation was as much a reality as the State—would long survive the enactment, not to mention the introduction, of any such scheme. To undertake Devolution would be to fight out the entire Irish question, and this the Liberals were not prepared to do in their first year in office. To raise the issue of the anomalous position of Trinity College, however, was altogether congruent with Liberal interests, and accordingly MacDonnell was set to work arranging for a Royal Commission on this subject. Perceiving that such an approach to the university question might well lead to the particular solution he preferred—the erection of a Catholic college in the University of Dublin—MacDonnell took up his assignment with alacrity. Though he avoided discussion of a possible Catholic college when he broached the subject of an inquiry with Trinity's Provost, Dr Traill, on 8 March, MacDonnell clearly hoped that the investigation would go beyond the questions of the College's 'finances, method of government, and system of education', which the Provost admitted were in need of study.[36] The Under-Secretary was elated when he reported to Bryce a month later that 'Archbishop Walsh with true appreciation of the situation, welcomes the reference of the general question.'[37] Arguing in favour of broad terms of reference for the new Commission, Sir Antony assured the Chief

6

Secretary that though in the past opposition from the hierarchy had been 'one of the greatest stumbling blocks in the
way of a settlement', the bishops would accept 'the solution in
our minds'.[38] On at least two occasions MacDonnell felt it
necessary to reassure Bryce that rumblings from O'Dwyer
(whom he described as 'an irresponsible vituperative politician') which ran counter to his ideas were unrepresentative of
the whole hierarchy's views.[39] On 5 June a Royal Commission,
under the chairmanship of Sir Edward Fry, was appointed

to inquire into and report upon the present state of Trinity
College, Dublin, and of the University of Dublin, including the
revenues of the College . . . the method of government . . .
the system of instruction . . . the system of University examinations, and the provision made for post-graduate study . . . and
also to inquire and report upon the place which Trinity College, Dublin, and the University of Dublin now hold as organs
of the higher education in Ireland, and the steps proper to be
taken to increase their usefulness to the country.[40]

The Commission was permitted to consider the evidence collected by the Robertson Commission, but not to take new
evidence on the matters into which that Commission had
inquired. In other words, everything possible was done to
increase the likelihood of the Commission's recommending
a university settlement along the lines favoured by Mac-
Donnell and Walsh.

Meanwhile MacDonnell was permitted to develop his
scheme for constitutional reform—embodying as it did major
changes in the primary and secondary education systems—
but nothing was said publicly to commit the government to
his ideas. Late in March in a Commons debate on Irish education, Bryce made a speech which was characterised mainly
by postponement to the indefinite future of the vexatious
issues which educational reformers had been raising. An
education department, for example, was a good idea, but unacceptable because of nationalist objections to another Castle
board. On the other hand, the government might create a
responsible, elected body, but 'How could they do that for
education only? (*Nationalist cheers.*) If they went as far as
that they would have to go a great deal further (*an hon.
member*—"Home Rule").'[41] With that the Chief Secretary

scampered with agility away from this topic. He had succeeded in creating the impression that he was not (in the
words of the Episcopal Standing Committee's January letter)
'in a hurry' to reform Irish primary and secondary education. His performance earned from the semi-official *Irish
Catholic Directory* the description 'an important and sympathetic speech'.[42] By the late spring of 1906 the Liberal Party's
Irish policy (or lack thereof) was creating increasing unease
in the Nation but seemed to be practically identical with the
policy proposed by the Church in the Standing Committee's
January letter.

The Liberal Party's English policy was another matter.
The Education Bill was to be the principal item of business
for the 1906 session, and early in April Birrell tried to persuade Redmond to give him 'some moral support' when the
bill was introduced.[43] Though Birrell leaned over backwards
to offer terms favourable to Catholics, Redmond decided,
upon consultation with Bourne, that the party should say
nothing at the bill's introduction.[44] The much-heralded bill,
which Birrell introduced on 9 April, provided that after 1
January 1908 all elementary schools in receipt of funds from
rates or taxes must come under the jurisdiction of local education authorities. The local education authority was empowered to make financial arrangements with the owner of a
voluntary (i.e. denominational) school whereby the authority
would control the use of the schoolhouse during regular hours
of instruction and would be responsible for the entire cost
of upkeep. Ordinarily, religious instruction in schools controlled by local education authorities remained limited to
simple Bible teaching—the so-called 'Cowper-Temple' teaching specified in the 1870 Education Act. The new bill provided, however, that in the agreement between a local education authority and the owner of a denominational school
for the purchase or hire of the schoolhouse, the contracting
parties might arrange for the continuance of the particular
denomination's religious instruction. Such instruction might
be given only outside the hours of compulsory attendance,
only on two mornings a week, only to those children whose
parents desired it, and only by someone other than the regular teaching staff. Birrell indicated the anticipated result by

noting that 'If it should happen to be given by the clergyman of the parish, that, after all, would only be restoring to that important person what has always been his canonical duty.'[45] These provisions were intended as a settlement of the controversy between Nonconformists and Anglicans.

The problem of Catholic schools was, in effect, separately treated in Clause 4, though Birrell was quick to point out that the Clause 4 provisions also extended to the schools of Jews and High Anglicans in the large towns.[46] Clause 4 permitted (but did not require) a local education authority in an urban area whose population exceeded 5,000 to afford 'extended facilities' for denominational instruction if (1) the parents of four-fifths of the pupils in the school desired the extended facilities and (2) there was accommodation available for the rest of the children in some school not having extended facilities. Under extended facilities a denomination might conduct its religious teaching during regular school hours and might, if the local education authority agreed, employ its regular teachers for such instruction. Nevertheless, the religious instruction must not be at the expense of the authority, and, contrary to what Redmond had understood from Birrell during the preceding week, no religious tests could be applied in the employment of teachers.

The Irish Party had now to decide what tactics to adopt on the second reading of the bill. On 26 April Bourne called Redmond to the Archbishop's House[47] and handed him a resolution of the English Catholic hierarchy marked 'PRIVATE' which urged 'that the Second Reading should be strongly opposed by all interested in Catholic Education'.[48] On the same day, speaking before the Catholic Truth Society, Bourne announced that the bishops endorsed a statement of the Catholic Education Council which criticised the bill in detail but which was less specific on the question of tactics, declaring only that 'the present Bill should be resisted at every stage'.[49] Redmond was thus enabled to appear to be acting as a free agent. On 27 April he granted an interview to the parliamentary correspondent of the *Times* and condemned the bill as it stood, saying that the Irish Parliamentary Party had been reserving comment until the English Catholic clergy and laity had taken a stand but that the party 'never had any doubt as to the injurious effect which the Bill as introduced would have on the interests of Catholic education'. Nevertheless, he stated that they had not yet decided what they would do at the second reading stage.[50]

Meanwhile, in Ireland, Logue had been speaking of the bill in especially strong terms. On his return on 1 April from a trip to Rome, he referred to the 'grave danger' threatening the Catholic schools in England in the course of remarks on the 'present trials' of French Catholics,[51] and on 16 April, referring to the bill in an address at Drogheda, he spoke of 'the banishment of God from the schools' which 'was the first sign of material decay in a nation'.[52] In his speech on 26 April Bourne announced that Logue had assured him of the 'fullest and most hearty co-operation' of the Irish hierarchy, and on 1 May the Standing Committee of the Irish hierarchy concurred with the position of the English hierarchy and urged 'resistance to the utmost limit of constitutional action'.[53] The Irish bishops thus avoided the mistake of 1902 when they had acted privately and thereby made it possible to infer publicly that they were unconcerned over English education questions. They expressed confidence that 'Our representatives in Parliament will not fall short of what their countrymen in Ireland, as well as in England, expect of them.' On the following day the Irish Party met and voted unanimously to oppose the bill's second reading.[54] Redmond's publicly expressed hope was for 'an arrangement which would enable [the party] to do what they were most anxious to do, which was not only to withdraw their opposition . . . but to support the Bill'.[55] Privately, he expressed to Joe Devlin, who was on a fund-raising tour of Australasia, the more modest hope 'that we will be able to extract ourselves from the difficulties of our position' on the bill, and he seemed fairly confident that this hope would be fulfilled.[56]

During Committee debates, which lasted for nearly two months, Bourne forwarded to Redmond instructions on specific tactics drafted by the Watching Committee of the Catholic Education Council,[57] a group of prominent Catholics set up by the English Catholic hierarchy. In certain important instances, however, Bourne conveyed advice at variance with the Committee's instructions, which were sometimes informed more by a desire to make a righteous stand than by a concern for winning practical concessions. Bourne had no interest in scoring a partisan victory, but rather was determined to secure the maximum concessions possible for Catholic schools. As he wrote to Redmond in June,

Anything is better than the dilemma which Mr. Birrell proposed to me last February: 'Accept my Bill or be starved out of existence.' We may in certain cases owing to local bigotry be unable to accept the provisions of the Bill, however much it may be amended; at the same time we have a very natural aversion to starvation.[58]

The party's policy in Committee debate was to support amendments offering tangible benefits to Catholic schools but to vote with the government or abstain on trivial points over which the Conservatives provoked divisions. It must be remembered that on most divisions the action of the Irish Party meant only the difference between a government majority of some 150 and one of over 200. The only time when opponents of the measure came within striking distance of a victory was on a minor point on which Birrell did not issue a government whip. The opposition move was lost by a majority of only sixteen, and the *Irish Catholic* complained bitterly of the absence of thirteen 'paid Catholic members of Parliament' on this occasion.[59]

Catholic interest in the bill centred on Clause 4, for the Clause 3 provisions for denominational instruction outside regular school hours were regarded as useless from a Catholic point of view. The Watching Committee had prepared an elaborate series of amendments to Clause 4.[60] The government, however, offered a compromise proposal which would allow owners of an eligible denominational school which had been refused extended facilities by the local education authority to appeal to the Board of Education. The Board might either order the authority to take over the school under specified terms or provide for the school to continue to receive State grants without receiving any rate aid (the pre-1902 position). The Watching Committee was adamantly opposed to acceptance of any proposal[61] which allowed return to the pre-1902 position, but Bourne and the rest of the English Catholic hierarchy were privately willing to allow Redmond somewhat more freedom to manoeuvre.[62] Bourne wanted assurances that the pre-1902 position would be imposed only 'while the Board of Education are endeavouring to bring an unfair local authority to its senses'.[63] On 27 June, when the government amendment came up for consideration, Redmond and his colleagues abstained.[64] After the amendment had been carried, they voted with the government on the motion 'That the clause, as amended, stand part of the Bill.'[65] Whether Redmond received assurance on the point Bourne had raised is not clear. He wrote a letter to Bourne which appears not to have been preserved in the papers of either Bourne or Redmond, and Bourne's reply, dated 29 June, is cordial and gives no hint of any disapproval of the party's action.[66] Bourne was obviously looking for a feasible compromise and not insisting upon the hard line recommended by the Watching Committee. The party was thus enabled to distinguish its selective, pragmatic opposition to the bill from the indiscriminate, irreconcilable Conservative opposition—a distinction which was not only vital to the Irish Party's larger political strategy, but which was important if the party was to carry on fruitful negotiations with the government on this very bill after the inevitable hostile action by the House of Lords.

The government showed no interest in making serious concessions on other points of concern to Catholics, such as religious tests for teachers, and during most of July Committee debates were devoted to points of no special importance to Catholics. At one stage Bourne expressed concern over a provision of the bill establishing a representative 'Council of Wales' to have jurisdiction over Welsh primary and secondary education. Wales with its Nonconformist majority had been a centre of passive resistance to the 1902 Education Act. Bourne realised that the issue would be an extremely delicate one for the Irish Party, but he tried cautiously to sound Redmond out on it.[67] The Irish leader settled the issue with the curt comment, 'You will, of course, understand that it would be utterly impossible for us to show even the appearance of refusing Home Rule to Wales.'[68] Apart from this touchy issue, the party followed the admonition of Bourne on 9 July that they should now make plain that, because of government action on Clause 4, the bill was 'radically unjust and unworkable' for Catholics.[69] On 18 July T. P. O'Connor told the House that they did not consider Clause 4 'in its present shape by any means satisfactory; on the contrary, it imperilled a very large number of their schools, and they hoped that before the measure passed into law the defects of the clause would be remedied'.[70] Several days later he alluded to the basis of their hopes for such a remedy which lay in the House of Lords, saying that 'they must wait for another opportunity which he need not exactly specify, because everybody knew exactly what he meant'.[71] On the same day Redmond wrote to Dillon of the 'universal impression here . . . that the Government will accept amendments satisfactory to us when the Bill comes back from the Lords'.[72] On 30 July the bill passed its third reading by 369 to 177 and was dispatched to another place.

Both Redmond and Bourne had been in difficult positions throughout the bill's progress through the Commons. English Catholics were naturally suspicious of Bourne's dealings with the Irish Party. One of them, a Mr Mountain of Thornton Heath, Surrey, complained bitterly, in a letter to Bourne in May, of a suggestion in the *Catholic Herald*, an Irish nationalist paper in England, that English Catholic ecclesiastical authorities should sanction collections for Irish Party funds. He accused the United Irish League of Great Britain of 'getting our poor people *to return well known socialists and atheists* to Parliament'. 'The two or three speeches recently made in the House of Commons', he argued, 'do not seem to go far to palliate such awful work *as this*; indeed, His Eminence Cardinal Logue some time ago described it as the favourite device of the Irish Members to make eloquent speeches in the House of Commons after they had grievously misbehaved themselves elsewhere.'[73] Such attacks upon the party were not always private. In a letter to the *Irish Catholic*, 'A Plain Spoken Catholic' of London spoke of T. P. O'Connor's election tactics as 'an awful spectacle. . . . On the one hand, our good priests fighting for our little ones as only good priests can fight; on the other, Mr. O'Connor's agents hurling insult after insult at them.'[74] In Limerick Bishop O'Dwyer lamented the fact that Redmond had not ordered

Irish voters in Great Britain to switch sides during the general election when it was evident that the Liberals were getting a large majority. 'Oh for a touch of the vanished hand, said his Lordship pathetically. Did they think that Parnell, if he was alive, would ask the Irish nation to abandon the interest of religion and allow the Catholic schools to be trampled upon?'[75]

Although in the month following O'Dwyer's speech the party had acquitted itself well enough to earn the praise of the Catholic Education Council,[76] of Archbishop Bourne himself,[77] and even of the Catholic Clerical Managers' Association of Kerry diocese,[78] the commendation it received from Cardinal Logue was so hedged about with unflattering remarks as to make it scarcely worth having. In addition to complaining about the number of Irish Parliamentary Party absentees at divisions, the Cardinal observed that 'the battlefield selected necessarily entailed failure'. 'The fight', he continued, 'should have been at the polls,' where the Catholics of England had made the mistake of

voting for all kinds of persons, for Nonconformists and for Labour members, with whom they had the greatest sympathy as long as they confined themselves to the interests of the labourers in whom the priests and people were deeply interested, but who unfortunately had shown since they had been elected—many of them by the votes of Irish Catholics—that they were the worst of their enemies.[79]

If 'instead of making a fight for these people', His Eminence maintained, they had been primarily concerned for Christian education, there would not have been so many 'heirs of Cromwell' elected.

CHAPTER VIII

The Art of the Improbable

PERHAPS more circumspect Irish bishops than O'Dwyer and Logue refrained from giving vent to their feelings about the government's English education programme because the same government seemed to be moving toward an Irish university settlement. The Fry Commission was now deliberating and had solicited statements from interested parties. A group of Trinity dignitaries headed by the Provost and six Senior Fellows submitted a statement resolutely opposing the establishment of a denominational college within Dublin University but renewing their 1903 offer to grant facilities for Catholic religious instruction and a Catholic chapel within the walls of the College.[1] A more serious attempt to meet the Church's demands without creating a new college was put forward by a group composed mainly of Junior Fellows (including Dr Starkie, a retired Junior Fellow). In addition to the concession of a Catholic chapel and Catholic religious instruction, they proposed a method for involving the Catholic bishops in the visiting body of the College and a complex reconstruction of the College's governing body. Under this scheme, Catholics would be allotted nearly twenty-five per cent of the seats on the governing body at the beginning of a twenty-five-year transitional period. That representation would grow as Catholic membership in the College increased, and at the end of the period they might hold as many seats as their academic achievement within the College merited.[2] Despite its sincerity, the scheme could not have satisfied the hierarchy, whose more conservative members were already making a considerable sacrifice of sentiment by acceding to Walsh's desire for a settlement within the University of Dublin. Walsh knew they would never acquiesce in a solution which did not produce some actual institution—college or university—explicitly or implicitly labelled 'Catholic'. Recognition of a Catholic interest in an institution which would continue to possess a substantial Protestant interest as well was simply not good enough.

The Junior Fellows' scheme was communicated immediately to a group of Catholic laymen who began to circulate a petition which, in a roundabout way, endorsed the scheme. This petition came to the attention of Archbishop Walsh on 25 July,[3] the day after the Junior Fellows submitted their scheme to the Commission and the day before the Standing Committee of the hierarchy submitted a statement of their own to the Commission. The implication of the Junior Fellows' scheme and the laymen's petition was not lost on the bishops. Though the Standing Committee could not, of course, refer directly to schemes which others were submitting independently to the Commission, they pointedly devoted most of their lengthy statement to a demonstration not only that Trinity College was unacceptable to Catholics, but that any changes in its constitution to render it acceptable to Catholics would be unwise if not futile. On the other hand, they stressed that a second college in the University of Dublin was 'quite another thing' which they were willing to consider 'with open minds'. In summary, they reiterated the three solutions they (or, in their words, 'the Catholics of Ireland') could accept: '(1) An University for Catholics; (2) a new College in the University of Dublin; (3) a new College in the Royal University.'[4] Walsh moved quickly, even before the publication of the Junior Fellows' scheme, to demolish any hope of episcopal sanction for it. In an interview on 29 July he subjected the laymen's petition to intense ridicule, refusing even to take it seriously,[5] and after the Junior Fellows' scheme was leaked to the press,[6] he had simply to publish the Standing Committee's statement[7] in order to preclude the rallying of public opinion to the plan. Six of the laymen who had signed the petition went to the length of formally withdrawing their signatures after Walsh's position became clear.[8]

During the following five months MacDonnell and Bryce went ahead with plans for the enlargement of Dublin University without much thought for the deliberations of the Fry Commission. In the middle of August MacDonnell had an interview with Walsh to sound his views on certain points in their scheme. On what was regarded as a particularly delicate point, the Under-Secretary reported to Bryce that Walsh 'agreed that the nomination of a Bishop quâ Bishop to the Visiting Board or to the Senate [presumably of the University, not the Catholic college] wd not be practicable: and said he shd be quite satisfied with a promise that a Bishop should be nominated to the Bd of Visitors'. Sir Antony was pleased to find that 'The Archbishops views were, as I could have expected from my dealings with him in 1903–04, Quite liberal and on the lines of our drafts.'⁹

Walsh had so far been able to maintain the appearance of episcopal unity, presumably by arguing that, as the new government seemed inclined toward a Dublin University solution, the bishops should not place obstacles in the way of that solution and endanger the chances for any settlement. Outside the hierarchy, clerical ranks were not so serried. Mgr Molloy, Vice-Chancellor of the Royal University and Rector of the Catholic University, published a long letter in September (shortly before his own death), paying lip-service to the July statement of the Standing Committee, but making plain his own distaste for the incorporation of a Catholic college into Dublin University and his preference for the plan of the Robertson Commission, barring an independent university for Catholics, which he dismissed as 'too good to be hoped for'.¹⁰ Though the publication of Molloy's letter obviously called for some clarification of the hierarchy's position, the bishops, at their October meeting resolved that, as things then stood, they did not see the utility of offering evidence before the Commission beyond the Standing Committee's July statement.¹¹ Walsh did what he could to patch up the situation on 20 October by providing MacDonnell with a letter, to be submitted to the Commission, in which he reiterated the bishops' prior public concessions on the questions of religious tests and the proportion of ecclesiastical representation on the governing body of a Catholic college. He stated, moreover, in the most explicit fashion, that the bishops, when consulted by Wyndham, had agreed to a settlement on the lines of Dunraven's scheme, and he stressed the provision of that scheme that the governing body of the new college would be 'selected *exclusively* on academic grounds'.[12]

A few days after Walsh had again put his prestige on the line by reiterating to the Commission through MacDonnell the bishops' concessions to Wyndham, his opponents found another occasion to embarrass him. The Senate of the Royal University unanimously adopted a resolution proposed by the Rev. William Delany, S.J., President of U.C.D., and seconded by Archbishop Healy:

That in the judgment of the Senate of the Royal University, it would be disastrous to the interests of education in Ireland, and gravely injurious to the welfare of the country to concentrate the control of higher education in one University.[13]

No doubt the senators, representing such diverse interests as they did, had differing reasons for voting for the resolution, which technically referred only to the Dunraven scheme and did not rule out a second college in Dublin University, leaving the Queen's Colleges within the Royal University scheme or under some other arrangement. Nevertheless, initiated as it was by two prominent ecclesiastics, the resolution was a direct slap at Walsh. Delany, who was also organising a 'Catholic Defence Society' to oppose a single-university solution,[14] was the only Catholic ecclesiastic to testify before the Commission, and he rendered the Senate's resolution even more damaging to Walsh's position when he told the Commission that in discussion of it

the Archbishop of Tuam, who seconded my motion, said that he might tell the Senate that he represented in those views the views of substantially the whole of the Episcopate of Ireland with just one possible doubtful exception.[15]

This remarkable generalisation by the Archbishop of Tuam, though not mentioned in the very brief press notice of the resolution, inevitably got into circulation in garbled forms by word of mouth. On 13 November, the day after Delany had been examined privately before the Commission in London, Walsh felt obliged to grant an interview to the *Freeman's Journal* to deny rumours that he had changed his views on the acceptability of a second college within Dublin

University. Pressed by the interviewer as to whether all or most of the other bishops were not opposed to that solution, the Archbishop replied:

I am perfectly aware that the statement is being made, and made with great confidence and very persistently. It is one of a number of falsehoods that have been put in circulation by certain people whom we may call 'wreckers'. It certainly is by no means respectful to our Episcopal Body to say that we are opposed, as a body, to a thing that was put forward by us as worthy of the favourable consideration of the Royal Commission. . . .

But [Walsh added] you must look at the case all round. I must not lead you to suppose that this particular line of settlement would be preferred by the Bishops to any other. Some Bishops, of course, would prefer one of the three solutions mentioned in our statement, some would prefer another. I really do not know how many of us would regard the establishment of a new college of the University of Dublin as the best. That is not a practical matter just now. For the sake of bringing out what I mean, I will put the case at the lowest. Let us suppose, by way of illustration, that I alone among the bishops regarded this as the best solution. This would not, in the slightest degree, affect the really important fact, that, whether this might be regarded as the best conceivable solution, or as only the second best, or the third best, it is a solution which the Bishops, with a united voice . . . have assured the Royal Commission that they are prepared to accept.[16]

Walsh concluded his remarks with an argument that, of the three solutions which the Standing Committee had offered to accept, only the establishment of a new college within Dublin University was within the Commission's terms of reference.

The fact that the Fry Commission was deliberating thus seriously magnified divisions within the hierarchy as well as diverting the bishops' attention somewhat from the government's English education programme. Dillon, however, wisely spent a good deal of the four months that the English Education Bill was in the House of Lords mending the Irish Party's educational fences in Ireland. In its last three years in office, the Unionist government, to apply pressure for educational reform in Ireland, had offered no significant increases in appropriations for Irish education. As a result, the Irish teachers were beginning to feel the pinch, but this time,

instead of lashing out at the clergy, they allowed their grievances to be worked into a revival of the clerical-Gaelic League
agitation for episcopally sanctioned reforms of the National
system. Dillon participated with Bishop Lyster of Achonry
at the large meeting at Ballaghaderreen on 22 September 1906
at which the revived agitation was launched. A few weeks
later, speaking before the annual conference of the Catholic
Truth Society of Ireland, he was emphatic in his defence
of Catholic educational principles which had just been expounded in a speech by Bishop Clancy of Elphin, who had
high praise for the Irish Party's efforts on the English education question. Dillon then took the opportunity to venture
onto the dangerous ground of the relations between the Irish
hierarchy and the party over Balfour's 1902 English Education Bill. He argued that, had the party's advice not to support that bill but to press for greater exchequer grants been
taken, the present danger to Catholic schools in England
would not have arisen. The implication that the Church
should allow the party considerable freedom in political
tactics was clear, and Dillon must have breathed a sigh of
relief when Logue rose and acknowledged that 'Though he
[Dillon] may not know more than the generality of us, perhaps, about the principles of education—though I am sure
he understands them fully—he has shown us in his eloquent
address that he knows better how to fight for those principles
than we do.'[17]

The policy which the House of Lords followed, at the
the direction of Balfour, was not to reject the bill, but to
return it to the Commons so amended as to be virtually
unrecognisable. Though this action was not completed until
6 December, the basic elements of the new situation were
well enough perceived by the last week of November for the
Irish Party to resume negotiations with the government.
Redmond arranged for an interview between Bourne and
himself and Dillon on 26 November.[18] The Irish leaders apparently reported that they had been in touch with cabinet
ministers and had found them ready to consider amendments
to satisfy Catholic claims.[19] After conferring with the Archbishop, Redmond and Dillon began to negotiate in earnest
with the government. The Lords' amendments went a good

deal further than Catholic interests demanded, and in many cases were inspired by purely political considerations having no bearing on religious interests, Anglican or Roman. Their Lordships were, in fact, taking the first step toward the grave constitutional crisis of 1909–11. By acting as they did, the Lords placed Redmond and Dillon in a strong bargaining position, for they could now offer Irish Party support to the government in return for concessions considerably less sweeping than those demanded by the Upper House.

On Tuesday, 27 November, the two Irish leaders met the Prime Minister and Birrell. The ministers indicated willingness to change the four-fifths criterion for extended facilities to three-fourths and to do away with the requirement that a school be in an urban area with a population of more than 5,000 to qualify for such facilities. On the sensitive question of appointment of teachers, Redmond came away from the interview with the impression that the government would agree to a consultative role for a parents' committee, but would balk at giving such a committee veto powers. The Irish leaders offered some compromise language on this point, and Redmond told Campbell-Bannerman that they would support the bill if they 'were completely satisfied upon these points and some minor ones, such as making the ballot a reality'.[20] This latter stipulation reflected Catholic fears that existing provisions of the bill would allow apathetic parents who failed to vote on extended facilities to be counted as opposed to such facilities. These negotiations were apparently conducted with some uncertainty as to what course would be followed when the bill actually returned from the Lords. Redmond told Bourne that he thought no one knew whether a compromise might be made with the Lords.[21] Dillon seems to have contemplated the possibility of an election, for in a letter to Birrell in which he put in writing the points discussed at the interview of 27 November, he laid stress upon the electoral consequences which would follow if he and Redmond were not given enough concessions to be able 'to take the *field vigorously* in support of the Bill'.[22]

Just at this point a group of English Catholics took a step which threatened the Irish Party's delicate position. Without consulting either Redmond or Archbishop Bourne, the Duke

of Norfolk and other Catholics organised a deputation to
Lord Lansdowne, the Unionist leader in the Lords. Purport-
ing to speak for 'Catholic feeling throughout the country',
the deputation urged the Lords to insist upon their amendments. Redmond immediately repudiated any connection
with the deputation[23] and wrote to Bourne that it had made
the party's task much more difficult.[24] Bourne, in his reply,
assured Redmond that he himself had not been informed of
the deputation 'until all the arrangements had been made'.[25]
The Archbishop was angrier over this 'lamentable oversight'
than he intimated to Redmond. In a letter to the Duke of
Norfolk a month later he complained bitterly of the fact that
'While Mr. Redmond was loyally consulting me at every
critical moment, my opinion and legitimate influence were
neither sought nor considered as far as other Catholic representatives were concerned,' and, the Archbishop observed,
'At the most critical moment of all a deputation was promoted to Lord Lansdowne. I was not informed of it until
all the arrangements had been made, and I had to undo the
mischief which was thereby wrought, as best I could.' It was,
in Bourne's view, 'the first evidence of any want of unity
among Catholics'.[26] In his letter to Redmond concerning the
deputation, the Archbishop had mentioned plans which were
under way for a similar deputation to the Prime Minister, and
he asked the Irish leader's advice on the matter. Redmond
opined that such action would be 'most mischievous' and
would make it difficult for the government to accede to the
limited Catholic demands which he and Dillon were pressing.[27] He also wrote to Birrell, urging the government not to
receive such a deputation,[28] and apparently he succeeded.

On Tuesday, 4 December, the English Catholic hierarchy
met to consider the amendments Redmond had discussed
with Birrell and Campbell-Bannerman on 27 November. In
a confidential resolution the bishops guardedly advised Redmond that government acceptance of the amendments he had
outlined would be sufficient justification for Catholics not
actively demanding the bill's withdrawal.[29] They made this
decision, however, not because the proposed amendments
would make the bill satisfactory, 'but because it seems the
safer course in the present very critical situation', and they

stressed the importance of further efforts to obtain guarantees that in future new Catholic schools might be built and not be 'treated as unnecessary at the will of the Local Education Authority'. Two weeks later Bourne revealed to Redmond that while two or three of the bishops at this meeting favoured 'wrecking the Bill', the remainder agreed with Bourne that, if the Irish Party got the terms for which they were negotiating, 'they would be well out of it and that the proper policy would be to facilitate [the bill's] passage'.[30] This account of the proceedings at the meeting is substantially confirmed by a letter from Bishop Burton of Clifton to the Duke of Norfolk early in January 1907. 'The Bishops, with one silent exception (which was not myself),' wrote the Bishop of Clifton, 'consented to leave the Irish Party unfettered, but carefully abstained from bestowing explicit sanction upon their action.'[31]

The night before the bishops met, Redmond heard a report that a movement was afoot to organise Catholic Associations in London. With Bishop Henry's Belfast Catholic Association a fresh memory and with the deputation to Lord Lansdowne and even fresher memory, Redmond was understandably alarmed. He presumed that the Catholic Education Council, which represented approximately the same forces that had deceived him over the deputation, was behind the new movement. 'I think I ought to let you know', he wrote to Archbishop Bourne, 'that we would regard such a move as a hostile one to our political organisation.'[32] Bourne, who had gone to Paris for a few days, replied after a short delay that he himself was responsible for the new movement. He explained that its aim was merely to protect Catholic interests in local government affairs, implied that it would not be antagonistic to the Irish Party's interests, but insisted rather firmly that it must not be opposed.[33] Fortunately, no crisis was precipitated by this matter, but the misunderstanding was indicative of the tensions which had been created by the uneasy alliance of Irish and English Catholics.

Perhaps fearing that the incident might dampen Redmond's zeal to press for the compromise solution, on the same day that he replied to Redmond the Archbishop wrote to Lord Ripon, a Catholic peer who was Lord Privy Seal,

giving him in confidence the substance of the bishops' resolution of 4 December and an outline of the proposed amendments as he understood them. Ripon passed the information
on to Birrell with the advice that they should not 'lose this
chance of a settlement with the R.C.s', adding candidly:
'Putting aside all other considerations we do not want to
lose their votes at elections if it can be avoided.'[34] Two days
later Birrell spoke to Redmond after a cabinet meeting and
gave him 'a positive assurance' that any compromise would
contain all the amendments in question including one to
require the concurrence of a parents' committee in appointment of teachers to Clause 4 schools. In addition, Birrell
indicated that the four-fifths criterion would be lowered, not
just to three-fourths, but to two-thirds and that some arrangement would be made for new schools.[35] The available evidence suggests that, after dispatching this news to Bourne,
Redmond and Dillon acted on their own later that evening
when they led the Irish Party into the government lobby on
the critical division over the government's motion to reject
the Lords' amendments *en bloc*.[36]

During this crucial week the split in the ranks of Catholic
members of parliament came clearly into public view. Much
to the consternation of Bourne,[37] Lord Edmund Talbot, chief
English spokesman for Catholics in the House of Commons
and brother of the Duke of Norfolk, had made a speech in
the Commons on 11 December calling for even stronger
amendments than those of the Lords and quoting, 'as a
warning to His Majesty's Government', an extract from a
speech by the Catholic Bishop of Liverpool which called for
resistance 'not in any passive sense, but in an active sense'.[38]
Dillon, feeling he could not let Talbot's statement of the
Catholic position go unchallenged, answered him on the
following day, before the critical division. In his speech,[39] and
in a public letter[40] after Talbot carried the matter into the
press on 13 December, Dillon revealed that the Irish Party
had succeeded in obtaining four-fifths, possibly nine-tenths,
of the concessions which were vital to Catholic interests. He
accused Talbot and his brother of being more anxious to
wreck chances for a settlement on political grounds than to
gain genuine safeguards for Catholic schools. In this judge-

ment Dillon was absolutely correct; from published accounts of the Church of England's involvement in this controversy —which has been much more adequately documented than the Catholic side—it is quite clear that the Conservative Party, led by Balfour and Lord Lansdowne, with the enthusiastic seconding of Norfolk, were out to make a show of strength on the issue regardless of the desires of Anglican ecclesiastics.[41] 'A characteristic outburst' by Lord Salisbury 'as to how he wished the Bishops would leave politics to the politicians'[42] was typical of the reaction of Conservative leaders to suggestions from Church of England authorities for compromise.

The vote of the Irish Party to reject the Lords' amendments together with the revelations of Dillon's exchange with Talbot sparked reactions from three distinct clerical quarters. The Revs John Clifford and J. Hirst Hollowell, two leading Nonconformist spokesmen, wrote to the press in outrage that the government would contemplate further concessions to the 'sectarians'[43] (a curious reversal of the ordinary sense of that term). From the Anglican camp, the Bishop of Manchester charged that the House of Lords would be 'asked to save Roman Catholic schools and abandon the Church schools'. He revealed, however, that he did not represent Anglican episcopal opinion on the recent course of events by prefacing his remarks with the 'hope that English Churchmen, and especially English Bishops' would realise what was occurring.[44]

The third, and for our purposes most significant, reaction came from O'Dwyer. Two weeks earlier the Bishop of Limerick had written to the press regretting the *Freeman's* statement that the Irish Party had 'repudiated' the deputation to Lord Lansdowne and expressed confidence that, while Redmond could not associate himself with a plea to such an ardent Unionist, he would not sanction such strong abuse of the English Catholics who made it. As we know, the Bishop was wrong in his interpretation of Redmond's feelings. In this early letter he enunciated a policy identical with that which Norfolk and Talbot were in fact following.[45] When the Irish Party, then, voted with the Liberals on 12 December, O'Dwyer was, he would have us believe, thunderstruck. After a full day of 'thinking and thinking' of the party's action, 'turning it over on every side', the Bishop composed a public letter which must rank, in historical significance as well as rhetorical exaggeration, with his more famous letters which appeared a decade later. He had for some time been disturbed by 'rumours of negotiations, that is, in more accurate language, of Liberal intrigues to sap the fidelity of the Irish Party'.[46] Recognising that in the summer the party had acted in accord with the desires of the English Catholic bishops, he nevertheless hardly even paused now to consider the possibility that the party might still be acting with episcopal sanction, but cited a recent public declaration of the English hierarchy welcoming the Lords' amendments and asserted: 'If the Bishops of the Catholic Church have not, by Divine right, a determining voice on such a question, then we might as well be Protestants.' The party's action in the Committee stage had been, the Bishop suggested, 'an elaborate imposture', for the government majority was large enough that 'there was no harm done by fine speeches and harmless divisions. But now,' O'Dwyer continued, 'is the crisis,' for

Their votes are wanted. Their Liberal masters are in a difficulty. Their iniquitous Bill is in danger, and so the screw is put on, and the Irish Party, by a vote that will never be forgiven, rat upon themselves, and forswear their own professions.[47]

The Bishop of Liverpool, whose call for active resistance to the law if the bill should pass had been quoted by Lord Edmund Talbot, had, according to O'Dwyer, 'stirred a chord of sympathy in all our hearts'. Dillon, in O'Dwyer's rogue's gallery, was 'the man who, with canine servility, licks the hand of Mr. Birrell'.

The Bishop then broadened his attack and questioned the whole basis of the Irish Party. Was there, he asked, a party meeting to consider the vote on this issue? 'Or, was it all settled in the Eighty Club by one of the political brokers who carry the Irish vote in their breeches pocket?' He was consoled, however, by the 'manifest signs of political break-up' in Ireland. Although, if the Catholic schools of England (the 'outposts' of Catholic schools in Ireland) should be 'taken by storm', then Ireland would also 'be threatened with the French system', O'Dwyer was nevertheless confident that no Irish bishop need have any grave apprehension on account of the irreligious blackguardism which any Irish Clemenceau may attempt to bring to bear against him. It is premature to talk of Clemenceau in this country. The hearts of the people are sound and true. But if anyone doubts the opinion he might hold a meeting in this city to denounce me for my action on this English Education Bill, and see, and possibly feel, the result. As far as I can judge, the Irish Party have nothing behind them. They represent no opinion—Catholic or Irish—but are the puppets of the English Liberals in this matter.[48]

This same subservience to the Liberals, the Bishop charged, had led already to the party being ' "squared", to use a slang but expressive word, on Devolution, as on Mr. Birrell's Bill. We shall have plenty of fine speeches, and green flag waving; but Devolution will be imposed upon us by similar artifices to those which we now deplore on the Education question.' This playing upon the political sentiments of doctrinaire and uncompromising nationalists as a means of attacking political moderates deemed to be acting contrary to the Church's interests foreshadowed the way in which ecclesiastical authorities would deal with the Irish Council Bill five months later. The party, O'Dwyer asserted—in a passage which more ominously foreshadowed a famous utterance ten years later—was 'losing touch with the healthy opinion of their own country', and, he suggested,

If just now they could separate themselves from Mr. Birrell and Mr. Lloyd George and the rest of the Eighty Club, and come over to Ireland and inquire why the fine generation of young Irishmen that is growing up is turning away from them en masse for the Gaelic League, or Sinn Fein, or some other policy, they would learn some salutary truths.[49]

Dillon, who had returned to Dublin after the crucial vote, had mixed feelings over the Bishop's action. On 15 December, the day the letter appeared, he wrote to Redmond: 'I think it is rather fortunate that O'Dwyer has come out in such an outrageous manner—It will make the others unwilling to follow such a lead,'[50] and four days later he was more confident in his opinion that the bishop was actually helping the party. He reported that O'Dwyer had provoked some clerical replies, and he indicated, interestingly, that the 'others' whose reactions he had feared were 'Dublin and Armagh'.[51] Dillon's initial optimistic reaction was tempered, however, by concern over dangers from another quarter. 'It would be a mistake', he warned in his letter of 15 December, 'to underrate the risk of Episcopal action against the Party— There cannot be a doubt that the wires will be pulled most vigorously by the Duke of Norfolk and his gang to get the English Bishops to declare in some way against us.' He was, it is clear from the tone of his remarks, by no means confident of Bourne's continued support.

I am strongly of opinion [he emphasised] that you ought at least to offer to see the Archbishop of Westminster as soon as possible —In matters of this kind a personal interview often checks mischief—If you do see him I would not raise the question of the Catholic Association at all—That had better be allowed to slide for the present.[52]

These misgivings were unjustified as far as Bourne was concerned. In 'a long and a most friendly and satisfactory interview' with Redmond on 17 December the Archbishop expressed his distress over the Bishop of Limerick's letter and indicated that he was writing to O'Dwyer 'remonstrating with him and telling him substantially how the matter stands'.[53] He told Redmond, moreover, that he regarded the party's vote on the crucial division as purely a tactical matter, and he assured the Irish Party leader that in his opinion they had done the right thing. Redmond then sent copies of the relevant documents to Bishop O'Donnell to demonstrate that the party had not ratted, but had acted in consultation with Bourne. The Bishop of Raphoe was obviously pleased by the correspondence which Redmond sent to him, and in reviewing the controversial points of the bill he made it clear that he shared Bourne's view of the strategy to be followed.[54]

On 19 December the Earl of Crewe, Lord President of the Council and chief government spokesman in the Lords, outlined in the Upper House the concessions the government were prepared to make in reply to the Lords' amendments.[55] With the government thus publicly on record in support of the concessions previously made in private, the Catholic ecclesiastical authorities in England were able to give Redmond in public the support which they had been giving only privately. An interview with Mgr Brown, Vicar-General of the diocese of Southwark, was published on 20 December. With the government amendments, Mgr Brown said, the bill would have been workable, and, barring administration 'in a hostile spirit by the local authorities the Catholic schools would have remained Catholic in every sense of the word'.[56] On the same day Bourne wrote Redmond a letter for publication thanking him for the Irish Party's efforts. 'Knowing as I do the negotiations which have taken place,' the Archbishop concluded, 'I am satisfied that you have done your best to deal with a very delicate situation.'[57] Redmond was able to state in the House of Commons that evening that the Irish Party had acted 'not only in consultation with, but with the concurrence of the responsible heads of the Catholic Church in England'.[58]

Dillon's fears of wire-pulling by 'the Duke of Norfolk and his gang' were amply justified. Norfolk reacted to Redmond's statement of 20 December by writing in dismay to all the Catholic bishops of England. While he agreed that gratitude must be expressed to the Irish members for their action during the summer session, he suggested that the bishops should add 'some expression of regret or disavowal in regard to the latter course adopted'.[59] By writing to each bishop without first consulting Bourne as to his dealings with Redmond, the Duke acted with questionable propriety, but the correspondence which he provoked among the members of the hierarchy is most revealing. In his reply to the Duke, Bourne was scrupulously careful to assure Norfolk of his confidence that he and Lord Edmund had conducted themselves honourably, but he did not conceal his anger with

others who politically sympathise with you who have never acted fairly towards me from the day that they realised that I valued my independence of party politics, that I was not prepared to play any tune for which they might be pleased to call, and that I was determined to deal impartially, to the extent of my ability, with all my flock irrespectively of their political opinion, nationality, or social position.[60]

Moreover, the Archbishop argued, 'In face of the ill-informed attack of the Bishop of Limerick, I should indeed have played a mean and cowardly part had I not publicly assured Mr

Redmond that I was satisfied "that he had done his best to deal with a very delicate and critical situation".'

At least one of Bourne's episcopal colleagues, Bishop Casartelli of Salford (i.e. Manchester), did not share his feelings toward O'Dwyer. Casartelli confessed his own sympathy with Norfolk's attitude and expressed grave dissatisfaction with the statements and actions of the Irish Parliamentary Party. 'I feel', he wrote, 'that the attacks made upon the Catholic Peers by some of the Catholic members of the Lower House & by a section of the Catholic press, put forward too under the aegis of the Bishops of England, & so bravely repudiated by the Bishop of Limerick, have had a disastrous effect in causing at least apparent disunion in our hitherto so serried ranks.'[61] Bourne's answer to Casartelli and two other prelates who were concerned over his action is a concise summary of the essential elements of the situation:

On Dec. 4th we could give only a hesitating consent to Mr. Redmond's negotiations. By Dec. 20th he was entitled to say that he had acted with *my concurrence*, for, step by step, consulting me at every stage, he had with no ordinary skill definitely won practically all that we had asked him to work for last spring.

The Bill was wrecked by Balfour as a political move; and by the Anglicans because, they were getting too little and the Romanists, in their judgment, too much. I have good authority for what I say.[62]

Bourne was attempting a major feat of ecclesiastical statecraft—to wean the Roman Catholic Church in Great Britain from its tendency to depend upon the Conservative Party in political matters.

The Irish Party had managed to avoid serious immediate consequences in the affair. Devlin reported from New Zealand that 'cables from home saying that the Bishops of Ireland were up in arms against the Party' had put a 'slight damper' on proceedings, but that his fund-raising had not been perceptibly affected.'[63] Once Bourne had endorsed Redmond's action, public episcopal criticism was silenced. Nevertheless, by his precipitate action O'Dwyer had made it difficult for the Irish hierarchy to offer congratulations to the party. There was some effort on the part of individual bishops, however, to obtain some expression of high ecclesiastical sanction for the party's action. When Bishops Mangan of Kerry and Fogarty of Killaloe visited Rome in May 1907, it was announced that Cardinal Merry del Val, the Papal Secretary of State, 'expressed his admiration of the able work done by the Irish Parliamentary Party in connection with the Catholic Education question in England'.[64] No expression of ecclesiastical endorsement of the Party's action, however, could dispel from O'Dwyer's mind the conviction that the Irish Party leaders had become contaminated through contact with liberal, secularist politics and opinion in England.

The Lords' rejection of the Education Bill had cast in high relief the seemingly intractable constitutional problem which bedevilled Anglo-Irish relations. The glee with which the Conservative Party, driven out of power in the Commons by the electorate, had used its permanent majority in the Upper House to mangle the Education Bill would become veritable ecstatic abandon if they were offered any measure for self-government in Ireland. Few Liberal statesmen, however friendly to the claims of the Irish Nation, could view with equanimity the prospects for the Liberal Party in the grave crisis of State which would ensue. Nevertheless, refinement and elaboration of MacDonnell's Devolution scheme had been going on now for a number of months, and pressures from Irish Party leaders were changing its character slightly.[65] The scheme had started out in 1903 as a meeting of the minds between MacDonnell, who believed that administrative efficiency would be enhanced and sectarian animosities assuaged by a modest popular voice in the Irish government, and a few Irish Unionists, who fancied that such a move might provide them with a new paternalistic role to replace the old exploitative landlord role of which they were now, happily, divesting themselves. The scheme was now becoming more of a compromise between what the Nation's representatives wanted and what the Liberal leadership thought it might possibly enact without provoking a crisis which would deprive it of power in the State for the indefinite future.

In January 1907 the Devolution scheme was still in a state of flux, but another rather less dangerous concession to Ireland was almost ripe for enactment. On 12 January the

Fry Commission reported. Eight of the nine commissioners (the dissentient being a Catholic Fellow of T.C.D.) called for the establishment in Dublin of a college acceptable to Catholics. Disappointingly, the majority was divided on the crucial question of the university to which the new college should be attached. Four commissioners favoured the inclusion of the new college along with the Queen's Colleges in a reconstructed University of Dublin.[66] Another commissioner, Professor Jackson, agreed in principle with this recommendation but felt that it was inexpedient to effect the scheme immediately.[67] The three other members, including the Chairman, rejected the enlargement of Dublin University in favour of essentially the same plan that had been recommended by the Robertson Commission. In explaining their position, these three commissioners relied heavily on the letter of the late Mgr Molloy, the evidence of Dr Delany, and the action of the latter together with Archbishop Healy in the Senate of the Royal University, as evidence

that whatever may have been the opinion of the Irish Roman Catholic Hierarchy at an earlier date, the full consideration of Lord Dunraven's scheme has led them rather to condemn than to approve of it: and we know from past history the power of such a condemnation.[68]

Nevertheless, MacDonnell and Bryce were undeterred in their resolve to effect a scheme along the lines of Dunraven's proposals. Even before the Commission's report was published, they seem to have been in touch with Archbishop Walsh about strategy to forestall difficulties with the hierarchy.[69]

By this time, however, Bryce was a lame duck. Late in December Campbell-Bannerman had offered him the Embassy at Washington, and as the United States, unlike Ireland, was a subject upon which he had special expertise, he accepted the new assignment eagerly. The Prime Minister decided to fill the Irish vacancy with Augustine Birrell, whose position at the Board of Education had been rendered somewhat uncomfortable by the Lords' action on his Education Bill. Birrell's appointment was not officially announced until well into January, and Bryce was anxious to use his last few days at Dublin Castle to commit his cabinet colleagues to the enlargement of Dublin University. He secured Birrell's approval to announce the scheme as government policy to a deputation from the Presbyterian General Assembly which proposed to wait on him on 25 January. Prompt action was necessary, Bryce wrote to the Prime Minister, because

> Those here who wish to block our course have been shewing that their one hope is that the R. C. bishops may be induced to withdraw from the consent they gave to the plan which approved itself to us: and the chief Tory organ accordingly deprecates any declaration of policy. This makes it all the more desirable that our view should be declared before the bishops are tempted to withdraw, so the policy I suggested to you of pinning the bishops at once becomes all the more necessary.[70]

When the Presbyterian deputation arrived, along with a separate deputation of Catholic laymen, Bryce made his announcement in a long, carefully phrased speech which proposed to establish within the University of Dublin three additional colleges—the Belfast and Cork Queen's Colleges and a new college in Dublin mainly for Catholics, but open in all respects for Protestants. The possibility was mentioned that Galway, Magee College and the arts faculty of Maynooth might be affiliated to the University without the rank of constituent colleges. The choice of Bryce to be an ambassador was, no doubt, well advised, for he demonstrated all the skills of the diplomat in presenting the scheme simultaneously to Presbyterian and Catholic deputations.[71] Two days later he reported to Campbell-Bannerman:

> With a view to our English Noncon. friends, I emphasized its non sectarian character as far as was possible without actually frightening the R. C. bishops, who, tho they had formally committed themselves to accept a new College in Dublin University scheme might be alarmed by our dwelling on the fact that we don't intend to confine the governing body of the new college to R. C.s, and that we mean the University Governing Body to be entirely academical in its constitution.[72]

MacDonnell did not hear from Walsh immediately,[73] and apparently wrote to the Archbishop suggesting an immediate meeting of the hierarchy. Walsh's reply of 4 February illuminates the precise extent to which the Archbishop was able to govern his colleagues in this matter. He first pointed out that a meeting could not be called on as short notice as Sir Antony had suggested and that, in particular, the approach of Lent made the bishops far too busy to assemble.

But, in addition to all this [he wrote], I should regard the holding of a meeting just now most injudicious. There are points in the scheme, (for instance, the inclusion of the three Provincial Colleges, the inter-Collegiate arrangements in Dublin, &c) to which many would object, and it is at least possible that the objectors might be in the majority, and might insist on the publication of the objections.

In a word, the whole thing, if it was to be dealt with now (when the scheme as to details is more or less in a state of fluidity), would have to be dealt with on the merits. The Bishops, if considering it, could not deal with it otherwise. Later on, things will have developed a little, and then the question to be considered will be quite a different one. It will be: is there anything in this that cannot be put up with, or acceded to by way of concession. At that stage the upholders of the Robertson scheme will be practically powerless. They are by no means powerless now, and they would on many grounds wish to show their *comparative* dislike of *any* University of Dublin scheme.[74]

Walsh, in other words, could be certain of an episcopal consensus in favour of tolerating a Dublin University solution only if he was backed by a firm offer from the government to enact a specific, detailed scheme into law. Bryce had deliberately avoided setting a date for the introduction of his scheme or spelling out many details. It would be necessary, he had written to the Prime Minister on 27 January, to give careful attention to details and 'possibly to resist some prelatical demands'. He had been assured, however, 'that they are so impatient to have something done that they will not let this chance slip'.[75]

It was true that the bishops were desperately anxious that this opportunity for settlement should not be lost. In his letter to MacDonnell on 4 February, Walsh noted with satisfaction that a statement by Bryce that the scheme accorded with the bishops' views had 'not evoked a whisper of questioning in any quarter, and is thus taken as having been tacitly assented to'.[76] Though Walsh was prevented 'by a useful provision of our domestic discipline' from publicly pronouncing in favour of the scheme before it should be formally accepted by the hierarchy, he was 'quite free to *act*', and was already taking steps to rally public opinion in favour of the plan. By 13 February he was becoming more optimistic and told Mac-Donnell: 'You may take it from me that there never was so clear a case of unanimity in Ireland (at the side of the people who have the grievan[ce], i.e. Ireland outside T.C.D.) coupled with an outspoken determinati[on] to suppress all individual divergences of personal views as to details for the sake of combination in support of the splendid scheme now before us.'[77] Even the Senate of the Royal University, which less than four months earlier had deprecated any single-university settlement, now passed a resolution which cordially welcomed Bryce's announcement.[78] The importance of 'pinning the bishops at once', as Bryce had put it, was made plain by a public letter from Father Delany denying that the Senate's action constituted 'approval or disapproval of any scheme' and pointedly remarking that he would welcome Bryce's plan only 'when the Catholic Hierarchy shall have recommended it as worthy of acceptance by the Catholics of Ireland'.[79]

In Balfour's words, Bryce had 'nailed his flag to another man's mast and sailed for America'.[80] The other man, Birrell, had his own set of priorities. The Speech from the Throne on 12 February had promised both university reform and 'measures for further associating the people of Ireland with the management of their domestic affairs, and for otherwise improving the system of government in its administrative and financial aspects'.[81] Though MacDonnell was permitted to draft a University Bill embodying Bryce's scheme, the government decided to try to appease the Irish Party by going ahead first with the governmental reform scheme. Despite the fact that the government had no mandate for Home Rule, hope sprang eternal in Irish breasts. In April, when the hierarchy's Standing Committee passed a resolution imploring the government to enact a university settlement, they deferred to the widespread, albeit groundless, expectation of something close to Gladstonian Home Rule. While acknowledging that much of the parliamentary session was already committed 'to another Irish measure of still greater importance', they argued that a university settlement should accompany 'the grant of self-government now about to be made to the people of Ireland'.[82] Redmond and Dillon, who were in earnest negotiations with cabinet members over the scheme, knew that it would be far less than a 'grant of self-government . . . to the people of Ireland'. Nevertheless, by early May they had won considerable ground.

On 7 May Birrell introduced the scheme in a measure entitled the Irish Council Bill. The bill provided for the establishment of a Council of eighty-two elected and twenty-four nominated members plus the Under-Secretary. This Council was to have cognisance over eight of the authorities of the existing Irish government, and the government might at some future date transfer to the Irish Council the powers of certain other minor authorities. The Council was to have no taxing powers, but was to administer an annual grant from the exchequer which, for the first five years of the act's operation, was set at £4,164,000 plus certain other revenues already assigned to the authorities to be placed under it. In replying to Birrell's speech, Redmond was careful not to commit himself until he could study the text of the measure (a disingenuous remark, as he had been negotiating over it clause by clause for a month) and assess opinion of it in Ireland.[83] He indicated that it would be submitted to a Nationalist Convention scheduled for 21 May and that the party leadership would advise the Convention whether they felt it would advance or hinder the cause of full Home Rule—for which, he stressed, the bill could be no substitute. Redmond and Dillon, no doubt, sincerely hoped that they could garner enough support in Ireland to make it safe for them to endorse the bill, but they were choosing their steps very cautiously.[84] Redmond's task was complicated the following week when the sudden death of Dillon's young wife deprived the party leader for the moment of his principal confidant and listening-post in Ireland. The bill was greeted in Ireland by a wave of disappointment, which was all the more difficult to control because the party leaders had failed to consult even the rank-and-file party members during their negotiations. Individual churchmen undoubtedly shared in the general disillusionment on nationalist grounds. From the standpoint of the Church as an institution, however, the bill was something other than a watered-down Home Rule Bill and an insult to nationalist sentiment. It was the long-awaited Irish education reform bill.

Ever since Starkie's Belfast speech in 1902, the Church had been mobilising herself for a possible showdown over 'reform' of Irish education. The prospect of a university settlement at the end of 1903 and again during the year preceding the Irish Council Bill's introduction had moderated ecclesiastical criticism of the government, but it had not allayed clerical fears. The Dale Report in 1904, Rule 127(b) in 1905, and the fact that in 1906 the Liberal government had failed to relieve the financial pressure which the Unionists had maintained in an effort to force surrender to the reform demands had all kept the issue alive. As recently as February 1907 the Church had been actively sponsoring a nationwide agitation, particularly by teachers, for a kind of reform which would undercut the plan of the reformers in Dublin Castle.[85] Moreover, the English Education Bill had been deeply disturbing to Irish clergy even though it did not affect their own interests. After his transfer to the Irish Office, Birrell, who was himself the son of a Baptist minister, had carefully avoided secularist rhetoric on education, admitting in one speech that the 'sacred words "popular control" which were so often on my lips once, do not reverberate through Ireland'.[86] The introduction of the Irish Council Bill, however, meant that once again the high hopes of churchmen for an immediate university settlement, which had no doubt bought Birrell an initial period of ecclesiastical tolerance, were once again probably to be disappointed. While the Irish Parliamentary Party leaders' negotiations had shifted the Irish Council Bill in a more democratic direction than MacDonnell had intended, they had not effaced one of the Under-Secretary's primary purposes: to move the education systems markedly toward popular control. Education would far outweigh all other matters over which the Irish Council would be given superintendence. In addition to the National and Intermediate Education Boards, the new Council was to acquire jurisdiction over the Department of Agriculture and Technical Instruction, which carried on extensive educational activity, and the Inspector of Reformatory and Industrial Schools, whose responsibilities were at least in some sense educational. Of the other four authorities, the Registrar General had only trivial powers from a political standpoint, and the Commissioners of Public Works, the Local Government Board and the Congested Districts Board, though their responsibilities were rapidly growing as successive governments tried to solve some of Ireland's pressing social problems, involved only a fraction of the personnel and dispensed only a fraction of the funds of the authorities primarily or partly concerned with education. Though the Council and the Lord Lieutenant, acting together, were allowed some freedom to reorganise the framework of the Irish government, one such reform was definitely spelled out in the bill. The Lord Lieutenant was directed to constitute an Education Department for Ireland to replace the National and Intermediate Education Boards. This provision alone would have been enough to convince most churchmen of the government's pernicious intent.

Walsh's first comment to the press—'I expected little, and consequently am not disappointed, as people generally seem to be'—shrewdly gave first place to the arguments which would appeal to lay nationalists. While reserving detailed judgement until copies of the bill were available, he observed that 'What is offered to us is very little indeed.'[87] Probably no member of the hierarchy was more genuinely devoted to the Home Rule cause than Walsh, though he had become privately dissatisfied with the Irish Party. His objection to the bill on purely secular grounds was no doubt sincere. Nevertheless, his specific criticisms focused upon issues in which the Church had definite interests. Of the existing Education Boards, he said:

They are commonly spoken of as 'Castle Boards'. Well, up to this there has been one safeguard: the Castle had no power of initiative. It might veto what either Board had done. It had no more authority than the tsar of Russia to order either Board to do anything. Let us hope that the power of the Castle in this respect is not going to be extended and that the new Council of Education may not be in a worse position than the old Boards. Mr. Birrell's speech is not reassuring.[88]

Here too, by introducing the concept of Castle interference, he made skilful use of the sentiments of lay nationalists, and

he followed the pattern which, since Wyndham first suggested a Department in 1904, the hierarchy had adopted in opposing co-ordination schemes. But the new proposal was
fundamentally different from anything a Conservative government would have introduced, for the new Department was
to be responsible not to the Castle, but to a popular assembly
in Dublin. In particular, the direct supervision of the Department was to devolve upon an education committee of the
Irish Council, and it was specially provided that the Lord
Lieutenant might appoint as additional members of this
committee 'persons having experience in education', including women. This was apparently the 'Council of Education'
to which Walsh referred, although that term does not occur
in the bill, and the spectre of a Castle initiative in its deliberations was nothing more than a pure fiction which had no
foundation in Birrell's speech or in the bill. A few days later,
after he had read the bill, Walsh, in a more careful statement, made no reference to Castle initiative but shifted his
ground slightly and asked: 'Is there not still to be a Castle
veto over everything that the new "Education Department"
as well as the new "Irish Council" can do?'[89] There was,
indeed, to be such a veto, though why this should inhibit
Walsh from 'saying anything that could tend to induce the
coming Convention to give it any countenance' is not immediately evident, for he himself conceded that one admittedly salutary reform specified in the bill—abolition of the
results system in the Intermediate Schools—had been blocked
in the preceding few years by the veto of the Castle upon
Intermediate Board actions.

The bill contained two features of educational reform
which the Church most feared: a Department and popular
(albeit not local) control. However, the nature of the measure
made it difficult for the hierarchy to attack these features in
the same way as they had been attacking them during the
preceding three years. The first line of defence against a
Department had been the charge that it would be merely
another 'Castle Board' unresponsive to Irish opinion. Such
a defence was logically undermined by the fact that the Department was to be under the jurisdiction of the Irish Council, and, had logic not been abandoned in the wave of

popular disappointment which greeted the bill, Walsh would have had to resort to even more tortuous argument than he found necessary in the statements quoted above.

Similarly the first line of defence against popular control had usually been to denounce the local taxation which was put forward as a prerequisite of such control and to cite the supposed financial grievances of Ireland which would be even further aggravated by this increased burden on the ratepayers. The bill embodied an unexpected tactic, for it granted popular control over education without giving the new popular body the power or obligation to raise funds on its own responsibility. The financial implications of the bill were rather complex, and Birrell's speech did little to clarify them, for he was trying simultaneously to demonstrate his generosity to the Nationalists and to convince Unionists of his parsimony. From examination of the relevant financial accounts, it appears that the Irish Council could spend as much as £100,000 annually on its own establishment and the administrative expenses of the new Irish treasury and still have about £300,000 per annum during its first five years to apply, if it so chose, to the needs of education. In addition, it might devote a large part of an annual supplemental grant of £114,000 to the construction of new school buildings.

In a letter to the press Bishop Foley presented figures, presumably from Education Office sources, indicating that the amount required was an additional £676,000 per annum plus a capital sum of £1,000,000 for building, etc. In his view, it was absurd to regard the financial provisions as adequate, though he raised, without answering, the very pertinent question of whether they were as good as could be obtained.[90] As things turned out, better financial arrangements than had pertained during the preceding few years were in fact forthcoming through ordinary parliamentary operations. Birrell, for all his supposed anticlericalism, did not perpetuate the financial squeeze which the Conservatives had begun in the interest of local lay control and at the expense of the hard-pressed teachers. In 1907, however, Birrell's good intentions were not so clear. Bishop O'Dwyer, for one, regarded the bill as the first assault by 'our Non Conformist Chief Secretary . . . upon the position of religion in our schools'.[91]

The new Education Department would bring in its train all the evils of secularism, and O'Dwyer dwelt at length upon the fact that under the bill the Irish Council would not be empowered to make the actual appointments of individuals to the Department.[92] He was undoubtedly afraid that the scheme would have the effect of putting Starkie in an even stronger position, and his fears on this score apparently outweighed financial considerations, for he seems to have felt that the teachers' interests would be better served by reviving their claims to the Equivalent Grant.[93] The Equivalent Grant, even if devoted entirely to education, would be only £185,000 —considerably less than would become available under the bill to augment the provision for education.

O'Dwyer's suspicion of the Liberals' intentions was echoed by Logue, who called the bill 'ludicrously disappointing . . . and in some of its provisions mischievous' and stated his belief that 'Any politician who will try to secure its acceptance at the forthcoming Convention will incur grave suspicion of endeavouring to deceive his countrymen in the interests of the Ministry.'[94] Dr Boylan, the new Bishop of Kilmore, declared: 'The new and long-expected Bill is not very encouraging; the present generation of Liberals appears to labour under a most distressing nightmare of cowardice and confusion.'[95] Bishop Foley, who had long been dissatisfied with the provision of the 1898 Local Government Act, which excluded Catholic clergymen from serving on local councils, used the extension of these disabilities to the proposed Irish Council as an argument against the bill. No Catholic clergyman, he argued, would be allowed to serve on the Council's Education Committee. It was true that three-fourths of the membership of that Committee was to be drawn from the Council itself, from which clergymen were excluded, but the provision for appointment of additional members was undoubtedly framed with a view to involving ecclesiastics in the new scheme. Foley was obliged to engage in some special pleading to explain away that loophole in his argument. 'I assume', he wrote, 'that no Catholic clergyman would care to become a member of it on the nomination of the Lord Lieutenant,' to which one might reasonably reply by pointing out that the Bishop himself currently held such an appointment on the National Board. To this argument Foley's rejoinder was that the National Education Commissioners were all nominated, and 'therefore equal in point of authority. . . . This would not be so in the case of a Committee, three-fourths of whose members were appointed by such a representative body as the Irish Council.' Though this may not seem a very compelling argument, Foley thought it grounds for urging 'the Catholic clerical body to be strongly represented at the coming Convention, and to insist upon the rights of ordinary citizens'.[96]

The views of the bishops were shared by the lower clergy. Among the resolutions adopted unanimously by the Munster Council of Catholic Clerical Managers was one declaring 'That whilst we, as a body, abstain from pronouncing any opinion on the Irish Council Bill now before the country, we regard the portion of it referring to Education as entirely unsatisfactory.'[97] One of the Irish Party's strong supporters, Alderman Joyce of Limerick, wrote to Redmond that he had spoken to 'a great many men both Cleric & lay & 95 per cent of them are dead against the Bill'.[98] The mere fact that Alderman Joyce specified 'both Cleric & lay' suggests that the clergy were an especially prominent element in the opposition.

Redmond appears to have intended, up until a short time before the Nationalist Convention assembled, to move acceptance of the measure in principle, and without prejudice to the larger claim. On his return from London to Dublin, however, he discovered how serious a popular reaction had set in against the bill. When he rose to address the Convention, he moved the rejection of the bill, and his motion was adopted unanimously. Among the many messages read to the Convention, the only one from a bishop was from O'Donnell, the party's stalwart, who noncommittally said only: 'My thoughts are with the Convention today. I believe it will signally advance the interests of Ireland. United, under God's blessing, we can carry what we want.'[99] It is unlikely that, if other bishops had been asked for messages, they would have withheld them. The party leadership probably felt that its prestige in England would not be advanced by a long series of letters from bishops in terms similar to those which had appeared in the press. It would not do for the Convention to appear to be acting under clerical dictation, and when Father David Humphrys attempted to make a speech which contained several impolitic remarks about Protestants and Catholic 'tolerance provers' he was shouted down.

Given the popular reaction against the bill, it is difficult to say how far its rejection was the result of ecclesiastical opposition. In evaluating the force of clerical opposition, however, one should remember that the clergy were already organised and on the alert to move against the feared educational reform, which, in their eyes, was precisely what the Irish Council Bill was. Had the clergy not been so overwhelmingly opposed to the bill, and had the Church not been on its guard and backed up by an existing popular movement against reform in education, it is possible that Redmond would have been both willing and able to influence the Convention to accept the bill. This, however, is mere speculation. What is important is that both Birrell and MacDonnell, the two officers of state most directly concerned, *believed* that clerical opposition was crucial in defeating the bill. The Chief Secretary, who was licking his wounds in Dieppe, was reluctant, as he wrote the Prime Minister 'to obtrude my melancholy visage upon the sight of our faithful but embarassed Commons'. From what he had heard, there were two main reasons for the bill's rejection by the Convention:

(1) The opposition of the Bishops & Priests to the Education Department—Jealousy of the Teachers &c &c.

(2) The *disaffection* of a number of the Irish M.P.s who resent (& I think justly) having been kept in *complete* ignorance of the contents of the Bill by *Redmond & Dillon.*

'Our poor dear Sir Antony', Birrell exclaimed, 'still thinks that if the Bill had been *much less* it would have got through!!' 'Our mistake was even to have touched *Devolution* at all,' the Chief Secretary reasoned. '*Home Rule* we could not give. We should have contented ourselves with *Land* Reforms & the *University* Question, & in both we should have taken altogether our own line & left Sir Antony in the lurch.'[100]

CHAPTER IX

Leaving Sir Antony in the Lurch

IN the minds of late nineteenth-century Unionist politicians the Irish university question existed primarily as a weapon in the struggle to 'subdue' Ireland. The question was to be raised in times of popular agitation in hopes of dividing the forces of the country by playing upon the bishops' fondest desire. In a larger context, all Irish reforms were, in a sense, bones thrown to a snarling dog. Wyndham and Bryce, under the influence of MacDonnell, represented a transitional stage in which reforms were conceived as a carefully planned diet designed to bring a child to maturity. Ireland was not bestial, simply immature. Her childish appetites were not to be appeased too freely by her guardians, who would see to it that she got what was good for her. What was good for her, in MacDonnell's view, was a university settlement designed to maximise interdenominational contact, a greater lay interest in the primary and secondary education systems, and just a taste of the responsibility of governing the country. When Birrell became disillusioned with his Under-Secretary, Irish policy entered a new phase. The Chief Secretary began to formulate policy with a view not to what might seem to the outsider to be good for Ireland in the long run, but rather on the basis of what the Irish wanted. One thing that the Irish did not particularly want was Bryce's university scheme.

Trinity College had already initiated what Birrell described as a 'fierce agitation . . . throughout the University world, at home and abroad, against the New National University'. The Chief Secretary, according to his own reminiscences, saw two important objections to the Bryce scheme: (1) 'It involved laying violent hands on the only English Institution

that has ever taken root in Irish Soil,' and (2) he was con-
vinced that such a proposal had no chance of being enacted.[1]
Underlying these considerations, which Birrell recorded
many years later, was a feeling that his Under Secretary's
carefully nurtured consensus of all parties outside Trinity
College was insubstantial. He had, Birrell wrote to Sir
Antony on 25 August, received two private letters from
Presbyterian leaders 'casting Bryces scheme to the wolves—
All they want is *money for themselves.*' Moreover, another
informant had told him '(with huge solemnity & vows to
secrecy) that Walsh is of the same way of thinking & *never
cared* for Bryce scheme'. 'Good heavens,' he exclaimed, 'what
a country.'[2] If the rumour about Walsh had any foundation
in fact, which is doubtful, perhaps it indicated no more than
despair on the Archbishop's part that, after he had come so
close to carrying both his colleagues and the government in
support of the solution he desired, the matter had been postponed again. If the Dublin University plan were put forward once more, Walsh would probably have even more
difficulty in persuading the hierarchy to accept it than he
had anticipated in February. MacDonnell tried to convince
Birrell that he had been misinformed about the attitudes of
the Presbyterians and the Catholic bishops, and, minimising
the obstructive power of Trinity College, he pleaded with
the Chief Secretary to persist with Bryce's scheme. The only
alternatives were the Robertson scheme and a scheme of
'Multiplex Universities', which had 'only been noticed to be
rejected by every responsible authority'.[3] The Robertson
scheme, Sir Antony argued, 'would be a fatal blow to the
future not only of Irish Higher Education but to our hopes
of the friendly co-operation of Protestants and Catholics in
common work for Ireland'. A year at the Board of Education and eight months at the Irish office had been enough to
dispel any idealistic notions Birrell might have entertained
about promoting friendly interdenominational co-operation
through educational reforms.

MacDonnell was also urging Birrell to undertake negotiations with the Bishops to secure a *'modus vivendi'* which
would make possible another attempt at educational reform
within a scheme of Devolution. 'If we had known their ob-

jections earlier we might have met them,' the Under-Secretary reasoned, 'but the Irish leaders led us to believe that the Bishops, although they might not admire the Educational provisions of the Bill, would not oppose them. We never dreamt that their secret opposition would have been so effective with these leaders.'[4] The Chief Secretary, however, had decided not only that he would propose no more half-measures of Home Rule, but also that educational reform in a secularist, democratic direction was too costly a creed for a politician to practise in Ireland. Secularism had led him into two ignominious defeats in the course of a year: the first at the Board of Education and the second at Dublin Castle. Moreover, his fundamental good sense overrode doctrinaire considerations, and he recognised that the financial squeeze on Irish education, begun under Wyndham, was having a disastrous effect upon the teaching profession and offered no hope of success in its main object, to force the ecclesiastical authorities and the nationalist politicians to consent to rate-aid and popular control. Since 1903 there had been practically no increase in the annual vote for National Education in Ireland. Indeed, shortly after assuming office Birrell, addressing the I.N.T.O. Annual Congress, had paid lip-service to the need for more money for the National system,[5] but so had Bryce a year earlier in the Commons, and to no effect. The financial squeeze on Irish education had, for practical purposes, remained in force. Late in the year, however, Birrell in effect announced his intention of abandoning this policy in a speech in Belfast before a meeting sponsored by the Ulster Liberal Association. With characteristic wit, he declared himself 'no admirer of this so-called Irish system (*applause*), which is no more Irish than I am (*laughter and applause*)'. This educational system was, he continued,

one of those ill growths of English ideas planted without due consideration upon Irish soil, and left to grow, and what it is grown to you can see. A more ridiculous history I have never heard in all my life. Were I to stop to give you my notion of it, I should be, I am sure, immediately called to order by my excellent predecessor, Mr. Walter Long (*laughter*)—a very excellent gentleman—in big type in the 'Times' for indecent jocularity (*laughter*).[6]

Assuring his audience that as a Protestant Nonconformist he was no friend of the managerial system, he went on to ask rhetorically whether any responsible man in Ireland would urge him to postpone improvements in school buildings and in teachers' salaries until the Irish people were prepared to discard the managerial system. Ireland, he conceded, was a religious country, and, he added,

For my part, I wish she may ever remain so; and when the Managerial System comes to be condemned, as I dare say some day it will be, it will not be condemned by any such argument as I have lately seen suggested, but by the educated force of a free people (*applause*).[7]

Birrell had carried a Liberal audience with him in postponing the application to Ireland of a cardinal feature of Liberal ideology until the Irish themselves should become secularists —an event which could be expected simultaneously with the conversion of the Jews. He did not linger on this reversal of policy, but proceeded immediately to outline the practical measures which he proposed to initiate including a grant of £40,000 a year for an unspecified period to rebuild schools and another annual sum to improve the pay of teachers. This latter grant turned out to be £114,000.[8] There was some wrangling over the exact formula for distributing it among the teachers, for the treasury wanted to exclude teachers in very small schools as further pressure toward amalgamation, but Birrell made a great show of getting the treasury scheme revised so that all National Teachers could share in the grant.[9] Moreover, in a less publicised, but very important, change of policy during Birrell's years at the Irish Office, the dispensing power of the Board to waive the stringent length-of-service requirements in promoting teachers to higher salary grades was 'liberally availed of in the years from 1907 onwards'. In 1913 the treasury was persuaded to alter its limitations on the numbers of teachers allowable in the higher salary grades so as to facilitate this process of special promotion.[10]

At the same time that he thus abandoned the policies of his predecessors and his Under-Secretary on the issues of Devolution and reform of the primary and secondary education systems, Birrell was developing his own university settlement. When the Chief Secretary discussed the matter with his cabinet colleagues, Richard Haldane, now Secretary for War, called his attention to a scheme he had worked out, with the approval of Logue and Walsh and of the Presbyterian General Assembly in 1898. Haldane's plan, which called for two new universities in Dublin and Belfast, both formally nondenominational but actually dominated by Catholics and Protestants respectively, had been encouraged as a private member's bill by Balfour. After a bill and two charters had actually been drafted, however, Balfour had been unable to persuade his own colleagues to give facilities for the measure. Birrell eagerly seized upon the scheme, communicated with both Presbyterian and Roman Catholic authorities, and received assurances that both stood by the agreement of 1898.[11]

The Chief Secretary promptly began to adapt Haldane's scheme to present conditions. He was already in touch with Archbishop Walsh by the end of December, when he sent him a printed outline for a bill. Walsh assured the Chief Secretary that he thought it a good scheme, an improvement upon the scheme of the Robertson Commission and surpassed only by schemes 'that would give us equality with T.C.D. in point of university status' such as the Bryce scheme or by the simple inclusion of a second college in Dublin University. Since equality of status was to be withheld, the Archbishop made plain his intention to drive a hard bargain for financial equality. Were Catholics to get as much from public sources as Trinity College, he asked, or as Trinity and Belfast together? 'If so,' the Archbishop remarked, 'we have equality in one substantial point. If not, not.'[12]

While the scheme 'was being incubated and embodied in a bill,' Walsh's biographer records, Birrell 'was in constant communication with Dr Walsh, and many of the Archbishop's suggestions were adopted by the Chief Secretary'. Moreover, he states that between the introduction of the bill on 31 March 1908 and the royal assent on 1 August 'The Chief Secretary not only sought and obtained from the Archbishop constant and valuable help, but he also made the Archbishop the depository of his apprehensions and worries—of his triumphs and failures in strategy and diplomacy.' This account, based upon the archdiocesan archives, seems at first glance to conflict with Birrell's own recollection, nearly thirty years later, that Walsh 'was in no way friendly to my scheme'. Birrell probably meant no more than that Walsh was disappointed at the breakdown of Bryce's policy and was determined to secure the most favourable financial terms possible. The Archbishop seems to have done his best to smooth the way for Birrell's settlement of the question.

In explanation of Walsh's feelings, Birrell wrote that the Archbishop entertained

a deep-rooted jealousy of the wealthy foundation and glorious site of Trinity College, Dublin. To live in a Catholic city, as a Catholic Archbishop, with this Protestant Elizabethan Institution for ever staring you in the face, was no doubt galling to a proud prelate, who had, besides, made a serious study of University Education in Ireland.[13]

Jealousy, it need scarcely be noted, is not an adequate explanation of Walsh's attitude. The Archbishop was motivated by a genuine desire to secure for Irish Catholics a centre of learning which would command the kind of respect accorded to the ancient universities of England and Scotland. Such respect would most readily be granted to an institution in some formal relationship with Trinity College, Dublin. Walsh had to fight for his ideal encumbered by less idealistic and in many cases less learned ecclesiastics who did not worry how their university would be regarded at Oxford, Tübingen or the Sorbonne but only concerned themselves with whether the faith and morals of their flocks would be adequately safeguarded. The bugbear of 'mixed' education no doubt haunted Walsh's efforts to convince his colleagues, though Walsh always carefully avoided any suggestion that his advocacy of a Dublin University solution was motivated by a desire to promote ecumenicity. The aggressive opponents to Walsh's ideal, among whom O'Dwyer was the most outspoken, did have an arguable case on educational grounds against association with Trinity. The kinds of learning fostered in that Oxbridge-style institution—classical studies and pure mathematics—were not suited to modern economic and social conditions, and Ireland, it was maintained, required a more practical type of higher education. Most of the bishops, however, though they did not share Walsh's zeal for a Dublin

University solution, had been willing to go along with the Archbishop so long as he seemed to be making progress toward the actual achievement of a settlement. Their consent to Dunraven's scheme in 1904 had contained an implied deference to the wishes of Trinity and the political forces it represented—a deference which probably indicated a hope on the part of some prelates that Protestant pressures would kill the scheme. Now that those pressures, together with Walsh's inability to dispel the notion that the hierarchy was lukewarm if not hostile to the plan, had killed the Dunraven plan in its revived form, Walsh no doubt realised that his preferred solution must be abandoned.

The bill which Birrell introduced at the end of March 1908, together with charters which were presented about a month thereafter, provided for the dissolution of the Royal University and the establishment of two new universities. The Queen's College, Belfast, was, in effect to be raised to university status and provided with a more autonomous governing body rather than remaining under the direct jurisdiction of the Crown. The other university was to have three constituent colleges, the Queen's Colleges of Cork and Galway and a new college in Dublin. Both universities were to be formally nonsectarian. No religious test might be imposed as a condition for any office, emolument or degree in either university or any of their constituent colleges. No ecclesiastical authorities were to have *de jure* representation on the governing bodies and no public funds might be used for chapels or religious instruction in the new institutions.

Birrell proposed to establish annual parliamentary grants totalling £72,000 (including certain sums previously voted annually for the Queen's Colleges and the Royal University) for the new university based in Dublin and its constituent colleges. The Belfast university was to receive £28,000 annually. In the light of their relative proportions in the total population, the Catholics (74.3 per cent) were obviously being treated less favourably than the Presbyterians (10 per cent), though it could be argued that there was a greater demand *per capita* for university education among Presbyterians than among Catholics. Both Presbyterians and Catholics could continue to feel aggrieved at the level of public support of university education for Protestant Episcopalians (13 per cent of the population) since Trinity College's estimated annual income from what may be called 'public' sources was approximately £50,000. (In making comparisons with Trinity, however, one must remember that one of that college's main functions was to train Church of Ireland clergy and that Maynooth received considerable income from 'public' endowments—probably more than £11,000 annually —for training Catholic clergy.) Difficulties arose, however, less from the annual grants stipulated in the bill than from the maximum initial grants which the bill allowed for the establishment of the new universities. Belfast was to be granted up to £60,000 for capital improvements to its physical plant. The three constituent colleges of the Dublin-based university were to be allowed a total of up to £170,000 of which £150,000 was allocated to establish the new college in Dublin, the only one virtually without physical facilities. This amount was reckoned to be sufficient to provide the necessary teaching facilities, but was not intended to cover the cost of residences for students or faculty. The new university was to be nonresidential as had been the Queen's Colleges before it.

Initial episcopal reaction focused upon these financial provisions. The *Catholic Times* asked the opinions of various members of the Irish hierarchy on the bill immediately after its introduction and received telegraphed replies from five of them. Though all five welcomed the bill, only one, Bishop Boylan of Kilmore, said without reservation: 'The Bill is well worth favourable consideration.'[14] Each of the other four— Archbishop Fennelly of Cashel, Bishop Foley of Kildare and Leighlin, Bishop McHugh of Derry and Bishop Owens of Clogher—pronounced the financial provisions inadequate. Owens went so far as to say: 'Trinity . . . should not be allowed to go scot-free.' The only reference to religious safeguards was made by McHugh, who described as 'dangerous' a provision of the scheme which permitted a professor dismissed by the Senate to appeal to the Crown for the appointment of a Board of Visitors to decide the particular case. The scheme allowed, but did not require, the Senate to affiliate Maynooth to the university. Owens, who said: 'Maynooth

ought to be affiliated,' apparently felt the affiliation ought to
be written into the bill or perhaps wanted the seminary raised
to the rank of a constituent college with a direct voice in
the government of the university.

The precise composition of the University Senate and the
governing bodies of the constituent colleges was not published until several weeks after the bill was introduced,
though Birrell had discussed their composition in general
terms. During the first five years of its existence, the Senate
was to be composed of thirty-six persons named by the Crown
in the University Charter. Seven of these individuals were
Protestants; five were Catholic ecclesiastics—Archbishops
Walsh and Healy, Father Delany, a Father Andrew Murphy
who represented Catholic headmasters, and Mgr Mannix, the
President of Maynooth (afterwards Archbishop of Melbourne). After the first five-year term, the Senate was to be
constituted according to the following scheme: [15]

Chancellor	1
Presidents of the constituent colleges	3
Persons nominated by the Crown of whom at least one shall be a woman	4
Elected by the governing body of the Dublin college (at least three to be members of the Academic Council of the College)	6
Elected by the governing body of Queen's College, Cork (at least two from its Academic Council)	4
Elected by the governing body of Queen's College, Galway (at least two from its Academic Council)	4
Registrar	1
Elected by Convocation	8
Co-opted	4
	35

The governing bodies of the constituent colleges were to be
constituted along similar lines, except that local government
bodies were to be given a share in their selection.

To these provisions O'Dwyer vehemently took exception.
In the May number of the *Irish Educational Review*[16] he

published an article noting the 'attitude of reserve and expectancy' with which the bill had been received in the country—an attitude which he characterised by the words: 'We don't like it, but ought we to refuse it?' The people were reticent, not only because of their own perplexity, but also because they were awaiting a clear lead from the bishops, O'Dwyer maintained, skirting very close to the bounds of propriety in episcopal relations. He then called the constitution of the new university 'as applicable to a Mohammedan as to a Catholic country', and regretted 'that persons who pretend to speak in Parliament for Irish Catholics are not slower in divesting themselves of every shred of Catholic principle'. True, two bishops had seats for five years on the temporary Senate, but, O'Dwyer maintained, 'At the expiration of that time they disappear, just as the representatives of the old Grand Juries did after the first term from the County Councils.' It was, the Bishop lamented, 'a great descent from the ideals set up in Newman's time',—a descent which had not been made at the instance of the Irish laity. The first concession demanded by the English Liberals had been that the governing body not have an ecclesiastical majority. After acceding to this demand by Mr Morley, the bishops yielded to a demand from Mr Lecky that the laity have a working majority. Then the Robertson Commission had proposed 'that two, but only two, Catholic bishops should be *ex officio* members of the Senate. In their anxiety to secure a university for their people the bishops agreed even to this.' 'But now', O'Dwyer charged, carefully ignoring the hierarchy's private concession of even *de jure* representation in 1904, 'Mr. Birrell, who, being a Liberal, can command exceptional support on the Irish side, carries the whittling process to the last, and in his bill gives no place at all to a Bishop or priest in the New University.'

The Bishop of Limerick viewed the bill as but another stage in the Irish Party's betrayal of Catholic interests in an effort to gain Liberal and Nonconformist support for Home Rule. In a public letter in June, during Committee debates on the bill, O'Dwyer spoke of 'the decree of Mr. Birrell and the couple of gentlemen in the Irish Party who undertake to represent Catholic interests'—a decree that after five years the university and its colleges would 'put the pilots ashore, and dispense with the services of the clergy'.[17] He went so far as to imply that the bill would deprive the clergy of 'every chance of being sent back again by free election' after the initial period had ended. This innuendo was too much for Stephen Gwynn, Protestant Nationalist M.P. for Galway, to bear silently. Under the terms of the measure, Gwynn pointed out, any bishop might be elected to the Senate by either the graduates or the professors and, moreover, 'any Bishop or clergyman may be made the representative of any one of seven local bodies'.[18] O'Dwyer's allegation was particularly galling to Gwynn because in Committee debates 'the fact has been cast in our teeth that these local bodies elect a disproportionate number of clergy on the Technical Education and Agricultural Committees'.

O'Dwyer's episcopal colleagues, if not O'Dwyer himself, no doubt realised how firm a security they really had in the proposed constitutions of the various governing bodies. It had not escaped the attention of bishops that the local government bodies set up in 1898 had been quite deferential to clerical wishes on questions relating to education. The general expectation that ecclesiastical representation would not lapse at the end of the first five years has, it should be noted in passing, been fully justified by events. In the eleven five-year terms from 1914, when the original government appointments expired, to 1969, there were never (except for brief intervals caused by death or resignation) fewer than five ecclesiastics on the Senate. At one point there were as many as nine. Two of these were always prelates, and the President of Maynooth was always co-opted to membership as soon as he assumed his office. Ecclesiastics have become members of the Senate by almost every possible method of selection: by government appointment, through appointment by college governing bodies, through election by the Convocation, by co-optation and by holding the office of chancellor or president of a constituent college.[19] If the present composition of the governing bodies of the constituent colleges is any guide, ecclesiastics have not been deprived of representation on these bodies either. While no bishop sits on the U.C.D. governing body at present, one of the government nominees is a Vicar-

General of the Dublin archdiocese, and one other priest as
well as one nun are members of the body. Three Catholic
prelates sit on the Cork college governing body and four are
members of the Galway body.[20]

The Bishop of Limerick did not confine his opposition to
public protest. Birrell refers to the 'dangerous machinations
in Rome of the late Catholic Bishop O'Dwyer, who was
honestly convinced that the bill was a Nonconformist conspiracy to obtain control of the education of the Irish laity',
and he adds that John Dillon's brother, a Franciscan monk,
rendered great assistance by 'keeping the Vatican well informed both as to the actualities and potentialities of this
theologically harmless measure'.[21] Although Logue, on his return from a visit to America, complained bitterly that the
bill would exclude the clergy from participation in the working of the new university,[22] he carefully avoided joining
O'Dwyer's assault upon the measure and the government. In
general the bishops were remaining remarkably quiet while
the bill went through its second reading and into a Standing
Committee of the House. When the committee of the Catholic Graduates Association prepared and sent to Archbishop
Walsh (and other interested parties) a long memorandum
criticising the bill in great detail,[23] the Archbishop expressed
his 'general concurrence' with their views but carefully confined his specific remarks to a relatively trivial point which
they had raised concerning the role of external examiners.[24]
In fact the hierarchy was remaining so quiet that *The Times*
could raise doubts over whether the bishops would accept
the measure at all.[25] In June, however, they decided to take
action. Professor Butcher, M.P. for Cambridge University,
who had sat on both the Robertson and the Fry Commissions,
proposed an amendment to the bill in Committee to provide
that a student of an institution to which the Senate of either
of the new universities chose to grant affiliation would be
required to spend two academic years in residence in one of
the constituent colleges before taking a university degree. The
amendment was frankly aimed at Maynooth. It was correctly
assumed that one of the first acts of the Senate of the university in Dublin would be to make Maynooth an affiliated college. Proponents of the amendment believed that university

degrees should only be awarded to persons who had been in contact with the more cosmopolitan culture of a university rather than just the limited environment of an ecclesiastical seminary.

The bishops themselves were divided on this issue. In his evidence before the Robertson Commission, O'Dwyer had expressed the hope that at least 200 of the 600 students at Maynooth would live in a separate residence hall in connection with a new university for the necessary period to obtain arts degrees. He believed that the clergy should come into contact with the laity during their education, but he was careful to add 'that in that respect all the bishops are not of the same way of thinking as I am. . . . Some bishops hold strongly the view that an Ecclesistical Seminary should be a place apart.' Perhaps as a compromise with these bishops, O'Dwyer added a footnote to his evidence, before it was published, to the effect that the 200 or more Maynooth candidates for arts degrees would not reside in Dublin but that in his opinion a certain number of clerical students which would steadily increase would 'prosecute their higher Art studies in the University itself'.[26] When the Commission examined O'Dea, the Vice-President of Maynooth who became Bishop of Clonfert in 1903, they found him much less enthusiastic about residence of clerical students in Dublin, and when Professor Butcher pressed him on the discrepancy between his own views and those of O'Dwyer, O'Dea cited O'Dwyer's footnote, admitted the desirability of 'bringing even the body of the clergy into direct connection with the life of the University', but dismissed the idea as impracticable 'at least for the present'.[27]

With opinion somewhat divided on this point, it is perhaps surprising that the hierarchy chose this point out of all the possible objections to the scheme upon which to make a stand. Nevertheless, Logue protested strongly against the amendment on 15 June,[28] and the bishops held a special meeting on the following day—the day before Butcher's amendment was to be considered in committee—and adopted a resolution agreeing to accept any suggestions by the Senate for the regulation of the arts curriculum of Maynooth or for any necessary strengthening of its staff, but flatly refusing to send Maynooth arts students to reside in Dublin. This resolution was immediately dispatched to Redmond, who flourished it in the Committee debate. Faced with the uncompromising stand of the bishops on this point, but apparently heartened by the tacit acceptance of the bill implied by the hierarchy's action, the Committee rejected Butcher's amendment by 32 to 16.[29]

The hierarchy's acceptance of the bill turned out to be more than simply tacit, for they had adopted another resolution declaring the bill to be 'constructed on a plan which is suited to the educational needs of the country and likely to lead to finality on the University question'. They were most gentle in criticising the outward nondenominationalism of the bill, and though they protested at the lack of residential facilities, they gave no indication that they intended to go beyond verbal protest. This resolution (along with the Maynooth resolution) apparently was not published until the Maynooth resolution had had its intended effect upon the Committee deliberations at Westminster.[30]

During the next six weeks, while the bill passed through its final stages, the bishops generally held their peace, though O'Dwyer did take the opportunity of a speech at the Laurel Hill Convent on 30 June to berate the co-operation between the Irish and Liberal Parties which had produced 'a lodging-house University on Nonconformist principles'.[31] When the bill finally emerged from Committee, Birrell wrote to Walsh: 'My illustrious predecessor, the Bishop of Hippo, was a saint and a doctor, but the honours of *martyrdom* have, I think, been reserved for his unworthy namesake.'[32] Of the Committee debates, he added: 'I have never heard greater nonsense talked in all my life.' Walsh, speaking four days later at Greystones, had kind words for the Chief Secretary. The drawbacks of the bill were 'not very numerous', though the lack of a residential college for laymen was of a 'terribly serious'—the Archbishop shrank 'from saying a fatally serious'—character. He remarked facetiously that if he were Chief Secretary for a week he could find £100,000 somewhere, but he added that 'he was not going to raise any outcry against the present Chief Secretary', who, he assured his audience, had worked hard, though unsuccessfully to gain a residential college.[33]

On 25 July the bill passed its third reading in the Commons and was sent to the Lords, who heard a speech of regret tinged with bitterness from Lord MacDonnell of Swinford, formerly Sir Antony MacDonnell. Referring to the Bryce scheme, he said:

I myself will never cease to regret that the plan, which was not only a measure for the advancement of education in Ireland, but for the mutual reconciliation of contending parties did not commend itself to the authorities of Trinity College. . . .

But as the Government deemed the support of Trinity College necessary to any Bill which could pass through Parliament, and as Trinity College would only give its support on condition of 'Hands off Trinity,' I admit that the Bill now before your Lordships is as good as any that could be accepted from that unholy alliance.[34]

On 1 August 1908 the bill received the royal assent.

'Mr. Birrell's happy solution of the University question' —as Walsh described it on the following day[35]—had been effected along lines which had for years been dismissed as impossible. The bishops had always stated that their first choice among possible solutions was a separate Catholic university. Yet even they had come to believe that no government would so defy Nonconformist opinion as to propose such a settlement. Birrell had so framed his bill that he could insist in the House of Commons that the new university was 'as undenominational . . . as any law could make any body of men undenominational', while Balfour, who supported the bill throughout, could assert with equal force a few moments later that the university was denominational.[36] Balfour was correct, and Birrell knew it. The undenominationalist phrasing of the bill was only a sop to secularist opinion. Birrell had given the bishops what most of them really wanted, while loudly protesting that he was doing precisely the opposite. It is not without significance that the solution which was supposed to be unpalatable to Nonconformist opinion had been originally drafted by Haldane, a Scottish Presbyterian, and was carried into effect by Birrell, the son of a Baptist minister.

The settlement reflected a fundamentally democratic postulate: that in the formation of Irish policy the wishes of the

Irish were to be consulted first. What the Irish—Archbishop Walsh and a few socially-aspiring Catholics and liberal Protestants apart—wanted was separate development for the two Irish communities. The Nation's territory, as was clear in the Gaelic League's affairs around 1900, simply did not extend to Belfast. The university settlement was the first act of State which clearly recognised this reality. The very word 'national', which in 1831 had been attached to a primary education system intended to unify the two communities, was now applied to a university specifically intended for the separate needs of the majority in the South and entirely distinct from the Queen's University of Belfast. MacDonnell had hoped, through Bryce's university scheme and the Irish Council Bill, to begin changing that reality—to induce Catholics and Protestants to learn and work together for the common good of their common island. In the years that followed, the Irish question would be approached on Birrell's principles rather than MacDonnell's. The majority would be asked what they wanted, and an attempt would be made to give it to them. If the minority objected too loudly, a compromise would be attempted between the two demands. No attempt would be made to change the character of the demands. MacDonnell's policy had been highly optimistic, if not visionary. The Irish had a great gift for taking institutions such as the National Education system or the non-statutory General Council of County Councils which were intended to foster interdenominational co-operation and adapting them to the realities of Irish life. Birrell had decided to accept those realities, and Ireland was well pleased.

CHAPTER X

The Ebbing Tide

FOR as long as the Nation's avowed enemies had held power in the State, the Irish Parliamentary Party had an irrefragable excuse for not successfully pressing home its demands for Home Rule. Now, however, with the Nation's professed friends in office, the party could engineer nothing better through the Liberal government than the Irish Council Bill. There was a deeper problem than the objective disappointment at the paltry Liberal offer. While the land question was still alive, there had been plenty of roles for young, politically aspiring men to play which provided a sense of active participation in the movement. Indeed, the existence of an agitation which pressed beyond the formal demands of party leaders and over which their control was limited could be a positive asset to them. The authorities at Westminster were thus given to understand that if they did not make terms with the Nation's accredited representatives, they might face other, more difficult, spokesmen. After Wyndham's Land Purchase Act, however, the achievement of Home Rule became the Nation's sole popular objective, and it was to be achieved primarily by concentrating power in the hands of the party leadership.

This principle meant, for one thing, that Healy, who proposed to disperse political authority in the (often clerically dominated) constitutencies, and O'Brien, who wanted the nationwide grassroots movement to dictate tactics to the party leaders and who was specifically offering a different national objective in some kind of settlement that might be worked out with the ex-landlords, were to be excluded from real power in the movement. The party's preparations for the 1906 general election had made plain that each was *persona non grata*, but both retained their seats in parliament and were being drawn together in their mutual isolation. Three other M.P.s, D.D. Sheehan, Augustine Roche and John O'Donnell, had come under O'Brien's sway. In addition, Sir Thomas Grattan Esmonde, after failing to persuade Redmond to demand an immediate government commitment to make Home Rule a leading issue in the next general election or to grant Home Rule by letters patent on the analogy of the recent establishment of self-government in the Transvaal, resigned his post as the party's Chief Whip.[1] There was growing pressure in the country in 1907 for an end to party disunity. The executive of the Mid-Tipperary U.I.L. wrote to Archbishop Walsh asking him to invite Redmond, Dillon, O'Brien and Healy to a conference to reconcile their differences. Walsh replied that no intervention of his could really help in ending the disunity. 'For some time past', the Archbishop explained, 'I have found it impossible to fall in with a line of action which I could not but regard as in great measure responsible for the division that exists in the country.' Alluding to the fact that he had ceased to contribute to party funds, he pointed out: 'I have consequently felt myself debarred from being free to give to the Parliamentary Party even the moderate measure of practical support which, moderate as it was, I had previously felt it a duty as well as a pleasure to give.'[2] Several weeks later the Tuam District Council sent Cardinal Logue a similar request to mediate among the party factions, and he too refused.[3]

Demonstrations calling for unity continued in several southern counties, and late in the autumn the party leaders decided to respond to a set of unity principles which O'Brien had proposed. Arrangements were made for a conference of two men from each side. Redmond shrewdly asked Bishop O'Donnell to accompany him, and O'Brien chose perhaps the highest-ranking ecclesiastic he could command, Father James Clancy, P.P., Kilkee. Clerical participation was therefore on a different footing from that envisioned in the earlier proposals to Logue and Walsh. Two churchmen sat on opposite sides of the negotiating table rather than acting as mediators. Redmond did not fundamentally disagree with most of O'Brien's proposals, and the issue which dominated the conference was the party pledge. O'Brien insisted on a clarification of whether or not the pledge bound members to support party policy publicly in the country as well as in the division lobbies. Healy was notoriously unwilling to be silenced by a party majority, but O'Brien maintained that Dillon had been equally guilty of this offence because of his opposition to the land settlement in 1903. Professor Lyons analyses this point of contention very thoroughly[4] and correctly concludes that the settlement which grew out of the negotiations did not long endure because the dispute over the pledge did not touch the deeper causes of dissension. It was easy enough for party leaders to give lip-service to the platitudes which O'Brien put forward as a basis for settlement and which included his philosophy of conciliation and co-operation with moderate Unionists. By 1908 the party had such a lively expectation that Home Rule would result from the Liberal alliance that O'Brien's policy was a practical anachronism. Moreover—a point which Lyons does not stress —the character of the party and of its organisation was changing in ways which were impossible to treat in formal terms of settlement. As has been noted, O'Brien's concept of public opinion, as expressed by the U.I.L., governing the party's decisions was simply not a workable method of achieving the stated goal of nationalist politics. O'Brien was a threat precisely because he persisted in stirring up public opinion in his efforts to gain his points, rather than trying to make his voice heard privately on the same basis as Dillon, O'Connor and Devlin. As Dillon remarked to Redmond just before the conference, 'If O'B would only shut up & give up "unity" meetings there might be a chance of a genuine reunion.'[5]

The conference met once on 13 December 1907 and quickly broke down. O'Brien, while, as usual, attributing honourable intentions to Redmond, blamed the breakdown on Bishop O'Donnell, whom he depicted as a puppet of Dillon. 'It would be painful and futile to recall', he recalled in 1910, 'the ungenerous spirit Dr. O'Donnell imported into these negotiations. A determination was only too plainly evinced from the first to shut Mr. Healy out from any accommodation by the device of sticking to the interpretation of the pledge which it was believed Mr. Healy would refuse to accept.'[6] The really significant point of contention, however, was not Healy's readmission but the suggestion, which O'Brien attributed to Father Clancy, that the questions before the conference should be placed before a Nationalist Convention. Several days before the conference Redmond had anticipated this problem and made clear in a letter to Bishop O'Donnell his opposition to an *ad hoc* Convention, which 'would lead to recrimination and endless mischief'.[7] The Bishop concurred and implied that any reference of the matter to a Convention should, in his view, take the form of a *fait accompli.*[8]

When the conference broke down, O'Brien cast the blame on O'Donnell, who 'brusquely broke off relations . . . and on the suggestion that we should reassemble later on . . . responded with the almost rude taunt that "my time is of some value".'[9] O'Brien, typically, carried the issue to the country, getting a public meeting at Buncrana to endorse his view. When a party meeting and a U.I.L. National Directory meeting in mid-January endorsed Redmond's position and Dillon made the conciliatory gesture of proposing a resolution at the party meeting calling for the dissidents to take the pledge and rejoin the party, O'Brien realised that his plea for a Convention would not be granted. He and his three followers as well as Healy and Sir Thomas Grattan Esmonde accepted the truce.[10] The defeat of the Convention proposal had been, in effect, an endorsement of the party's method of doing business, and the episode demonstrated that, within the hierarchy, at least O'Donnell understood and agreed with the leaders' political style.

The party's attempts to crush out Healyite and O'Brienite 'factionism' were carried out through its national organisation, the U.I.L. In the North, Joseph Devlin was building another party organisation to supplement the U.I.L. Though branches of the League had been formally organised throughout Ulster when the U.I.L. was constituted the official Nationalist organisation, they had been artificially introduced. The League's social appeal to the land-hungry peasantry of the West was not really applicable to Ulster, where the pressing grievance of Catholics was not the grazing system but the domination of Orange bigotry over the political and economic life of the province. Any threat to the party's hegemony over Catholic politics in the North would be likely to come from some organisation which might play upon this grievance. Bishop Henry's Catholic Association had offered such a threat, but the party organisation had managed to defeat this clerically directed machine and drive it from the field. Devlin's approach to another potential political threat, the Ancient Order of Hibernians, was not to eliminate it, but to capture it for the party's purposes.

The A.O.H. claimed to be in some sense a descendant of the various secret societies which figured prominently in Irish social history during the eighteenth and nineteenth centuries.[11] For practical purposes, however, the society dates from 1838 when the name Ancient Order of Hibernians was adopted by groups of Irish immigrants in the United States. It became an important focus of Irish-American political activity. Though groups in Ireland gradually adopted the name, the Order was never a significant political force in Ireland during the nineteenth century. In 1884 both in Ireland and in the United States the society split over the question of admission of members of Catholic-Irish descent as well as those who could claim birth in Ireland. The breach was healed in America in 1897,[12] but in Ireland the split remained until 1902 when a probationary joint executive known as the Board of Erin was formed. This reunion marks the beginning of the Order's political significance in Ireland.

In America the society had had difficulties with the ecclesiastical authorities a generation earlier because of its close resemblance to a secret society and its suspected ties with both Fenianism and the Molly Maguires of the Pennsylvania coalfields. After a protracted controversy within the American Catholic hierarchy and deliberate efforts by the Order to reform itself to the satisfaction of the ecclesiastical authorities, the Hibernians in America had achieved at least *de facto* toleration as a Catholic benefit society. Non-Catholics were, and apparently always had been, excluded from membership both in America and in Ireland, and the Order, where permitted to do so, emphasised its Catholic character by enrolling chaplains and by attending Mass in a body, the members decked out in an elaborate regalia.

Although the A.O.H. in America had at one point eschewed

political activity in its efforts to gain episcopal sanctions, the political potentialities of a revived and reunited A.O.H. in Ireland were obvious. Accordingly, Devlin moved quickly and effectively to gain control of the united organisation and in 1904 was elected its first President. Shortly thereafter numerous branches were organised, mainly in and around Ulster. A National Chaplain, the Rev. J. J. McKinley, C.C., was appointed,[13] and at least in certain dioceses the Order gained the approval of Church authorities. From O'Donnell's diocese of Raphoe the police reported an A.O.H. organising meeting at Glenties on St Patrick's Day 1905 chaired by Canon McFadden, and they added: 'Since the Order received ecclesiastical sanction great numbers are joining.'[14] On the same day in Sligo, Bishop Clancy addressed a procession of 260 A.O.H. members wearing their badges and accompanied by two bands,[15] and three months later a procession of seven hundred members of various Sligo A.O.H. divisions as well as eight divisions from Leitrim and Roscommon was addressed by Father Conry, C.C., in the Sligo Town Hall.[16] In the diocese of Dromore a division was organised in February 1905 at a meeting presided over by Father Lupton, C.C.,[17] and in July it was reported that a division was formed at Newry 'with the sanction of' Bishop O'Neill of Dromore.[18] Enthusiastic and widespread clerical support for the A.O.H. seems, however, to have been confined to these three dioceses—Raphoe, Elphin and Dromore. Moreover, Dromore was an ambiguous case, for ecclesiastical sanction in that diocese appears to have been extended to the so-called Scottish Section of the A.O.H. The unity achieved in 1902 was breaking down in 1905 while Devlin was consolidating his influence within the Order. This splinter group, which was distinguished by its desire to 'register' its divisions with the civil authorities as friendly societies, was drifting outside the much larger political machine Devlin was building. After early reports of clerical support for the Scottish Section 'registered Divisions' in Dromore diocese, that support seems to have disappeared.

Ecclesiastical support for Devlin's branch of the Order continued unabated in the diocese of Raphoe. Donegal clergy actively fought the Scottish Section[19] as well as endorsing the Board of Erin. In the diocese of Elphin ecclesiastical sanction also continued for some months. In October 1905 Canon Sloan, P.P., precipitated a special order from the National Education Board when he permitted A.O.H. meetings in the Ballyweelin Male National School,[20] and on St Patrick's Day 1906 Bishop Clancy again addressed an A.O.H. procession, which this time numbered 350 members and included three bands.[21] Clancy's confidence began to be undermined shortly thereafter by the President of the Sligo A.O.H. Division, Dan O'Donnell. O'Donnell, according to a police informant, told an A.O.H. meeting in June that 'if the A.O.H. were to be a success, it should be more secret and the Roman Catholic Clergy [should] be kept in the dark as to its working unless they became members'.[22] In March 1907 Bishop Clancy censured the Order in Sligo,[23] and it was later reported that he had communicated with Dan O'Donnell 'in reference to some disrespectful remarks made by O'Donnell about clergymen collecting money from the A.O.H. in America for the building of Churches and who when they return do not support the Order'.[24] The 1908 St Patrick's Day procession in Sligo included only two hundred A.O.H. members and was pronounced a failure by the police, who reported: 'It did not receive the countenance of the clergy as in previous years, owing to some differences between them and the President of the Division.'[25] A decrease in membership in Sligo noted by the police[26] was discussed at the Co. Sligo A.O.H. Board meeting in June 1908 and was attributed to clerical action.[27]

Clancy's disillusionment with the A.O.H. brought his sentiments into line with those of many other churchmen in areas (outside Donegal) where the Order was active. In Drumkeeran, Co. Leitrim, an A.O.H. division founded in August 1905 was strenuously opposed by Father McMorrow, P.P.,[28] until the Division President resigned 'owing to abuse which he received' from the priest.[29] At Lavey, Co. Cavan, and Claddy, Co. Armagh, clerical opposition to the founding of A.O.H. divisions was reported, and at Carrickmore, Co. Tyrone (Armagh diocese), the attempt to start an A.O.H. division failed at least temporarily because of the Parish Priest's opposition.[30] Elsewhere in Co. Tyrone, Father O'Kane, P.P., Clogher, 'denounced the A.O.H. as a secret Society, remarking that any Society having Secret signs and passwords not known to the general public was a secret Society'. He declared that 'the A.O.H. would not receive his sanction, nor had it the sanction of the Roman Catholic Church'.[31] Canon McGlone, P.P., Magherarney, Co. Monaghan, warned his parishioners after Mass against a branch of the A.O.H. which was being established,[32] and one parish priest, Father McKenna of Park, near Limavady, Co. Derry, succeeded in getting a division abolished after discovering 'that some secret rules existed in reference to it'.[33] Father Fox, C.C., Knockmoyle, Co. Tyrone, was so strongly opposed to the local A.O.H. division that he 'on more than one occasion visited their hall and turned their members out by force'.[34]

The police understood in 1908 that Cardinal Logue 'for a considerable time past' had been hostile to the A.O.H.,[35] and at a meeting in Armagh, apparently in the early summer of that year, the Ulster bishops decided to forbid the wearing of A.O.H. regalia in churches.[36] The decision has the appearance of a compromise between O'Donnell, who undoubtedly did not want to disturb the organisation, and Logue, whose later public statements showed him inclined to much stronger measures. The impression of the compromise character of the action taken is strengthened by the fact that the ban on regalia in churches extended as well to the Irish National Foresters, an innocuous society whose activities seem to have been purely social and athletic.

Why did the A.O.H. excite so much clerical hostility? In the first place it was in some sense a secret society, and such societies always aroused clerical suspicions. In fact, the most objectionable features of secret society activity were more associated with the dissident Scottish Section divisions, which, ironically, were more anxious during the early part of this period to register as friendly societies, than with Devlin's Board of Erin. In 1907 Robert Johnston of Belfast, an old Fenian leader, wrote to John Devoy that 'a considerable number of our friends' had recently joined the registered divisions, which he carefully distinguished from the 'Board of Erin people' whom he described as 'solely in the hands of the Parliamentarians'.[37] Nevertheless, when one of the prominent Board of Erin Hibernians,[38] while not regarding himself as a secret society man, could affirm that he still 'believed physical force was the only method to secure the freedom of Ireland', it is understandable if ecclesiastics did not draw very fine distinctions between the different sections of the Order. In contrast to the attitudes of the Ulster bishops, however, some of the Roman Catholic bishops of Scotland were quite able to perceive the distinction. A Board of Erin Hibernian in Glasgow had complained in 1906 that the Scottish Section's efforts 'to foster a Secret Physical Force Movement' were depriving the Board of Erin in Scotland of full ecclesiastical sanction.[39] After a long legal battle with the Scottish Section, the Board of Erin in 1907 won the right to register as a friendly society,[40] and the change was especially welcomed by Board of Erin Hibernians in Scotland who hoped it might be 'the means of removing the ban which the R.C. Bishops have placed upon the Society there'.[41] Their hopes for gaining favour with the Scottish hierarchy were fulfilled at least to the extent that five bishops sent a memorial to the Holy See asking for the removal of the ban on the Order in Scotland.[42]

The leaders of the Armagh Division of the Board of Erin A.O.H. hoped that the hostility of Logue and his clergy would similarly abate when they undertook to register as a friendly society in December 1908.[43] Logue's hostility was undiminished, and on his triennial visitation to Carrickmore a few months later he made an interesting statement in denunciation of the Order in that particular parish, where Hibernians were allegedly trying to gain members through intimidation. Noting that, some time before, the A.O.H. had submitted its rules to the Irish hierarchy, who had not approved but 'merely tolerated' it, the Cardinal declared that 'There was nothing in the rules to which anyone could object. That, indeed, was one of the greatest dangers of the Society, because the members boasted that they were all good Catholics, and they boycotted, threatened, waylaid, and beat their neighbour for the honour of religion.'[44] Though Logue's charges of boycotting, waylaying, etc., were probably well-founded for this particular parish, the real danger in the growth of the A.O.H. from a clerical point of view was represented not so much by the waylaying as by the members' boasts that they were 'good

Catholics'. The Order threatened to become an established institution clearly labelled 'Catholic' in everyone's mind but remaining effectively outside clerical influence.

The charges of waylaying, boycotting, etc. could have been directed, with more justice, at the party's other organisation, the United Irish League, in this period. The U.I.L. differed in several essential respects from the A.O.H. It made no claim to be a Catholic organisation, though, in fact, the parish priest would ordinarily be a key figure in a local U.I.L. branch. A diligent Unionist observer in late 1907 pointed out that in a period of slightly more than one month 'between Aug. 8 and Sept. 16, 71 meetings of the U.I.L. have had priests as chairmen, and these have been supported by the speeches or the presence of 70 of the Roman Catholic clergy'.[45] The difference between the clergy's roles in the U.I.L. and in the A.O.H. suggests a possible difference between the social structure of a typical parish in the West where the U.I.L. had its origin and that of a Catholic community in Ulster. In a Connacht parish, the priest very often assumed a leading position in the League branch as a matter of course. There might be a few rebellious souls who would flaunt the clergy by some sort of secret society activity, but they would not seek and could not in any event obtain clerical sanction. Perhaps the fact that Ulster Catholics could be organised by an agency—the A.O.H.—which neither fell naturally under clerical influence, like the western League branches, nor deliberately spurned clerical participation, like the revolutionary secret society, reflects contact with working-class Protestants who demonstrated that religious devotion need not imply deference to the clergy. The A.O.H. sought clerical sanction but could operate successfully without it.

On the fringes of Ulster, where both U.I.L. and A.O.H. organisations were active, relations between the two groups were not always friendly, in spite of their common allegiance to the party. When a vacancy was created by the retirement of the M.P. for North Monaghan in 1907, a conflict developed between 'the great majority of the priests and the branches of the League wh are controlled by the priests'[46] on the one hand and the A.O.H. on the other. At the convention, the clerical and U.I.L. delegates voted against the candidate supported by the party leadership, a Mr Donovan, but he won by the votes of the numerous A.O.H. delegates, whose divisions outnumbered League branches in the constituency. In the end Redmond, no doubt fearing a Unionist *coup* if two Nationalists were nominated, compelled Donovan to withdraw.[47] In East Cavan, where the A.O.H. also threatened to become stronger than the U.I.L., the local League executive attempted to reduce A.O.H. representation by the device of requiring delegates from A.O.H. divisions to present the written consent of their parish priests for admission to parliamentary conventions.[48]

The social and economic goals of the United Irish League gave it a claim to clerical sympathies which the A.O.H. did not possess. Though the Wyndham Land Purchase Act had established the principles upon which the landlord-tenant relationship would be finally abolished, the U.I.L. had been founded five years before Wyndham's Act on an agitation for a much more fundamental and sweeping reform—the division of large grazing farms among the tenants of small, uneconomic holdings. Only by such a process, Sir James O'Connor observed with bitter sarcasm, could 'the millenium of 20 millions of industrious Irish agriculturists be evolved, and the Heaven-sent principle that every man has a right to land be established'.[49] The clergy generally shared the vision of this millenium, and, as has been demonstrated in Chapter III, entered enthusiastically into efforts to realise it. Such efforts continued in the period of the present chapter, and while clergy were sometimes involved in the questionable means by which division of farms was attempted,[50] they were able in some cases to moderate popular forces and avert violence in the achievement of this goal.[51] Late in 1906 this agitation entered a new phase represented by the technique of cattle-driving, promoted by Laurence Ginnell and several other Nationalist M.P.s. The cattle on a large farm would be driven off at night to some remote place, to the considerable inconvenience of the harrassed owner or tenant of the farm. Though the new species of agitation did receive some clerical encouragement,[52] ecclesiastical reaction against it quickly set in. The Provincial Synod of Tuam in 1907 placed cattle-driving upon the list of sins for which absolution was

8

reserved to the bishop.[53] Archbishop Healy of Tuam, Bishop O'Dea of Galway, and Bishop Clancy of Elphin spoke out in strong terms against the practice,[54] and some of the lower clergy also denounced it.[55]

Two features of clerical opposition to cattle-driving and concomitant forms of agitation deserve mention. Firstly, there was no disagreement with the goals of the agitation. 'The end of your agitation', said Bishop Hoare of Ardagh, speaking in a parish plagued by boycotting, 'is good; your methods are sinful.'[56] Archbishop Healy stressed the possibility of achieving these aims by legal means in a sermon in which he 'pointed out that cattle-driving was not only *an unjust and immoral practice* but that it was the most lamentable folly at the present time, when a sympathetic Chief Secretary had declared himself ready to do all in his power . . . by providing more money, to hasten the splitting up of the non-residential grass farms, which is the chief aim and anxiety of the cattle-drivers.'[57] As the Rev. P. Kelly, C.C., President of the Castlepollard and Finea branches of the U.I.L. pointed out, 'The difficulty which towers over all others was that of finance—the question of ways and means. Breaking down gates and fences, brandishing camans and blackthorns, to the tune of "God save Ireland"', he maintained, 'would never solve the vital question.'[58]

The second significant feature of clerical denunciation of the agitation associated with cattle-driving is that it did not take the form of a concerted attack upon the U.I.L. itself, despite the close association of U.I.L. branches and Nationalist politicians with the agitation. The denunciation, unlike the attack on the A.O.H. at the same time in Ulster, has the character of internal criticism within an institution, the U.I.L., whose overall acceptability is not questioned. When the Rev. Michael Dillon, C.C., condemned cattle-driving after Mass on 24 November 1907 he apparently did not threaten to resign his presidency of the Kinnegad branch of the U.I.L.,[59] and when Laurence Ginnell, M.P., advocated cattle-driving at a Myles the Slasher anniversary demonstration sponsored by the U.I.L. in Finea, Co. Westmeath, in 1908, two priests along with J. P. Hayden, M.P., spoke from the same platform but felt free to dissociate themselves from

Ginnell's advice and to deny that cattle-driving was the Irish Parliamentary Party's policy.[60] In areas where the 1903 Land Act had not yet relieved agrarian grievances, the party, through the U.I.L. branches, was able to sustain the kind of relationship with the clergy which had been built up between 1898 and 1903. The extent of such areas was dwindling, however, through the operations of the act, and, although the U.I.L. continued to be the official Nationalist organisation, in more and more areas the only organisation through which the party could muster much enthusiasm was the clerically disapproved A.O.H.

The party's need for the A.O.H. and its consequent 'Tammany Hall' image, like its treatment of Healy, O'Brien and their partisans, were evidences of the concentration of authority in the hands of the leadership which necessarily followed the land settlement. This concentration was particularly vexatious because it came late in a generational cycle of the Nation's politics. The men in the party leadership had entered politics nearly thirty years earlier, with the rise of Parnell. They were now in their fifties and the younger generation of nationalists were increasingly restive over their exclusion from political affairs. Probably the majority of the politically conscious members of the Nation's younger generation still concentrated their energies on the marginally political Gaelic League efforts to gain a more favourable position for Irish in the schools while continuing to give tacit support to the older generation—as embodied in the Irish Parliamentary Party—in the serious politics of Home Rule. In local government, however, where younger men could compete without being accused of splitting the Nation's forces in the face of the enemy, Sinn Féin was making some significant inroads. Sinn Féiners had won seats on the Dublin Corporation, for example.[61] No doubt Dublin was their most secure foothold, but a careful study of the politics of local government in this period might well reveal other areas in which young critics of the Irish Party were strong. Dillon wrote to Redmond in September 1906 that he had always 'been of the opinion that this Sinn Fein business is a very serious matter and it has been spreading pretty rapidly for the past year. But', he counselled, 'if the party and the movement keep on [the] right lines it will not become very formidable, because it has no-one with any brains to lead it.'[62] If he mistook impractical youthful idealism for brainlessness, Dillon nevertheless correctly perceived a potential danger—a danger with which Bishop O'Dwyer was to taunt the party leaders several months later in his allegation that 'The fine generation of young Irishmen that is growing up is turning away from them en masse for the Gaelic League, or Sinn Fein or some other policy.'[63] Young nationalists were prominent among the critics of Redmond's tentative association with the Irish Council Bill: when Pádraig Pearse, the editor of *An Claidheamh Soluis*, endorsed the bill on the plausible ground that it gave Ireland control over her educational systems, there was a storm of protest from the Gaelic League leadership and rank and file.[64] The bill precipitated the decision of a young Irish Party M.P. for North Leitrim, Charles Dolan, to announce his own conversion to the Sinn Féin policy and his intention to retire from parliament (at some unspecified date) and stand again for the seat as a Sinn Féin candidate.

Dolan's prospects for some clerical support looked good, for his uncle was Vicar-General of the diocese in which most of the constituency lay,[65] and Dolan had himself been a lay student at Maynooth a few years earlier.[66] Accordingly, the party organisation sprang into action to consolidate its position with the local clergy. On 27 June the report of a party organiser 'that all the parish priests in the Division are against Dolan' was forwarded to Redmond.[67] At a meeting of the Glencar Branch of the U.I.L. on 23 June the Rev. Michael Maganran stressed the necessity of firm, cautious adherence to the League's principles, and the Rev. Father O'Reilly presided at a meeting of the Killasnett Branch which passed a resolution unanimously endorsing the party.[68] In this early round of campaigning Dolan cited a speech by a Father Brennan of Killarney who told the Maynooth Union: 'There are times when unity is a great evil.' In reply, P. A. McHugh, M.P. for North Sligo and the party's leading local figure, ridiculed Dolan for relying upon the endorsement of a 'Kerry curate' and claimed the support of Cardinal Logue, on the dubious basis of a statement urging unity; of the local

bishop, Dr Boylan of Kilmore, on the basis of his recent
contribution to party funds; and of Father Flynn, P.P., Killargue, who, according to McHugh, was 'against this childish,
babyish, and ridiculous policy'.[69] McHugh's newspaper did,
however, admit that Dolan had received the 'patronage' of
the Rev. Terence Connolly, C.C., 'whose factionist record is
known to every elector in the constituency'.[70] McHugh's report to Redmond was optimistic. 'There are two little curates
in the constituency', he wrote on 1 July, 'who will, in an
underhand fashion support Dolan; but they have little sense
& less influence, & they will be affraid [sic] to come out in
the open as their Bishop Dr Boylan (Kilmore Diocese) has
nailed his colours to the mast in support of the party.' To
back up his conclusion he enclosed a letter from Father
Flynn, 'by long odds the most powerful priest politically in
North Leitrim'.[71]

While Dolan procrastinated his decision to apply for the
Chiltern Hundreds, Redmond decided that some efforts to
counter Sinn Féin in the city of Dublin were advisable. In
August he wrote to his old Parnellite colleague, T. C. Harrington, who was still M.P. for Dublin Harbour, but who
was drifting out of the party's ruling circle. Redmond tried
to persuade Harrington to join in the new effort and added:
'I am convinced that a reaction is setting in in Dublin against
these Sinn Fein people, and that a reorganisation of the
National forces is possible.'[72]

You may take it from me [replied Harrington], Dublin is really
as sound as ever it was but it requires a little special treatment.
The Sein [sic] Fein have no real grip in the City. They are
composed of two classes who were always hostile to us and who
are not a bit more influential today than they ever were only that
owing to mistakes on our own part they have been allowed to
become a little more prominent. The really active force in it are
the representatives and the agents of the Clan na Gael, such as
P. T. Daly and Griffith and Henry Dixon. They have for the
moment been joined and supported by the doubters and censors
both lay and clerical who have always been on the track of the
Parliamentary Party to decry them and the movement. A little
activity on our part and particularly the disappearance of all
differences amongst ourselves would in a few weeks extinguish
these forces.[73]

Within the next few months the party's differences with Healy, Esmonde and O'Brien and his friends, were papered over, as recounted above, but Dolan refused to be mollified. As late as December 1907 the Sinn Féin forces decided to postpone the North Leitrim contest again because the consituency was 'not yet fully educated in the Sinn Fein policy'.[74] According to police intelligence, the Leitrim clergy were opposing the spread of Sinn Féin and 'advising the people not to attend meetings addressed by its organizers on Sundays'.[75] Dolan finally vacated his seat early in 1908. At a convention in Drumkeeran on 11 February to select the Irish Party candidate, the Very Rev. Patrick McMorrow, P.P., V.F., presided and at least two other parish priests and one curate were present as delegates. A letter wishing success to the convention was received from Canon Hourican, P.P., Killinumery. The nominee, F. E. Meehan, was proposed to the convention by Father Flynn of Killargue.[76] Support of senior clergymen for the party was sustained during the campaign, and although Bishop Boylan did not intervene in the contest, party speakers felt free to invoke his name.[77]

Dolan's uncle, the Vicar-General, left his position sufficiently vague that P. A. McHugh could claim, apparently without fear of contradiction, that if the Vicar-General took a side in the contest it would be the side of the party candidate[78] (though at the declaration of the poll it was noted that Dolan was accompanied by his uncle).[79] Nevertheless, there was enough private clerical support for Dolan that McHugh felt obliged to refer to reports 'that some young clergymen throughout the constituency had felt it their duty out of personal friendship to Mr. Dolan to give him their support'. Belittling the influence of these clerics, McHugh added that

It would be a fatal day for religion and for the country if the people were led to believe that faction was promoted in the great College of Maynooth. They were school fellows together at Maynooth. . . . Was it there they learned to be factionists? That was a question of grave importance for the future of religion in this country.[80]

'If men tried to make decent electors go wrong now in order to support what was called the Hungarian policy,' continued McHugh, in a truly masterful muddling of the issues, 'with what voice could they stand up hereafter and oppose doctrines hostile to their religion which were introduced from France and elsewhere?' In spite of opposition from many of the older clergy and the concerted efforts of the party organisation, Dolan made a surprisingly strong showing. Eight months earlier a party official had predicted that he would get less than three hundred votes.[81] In the event he polled 1,157 votes against 3,103 for the party candidate, and McHugh admitted after the polling that 'amongst the younger clergy, who were his class-fellows in Maynooth' Dolan had 'found active and ardent supporters'.[82]

It was clear in the North Leitrim contest that the Church, as represented by the bishop and his senior clergy (but for the special case of Dolan's uncle), saw no cause to abandon the Nation's accredited representatives. There is no reason to suspect that their counterparts in most other dioceses would have reacted differently. Significantly, however, there was no ecclesiastical suggestion that Sinn Féin was not a potentially legitimate claimant to national leadership. The movement was not stigmatised by the clergy as revolutionary, but was simply opposed on pragmatic grounds. Equally clear was the fact that the generational division of the Nation was mirrored in the Church itself. When the inevitable transfer of power from the party to its successor should take place, the Church would already have the benefit of strong ties with the Nation's younger generation through its own younger generation. For the transition to take place smoothly it was important that the younger generation of the Nation should not lose sight of the conventions between Church and Nation. It must eschew violence as a means of supplanting the State, and it must continue to recognise the Church's rights in education. The former of these conditions was no problem for the moment: few if any nationalists were seriously contemplating revolution in 1908. The latter, however, was more delicate. In the nature of things, education is a preoccupation of the generation which includes students and those who have recently been students. As year after year rolled past, in which Redmond's and Dillon's generation continued to occupy the centre of the stage in the Nation's politics, younger nationalists found it more and more difficult to restrain their desires to play a role in the lesser arena of educational politics. This situation explains the curious ambivalence of several young Irish Irelanders—notably P. H. Pearse and Terence MacSwiney[83]—toward the Irish Council Bill. Another young Catholic journalist, W. P. Ryan, editor of the *Irish Peasant*, a paper backed by a wealthy Irish Party M.P., James McCann, in connection with an agricultural and industrial colony in Co. Meath, opened his columns to articles critical of clerical control of education. Although the paper was published in Navan, in the diocese of Meath, Cardinal Logue wrote to McCann late in 1906 describing the paper as 'a most pernicious anti-Catholic print' and threatening to ban it in his archdiocese. Ryan was obliged to close down his paper, and after a brief revival of it in Dublin, he left Ireland for a career in England.[84]

The confrontation between Ryan and Logue illustrates the difficulties which might easily have wrecked relations between the Church and the Nation's younger generation had there not been men on both sides more cognizant than Ryan and Logue of the mutual advantages of making the conventions between Church and Nation work. Early in 1908 Pádraig Pearse was contemplating the establishment of a bilingual school under lay management in Dublin. In writing to Eóin Mac Néill of his idea, Pearse was obviously aware of possible difficulties with the clergy. He contemplated having a chaplain and clerical extern lectures and hoped that Walsh might be persuaded to be a patron of the school, which he proposed to advertise as 'An Irish school for Catholic Boys'.[85] Mac Néill's revealing reply began by deploring the anticlerical campaign in Ryan's paper. 'The moving principle of that crusade', Mac Néill wrote, 'is that the clergy have deliberately arrogated & continue to usurp exclusive control of Catholic schools.'[86] This proposition, he believed, was quite untrue. The clergy had been 'compelled' to assume their present position in education by the 'helplessness' of the laity and the action of the State, and in this 'natural historical result' the laity generally had 'fully acquiesced & *still acquiesce*'. It was no wonder, he maintained, that some of the clergy 'are shocked at the criticism the whole body receives, & feeling it to be unfair, find only anti-religious tendencies in it'. Mac

Néill hoped that reform would come, but added that 'In seeking this reform, Irish Catholics ought to maintain a wholly friendly & sympathetic attitude toward their clergy, by whose aid alone a salutary reform can be effected.' Applying these philosophical reflections to the problem at hand, Mac Néill observed that Pearse's project, 'if it goes forward, ought to be kept entirely clear of anything savouring of Laity v. Clergy'. 'In short,' he maintained, 'it ought to start with the active approval of Archbp. Walsh, unless that approval be *unreasonably* withheld.' The Archbishop had encouraged Mac Néill's own brother, Mac Néill confided, to start a school under lay management some years earlier, a fact which suggested 'that His Grace may possibly be counted as a friend to a similar undertaking, though the crusade I have mentioned is likely to increase the natural timidity of ecclesiastics *towards each other*'. However, he thought the time was opportune for creating such a school as Pearse contemplated. 'Indeed,' he remarked, 'I have for some time thought of consulting Dr. Walsh on the point.'

Mac Néill did consult Walsh, though only after a delay of three months and then through an intermediary, Father Michael Curran, the Archbishop's secretary. Perhaps Walsh's advancing age was causing him to restrict his personal correspondence, for after 1905 or so he often communicated with Mac Néill through his secretary, and probably Mac Néill postponed raising the issue because the university question would at this moment be uppermost in Walsh's mind. Father Curran informed Mac Néill that the Archbishop, predictably, would not lend his name to such a risky venture, 'however much he would like to see such a school succeed'.[87] From the tone of the letter it was clear that Walsh would permit the project to go forward, and in September St Enda's School was established under Pearse's direction. From the episode it is clear that in Mac Néill the Nation's younger generation had a leader who sympathised with the feelings of frustration which impelled them to work for change in the educational systems, but who quite sincerely accepted the clerical position on education and had a realistic sense of how to work with rather than against the ecclesiastical authorities. Moreover, his lines of communication with Archbishop Walsh, while not quite so direct as they were a decade earlier, were still quite open. That was more than Redmond could have said.

The Irish Parliamentary Party leaders were in an uncomfortable predicament, for they had to retain and cultivate the Liberals' friendship in hopes of gaining Home Rule while avoiding the taint of Liberal secularism. The Lords were continuing their gleeful wrecking of Liberal programmes, and, as the government's claim that the Upper House was abusing its powers rested on the assertion that a popular mandate was being defied, the numerous by-elections of 1908 were regarded as tests of the validity of that claim. The most celebrated of these contests resulted from the cabinet reshuffle when rapid decline in Campbell-Bannerman's health necessitated his retirement from the premiership. On 8 April the King asked H. H. Asquith, the Chancellor of the Exchequer who had never been more than a lukewarm Home Ruler, to form a government. When the new Prime Minister moved David Lloyd George from the Board of Trade to the Exchequer, he filled the resulting vacancy with his party's most colourful figure, the young Winston Churchill, thereby obliging the latter to stand again for his seat in North-West Manchester. Churchill had captured the traditionally Conservative seat in 1906 by a remarkable 1,200-vote margin largely because of Unionist flirtation with protectionism. Manchester still worshipped at the altar of Free Trade.

By 1908, however, Joseph Chamberlain, the chief exponent of tariff reform, had been removed from politics by illness, and the issue which had swung North-West Manchester to the Liberals in 1906 was no longer paramount. Redmond advised Churchill that he could not deliver the Irish Catholic vote (some nine hundred electors) without 'a very strong and explicit Home Rule declaration' and that even with such a declaration only part of the vote could be secured. With striking candour the party leader added: 'You probably would lose quite as many votes because of your declaration.'[88] In his election address at the opening of the campaign, Churchill made no reference to Home Rule, but on the education question he affirmed his support of popular control and the abolition of tests for teachers, adding a proviso, which was unsatisfactory to the Catholic clergy, that provision had to be made for Catholics who might well demand 'a special type of school'.[89] Members of the local U.I.L. branch had an interview with Churchill at which he gave them certain verbal assurances on Home Rule and education, purportedly formulated in consultation with T. P. O'Connor before Churchill left London for the constituency.[90] There being some doubt as to how far Churchill spoke for the government, a deputation was sent to London to confer with O'Connor and spokesmen for the ministry.[91] While the Manchester Catholic Federation deferred action pending a firm decision by the U.I.L., the clergy of the division, on their own, drew up but did not yet publish a declaration opposing Churchill and favouring Mr Joynson-Hicks, the Conservative candidate.[92] The local U.I.L. branch, acting on advice from Redmond, published a statement asking Irish voters not to commit themselves to either candidate for the time being and affirming their own friendly working arrangement with the Catholic Federation.[93] Churchill and T. P. O'Connor were working furiously to come to some formula to which Churchill could commit the government and thereby enable the party to endorse his candidacy.[94] The U.I.L. managed to forestall hostile action by the Federation and to keep the priests' manifesto from being distributed on Sunday, 19 April, 'except at one church which was in ignorance' according to a clerical apologist.[95] 'It is no joke fighting such a contest as this,' Churchill commented in a report to Asquith.[96]

On 20 April Churchill spoke at the St John's Schools, Gartside-street, on the education and Irish issues. In both cases his statements were vague, but he did claim Asquith's 'full concurrence and approval' in the opinion that at the next election the Liberals 'should claim full authority and a free hand to deal with the problem of Irish self-government'. He made it plain that he was not referring to a scheme like the Irish Council Bill.[97] Redmond and T. P. O'Connor immediately directed the local U.I.L. to declare for Churchill,[98] and Irish politicians commenced a whirlwind campaign during the few remaining days before polling.[99] 'Jews, Irish, Unionist Free Traders, & Protestant League are all now safely penned in the same cage together,' Churchill reported to the Prime Minister. 'Please God they do not fight before Friday evening. I am rather battered.'[100] The Irish were slipping out of the cage already, however. Just before Churchill's crucial speech, Bishop Casartelli sent to the Federation's executive a letter embodying 'a dignified, gentle, yet firm assertion that Catholics could vote for Mr. Joynson-Hicks, but not for Mr. Churchill, on the Education question alone'.[101] Despite a telegram from Devlin pleading for further delay, the executive decided to publish the letter as a 'direct expression' of its views. Not many Unionist Free Traders had got into the cage—perhaps others had broken out after Churchill's pro-Home Rule gesture—and too few Irish were sufficiently impressed by his gesture to defy their priests and save his seat. The new cabinet minister lost by 429 votes and was forced to seek refuge in a safe Liberal seat, Dundee.

Redmond's pessimism had been fully justified, but Churchill's filial biographer has missed the point.[102] The Irish Party leader wanted Churchill to believe that the government's lack of an explicit Home Rule policy was the principal reason he could not deliver Irish votes. Nevertheless, he discouraged Churchill from declaring for Home Rule (although T. P. O'Connor, chief organiser of the Irish in Great Britain, no doubt took a different attitude). Apparently Redmond did not point out that the issue upon which the Irish vote would turn was not Irish policy but English education policy. How can we account for Redmond's strange behaviour? Quite simply, the party leader knew that if Churchill tried to win Irish votes at this juncture English liberalism would be treated to a spectacle of clerical dictation in 'Irish' politics—as indeed it was. It would be better to pass up the chance for a declaration—easily repudiated in any event—in favour of Home Rule than to call attention to this aspect of the national movement. The mind of English radicalism, however much it might incline toward granting the aspirations of an oppressed nationality, still harboured the fear that a self-governing Ireland would become a theocratic rather than a democratic state. The popular image of the Irish as a priest-ridden people and the raucous cry 'Home Rule means Rome Rule' might not be so openly expressed by English Liberals as by Irish Unionists, but, in a House so dominated by Nonconformist and secularist opinion as that of 1906–09, the effect of such stereotypes among government backbenchers could not be ignored. Dillon had written to Redmond shortly after the Nationalist Convention which rejected Birrell's Irish Council Bill: 'You and T.P. and the members . . . of the Party ought to be able to do a good deal to remove the ridiculous impression that the Council Bill was killed by the priests.'[103] Dillon had been temporarily removed from the arena of active politics by the death of his wife just after the introduction of the bill. The accuracy of his contention that the impression was 'ridiculous' is to be judged in light of the discussion of the bill in Chapter VIII, but his assessment of English political facts was unimpaired by the effects of his domestic tragedy. 'If that impression gets fixed in the minds of the Radicals,' he wrote, 'it will do a great deal of harm.'

After the Manchester debacle the party leaders took steps designed to persuade the radicals that at least they themselves were not priest-ridden. In Leeds on 6 June 1908 the annual convention of the United Irish League of Great Britain passed a resolution 'condemning the action of the Catholic Federation in asking Irish Catholic electors to vote against certain Liberal candidates who were pledged to support the Government Bill on Primary Education'.[104] Both Redmond and Dillon made speeches which outraged the editors of the *Irish Catholic*. The offending passage in Dillon's speech was an attack on English Tory priests whose 'INSENSATE CONDUCT' had 'to a great extent paralysed' the party in its dealings with the government over the education question. The passage from Redmond's speech to which the *Irish Catholic* took exception was more interesting, for in it the Irish leader attempted to sketch out his conception of Irish nationality and the party's function:

We are told that the Irish people of Great Britain owe a divided duty; they owe a duty, no doubt, to their country's freedom; but that alongside there is another duty which occasionally may be held, rightly, to over-ride the first, a duty due to the Catholic religion and the Catholic Church. I say that THIS NATIONAL MOVEMENT IS NOT A CATHOLIC MOVEMENT. It is a National movement. It is not in conflict with the interests of the

Catholic religion—God forbid—that is the religion of the over-whelming majority of our people. But the National movement is a National movement embracing within its folds men of all religions, and those who would seek to turn this National move-ment simply into a Catholic movement would be repudiating some of the brightest pages of our National history and forgetting the memory of some of the greatest of our national heroes, who PROFESSED THE NEWER AND NOT THE OLDER CREED OF OUR COUNTRY.[105]

Dillon went so far as to accept a Sunday speaking engage-ment at Whitefield's Central Mission Church, a Noncon-formist centre in London, and paid tribute to Birrell and the government's Nonconformist supporters for the friendly attitude they adopted toward the Irish Universities Bill.[106]

Such gestures as these, designed to calm Nonconformist fears of 'Rome Rule' in Ireland, were costly for the party, and their cost was increased by government sensitivity to Nonconformist prejudices. This sensitivity was highlighted in September when Bourne announced plans for an elabor-ate procession through the streets of Westminster as part of a Eucharistic Congress in London. The public display of the Host, to be carried by Cardinal Vannutelli, the Papal Legate, and the wearing of vestments as planned were technical violations of the Catholic Emancipation Act of 1829, though a government less sensitive to Nonconformist opinion than the present one would probably have treated the law as a dead letter. Reacting to threats of violence by Free Church-men, who were perhaps understandably offended by the announcement that the Congress was 'an act of reparation for the English Reformation', Asquith requested Bourne to abandon the illegal elements of ceremony, and Bourne, though he made a very sound case for being allowed to pursue his original plans in private correspondence with Asquith, subsequently published, agreed to comply if al-lowed 'to state that he did so at the Prime Minister's re-quest'.[107] The curtailment of ceremonial elements in the procession caused intense resentment among Catholics. On the following Sunday in a letter read in Catholic churches in Newcastle urging voters, in effect, to vote against the Liberal candidate in an upcoming by-election, the clergy took the 'opportunity also to protest publicly against the action of the government in prohibiting the Procession of the Blessed Sacrament last Sunday', which they considered 'a grievous indignity offered to this holiest mystery of your Faith'.[108] The Irish Party did not attempt to resist the clerical directive in this case but instructed electors to vote against the Liberal candidate in protest over the procession incident, and the government lost the seat.[109]

Three days after the election, Dillon tried to repair some of the damage to the party's relations with the Liberals in a speech at Clara in which he pointed out that Asquith had not forbidden the procession but had merely suggested to Bourne that it was unwise. Dillon was roundly attacked by the *Irish Catholic*, which exulted in the Liberal defeat at Newcastle,[110] and Bishop O'Dwyer, in answer to a resolution of the Limerick Guardians against Asquith's action, took the opportunity to denounce Dillon's apology for that action.[111] When the Limerick Borough Council sent O'Dwyer a similar resolution, he replied with another full-dress tirade against 'the alliance which enables Mr. Winston Churchill to count the eighty Irish members as a Liberal asset'.[112] Belittling the efficacy of such resolutions as the Borough Council had passed, the Bishop predicted that the party would not attempt 'to force the hand of the Government', for the party was 'at the disposal of two or three political "bosses", whom Mr. Asquith and the Liberal Whip have no difficulty in "squaring"'. Deploring the party's support of a government pledged not to introduce Home Rule during the present parliament, he charged the party with a systematic attempt to deceive Irishmen into believing that Churchill's statement in Manchester constituted a Liberal commitment to deal with the Home Rule issue. The party might make a 'pretence . . . of resentment while feeling runs high amongst Catholics against Mr. Asquith and his Government on the religious question.' O'Dwyer went on to predict with heavy irony:

But mark my words for it, it is all a sham and humbug. These Penal Laws will stand. We are only 'Papists', whom it is safe to insult; and while one of our Catholic leaders does not think himself degraded by going to act as temporary curate to a Nonconformist parson in London, who is one of the loudest of the bigots that call for our humiliation, we had better hold our tongues, if we have not the will nor the power to make our representatives represent us.[113]

That O'Dwyer's hyperbole was atypical of the whole hierarchy could be small comfort to the party leaders, for even the more reserved Bishop Clancy took up the same theme in answer to a resolution of protest over the Eucharistic Procession incident from the Roscommon Rural District Council. 'I do not hope for much practical result', he wrote, 'from these resolutions which have been passed all over the country unless we see our way to make things hot for Mr. Asquith through our Parliamenatry representatives.'[114]

Ironically the party was now in greater jeopardy of guilt by association with the Liberals' other allies—the English Nonconformists—because the Liberals had been so evenhanded in satisfying the contradictory demands of their two theologically incompatible allies. The government's attempts to expand popular control in English education, which it still continued in a halfhearted way, and its surrender to Nonconformist prejudice in the procession episode were counterparts in England of an Irish policy which had gratified the episcopal desires with a virtually Catholic university and the removal of financial pressure for popular control in primary and secondary education. This Irish policy had met the demands which the bishops had asked Redmond to press in January 1906, and, in the absence of an imminent prospect of Home Rule, there was no further reason for the Church to be indulgent of the Liberal alliance.

PART THREE

Hiatus, 1909-1916

CHAPTER XI

The Strange Ailments of Nationalist Ireland

FOR technical reasons the finance of the Wyndham Land Purchase Act had broken down. Since 1907 the Irish Parliamentary Party leaders had been prodding the ministry to bring forward a bill to enable the process of land purchase, which had now virtually ceased, to go forward as originally contemplated. When, late in 1908, Birrell finally did bring in such a bill—which incidentally would enlarge the geographical scope of the C.D.B. as was urged by the Connacht bishops in 1903—the party leaders called a Nationalist Convention to consider it. On the morning the Convention opened, 9 February 1909, the *Freeman's Journal* carried messages to the gathering from twelve bishops under the heading 'Tributes to the Party's Work'—a description which fitted most, but not all, of these gestures.[1] As perfunctory resolutions of support for the party and its policy were being passed, members of the Young Ireland Branch of the U.I.L.—a group of U.C.D. students formed several years earlier to work within the party's organisation—offered an amendment mandating the party 'to accept no responsibility for any further minor measures' after the Land Bill but to do all in its power to embarrass the government which had failed to introduce a Home Rule Bill.[2] They were shouted and, according to one account, 'bludgeoned'[3] down by the assembled delegates, and their arguments ridiculed by Devlin. Next Laurence Ginnell, M.P., one of the leaders of the cattle-driving agitation, tried to move an amendment calling upon the party to return to the country to organise the people rather than 'supporting in England a renegade and treacherous Liberal Government'.[4] He tried to make himself heard for some ten minutes, but was shouted down, as was another delegate who wanted party members to resign from the National Liberal Club.

When Redmond, who was presiding, offered a resolution endorsing the party's acceptance of the new Land Bill, subject to certain amendments, William O'Brien came forward to speak against the motion. O'Brien had been defeated in a meeting of Nationalist M.P.s nearly a year earlier on a motion to have the land question referred again to a landlord-tenant conference. When he tried now to depict the Land Bill as subversive of the 1903 settlement, pandemonium broke out. O'Brien tried vainly to make himself heard for an hour, during which some of his followers were roughed up by the stewards—specially recruited, according to his version, from Devlin's A.O.H. followers in Belfast. Finally he defiantly stalked out, and Redmond's motion was carried overwhelmingly.

On the preceding evening, Dublin had been treated to a torchlight parade organised by students in favour of requiring a knowledge of Irish for admission to the new National University.[5] On the second day of its deliberations, this issue was injected into the debates of the Nationalist Convention. Dillon rose to oppose a compulsory Irish motion and found himself facing almost as much hostility as O'Brien—the party's outcast—had faced the previous day. Douglas Hyde then spoke in favour of the compulsory Irish proposal, which was thunderously carried by about a three-fourths majority.[6] Though O'Brien gave the 'baton convention' a certain immortality by returning *ad nauseum* in his subsequent effusions to his rough treatment at the hands of Devlin's 'Molly Maguires', one need not share O'Brien's peculiar point of view to recognise in the Convention some symptoms of serious disorders in the Irish political system in 1909.

The issue of Irish in the new university had come into prominence at a meeting at U.C.D. on 29 November 1908 at which a 'quiet and scholarly' paper arguing that Irish ought to be an integral part of the curriculum was read.[7] Several Gaelic Leaguers then expressed themselves more vigorously on the subject, and the chairman, Eóin Mac Néill, with more fairness than prudence, called upon Father Delany, S.J., the President of U.C.D. and a member of the new University

Senate, to respond. Delany, feeling that silence might imply agreement with the speeches, replied that he 'would give Irish a privileged, a predominant place in the University, but he would stop there'. Compulsion would, in his opinion, be harmful to both university and country. The views of Delany were taken as representative of the Senate. The following week Gaelic Leaguers took up the issue at a meeting in the Rotunda at which 'essential Irish' was defended by Hyde, Mac Néill, Griffith and others, and the Dublin papers were deluged with letters on the subject.

Within a few days Mac Néill, himself (along with Hyde) a member of the Senate, learned that he could not count on the unequivocal support of Archbishop Walsh, who was about to be elected Chancellor of the University, and who told Mac Néill quite pointedly that he was not inclined to take the Gaelic League view of this issue.[8] Originally, the Archbishop assured Mac Néill, he had been 'unconvinced, but anxious to be convinced', but he had been alienated by 'the shocking vulgar abuse in which a number of them [Gaelic Leaguers] seem to revel and the utterly irrelevant arguments they bring forward', and he discerned 'a determined, and to judge by some of the language used, a vicious attempt to intimidate and terrorise'. Bishop Clancy of Elphin took up the same theme in a public letter to a Gaelic League meeting in Sligo, one of the numerous gatherings that had been organised around the country to press the essential Irish demand. In Clancy's view, 'Certain members of the Gaelic League, while acting as if they themselves were obsessed by a rabid form of Anglophobia, are disposed—if they can—to "bulldoze" the country, believing her to be suffering from a bad attack of Anglomania.'[9] There was, however, a substantive issue troubling ecclesiastics as much as the tone and tactics of the Gaelic League agitation. The bishops had worked and waited for half a century to gain a Catholic university, and they were quite suspicious of a proposed admission requirement which might tempt Catholics who did not know Irish to go to Trinity. Clancy, after expressing this fear, offered a practical suggestion for compromise: that a four- or five-year period be allowed for the secondary schools to prepare for an Irish matriculation requirement at the new university.[10] Influential advocates of the language revival were already working on compromises along these and other lines,[11] but the movement to press for immediate compulsory Irish had already gained momentum with the support of a number of the lower clergy.[12] The Gaelic League, according to one of their young leaders, was 'dying for a fight'.[13]

The fight was not long coming. In the middle of January the Episcopal Standing Committee issued a statement declaring the question was one for 'fair argument' but making plain their own opposition to compulsory Irish in the university. They looked forward to the day when Irish would become the medium of instruction in the university. They maintained, however, that this goal would best be attained by establishing 'bright centres of Gaelic study' in the colleges for voluntary instruction.[14] When Dillon faced the heckling delegates at the Nationalist Convention three weeks later, he was acting in accordance with that rule of the Irish political system that the Nation's representatives must always defer to ecclesiastical wishes—clearly and officially articulated as they had now been—in matters affecting education in Ireland. Many of the Gaelic League leaders were quite aware that they too should respect this rule if they wanted to enlarge their role in the political system, though the enthusiasm with which the cause had been taken up meant that they must beware lest they lose their role within the League. On the Church's side, at least Walsh was anxious for a compromise settlement, though he too was obliged to move cautiously to protect his position within the hierarchy. In a letter to a Gaelic League leader dated 20 February he discussed some research he had done in the history of language requirements in the old Royal University with the apparent intent of finding a compromise solution defensible on conservative grounds. Significantly, he concluded by saying: 'There is, as you can see, nothing confidential in all this. But I would ask you, if you have occasion to make any public use of it to take the information from the Calendars &c. yourself.'[15]

Tempers within the hierarchy seem to have been running high because of the persistence with which some of their clergy supported the agitation. A Co. Galway priest had used the 'fair argument' clause of the Standing Committee's state-

ment to speak in favour of compulsory Irish at the Nationalist Convention, and the *Times* correspondent reported that
many, though not most, of the priests at the Convention
voted for the resolution.[16] The implications of the Standing
Committee's phrase 'fair argument' for clerical freedom of
speech were hotly disputed, proponents of essential Irish
citing a statement by Cardinal Logue that people were 'free
as the winds' to take whatever position they preferred in the
controversy.[17] Archbishop Healy, on the other hand, rendered
the interpretation that 'It was a matter for fair discussion
before they [the bishops] spoke, but not since, and [he candidly added] I can't understand how the Cardinal can maintain that it is not a matter of conscience, for I hold it a
serious matter of conscience to do anything which would
drive Catholic students to Trinity College.'[18] At least in
Tuam archdiocese the priests were explicitly silenced,
though elsewhere ecclesiastical policy seems to have varied
markedly.[19] Tension was increased by a League campaign
directed toward the local government authorities which were
empowered to levy rates to provide scholarships in the new
universities and over which churchmen were accustomed
to exercise considerable influence. By the middle of February
nine city and county councils had resolved not to levy the
rates unless Irish were made compulsory.[20]

Cardinal Moran, the Archbishop of Sydney and formerly
Bishop of Ossory, seemed to be trying to facilitate a compromise when he gave an interview to an Australian Catholic
paper advocating compulsory Irish in the university, but
adding: 'Still I fully agree with the Senate of the National
University and with the Committee of the Irish Bishops
that an exception might be made for the first or second year
of matriculation.'[21] Of course, neither the Senate nor the
Standing Committee had said any such thing, but it was
hard to argue with a Cardinal in the antipodes and easy to
see the logic of such a compromise as he was suggesting. Early
in May, Col. Maurice Moore (brother of the novelist George
Moore), a Catholic gentleman active in the language movement tried to establish negotiations with the hierarchy
through his old classmate at Oscott, Canon Arthur Ryan of
Tipperary, one of the outspoken proponents of compulsory

Irish prior to the Standing Committee's pronouncement. Moore's proposed terms were

　　1. Irish not to be compulsory for 3 yrs. but to be from the beginning a well marked voluntary subject.

　　2. After 3 yrs. Irish to be compulsory on the following lines. . . . The Saxon & Early English questions in the present. . . Royal University English examination papers to be dropped out & an Irish examination on similar lines substituted.[22]

Moore stressed that the League would not yield to pressure either to postpone the question beyond the the five-year life of the first University Senate or to accept the endowment of Irish professorships, scholarships, etc., in place of a compulsory matriculation examination. Canon Ryan raised the matter with his own archbishop, Fennelly, who was quite friendly but wanted assurance that these proposals came from an authorised Gaelic League spokesman.[23]

　　Moore communicated with Mac Néill and Father Michael O'Hickey, who had also been a Vice-President of the League until recently, and both agreed that the terms he offered were acceptable.[24] They felt unable to grant plenipotentiary authority but were anxious that negotiations proceed. Moore summed up for Canon Ryan the views of several influential Gaelic Leaguers to the effect that they would like Irish compulsory from the beginning and thought two years would be an ample warning period, but, as a gesture to encourage their opponents to compromise as well, they would accept a three-year postponement. Perhaps as an answer to Fennelly's query about his authority to negotiate, Moore stated:

All agree that if this is agreed to in a straightforward way, the G. League will be practically unanimous in accepting the settlement as a definite solution of the problem; & that everything will be done to make the road smooth & easy. We will do all we can to get the County Councils to levy a vote for the University &c &c.[25]

By the end of May Canon Ryan was able to report to Moore: 'So far your proposals have been met kindly enough & personally I am very hopeful.'[26] The proposals were, he confided, in Walsh's hands, and he was anxiously awaiting a reply. At this point a settlement might indeed have been reached between the Church and the Nation's younger generation.

Three years' delay was a reasonable compromise between the popular cry for instant—even retributive—compulsion (which the League leaders themselves privately disclaimed), and the four- or five-year delay suggested by Bishop Clancy some months earlier. Nevertheless, in the middle of June Father O'Hickey was writing to Col. Moore: 'I am very grieved to hear of the failure of your efforts to bring about a settlement.'[27]

This failure was in all probability related to O'Hickey himself, who was Professor of Irish at Maynooth. Early in the controversy, before the Standing Committee's action O'Hickey had entered the agitation with a number of sharply worded public letters branding opponents of compulsory Irish as 'West Britons'—a term of derision which he applied to Catholics who aped English fashions in hopes of social advancement. On 13 December 1908 he had given a lecture to a Maynooth student audience in which he referred to the five Catholic churchmen whom the government had appointed to the Senate. After singling out Walsh as a friend of Irish Ireland, he commented: 'As for the other Clerical Senators, I shall say nothing farther than to recommend them to your earnest prayers.'[28] O'Hickey's later plea that this remark deserved to be treated as mere 'banter'[29] is perhaps undermined by the fact that O'Hickey allowed the lecture to be published in *Sinn Féin*, and, after the Standing Committee's action, defiantly republished it along with his public letters in a pamphlet entitled *An Irish University, or Else—*. O'Hickey further angered leading ecclesiastics with an entire pamphlet attacking the hierarchy in even more unmeasured language, though this time he identified himself only as 'An Irish Priest'.[30]

Father O'Hickey's actions gave the conflict a new dimension. As the Church and the Nation's younger generation were moving cautiously toward a compromise in the late spring, the process was upset by a dispute within the Church itself which overshadowed for the time being the larger issue. By early May the bishops in their capacity as trustees of Maynooth had forced O'Hickey to cease his public attacks.[31] Nevertheless, Mgr Mannix, the President of Maynooth, who as one of the clerical senators for whom O'Hickey had recommended earnest prayers was understandably enraged, seems to have persuaded members of the hierarchy of the need for even sterner measures against insubordination within the College on occasions which presented themselves at the end of the spring term. On 12 June, the day on which the list of orders to which each student was now deemed worthy was read, half a dozen students, the committee of a student organisation which had telegraphed a message of sympathy to the Dublin students' demonstration the day before the Nationalist Convention, found that they were not to receive the orders which students normally obtained at their respective stages in seminary training.[32] The priesthood was withheld from the group's president. A few days later the bishops held their annual June meeting, and at the sitting to transact their functions as Maynooth trustees they called O'Hickey before them and demanded that he withdraw certain of his remarks on pain of loss of his professorship. O'Hickey refused and wasted away the remaining five years of his life in fruitless appeals of his case through the various ecclesiastical courts in Rome.

His colleague Father Walter McDonald acted as an informal advisor to him on canon law and provides the fullest account of the whole affair in his *Reminiscences of a Maynooth Professor.*[33] McDonald himself had been denied an international reputation because the Irish bishops were so afraid that any new theological idea might be infected with modernism that they forced him to send his books to the Roman authorities before they were published. Rome, faced with the choice of endorsing novel ideas untested by scholarly controversy or refusing permission to publish, repeatedly chose the latter course, even though theologians from most Catholic countries would not have had to go through this disheartening procedure unless *after* publication a charge of heresy had been made. In the process McDonald had gained some intimate knowledge of canon law and an obsession with trying to force the Irish bishops to act according to its letter and spirit. McDonald was probably correct in suspecting that the bishops in O'Hickey's case, as in his own, resorted to unfair wire-pulling to bias the judicial procedures. The hierarchy treated dissent within the Church with the same heavy hand that the party leaders treated dissent within the Nation, though the bishops' methods may have had more apparent dignity. O'Hickey was up against a situation very similar to William O'Brien's. The bishops were accustomed to compromise, mutual accommodation and respect for established rules and conventions in Church-State and Church-Nation relations, but no such constraints applied to intra-Church relations.

Such a message was implicit in a statement the bishops published shortly after their confrontation with O'Hickey. Their decision, they explained, was purely a matter of ecclesiastical discipline and 'had no connexion whatsoever with the views of anyone as to whether the Irish language should or should not be an obligatory subject at certain examinations, or in certain courses of the National University of Ireland'.[34] In this disclaimer the bishops were no doubt quite sincere, for they quite genuinely needed a settlement. The subtleties of the situation escaped the more radical Irish Irelanders. Pearse had already bitterly attacked the dismissal of O'Hickey in *An Claidheamh Soluis*, to the consternation of one moderate Gaelic Leaguer, who warned Mac Néill that the article would 'do us no end of harm and delight the enemies of the Gaelic League'.[35] The affair probably breathed new life into the agitation, which climaxed in September with a procession in Dublin that took three hours to pass any given point. A deputation from the General Council of County Councils appeared before the University Senate to demand compulsory Irish.[36] Fortunately the complex procedure for establishing the curriculum prevented any action by the Senate for some months during which tempers had a chance to cool. Early in the spring of 1910 the Senate—on the motion, significantly, of Mac Néill—adopted by a one-vote margin the suggestion of the U.C.D. Academic Council that no specific subject be obligatory at the 1911 matriculation examinations but that students who did not take the Irish examination be required to follow 'to the satisfaction of the Professor' certain non-examination courses in the Irish language and Irish history. This action made possible a smooth transition to the further enactment on 23 June 1910 of a requirement that, from 1913, Irish should be compulsory for matriculation.[37]

This arrangement was consistent with Bishop Clancy's suggestion at the end of 1908 for a four- or five-year period of transition. By 1913 the secondary schools would be able to prepare all candidates for matriculation examinations in Irish. Although some churchmen would no doubt have preferred not to be bothered with arranging for universal Irish instruction in the primary and secondary schools, the arrangement was one they could live with. Moreover the language enthusiasts were appeased and the county councils began immediately to provide scholarship money.

Certainly the relations between the Church and the Nation's younger generation were strained by this entire episode. Yet it would be a mistake to overestimate the damage. Precisely because the pattern of political division was more generational than ideological there was a certain resiliency in Church-Nation relations. Churchmen knew the young men would eventually lead the Nation and the young men knew the Church was there to stay. Moreover, if it is the role of fathers—for that is how ecclesiastics are addressed—to chasten and correct, it is the part of sons to resist and rebel. The rage of adolescent and parent need not preclude the mutual respect of adult and parent a few years later. It was far otherwise between the two generations of the Nation itself. Here the analogy of a literal family breaks down. From 1909 the 'sons' were clearly set upon a course not just of establishing their own identity, but of actually, and in literal fact, supplanting the Irish Parliamentary Party. The party was cast in the role not of a metaphorical father who chastens and corrects, but of a real political opponent with whom there would eventually be a fight to the finish. In the autumn of 1909 Redmond refused a request from Hyde that he join the essential Irish agitation in a letter cataloguing instances of friction between Gaelic League forces and his own supporters.[38] Some months later Hyde regretfully admitted to John Horgan, a staunch Redmondite who was becoming uncomfortable within the Gaelic League, 'that all the best Gaelic League workers are also advanced politicians while the language gets little or no help from the M.P.'s, the United Irish League or the Ancient Order of Hibernians'.[39] For our purposes, the most serious result of the essential Irish agitation was not the memory of the Church's opposition but the memory of Dillon's support for that opposition at the 'baton convention'.

After the Nationalist Convention in February, O'Brien had once more flamboyantly vacated his seat for Cork City, but this time instead of standing again he went to Venice and underwent serious surgery.[40] O'Brien had such a hold upon Nationalist politics in Cork that his forces would inevitably dominate any nominating convention that might be called. A convention met and nominated Maurice Healy, brother of O'Brien's new-found ally, T. M. Healy. After failing to produce an opponent to Healy by means of an *ad hoc* committee,[41] which might confer at least some of the sanction of a popular convention, the party's forces resorted to a simple deputation—headed by an M.P. and one of the cathedral clergy—which called upon George Crosbie, proprietor of the *Cork Examiner*, and invited him to stand. Although the Bishop of Cork did not become publicly involved, his dean and clergy joined enthusiastically in the party's efforts,[42] thus sanctioning disregard of proper democratic forms in the interest of crushing out faction. In spite of overwhelming clerical opposition and the party's strenuous efforts, however, Maurice Healy won by 4,706 votes to 3,547. The views of the Cork clergy, however, were not shared by Archbishop Walsh, who, on the day following the election, called on T. M. Healy at his home in Chapelizod to offer congratulations. Healy, who with tongue in cheek still regarded himself as a party member by virtue of the 1908 reunion, wrote to Maurice: 'The Archbishop inquired would there be any effort to exclude you from the Party, and said it would be "very funny if the terrible member of the family were included and they excluded you." '[43]

As Walsh had supported the party in 1900 when it crushed Healy's influence and rudely thrust him out of power, it seems passing strange to find him now dropping in upon Healy to exchange jokes at the party's expense. Yet the Archbishop had made plain to Redmond at the end of 1905 his dissatisfaction with the way the party was conducting its business, and he never wavered in his resolve to have nothing more to do with the party. His secretary, Father Curran, wrote of him after his death:

Democratic in the best sense of the word, he believed in the capacity of popularly elected bodies and had faith in the ultimate judgment of the people. He knew they might go astray for a time, but that it was impossible to deceive them for ever. What he did dread was the machine in politics operating through the bogus convention.[44]

'Legalistic' or 'constitutional' might describe Walsh's ideals more accurately than Father Curran's word, 'democratic'. He possessed the canon lawyer's exaggerated respect for precisely defined procedures for reaching decisions. The application of such ideals to an ostensibly democratic mechanism, such as the party organisation, demanded the free, unfettered interaction of political ideas in the popular arena. The encouragement of public debate, however, was incompatible with the unity and discipline deemed necessary to extract a Home Rule Act from the imperial parliament. Although the leadership—and especially Devlin—may have put down dissent with a bit more gusto than was really necessary, one should not forget the vivid memories of national powerlessness in the 1890s when everyone was free to say and do virtually whatever he pleased. It no doubt seemed self-evident that so long as the overriding political aim of Irish Catholics was to force the English to grant self-government to their country, differences must be suppressed and political power concentrated in the hands of the Nation's accredited spokesmen. Walsh was not content with this arrangement.

Walsh's lack of confidence in the Irish Parliamentary Party was shared by Logue, O'Dwyer and Archbishop Healy, though for somewhat different reasons. Logue was not subject to the fine legal scruples of Walsh, but he did know that the party had isolated his kept politician, T. M. Healy, and he had never reconciled himself to the reality represented by this fact—that ecclesiastics must make their influence felt in politics through subtler means than overt dictation and the sponsorship of sycophants. The same stubborn inability to adjust governed the Cardinal's relations with the A.O.H., against which he spoke out strongly in his 1909 Lenten pastoral.[45] When delegates from the American A.O.H. came to Ireland a few weeks later to mediate between Devlin's Board of Erin Hibernians and the Scottish Section of the

Order, Logue did grant them an audience (perhaps because one of them was a priest) and they reportedly went away pleased at the reception they were accorded.[46] Nevertheless, on his triennial visitation to Carrickmore in the following month, Logue referred to the A.O.H., at least in that parish, as 'a pest, a cruel tyranny, and an organised system of blackguardism'.[47] Not only did he suspect that in A.O.H. halls there was 'drinking and dancing till the small hours of the morning', but in Carrickmore and elsewhere, he charged, Hibernians used boycotting, waylaying and beating to compel people to join the Order. Therefore, Logue announced, he would forbid his priests to give absolution to persons who attempted to coerce anyone to join the A.O.H., and if this remedy did not end such practices he would excommunicate all Hibernians in his diocese. At the Armagh A.O.H. County Board meeting in June some delegates suggested a deputation to wait upon Logue in reference to his action, but the suggestion was not adopted.[48] At about this time Father McKinley, whose presence at meetings had in many cases been the Order's sole claim to ecclesiastical respectability, resigned the National Chaplaincy of the society. The police believed that the resignation had been ordered by Father McKinley's bishop, John Tohill (who had succeeded Bishop Henry in the see of Down and Connor) in response to Logue's denunciation of the A.O.H.[49] Though the police analysis has the appearance of conjecture, the replacement of McKinley with Bishop O'Donnell's own administrator, Father J. Cannon,[50] does suggest that outside the diocese of Raphoe all traces of ecclesiastical sanction were being withdrawn. Nevertheless, the Order prospered. Unlike McEvilly, who had been able to respond skilfully to the challenge of the U.I.L. in Connacht a decade earlier, Logue failed to lead the bishops and clergy of his province to a constructive policy toward the Ancient Order of Hibernians.

Although perhaps the Cardinal did not think of the Order primarily as a component of the party's political machine, his attitude toward it did deepen the rift between himself and the party. So also did his deep suspicion of the Liberal alliance because of Liberal sponsorship of secularist legislation for the English schools. Such suspicions had little or no part in Walsh's attitude (though the latter came to dislike the alliance on nationalist rather than Catholic grounds), but they were uppermost in the attitude of O'Dwyer. The Bishop of Limerick was so obsessed with the maintenance of Catholic claims in education that he was unwilling to distinguish between the Irish Church's direct interests—which in fact the Liberals had been surprisingly willing to respect—and the interests of the Catholic Church in England to which most Irish bishops were content to pay little more than lip service. He clung tenaciously to the opinion that the university settlement, even though it satisfied his colleagues, must be some sort of Nonconformist plot simply because it was sponsored by Birrell. Perhaps the fact that he was hard of hearing increased the difficulties of anyone, cleric or layman, who tried to soften the conclusions he relentlessly drew from the printed page. He professed, however, to be a sincere nationalist, and the secularist drift of England only increased his desire for Home Rule, though it did not allay his distrust of the Irish Party. This fact distinguished him from the one other member of the hierarchy, Archbishop Healy, who along with himself, Logue and Walsh was alienated from the party. Unlike the party's other episcopal detractors, Healy, despite fairly advanced views on the land question, had never made any pretence of being a Home Ruler. His endorsement of the party in 1905 had been grudging and perfunctory, and he even told a congregation in 1909 that some of them were not yet 'fit for Home Rule'.[51]

By 1909, therefore, the older generation of the Nation's leadership was in trouble with four prelates—Walsh, Logue, Healy and O'Dwyer. Only one, Healy, even tacitly denied the political claims of the Nation itself, though perhaps Logue was not wildly enthusiastic for Home Rule either. Only one, O'Dwyer, seems to have made any public gesture of support for the succession of the younger generation to national leadership,[52] though Walsh did maintain fairly good channels of communication with the younger leaders. No bishop was attracted to the only alternative leadership within the older generation—O'Brien—though T. M. Healy hoped to woo some of his clerical friends into the camp of his new ally. The average bishop was content to continue endorsing the party, if requested, much as he might endorse the products of a manufacturer of vestments or stained glass. Most churchmen, in supporting the party were essentially simply staying within the convention established in the 1880s of sanctioning the legitimacy of the Nation's claim so long as the Nation's spokesmen abjured revolutionary methods and defended the Church's educational claims. Few of them yet stopped to consider alternative spokesmen.

At the other end of the spectrum from the party's detractors, Bishop O'Donnell remained actively involved in the party's affairs and was described by Birrell as 'frankly a Nationalist politician with a tinge of enthusiasm in his nature'.[53] Dillon was recognising O'Donnell's close identification with the party when he wrote to Redmond that if they allowed a party member and O'Donnell to serve on a Commission to inquire into the C. D. B., they would 'be bound by its report'.[54] Moreover, the Bishop of Raphoe became quite alienated from the younger generation of potential national leadership. Though he was a consistent proponent of the Irish Language revival, as early as 1906 there was serious friction between O'Donnell and his clergy on the one hand and the Gaelic League on the other. The immediate cause for this bad feeling was the fact that League efforts to raise funds for a training school in Irish were conflicting with O'Donnell's campaign for funds for his almost completed diocesan seminary, St Eunan's College.[55] When he climaxed this campaign with a Gaelic Festival, which he called Aonach an Dúin, and which ran for ten days in Letterkenny,[56] prominent Gaelic Leaguers seem to have been notable by their absence.[57] Indeed, at about this time O'Donnell established his own training college for teachers of Irish, the College of the Four Masters, and in succeeding years it was charged that Gaelic League leaders in Dublin tried to suppress news about the college and connived to get it into trouble with the National Education Board.[58]

During the essential Irish controversy, some language enthusiasts easily persuaded themselves that O'Donnell was their prime enemy within the hierarchy. Patrick O'Daly, the General Secretary of the Gaelic League, told a meeting at Edenderry, King's County, that St Adamnán, 'a great church-

9

man from Donegal', had made perhaps the first attack upon the language by calling it 'the harsh and barbarous Irish tongue'. 'History had a curious knack of repeating itself,' O'Daly continued. 'It was said that a great deal of the present opposition to Irish hailed also from the meridian of Donegal.'[59] One moderate Gaelic Leaguer reported to Mac Néill in June that a League organiser in Co. Donegal had gone out of his way to antagonise O'Donnell and his clergy by bringing two notorious anticlericals into the diocese 'not to get weight for Comp. Irish demand with the Senate, but merely to contradict them [—] the Bishops and priests—to shake a fist at them in their own territory without any expectation of helping a decision of the question'.[60] Small wonder, then, that the Bishop of Raphoe organised his own local version of the Gaelic League, called Crann Eithne, a few months later.[61] Whether O'Donnell's antagonism to the Gaelic League organisation (though not to its stated aims) was complementary in his own mind with his active involvement with the Irish Party organisation is not clear. It should not be surprising, however, if some members of the younger generation drew such a conclusion, especially after Dillon placed the Irish Party in opposition to compulsory Irish in the university. In trying to account for the bishops' decision, after some hesitation, to reject Col. Maurice Moore's overtures in June 1909, Father O'Hickey wrote: 'The Bishop of Raphoe is no doubt a disturbing element, his motives being political; and behind him and inspiring is Mr. Dillon M.P.'[62]

The only other prelate who was as deeply involved as O'Donnell in the party's affairs was Denis Kelly, Bishop of Ross. Prior to the 1906 election he had unashamedly worked as a sort of party organiser in the heart of O'Brien's stronghold.[63] The administrative duties of his tiny south-western diocese cannot have been onerous, and he had made himself the hierarchy's expert on matters of public finance. Probably both this fact and the fact that he was on good terms with the Irish Party leaders contributed to his appointment in 1906 to fill a vacancy on a Royal Commission set up in the last days of Balfour's administration to study the Poor Laws and other means for the relief of distress throughout the three kingdoms. Early in 1909 the Commission issued its voluminous report together with the celebrated minority report of Beatrice Webb and three other commissioners who presented, roughly, the Fabian socialist view. It was a propitious time to bring forward major social reform proposals. With the 1908 cabinet reshuffle, the government acquired a more radical thrust which had already resulted in a modest but significant scheme of old age pensions. The government was making a new departure, leaving behind its preoccupation 'with the troubles of the dissenting schoolmaster or preacher, or with those of the temperance reformer and frugal manufacturer' and turning to 'the unemployed artisan, the casual labourer, the sweated or infirm worker, the worker's widow, the underfed child, the untrained, undisciplined and exploited boy labourer'.[64] Naturally, a decrease in government attention to Nonconformist grievances could be expected to allay some of the anxieties of Irish Catholic churchmen, but whether the 'new liberalism' might capture their enthusiasm was another question.

The Poor Law Commission reports are a good place to begin answering this question because the volume of the majority report devoted to Ireland seems to have been the work of Bishop Kelly and one other commissioner, a senior civil servant from Dublin Castle.[65] The majority and minority reports agreed in principle that workers in England and Wales should be protected against unemployment by some form of unemployment insurance[66] together with a system of labour exchanges which would help match unemployed workers with available jobs in their own communities or elsewhere. The minority argued that the programme ought to be applied to Ireland as well, but the majority went along with the Irish commissioners' opinion that such measures as labour exchanges and unemployment insurance, recommended for dealing with unemployment in Great Britain, did not seem 'adapted to the conditions of Ireland, which is almost exclusively an agricultural country'.[67] Therefore, they should not be applied to Ireland, at least until they had been tested in Great Britain. The minority retorted that the unemployment problem in the larger towns of Ireland was little different from that in Great Britain and that in the poorer agricultural districts such as Connacht and Donegal recurrent crop failures caused periodic distress virtually identical to periodic industrial unemployment in its effects. They were unable to see that 'the urgent need of grappling with the whole problem is any less in Ireland than in Great Britain'.[68] It is hard to escape the logic of the radical minority's argument. What could be more sensible than a system whereby, when the crops failed in West Mayo, a destitute young man might go to a labour exchange in Castlebar and be told that there was a labour shortage in, say, Sheffield, and be given assistance to migrate there and find a job when he arrived. Churchill, who had been in communication with the Webbs before the reports were published,[69] was already drafting a Labour Exchanges Bill which, sensibly, applied to the entire United Kingdom, and it was enacted during the 1909 session. Bishop Kelly's suspicion of such a scheme represented a fundamental divergence between the ideals of the Irish clergy and those of the new liberalism. It was clear from clerical discussions at the time of the land agitation a few years earlier[70] that what most Irish churchmen wanted for the young man in West Mayo was some method of keeping him in West Mayo. Any enticement which might lure him to Sheffield would, they feared, place his faith and morals in grave jeopardy. Still, this kind of consideration was more an ideal of many churchmen than one of their direct interests.

Some Irish churchmen, in common with the well-to-do classes throughout the United Kingdom, did perceive a threat to their interests in another government measure in 1909. Both to pay for new programmes such as the pension scheme of the preceding year and the naval building programme being demanded by public clamour, and to precipitate a crisis with the House of Lords, which had continued to frustrate the wishes of the Commons majority on a number of issues, Lloyd George, the new Chancellor of the Exchequer, brought forward his famous 'People's Budget'. The budget infuriated the propertied classes by introducing, at quite modest levels, the principles of a graduated income tax and a tax on the unearned increment of land values. Moreover, death duties and tobacco taxes were to be raised along with liquor taxes and liquor licence duties. These last proposals looked very much like retribution upon the liquor interests for having

recently rallied the House of Lords to their cause to reject a
government measure for tightening up restrictions on the
granting of liquor licenses. Unfortunately, although the
British liquor trade was allied to the Conservative Party, the
Irish liquor trade was allied to the Irish Party. The Irish
Party's alliance with the Liberals suddenly offended one
more important body of its supporters. In addition, land
taxation was not a pleasant thought for peasants who were
being converted into proprietors. Most important, however,
William Martin Murphy, whose economic interests were
little different from those of a wealthy English businessman
and whose friendship with Healy gave him an incentive to
embarrass the Irish Party at every opportunity, launched a
concerted attack on the budget in the columns of his *Irish
Independent*, which was rapidly becoming the dominant
Catholic paper in Ireland. Soon Irish public opinion was
convinced that the budget embodied some sort of plot to
wreck the Irish brewing and distilling industries and to
overtax the average Irishman into the workhouse. The party
gained small comfort in its difficulties from the members of
the hierarchy who spoke out. Bishop Boylan of Kilmore, in a
letter to the Cavan Urban District Council urging unity
behind the party, described the proposed taxation as 'oppressive',[71] and some months later Bishop Foley went so far as to
charge that the burden of taxation proposed by the budget
would make it 'extremely difficult for the people to subsist'.[72]
Cardinal Logue told an audience at Derry that 'England had
not only robbed us, but continued to rob us, and the heaviest
hand laid on for years was laid on us at present, and by a
party about which we were all so enthusiastic—the grand old
Liberal Party of England.'[73] The Cardinal predicted that as
a result of the budget 'a number of traders in the country
will be stopped (*hear, hear*)'. He expressed concern about the
fate of barley-growing in his archdiocese, and with the kind
of silliness which informed Tory criticism of the budget, he
worried that snuff might be priced out of the range of his
own pocketbook. Echoing the popular Irish opinion, he
charged: 'All this has been done to the Irishman, while
nothing has been put on the Englishman, except perhaps in
the case of tobacco.'

In general, the Church's attitude toward the reforms of the new liberalism was not yet defined. The Pension Bill seems to have drawn little clerical comment, though as early as 1903 Walsh had suggested such a plan.[74] The Labour Exchanges Bill conflicted with clerical ideals but drew no notable ecclesiastical opposition apart from Bishop Kelly's demur before the fact. The budget ran counter to the interests of individual bishops in their capacities as comparatively well-off Irishmen, and a few of them added their voices to W. M. Murphy's campaign to persuade the Irish public that it somehow ran counter to their country's interests as well. As yet, however, the new liberalism had produced no apparent threat to the vital interests of the Church as an institution. Such a threat would arrive in due course, but it would be delayed and the Church's response would be muted by the momentous events about to transform the whole nexus of Anglo-Irish relations.

Redmond had condemned the whiskey and tobacco proposals on budget night, and the party voted against both first and second readings of the budget. Good relations with the Liberals were of vital importance if the party was to be able to take advantage of the unprecedented constitutional crisis which would be precipitated if the Lords rejected the budget. Redmond tried vainly to secure amendments which would blunt criticism of the Liberal alliance on this issue at home.[75] By the time the bill came up for a third reading, in November, the impending confrontation between the two chambers —which might result in abolition of the Lords' power to veto Home Rule—was a much more credible possibility, and the party abstained rather than vote against the government. When Redmond tried to defend his attitude toward the budget on the ground that the increased taxation for Ireland was more than compensated by the benefits which the Liberal government had conferred on Ireland, Archbishop Walsh wrote a very sarcastic public letter—described by T. M. Healy as 'a nasty pill for Redmond'—attacking the party leader's use of the university grant as evidence to support his thesis.[76] This nasty pill had no ill effects, however, for within a week the House of Lords had, in violation of constitutional precedent 250 years old, rejected the budget. Parliament was dissolved, and when a new parliament assembled, Redmond would be its master.

On the eve of this great transformation of Anglo-Irish relations, the bonds of the Irish political system had become rarefied in a way which diminished perceptibly the Church's range of political action. Let us review how that system operated. Its dynamic element was the assumption that the Nation would ultimately displace the State in Ireland; but after a decade of Unionist rule and more than three years in which the supposed friends of Home Rule in the Liberal Party had produced nothing better than the Irish Council Bill that assumption had never been less convincing. The disheartening spectacle of the Nationalist Convention in February 1909 was a symptom of this fact. The system had two sets of conventions governing the Church's relations with the State and the Nation respectively. The Church sanctioned the State's present legitimacy in return for concessions to her own claims mainly in the realm of education; yet after the Universities Act of 1908 and Birrell's relaxation of financial pressure for reform the Church had few such claims to press. The Church also sanctioned the future legitimacy of the Nation in return for renunciation of revolutionary methods and protection of her educational interests on the part of the Nation's representatives; yet in 1909 revolutionary nationalism seemed at its lowest ebb, and the waning cattle-driving campaign was even less of a threat to public order than the U.I.L. agitation a decade earlier had been. This fact, together with the party's remarkably faithful obedience to clerical directives regarding Irish education (though not English education, which was outside the system, whatever a maverick like O'Dwyer might say), made this sanction too inflexible to have political utility. Finally, the system reinforced a natural tendency in Irish history for the Nation's leadership to remain in the hands of one group for the span of a single generation, about thirty years, and then to change hands abruptly. Such a change, but for the spectacular events of January 1910, ought now to be almost at hand.

At such a time the Church should hope to be on good terms with the younger generation, whose day could not long be delayed. For the moment the Church seemed estranged from the younger generation through the essential Irish controversy. This estrangement, however, was more apparent than real, and the real causes of the weakness of the Church in influencing political events in the next few years were the other conditions of the Irish political system which I have just described. Only one of these conditions—the credibility of the assumption that the Nation would supplant the State—would be changed markedly in 1910. The others would change spectacularly in the next few years.

CHAPTER XII

Redmond Imperator

IF the gentlemanly division of English politics into Liberal
and Conservative had pertained in Ireland, the Liberals
would have been trounced from Clonakilty to Coleraine.
Lloyd George's budget struck few responsive chords in Ireland. However, few Irish electors ever had an opportunity to
register an opinion on the great issues which divided Conservatives and Liberals except as those issues filtered through the
peculiar polarisation of Irish politics into Unionist and Nationalist. If the budget were to become the occasion for restricting the veto of the Lords on general legislation, then the
matter would be relevant to that principal concern of Irish
politics, Home Rule, for the Lords' veto was the insurmount-
able barrier which had hitherto made discussion of Home
Rule largely academic. Would the enactment of the 'People's
Budget' and the restriction of the peers' powers, for which
the Liberals now asked a popular mandate, be followed by
the introduction of a Home Rule Bill? Asquith was equivocal. The present parliament, he told an Albert Hall audience
on 10 December 1909, had been 'disabled in advance' from
proposing what he regarded as the only real solution to the
Irish question, viz., 'a policy which, while explicitly safeguarding the supremacy and indefectible authority of the
Imperial Parliament, will set up in Ireland a system of full
self-government in regard to purely Irish affairs'. Choosing
his words very carefully, he declared that 'In the new House
of Commons the hands of a Liberal Government and of a
Liberal majority will, in this matter, be entirely free.'[1] Although this was not an ironclad commitment to Home Rule,
it was the closest any responsible minister had come to such
a commitment for seventeen years, and for most Irish voters

it outweighed the distasteful features of the budget.

In Ireland the Irish Parliamentary Party faced, for the first time, in a general election, the united opposition of O'Brien and Healy, acting together. O'Brien had been making concerted efforts since the land settlement of 1903 to shed the public image of a left-wing agitator and to assume the role of the great conciliator among the classes and creeds of Ireland. After the brief reunion of his own and Healy's forces with the main Nationalist body in 1908—a reunion which had virtually come to an end at the 1909 Nationalist Convention—O'Brien began to prepare for a fight with the party under the banner of a new organisation which he dubbed, quaintly, the All-for-Ireland League. This new League's programme consisted of several rather incongruous points: (1) extension of the conciliatory spirit of the Land Conference to the larger problem of Irish self-government; (2) distrust of the party's alliance with the Liberals and specific opposition to Lloyd George's budget and Birrell's 1909 revision of the land settlement; and (3) hostility to the Ancient Order of Hibernians.

The coalition which O'Brien built upon this platform consisted of himself, Healy, and their parliamentary hangers-on, together with a handful of Southern Protestants such as Lord Dunraven and Moreton Frewen. For electoral support the new League depended almost entirely upon O'Brien's personal following among the farmers and labourers in Co. Cork. O'Brien attempted unsuccessfully to enlist the Sinn Féin organisation in his new movement. In later years he tried to create the impression that since he had gained the support of a few members of the Protestant gentry and commercial classes of Munster, the All-for-Ireland League could somehow have attracted Northern Protestants to the Nationalist side and prevented partition. In 1910, however, he realistically made little effort to win the affections of the Ulster Protestants.

One group he did hope to win over to his new movement, on the other hand, was the Catholic clergy. His new daily paper, the *Cork Accent*, referred to A.O.H. branches as 'Ribbon Lodges', with the tacit implication that the ecclesiastical ban on secret societies applied to them. Logue's de-

nunciation of the Order some months earlier was reprinted
and discussed under the heading 'The Cardinal on the
Mollies'.[2] Prominent coverage was given to clerical attacks
upon the Liberal alliance and upon the Irish Party's attitude
toward Healy.[3] The *Cork Accent* maintained that Asquith
had not pledged to introduce Home Rule, but had pledged
to revive the Education Bill, 'which the Catholic Bishops
declare with one voice would be fatal to their schools'.[4] Campaign efforts by Redmond in Manchester, O'Brien's mouthpiece argued, were intended to counteract a recent manifesto
by the English hierarchy declaring 'that for Catholics the
supreme question is the maintenance of their schools'.[5]
Though the party was certainly vulnerable on these points,
O'Brien was scarcely the man to capitalise on them. Earlier
in his career, he had defied ecclesiastical authority at least
as blatantly as the A.O.H. did now, and, at all events, his
principal line of attack against the Order was to fault it as
anti-Protestant, which was scarcely the reason for Cardinal
Logue's denunciation of it. Moreover, O'Brien's record on
the education question was far from spotless from a clerical
point of view; he had been blamed in 1902 for the party's
abstention during debates on Balfour's Education Bill.
O'Brien was simply disqualified by past indiscretions from
becoming a rallying-point for ecclesiastical forces. No doubt
he hoped that his new-found ally, Healy, would keep the
clerics happy while he busied himself with Cork artisans,
former landlords and evicted tenants. The events of 1910
were to prove that Healy was unable to fulfil his assignment.

In nineteen Irish seats the party candidates faced opponents
styling themselves Nationalists. Though not all these dissidents adhered to the A.F.I.L., the *Cork Accent* was willing
to claim as an ally almost any Nationalist enemy of Redmond
and Dillon. Twelve of the contests were in the Munster
counties of Cork, Kerry, Limerick and Waterford, where
O'Brien's personal influence was strongest. Throughout this
region O'Brien could nearly always find a few priests who
would support his candidates, and, with few exceptions, the
clergy seem to have been free to express their convictions.
Nevertheless, in most divisions the O'Brienites failed to win
the concerted support of the clergy as a body. In the two-

member constituency of Cork City, for example, in which O'Brien himself and Maurice Healy stood in the All-for-Ireland interest, it became clear very early in the campaign that the influential clergy of the cathedral parish were united behind the Irish Party candidates.[6] O'Brien's clerical support was virtually limited to two curates, Father Barrett and Father O'Flynn, whose names were frequently invoked on his behalf.[7] Similarly in Mid-Cork, North Cork, West Waterford, Limerick City and North Kerry the clergy were substantially united behind the official Irish Party candidates.[8] In East Kerry the clergy seem to have remained aloof from a contest which was provoked more by the traditional hostility between O'Sullivans and Murphys than by national issues.[9] In three constituencies—South-East Cork, West Cork and North-East Cork—the clergy were so badly divided between the O'Brienite and Irish Party candidates that one cannot speak of a consistent ecclesiastical policy.[10] In only one Munster constituency, East Limerick, was there an organised, clerically led revolt against the party organisation reminiscent of the 1900 general election. Several priests and laymen walked out of the official party convention, protesting that it had been rigged, and held their own convention which nominated an O'Brienite.[11] Even here, however, there was no clerical unity, for, though ten priests attended the O'Brienite convention, eight priests signed the nomination papers of the party candidate.[12] The constituency was divided between O'Dwyer's diocese of Limerick and the archdiocese of Cashel, and the *Cork Accent* indicated, significantly, that the clerical opponents of the party candidate were concentrated in Limerick diocese.[13] In the event, the party won this seat (though by a very narrow margin) as well as all the other Munster contests outside Co. Cork except the O'Sullivan-Murphy battle in East Kerry. Within Co. Cork the O'Brienites won every seat which they contested except for one of the two Cork City seats. O'Brien himself obtained two seats and resigned one of them in favour of Maurice Healy, who had stood third in the Cork City poll.

In most cases, whatever attraction O'Brienism had for the clergy was founded more on personalities than on policy, as is illustrated by the contests outside Munster. In North

Mayo there remained bitter memories of the 1900 election
in which Conor O'Kelly, the United Irish League candidate,
roundly defeated William Martin Murphy, the Healyite
candidate, who enjoyed the organised support of the Bishop
and clergy of Killala diocese—the only Connacht diocese
whose clergy had resolutely refused to come to terms with
the U.I.L. at that time. O'Kelly continued to be offensive to
the clergy, who, in December 1909 brought a U.I.L. organiser, Dermot O'Brien, into the constituency and began to
groom him as an opponent to O'Kelly. Redmond was asked
to intervene, both candidates withdrew, and the party leader
named Alderman Daniel Boyle of Manchester as the official
candidate. The clergy loyally supported this compromise,
though another candidate, Bernard Egan, contested the seat
as an Independent Nationalist and came within forty votes
of defeating Boyle. One of Egan's supporters was Dermot
O'Brien, who no doubt felt cheated when he learned that
another part of the bargain was that Conor O'Kelly was to
be adopted as the official party candidate to oppose John
O'Donnell in South Mayo.

O'Donnell and O'Kelly had both started in politics as
protégés of William O'Brien in the early organisational activity of the U.I.L. in Mayo during 1898–1900, but while
O'Kelly was remaining loyal to the party despite O'Brien's
defection, O'Donnell had recently announced his intention
of standing for re-election in his South Mayo constituency
as an O'Brienite. Thereupon his constituents, lay and clerical,
had begun to seek a suitable candidate to oppose him in the
Irish Party interest. Although Redmond's arrangement in
North Mayo was successful, its effects upon South Mayo were
disastrous. O'Kelly already had an anticlerical reputation in
the latter constituency, for as a county councillor for Mayo
he had come into open conflict with Archdeacon Kilkenny of
Claremorris in a dispute which has been recorded in colourful detail in W. P. Ryan's *The Pope's Green Island*.[14] Moreover, his speech accepting the nomination in South Mayo was
unnecessarily abusive toward the clergy. The Church's forces
were therefore thrown to O'Donnell, toward whom the clergy
had hitherto shown no particular attraction. In consequence
the O'Brienite won by 2,667 votes to 2,226, and on the day

following the declaration of the poll Archdeacon Kilkenny's sodality clubhouse in Claremorris was set on fire. A wave of strife between clerical and anticlerical partisans was set off.[15] The clergy extracted a pledge analogous to the party pledge from O'Donnell and tried to persuade Redmond to have him readmitted to the party. They made it clear, however, that their main desire was not to buttress O'Donnell's position, but simply to have Conor O'Kelly renounced by the party. Father James Stephens of Ballinrobe assured Redmond that if O'Donnell 'is not faithful to the Party and faithfully uphold [*sic*] the policy of the Party the remedy is not far to seek —and South Mayo would send you in his stead any man of your choice—*but one*'.[16] Early in April an arrangement was worked out by which the party would withdraw all moral and financial support from Conor O'Kelly without, apparently, committing itself to support O'Donnell. The clergy were happy with this arrangement,[17] and in the December election O'Donnell, realistically, did not contest the seat against the party nominee, a Mr Fitzgibbon.

The South Mayo election is significant, for it illustrates how little appeal O'Brienism made to the clergy outside the area where he had real popular support. Only when the party offered an extremely offensive candidate did the South Mayo clergy throw their support to an O'Brienite candidate. As one horrified priest explained to Redmond, this was done

not against the Party, but against a species of Atheism worse than that which obtains in France. Our Vindication came but too soon in the rushing of the House of God at the time of Mass and the arson of the Reading Room of the Sodality of the Sacred Heart and the burning of the statues of the Sacred Heart and of the Blessed Virgin Mary at Claremorris—profanation without parallel in elections all over the civilized world.[18]

Nevertheless, even in the face of such sacrilege as the party's followers had committed, the clergy were prepared to make generous terms with the party to the disadvantage of O'Brienism.

In the East and North-east, where Healyism had once been strong, the party undertook to displace four recalcitrant sitting members: Healy himself in North Louth, Laurence Ginnell in North Westmeath, John McKean in South

Monaghan and G. Murnaghan in Mid-Tyrone. In two of
these contests the clergy were split and no consistent ecclesiastical policy was evident. In South Monaghan, McKean was
a personal friend of Archdeacon McGlone who worked on
his behalf, but Canon O'Connor and a number of curates
were active on behalf of C. Laverty, the party candidate,
who nevertheless lost by 2,611 to 1,903.[19] In North Westmeath Ginnell may have profited slightly from the local
clerical distrust of the party organisation, which in 1900 had
worked to his own disadvantage. Only one clergyman attended the party convention which nominated an opponent
to Ginnell. On the other hand Ginnell was known mainly
for having promoted the widespread use of cattle-driving as
a means of protest against graziers, and Father Murphy, P.P.,
speaking at an Irish Party meeting at Multyfarnham, said of
this policy: 'No clergyman could approve of these doctrines,
not merely landlords but tenants they were attacking.'[20] At
least two clergymen, undeterred by this argument, signed
Ginnell's nomination papers, and he won by 1,996 votes to
1,379.[21] The existence in South Monaghan of a strong Unionist minority which may have deliberately voted for the candidate disliked by the national organisation might account
for McKean's victory. Ginnell on the other hand was able
to stand alone against the party because of his very considerable local popularity in a district where extensive grazing farms offered ample opportunity for the talents of a
skilled agitator.

Murnaghan, who had sat for Mid-Tyrone since 1895, had
been identified with Healyism early in his parliamentary
career[22] but had been left undisturbed by the U.I.L. in 1900
and 1906, presumably because the constituency contained a
strong Unionist minority eager to take advantage of any split
in the Nationalist vote. When it became clear at the convention for the January 1910 election that a Mr Valentine
would be nominated, the clergy and other supporters of
Murnaghan withdrew and placed the sitting member's name
in nomination in defiance of the convention.[23] Predictably, a
Conservative candidate was nominated and captured the seat
because of the Nationalist split.[24]

Once again the division which attracted the most attention was North Louth where the party put forward R. Hazelton, M.P. for North Galway, as an opponent to T. M. Healy. Though most of the clergy of the division were staunch supporters of Healy, a few priests openly associated themselves with the attempt to unseat him.[25] At a public meeting in support of Hazelton on 2 January, the Rev. M. J. Quin, Adm., Dundalk, who presided, announced that he wanted to correct a possible misconception which might arise from his presence. It would be, he stated, 'most unfair and most unjust' to associate Cardinal Logue with his own presence at the meeting. 'It would be most painful to me to have the venerated and honoured name of our beloved Cardinal through me, dragged into this contest (*hear, hear*).' The Cardinal had, according to Father Quin, given his priests 'the fullest liberty to take whatever side they please (*loud cheers*)'.[26] When Healy's local organ, the *Dundalk Examiner*, claimed Logue's support for Healy and attacked the Dundalk clergy as having set themselves in opposition to the Primate, Hazelton retorted by citing Father Quin's statement that Logue had left his clergy free to support either candidate. 'In the absence of Direct Evidence from the Cardinal himself', Hazelton asked the voters to consider the *Examiner*'s statement false, and he claimed that 'In common with the Bishops of Ireland, his Eminence is in sympathy with the Irish Party (*cheers*).'[27] This allegation was enough to give His Eminence second thoughts about his policy of aloofness from the contest, and within a few days he provided one of Healy's friends with a letter stating that he would 'endeavour to be in Dundalk on Thursday . . . to vote for Mr. Healy'. He added: 'You can make any public use of this fact which you find necessary for the purpose of contradicting rumours or allegations to the contrary.'[28] This latter suggestion was, needless to say, enthusiastically adopted by Healy, who also produced a telegram from Archbishop Walsh congratulating him upon a successful suit to enjoin a certain Irish Party M.P. against publishing an allegation that he (Healy) had taken fees from a landlord to oppose the restoration of an evicted tenant.[29] With the public support of both Primates, Healy narrowly defeated his opponent by 2,432 votes to 2,333 and received another congratulatory telegram from Walsh.[30]

The eighty-two Nationalists who were returned to West-minster included only seventy-one who formally acknowl-edged Redmond's leadership, most of the other eleven being aligned with O'Brien openly or privately. The O'Brienite defection, however, did not weaken Redmond's hand, for the Unionists returned with 273 seats and the Liberals were reduced to 275. Even with the support of the forty Labour members, Asquith could only govern with Redmond's con-sent. The issue upon which that consent would be granted or withheld was, for the moment, not Home Rule, but the question of the House of Lords. Liberal ardour for a direct clash with the Upper House had been dampened considerably by the discouraging election results. Moreover, the willing-ness of the King to co-operate in the wholesale creation of peerages which might be necessary to effect reform was in doubt, and the Lords themselves were beginning to exhibit signs of repentance for their unprecedented behaviour. Asquith vacillated over whether legislation to restrict the Lords' veto powers would necessarily follow enactment of the budget which was so cordially disliked in Ireland. Redmond insisted that Irish support for the budget would be forth-coming only upon receipt of guarantees that the government would also bring forward a measure to reform the Lords. After two months of indecision, the cabinet yielded, and Asquith brought in a series of resolutions and a bill (1) to abolish the Lords' veto over money bills, (2) to permit other legislation to become law without the Lords' consent if passed by the Commons in three consecutive sessions, and (3) to require a dissolution at least every five years. With the Parliament Bill before the House, Redmond could and did safely lead his party into the government lobby a few days later to enact the famous budget, while the Healy-O'Brien connection voted with the Conservatives. This time the Con-servatives acquiesced in the budget and parliament adjour-ned for Easter. During the recess, the King died suddenly on 6 May, and all the politicians' careful calculations were thrown into disarray.

During these early months of 1910 the party had prevailed upon some of the bishops, including O'Dea (Galway), Kelly (Ross), Mangan (Kerry), Browne (Cloyne), Sheehan (Waterford), Clancy (Elphin), and McHugh (Derry), to double their usual subscriptions to the Parliamentary Fund as a gesture of renewed confidence.[31] No doubt the gesture augmented Redmond's prestige, but the fact that not even all the bishops who ordinarily contributed made the gesture is evidence that the hierarchy was not extraordinarily enthusiastic. T. M. Healy wrote to O'Brien in May that recently when one of Logue's canons remarked 'that the Bishops were supporting the Party & doubled their Subscriptions', the Cardinal had retorted, ' "Only 9 out of 28" (or whatever the total number is)'.[32] O'Brien and Healy hoped to capitalise upon Logue's dissatisfaction with the party to gain a broader basis of clerical support for the All-for-Ireland League, but Logue persistently refused to give concrete expression to his opposition to the party beyond extending his personal protection to Healy. A letter from O'Brien to Healy in the middle of March suggests that overtures were made to the Cardinal urging him to sanction O'Brien's plans to extend his League into Ulster and that the Cardinal declined on the grounds that co-operation between Catholics and Protestants was not a very realistic political programme in the North.[33] No doubt Logue remained suspicious of O'Brien and realised as well that the Church could only suffer from backing a rival party (as opposed to an individual dissident) at a time when the Irish Party was riding the crest of the wave. Early in May Healy wrote to his brother: 'The Cardinal has been expressing himself against O'Brien's League again, and wrote me against it.'[34] Healy tried to gain Logue's support for the new alliance, but the Cardinal, he reported to O'Brien, was 'so scrupulous' that he had deliberately promoted Father Quin, who had strenuously opposed Healy in the January election, and was about to fill Father Quin's place as Administrator of Dundalk with another of Healy's enemies. 'So you cant expect he will do anything with a merely political motive,' Healy concluded.[35]

Although Healy was plainly pessimistic over gaining more active support from the Cardinal, he and O'Brien did hope that the A.O.H., which they dubbed 'the Molly Maguires' and which was now beginning to displace the U.I.L. as the basic party organisation in parts of the South as well as in

Ulster, would precipitate a clerical reaction against the party. In the letter just quoted, Healy said of plans for a great nationalist demonstration at the primatial city: 'Devlins going to Armagh next Sunday to parade the Mollies under his [Logue's] Cathedral, is of course to intimidate, but will only have the opposite effect.' The demonstration—at which Healy was burned in effigy—was no doubt disconcerting to the Cardinal, but, far from making an issue of it, he gave permission to the organisers to hold the demonstration on his Cathedral grounds. Though clergy seem to have been notable by their absence from the affair, the meeting could be called anticlerical only on the assumption that attacks upon Healy were aimed at his clerical supporters.[36] So far, though the Healy-O'Brien alliance was common knowledge, Healy had not formally acknowledged his connection with the All-for-Ireland League. In the autumn, however, Healy decided to join O'Brien's forces openly at a meeting at Dungarvan. Logue could not overcome his aversion to O'Brien and urged Healy to remain aloof and 'fight a "lone hand" in Parliament'. Healy chose to ignore Logue's advice.[37]

The accession of the new King, George V, had produced a brief pause in the extraordinarily bitter constitutional struggle between the two Houses, and in June the King convened a constitutional conference at which it was hoped that four representatives from each of the two principal English parties could agree privately upon some settlement of the House of Lords issue. The conference dragged on for nearly five months before its members decided on 10 November to announce publicly that they had reached a deadlock. The cabinet decided to call another general election at which the voters would determine the fate of the Upper House.

Cardinal Logue, too, had made a decision. On 22 November he called a conference of his clergy in Dundalk and expressly forbade all his priests from interfering in the forthcoming North Louth election by going on any platform in support of a candidate, by writing to the press or by canvassing.[38] The party again sent Richard Hazelton to oppose Healy, and though the Cardinal's ban was strictly observed, each candidate ostentatiously visited his clerical sympathisers while campaigning in their respective parishes.[39] Deprived of the Cardinal's public blessing, Healy was defeated by 2,509 votes to 2,021. Although, he succeeded in unseating Hazelton by lodging a petition charging his opponent with intimidation and bribery, Healy made no attempt to stand against the candidate which the party offered in Hazelton's place. Realising that without the Cardinal's patronage North Louth was hopeless for him, he took refuge in a safe Cork seat provided for him by O'Brien.[40]

In Cork O'Brien consolidated his position, holding all the seats won in January and picking up two which had previously been held by the party. The Church's forces, however, were mobilised even more thoroughly against him this time. Bishop Kelly of Ross signed the nomination papers for the Irish Party candidate in South Cork, and Bishop Browne of Cloyne made the same gesture for Captain Donelan, the Protestant Nationalist M.P. for East Cork, the only division in the county which O'Brien's forces never captured. O'Brien felt as if he were under siege from clerical forces, and began exhibiting the anticlerical side of his personality rather more openly than he had done in January. When Father O'Flynn, one of his clerical supporters, was prevented from attending one of his meetings in Cork City because the local parish priest refused to grant permission, O'Brien denounced the 'one-sided Penal Code' which allowed such action—hardly a politic way to describe legislation of the National Synod.[41] At the end of the election, the leader-writer for O'Brien's organ, the *Cork Free Press* (which had replaced the *Cork Accent*), wrote bitterly: 'We have to deal with a confederacy of the priests of this county to strangle the All-for-Ireland League and to strike down its standard-bearers.'[42] The writer might have added that outside the county, as well, the All-for-Ireland League candidates in fourteen constituencies received only scattered clerical backing. In general, when the clergy acted in any concerted fashion, they did so on the Irish Party side.[43] In South Mayo, John O'Donnell did not try to retain his seat. In East Kerry, the O'Sullivans returned to the party fold. No opposition was offered to the two non-aligned independents of the North-east, Ginnell in North Westmeath and McKean in South Monaghan, but according to rumour McKean had made an arrangement whereby he would be taken into the party after his unopposed return.⁴⁴ O'Brien's party was reduced entirely to a local connection of eight members from Co. Cork.

O'Brien felt cheated by the Church, for he had taken up a position which should have been attractive to clergy. 'In the hour of need', lamented his mouthpiece, the *Cork Free Press*, the Irish Party had 'betrayed' the Catholic schools of England and Wales. The proposed limitations of the Lords' powers, which the party approved, would result in the immediate revival of the 1906 English Education Bill. By its alliance with the Liberals, the party had not only imposed on Ireland 'Mr. Lloyd George's Robber Budget', but had brought about 'such a state of things in England as will ensure at no distant date the triumph of Socialism and Secularism in that country'.⁴⁵ O'Brien had correctly pinpointed the sources of clerical uneasiness with the party, but the shortcomings he cited were not violations of the conventions between Church and Nation. The party could not be charged with any dereliction of its duty to protect the Church's interests in *Irish* education; indeed O'Brien, who continued to sing the praises of the Irish Council Bill, was more vulnerable on that score. Moreover, the party was manifestly a constitutional movement, and it had now demonstrated in two general elections that it possessed the confidence of the people. These considerations outweighed O'Brien's charges against the party in clerical minds, and even if they had not, O'Brien was hardly the man upon whom the Church would confer the mantle of national leadership.

Above all, however, it was now an active, working assumption that the Nation would indeed supplant the State in Ireland, and in the foreseeable future. The second general election of 1910 had produced practically no change in the parliamentary situation: Liberals, 272; Unionists, 271; Labour, 42; Redmondites, 72; O'Brienites, 8; other Nationalists, 2. The millenium had arrived: the Nation's representatives could dictate their terms. Throughout the rest of the period of this study it was reasonable to assume that some form of self-government for at least the major portion of Ireland was now on its way. No hard-headed businessman would have based transactions involving Ireland on any contrary assumption—neither would any bishop.

CHAPTER XIII

Home Rule Politics

WITH the opening of the 1911 session, Asquith proceeded with his Parliament Bill, which the Lords finally accepted in August rather than be swamped by five hundred hastily ennobled Liberals. As the peers' choice, in Lord Selborne's words, was simply whether they should 'perish in the dark, slain by our own hand, or in the light, killed by our enemies',[1] Home Rule and the shape it would take were uppermost in the thoughts of public men in both islands from early in 1911. Some Irish bishops were plainly apprehensive about the Church's position in the new order. Bishop Hoare of Ardagh declared:

There are forces making for secularism in holy Ireland, as well as in Portugal and France, and indeed, in all the countries of Europe. It is the boast of our politicians that they have, Samson-like, pulled down the Gaza of the Lords, and that they are staunch followers of the present Government, because they will win for their country Home Rule. The end and the reward command the sympathy of all of us. But the question is: Are they not as likely, or more likely, to have as their reward Secularism in the Schools?[2]

'As a matter of fact,' he warned, 'we know that a majority of the Bloc looks rather in this direction, and our countrymen who see this with a light heart do not recognise that such secularism would be a greater curse than any we inherited from the Dane or the Norman.' Did Hoare's comments represent widespread clerical fears that the particular politicians who now led the Nation had been so corrupted by Liberalism that they would betray the Church's educational interests?

Indeed, occasional speeches by leading Nationalists designed to allay Liberal fears that Home Rule really would be

'Rome Rule' were clearly making some churchmen anxious.[3] The most deep-seated cause for alarm, however, was not that the current national leaders would wilfully disregard their obligations within the Irish political system. Rather, many clerics feared that two peculiar circumstances—one social and the other economic—which had hitherto made the system work so nicely were now endangered. The social circumstance was the extraordinary devotion of the Irish people to their religion, which enhanced the Church's ability to act as moral arbiter between rival claimants to sovereignty. The economic circumstance was the existence of a reservoir of funds—in particular the British exchequer—which could be drawn upon to support the Church's interests in education without making the Irish taxpayer (or ratepayer) feel the bite directly. Although the generalised anxieties voiced by Hoare in the speech quoted above were no doubt widely, if not deeply, felt, he was closer to the mark in pinpointing the real difficulties the Church might face in his letter forwarding his 1911 subscription (£5) to the Parliamentary Fund. When he expressed his fond hope that 'the coming Home Rule Bill may satisfy our desires', he added, significantly, 'especially in the financial clauses'.[4]

Simultaneously with the emergence of Home Rule into the arena of practical politics, the British Isles were being wracked by a series of strikes whose leaders espoused socialism, and the government itself was sponsoring measures which were viewed by conservatives at the time as full-blooded socialism, though in retrospect they seem comparatively short, halting steps toward the welfare state. Of course, the labour agitation and the reforms of the new liberalism were quite distinct phenomena, set in motion by men of very different backgrounds and interests. Nevertheless, they reinforced each other to create anxieties in Irish churchmen that Home Rule might come under somewhat inauspicious circumstances. The confrontation between socialism and the Irish Church in the years 1909–14 has been described in detail by Emmet Larkin.[5] Mr Larkin notes three spates of somewhat hysterical verbal attacks by clergymen against socialism and the leaders of the small Irish labour movement, followed in each case by groping clerical attempts to come to terms with the new and unfamiliar forces which were associated in the public mind with Jim Larkin, a Liverpool Irish labour organiser who had brought his considerable talents to Dublin and Belfast in 1907. In a rather basic sense, of course, the socialist argument that wealth should be distributed more equally throughout society was not new in Ireland. Such an idea had been the driving force behind the land agitation, with which the Church had so successfully accommodated herself—carefully distinguishing 'between the main aim, social justice, and the attendant excesses'.[6] What was new was the espousal of such ideas in an urban setting. There was, in clerical minds, an enormous difference between the demand for a patch of land for every Irish peasant and the demand for a share of the profits for every employee of the Dublin United Tramway Company. Father Walter McDonald attributed the clergy's greater sympathy with the agrarian than with the labour movement to the fact that priests were the sons of farmers more often than of hired labourers. 'We are all, naturally, disposed to favour the class to which we belong,'[7] he noted. This shrewd piece of observation is perhaps less than satisfactory as explanation, for the hired labourer in Dublin very likely came from the rural society just like the priest.[8] More to the point was the fact (set forth in Chapter III) that most priests were convinced that life in cities would corrupt the simple piety of the peasantry. To obtain 'land for the people' would have the desirable result of keeping the people on the land, while to achieve better wages for the tramway workers would create an incentive for them to stay in the cities.

The basic thrust of the socialist agitation—to make urban life liveable—ran counter to a dominant clerical ideal: to make rural life more attractive than life in cities. This ideal was rooted in the assumption that in an urbanised society the people would no longer respect so implicitly the clerical view of public affairs and private morals—thereby undermining one of the foundations of the Irish political system. The labour leaders seemed themselves to confirm these fears. Perhaps the most extravagant allegations against socialism—that it denied Christ's divinity, advocated free love, etc.—were not believed by most clergy.[9] As early as 1907, however, Cardinal

Logue, while declaring his sympathy with lawful combinations to secure just wages, expressed apprehension, 'because I find when these people get together as they did a few days ago in England, and earlier still at Stuttgart, and even at meetings in Dublin of our own people, one of the cries I find coming up from amongst them is THE CRY FOR SECULARISM IN THE SCHOOLS'. There was no reason, the Cardinal maintained, why the labourers should not organise to assert their rights without adopting 'this very dangerous cry', which 'would lead finally to the destruction of religion amongst the people'.[10] The Irish Trades Union Congress had previously avoided carefully any religious issue, such as school secularisation.[11] At the 1908 Congress, however, Jim Larkin provided confirmation for Logue's fears by bluntly telling the delegates that there would be no improvement in education 'until they would get rid of the clerical power'.[12] Though Larkin apparently soon learned that this was one reform that he dare not advocate in Ireland, churchmen retained the impression that the new militancy in the labour movement with which he was associated was opposed to what they regarded as the foundations of Irish piety. In September 1910 Bishop McKenna of Clogher, told a congregation in Monaghan that at a recent Trades Congress 'the trend of modern thought was fully demonstrated'. The delegates had 'openly proclaimed' that religious teaching in the schools hampered proper education—'that it took up too much time that could otherwise be better spent, according to their ideas, in teaching reading, writing and arithmetic. What did it profit a man', the Bishop asked, 'if he gained the whole world and lost his own soul?'[13]

The fact that Larkin, although he was of Irish Catholic extraction, had been born and raised in Great Britain confirmed clergymen in their suspicion of socialism as a 'foreign' doctrine. When Ireland was hit by a wave of strikes in the late summer and early autumn of 1911, one priest attributed them to 'English dictators'.[14] At Clonmel Archdeacon Flavin denounced 'these imported Socialistic ideals' and said he had been told by a Liverpool priest that Irish workers in that city 'regretted having taken the advice of the strike-makers, and would never come out again, because they were put in the front, while none of the Englishmen suffered'[15]—an altogether believable story about Liverpool, but hardly one relevant to Clonmel. For some ecclesiastics, the strikes seemed to threaten one of their cherished visions—the fostering of local industries to forestall emigration. 'How lamentable', said one Dublin priest, 'if from the healthy, once prosperous, and truly Catholic town of Wexford Catholic families in search of work must emigrate to the unhealthy and immoral slums of great English manufacturing towns.'[16] The bishops, at their October meeting, tied these themes together in the course of a statement decrying the strikes:

> The worst aspect of this sad business is that the main crisis was precipitated under the guidance of mischief-makers who have shown themselves as reckless about the fate of the Irish working-man as they have been indifferent to the life of our rising trade and nascent industries. A more glaring instance of the evil of being tied to Great Britain in our local affairs could not well be found.[17]

Clerical fears that socialism was a plot by the wicked outside world against the spiritual and temporal interests of Irish Catholics received a kind of confirmation two years later, when, after a lull in strike activity, the great Dublin transport dispute of 1913 brought Jim Larkin to prominence again. Again he was depicted as 'an importation from England'.[18] As the long weeks of strike and lockout dragged on, the desperate straits of many Dublin working-class families prompted a group of well-intentioned English people to organise a programme whereby Dublin slum children would be placed in English homes for the duration of the dispute. Archbishop Walsh protested at once against the sending of children 'to be cared for in a strange land without security of any kind that those to whom the poor children are handed over are Catholics, or, indeed, persons of any faith at all'.[19] Unseemly incidents followed, in which bands of priests battled with social workers on the quays, on the railway platform and in the Corporation Baths to capture the children who were, it was alleged, being 'kidnapped' so that they might be proselytised in the homes of English socialists.[20] Father Fleming, C.C., preaching to the Women's Sodality at Westland Row a month later, summed up—albeit rather hysterically—much of the clerical anxiety over the socialist movement in these years by comparing the lot of contemporary Ireland to that of St Laurence O'Toole trying to fight off the invaders:

Formerly their enemies came with the open intention of exterminating them, of crushing out the Faith, and of putting to death the priests. They knew where they were. They came as the avowed enemies of the Irish race; they came as wolves, but nowadays the wolves came in the sheep's clothing; the socialist and the syndicalist and the rest of the anti-Catholic crowd came to persecute Ireland—under the pretext of uplifting the working man.[21]

It is safe to say that few of Father Fleming's colleagues actually feared that they would be put to death by the socialists. As Emmet Larkin has pointed out, the confrontation between socialism and Catholicism in Ireland was an entirely unequal contest in which the Church was by far the stronger combatant. Moreover, the contest was brief, for by the end of the First World War revolutionary nationalism had 'swallowed and digested whole, without any visible after-effect, revolutionary Socialism'.[22] Nevertheless, the reactions of churchmen to the movement are interesting, for they illustrate that the social ideals discussed in connection with the land agitation (Chapter III) were still a crucial element of Irish clergymen's vision of the future—crucial because they were a programme for preserving the features of Irish society which made the Irish political system work.

Although the threat that socialism would undermine the popular piety which gave the Church its political influence was probably a phantom, the possibility that the legislative programme of the new liberalism might affect the Church's interests prejudicially was quite real. The reform programme begun with the pension scheme and the labour exchanges had been interrupted by the conflict over the budget and the crisis over the Upper House which that measure had precipitated. In May 1911 Lloyd George took up where Churchill (now Home Secretary) had been forced to leave off by introducing an insurance scheme to complement the labour exchanges. In addition to unemployment insurance, the bill included health insurance, and the health provisions were to extend to a much larger segment of the population than the unemployment provisions, in which only workers in certain precarious trades would participate. Because the health insurance called for compulsory contributions from both employees and employers, the Chancellor found himself attacked by a wide spectrum of opinion. Agricultural interests, which included most of the Irish population, objected to being charged at the same rate as the city dwellers for a scheme of which they had much less need, because of healthier living conditions, to cite only the most obvious distinction. Irish labourers, indeed, had the further grievance that because their wages were far lower than English wages they would be paying a higher proportion of their income for the insurance.

The Irish segment of the initial wave of protest against the bill included a resolution passed by the hierarchy at their June meeting.[23] The bishops acknowledged that the bill was 'a great and beneficent provision' for the needs of industrial England and Wales, but cited the predominantly rural character of Ireland and the fact that 'only a mere fraction' of Irish workers were wage-earners as evidence that the measure was inapplicable to Ireland. In support of this view they raised a very valid objection to the bill as it stood. Tradesmen and farmers (except farmers with holdings having annual valuations under £20) would be obliged to insure their sons and daughters, over sixteen years of age, working without wages, and to pay both the employer's and the employee's contribution, but in such cases (which the bishops believed would constitute the majority of cases in Ireland) the insured persons would ordinarily be in receipt of room and board from their 'employers' and would therefore, under the terms of the bill, not be entitled to sick-pay or disablement benefits (though they would receive free medical attention and free medicine). The same unfairness was to be practised against 'a great proportion' of the wage-earners in Ireland who, the bishops believed, were boarded and lodged by their employers. In this category the bishops placed 'female domestic servants, shop-assistants, farm hands and artisans' apprentices', who 'could receive only free medical attendance and free medicine of the very same character which they now receive through the existing dispensary system'. Here the hierarchy was on somewhat more debatable ground. It was true that in Ireland medical benefits not available in England were already provided under the Poor Law, but the dispensary system, while quite satisfactory to the bishops, was very distasteful to labour spokesmen and to many Liberals. Its benefits were only available to those willing to accept the status of paupers and apply for a 'red ticket'.

Even as applied to the manufacturing segment of the Irish economy, the bill disturbed the bishops, for it would be

a heavy burden on many of our small, struggling industries, and would, in our opinion, increase unemployment, whereas a great need of Ireland is more employment and better wages, and not a provision designed for the wounded members of a wealthy and powerful industrial system.[24]

For these reasons, the hierarchy called, not for amendment of the scheme's details, but for the total exclusion of Ireland from the bill, and requested the Chancellor of the Exchequer 'to set aside the State contribution necessary for financing this scheme to the credit of Ireland, either for an insurance scheme specially devised for the needs of this country, or for some other purpose that may be deemed more beneficial to the general welfare of our population'. The bishops concluded by asking the Irish Party to take up this policy, and though the party could scarcely ignore so explicit a directive from their Lordships, men like Devlin and Dillon could hardly be expected to throw away such a sweeping piece of social reform. Queues were already forming outside Lloyd George's office, and diverse interest groups were pressing with notable success their special claims upon the obliging Chancellor. Redmond and his colleagues, as well as representatives of English agricultural interests, simply joined the queue, so to speak, and without apparent difficulty secured amendments which met all the difficulties the bishops had raised but avoided the drastic step of total exclusion of Ireland from the bill. All unpaid farm labour and all persons working without pay for their parents were exempted from the scheme. The rates at which both Irish employers and Irish employees would contribute were lowered, and medical benefits (though not sickness and disability benefits) were eliminated for Ireland, thus leaving the dispensary system unaffected. Finally, a separate administrative structure and a separate financial account for the health insurance scheme were established for Ireland, and provision was even made for the contributions of Irish migratory workers employed in England to be credited to the Irish account. The groundwork was thereby laid for eventual assumption of the scheme by a Home Rule parliament in a more modest form which might be deemed suitable to the peculiar circumstances of the country. The O'Brienites did their best to embarrass the party during debates on the amendments in November by repeatedly pointing out that what the bishops had requested was not amendment of detail, but total exclusion of Ireland and the earmarking of the resultant savings for some other scheme for Ireland.[25] O'Brien and Healy were probably reflecting accurately the sentiments of most of the hierarchy, but the bishops wisely refrained from pressing the issue. Opposition to the scheme in its amended form would have been much more risky than had been the hierarchy's action in June, in the full tide of initial popular reaction against the bill.

The bishops' statement followed logically from the argument against the extension of labour exchanges and unemployment insurance to Ireland in the Irish volume of the Poor Law Commission's majority report two years earlier. That argument, as was observed in Chapter XI, was probably in large measure the work of Bishop Kelly, but at that time the hierarchy did not apparently feel it necessary to protest against the enactment of the Labour Exchanges Bill. Why did they now enter the lists so boldly against the insurance plan? Unlike the celebrated Browne episode in 1951, this action took place years before public health measures had become charged with significance for faith and morals in Catholic thinking because of such issues as contraception and Freudian psychiatry. Rather, churchmen perceived a threat to the Church's interests which can only be understood in the context of the financial relations between Great Britain and Ireland. As has frequently been pointed out, churchmen regarded clerical control of education as dependent upon the continued exclusion of local authorities from the finance of primary and secondary education. Indeed, the recent use by the county councils of their power to provide scholarships in the National University as leverage to frustrate the hierarchy's desires for its matriculation requirements provided disquieting evidence of the dangers churchmen feared (though churchmen were not so unanimous on the issue of Irish in the University as they were on the more general issue of clerical control in primary and secondary education). Nothing had been more useful in support of clerical claims for the increased exchequer grants needed to forestall popular control than the Royal Commission on Financial Relations. That Commission had declared in 1896 that Ireland was shamefully overtaxed in proportion to her capacity and in relation to expenditure on government services in Ireland. In the fiscal year 1895–96, Irish 'true' revenue—a figure based upon the revenue collected in Ireland but adjusted to account for certain payments originating in one country but actually tendered in another—was £8,034,000, while Irish local expenditure was £5,938,000. During the fifteen years following that report, 'true' Irish revenue had risen to about £10,300,000,[26] in 1910-11 while the expenditure upon Irish services had risen to £11,344,000. In other words, Ireland's financial grievance, except for impractical historical claims, had been completely eradicated. The *increase* in Irish expenditure was distributed as follows (round figures):

	£
Aid of Local Taxation	850,000
Post Office Services	600,000
Collection of Taxes	70,000
Department of Agriculture	365,000
Land Commission	350,000
Educational Votes	600,000
Old Age Pensions	2,400,000
Ireland Development Grant	185,000
Total	£5,420,000

The other services, taken together, showed a small saving.)[27]

Clearly, the greatest single cause for the reversal of the financial balance was the first of the Liberals' welfare state measures, the Old Age Pensions Act. The financial effects of this scheme were particularly marked in Ireland because emigration of young people had left the country with a disproportionate number of aged and, perhaps, as Birrell genially suggests, because the lack of official birth records for Ireland prior to 1860 made it easier 'to persuade yourself that you are two years older than you have any good reason to believe you are'.[28] At all events, the welfare state had introduced into Irish accounts an immense new item of expenditure in 1908 and was now about to introduce another huge item, state contributions to a health insurance scheme.

At the same time that the bishops were reacting to the Insurance Bill, one of their number was actively engaged in an inquiry into these larger questions of Irish finance. To help him arrange the financial provisions of the Home Rule Bill which the Irish Party would demand as soon as the Parliament Bill became law, the Prime Minister had quietly appointed an *ad hoc* committee, under the chairmanship of H. W. Primrose, which included Lord Pirrie (the Belfast shipbuilder), Henry N. Gladstone, a city banker, a prominent accountant, an Oxford don, and Bishop Kelly. During May, June and July of 1911, this committee took evidence from a large number of civil servants and other experts and by mid-September had drafted a report which all members signed, though one member, W. G. S. Adams, the Oxford don, had private misgivings.[29]

Apart from the abortive Irish Council Bill of 1907, three schemes for rearranging the financial relations of the two countries in connection with Irish self-government had previously come to public attention: the financial provisions of the 1886 Home Rule Bill, those of the 1893 Home Rule Bill, and those of the latter bill as amended in Committee. Each of these schemes had been propounded before the great shift in the Anglo-Irish balance of revenue and expenditure. Each presupposed, therefore, that Ireland would continue to make a substantial contribution to 'imperial' expenditure and was primarily concerned with means whereby Ireland's proper imperial contribution could be ascertained, collected and, with the passage of years, adjusted. The 1886 bill provided that the imperial parliament should continue to levy customs and excise in Ireland and that the Irish parliament should levy

all other taxes. A certain sum from the revenue collected in
Ireland, calculated at one-fifteenth of total imperial expenditure was to be Ireland's imperial contribution. Under the
first 1893 scheme the distribution of financial powers between
the two parliaments was to be approximately the same as
under the 1886 scheme, but the imperial contribution was
sensibly fixed at the total of the *customs* revenue collected in
Ireland plus £1,000,000 toward the cost of police, which was
to remain temporarily an imperial service. The second 1893
scheme provided for one-third of the 'true' revenue of Ireland to be alloted to imperial purposes and two-thirds to
Irish expenditure.[30]

In 1911, however, the question before the Primrose Committee was not how to maintain a fair contribution by Ireland
to imperial charges, but how to provide Ireland with sufficient revenue to meet its own local charges. The committee's
proposal was that the new Irish parliament be granted full
powers to impose and levy all forms of taxation in Ireland
(subject to safeguards against the raising of tariff questions
prejudicial to foreign relations or to trade between the two
islands) and full responsibility for Irish expenditure. The
new Irish government could expect to take over a fiscal system yielding £10,350,000 revenue to meet an estimated
£12,400,000 expenditure in 1913–14—obviously an inauspicious beginning. The imperial exchequer should therefore provide at the outset some sort of subsidy to get the new government fairly on its feet, but the subsidy should diminish and
eventually disappear (the pious hope being held out that
Ireland might one day make some token imperial contribution). The mechanism by which the committee proposed to
accomplish this purpose was disarmingly simple. Those old
age pensions already granted before Home Rule went into
effect should continue to be paid out of imperial funds. This
item would total about £3,000,000 at the outset, but would
steadily diminish as the beneficiaries of Westminster's mis-
placed benevolence died off. The Irish parliament would
thus begin its operations with a comfortable budget surplus
of £950,000. But what of old age pensions for those who had
not reached the age of seventy before Home Rule went into
effect? The united voice of London finance, Belfast ship-

building, Hawarden Liberalism and Skibbereen spirituality declared that old age pensions were 'an item of expenditure on which reduction would be not only legitimate but desirable in the new conditions to be established in Ireland—of course, in respect of future pensions only'.[31] In other words, in Ireland Home Rule was to be made the occasion for stopping the welfare state dead in its tracks.

Kelly, who had informed Primrose at the committee's first meeting that he intended to consult Redmond from time to time, was jubilant when he wrote to the party leader in September, explaining the provisions of the draft report which was being circulated among committee members for their approval. He evidenced no misgivings when he pointed out that 'all Old Age Pensions coming on lists after the birth of Parliament would fall on Irish Funds'. 'If we put them on at same rate,' he continued, 'the balance of £950,000 would rapidly disappear. Hence we must draw the net more tightly.'[32] A few years earlier Kelly might have found it difficult to justify before his episcopal colleagues a policy which would cut Irish education off from all hope of assistance out of the resources of the imperial exchequer. Under the new, post-1908, dispensation, the fiscal aspect of the British connection was beginning to look much less advantageous to the Church, for new benefits, unasked by ecclesiastical authorities, were being heaped upon the country on such a scale that future claims for more money for education were likely to be swamped by the needs of hitherto undreamed-of public services. For education, that unthinkable recourse—the rates—might once again become a possibility. Better, therefore, to rely upon a fiscally independent parliament having access only to Irish funds, than to have Ireland's fiscal policy permanently integrated with that of the growing British welfare state. An Irish parliament would be naturally more conservative if its fiscal policy were not dictated by a joint Exchequer Board (or some other institution which would have to be created if fiscal autonomy were not granted) and would not vote social benefits on such an 'extravagant' scale as did the present imperial parliament. 'The only answer that has ever been given to our claims for the adjustment of the financial relations between Great Britain and Ireland', Bishop

Foley had written two years earlier, 'is that we get back almost as much as we contribute in the shape of taxes. But what good is this seeing that we have no voice in the allocation of that bloated expenditure?'[33] 'The only radical remedy', in Foley's view, was Home Rule, and from the logic of his argument it is clear that he would prefer Home Rule with the widest possible fiscal autonomy.

Of course, Kelly in a sense represented both the hierarchy and the party in the Primrose Committee's deliberations, and his views reflected a genuine nationalism as well as specifically ecclesiastical interests. While popular opinion favoured fiscal autonomy, however, so far as the public understood or was even aware of the issues involved, few laymen were as concerned as were certain higher ecclesiastics over the matter. 'Is Home Rule Coming?' Mgr O'Riordan, Rector of the Irish College, Rome, wrote to John Horgan, a party supporter in Cork early in 1912.

One of your politicians was here recently—not an M.P.—who says it is to come, and this present year. I asked him about the financial provisions and if we could start house-keeping with a sound capital. He had no doubt about that but I fear he did not know enough about the point to have doubts. Happy man! I fear he has great trust in the Liberals—happy man also! I have no trust in them where things Irish or things Catholic are concerned.[34]

O'Riordan's own former bishop, O'Dwyer, presented the financial issue more clearly in a speech on education early in February 1912 before an audience which included, significantly, three Irish Party M.P.s. The Bishop of Limerick conceded willingly that specifically educational issues should not, in the coming parliamentary session,

be allowed to interfere with the higher interests of the country (*hear, hear*). But, at the same time, it may be well to point out that it would be a great misfortune if the present wretched condition of our schools should be stereotyped under a new form of government. If we are to set up house for ourselves it is not unreasonable for the teachers and others who are interested in education to claim that we should be provided with sufficient means to keep the house properly (*hear, hear*). I am quite confident that the Irish Parliamentary representatives will see to it that in the financial settlement between the two countries Irish education is not left in a half-starved condition.[35]

This expression of confidence is indicative of the urgency with which O'Dwyer viewed the question. The stakes were too high for him to engage in the carping, often irresponsible, criticism of the party which had been his usual style since 1906.

Early in 1912 the financial question was discussed intensely by Redmond and Dillon and Bishops Kelly and O'Donnell. Kelly was bursting with enthusiasm for fiscal autonomy and O'Donnell only slightly less so. It 'would never do', O'Donnell advised Dillon, for the party not to ask for the measure of autonomy recommended by the Primrose Committee.[36] Dillon himself was doubtful that the government would accept the committee's recommendations and apprehensive that, if the issue of fiscal autonomy were raised unsuccessfully, the restricted fiscal powers which were more likely to be forthcoming might be received with disappointment in the country. Though O'Donnell was not so apprehensive on this score as Dillon, he apparently was more easily reconciled to the more restricted measure of autonomy than was Kelly, who continued to urge the party leaders to press for the fullest possible autonomy.[37] Dillon's judgement of the government's intentions proved correct. The cabinet rejected the proposals of the Primrose Committee before it even allowed their report to be published. Acceptance of the proposals would, indeed, have been most embarrassing to leading members of the government, for it would have constituted an admission that, at least in reference to Ireland, they merited Tory charges of extravagance in social welfare spending. In the Home Rule Bill, which Asquith introduced on 11 April 1912, the Irish parliament would be allowed to vary, within certain limits, the rates of taxation established at Westminster, and to levy taxes on previously untaxed items. Revenue would continue to be collected by the imperial authority, and old age pensions along with national insurance, and labour exchanges, land purchase and constabulary would remain, at first, imperial services. The Irish exchequer was to receive each year a certain 'transferred sum', calculated to provide a gradually diminishing surplus (at the expense, of course, of the British taxpayer) of receipts over expenditure upon the services placed under Irish control. The Irish parliament would therefore be encouraged to make retrenchments and bring its accounts into balance, but *not* in the area of the new social welfare services. The bill provided that the Irish parliament could take over the pensions, the health insurance or the unemployment insurance and labour exchanges at any time it wished (on twelve months' notice), but a Home Rule government would obviously think twice before assuming any of these services if its first act in connection with such a service would have to be a reduction in its benefits. Home Rule was not to be an easy escape from the welfare state.

At a Nationalist Convention in Dublin on 23 April a letter from Bishop O'Donnell stressed that under the bill the Irish deficit might be eliminated through increasing Irish prosperity[38]—a clever argument, as it was an article of nationalist faith that the British connection was the primary impediment to a prosperous Ireland. The Convention readily accepted the bill, and it was clear that the bishops now had little chance of gaining a financial settlement more to their liking. Bishop Foley was reduced to lamenting that school attendance in many parts of the country—though his own diocese was an exception—had been so low in the past: if it had been higher the treasury would have provided more money, which would thus have favourably influenced the calculations on which the bill's financial clauses were based. Perhaps even yet, he mused, if they could raise attendance by fifteen per cent they might get some more money under the bill, which might not become law for two more years.

Anyhow, of one thing they might be convinced [he continued], that for the first ten or fifteen years after 'the appointed day' there would not be an additional penny available for primary education unless in the shape of additional taxation or of local rates, neither of which would be welcome to any large section of the community. . . . Some would say that great savings could and would be effected in the administration of the country; and so, doubtless, there would be, but not during the first ten or fifteen years, which would represent the necessary period of transition from the present extravagant system to one that would be more in harmony with the requirements of a country like theirs.[39]

The resignation which characterises Foley's lament was probably typical of the hierarchy's response to the bill. In the absence of a tide of popular disapproval such as had greeted the Irish Council Bill in 1907, there was little they could do apart from hoping for the best. Indeed the Home Rule Bill was not a bad bargain as far as the Church was concerned. It did nothing to upset the status quo in education except to interpose an Irish parliament between the existing systems and the British parliament.

Redmond hoped to capitalise on the crest of popularity the party was enjoying to regain some of the episcopal support he had lost early in the Liberal alliance. Perhaps encouraged by O'Dwyer's friendly remarks in February, he wrote to both O'Dwyer and Walsh in March asking for contributions to the Home Rule Fund—gestures which both had long ceased to make. Walsh's reply was predictably curt: 'As t[o] the matter about which you have written I can only say that it is now some years since I made up my min[d] to have nothing more to do with Irish politics and that nothing in the world cd now induce me to change my mind in the matter.'[40] O'Dwyer, on the other hand, replied with surprising candour and cordiality. He began by declaring his desire to act on Redmond's suggestion, but he then offset this personal inclination with three other considerations. Firstly, he hesitated to participate 'now for the first time, since I became Bishop, in a purely political movement', but this, he assured the party leader, would not in itself stop him in the present, quite exceptional, crisis. A much more serious obstacle, in his mind, was the growing power of the A.O.H. 'within or under the regular political organisation of the United Irish League'. Under Home Rule he would 'dread the existence of such an irresponsible power'.[41] His third concern was prompted by the debate two days earlier in the Commons on a Liberal private member's Single School Areas Bill, which would require popular control of any publicly subsidised English school which was the sole such school in its community. Only a very few Catholic schools would be affected, and Dillon had promised the Irish Party's hearty support to this measure which would rectify the clearest example of discrimination against Nonconformists.[42] This bill was not a great attack upon denominationalism but an implicit admission of the government's inability to enact the kind of sweeping reform it proposed in 1906. For O'Dwyer, however, it foreshadowed a fresh assault:

There are indications . . . that the Government are about to renew their attacks on the denominational schools in England, and I should like to be sure that Catholic children will not be made a price for Nonconformist fulfilment of their pledges on Home Rule. Mr. Dillon's speech on Friday last is not reassuring, and makes me anxious as to the concessions which the Catholics of England may be coerced into accepting.[43]

O'Dwyer concluded then that he felt prevented from openly supporting the party, though he assured the party leader that for the latter personally he had 'the highest respect'.

A few days later *The Tablet* published a notice that it was authorised to state that the Irish Party's action on the Single School Areas Bill 'was taken in direct opposition to the clearly expressed opinion of the Cardinal Archbishop of Westminster, who regards the Bill as full of menace to the interests of definite religious education'.[44] Fortunately for the party, Bishop O'Donnell was in Rome when the article appeared, and he telegraphed immediately to Redmond asking for copies of the relevant correspondence which took place at the time of the 1906 Education Bill.[45] Redmond quickly obliged with an eighteen-page memorandum quoting not only the critical correspondence between Bourne and himself but extracts from speeches by Irish leaders on the Single School Areas question as well. The memorandum was an able demonstration that the English Catholic bishops had sanctioned the party's acceptance of the 1906 bill, if amended as the cabinet finally agreed to amend it, that the present bill would interfere far less with Catholic schools than did the 1906 bill even in its final amended form, and that the party had repeatedly pledged itself to support the Nonconformists in their claims for redress of the Single School Areas grievance. Moreover, it was argued, the removal of this main grievance which was 'admitted by all parties' would 'effectually diminish, if it does not entirely destroy', the clamour for secularisation of the entire system.[46] O'Donnell was pleased with the memorandum and assured Redmond on 24

March that there was 'even an important Englishman' in Rome who understood and appreciated the party's position.[47]

Eventually the Single School Areas Bill died in Committee, but during 1912 Birrell took some actions which fanned into life clerical fears of secularist designs on his part which had been nearly extinguished by his generosity to primary education and his Universities Act four years earlier. In July he announced a plan to distribute a new grant of £40,000 per annum to benefit the *lay* assistant teachers of secondary schools. This plan, by substituting the carrot of cash for the stick of financial stringency in hopes of forcing acceptance of rate-aid, was a much shrewder, if more modest, attack on clerical domination in education than the one the government mounted between 1901 and 1907. The Catholic Headmasters' Association protested, predictably, that the plan demanded for 'outsiders, merely because they are lay persons, the right to thrust themselves into the schools', and required 'the dismissal of religious teachers to make room for them'. They compared this demand with 'the claim of the governments of France and Portugal to the right of forcible confiscation'.[48] At their October meeting, the hierarchy issued a statement which protested 'against the discrimination between lay and clerical teachers', but adopted a more conciliatory tone than that of the headmasters.[49] The hierarchy seems to have allowed the headmasters to handle the issue, and the secretary of the Catholic Headmasters' Association, Canon Murphy of Limerick, negotiated with Birrell in a correspondence which dragged on for a number of months[50] and ultimately resulted in Birrell postponing the entire matter in the summer of 1913.

Late in October 1912, during Committee debate on Clause 3 of the Home Rule Bill, which was intended to prevent religious discrimination by the Irish parliament, Birrell took action which intensified the clerical suspicions he had already aroused with his lay teacher scheme. The cabinet had drafted the clause in very general language, no doubt intending to leave ample opportunities to appear generous by accepting clarifying amendments from the Opposition. Several such amendments were offered, including one which would prohibit Irish legislation that might 'affect prejudicially the right of any child to attend an elementary school receiving public money without attending the religious instruction at that school'.[51] In accepting this amendment, Birrell stated that he thought the required safeguard was already provided in the general wording of the original clause, but suggested that, if this additional safeguard be desired, the word 'elementary' be omitted, because it was the government's intention that such protection for minorities should apply in secondary as well as elementary schools.

This change was not so trivial as it might appear. In the National Schools religious instruction took place at a fixed hour, at which time any children of a different denomination from that of the school would withdraw, and religious emblems, forbidden during secular instruction, would be brought out. This curious procedure was enforced through regular inspection by the National Board's staff. Although enforcement may have occasionally been lax in those schools where every single child was a Catholic, the Church was reconciled to the principle of not offending the religious sensibilities of the one or two Protestant children who might be enrolled in an isolated National School under Catholic management. Matters were quite different, however, in the secondary schools. The Intermediate Board had virtually no cognisance over the day-to-day operations of these schools, and in Catholic secondary schools secular instruction was much more closely interwoven with the organised devotional life of the students than was possible in the primary schools. Protestant enrolment in Catholic secondary schools was virtually unheard-of, and any Protestant student would, no doubt, have been uncomfortable in such a school. The same was true of the Catholic training colleges for which the bishops had succeeded in obtaining government grants after years of official efforts to maintain a nonsectarian system for the training of teachers.

Birrell's expressed desire to extend the 'conscience' provisions to non-elementary schools, together with his initiative on behalf of the lay teachers, seems to have panicked Cardinal Logue. Early in November the Cardinal wrote to Bishop O'Donnell, expressing concern over Clause 3, and suggesting that an attorney, James Murnaghan, should be asked to give a detailed opinion on the bill. The brief available summary of Logue's letter to O'Donnell refers obscurely to 'Birrell's mania for denominational education'.[52] The Cardinal seems to have been particularly concerned about the training colleges, for in addition to contacting Murnaghan,[53] O'Donnell obtained, through Redmond, a written assurance from Birrell, dated 7 November, that the exclusions in Clause 3 would not interefere with existing grants to denominational colleges.[54] 'His Eminence, who is very anxious on this head,' O'Donnell later confided to the party leader, 'was pleased to have the letter, and said it would be very important to have Mr. Birrell's interpretation made secure in law.'[55]

The text of the clause upon which Murnaghan's opinion was requested was as follows (the passages in brackets consisting of amendments which had been either accepted or promised by the government):

In the exercise of their power to make laws under this Act the Irish Parliament shall not make a law so as either directly or indirectly to establish or endow any religion, or prohibit [or restrict] the free exercise thereof, or give a preference, privilege, or advantage, or impose any disability or disadvantage, on account of religious belief or religious or ecclesiastical status, or make any religious belief or religious ceremony a condition of the validity of any marriage [, or affect prejudicially the right of any child to attend a school receiving public money without attending the religious instruction at that school, or alter the constitution of any religious body except where the alteration is approved on behalf of the religious body by the governing body thereof, or divert from any religious denomination the fabric of cathedral churches or, except for the purpose of roads, railways, lighting, water, or drainage works, or other works of public utility upon payment of compensation, any other property].

Any law in contravention of the restrictions imposed by this section shall, so far as it contravenes those restrictions, be void.[56]

Two of the eight questions[57] posed to Murnaghan by the bishops dealt with possible repeal of remaining Catholic disabilities and with phrasing in the clause intended to prevent the Irish parliament from giving civil effect to two recent papal pronouncements. Murnaghan suggested an amendment to repeal remaining disabilities, but he noted that it might be better to avoid raising the issue of the section of the 1898

Local Government Act prohibiting election of clergy as county or district councillors. In forwarding this amendment to Redmond, Bishop O'Donnell was quite ambiguous as to whether he thought the party ought to attempt to repeal the 1898 provision.[58] The two papal pronouncements dealt respectively with civil jurisdiction over clergy and with marriage. Murnaghan ignored the former issue, and on the latter he offered only very minor verbal changes designed to allow the Irish parliament to provide for religious marriages if a civil alternative were also provided. Logue admitted to O'Donnell that the marriage question was 'of secondary importance',[59] and O'Donnell, in turn, described Murnaghan's amendment to Redmond as 'a suitable improvement', but added realistically: 'At the same time, I do not think there is much desire that the Irish Parliament would legislate on this subject.'[60]

Six of the eight questions submitted to Murnaghan concerned education. It was education, not marriage or civil disabilities, which was troubling the Cardinal. The first education question Murnaghan treated was: 'In preventing an indirect endowment of religion does Clause 3 bar any law giving such grants as are now allowed to Denominational Training Colleges, whether Catholic or Protestant [?]' Murnaghan, replying on 14 November, minimised the danger to Catholic training colleges, and, while suggesting an amendment to clear away doubts on the point, did not feel that the amendment was absolutely necessary. In the next instalment of his replies, submitted to the bishops four days later, the attorney dealt with the five other education questions, and several of these questions were phrased in a way that suggests that Logue was not satisfied with the answer to the first one and was pressing for clarification. Did the clause 'impose any fresh restrictions' on intermediate schools and training colleges? Must they be 'less denominational than before'? Would the status of secondary schools be affected 'in the direction of secularisation'? What really concerned the Cardinal apparently was not so much the right of the Irish parliament to provide money to Catholic institutions as the possibility that such grants might entail modifications in the programme of the secondary schools and training colleges and the admission of Protestants to such institutions

upon demand. Murnaghan's opinion was that the clause
would not require the removal of religious emblems from
such schools or any change in the character of the teaching.
He pointed out that the clause did confer certain advantages,
for under its terms neither the National Board's rule prohibiting monks and nuns from teaching in ordinary National
Schools nor Birrell's scheme for lay secondary teachers could
be enacted into law. He did believe, however, that Protestant
students would have the right to attend any school receiving
public money, and to safeguard the Catholic character of
Catholic colleges and secondary schools he drafted an amendment somewhat stronger than the one he had suggested on
14 November. A few days later he revised the amendment to
give it even stronger wording:

Nothing in this section shall be construed so as to hinder any
Training College or School from receiving public money, because such Training College or School is founded or maintained
by persons belonging to a particular church or denomination
for the benefit solely of the members thereof.[61]

The two further education questions revealed episcopal hopes
that Home Rule might make it possible to move toward
greater denominationalism. Could the Home Rule parliament 'establish a system of denominational education giving
equal advantages to all parties if all parties wished for it'?
Could the parliament permit religious services and religious
instruction in the National University? Murnaghan answered
both questions in the affirmative, with certain qualifications,
and did not suggest amendments.

On 20 November, after most of Murnaghan's answers had
been received, Logue was still dissatisfied. He complained to
O'Donnell that Murnaghan was 'vague', and he lamented
that Clause 3 was a net to drag in everything. He decided to
send the attorney's memorandum to Walsh.[62] The Archbishop
of Dublin offered the none-too-helpful opinion that the Irish
Party would have to take what they could get.[63] Though the
last instalment of Murnaghan's memorandum was completed
on 30 November, another week elapsed before it was forwarded to Redmond for action. As time was obviously running out, it is likely that a rather intense discussion among
the prelates was preventing prompt action. Perhaps the

Bishop of Raphoe was trying to persuade Logue that the financial provisions were more important to the future of Irish education than were the statutory limitations upon the Irish parliament's powers, for the Cardinal confessed to O'Donnell on 3 December that he understood little of the financial clauses.[64] On 6 December Logue wrote to O'Donnell that like Walsh he thought there were a great many doubtful things in the bill. In regard to religious interests he would rather live under an imperial parliament than under a Home Rule parliament.[65] Apparently, however, he told O'Donnell to go ahead and send Murnaghan's suggestions to Redmond, for on the following day the Bishop of Raphoe transmitted the memoranda to the party leader with apologies for the 'unavoidable' delay. The Bishop no doubt realised that from considerations of both timing and policy the entire project was hopeless, when he commented: 'I know your Committee will give earnest attention to these opinions and that you will turn them to best account as circumstances permit.'[66]

As O'Donnell probably anticipated, Redmond replied after several days that although he had carefully studied the suggested amendments, there was 'a preliminary and fatal objection' to acting upon them—Committee debate was substantially complete when the amendments were received. Three or four months earlier it might have been possible to have carried out some of the suggestions in consultation with the government. The amendments were of such a character, however, that to raise them at this stage 'would instantly arouse all the latent anti-Catholic feeling in England, and would create a storm round our heads which would in all probability wreck the Home Rule Bill'. In the party's opinion, however, most of the suggested amendments were unnecessary, as the bill would provide the Irish parliament with the powers the amendments sought to confer. With reference to the denominational training colleges, Redmond was satisfied that Birrell's letter accurately conveyed 'the meaning and intention of the Bill, and that his Eminence and you can be easy in your mind about that point'.[67] Though Logue told O'Donnell he was resigned to take the bill with its defects,[68] he was not 'easy in his mind'. Within a few days he was complaining again to O'Donnell that excessive safeguards for

Protestants in the bill would ruin freedom.[69] O'Donnell, however, in his reply to Redmond made clear his own sympathy
with the party's position: 'Our Committee . . . knowing it
was late in the day wished you to have the papers so that you
could make the most of an opportunity if any should offer
in connection with amendments accepted from the Unionists
and not yet finally formulated.'[70] At this stage, as both O'Donnell and Redmond knew, concessions by the government to
the Unionists did not call for any compensating concessions
to their Nationalist allies. The debate droned on until the
middle of January 1913, when the bill received its third
reading and was sent to the Lords, who, to no one's surprise,
rejected it. Under the new constitutional procedure, the
Home Rule Bill ought now to be entered on the statute
book sometime in 1914, provided only that the House of
Commons would twice go through the ritual of passing it
again without altering a comma.

The Nation, to all appearances, was now really going to
become the State in Ireland. Some churchmen were apprehensive, but the Church had loyally adhered to her obligations under the Irish political system. She was committed to
sanctioning the Nation's claim in return for the adherence of
the Nation's leaders to constitutional methods and their faithful defence of her own educational interests. As there was no
question of the party not possessing the Nation's confidence
(unlike the 1907 situation) or of the bill not being an embodiment of that claim, there was no question of the bishops
doing anything to impede its enactment. Even Bishop
O'Dwyer, who was often unwilling to play by the rules,
realised that at this juncture they must be obeyed. In a speech
at the Laurel Hill Convent in December 1912, he lamented
a speech by Dillon suggesting that under Home Rule Irish
education might be 'recast', but he quickly added that he
did not want to say or do anything 'that at the present time
might embarrass Mr. Redmond in the great task which he is
prosecuting with such conspicuous ability and statesmanship'.[71] The Irish political system seemed to be working like
clockwork, except in one respect. The territory within which
the Nation was to supplant the State did not exactly coincide
with the territory of the Nation as defined by that system.

CHAPTER XIV

The Protestant Rebellion

EVEN before the Lords' veto was abolished in 1911, the Unionists of Ulster had been organising to resist Home Rule. A great deal of rhetoric and some sectarian rioting in Belfast —as had accompanied the 1886 and 1893 Home Rule debates—was, of course, to be expected. On 23 September 1911 the 50,000 men from Orange Lodges and Unionist clubs throughout Ulster who gathered outside Craigavon, the suburban Belfast residence of Captain James Craig, heard what they had come to hear. Sir Edward Carson, the Dublin barrister who had recently been chosen leader of the Ulster Unionist Party declared: 'We must be prepared . . . the morning Home Rule passes, ourselves to become responsible for the government of the Protestant Province of Ulster.'[1] It turned out to be more than crowd-pleasing rhetoric. Two days later a group of prominent Ulster Unionists began drafting a constitution for a provisional government in Ulster. More to the point, for the moment, the Craigavon crowd's attention had been captured by an Orange contingent from Co. Tyrone which seemed to march with unusual precision. It turned out that this group had been practising military drill, and their example was soon being widely imitated. It was discovered that a loophole in the law permitted any two Justices of the Peace to authorise military drilling within their jurisdiction if 'the object was to render citizens more efficient for the purpose of maintaining the constitution of the United Kingdom as now established and protecting their rights and liberties thereunder'.[2] That citizens might strive to maintain 'the constitution of the United Kingdom as now established' by conspiring to set up a revolutionary government to thwart the enforcement of an act of parliament was only one of the ironies of these troubled years. On 28 September 1912 some 100,000 Ulstermen affixed their signatures —some of them in blood—to a new 'Solemn League and Covenant'. They pledged to use 'all means which may be found necessary to defeat the present conspiracy to set up a Home Rule Parliament in Ireland'. In deference to Presbyterian clerical sensitivities, the obligation was undertaken not for all time, but only 'throughout this our time of threatened calamity'.[3]

The antics of the Ulstermen might have seemed little more than a joke—at worst a bluff easily called—had not the Conservatives in Great Britain made themselves a party to the whole grim business. Balfour had come to be regarded as a bit too gentlemanly, and his replacement in the Conservative leadership by Andrew Bonar Law, a dour, unimaginative Canadian of Ulster-Scots extraction, was symbolic of the change which was overtaking British politics. In the years before 1910 one might expect the Prime Minister and the Leader of the Opposition to engage one another in the most hostile debate in the Commons, only to show up later the same evening at some London hostess's party in the same cab. Politics was a game governed by the rules of sportsmanship, not by malice. Suddenly all this had changed. At one point in the debates on the Home Rule Bill an Ulster Unionist member became so angry that he threw a heavy book—the Standing Orders of the House—at Churchill, drawing blood. If, for the most part, parliament did not forsake verbal debate for physical combat, it did seem to become less and less the real arena of politics. During 1913 the Commons went through the form of passing the Home Rule Bill a second time, and the Lords the form of rejecting it again. Though this procedure, in principle, brought enactment of the Commons' will closer, it also reinforced the eerie impression that what went on in Westminster Palace actually was no more than meaningless ritual—that the real decision was to be made by force, or at least threat of force, outside the walls of either House. Carson's infrequent appearances in the Commons were calculated displays of contempt for parliamentary institutions—mere interludes in his real business of organising an army.

During 1913 Catholic ecclesiastics had relatively little to say in public about the Ulster agitation against Home Rule. Cardinal Logue, optimistically asserting that Catholics would not provoke a civil war by resisting Carson's army and their 'cast-off Italian rifles', quipped that 'between the quality of the rifles and the skill of the gunmen he did not think there would be much danger'.[4] Influential secular politicians, however, were beginning to take a less sanguine view than that of the Cardinal. Lord Loreburn, a staunch Home Ruler who had retired from the Lord Chancellorship in 1912, wrote to *The Times* in September expressing fears of serious violence when the Home Rule Bill became law and calling for a conference or some direct communication between the respective Irish leaders in hopes of reaching a settlement by consent.[5] The King himself was trying desperately to promote some such settlement, and the air was full of suggested concessions which might appease the Orangemen. Lord Loreburn and other advocates of sundry compromises, including the King, could safely be ignored by the Nationalists, but Churchill's speech at Dundee on 8 October 1913 was another matter. The latter, now First Lord of the Admiralty, presumably speaking for the government, expressed the hope that Ulster leaders would put their case more temperately rather than trying to impose a 'bully's veto'. 'Their claim for special consideration,' he declared, 'if put forward with sincerity, could not be ignored by a Government depending on the existing House; there was no advance that they could make which would not be more than matched by their Irish fellow-countrymen and the Liberal party.'[6] On the following day, Bishop O'Donnell wrote to Redmond of 'a growing apprehension on the part of a good many Catholics and Nationalists in Ireland in reference to conference schemes'. Churchill's speech, the Bishop predicted, would not allay such fears, for following certain recent statements by F. E. Smith, one of the more opportunistic of the Conservative leaders, the First Lord's words would 'be taken to imply something more than a display of sweet reasonableness towards N. E. Ulster'. Though O'Donnell was willing to make concessions to satisfy the Orangemen, 'provided Ireland did not suffer seriously, and provided also that the Nationalist minority in the N. E.

did not suffer badly', he did not suggest specific terms of compromise. Talk of special treatment for the Protestant counties naturally excited apprehension about the fate of the Catholic minority in those districts. O'Donnell reported widespread feeling that a special committee should be established to agitate on behalf of the Ulster Nationalists and claim representation at any conference that might be called. As such an organisation might be very troublesome to the party leaders in their negotiations with the government, O'Donnell was opposed to its formation, but he obviously wanted to impress on Redmond's mind the need to press the claims of Ulster Catholics.[7]

There were essentially two possible lines upon which concessions to the Carsonites might be formulated: (1) a large degree of local autonomy in Ulster upon certain sensitive matters, combined, perhaps, with some sort of veto powers for Ulster over certain categories of legislation in the Irish parliament and/or some reduction of the powers of that parliament (this solution came to be known as 'Home Rule within Home Rule'); (2) the exclusion, temporarily or permanently, of all or part of Ulster from the jurisdiction of an Irish parliament.

Redmond's initial inclination was that if concessions had to be made, they should be along the lines of 'Home Rule within Home Rule'. In an interview with Asquith on 17 November, he indicated a willingness to proceed along such lines, though he stressed in a subsequent letter that he thought the government should not make offers to the Conservatives at that particular time.[8] Early in 1914 the Prime Minister was leaning toward Home Rule within Home Rule, a proposition which could only arouse serious episcopal misgivings. Local autonomy in the Protestant districts was quite a different matter, in ecclesiastical eyes, from continued government from Westminster, for a Protestant government in Ulster could be expected to make short work of the status quo in education. In his letter to Redmond of 9 October 1913 Bishop O'Donnell had given an indication of what came first to the minds of churchmen when they contemplated such schemes; in reference to the nationalist minority he had written: 'Autonomy in Education &c for the N.E.

would be queer autonomy for them.'[9] Early in January he indicated his continued abhorrence of local autonomy by writing to Redmond: 'I dislike this talk of withdrawing the separate Post office, [some?] control of Customs, and the appointment of certain judges, from Ireland, only less than the "concession" of an "administrative Council" to N.E. Ulster.' The concession which he favoured was some modification in the constitution of the Senate, which under the bill was to be (after an initial period of nomination) an elected body in which Protestants would have scarcely more weight than they would in the Irish House of Commons.[10]

In an interview on 2 February the Prime Minister outlined for Redmond the government's plan to offer a scheme of Home Rule within Home Rule, to which Redmond gave grudging and conditional approval, still urging the Prime Minister to avoid making a public offer.[11] During February, forces within the cabinet, together with pressure from the King, forced Asquith to reconsider his plan, and intimations of the shifting situation were reaching Redmond by the middle of the month, when Bishop O'Donnell came to London to confer with the party leaders.[12] The Bishop and the politicians agreed that if an exclusion scheme was called for, the one to press upon the government was a plan suggested by Sir Horace Plunkett in a letter to *The Times* of 10 February. Plunkett had argued that Ulster Unionists should accept the bill under several conditions, the most important of which was that a definite area of Ulster should have the right, by plebiscite, to secede from Ireland after a certain number of years. Such a plan was much less distasteful to nationalists than any scheme for excluding the Protestant districts from the start, even if some mechanism were provided for possible inclusion at a later date. Even very intelligent nationalists had a naïve belief that Protestants, if once forced to accept Home Rule, would quickly come to like it and refuse to be excluded from it. In Bishop O'Donnell's opinion, an offer of an immediate plebiscite would make the Carsonites more zealous to reduce the powers of the Irish parliament because the people of the disputed counties would be less likely to opt for the Irish parliament if it was obviously a very weak body.[13] Moreover, for the party, im-

mediate inclusion with an option of exclusion at a later date
had an obvious advantage over immediate exclusion under
any conditions, for the former plan would not have such serious repercussions on the party's support in the country.

O'Donnell's intuition, expressed to Redmond in October
1913, that the fluid state of the Ulster question might well
call forth auxiliary nationalist bodies which would prove
embarrassing to the party was already being vindicated beyond even his expectations. In the 1 November issue of *An
Claidheamh Soluis*, Eóin Mac Néill published an article
entitled 'The North Began', calling for the formation of a
nationalist Volunteer movement on the pattern of Carson's
Ulster Volunteers.[14] The idea was enthusiastically taken up
by nationalists of varying opinions. Although some of those
attracted to the new movement were, like Mac Néill, generally supporters of the Irish Party, the Volunteer organisation
quickly provided an outlet for the political energies of Irish
Irelanders who had become disenchanted with the party.
This much was obvious even to casual observers. What was
not publicly known was that the leaders of the Irish Republican Brotherhood also became involved in the highest councils of the movement. The I.R.B., or Fenians, as its members
had earlier been known, represented the revolutionary nationalism which had been prominent in the generation
between O'Connell and Parnell and which the Church had
ruled out of the Irish political system. From the 1860s on-
ward, the Brotherhood was under a most explicit ecclesiastical
ban, frequently reiterated from the altar and enforced in the
confessional. Its membership had declined from an estimated
80,000 in the early 1860s to about 1,500 in 1911.[15] That the
ban remained a stumbling block to recruiting for the organisation is attested by Diarmuid Lynch, one of its leaders in
the early twentieth century, who recalled that 'Often when
after tedious investigation a man was deemed fit in every
respect the inquisitor found himself "up against a stone wall"
—that of religious scruples in the matter of joining a "secret
organisation".'[16] The brotherhood had recently been reorgan-
ised and revitalised under the leadership of Tom Clarke, who,
after a period of penal servitude for dynamiting activities and
a stay in America, had returned to Ireland in 1907. An older,

more cautious, leadership was forced to retire about 1910–11 and was replaced by Clarke and a group of younger militants. Though the Brotherhood probably did not grow spectacularly —numbers were in any event a threat to secrecy—the Volunteer movement provided it a golden opportunity to work for its aims through a 'front organisation'. It was not slow to seize the chance.

Something closer to what the Bishop of Raphoe had had in mind was waiting for him when he returned to Letterkenny from his visit to London. The Nationalists of Derry were making plans for a great demonstration on 14 March to 'strengthen the hands of Mr. Redmond and the Irish Party'. Bishop McHugh of Derry went to Letterkenny on 22 February to consult O'Donnell about the demonstration.[17] McHugh represented the ghetto mentality of the Northern Catholics far more authentically than did O'Donnell, whose diocese contained only a small minority of Protestants and who was capable of considerable emotional detachment in discussing the Ulster question. In particular McHugh feared that the Northern Catholics were a forgotten group in the manoeuvrings taking place at Westminster. Apparently McHugh had already communicated his misgivings to Devlin, for three days later, in a letter to Redmond, O'Donnell mentioned a letter in which Devlin had assured the Bishop of Derry 'that no concessions would be made in regard to Ulster against the mature judgment of the Nationalists concerned when they knew all the circumstances'—an approach which O'Donnell regarded as 'the right line to steady the situation in Nationalist Ulster'.[18] We do not know exactly what O'Donnell said to McHugh, beyond McHugh's own, rather defensive, later statement to Redmond that the Bishop of Raphoe agreed with him that 'the contemplated meeting could do no harm and might do much good'.[19] Probably it was a case of O'Donnell yielding against his better judgement to the strong sentiments of his brother bishop. About the only piece of solid information he could have given McHugh at this point would have been that the government's latest concrete proposal to Redmond, that of 2 February, was for Home Rule within Home Rule, which, with its implication of Protestant control over Ulster education, could hardly have been reassuring to the Bishop of Derry. When Redmond heard of the proposed demonstration, he thought immediately of a 1912 Hibernian demonstration at Castledawson, Co. Derry, which had led to a clash with local Presbyterians and to serious anti-Catholic rioting in Belfast. Believing that repetition of such incidents could only weaken the party's hand, Redmond wrote to the Bishop, Dr McHugh, remonstrating with him to cancel the event. The Carsonites, Redmond pointed out, 'would welcome an outbreak of riot and disorder in Ulster', and, having consulted the Nationalist members for Ulster constituencies, the party leader believed that the demonstration would be 'a great mistake in tactics at the present moment, when parties are practically manœuvring for position'.[20] Though McHugh reluctantly acquiesced in Redmond's request, on condition that the latter take responsibility for the cancellation, he was not convinced by the leader's arguments.

The Orange faction [he wrote] is never done crying out intolerance and publishing what they would suffer under Home Rule, but there is not a word about what Catholics and Nationalists in Ulster would suffer if the Orangemen got control, and what they have already suffered at their hands. The great object of the meeting was to give the Liberal Party to understand that the Nationalists of the North have their rights as well as the Orangemen, and that, while agreeable to make concessions, they were not prepared to accept a state of things that would be worse than if they had never stood up for Home Rule.[21]

Rather than doing harm, the Bishop believed that 'the meeting would in all probability have improved the proposals of Mr Asquith, and opened the eyes of the English people generally so as to see that there were two sides to the Ulster question'. He was at pains to minimise the danger of disturbance, but in a closing reflection he wrote, significantly: 'If the Orangemen did attack our people coming or going it would only expose their intolerance and show the hollowness of their cry against the treatment they would receive under Home Rule.' Though there was no direct contradiction between the respective positions of Bishops McHugh and O'Donnell, this last statement reveals a rather considerable

difference in temper from some reflections O'Donnell had
sent to Redmond several weeks earlier:

Fighting is not in the mind of the 'Ulster' army. But if they
wanted to fight or riot, the way in which Nationalists in Ulster
would suffer least is by offering no show of resistance, and they
can take that course now for Ireland's sake without any impu-
tation on their manhood. . . .

Ulster Nationalists of the rank and file can grasp the situation
and even in Belfast under Mr Devlin's leadership would keep
to their houses and leave defence to the police and military.[22]

Such a strategy of impeccably good behaviour, and not provocative monster demonstrations such as McHugh favoured,
was O'Donnell's idea of how to strengthen the party's hand
in negotiations with the government.

Those negotiations soon focused upon a new scheme prepared by Lloyd George, under which counties would be
allowed to opt out of the jurisdiction of the Irish parliament
for a certain term of years. At the end of that period, which
would be after the next British general election, the excluded
counties would be automatically included in the jurisdiction
of the Irish parliament, unless the imperial parliament, which
by that time might well have a Unionist majority, provided
otherwise. The Lloyd George scheme had not apparently
been before the Irish leaders at the time of Bishop O'Donnell's visit to London, and when it was given to the party
leaders and forwarded to the Bishop, he noted at once the
political risks it might entail for the party. While acknowledging that the leaders must give a hearing to all schemes, he
urged continued advocacy of the Plunkett scheme.[23] Devlin
had already done precisely that in a memorandum submitted to Liberal leaders,[24] but Lloyd George was rapidly gaining
the upper hand in cabinet deliberations. On 2 March Asquith
outlined for Redmond a new government plan. Instead of
'Home Rule within Home Rule' the cabinet now proposed
to offer the Lloyd George scheme to Carson with three years
as the time limit for exclusion. Redmond acquiesced in this
proposal 'as the price of peace' and agreed to have the Irish
Party abstain on the question, leaving to the Conservatives
the onus of accepting or rejecting it, but he insisted that it
must be the government's final offer.

Redmond then dispatched several of his lieutenants to Ulster to secure support from leading local figures—especially ecclesiastical figures. The four counties with clear Protestant majorities—Antrim, Armagh, Derry and Down—were included within the Catholic dioceses of Armagh, Dromore, Down and Connor, and Derry. It appears that Redmond's emissaries went to Ulster with the impression that in plebiscites the boroughs of Belfast, Derry and Newry would be treated as separate counties. This feature of the scheme, though apparently not yet formally stated, would have been most important in securing Catholic support. Belfast was overwhelmingly Protestant, and would, without question, opt for exclusion. Derry and Newry, however, had Catholic majorities, and were so close to the borders of the potentially excluded area that their separate treatment would be an important issue. Moreover, both towns were Catholic episcopal sees. When, on 6 March, the cabinet's proposals were formally drafted, Derry and Newry were not treated separately, but Redmond successfully insisted that they be accorded the same status as counties. Devlin conferred with McHugh in Derry on 4 March, and went to Letterkenny with him to consult O'Donnell. McHugh acquiesced in the scheme, and even told Devlin, in reference to the Ulster prelate with whom the party's relations were coolest, 'that if there was no other method by which it could be done, he himself would go to Cardinal Logue & put the situation before him'.[25] The sharp contrast between McHugh's mood at this time and his grave apprehensions of the previous week was due partly, no doubt, to the fact that under the scheme a large proportion of the Catholics in his diocese, in Derry City and Co. Tyrone, would be able to vote themselves into the Irish parliament's jurisdiction. Nevertheless, his change of mood and the favourble reaction which was found among the other bishops whose dioceses were not so fortunately placed must be attributed in significant measure to a sense of relief that, unlike 'Home Rule within Home Rule', the scheme involved no new local, Protestant-dominated governing authority able to shape educational policy in the province.

Devlin then returned to Belfast where he held a meeting of influential laymen and clergy, including a priest from Newry who had been sent to represent Bishop O'Neill of Dromore, with instructions to 'fall in with any arrangement we decided upon'.[26] The meeting endorsed the party's position, and on 7 March Devlin contacted Bishop Tohill of Down and Connor. He, too, was quite satisfied and agreed 'that the best that could be done has been done'.[27] The task of dealing with the Cardinal had wisely been delegated not to Devlin, but to Jeremiah MacVeagh, M.P. for South Down, and J. C. R. Lardner, M.P. for North Monaghan. Bishop O'Donnell had already broken the news to Logue in a letter, and Bishop McHugh's proffered assistance was not required. MacVeagh and Lardner achieved 'splendid results' in Armagh. The Cardinal was 'most gracious', MacVeagh wrote to Redmond,

and said he thought you had done the best possible under the circumstances. He prefers the Plunkett scheme, but would not let the other scheme stand in the way of peace. 'The Bill must be saved,' was the last thing he said to us. It was well we went for he was restive until everything was explained to him. Of course he doesn't love the concessions, but will not object.[28]

The two M.P.s then drove to Newry where they found Bishop O'Neill willing to agree as well.

Despite the apparent ease with which episcopal agreement was obtained, the party had mortgaged a significant share of its prestige among Ulster ecclesiastics to gain a consensus upon what Redmond described, on 9 March when Asquith proposed the plan in the Commons, as 'the very extremest limit of concession'. The time limit had been extended from three years to six, but Carson brushed aside the proposal as a 'sentence of death with a stay of execution for six years'. The party's careful efforts in Ulster had not only come to nought but had raised expectations in the minds of ecclesiastics which later, when the party would have to make further concessions, would greatly complicate their relations with the Ulster bishops.

From the moment Carson spurned 'temporary' exclusion, the country began a plunge into anarchy which was only halted by the declaration of war. Up until this time it had been possible to believe that the whole Ulster movement was a gigantic bluff. The situation took on an entirely new aspect late in March. The government was now obliged to go forward with the enactment of the bill, and to forestall trouble certain discreet and precautionary deployments of military forces in Ulster were ordered. Through a combination of verbal ineptness and wilful partisanship several senior officers at the Curragh—the major military camp near Dublin—gave their subordinates the impression that they had been ordered to initiate hostilities against the Ulster Volunteers and that within twenty-four hours the entire country would be 'ablaze'. They were able to report to the government, with scarcely concealed delight, that most of the officers under their command had chosen to accept dismissal rather than to obey their orders. This was the so-called 'mutiny' at the Curragh. As if the situation was not bad enough, when the ring-leader, Brigadier Gough, was ordered to London, he managed to extract from a bumbling cabinet a statement which could be interpreted as virtually ratifying the officers' intervention into politics. The wording which allowed the impression that the government would not use force to suppress the Ulster Volunteers was added to the cabinet statement without Asquith's knowledge and was repudiated by the Prime Minister who dismissed the irresponsible Secretary for War and assumed his office himself. Nevertheless, the impression that the government could not rely on the army to enforce its policy could not be removed. A month later, the Ulster Volunteers successfully defied a ban upon importation of arms by running a large quantity of weapons at Larne. Although a grave offence had been committed, the government chose not to risk the political dangers of a prosecution.

These two incidents not only increased the arrogance of the Carsonites, but gave a new impetus to the Irish Volunteer movement, which had not yet achieved the imposing military stature of its Ulster counterpart. The clergy were instinctively wary of these bands of armed Catholics which were springing up throughout the country, even if they possessed nothing more deadly than a few pistols for their officers. When Redmond learned that Irish Volunteers in Derry were planning a route march for Sunday, 22 March, he wired Bishop McHugh urging him, for much the same reasons as he had advanced a month earlier against the Derry demonstration, to 'take immediate steps to stop it'.[29] The Bishop's response contrasted sharply with his reaction to Redmond's earlier plea. Far from complaining that this event would strengthen the party's hand, he immediately dispatched his administrator to the Volunteer drill field to read Redmond's telegram and urge compliance with it, but the priest received distressingly little co-operation. The most the Volunteers would do was to change the proposed route from the Protestant to the Catholic quarter of the city and to send a deputation to wait upon the Bishop. Despite an hour and a half of arguments from the Bishop, the deputation refused to make further concessions. Finally they announced that they would go back and put the matter before the whole Volunteer body. At this point McHugh delivered an ultimatum: as soon as they left his room he would wire Redmond that he had failed to dissuade them and on the following day, Sunday, he would have the route march denounced from every altar in the city and suburbs. 'It was only then they yielded,' the Bishop wrote. 'After this we got matters patched up agreeably. They have a body of 2,000 men drilled by ex-soldiers and are all armed with revolvers. I must say the situation seemed very serious.'[30] The situation was indeed very serious for both the Church and the party. The demonstration which Redmond had persuaded McHugh to cancel in February might have created a threat to the party's influence, but it was being organised under ecclesiastical sanction. The Volunteer movement, as the Derry incident made painfully evident, was not only outside the party's control, but could be influenced by the Church only through the threat of public condemnation.

During the ensuing months, the common danger perceived by both Church and party in the Volunteer movement caused clergy and politicians to draw closer together at a time when disillusionment with the party might otherwise have driven many ecclesiastics to look for alternative political leadership. During May Redmond and his colleagues attempted, in negotiations with Eóin Mac Néill and Sir Roger Casement, two of the more moderate Volunteer leaders, to gain representation for the party on the Volunteers' governing body. When these negotiations broke down in June, Redmond delivered a public ultimatum demanding equal representation for party nominees on that body. The party's prestige was still great enough that the Provisional Committee of the Volunteers had to acquiesce. More significant than these arrangements, which broke down soon after Redmond's announcement of support for the war effort, was the fact that the clergy throughout the country joined in the party's attempt to gain control of the movement on a local level. The Inspector-General of the Royal Irish Constabulary, in his report for June, noted that 'Following the action of Mr. Redmond, the Roman Catholic clergy as a body joined the Movement and are taking an active interest in it.' The I.-G. continued by citing the most remarkable case of clerical involvement:

The Archbishop of Tuam, Doctor Healy, who is strongly opposed to unconstitutional agitation, has given his approval. The districts round Tuam and Athenry, and other Western areas, are famous for turbulent agitation, and it is not at all improbable that the clergy there, and elsewhere, have associated themselves with the Volunteers partly with a view to lessening the danger of this huge Force, drilled and trained without a sufficient number of persons of responsibility and influence to exercise control.[31]

Dr Harty, the new Archbishop of Cashel, also signified public support of the Volunteers, 'if they are organised under leaders whom the Irish people can follow'. Warning that if they were organised on different lines they might destroy 'our National hopes', he remarked—somewhat ominously, it might seem in retrospect—that 'At the present time there are no leaders whom the people can follow except the Irish Parliamentary Party,' but he made clear his confidence 'in the prudence of the Irish Party, under the leadership of Mr. Redmond'.[32] Eighteen of the county inspectors of police, in their monthly reports for June noted clerical support for the Volunteers ranging from mere approval to active and enthusiastic participation.[33]

While the clergy and the party worked furiously in Ireland to capture the menacing new nationalist organisation, the Home Rule Bill was passing through its final stages, and Asquith announced his intention of introducing an Amending Bill on the same lines as the compromise Carson had rejected in March. As the fate of the Amending Bill obviously depended on the attitude of the Lords, it was first introduced in the Upper House. In that House it was drastically amended so as to exclude the whole of Ulster with no plebiscite and no time limit. In an effort to break the impasse, the King called a conference at Buckingham Palace under the chairmanship of the Speaker. Asquith, Lloyd George, Redmond and Dillon spent four days in fruitless negotiation with Bonar Law, Lansdowne, Carson and Craig over bits and pieces of the two Ulster counties with nearly equal Catholic and Protestant populations—Tyrone and Fermanagh. It was quite impossible to partition those counties equitably between the two religions, and the conference broke up with no tangible result.

Meanwhile, the more intrepid spirits among the Irish Volunteer leadership had managed to acquire a few rifles and some ammunition on the continent, and on Sunday, 26 July, in broad daylight, they landed the arms at Howth, outside Dublin. As 1,000 Volunteers marched back to Dublin with rifles, the police and military were called out. A detachment of Scottish troops marching along the quays was jeered and a few stones were thrown. When they reached Bachelor's Walk, their exasperated commanding officer ordered them to fire on the crowd, and three civilians were killed and over thirty wounded. The unhappy contrast between this action and the government's vacillation over the identical exploit by Protestants three months earlier caused an outraged reaction throughout Catholic Ireland against what seemed to Archbishop Walsh to have been an 'unprecedented action of a portion of the military forces garrisoned in Dublin'.[34] On the following Sunday, while memorial Masses for the victims were held 'up and down the country',[35] an ultimatum demanding free passage for the armies of Germany was served upon the government of Belgium.

CHAPTER XV

The Catholic Rebellion

As the war-clouds gathered, the problem of what political strategy to pursue must have occupied Redmond's thoughts. On the evening of Saturday, 1 August, Margot Asquith, the Prime Minister's wife, characteristically wrote to Redmond urging him to make the dramatic gesture of offering all his soldiers to the government (or to the King) in hopes that he 'might strengthen the claim of Ireland upon the gratitude of the British people'.[1] Redmond acknowledged her letter on Sunday and indicated that he hoped to be able to follow her advice. The course he adopted, however, was somewhat different from Margot Asquith's suggestion. On Monday, 3 August, after Sir Edward Grey, the Foreign Secretary, had addressed the Commons at length on the very grave international situation, Redmond rose to speak. Amid cheers from all benches, he declared that the government might immediately withdraw all its troops from Ireland and rely upon the Volunteers to defend their country from foreign invasion. 'And for this purpose', he promised, 'armed Nationalist Catholics in the South will be only too glad to join arms with the armed Protestant Ulstermen in the North.'[2] Though Redmond unquestionably sympathised instinctively with the cause of the Allies, his action was not a spontaneous and reckless commitment, but a carefully calculated gesture designed to win English gratitude at minimum cost to his party's prestige in Ireland. He did not at this point offer to send a single Irish soldier overseas.

After six weeks of intense negotiations between the party and the government, it was agreed that the Home Rule Bill would be placed on the statute book immediately, together with a Suspensory Bill preventing its operation for the duration of the war. Asquith gave assurances that Ulster would not be coerced and that parliament would have an ample opportunity to modify the Home Rule Act 'in such a way as to secure the general consent both of Ireland and of the United Kingdom'.[3] The entire Unionist Party filed out of the House in protest after Carson and Bonar Law had denounced this arrangement, but Redmond welcomed the plan. In doing so the Irish Party leader was striking the best bargain possible under the circumstances. Naturally the war effort overshadowed all other considerations in the government's policy, and that effort could be carried on without Ireland's support, but not against active Tory opposition. Redmond's task was so to demonstrate Ireland's loyalty in the crisis, while maintaining his position in Irish politics, that he might win the most favourable settlement of the Ulster question possible in the unforeseeable circumstances which would follow the war. Indeed, he hoped that Irish participation in the war effort might even break down the prejudices of the Ulstermen and thus alter the whole political equation. On the strength of 'Home Rule on the Statute Book' he made his first public reference to Irishmen serving overseas while reviewing a Volunteer unit at Woodenbridge on 20 September. In moving towards active participation in the recruiting campaign at this point Redmond probably had the support of the overwhelming majority of his countrymen. It is true that a majority of those members of the Provisional Committee of the Volunteers not nominated by Redmond signed a manifesto dissociating themselves from his recruiting activity. In the split which followed, however, approximately 160,000 men remained loyal to Redmond under the name 'National Volunteers', while only some 11,000 seceded to join Eóin Mac Néill's 'Irish Volunteers', popularly dubbed the 'Sinn Féin Volunteers'.

Meanwhile, on 26 September Redmond formally endorsed the recruiting campaign by joining Asquith on a recruiting platform where the Prime Minister made a most explicit promise to form a distinctive Irish unit and implied that the Volunteer units themselves would be accepted into the Crown forces.[4] Had Asquith's intentions been fulfilled, it is possible that the initial wave of public support for Redmond's policy might have been sustained. In the event, however, Kitchener and other military leaders, suspicious of both Asquith and the Irish and lacking in imagination, effectively blocked efforts to organise Irish units in ways that would command Catholic and nationalist enthusiasm. While an Ulster division was being raised under its own distinctive emblems and with other special privileges, Nationalist leaders seeking similar privileges met only infuriating bureaucratic delays and obstinacy on the part of the military authorities. Although some improvement took place in 1915, by that time public enthusiasm had waned and could not easily be revived.

During the early weeks of the war, Redmond received some fairly encouraging episcopal support. Bishop McHugh declared that 'the sympathy of our people one and all is with the arms of England' and alluded to Germany as 'a Power that would set at nought the very foundations upon which civilisation rests'.[5] Bishop Morrisroe of Achonry, preaching at Ballaghaderreen on 16 August, identified the Allied cause with 'the interests of liberty and humanity'.[6] Redmond was able to write to Asquith on 22 August that when he attended Mass at Baltinglass on the preceding Sunday a pastoral from Bishop Foley had been read urging prayers for the success of British arms. In the sermon which followed, the justice of England's cause had been defended, and Redmond observed that the priest 'mentioned only England, he never referred even to France, showing that it was England and not France that appealed to him'.[7] Ecclesiastical support for the war effort, however, was by no means unequivocal. The death of Pius X in the early days of the war had necessitated Cardinal Logue's absence from Ireland for several weeks. When, returning from the Conclave, he landed at Plymouth on 28 September, the Cardinal was met by a newspaper reporter. Exactly what was said in the ensuing interview is not clear. When he arrived in Dublin on the following day, Logue insisted that his remarks had been limited to 'a few words . . . denouncing the barbarism of the Germans in burning Rheims Cathedral'.[8] Much to his disquiet the press had elaborated on his remarks and various versions appeared in the daily papers. The *Independent* ran the story under the heading 'The Loyalty of Ireland—Cardinal Logue and the

War', and attributed to the Cardinal such sentiments as that 'there was no more loyal country than Ireland' and that 'Irishmen throughout the world would stand by the Empire in the crisis, and were prepared to fight shoulder to shoulder, petty animosities being forgotten'.[9] Logue did not explicitly disavow particular statements or even indicate which of the morning papers had offended. Nevertheless, it is clear that by the time he arrived in Dublin he did not want his condemnation of German excesses to be construed as more than very cautious support for England. In his Dublin interview he referred to the Home Rule Act and 'said it would be time enough to praise the measure when they saw what its ultimate fate would be', adding: 'I don't trust your politicians in England very much. . . . They have an Amending Bill to bring in. What that will be I don't know.' Three months later Archbishop Walsh, who was avoiding public comment on political matters, confided to T. M. Healy that he thought the recent appointment of Sir Matthew Nathan, a highly-regarded Jewish civil servant, as Under-Secretary 'evidenced an intention to diddle us on finance'.[10] Walsh was also worried over the possibility of a coalition government under which Home Rule would become 'whatever the Tories cared to offer'. Healy summarised the conversation in a letter to O'Brien by saying: 'He is evidently no swallower of Redmondite promises.'

Despite the misgivings of Logue and Walsh, the party was probably still profiting from the alarm with which many clergymen had viewed the Irish Volunteer movement before Redmond had gained a voice in it. At the end of 1914 a police report stated that 'the Catholic Clergy throughout the country in general supported the policy of the Irish Parliamentary Party in relation to the war and recruiting'.[11] There were exceptions to this generalisation, however, and the report listed twenty-four priests (five parish priests, eighteen curates and 'an American on leave') who had made anti-recruiting or pro-German speeches since the outbreak of the war. This number was, of course, less than one per cent of the Irish clergy, and therefore cannot be taken as evidence of any widespread clerical revolt against Redmond's policy. Nevertheless, clerical sentiment in favour of the war effort was not very enduring, as was demonstrated in a controversy over the provision of Catholic chaplains for the forces. Shortly after the outbreak of the war, reports from the front that Catholic troops were dying without attendance of priests provoked an angry public outcry and strong protest from the hierarchy. The initial problem of a simple numerical deficiency of Catholic chaplains was complicated by failure of Protestant military authorities to appreciate Catholic desires for priests to accompany troops into the thick of battle to administer last rites to the wounded, and by disedifying rivalry behind the scenes between the English and Irish Catholic hierarchies over who should appoint the chaplains. By late 1915 the difficulties over appointment and deployment of chaplains had been smoothed over, only to reveal that there was no stampede of Irish priests to fill the posts created by the army. Logue was obliged to make urgent appeals and had to admit that 'In justice it must be said that any deficiency in the supply of chaplains cannot be attributed to the War Office Authorities who are quite willing to make appointments wherever they are required.'[12]

Whatever enthusiasm the clergy may have had for the war effort at the outset was largely dissipated before the end of 1915. As late as April 1915 Bishop Brownrigg sent a letter to a local recruiting meeting heartily endorsing the Allied cause and appealing in the name of fallen and captured Kilkennymen for more Kilkenny recruits,[13] but such impassioned episcopal support for the recruiting drive was already uncommon. At a recruiting conference at the Viceregal Lodge in the autumn of 1915 Catholic bishops were notable by their absence.[14] The police list of clergymen 'who have come under notice owing to their disloyal language or conduct during 1915' was about twice as long as the 1914 list—still an insignificant fraction of the Irish clergy. The prevailing clerical mood was not hostility to the war effort and Redmond's policy, but simple apathy. A police memorandum dated 10 April 1916 stated that 'The R.C. Clergy as *a body* are, on the whole, lukewarm on the subject of recruiting.'[15]

The shift between late 1914 and early 1916 from 'general support' to a 'lukewarm' attitude toward the war effort on the part of the clergy was, no doubt, partly a reflection of a general waning of popular enthusiasm for the war. Certain factors, however, were particularly damaging to clerical support for the war. Recruiting advertisements on the theme 'Save Catholic Belgium' raised the awkward issue of which group of belligerents was more deserving of Catholic sympathies on religious grounds. 'The young priests', T. M. Healy wrote to William O'Brien in December 1914, 'hate the French Anticlericals & talk of Austrias Catholicity,'[16] and according to the police, one of the cries of clergymen opposed to the war effort was 'that the anti-clerical policy of the French Government should not be forgotten by the people of this country'.[17] Indeed, French officialdom seemed determined to jar the memories of any devout Catholics who might have momentarily forgotten French anticlericalism. It was reported early in the war that any wounded Irish soldier in a French hospital who requested the services of a priest was required first to sign a declaration, in French, that he was a Catholic and expressly demanded the sacraments. The hierarchy, at its October 1914 meeting, protested against this 'miserable French device',[18] and as the issue seems to have soon faded away, presumably some sensible arrangement was made to adapt French legal requirements to the religious sensitivities and linguistic limitations of Irish soldiers. Nevertheless, the episode is indicative of suspicions and memories which inhibited clerical zeal for the war effort.

As the manpower drain caused by the war became more evident, some ecclesiastics reacted in ways similar to those in which they customarily reacted to ordinary emigration. At an industrial exhibition held in Dundalk during July 1915, Logue said that 'the Government that killed their Irish industries, and forced the people to emigrate were looking out for men now to fight for them, and the men were not there to be got (*cheers*)'.[19] He did admit that there were 'a good many' men in the country still, but he stressed that the country should not be depleted of men and then reverted to the theme of what a 'grand thing' it would be for Ireland and for the Empire if industries had been encouraged and the people kept at home. Bishop Foley was probably thinking along similar lines when he wrote to a recruiting meeting in Carlow that, although he supported its purposes, he felt that

Carlow had already contributed her fair share of recruits when compared with many English or Scottish towns. In his view the fair quota of troops to be contributed by Ireland should be a smaller proportion of total population than the quota for England or Scotland.[20]

The coalition government which Walsh had feared at the beginning of 1915 materialised in May, when Asquith reconstructed his administration as a 'national' government. Several days before the new administration was formed T. M. Healy had tried unsuccessfully to persuade the Archbishop to write a public letter on the political situation. On 21 May, when plans for the coalition were becoming common knowledge, Healy suggested to O'Brien that, given the new situation, the latter might be able to move Walsh to action, but apparently nothing came of the suggestion.[21] Not only did the new ministry contain Unionists, but it included the one Unionist most detested in Catholic Ireland—Carson—and the post of Lord Chancellor of Ireland was offered to another Irish Unionist diehard, James Campbell.[22] Redmond was also offered a place in the new ministry. To have accepted would have been an even bolder step than his action in supporting the war effort. He had hoped that his earlier action, combined with the prevailing sense of crisis, would call forth reciprocal gestures of good will from the old enemies of Irish nationalism and usher in an era of good feeling. By May 1915 it was clear that nothing of the sort was happening. Unionist leaders had remained personally hostile to Redmond and his colleagues. An Ulster division had been organised on the basis of rigid exclusion of Catholics from its ranks. Military leaders had abandoned little or none of their instinctive suspicion of Irish nationalists. In short, no one but Redmond had made a serious effort to free himself from old patterns of political behaviour. Therefore, Redmond had no ground for making another bold gesture, and in keeping with an established rule of the Irish political system, he declined to join the ministry.

The formation of the coalition was a turning point in the development of at least one bishop's political attitudes. For years Bishop Fogarty of Killaloe had backed the Irish Party, but on 3 June 1915 he wrote to Redmond:

This Coalition with Carson on top is a horrible scandal and intolerable outrage on Irish sentiment, and now expelling Irish L. Chancellor to make a place for Campbell! Such hideous jobbery!! The English having got all they wanted from Ireland, don't care two pence about her feelings. Such is our reward for her profuse loyalism and recruiting. The people are full of indignation, but are powerless. The Party, to my mind a great mistake, have taken the whole thing lying down, without a bit of fight. Worse still in their proclamation when immediately after it they declared they would support conciliation and Carson, and indulged in the usual nonsense about England's solicitude for small nations. Little she cares for small nations. As far as Ireland is concerned, there is nothing to choose between Carsonism and Kaiserism. Of the two, the latter is lesser evil; and it almost makes me cry to think of the Irish brigade fighting, not for Ireland, but for Carson and what he stands for, Orange ascendancy here.

Home Rule is dead and buried and Ireland is without a national Party or National Press. The 'Freeman' is but a Government organ, and the National Party but an Imperial instrument.

What the future has in store for us, God knows: I suppose conscription, with a bloody feud between people and soldiers. I never thought that Asquith would have consented to this humiliation and ruin of Irish feeling. There is a great revulsion of feeling in Ireland. But all this you know and feel yourself, I am sure, without my sad and angry tale.

May God guard you.[23]

Redmond forwarded a copy of the letter to Asquith, describing the author as 'one of the most able and broadminded Irish Catholic Bishops, and a man who has always been a strong supporter of the Irish Party'.[24] He took pains to point out to the Prime Minister that the letter was indicative of the mood in Ireland not only of the 'unthinking crowd' but of 'intelligent men' as well.

Bishop O'Dwyer had been quite silent on political issues during the first year of the war, but early in August 1915 he appealed to Redmond in a long, carefully worded letter to apply pressure to the government to honour the recent papal proposal for peace. He raised the question whether Germany could be crushed without costs more ruinous than defeat, and argued that even one hour's prolongation of the war would be a crime against humanity. Moreover, he maintained, the

war was creating an intolerable war debt for Ireland and
would be followed by the collapse of prices and attendant
economic evils which would condemn Home Rule—if indeed
Home Rule were forthcoming—to 'hopeless poverty and
impotence'. Finally, in the Bishop's view it was inexcusable
for Irish Catholics to ignore the Pope's appeal, and Redmond
was the man to initiate action upon it.[25] Although in 1912
O'Dwyer had expressed his confidence in Redmond personally in a private letter to the party leader, he had refused to
give any public countenance to the party since the formation
of the Liberal alliance in 1906. The Bishop of Limerick had
jealously guarded his independence of the party and reserved
the right to attack it with great gusto on the slightest provocation. Thus his courteous appeal to Redmond at this time
was a definite departure from his usual form. Perhaps
O'Dwyer was giving Redmond one last chance to disprove
his belief that the party valued their English political friendships more than they respected the admonitions of ecclesiastical authority—in this case the highest ecclesiastical authority.
Of course, if Redmond had acceded to the request, he would
not only have forfeited whatever advantages had been gained
by his policy of loyalty to the Empire in its hour of danger,
but he would have lent credence to Ulster Protestant charges
that the Catholic Irish owed allegiance to a foreign ecclesiastical prince in secular matters. When Redmond tersely refused
to do as the Bishop suggested,[26] he was following the policy
which he and Dillon had been trying to pursue for some
years—to do nothing which would strengthen the argument
that Home Rule meant Rome Rule. Though by his refusal
of O'Dwyer's request he avoided stirring up anti-Catholic
feeling, he lost a genuine opportunity for a *rapprochement*
with the Bishop of Limerick. No doubt the choice seemed
easy in 1915, but within a year he would have cause to regret
his decision.

O'Dwyer apparently regarded Redmond's rejection of his
suggestion as a release from the self-imposed restraint which
he seems to have practised for the first year of the war. During
the following month, at the close of a speech in which he
criticised the Intermediate Education system, O'Dwyer went
out of his way to praise the educational system of 'our enemy',

avoiding the mention of Germany by name 'because of the Defence of the Realm Act'.[27] Several weeks later, when a group of Irish emigrants en route to the United States were attacked as shirkers by a mob in Liverpool, O'Dwyer cast aside all reserve and composed a fiery public letter, asking:

What have they or their forebears ever got from England that they should die for her? Mr. Redmond will say, 'A Home Rule Act is on the Statute Book.' But any intelligent Irishman will say, 'A Simulacrum of Home Rule' with an express notice that it is never to come into operation.

This war may be just or unjust, but any fairminded man will admit that it is England's war, not Ireland's.[28]

The letter escaped the censorship in the Limerick papers, but was suppressed in the Dublin papers. Nevertheless, it was quickly reprinted in leaflet form, and during November and December police found it in circulation in at least seventeen counties.[29] Of course, this most outspoken episcopal attack upon Redmond's policy since the outbreak of the war gave respectability to clerical participation in the Irish Volunteer organisation and in anti-war activities. After all, a priest could scarcely be disciplined by his ecclesiastical superiors for reading to his congregation a pronouncement of the venerable Bishop of Limerick or for expressing the opinion that his Lordship 'was one of the most fearless and disinterested of Irishmen'.[30]

Realising, no doubt, that its political position had been weakened by the events of the preceding year, the party seems to have systematically solicited expressions of support from various bishops in the form of letters to U.I.L. conventions during the latter half of 1915. O'Donnell, of course, produced a highly optimistic letter stressing such things as the friendliness of the 'democracy across the Channel' to Irish claims. He admitted that an Amending Act was inevitable, but implied that strong Nationalist organisation could influence the content of the act.[31] This optimism was echoed by Bishop Naughton of Killala.[32] McHugh did not venture a prediction on the Amending Act, but he stressed the need for Nationalists to unite behind their 'General-in-Chief'.[33] Archbishop Harty of Cashel managed to produce an almost naïvely optimistic letter.[34] Other prelates such as Sheehan of

Waterford, Finegan of Kilmore, and Brownrigg of Ossory produced straightforward, brief letters urging unity behind the party.[35] Bishop Hoare of Ardagh avoided direct mention of the party, contenting himself with a vaguer reference to 'keeping together the political forces of the country', and the tone of his letter was marked by depression over the war and 'the pitiable state of the hay and other crops'.[36] Foley apparently limited his remarks to thanks for the invitation extended to him by the Queen's County convention and formal regrets for his absence.[37] A predictably noncommittal letter was received by the Louth convention from Logue: 'I am sorry I cannot attend the Convention in Dundalk on the 5th Dec., as I have never hitherto appeared on a political platform, and cannot change my rule. I must therefore, content myself with wishing our Convention every success.'[38] Moreover, there were evidently a number of prelates whom the party did not choose to invite or who replied in terms which the party did not wish to publicise. In general, the party's standing with the clergy at the end of 1915 was as depressing as was the war itself.

Redmond's assertion of his authority over the Volunteers during the summer of 1914 had temporarily and in outward form absorbed into the party's organisational structure its only serious rival. This absorption had been more apparent than real, however, and after Redmond's Woodenbridge speech the Volunteer leadership which had existed in the spring of 1914 was able to secede almost intact to form the Irish ('Sinn Féin') Volunteers. While they probably lost a large number of the men they had commanded before Redmond's June intervention, the significance of the Irish Volunteers lay not in their numbers, but in a peculiarity of their structure which was unperceived even by some of their leaders. The President and Chief of Staff of the organisation was Eóin Mac Néill, who for twenty years had cultivated good relationships with a number of leading churchmen. On the other hand, a number of key positions in the organisation —indeed a majority of the places on its governing committee —were held by leading figures in the Irish Republican Brotherhood, which was regularly condemned by those same churchmen. Unknown to Mac Néill, the Supreme Council of the I.R.B. decided just after the outbreak of the war to mount an insurrection before the war was over. During 1915 a highly secret Military Council of the I.R.B., whose very existence was unknown even to some leading I.R.B. men, was given the responsibility of carrying the Supreme Council's resolution into effect.

The utility of the Volunteer movement as a 'front organisation' for the I.R.B. has been noted above (Chapter XIV). Since about 1911, moreover, advanced nationalists had come more and more to dominate the Gaelic League. Douglas Hyde had fought a losing battle to maintain the facade of non-political, nonsectarian policies, but here too the I.R.B., together with assorted other anti-Irish Party nationalists, were achieving a commanding position.[39] At the 1913 Gaelic League Árd-Fheis the left wing of the League secured a clear majority on its executive. Moreover, at the 1915 Árd-Fheis, the activists were able to carry unanimously a resolution that:

The Gaelic League shall be strictly non-political and nonsectarian, and shall devote itself to realising the ideal of a Gaelic-speaking and free Irish nation, free from all subjection to foreign influences.[40]

The demise of the nonpolitical, nonsectarian rule could no longer be disguised, despite the opening clause of this curious resolution. Hyde shortly resigned the League presidency, and the organisation as it had been known went into eclipse. The energies of its most zealous workers were now absorbed in Irish Volunteer activities. Through the Volunteer movement, a good deal of Irish Ireland was being placed at the disposal of the I.R.B. leadership.

By early 1916 the I.R.B. Military Council had decided to launch the rebellion on Easter Sunday of that year. The Irish Volunteers would be mobilised for 'manoeuvres', and, it was hoped, arms would be supplied from Germany. The I.R.B. men were so entrenched in the Volunteer organisation that practically the only bar to a mobilisation at their bidding was Mac Néill himself. Early in 1916 Mac Néill began to suspect that an insurrection was being contemplated, and he composed a long memorandum setting forth, in terms drawn from Catholic theology, why a rebellion would be unjustifiable at that time. Such a rebellion would attract no popular support and would be easily crushed, he argued, and without a reasonable prospect of military success, military action would be morally wrong—a consideration which to Mac Néill was 'final and decisive'.[41] The Volunteers should patiently continue to organise and do nothing to impede the tide of opinion which he believed was flowing in their direction. The only situation in which he admitted military action to be justifiable under present circumstances would be an attempt by the government to disarm the Volunteers. In such a case they were entitled to 'resist to death'.[42]

Mac Néill read the memorandum to his staff at a meeting in February, and in some sense the staff members indicated assent. Pádraig Pearse, one of the members of the I.R.B. Military Council, 'explicitly repudiated the suggestion that he or his friends contemplated insurrection or wanted to commit the Volunteers to any policy other than that to which they were publicly committed'.[43] Nevertheless, Pearse and his friends went right ahead with their deception of Mac Néill. With his argument that rebellion was militarily hopeless they apparently agreed, but from his moral conclusion—that it was therefore unjustifiable—they tacitly dissented. They had, in fact, abandoned traditional Catholic morality on this point —though several of them were obviously very devout Catholics—and concocted a new doctrine of 'blood sacrifice'. Bloodshed was seen as a means of cleansing and sanctifying the Irish nation. Theological terminology was made to serve purposes never contemplated by the theologians.

Although Pearse and his friends rejected Mac Néill's moral argument, they did not forget one point which he made—that he would support resistance to any attempt to disarm the Volunteers. As Easter approached, Joseph Plunkett, another of the Military Council members, contrived to take advantage of this feature of Mac Néill's position by having a certain document—purportedly smuggled out of Dublin Castle— printed and placed in circulation. The 'Castle Document' ordered government forces to prepare to arrest all members of certain nationalist bodies and to occupy or surround certain centres of anti-British activity in Dublin, including the Archbishop's House—a touch which should have immediately branded the document as at least partially a fabrication.

The document was probably based, in part, upon an actual document which had been drafted by someone in the Irish administration as a contingency plan. The deception carried out by Plunkett consisted in the implication that the specified measures were imminent.[44] Mac Néill was briefly taken in by the document and, in consultation with the Volunteer executive on Wednesday of Holy Week, drafted an order directing Volunteers 'to prepare themselves against suppression'. He dispatched messengers with copies of the 'Castle Document' to various influential persons throughout the country—including, characteristically, Catholic bishops.[45] On Holy Thursday Mac Néill discovered that orders tantamount to an insurrection had earlier been issued without his permission, and he told Pearse he would use every means short of informing the government to prevent the Rising.

Mac Néill briefly had second thoughts about this threat and elected not to disturb Archbishop Walsh who was quite ill at this moment. His brother James MacNeill, however, took the initiative to call on Father Michael Curran, the Archbishop's secretary, on the evening of Good Friday. James apparently hoped that Walsh might obtain some unofficial assurance from the authorities that no disarmament was intended. Father Curran suggested that he communicate with the Archbishop through Dr Cox, a physician who was attending him twice daily, and reported the interview to Walsh, who 'was more than ever depressed that day with his illness but he listened attentively & though he said little more than that he could hardly do anything & that he was not in the confidence of either party, he said he would talk on the matter with Dr. Cox'.[46] It was now Saturday, and news had arrived that a German submarine carrying arms for the Rising had been intercepted in Queenstown harbour and sunk by her own captain. Eóin Mac Néill had become convinced that the Castle Document was a forgery and reasoned that since the government had not acted as soon as the submarine was sunk, it was unlikely to act at all. He therefore took immediate steps to effect his earlier resolution to stop the Rising. He published a countermanding order in the *Sunday Independent* and communicated, he stated at his court martial a month later, with 'every person of influence who in my opinion would be able to use persuasion against any action of this kind', including 'a great many members of the clergy especially'.[47] Copies of the countermanding order were distributed through Father Curran to Volunteer units in the Dublin area by priests of the archdiocese.[48] The order did prevent the outbreak on Easter Sunday. The I.R.B. leaders, however, realising fully that the failure of the arms shipment together with Mac Néill's action had rendered any general, nationwide insurrection impossible, decided to rise in Dublin nevertheless on Monday.

No doubt those clergymen throughout the country through whom Mac Néill conveyed his countermanding order worked very effectively to prevent isolated outbreaks. Even militantly nationalist priests, such as Father O'Daly of Co. Tyrone, who was actually a member of the I.R.B., and Father Hennessy, O.S.A., a chaplain to the Irish Volunteers in Limerick, discouraged provocative action in the hopeless situation.[49] In Cork Dr Cohalan, the Auxiliary Bishop, acted as a mediator between the local Volunteer leaders and the military authorities. Together with the Lord Mayor he arranged for the Volunteers to place their arms in the Lord Mayor's custody in return for vague guarantees against arrest—an agreement which the military made no pretence of honouring after the Dublin insurrection had been suppressed.[50] In Dublin two Capuchin fathers spent the early part of the week ministering to wounded rebels, and at the end of the week, when rebel defeat was inevitable, they helped to minimise bloodshed by arranging a temporary truce in one area and persuading rebels in other areas to surrender.[51]

On Easter Monday, after the rebels had taken strategic points and before the government had been able to mount its counterattack, Mr (afterwards Sir) James O'Connor, a Roman Catholic law officer of the Crown, called at the Archbishop's House and asked Walsh to write a letter appealing to the rebels to lay down their arms. According to O'Connor, the Archbishop expressed detestation of the Rising,[52] but the only public appeal he issued was for the people to keep off the streets 'in this time of unprecedented excitement and danger'.[53] Walsh, according to the version of the interview which he related to one of his secretaries, declared O'Connor's suggestion 'preposterous'.[54] It was, in his view, 'absurd and foolish . . . to call on men who had actually taken up arms to lay them down unconditionally'. Though O'Connor's word 'detestation' was perhaps too strong a description of Walsh's feelings toward the Rising, the Archbishop did speak of 'the *folly* of the rising, which, he believed, could only end in defeat'. In his opinion, however, the fault lay with the government, 'which, with the ample resources of military and police at their disposal had allowed blood to be spilt'. Therefore, he upbraided O'Connor and the government for 'trying to make a cat's-paw of him' and told his visitor 'that he and his Government should resign, and that, if they did not, they ought to be superseded'.

The government, thwarted in its attempt to gain ecclesiastical intervention in Dublin against the rebellion, took heart when, later in the week, Pope Benedict XV directed the Papal Secretary of State to telegraph to Cardinal Logue 'requesting information as to the situation and expressing his hopes that that noble and dear country should be spared further sanguinary conflicts'.[55] Logue replied on about Sunday or Monday of Low Week: 'Insurrection happily terminated. Insurgents have surrendered unconditionally. Hope peace soon re-established.'[56] Though Logue's statement was sufficiently noncommittal to excite no enthusiasm in government circles, the news of papal interest in the rebellion gave rise to the hope that the resources of the Catholic Church would somehow be mobilised to pacify Ireland in support of British interests. Before Logue had replied, it had been reported in Italy that the papal message had urged him to recommend that Irish Catholics co-operate for the re-establishment of order and not thwart the measures of British government.[57] We do not know if Logue expressed to Vatican authorities any unwillingness to take positive steps urging co-operation with the British, but in the official communiqué (quoted above), released after Logue's reply had been received, they made no reference to this request. On 3 May Sir Henry Howard, the British Envoy to the Holy See, called the stronger wording of the papal message suggested by earlier press reports to the attention of Cardinal Gasparri, the Papal Secretary of State. The Cardinal replied 'that although the words in [the *Corriere della Sera* report of 29 April 1916] were not the same as those in the message to Cardinal Logue, they both "au fond" conveyed the same idea, namely "that the rebels should lay down their arms and make peace", and he added that he hoped HM's Govt would be pleased with the action of the Pope in this matter.'[58]

Armagh was rather less anxious than Rome to please H.M.'s Government; Logue made no public effort to secure the co-operation of Catholics with the government. When the *Irish Catholic* resumed publication after the holocaust with a combined 29 April-6 May issue it was operating virtually without episcopal guidance concerning the momentous events since its last issue, and it wisely made only very brief comment on 'the partially socialistic and partially alien outbreak' of the preceding week. Except for this short editorial and the acknowledgement that an issue had been missed, the paper gave no indication that anything untoward had occurred.

The Church would require some time to make up her collective mind about the Rising. She would need even more time to come to a decision about some larger issues with which she was now presented. Since about 1908 the Church's power within the Irish political system had been greatly constricted, first by the removal of her most pressing grievances in the realm of education around which she could rally her forces to bring pressure on the State or the Nation, and later by the extraordinary parliamentary situation which pertained after the 1910 general elections. The basis of the Church's power had been her extremely influential voice in the popular decision-making process over the legitimacy of political institutions. Between 1910 and 1914, however, that process was at a happy standstill. Those in power in the State no longer contested the Nation's legitimacy; those in power in the Nation were in the process of converting the *de jure* legitimacy of their institution for the future into a *de facto* sovereignty in the present—albeit the sovereignty would be of a rather attenuated sort and the future never did become the present. The Church had little to do but watch. Now, however, war and rebellion had decisively altered the whole political world. The Irish people would, in the next few years, have to choose between rival claimants to political legitimacy. The Church would have a role in the choice and, more important, would have a hand in shaping the alternatives between which the choice would be made. A perceptive Ulsterman told Lloyd George a few weeks after the Rising 'that the Church is the only organization which now really exists in the three southern provinces. The State & the League have both fallen to pieces.'[59]

PART FOUR

Resolution, 1916-1921

CHAPTER XVI

The Terrible Beauty

THE Nation's younger generation was in disarray. Virtually all its leaders—even those such as Mac Néill and Griffith who had known nothing of the Rising until it was almost under way—were in custody. Moreover, public reaction in Ireland was overwhelmingly against the rebels. Under these circumstances one might have expected the Church to issue a ringing condemnation of this violation of the most fundamental rule of Church-Nation relations—that the Nation's claim must be put forward only by constitutional methods. Such indeed seemed to be the tenor of comments by several prelates on 7 May, the first Sunday after order had been fully restored. Bishop Kelly of Ross referred to the Rising as an 'unlawful war' in which 'the killing of men . . . was murder pure and simple'.[1] 'The Sinn Fein section', declared Dr Higgins, the Auxiliary Bishop of Tuam, 'would have to render a fearful account for the blood they had shed.'[2] Archbishop Harty, congratulating the people of Cashel archdiocese on abstaining from the insurrection, expressed confidence 'that the people of Ireland at large do not want any revolutionary measures . . . that the people of Ireland believe that by constitutional means they can obtain substantial redress of their grievances'.[3] Bishop Mangan of Kerry alluded to the countermanding order of Eóin Mac Néill and urged that 'the young men who are members of the Irish Volunteers . . . not allow themselves on any account to be drawn into illegal courses by evil-minded men affected by Socialistic and Revolutionary doctrines'.[4]

By Sunday, 7 May, the military government which had supplanted the ordinary Dublin Castle administration had already begun executing these 'evil-minded men' one by one.

As the terse announcements of the firing squads' work appeared day after day the initial public disdain for the rebels changed into sympathy. This change was already perceptible in the sermon of Bishop Gilmartin of Clonfert, who, in contrast to the other prelates who were speaking out this Sunday, 'made a strong appeal that bloodshed might be spared, and urged that the authorities and the military must, above all, be guided by the principles of humanity'.⁵ By the following Sunday all seven signatories of the rebel proclamation, together with several other rebel commanders, had been shot, and the grim business had come to an end, but the shift in public mood was irreversible. It is reflected in the fact that on Sunday, 14 May, Bishop Hoare of Ardagh and Clonmacnoise, after pronouncing the Rising 'a mad and sinful adventure', expressed the hope that the authorities would eschew any policy of vengeance and added that 'the time had come for reconciliation'.⁶ Moreover, on the same Sunday Bishop Fogarty of Killaloe told a congregation that

He was not going to trouble them with a denunciation of the unhappy young men who were responsible for that awful tragedy. There are enough and plenty in Ireland ready to do that. He bewailed and lamented their mad adventure; but whatever their faults or responsibility may be—and let God be their merciful judge in that—this much must be said to their credit, that they died bravely and unselfishly for what they believed—foolishly indeed—was the cause of Ireland.⁷

Though this statement does in some sense oppose the Rising, the emphasis is more on condonation than condemnation. Just as public opinion shifted dramatically in the rebels' favour during the period of slightly more than a week in which the leaders were executed, the emphasis in the episcopal declarations the public heard changed—albeit more subtly—from the 'fearful account' the rebels would have to render, to 'let God be their merciful judge'.

Sympathisers with the rebel cause could take even more comfort in the action of Bishop O'Dwyer a few days later. General Maxwell, who, under martial law, had assumed all governmental powers in Ireland, had written to O'Dwyer on 6 May charging that two of O'Dwyer's priests, Father Michael Hayes and Father Thomas Wall, had created 'a dangerous menace to the peace and safety of the realm' and requesting that they be moved 'to such employment as will deny their having intercourse with the people'.[8] O'Dwyer directed one of his priests to reply on his behalf requesting further information, and Maxwell obliged with a list of reports implicating the two curates in Irish Volunteer activities. On 17 May O'Dwyer finally replied that he had read the allegations and found no justification for disciplinary action against Fathers Wall and Hayes.

They are both excellent priests, who hold strong National views [he wrote], but I do not know that they have violated any law, civil or ecclesiastical.

In your letter of 6th inst., you appealed to me to help you in the furtherance of your work as the military dictator of Ireland. Even if action of that kind was not outside my province, the events of the past few weeks would make it impossible for me to have any part in proceedings which I regard as wantonly cruel and oppressive.

You remember the Jameson raid, when a number of buccaneers invaded a friendly State and fought the forces of the lawful Government. If ever men deserved the supreme punishment it was they, but officially and unofficially, the influence of the British Government was used to save them and it succeeded. You took care that no plea for mercy should interpose on behalf of the poor young fellows who surrendered to you in Dublin. The first information which we got of their fate was the announcement that they had been shot in cold blood. Personally, I regard your action with horror, and I believe that it has outraged the conscience of the country. Then the deporting of hundreds and even thousands of poor fellows without a trial of any kind seems to me an abuse of power as fatuous as it is arbitrary, and altogether your regime has been one of the worst and blackest chapters in the history of the misgovernment of the country.[9]

The letter soon leaked out of the Bishop's study and, with the names of the priests left blank, was published in pamphlet form. This violation of confidentiality in his correspondence with Maxwell was typical of O'Dwyer's disregard of the rules of the game when it suited his purpose. Castle requests for bishops to silence troublesome priests were perhaps extraordinary, but this was not the first such instance.[10] No doubt

Castle officials felt that no bishop, even if he refused such a request, would be so ungentlemanly as to allow the correspondence to be published. If so, they reckoned without their host. The other bishops could have told them that O'Dwyer could not be relied upon to play the game by the rules. In 1891 he had embarrassed his colleagues by refusing to sign a manifesto against Parnell. In 1901 he had connived with Archbishop Healy to exclude Walsh's preference from the options open to the Robertson Commission. In January 1904 Walsh had summoned a meeting of the hierarchy very hastily precisely to avert the possibility that O'Dwyer would wreck the Dunraven university proposal by declaring unilaterally against it. His fiery public letter in December 1906, which virtually precluded the Irish hierarchy's joining with Archbishop Bourne in commending the Irish Party for its actions on the English Education Bill, was another item in the pattern of which his 1916 letter to Maxwell is the most celebrated. Although the statements of Gilmartin, Hoare and even Fogarty following the Rising may have been simply part of the general tide of public sympathy which accompanied the executions, O'Dwyer's action, in the context of his entire career, looks very much like a calculated political move. It certainly decreased the chances that at their scheduled June meeting the rest of the bishops might arrive at any consensus pronouncement on the Rising which O'Dwyer could be coerced into endorsing. At the time the Bishop of Limerick wrote to Maxwell it would have been reasonable to anticipate a pronouncement which, by condemning unconstitutional methods, would almost inevitably benefit O'Dwyer's old enemy, the Irish Party. Before the June meeting, however, the party had alienated another segment of the hierarchy as well.

The Rising had precipitated efforts at Westminster to secure a settlement which might remove the troublesome Irish question from British politics for the duration of the war. Asquith delegated to Lloyd George the task of trying to find some basis for agreement between the Irish Party leaders and the Ulster Unionists. Anxiety over the course of the war was growing, and because of it Lloyd George was able to induce both Carsonites and Redmondites to make sacrifices. By early

June, proposals had been worked out which provided for the immediate operation of the Home Rule Act in the provinces of Leinster, Munster and Connacht and the counties of Donegal, Cavan and Monaghan. The six excluded counties would be controlled by the Westminster parliament at which Ireland would continue to be represented at full strength. Carson accepted the embarrassment of repudiating the application of the Covenant to the three Ulster counties in which Protestants were in a hopeless minority—Donegal, Cavan and Monaghan—and Redmond took on the task of reconciling the Catholic majorities of Tyrone and Fermanagh to 'temporary' exclusion. Lloyd George was able to accomplish this piece of wizardry by negotiating separately with Redmond and Carson and not bringing them together in the same room. If the two Irish leaders had met face to face, there can be little doubt that they would have realised they were being told very different things. Redmond understood the arrangement to be temporary—for the duration of the war only—Carson believed that it would be permanent in the sense that it could be altered only by a new act of parliament.[11]

Just as he had done in March 1914, Redmond dispatched Devlin and Jeremiah MacVeagh to Ulster early in June to take soundings, particularly among the bishops. This time, however, they met with a wholly different response. Bishop McHugh of Derry, who had received the 1914 proposals with a sense of relief and had even offered to assist the party in dealing with Logue over them, treated the new scheme with contempt. He called the proposals 'rot' and apparently volunteered to Devlin some uncomplimentary opinions of the party for even entertaining them. When Devlin asked him to suggest alternatives, he mentioned the plebiscite by counties which had been embodied in the 1914 proposals. He was 'perfectly friendly', according to Devlin, but absolutely hostile to the new proposals. Moreover, he was still rankling over the abandonment—at Redmond's insistence—of the monster meeting in Derry which he had planned in 1914. He believed that his meeting 'would have demonstrated the strength of Ulster Nationalism, of which England apparently was ignorant'.[12] Bishop O'Donnell, the party's stalwart, examined the proposals carefully and 'appeared anxious to accept them if he could'. He concluded, however, that the exclusion of Fermanagh, Tyrone and Derry City without a plebiscite would be impossible to defend and would wreck the party. He 'appreciated the difficulties of the situation', but felt that the party should 'hold on' in hopes of some turn of events which would alter the situation.[13] Dr MacRory, the new Bishop of Down and Connor, refused to entertain the proposals, and Devlin observed that while he was 'not a politician in the sense of Derry or Raphoe . . . his opposition would influence a section of the clergy'.[14]

The most obvious point of objection to the proposals was the exclusion of Fermanagh, Tyrone and Derry City without a plebiscite. The bishops, realistically, were wary of assurances of the temporary character of the settlement. MacVeagh, who dealt with the Cardinal and the new Bishop of Dromore, Dr Mulhern, may have exhibited more optimism than Devlin over the posssibility of a plebiscite. He found the Cardinal willing to accept the proposals if a plebiscite at the end of the war were guaranteed and if his episcopal colleagues agreed.[15] Mulhern was anxious to find a *modus vivendi*, and suggested that Redmond should ask Logue to arrange for him to meet with the bishops of the affected area and should 'undertake to press resolutely for a period at which a plebiscite should be taken, whether at the end of the war, or in 5 years, or even in 10 years'. Mulhern hoped that the bishops would then support Redmond even if such pressure should fail.[16]

Redmond probably realised that there was no chance for the further concession of a plebiscite on Carson's part. In any case, if such a plebiscite were granted, it would give the settlement the stamp of permanence which he hoped to avoid at all costs. There was a fundamental, if subtle, divergence between the scales of priorities of Redmond and the bishops. Redmond was basically interested in keeping open the possibility of an eventual settlement without partition. The bishops thought first of how they might save as many as possible of their flock from the excluded area and were a bit less worried over the possibility that extreme eastern Ulster might never join the rest of Ireland. Redmond did, however, take up Mulhern's suggestion that he ask Logue to arrange for him to meet with the Northern bishops.[17] Logue agreed to call the meeting for 16 June at the Minerva Hotel in Dublin and discreetly noted that 'A meeting there—especially as some of the Bishops will be on their way to Maynooth—will attract less attention than if it took place at Armagh.'[18] In his reply Redmond asked the Cardinal his opinion on how the proposed conference of Ulster Nationalists should be constituted.[19] Logue obliged with the suggestion that attendance be restricted to members of elected (local government) bodies, representatives of U.I.L. branches and clergy. He specifically urged exclusion of representatives of 'Benefit Associations' as being self-elected and therefore likely to lay the conference open to the charge of being unrepresentative, and Redmond was thereby left to understand that Logue's hostility to the A.O.H. was unabated. The Cardinal also took the opportunity to offer a mild rebuke to traditional party methods of arranging such gatherings, distinguishing between 'a conference or deliberative body', which he clearly preferred, and 'a convention, at which things are generally carried by acclamation without much consideration'.[20]

Redmond's emissaries had also taken some soundings of opinion among the laity and parish clergy, and the results were not encouraging. Devlin's view was that the people outside Belfast would be as hostile as the bishops, although he expected some popular support among Catholics in his own political territory in the northern metropolis.[21] Mac-Veagh interviewed 'scores of priests & leading laymen' before concluding that the agreement as it stood had no chance of approval (and proposing the addition of county plebiscites). Such pessimism over popular lay and clerical support was fully justified by events. On 8 June agitation against the proposals was launched at Omagh, in the heart of the predominantly Catholic portion of the territory proposed for exclusion. The movement was organised under the auspices of a local clergyman and two attorneys, F. J. O'Connor and George Murnaghan,[22] and the meeting, at which a Mgr O'Doherty presided, adopted a series of resolutions (seconded by a parish priest and 'supported by several priests, magistrates, solicitors, and A.O.H. officials') which, while declaring loyalty to the party, called upon them to oppose resolutely 'any settlement, temporary or permanent, which would ex-

clude any part of Ulster'. Four bishops—McHugh, O'Donnell, MacRory and McKenna of Clogher—sent messages of
support.[23] Exclusion of any sort was condemned out of hand
by MacRory, McKenna and McHugh, whom Dillon described
to Lloyd George as 'the best of the Ulster Bishops—and possibly the most loyal ecclesiastical supporter the Irish Party
has in Ulster'.[24] O'Donnell stressed the party line—that a conference of Nationalists of the six counties must decide the
Nationalist strategy.

During the following two weeks similar protest meetings
took place throughout the country, and especially in Ulster.
Clergymen were prominent in proceedings at Derry, Enniskillen, Monaghan,[25] Armagh[26] and Coalisland.[27] At Enniskillen Canon Keown, P.P., V.G., said that 'if they were going
to allow Fermanagh to be cut off from the rest of Ireland the
ideal for which they had been striving for years would be
lost'.[28] At a meeting of the Knockbridge East (Co. Cavan)
United Irish League, the Rev. T. McCormack, C.C., declared
that

Every patriotic Irishman should do his best to prevent partition,
and they could no longer depend on the Irish Party, as they
were the principal accomplices, but exclusion would be defeated
in spite of them. It was the West British tendency in the Party
that repelled from it in recent years all that was young and intellectual, courageous and disinterested throughout the country,
and drove them ultimately into wild and desperate movements
of armed revolt and revolution. Could anything baser or more
treacherous be ever conceived than to conclude a separate peace
behind the backs and against the wishes of staunch Catholics of
the North?[29]

Devlin's prediction was being fulfilled, for the priests and
people of Catholic Ulster were rejecting the scheme spontaneously everywhere outside Belfast, where Devlin could
take at least some pleasure in reporting to the party leader
that a meeting of 2,000 persons including 'all Belfast important priests' backed the party's course of action with only
about twenty dissenting votes.[30] Outside the city, the generalisation made by Stephen Gwynn about Devlin's efforts at
this stage is correct: 'The whole force of the ecclesiastical
power was thrown against him. Apart from the detestation

of partition, the Catholic Church conceived that the principle of denominational education would be lost in the severed counties, where the dominant Presbyterian element was opposed to it.'[31]

On 16 June Redmond met the Northern bishops. O'Donnell and all the bishops whose dioceses lay wholly or partially in the six counties were present.[32] Predictably, the party leader found all the bishops hostile to the proposals. They predicted that the Northern Nationalist conference would reject them overwhelmingly. Dillon relayed from Redmond to Lloyd George the information that the bishops had

no *practical* alternatives to propose. The Bishop of Belfast [MacRory] however—at last proposed that the Conference should have a reasoned resolution putting forward County option as an alternative—And calling on the Party to press for this. Redmond said it would be useless.[33]

No doubt the Northern bishops spent the weekend together in Dublin, for the hierarchy's June meeting was to begin early the following week. On 19 June Bishop McHugh wrote a lengthy reply to an enquiry from a Derry alderman about the bishops' opinions concerning the exclusion proposals. He was happy to report 'that the Bishops, whose jurisdiction extends over the area in question'—a clause that excluded O'Donnell—'are absolutely unanimous in their opposition to the Lloyd George proposals and that they adopt, without reservation, the view of his Eminence Cardinal Logue that "It would be infinitely better to remain as we are for 50 years to come, under English rule, than to accept these proposals." '[34] As Irishmen, McHugh explained, the bishops regarded 'with feelings of deep regret' this 'admission of the principle of a divided Ireland'. In ecclesiastical eyes, however, there were more important issues at stake than national unity. 'What causes more alarm to the Bishops than the voluntary surrender of the National ideal', McHugh revealed, 'is the perilous position in which religion and Catholic education would be placed were these proposals, so imperfectly understood by the public, reduced to practice.' Since Carson and his followers were already publicly proclaiming the scheme to be a 'definite and final settlement', the Bishop could easily impugn the temporary character of the plan. If the provision was to be only temporary, he asked, reasonably enough, 'Why is a new Executive to be established in Belfast, with all the machinery of an independent body and without any connection with the Executive in Dublin?' 'Why is Belfast to have', he continued, specifying first the matters upon which the bishops were most sensitive, 'self-controlled branches of the Board of National Education, the Intermediate Board, the Agricultural Board, an independent Judiciary, and provision for cases where the two jurisdictions overlap or come into conflict?' There was an important distinction between the 1914 proposals and the present scheme beyond what Birrell would have called the question of 'acreage'.[35] On the subject of executive powers in the excluded area, the 1914 proposals had stated, rather vaguely: 'It may . . . prove necessary to make some new arrangements for the mode in which the authority of the Imperial executive is to be exercised in any excluded area.'[36] The 1916 scheme, though only a little more specific on this point, aroused serious episcopal misgivings by providing:

As regards the excluded area the executive power of His Majesty to be administered by a Secretary of State through such officers and departments as may be directed by Order of His Majesty in Council, those officers and departments not to be in any way responsible to the new Irish Government.[37]

It was the spectre of a Protestant-controlled Education Office in Belfast more than the concession of additional 'acreage,' which made the Northern bishops prefer to remain 'under English rule' for fifty more years. The new proposals, unlike the 1914 proposals, seemed to the bishops not to retain the Northern Catholics under English rule as they had known it, but to re-establish in the North the rule of bigoted Irish Protestants. McHugh conceded that the proposals had not been put forward by the Irish Party, but he maintained that 'to stand up in defence of them, to suggest the acceptance of them is just as bad as to be branded with the dishonourable reputation of having fathered them'.[38]

Clearly, then, the hierarchy had gathered at Maynooth in no mood to reach a consensus on the spectacular events of the past two months which might redound to the benefit of the

Irish Party. No public resolutions of any moment were forth-coming from the meeting. At a plenary session of the May-nooth Union, Logue did make a rather rambling speech defending the Irish priesthood against charges and anticipa-ting charges of disloyalty—which was, in a narrow sense, the issue raised in the O'Dwyer-Maxwell correspondence. In the course of the speech he made it plain that he regarded the Rising as 'foolish and pernicious', but he seemed to lay the heaviest blame on the government for the way in which it handled the situation.[39] More interesting perhaps than the Cardinal's speech was the fact that at the College's prize distribution the same week, O'Dwyer received an enthusiastic ovation as he left the hall.[40] Moreover, a newly formed organ-isation of Irish-speaking priests within the Maynooth Union, significantly, chose Father Thomas Wall to be its first presi-dent.[41]

Abandoned by the bishops of the six northern counties and with no encouraging gestures from the hierarchy as a whole, Redmond bravely faced a conference in Belfast, behind closed doors, of 776 Nationalists—including 130 priests—from the six counties on 23 June. Only by a threat to resign his leadership and the self-sacrificing efforts of Devlin[42] did he succeed in gaining acceptance of Lloyd George's pro-posals for 'temporary and provisional settlement of the Irish difficulty' by a vote of 475 to 265. At least five senior clerics were reported to have spoken on the issue—three of them in favour of the proposals and two against[43]—and it is an index of the efforts Redmond had to make to gain his majority that one of those who spoke in favour of accepting the proposals—Canon Quinn of Camlough—had the previous week chaired a meeting which protested against the 'outrage threatened to the six Ulster counties' and condemned the 'proposed mutila-tion of our country'.[44] Yet even as Redmond was mobilising every fibre of Nationalist organisation and party prestige in favour of what he took to be an agreed settlement, events in London were undermining the very basis of that understand-ing. Prominent Unionist members of the coalition were in revolt against the scheme and by early July had forced the government to alter those provisions of the agreement upon which the Irish Party leaders relied as safeguards of its temporary character. The original agreement provided for a bill which would remain in force until twelve months after the termination of the war and be extended beyond that time by action of the Privy Council if parliament failed to act. During all this time the Irish members were to remain at Westminster at full strength, thereby, it was hoped, ensuring their ability to force parliament to come to a settlement more favourable than the six-county exclusion scheme. During July Redmond was informed that these provisions had been cancelled, and on 24 July he repudiated the agreement under these altered terms.[45]

The Nation's representatives, unable to obtain the Church's sanction for their course of action following the Rising, had heavily mortgaged their own prestige to secure immediate implementation of some sort of Home Rule, and now they were forced to default. The Church, by her refusal to co-operate, had helped to weaken the one existing nation-wide agency which conformed to her own specifications for legitimate national leadership. For the moment the extent of this weakening was hard to gauge because there was quite literally no credible alternative leadership in the country. In addition to the fifteen rebel leaders who were executed, over 2,000 men and women were imprisoned in Great Britain, most of them without trial. In the succeeding two years, as the fortunes of the Irish Party continued to decline, the Church would have to find or create a new political movement which could be deemed to fit the constitutional mould. This process was already under way, but the fact that virtually all likely leaders for such a movement remained interned until late 1916 gave the process a certain air of unreality.

To understand the process, it is necessary to note one important result of the hierarchy's failure to take a united stance in condemnation of the Rising. With the solitary exception of Sir Roger Casement—an Anglo-Irishman of nationalist sympathies who had arranged the German arms shipment and had been captured in the West of Ireland just before the Rising broke out—the leaders of the Rising had been at least nominal Catholics, and shortly before his execution in an English prison in August Casement was received into the Catholic Church. Although several of the rebel leaders had suffered temporary lapses from religious practice in the past, all except apparently the old Fenian Tom Clarke[46] made their peace with the Church before their deaths. When one of the Capuchins who had been with the rebels during Easter Week called on Pearse the night before his execution, he mentioned that he had given communion to Connolly. 'Thank God,' Pearse reportedly exclaimed. 'It is the one thing I was anxious about.'[47] Pearse, Ceannt and Plunkett were extremely devout Catholics—Pearse a daily communicant.[48] It was characteristic of the rebel leaders that through Plunkett's father, a papal count, they had actually solicited the Pope's blessing upon the Rising.[49] The leaders' fervour was apparently typical of the religious life of lower-ranking rebel officers and many of the rank-and-file. During Easter Week the garrisons frequently recited the rosary together. When The O'Rahilly, a Catholic gentleman who had helped finance the Volunteers, realised that a sortie he was about to lead out of the G.P.O. on Friday evening meant almost certain death, he turned to one of the Pro-Cathedral priests who was serving as chaplain to receive a last absolution and blessing.[50]

Reports of such instances of the extraordinary piety of the rebels before, during and after the insurrection were soon in circulation. They were conferring upon the rebels the status not only of national heroes but of martyrs for the faith. Early in June T. P. O'Connor visited Dublin and heard of one little girl who began praying to 'St Pearse' when her mother refused to buy her a new hat. (The mother yielded.)[51] Another story he heard was that a priest giving Con Colbert, one of the rebel leaders, the last rites before his execution, assured him that he would go to heaven and begged his intercession to obtain an 'intention'. An 'intention', O'Connor explained to Lloyd George, 'means an unfulfilled though usually secret wish of a religious character.' The priest told Colbert that he had desired the fulfilment of this 'intention' for many years, but that if he obtained it within five days after Colbert's execution, he would know that Colbert's intercession had obtained it for him. The 'intention' was realised within three days after Colbert's execution.[52]

Since political demonstrations in Dublin were forbidden in

the weeks following the Rising, memorial Masses for the fallen and executed rebels became a focus for the growing public sympathy[53] and naturally added to the fascination with their religious lives. This fascination became a virtual hagiography when the July number of the *Catholic Bulletin*, a Dublin magazine carrying a selection of Catholic popular and devotional material, began a series entitled 'Events of Easter Week'. Interestingly, the *Bulletin* ceased with this issue to carry the imprimatur of the Dublin archdiocese, suggesting that perhaps Walsh did not want to be directly linked to the interpretation of the Rising which was being expounded.[54] Nevertheless, the cataloguing, month after month, of the religious virtues of the various rebels in a journal clearly labelled 'Catholic' no doubt made it more and more difficult to depict the Rising as opposed to Catholic principles. Clearly, if and when the survivors of the Rising were released from gaol, they would be a political entity for the Church to reckon with.

For the moment, however, the problem was how to bring about a new and acceptable focus for the Nation's politics. In July McHugh tried to institutionalise the June protest movement against partition into a nationwide challenge to the party. In a public letter on 11 July he urged 'a National Convention, summoned by the people, controlled by the people, and under the presidency of some great and fearless Irish layman chosen by the people'.[55] A great public meeting in Derry the following week including nearly a hundred priests passed resolutions condemning partition, temporary or permanent, pledging opposition to any attempt to set up a separate Northern government and resistance to any such government if it were constituted and calling on Nationalist M.P.s for Fermanagh and Tyrone 'to oppose exclusion or resign their seats'. McHugh sent a letter to the meeting attacking 'Irishmen calling themselves representatives of the people' who were 'prepared to sell their brother Irishmen into slavery to secure a nominal freedom for a section of the people'.[56] From the meeting came the nucleus of an Anti-Partition League based in Derry, Tyrone and Fermanagh, which was soon transmuted, with the addition of men from Belfast and Dublin, into the Irish Nation League.[57] It adopted a broad programme designed to appeal to nationalists throughout Ireland, began to spread its propaganda in England, and made plans to 'raise funds to contest Irish seats held by Nationalists who support the exclusion policy of Mr. Redmond and his friends'.[58] The new movement—which party orators aptly dubbed the 'League of Seven Attorneys'— suffered from the fact that it had little to distinguish it from the party itself. It was composed of middle-class, apparently middle-aged, Catholics, and proposed virtually the same strategy and programme as did the party, which, after all, shared its dislike for the idea of partition. The only experienced nationalists it attracted were the outcast and disaffected members of Redmond's own generation—Healy, O'Brien, Ginnell and William Martin Murphy[59]—who, indeed, were practically the only nationalist leaders outside the Irish Party still at large. For some months, however, it did provide a focus for opposition to the party.

Walsh, though he did not openly endorse the Irish Nation League, did choose the moment when it was germinating to break a political silence of over a decade. In a public letter on 25 July he pointed out that he had for some years indicated his 'strong view of the lamentable position of the Home Rule cause by what seemed to me to be a sufficiently striking indication of it—absolute abstention from everything that could be regarded as expressing concurrence in the course that was being pursued'.[60] The present helplessness of the Nationalist M.P.s was 'the necessary result of the abandonment of the policy of Independent Opposition'. During his years of silence he had been certain that disaster impended, but 'Nationalist Ireland, or to speak with accuracy, the preponderating majority of our people who still retain faith in the efficacy of Constitutional agitation, had become hopelessly possessed of the disastrous idea that "the Party",—or, to use the new-fangled term, its "leaders",—could do no wrong.' Any critic of its policies became a target for 'the easily handled epithets of "factionist", "wrecker", or "traitor"'. Thus Walsh took the step which, as we have seen, T. M. Healy—the arch-factionist—had urged him to take more than a year earlier, but he had the political acumen not to take it as a partisan of long-discredited Healyism, but rather to take

12

it at the precise moment when a new factionism was just coming into vogue. Moreover, at this moment the party's prestige was at such a low ebb that its epithets would have little force. The Archbishop avoided direct references to partition—although his timing made it inevitable that that issue would be read into his remarks—and he left his position on all substantive issues vague. The closest he came to an explicit statement on the possible contents of a Home Rule settlement was in a postscript:

The country has so long allowed its attention to be distracted with all sorts of side issues regarding the Irish Parliament that is to be, whilst an effective bar is kept up,—for that is what it comes to,—against all real consideration of the question whether the Parliament that is to come to us is to be a Parliament in any sense worthy of the name.

If Walsh's statement was encouraging to the organisers of the new movement, they could get small comfort from Bishop O'Dwyer, despite the latter's long-standing alienation from the party. When anti-partition organisers in Belfast solicited an expression of support from the Bishop of Limerick he replied with a characteristic torrent of abuse, prompted, it would seem, by the Belfast Catholic community's reputation for subservience to Devlin's machine. He could understand their 'anxiety and indignation', but he had 'very little pity' for them:

You gave up willingly the right to think and became puppets. You saw the interests of your religion sacrificed to the bigotry of the English Nonconformists, and never said a word. You thought it a grand thing for one of your idols to occupy the pulpit on a Sunday in a Protestant Conventicle in London. You have ceased to be men, and your leaders naturally think that they can sell you like chattels—but my sorrow in all this disgraceful business is for our poor country, that is being made a thing of truck and barter in the Liberal Clubs in London.[61]

O'Dwyer does not seem to have been very interested in the issue of partition. The actions of the party leaders with which he finds fault in this passage are precisely those most calculated to allay Protestant misgivings over Home Rule. It would have been quite in character for O'Dwyer to have felt that the loss of the predominantly Protestant counties would be good riddance. He had fought bitterly against any university settlement which might promote interdenominational fraternisation. His view of Protestantism was suggested in a revealing description by a friend shortly after his death: 'If he was considered intolerant in religious matters his motives were simple hatred of heresy and unbelief and a scorn tempered with pity for all outside the pale of the Catholic Church.'[62] These feelings gave him a sort of tunnel vision in political affairs. In the war, for example, 'his sympathies were altogether with the great Catholic Empire of Austria and the sixty million Catholics of Central Europe as against infidelity and Protestantism as represented by the Allies'[63]—as if Europe were at war over the same issues which had divided it in the seventeenth century.

O'Dwyer, then, did not ally himself with McHugh's effort to create another parliamentary party distinguished from the existing one mainly by a heightened concern to bring the Protestant-dominated North-east into the Home Rule settlement. Rather, in a speech accepting the freedom of the City of Limerick on 14 September, he made a new political departure. 'The national spirit', he declared, 'will yet vindicate our glorious country and not the petty intrigues of Parliamentary chicane.'[64] If the party had relied on this national spirit, rather than upon Asquith, Lloyd George and the Liberals, 'they would not be where they are today'. Some of them, the Bishop noted, had recently been asking for an alternative policy. Although he had no responsibility for 'the present deplorable condition of things', O'Dwyer offered to state his own alternative to 'trusting the Party, who trust the Liberals, and are now reduced to the statesmanship of Micawber—waiting for something to turn up'.

When war was being declared I would have said to the English Government 'Give us our national rights; set up a genuine Parliament in Dublin, and we are with you.' Again this very year, when the English government played false, I would have said to the Irish Members of Parliament 'Come home, shake the dust of the English House of Commons off your feet, and throw yourselves on the Irish Nation.' These are my alternatives. I think they would have been effective, but I fear that they would not be in favour with our present Parliamentarians.[65]

'*Sinn Fein is, in my judgement, the true principle,*' he declared to loud and prolonged applause. Although this declaration was explicit and unequivocal, just what it meant in terms of political organisation and leadership was quite vague. In the years between 1910 and the outbreak of the war, when Home Rule seemed imminent, Sinn Féin as an active organisation had practically disappeared, though it had survived as an ideology in Arthur Griffith's endless stream of periodicals. In the tumultuous events of 1913–15, Sinn Féin had been swept into the Volunteer movement and, after the split with Redmond, had donated its name—though little else—to the Irish Volunteers. 'Sinn Féin' had in fact become simply an emotive term used to describe almost any type of nationalist sentiment not associated with the older generation. In this vague sense the term had quickly been attached to the Rising; as far as the press was concerned, it was the 'Sinn Féin Rebellion', and any common vagrant arrested on suspicion of complicity in it was described as a 'Sinn Féiner'. When, therefore, the tide of popular sympathy turned toward the rebels, ordinary folk, with no very exact knowledge of the history of the term, described their new state of mind as 'Sinn Féin'. There was no active, nationwide organisation answering to the name of Sinn Féin, but there were every day more and more individuals willing to apply that term to their own political persuasions.

By the time of the hierarchy's October meeting, therefore, two bishops—McHugh and O'Dwyer—had taken rather different initiatives to encourage opposition to the party. Although, as will be seen, their initiatives pointed in rather different directions, they were able to unite, together with the party's inveterate detractors, Walsh and Logue, to prevent the hierarchy from giving even the appearance of unanimous support for the party. An attempt was made at the October meeting to consolidate a position on the current state of the country. The hierarchy, it was proposed, should (1) condemn conscription for Ireland, (2) oppose the continuance of martial law and (3) endorse 'the constitutional, as opposed to the physical force, movement'. There was agreement on the first two resolutions, but the proposals had to be dropped after 'several prominent members of the Hierarchy' objected 'that, if the series of resolutions were passed in their entirety, the portion referring to the constitutional movement might be interpreted as implying satisfaction with and approval of, the policy, and course of action, of the Irish Party'.[66] T. M. Healy wrote to O'Brien that the attack on the proposals was led by McHugh and backed by Logue, Walsh and O'Dwyer.[67]

Although Logue and Walsh were apparently simply waiting and watching, McHugh and O'Dwyer had been taking specific action which can be interpreted as their different ways of putting the Irish political system back into working order. As long as the Nation existed distinct from the State, the Church needed some national organisation which (1) did not rely on physical force to supplant the State, (2) respected the Church's vital interests and (3) enjoyed the Nation's confidence. McHugh's attempts to produce such an organisation were pedestrian and unimaginative—staying strictly with the rules of the game, narrowly conceived. O'Dwyer, by being willing to bend the rules—even to break a few minor procedural rules—was opening a new possibility for preserving the main structure of conventions through which the Church protected her interests within the Irish political system. By conveniently ignoring the question of whether the Rising was theologically justifiable—a moot point, in this world anyway, as its principal organisers had now gone to their rewards—it was now possible for the Church to take advantage of the memory of that event at minimum risk. Those who honoured that memory were now calling themselves Sinn Féiners, and if there was no clear definition of what Sinn Féin meant, the Bishop of Limerick would tell them: it meant shaking the dust of the English House of Commons off your feet. This you could find out by reading Arthur Griffith's writings over the preceding decade. Of course, you might find some other ideas and rhetoric not fully consonant with the Church's interests, but there was no need to go into that. Arthur Griffith was in jail, and when he got out he would see how the land lay quite rapidly. The point was that the concept of Sinn Féin need not involve physical force and that this was a uniquely favourable moment for the Church, by accepting the phrase Sinn Féin, to see that it did not.

If there was a chance that physical force could be defined

out of the concept of Sinn Féin, there was an even better chance that the movement growing up around that name could be taught to respect the Church's interests. Such at least would be O'Dwyer's opinion. The young men who would presumably lead Sinn Féin once they were released from prison, unlike John Dillon, had never been corrupted by dealings with the English Nonconformists. Unlike Redmond, the landed gentleman whom Birrell later described as 'from a purely political point of view . . . anti-clerical after the same fashion as many an English squire',[68] they were farmers' sons and shop assistants for whom the priest was by no means a social inferior. Unlike T. P. O'Connor, they went to Mass—some of them every day. It is true that they had defied episcopal authority over the question of essential Irish in the university, but so had the party in its conflict with Bishop Henry and its refusal to allow Logue to keep Healy in his seat. A few of them were implicated in a secret society, the I.R.B., but the A.O.H. was also a secret society in some sense, and if it seemed relatively innocuous to some bishops, it definitely did not appear so to O'Dwyer, as he had made plain in his letter to Redmond in 1912. On balance, then, from the perspective of a man like O'Dwyer, there was no reason to fear greater danger to the Church's interests from the Nation's younger generation, describing itself as Sinn Féin, than from its older generation as represented by the Irish Parliamentary Party.

On the third requirement, that the new national movement enjoy the Nation's confidence, O'Dwyer's course of action was clearly superior to McHugh's. The Irish Nation League had captured no one's imagination, and, more important, it lacked the vital element of youth. It was now clear that the party's time was running out. By the standards of Irish politics, its leaders were old men, and the generational succession was now at hand. Whatever would take the place of the party must be a movement of young men who, in some symbolic way, thrust aside the methods of their fathers. In the 1847 succession the symbol had been armed revolution; in the 1879 succession it had been parliamentary obstruction. Would the symbol of this generational succession be more armed rebellion, labelled by the police 'Sinn Féin', or the original Sinn Féin doctrine of abstention from parliament? In either case, the succession would take place, and the younger generation would be called Sinn Féin, but the Church had at least a chance to influence the symbolism the new movement would adopt.

The attraction the name held for politicians was illustrated in November when a by-election was held to fill a vacancy caused by the death of the O'Brienite member for West Cork. Two of the three candidates tried to claim the label 'Sinn Féin'. One of them, Frank Healy, had been detained at Bournemouth following the Rising, but other Easter Week prisoners disavowed his candidacy. The other, a Dr Shipsey, seems to have had equally shaky credentials. Probably realising that their influence might be negative, the party leaders refrained from openly endorsing the third candidate, a Mr O'Leary, who stood in the party interest and seems to have received the support of most of the clergy. Dr Cohalan, who was consecrated as the new Bishop of Cork during the campaign, stated in reply to an address from local government bodies that he was glad that a majority of the members of the municipal body were loyal supporters of Redmond and the party.[69] Actually, the election was fought along well-worn O'Brienite-Redmondite lines. Although O'Leary, the Redmondite, won, the two Sinn Féin candidates had a greater combined poll.[70] Perhaps the lesson of the election was that those interned rebels were very important political figures indeed. At the end of November Redmond wrote to Asquith about an amnesty movement under way to secure their release. If amnesty should be refused, he predicted the movement would promptly become very formidable and the party would be obliged to support it. Moreover, he added, it would be supported actively by the Church.[71]

Within a few weeks the parliamentary seat for North Roscommon fell vacant, and this time a Sinn Féin candidate with stronger credentials was drawn from the group arrested after the Rising. The candidate was a curious figure, George Noble Plunkett, Count of the Holy Roman Empire, formerly Director of the National Museum, once a Parnellite candidate for St Stephen's Green division, once even a candidate for the Under-Secretaryship. Overshadowing this chequered back-

ground, however, was the supremely important fact that the
Count was the father of Joseph Plunkett, signatory of the
Easter Week proclamation. Count Plunkett's cause was taken
up with extraordinary vigour by a young local curate, the
Rev. Michael O'Flanagan, who, with a few other delegates,
walked out of the party convention which nominated T. J.
Devine.[72] Father O'Flanagan was himself a curious figure,
for, although he had been associated with Irish Volunteer
activities before the Rising, he publicly advocated partition
during June 1916.[73] In North Roscommon he stressed the
theme that the Rising had prevented conscription and made
a strong appeal to young men of military age, urging them to
carry the old voters to the polls on their backs, for 'it was
easier work for them to secure these votes than to have to
go to Flanders digging trenches'.[74] The young curate's most
important contribution, however, was to enlist the support of
other priests in the constituency. It was reported that sixteen
priests, including two parish priests, actively supported Count
Plunkett.[75] Moreover, Father O'Flanagan reportedly obtained
from each parish priest in the division permission to address
a public meeting in his parish, although Bishop Morrisroe of
Achonry refused permission for him to speak in his own
episcopal parish in Ballaghaderreen,[76] just outside the division
and just outside Father O'Flanagan's own diocese of Elphin.
One parish priest, Father Monaghan of Fairymount, did endorse Mr Tully, a local newspaper owner who stood as an
Independent Nationalist,[77] but the vast majority of the clergy
who took any active part in the campaign supported Count
Plunkett. One parish priest had originally endorsed Devine,
the party candidate, but later switched to Count Plunkett.[78]
At the polling on 3 February 1917, the Count won easily,
with 3,022 votes against 1,708 for Devine and 687 for Tully.
Probably the very prominent clerical support of the Sinn Féin
cause helped to sway a significant portion of the voters, but
the really important feature of the election was that it
created an alternative course for the energies of priests disenchanted with Redmond.

The Irish Nation League had lent its support to Count
Plunkett's candidacy. During the weeks following the election
there was a good deal of discussion among leaders of the

League and spokesmen who had explicitly adopted the label
'Sinn Féin'. Count Plunkett had not clearly stated during
the campaign whether he would take his seat if elected,[79] and
his decision after the election not to take it caused consternation among his Irish Nation League supporters. Although
Griffith and Father O'Flanagan seemed willing to consider
compromise on the issue of abstention,[80] Count Plunkett was
adamant that all future candidates should be pledged to abstention. 'It is impossible to reason with him,' wrote one Irish
Nation League leader.

He thinks the I.N.L. should at once adopt his idea—Total Abstention. He wants to start a new organisation and he wants the
I.N.L. to merge in it. We of the I.N.L. are unanimous in believing that Plunkett's Policy would be ruinous—would be suicidal.[81]

The reason it seemed suicidal, presumably, was that the Irish
Nation League's *raison d'être* was to prevent partition, and
clearly abstention of nationalists from parliament could only
make partition more likely. Father O'Flanagan was already
regarded with suspicion in the League for his advocacy of
partition the previous year.[82] Count Plunkett called a convention in Dublin for 19 April and sent invitations to 'bodies
that commit themselves to the principle of Abstention from
Westminster'.[83] F. J. O'Connor, an I.N.L. leader from Co.
Tyrone, was indignant. 'I believe', he wrote to George Gavan
Duffy, 'a very large number of priests and some of the Bishops
would give the forward Programme at least a modified support. "Abstention" would be an obstacle to this. They would
join with us in opposing any Proposals for a sham settlement
and then we could bring them along.'[84] The bishops and
priests O'Connor no doubt knew best were those of the
Derry-Tyrone-Fermanagh area whose principal anxiety was
over partition.

It is possible to discern here a fundamental division in
what was being called the 'forward' movement which reflects
the different strategies of McHugh and O'Dwyer. The Irish
Nation Leaguers were pursuing the practical goal for which
McHugh was the principal ecclesiastical spokesman: the
defeat of partition. They were trying with scant success to
co-operate with those who had been imprisoned after the
Rising, for whom a symbolic gesture, such as abstention from

parliament, was more important than the partition issue. One of these young men, J. J. O'Kelly ('Sceilg'), the editor of the *Catholic Bulletin* who was still being detained in England, noted with pleasure that another impractical but symbolically potent idea, Irish representation at the Peace Conference, had been endorsed by Bishop Fogarty of Killaloe.[85] When Count Plunkett's convention met on 19 April it endorsed this idea, along with 'denying the authority of any foreign Parliament to make laws for Ireland'. There were some 127 priests among the 1,200 delegates,[86] and evidently other priests were prevented by their bishops from attending.[87] An organising committee including Count Plunkett, Father O'Flanagan, Arthur Griffith and William O'Brien of the Dublin Trades Council was established.[88] Apparently the Irish Nation League now died a quiet death.

Meanwhile another parliamentary vacancy occurred—this time in South Longford. Sinn Féin offered as its candidate Joseph MacGuinness, who was serving a sentence imposed by court martial after the Rising. Not one, but three candidates presented themselves as Irish Party supporters. During the preceding few years the established machinery for selecting a party candidate had fallen into desuetude. It was now to be expected that a decision would be made at the U.I.L. headquarters in Dublin, but before Dillon and his colleagues could act, the Bishop, Dr Hoare of Ardagh, took the initiative. Bishop Hoare had been rumoured to be backing one of the candidates, Joseph Flood.[89] On Easter Monday, 9 April, he held a deanery meeting in Longford and secured a resolution that the clergy should back an Irish Party supporter.[90] He then proposed that in the absence of a convention the clergy should back one of the candidates unanimously and that the majority should bind the minority. Apparently he expressed a willingness to accept any of the three Irish Party contenders but made plain his preference for Flood. Two of the three names were put before the meeting: Flood and Patrick McKenna, a local man who was a member of the National Directory of the U.I.L.[91] Nine parish priests, two administrators and four curates voted for Flood and one parish priest and one curate for McKenna. None of the priests serving parishes outside the constituency took part in the voting; four curates from within the division, known to have Sinn Féin leanings, abstained from voting. The Bishop announced that he would sign Flood's nomination papers.[92] McKenna, nevertheless, indicated to his friends on the U.I.L. Standing Committee that he would be supported by many priests.[93] He had in fact held one meeting at which a Father O'Connor, C.C., Newtownforbes, presided, before the deanery meeting took place.[94]

Dillon regarded the action of the Bishop as 'outrageous',[95] and the Dublin correspondent of the *Daily Mail* reported: 'I hear that Nationalists are criticising this action of the bishop quite fiercely. They declare that this intrusion of the clergy into politics, particularly on the basis that the decision of the majority should bind the minority is an impertinence and is presenting Ulster with the kind of argument Ulster wants to defeat Home Rule.'[96] Meanwhile, the third party hopeful, H. Garrahan, received the endorsement of the county council.[97] The party leaders were resolved not to resort to a convention,[98] and as matters seemed unlikely to sort themselves out, Devlin called Flood, McKenna and Garrahan together on 21 April and got them to agree to submit their respective claims to Redmond for a decision.[99] McKenna had all along been the favourite at U.I.L. headquarters, and would probably have been endorsed two weeks earlier but for the clerical action, for Dillon regarded him as the strongest candidate in the field.[100] Encouraged perhaps by a telegram from the Parish Priest of Killoe stating that many of the clergy favoured McKenna,[101] Redmond decided in his favour and courteously so informed the Bishop, who had evidently acquiesed in referring the matter to Redmond.[102] Hoare replied, with equal courtesy: 'We will all now obey your ruling and strive for Mr. McKenna,' and expressed his hope that Redmond's 'Policy and Party' would remain 'after the Physical Force has been tried and found wanting'.[103]

What the Bishop and his priests had tried to do was really rather singular in Irish politics. Reasoning that the party's main weakness was its public image as a Tammany Hall type of organisation, they proposed to strengthen it by offering— to carry the American analogy a bit further—a 'blue-ribbon' candidate. Instead of McKenna, the party hack, who was described in the press as 'of that type of education that suits his avocation in the pigdealing business' (but who could be relied upon to do as he was told by the party leadership), the clergy had offered 'a gentleman whose scholarship would shed lustre on a deliberative assembly'.[104] Flood, though of Longford origins, was an official in the Education Office in Dublin. He was involved in Catholic social work and had written historical and religious articles for various magazines. And who could question the Irish Ireland credentials of a man who had published a book on *Myths and Legends of Ancient Ireland*?[105] In proposing Flood, the clergy, argued Canon Reynolds, Adm., 'were not out to smash the Irish Party but to reform it and to revive in the Party the old fighting and independent spirits'.[106] To those who felt that clerical dictation was even worse than Tammany Hall dictation, it could be pointed out that the Bishop had leaned over backwards to act broadmindedly by choosing a man who was a Trinity College graduate[107] and a close colleague of that *bête noir* of Catholic ecclesiastics, Dr Starkie.[108]

Besides scuttling an imaginative attempt to give new life to the party, Redmond's decision had upset Hoare's carefully planned attempt to keep his clergy out of the Sinn Féin camp. Though the Bishop signed McKenna's nomination papers,[109] the principle of the majority of the clergy binding the minority could not be sustained when the majority decision no longer bound even the majority. On 28 April the *Roscommon Herald* reported that all but one of the young priests were backing Sinn Féin, as were also 'a large body of the P.P.'s'. A Sinn Féin procession at Longford on 29 April included a 'bevy of young priests who filled two or three motor cars',[110] and on 8 May the *Irish Times* noted the Sinn Féin campaigning of 'most of the young priests':

They do not conceal their views. Indeed they proudly proclaim them by sporting the Republican colours. Their attitude is undoubtedly doing harm to the Redmondite prospects, and their influence on voters is not counterbalanced by the fact that nearly all the older clergy are supporting Mr. M'Kenna.[111]

Dillon, campaigning for McKenna, was reduced to a rather intemperate attack on the younger clergy (and the school teachers), sarcastically observing 'that the young curates would apply to Rome for a Rescript to make them independent of their parish priests and their bishops'.[112]

Just before the polling took place, an event occurred outside the constituency which was to have serious implications for the election. The government had announced late in March through Bonar Law that another attempt at an Irish settlement would be made. As Carson was now back in the government as First Lord of the Admiralty it did not require any special knowledge to infer that some form of exclusion would inevitably be embodied in whatever scheme issued from the new efforts. The fact that Lloyd George, whose name was principally associated in Ireland with the abortive partition scheme of the preceding summer, was now Prime Minister, only intensified nationalist suspicions. Bishop McHugh circulated an appeal against partition among both Catholic and Protestant bishops. On 8 May the declaration was published over the signatures of sixteen Catholic prelates, three Protestant bishops and several laymen.[113] The appeal called for all opponents of partition, temporary or permanent, to send in their names for the purpose of demonstrating a national, rather than just a regional, protest.

The appeal was rendered particularly significant by an action of Archbishop Walsh. Less than two months earlier, when the Irish Nation League and Sinn Féin were engaged in their quiet tug-of-war, the Archbishop's secretary, Father Curran had written an interesting letter to Seán T. O'Kelly in which he sidestepped the main issues of the controversy but noted: 'I am sure things will come right enough in the long run, if we only get sufficient time, and I believe we will get an abundance of time. I am always preaching that we must give the Part[y] Leaders rope to hang themselves before attempting much in their place.'[114] Father Curran did not purport to be speaking for anyone other than himself, but he was describing fairly accurately the policy Walsh seems to have been following. The Archbishop apparently now decided that the party had enough rope to do the job, for on the day of the antipartition appeal he wrote to the press:

The question may perhaps be asked why a number of us, Irish Bishops, Catholic and Protestant, have thought it worth our while to sign a protest against the partitioning of Ireland. Has not that miserable policy, condemned as it has been, by the all but unanimous voice of Nationalist Ireland, been removed, months ago, from the sphere of practical politics?

Nothing of the kind. Anyone who thinks that partition, whether in its naked deformity, or under the transparent mask of 'county option' does not hold a leading place in the practical politics of today, is simply living in a fool's paradise.[115]

And he added in a postscript:

I think it a duty to write this although from information that has just reached me, I am fairly satisfied that the mischief has already been done, and that the country is practically sold.

The polling in South Longford took place on the following day, and leaflets containing Walsh's letter were 'lavishly distributed' at the polls.[116] The following comment was appended to the letter: 'This is a clear call from the great and venerated Archbishop of Dublin to vote against the Irish Party traitors, and to vote for Joe M'Guinness.'[117] When the votes were counted it was found that the Sinn Féin candidate had won by the narrow margin of thirty-seven votes.

In addition to turning the balance, in all probability, in favour of the Sinn Féin candidate, Walsh's timing of his letter had the effect of linking the partition issue to the Sinn Féin cause. Of course, opposition to partition and abstention from parliament were absolutely incompatible in the realm of logic. In the realm of symbol, however, the rules of logic need not apply. Partition was converted from a practical problem to be solved into a symbolic grievance to be trumpeted across the land. There would be no more of those embarrassing statements from Father O'Flanagan in favour of partition. On this issue the young bloods would speak with one voice—and do precisely nothing. Ironically, then, Walsh's letter can be seen as the final blow to McHugh's efforts to promote a new Irish party on the pattern of the old, and a seconding of O'Dwyer's bold alternative of conferring the mantle of political legitimacy upon the Nation's younger generation. It is interesting that O'Dwyer and Bishop Fogarty apparently did not bother to sign McHugh's antipartition manifesto until after Walsh's letter had linked it to Sinn Féin through the South Longford election.

Although it would be wrong to suppose that the hierarchy

as a whole was ready to associate itself with Sinn Féin, a process which might facilitate such action was already under way. Efforts were being made to stress the nonrevolutionary ideology which Griffith had been advocating for years. On 6 May a letter was read to a Sinn Féin meeting in South Longford from a Father O'Meehan of Kinvara, Co. Galway, attacking the 'great delusion' which had been instilled in some priests that Sinn Féin was 'some awful revolutionary, and not a constitutional, movement'.[118] He added: 'Obviously these worthy men have never taken the trouble to study for themselves the fifteen perfectly constitutional aims of the Sinn Féin programme.' Just before Count Plunkett's convention someone prepared a circular, headed 'The Socialist Party of Ireland', expressing support of the convention, and sent it out to Catholic priests, with the obvious intent of associating Sinn Féin with economic doctrines repugnant to the clergy. The incident only strengthened the position of Sinn Féin by offering Griffith and clergy of Sinn Féin sympathies[119] the opportunity to cite the circular as a transparent forgery. Eóin Mac Néill persuaded the editor of the *English Review* 'that there is nothing "treasonable" in the aspirations of Sinn Féin, and that the way of reconciliation and construction lies in the acceptance of the movement as a Party in the spirit of the age'.[120]

We should not pretend that people suddenly began to listen to Griffith as an oracle or that the subtleties of his 'Hungarian policy' were widely understood. Dual-monarchy theories and the economics of Friedrich List have little to commend them as electioneering slogans, but precisely the fact that primary efforts of Sinn Féin were now directed toward winning elections—and not any ideological apologetic —was the reason that Sinn Féin could take its place as a 'constitutional' movement in the eyes of ecclesiastics. There was, after all, no important violence in Ireland between May 1916 and early 1919, and in this two-and-a-half-year interval the involvement of forces labelled 'Sinn Féin' in the ordinary operations of a political party lent to the new movement the trappings of respectability it so sorely needed if it was to gain widespread clerical sanction. A by-product of this process was the relegation of the Ulster difficulty to the realm of rhetoric—or perhaps metaphysics. That the Church was willing to go along with this development was a consequence of the structure of the Irish political system. The Nation's territory manifestly did not include the North-east (give or take a county or two), a fact which was implicit in the conventions by which the younger generation's relations with the Church had been governed since the turn of the century. The interests which the Church sought to protect were those of the whole Irish Catholic Church, but ultimately the defence of those interests by the Nation could extend only as far as the Nation's territory. The Catholic Church in the North might have to fend for itself. There was, however, just at this moment, one ray of hope—a bare possibility that the ordinary operations of the Irish political system might be bypassed.

CHAPTER XVII

The Irish Convention

DURING the year following the Rising the hierarchy had been divided over what kind of change in national leadership the Church ought to promote. By May 1917 the tide was running strongly in favour of Bishop O'Dwyer's position of frank endorsement of the younger generation's claims, and against Bishop McHugh's efforts to whip up a new national movement which, by being willing, in Logue's words, 'to remain as we are for 50 years to come, under English rule'[1] rather than accept partition, could scarcely capture youthful imaginations. Both the Bishop of Limerick and the Bishop of Derry were operating on the assumption that the Irish Parliamentary Party would itself be supplanted in the national leadership before the great day when the Nation would supplant the State. In the early months of 1917, however, a new possibility arose. Lloyd George, capitalising on widespread dissatisfaction with the course of the war, had replaced Asquith in the premiership at the end of 1916. With the entry of the United States into the war, the new Prime Minister faced increasing pressures to settle the Irish question in deference to Irish-American sentiment.

Walsh's allegation on 8 May that partition was still being actively considered and that the country was 'practically sold' had at least this much basis in fact: a cabinet committee had been working on proposals for a temporary Irish settlement and Lloyd George was about to make an offer of immediate Home Rule for the twenty-six southern counties with the position of the six excluded counties to be reconsidered by parliament after five years. Far from having 'sold' the country on this basis, however, the party leaders had made it clear that they would not even enter negotiations. When, on 15

May, Redmond heard the terms of the impending offer from Lord Crewe at a banquet for General Smuts, he indicated that he could not accept it. He then posed the question whether 'it would be the right course to copy what had been done in the dominions and leave the constitutional question to a convention entirely Irish'.[2] Crewe took the hint and later in the evening conveyed the idea to Lloyd George at Downing Street. On the following day the cabinet approved adding the proposal of 'a convention of Irishmen of all parties' as an alternative to the offer of immediate Home Rule for the twenty-six counties. Response from the various interested groups in parliament—Northern and Southern Unionists, Redmondite and O'Brienite Nationalists—was, on balance, more favourable to the Convention idea than to the partition scheme. On 21 May Lloyd George announced that a Convention would be called to prepare a scheme for the government of Ireland within the Empire and promised that if the Convention reached 'substantial agreement' the government would see that its recommendations were enacted.

Bishop Kelly, who had been in London at least twice in the previous nine months to confer with leading politicians, arrived there again on the day after the Prime Minister's announcement,[3] and was asked by H. E. Duke, who had been made Chief Secretary late in 1916, to give advice to the government on the composition of the Convention. He counselled keeping the numbers below seventy—below fifty if possible—advice that ran counter to the desires of Irish Party leaders for a larger forum. He also urged, significantly, that no teachers' association be invited to send delegates.[4] The government, within a few days, settled upon a figure of 101—of which the largest component was to be representatives from local government bodies. Kelly took the rejection of his advice with good grace, and his enthusiasm for the Convention idea received encouraging seconding at the end of May when Archbishop Walsh joined in a public statement by several leading Irishmen expressing 'general agreement' with a pamphlet by the poet 'AE' entitled *Thoughts for a Convention*.[5] Within a few days Duke sent Sir James O'Connor to Armagh and Cardinal Logue agreed to confer with Walsh and arrange for the hierarchy to make nominations.[6]

Bishop McHugh was still desperately afraid that the Northern Catholics would be sold out. He was trying once again to organise a national protest against partition and apparently finding it difficult to work with Sinn Féin—his Irish Nation League having evaporated. Writing to T. M. Healy to urge that their party join in McHugh's efforts, William O'Brien unwittingly hit upon the fundamental reality of the new political situation: 'There would not be an atom of difficulty if the Sinn Féiners had only the sense to permit a big gathering in the Rotunda on the *single* issue —Partition or no Partition.'[7] That was not the single issue which fired the young men's imaginations. The composition of the Convention was publicly announced on 11 June,[8] and as it provided special representation for the Southern Unionists and none for Northern Nationalists, McHugh was outraged and added the 'partisan and pro-partition' Convention arrangements to the list of grievances for his national protest movement.[9] On 14 June Bishop O'Donnell told Sir Horace Plunkett that the bishops, who were scheduled to meet at Maynooth the following week, might decline to send a delegation, and Plunkett commented in his diary: 'They are evidently badly split.'[10] After the hierarchy met, however, they announced, with the usual *pro forma* declaration of unanimity, their decision in favour of sending a delegation.[11] Although McHugh went along with the decision, he refused to accept nomination,[12] and the delegates chosen were Kelly, O'Donnell, Harty of Cashel and MacRory of Down and Connor. As important as the specific personnel chosen was the fact that the four delegates pledged themselves to their colleagues to oppose 'Partition',[13] a term which, as will become clear, they construed very broadly.

O'Brien had tried to prevent the inclusion of the county council representatives in the Convention,[14] for the obvious reason that most of them were Redmondites. When his request was refused, he declined to send delegates from his own little party, despite the fact that for thirteen years he had been calling for a conference of all parties to settle the Irish question. Healy regretted the decision, arguing shortly before the hierarchy's meeting: 'If prelates like Dr M'Rory & Dr M'Hugh are chosen to fight partition, they will not forgive us for not standing by them.'[15] A more serious blow to the Convention's prospects was the refusal of Sinn Féin to fill its five allotted seats. The government tried to remedy the obvious deficiency by including among its own nominees two intellectuals—George Russell ('AE') and Edward Lysaght (afterwards MacLysaght)—who, it was hoped, might represent the Sinn Féin viewpoint, if not its organisation.

The Convention assembled in the Regent House of Trinity College, on 25 July 1917, and a good augury was apprehended in the fact that the Protestant and Catholic episcopal delegates spontaneously took adjoining seats.[16] Sir Horace Plunkett, despite the private opposition of several important delegates,[17] was elected Chairman. A Grand Committee of twenty delegates was appointed, and after a few days devoted to organisational details, the Convention adjourned to allow the Grand Committee to frame a method of procedure. The plan adopted was that the Convention should reassemble on 17 August for what was called the 'Presentation Stage', during which various schemes which had come to the attention of the Grand Committee would be presented to the Convention and discussed freely by all parties. Then the Convention would adjourn again, and the Grand Committee would be instructed to draw up a scheme which, it was hoped, would take account of the various viewpoints expressed at the Presentation Stage and which would meet the Prime Minister's stipulation that the future government of Ireland be within the Empire. The full Convention would then reassemble to consider the Grand Committee's scheme much as the House of Commons considers a bill.

When the Convention reassembled on 17 August, three distinct groups soon became evident. The largest was the Nationalist group led by Redmond and including the four other Irish Party nominees (Joseph Devlin, Stephen Gwynn, J. J. Clancy and T. J. Harbison),[18] the four Catholic bishops and a large but less articulate group composed mainly of representatives from local government bodies. Three of the government's nominees—Lysaght, Russell ('AE') and William Martin Murphy—were Nationalists but did not acknowledge Redmond's leadership. The second group was the Ulster Unionists, who chose H. T. Barrie, M.P., as their chairman.

They came to the Convention pledged to report back to a committee of the Ulster Unionist Council before committing themselves to any important proposition. A third group, the Southern Unionists, which emerged under the leadership of Lord Midleton, was quite distinct from the Ulster Unionists. These former landlords and professional men were responsible only to themselves and were the only party capable of truly independent action. A handful of delegates—Lords Granard and MacDonnell, Provost Mahaffy of Trinity and Archbishop Crozier of Armagh (C. of I.)—resisted firm alignment with any of the parties, and the seven labour members remained a separate and somewhat ineffective group.

During the six-week Presentation Stage all the delegates were given the opportunity to exercise their forensic talents without serious restraint. Though little substantial business was transacted, the 'Plunkett preliminaries', as Midleton scornfully called this stage,[19] did serve the useful purposes of allowing the various parties to become acquainted on a social basis and of breaking down the almost instinctive suspicion between Protestants and Catholics. The festive spirit of conviviality was augmented when the Convention accepted invitations from the Lords Mayor of Cork and Belfast to hold brief sittings in their respective cities. The contributions of the Catholic prelates to the discussions, however, did not always serve to further this salutary spirit of cordiality. Early in the debates Bishop MacRory of Down and Connor made a disastrous speech, 'raking up the past' and awaking 'some bitter memories of the Anglo-Irish conflict in the nineteenth century'. Nationalists were acutely embarrassed, and Bishop O'Donnell tried to patch matters up, taking 'the earliest opportunity to place his views before us in an altogether conciliatory way'.[20] The Bishop of Raphoe's talent for assuaging bitter emotions came into play again when Col. Wallace, the Grand Master of the Orange Order, raised the touchy issue of the papal decrees *Ne Temere* and *Quantavis Diligentia*. O'Donnell gave a very sensible and learned interpretation of the application of the decrees to Ireland which very much impressed the Ulster Unionists, who applauded Lord Oranmore's observation 'that the *odium theologicum* had been replaced by *divina caritas*'. Some months later Barrie, the Northern Unionist leader, recalled O'Donnell's speech 'as one of the things which they would never forget'.[21]

Bishop Kelly probably thought he was emulating O'Donnell's example and furthering friendly relations with the North when, during the sitting in Belfast, he spoke for an hour and three quarters on economic issues. His argument, buttressed by many statistics, was that far from benefiting from continued Union with Great Britain, Ireland stood to suffer immensely if she were saddled with a share of the war debt. He perhaps thought that the idea of Ireland repudiating her share of the war debt (though not, apparently, the principle of an imperial contribution) would appeal to the business sense of the Belfast men, but the suggestion had the opposite effect. Northern spokesmen denounced the proposition as a 'bribe', and insisted 'that Ulster considered it Ulster's duty and Ireland's duty to take a full share equally with the rest of the United Kingdom, in all the consequences of the war—even if it cost them their last shilling'.[22]

What the most sensible of the Ulster Protestants would have liked to hear from the Catholic bishops was not a disquisition on finance, but some indication that the Church might modify what they regarded as her unreasonable insistence upon absolute clerical control and rigid denominational segregation in the schools. On the day following Kelly's speech, Sir William Whitla, a prominent physician nominated by the government to represent the Methodists (who were not numerous enough to justify separate ecclesiastical representation), broached the question. He quoted Carson's statement that what Ulstermen dreaded was not legislation but administration, and, alluding to Kelly's argument, warned that 'to approach them with a proposal to shirk their sacred responsibility of sharing in the war-debt, in order to save wherewith to finance a Home Rule Government, would blight every hope of a settlement'. He then tried to face up to one of the most pressing financial difficulties. Before the war, he pointed out, the National Education Board had stated that another one and a third million pounds were urgently required to carry on their task in Ireland. It was futile, he argued, to look to the British exchequer in its present condition for further grants, and therefore local rate support and, in consequence, popular control appeared inevitable. This, he maintained, no doubt recalling the controversies which had raged a decade earlier, 'at once raised a fundamental Irish difficulty'. He did not conceal the preference of Ulster Protestants for mixed education. 'He himself had been educated in a mixed school. But now all was changed and the youths of Ireland were trained in different camps, with the result that the "old close and tender comradeship amongst men of different religious beliefs" was dying out.' He made no appeal to the bishops to reverse their decision, but he reminded them 'that the working of denominational education in recent years had made vastly more difficult the prospect of agreement on the national question'. His suggestion was that the Protestant and Catholic ecclesiastics in the Convention, together with a few laymen, 'should informally meet to discuss frankly and freely this great and vital problem'. Archbishop Harty rose immediately to reply. He made vague references to giving 'any concessions in reason' and working 'for the welfare of the whole country', but he rather spoiled the effect of this conciliatory gesture with some unnecessary criticism of the state of the Protestant educational system of Belfast. 'As for Sir William Whitla's main suggestion, he could only say that it was a principle of the Catholic Church that there must be a mingling of secular and religious education. The Church claimed the right to teach its own children, admitting, of course, the similar rights of others.'[23] No more was heard of Whitla's idea of an informal discussion of education, and virtually nothing further was heard from the bishops on the subject of education throughout the Convention.[24] The Archbishop had made plain that in the one important area in which the bishops were uniquely qualified to contribute to the easing of tensions, they had no intention of departing from those hardline attitudes that many Protestants believed had fostered the animosities which blocked a settlement.

On 25 September, just before adjournment of the Presentation Stage, the Grand Committee was reconstructed so as to contain the most important and capable figures from each faction. The members fell into the following categories:

Ulster Unionists
  H. T. Barrie, M.P.
  Lord Londonderry
  H. McD. Pollock
  Sir Alexander McDowell
  Rev. John Irwin, Moderator of the General Assembly

Southern Unionists
  Lord Midleton
  Lord MacDonnell[25]
  John Powell
  Most Rev. John H. Bernard, Protestant Archbishop of Dublin

Nationalists
  John Redmond, M.P.
  J. J. Clancy, M.P.
  Joseph Devlin, M.P.
  Stephen Gwynn, M.P.
  Most Rev. Patrick O'Donnell, Catholic Bishop of Raphoe
  Most Rev. Denis Kelly, Catholic Bishop of Ross

Independent Nationalists
  William Martin Murphy
  Edward E. Lysaght
  George W. Russell ('AE')

Labour
  James McCarron
  Robert Waugh

Plunkett was an *ex officio* member of the Committee, and
Lord Southborough, the Convention's secretary, presided
over its deliberations, which were scheduled to begin on 11
October. On 30 September Plunkett tried to persuade Redmond to draw up a scheme to be the basis for discussion in
the Grand Committee. The party leader declined for fear of
'falling foul of W. M. Murphy', but he advised Plunkett to
ask O'Donnell instead.[26] Plunkett took the advice, and the
Bishop replied that though George W. Russell would be his
own choice for the task, he was willing to undertake it.[27]

    T. M. Healy, who, though not a member of the Conven-
tion, was kept informed of its activities by William Martin
Murphy, had written to O'Brien early in August:

Partition is dead and buried. It is generally said that Carson & Redmond have agreed on a scheme of 4 provincial bodies with a central authority. The Northerners are to be tempted by tax exemptions & awed by the fear of a Socialist Republic in England. There is a general impression that some scheme other than Partition will 'emerge' from the Convention.[28]

Although there were certain fanciful features in this statement—Carson had certainly made no deal with Redmond—Healy had hit upon the main lines along which thoughtful men hoped to achieve a settlement of the Ulster difficulty: (1) Some measure of local control over Ulster affairs might be offered to the Ulstermen through such expedients as a subordinate provincial legislature, an 'Ulster Committee' in the Irish parliament with special powers over the application of certain types of legislation to Ulster, and special administrative arrangements in Belfast; (2) An attempt might be made to persuade the spokesmen for Belfast commerce and industry that their interests were identical with those of Murphy and to convince them, as he had become convinced, that an Irish parliament able to form an economic policy separate from that of Great Britain (as the parliament contemplated in the Home Rule Act could not do) would serve the interests of the propertied classes better than would the British parliament.

From the outset, the bishops resisted the adoption of the first, and more obvious, of these approaches.[29] During the Presentation Stage, for example, a scheme modelled on the federal system of Switzerland was brought forward. 'Our Bishops are against it,'[30] wrote Sir Bertram Windle, the Catholic, Nationalist President of University College, Cork, to his son-in-law, John Horgan. Essentially, the episcopal delegates were construing their pledge to oppose 'partition' as binding them to resist any measure of provincial autonomy for Ulster within an all-Ireland settlement just as strongly as definite exclusion. Whether the pledge which they made to their colleagues specifically called for this attitude cannot be determined from available evidence. However, McHugh, the most outspoken episcopal opponent of partition had made it clear in June 1916 that the fundamental cause of alarm among the Northern bishops was the danger of a Protestant-

dominated Ulster administration, especially in education.
This danger might be just as great if Ulster came into an
all-Ireland settlement with some measure of provincial
autonomy.

To circumvent the question of provincial safeguards,
O'Donnell embodied in the scheme[31] he was drafting an idea
which he had mentioned to Redmond nearly four years
earlier—that the best safeguard for Unionists would be 'some
modification of our strangely constituted Senate'.[32] The Home
Rule Bill had been drafted in the aftermath of the struggle
with the House of Lords, and ministers who had just spent
several years fulminating against the evils of an unrepresentative Upper House were hardly inclined to introduce an
unrepresentative second chamber into the Irish constitution.
After an initial period of nomination, the Irish Senate was
to have been elected. The constituencies for the Senate were
to be entire provinces, and Ulster was to be allotted fourteen
out of forty Senate seats. Obviously, this system did not provide any security for the Unionists against democracy. The
Bishop of Raphoe had a disarmingly simple plan. In place of
the elected Senate, the old Irish House of Lords would be
revived, with certain necessary modifications. In place of the
old Lords Spiritual of the Established Church, there would
be four Catholic and two Protestant prelates together with
the Moderator of the General Assembly. The Lords Mayor
of Dublin, Belfast and Cork and a Lord Chancellor would
also be given places. The remaining thirty-nine seats would
be filled by members of the Irish peerage. (The method for
selecting these Lords Temporal is not clear. Presumably the
approximately eighty Irish peers would elect them in the
same manner as representative peers were elected under the
Act of Union.) The effect would be to make the Irish Upper
House even more of a Tory preserve than the House of Lords
at Westminster. The Bishop also proposed that the House
of Commons (which on his plan would ordinarily have 168
elected members) should be augmented during its first ten
years with twelve nominated members 'to represent the industries, commerce and trade of the North-east of Ireland'
and twelve more to represent the Southern Unionists. In
other words the question of local autonomy was to be cir-

cumvented by undemocratic expedients in the constitution
of the Irish parliament, which to many members of the
Liberal cabinet which had framed the Home Rule Bill in
1911–12 would have been most unpalatable. From the
moment O'Donnell's scheme became the basis of discussion,
provincial federalism never figured seriously in the options
before the Convention.

In the area of finance, where Nationalists hoped to make
willing converts of the Unionists, the Bishop proposed full
fiscal autonomy for the Irish parliament, including control of
customs and excise. He drew up a plan whereby a joint
British-Irish Commission would negotiate a customs union
between the two countries, or, in default of such an arrangement, most favoured nation terms would apply to trade between Great Britain and Ireland. The principle of an imperial contribution was affirmed, but the amount was to be
left to the discretion of the Irish parliament, which would
take into account the financial ability of the population and
the protection received by Ireland from the army and navy.
O'Donnell was slightly more tactful than Kelly had been in
handling the vexatious problem of the war debt: 'The over-
taxation of Ireland in the past and her share in the national
debt may be set off against each other.'

In many other respects the Bishop's plan followed the 1914
act fairly closely. Police, however, were to be transferred immediately to Irish control, as were certain other expensive
services such as land purchase, pensions, insurance and labour
exchanges (which had been temporarily 'reserved' under the
1914 Act), unless the Irish parliament desired to defer acceptance of them. Irish representation at Westminster was to be
eliminated (until such time as a federal parliament for the
entire United Kingdom might be created). Though defence
was to remain under imperial control, the assent of the Irish
parliament was to be required for the imposition of conscription, and Ireland was to be allowed, under certain conditions, to raise a territorial force. Certain restrictions on the
powers of the Irish parliament (relating to such matters as
treason, coinage, weights and measures, international postal
service and copyright) were omitted from the scheme. To
meet Logue's misgivings, a clause was to be framed 'to annul

any existing legal penalty, disadvantage or disability, on account of religious belief'—a phrasing which apparently would not affect the prohibition upon election of clergy to local government authorities.

When the Grand Committee met on 11 October, it was decided that O'Donnell's scheme should be considered by a smaller subcommittee, while other subcommittees dealt with special problems such as land purchase, police and electoral systems. The main subcommittee was composed of Redmond, Devlin and O'Donnell (Nationalists), Murphy and Russell (Independent Nationalists), Barrie, Londonderry and McDowell (Ulster Unionists) and Midleton (Southern Unionist). For a few days, the deliberations of the 'Committee of Nine' were pleasant enough. A number of points in the Bishop's scheme were accepted, usually on condition that the final scheme should prove satisfactory, and other points were reserved for later consideration. Unionists insisted upon continued representation at Westminster, and Nationalists conceded the point. O'Donnell's 'House of Lords' was recast as a 'Senate' incorporating various sorts of dignitaries, but the idea of an elected Upper House was not revived, and the new Senate promised to be nearly as staunchly Tory as the proposed Irish House of Lords. It was agreed that by some means the Unionists were to get a forty per cent share of the House of Commons.

On 7 November, the Committee having reached provisional conclusions on a number of heads, the Ulster Unionists decided to confer with their 'advisory committee' on the proposed composition of the two houses of the Irish parliament. They reported on 13 November that the advisory committee disapproved of the nominated element in the House of Commons as a safeguard for Ulster (though it was conceded that the plan might have some value for the Southern Unionists). They undertook to bring forward their own proposals for safeguarding Ulster interests by means other than extra representation.[33] It was at this stage that the major blunder of the Convention's deliberations was made. This was the only point in the entire course of the Convention at which the Ulster Unionists gave any indication of a desire to bargain on significant issues. Instead of waiting eagerly for the Ulster proposals, the Committee (partly, it would appear, through Plunkett's ineptitude) continued its discussions on the financial question. The Nationalist hope that the Ulstermen could easily be persuaded that fiscal autonomy was in their own interests was an *ignis fatuus*. The Ulster Unionists, fearing that an Irish parliament would, at worst, undertake a tariff war with Great Britain, or, at best, adopt fiscal policies favourable to agricultural interests to the detriment of the industrial North-east, refused to contemplate any wider financial powers than those offered in the 1914 act. The Nationalists were equally adamant that continued fiscal union with Great Britain would not only be unacceptable to the country, but would give rise to needless friction between the two countries and bind Ireland to fiscal policies not adapted to her needs. Plunkett and Lord Southborough tried in vain to mediate between the two groups, but on 21 November the Committee of Nine decided to report to the Grand Committee that 'In consequence of the continued divergence of our views on the financial question, our endeavour to find a basis for agreement has not proved successful.'[34] The most important consequence of the impasse, however, was that it gave the Ulster Unionist delegates a perfect excuse to renege on their earlier undertaking to submit a scheme of their own.[35]

The Grand Committee reassembled on the following day and after several days of fruitless reiteration a new element suddenly entered the situation on 28 November. Lord Midleton, who had not committed himself on the fiscal issue in the Committee of Nine, submitted a compromise on behalf of the Southern Unionists. As a contribution to imperial charges Great Britain should continue to levy and collect customs in Ireland, but in all other respects, including the imposition and collection of excise, the Irish parliament was to be fiscally independent. Compromise along these lines had been suggested by Plunkett and Southborough, but put forward by the leader of a party which had always previously insisted upon fiscal union, the proposal now seemed to take on crucial significance. Lord Midleton and his dozen or so colleagues were trying to take a middle position so inherently sensible that reasonable members of both the Nationalist and

Ulster Unionist parties would join them, leaving only a few extremists on either side outside a consensus which might meet the government's 'substantial agreement' formula. William Martin Murphy, who, as publisher of the most widely read nationalist paper in Ireland, could not be ignored, made it plain immediately to his Nationalist colleagues that he intended to hold out for complete fiscal autonomy—a view which T. M. Healy understood was also receiving 'some countenance from "AE"'.[36] Redmond and Devlin were leaning toward aligning themselves with Midleton, and Bishop O'Donnell's position was in doubt. On 11 December, after a recess (during which M.P.s on the Grand Committee attended critical debates on a Redistribution Bill) Plunkett addressed the Grand Committee on the theme that the Nationalists ought to come to terms with the Southern Unionists and 'make the Irish Question 4/5th vs 1/5th instead of 3/4th vs 1/4th and the 1/5th will then come in!' He was pleased to note that the Ulster Unionists 'did not object to this way of putting things' and that privately Redmond and Devlin indicated their agreement. Redmond, however, added: 'But what of Murphy and O'Donnell?' 'He is a queer leader,' Plunkett observed in his diary.[37] No decision on the Midleton compromise was reached by the Grand Committee, which referred the matter to the full Convention, called to meet on 18 December.

On the evening before the Convention reassembled, the Nationalist leaders scheduled a meeting in Dublin with their 'backbenchers'. Just at this critical moment the group was deprived of very important leadership. Rapidly failing health together with a heavy snowstorm kept Redmond isolated in his Wicklow retreat. Less notable at the time, but very significant in retrospect, Bishop Kelly had become gravely ill. The caucus was in agreement that, provided that Ulster participated in Midleton's plan, Nationalists should accept it. Bishop O'Donnell and George Russell were adamant, however, that the claim to full fiscal independence must not be waived for anything less conclusive than an agreement among all sections of the Convention. If Nationalists acquiesced, and Ulstermen held aloof, they argued, the government would not regard the compromise as founded upon 'substantial agreement' and would treat it as a bargaining position to be reconciled with Ulster's views in legislation. Any measure which might come out of such a process would be rejected by the country and would precipitate another rebellion.[38]

The Convention met for only two days before adjourning for Christmas holidays. The Southern Unionists, unlike the other two parties, Lord Midleton told the Convention, were genuinely working for a settlement *within* the Convention, without considering pressures from the outside. They were committed to the Union, but they had made a sincere effort to go to the limit of concession without disturbing the essence of the Union. What could not be surrendered was a common defence and a consequent obligation upon Ireland to contribute to that defence. As customs powers entailed treaty-making powers, they were inseparable from defence, and therefore the most logical mode of imperial contribution would be the retention at Westminster of the power to levy and collect customs duties, which, in turn, implied the necessity of continued Irish representation in the imperial parliament. Although the total yield of customs was believed necessary as an imperial contribution during the war, the door was left open for an inquiry after the war into the proper level of contribution, and the prospect of a transfer of part of the customs yield to Ireland was held out. Redmond, still too weak to attend, was unable to reply or to mobilise Nationalist forces for compromise along Midleton's lines.[39] No serious response was made from either the Ulster or the Nationalist side, and Bishop O'Donnell was beginning to move into the leadership vacuum which Redmond's incapacity was creating. The Bishop argued for submitting a 'reasoned amendment' to Midleton's scheme, but Devlin managed to prevent this course, maintaining that no action should be taken for the time being in the hope that Ulster would make a move.[40] O'Donnell, apparently as an alternative, signed a lengthy memorandum, drafted by Russell, setting forth the arguments for fiscal autonomy (including customs) and circulated it to members of the Convention before they left for Christmas.[41] Though there was nothing new in the memorandum, the timing of it was hardly auspicious. Plunkett wrote to Redmond: 'The Bishop of Raphoe seems determined not to come to terms with Lord Midleton,'[42] and several days later Redmond received from the Bishop's own hand an explication of his position. As he had maintained in the Nationalist caucus, O'Donnell had little faith in the possibility of the Northern Unionists accepting Midleton's terms, and was wary of an agreement with the Southern Unionists which might be 'greatly diluted' by the government to meet Ulster demands. He argued that the Midleton financial proposal was not really an advance by the Southern Unionists, and he seemed to believe that further concessions could be extracted from the Southern Unionists despite protests to the contrary. Midleton himself, the Bishop conceded, was probably sincerely unwilling to claim separate customs, but he thought other leading Southern Unionists would prove more pliable[43] and had only taken a 'safe line in finance' to facilitate their dealings with Ulster. O'Donnell seemed to favour trying to draw the Southern Unionists further toward the Nationalist position, particularly along lines suggested by Lord MacDonnell, who favoured setting up a commission to ascertain Ireland's proper post-war imperial contribution with a view to transferring to Irish local purposes any excess yield from customs above that contribution. The Bishop implicitly discounted the possibility that Ulster might join in the Midleton compromise proposals and assumed that the government would eventually have to legislate on a middle course between a Nationalist-Southern Unionist position and an intransigent Ulster position.[44]

Redmond shared both the Bishop's pessimism over voluntary Ulster acceptance to the Midleton compromise and his hope of amending the Midleton scheme along MacDonnell's lines. His strategy, however, was to make a public offer to accept Midleton's proposal, with certain amendments, provided that the Ulstermen would accept it as well. Whereas the Bishop wanted to offer autonomist amendments to Midleton's motion immediately, Redmond felt that such amendments should be held in reserve until after Ulster's expected refusal of his proposed offer. Even if the offer were to be refused, he argued, 'Our position will be all the stronger for having made it.' Lloyd George had expressed to Redmond his hopes for a settlement on the basis of Midleton's proposals and he had verbally mentioned to Redmond and Devlin a plan to 'fight the Ulstermen on this issue' if they refused to join in the compromise. He had refused, however, to give written assurances that he would carry the plan into effect if Redmond came to terms with Midleton. The party leader enclosed copies of the relevant correspondence with Lloyd George in his letter explaining his strategy to the Bishop. No doubt when he spoke of strengthening the party's position by making the conditional offer of acceptance of the Midleton scheme, Redmond had in mind strengthening the resolve of the Prime Minister to precipitate a confrontation with Ulster.[45]

The Bishop of Raphoe was 'exceedingly doubtful about conditional acceptances until we know the North makes good the condition'. The Ulstermen, he argued in a letter of 27 December, would take the acceptance as a starting point for exacting further concessions. 'I am inclined to think', he wrote, 'that it is a question of either coming to an agreement with the North or stating the situation to the people. If the P.M. heard that, we might get more help.' 'These times,' he reflected, 'anything may happen to men or governments and rather than give anything away in a hurry I should be inclined to keep the Convention in session for a considerable time fashioning out a reasonable instrument of Irish government.' He arranged to meet Redmond on the evening of 1 January to discuss strategy for the Convention sessions which were scheduled to reopen on the following day.[46]

On New Year's Day Lord Midleton returned to Dublin from London with a written pledge, in the handwriting of Lord Curzon and initialled by Lloyd George, that if the Southern Unionist scheme were carried 'with substantial agreement—i.e. with the opposition of Ulster alone—the P.M. will use his personal influence with his colleagues, the sympathies of many of whom are well known, to accept the proposal and to give it legislative effect'.[47] Though this was not the kind of assurance Redmond had hoped for, it did encourage him. On 2 January Midleton offered his resolution with the further concession that the collection of customs should be handled by the Irish civil service, but without any weakening of the principle that customs must be levied at

13

Westminster. After two days of speeches, including one in which O'Donnell argued for Irish control of customs on the ground that this form of taxation most directly affected the interests of the poor, but conceded reservation of customs for a term of years and a subsequent free trade arrangement between the two islands,[48] Redmond rose on 4 January to speak. He made a moving appeal, asking: 'Is there a man in this room who can contemplate without horror the immediate future of Ireland if this Convention fails?' A 'maddened people, with no responsible control' would face 'a Government ruling by the point of the bayonet'. He and the party had taken a grave political risk in supporting the war effort, and had been reduced, he implied, to political impotence. Yet 'If the choice were to be made to-morrow,' he assured his audience, 'I would do it all over again. I have had my surfeit of public life. My modest ambition would be to serve in some quite humble capacity under the first Unionist Prime Minister of Ireland.'[49] At the close of the debate, Redmond quietly tabled a motion to adopt Midleton's proposals *provided* that they 'be adopted by His Majesty's Government as a settlement of the Irish question and legislative effect be given to them forthwith'.[50]

There was considerable feeling that the Convention was on the verge of a settlement. Even Ulster Unionist delegates were hinting that they might abstain rather than oppose the plan. Carson had intimated to Dr Crozier, the Protestant Archbishop of Armagh, that 'both of them must risk all their popularity in Ulster to obtain the settlement'.[51] On the evening before Redmond tabled his motion most of the delegates attended a party at Lord Granard's house, which, according to Stephen Gwynn 'marked the most festive moment of our comradeship'.[52] As Barrie left the party he said to Midleton: 'I think you may count on us. We shall certainly not be against you.'[53] Lord Southborough, who as secretary was in touch with all groups, believed that if a division had been taken at that point only two negative votes would have been cast and that, moreover, Ulster might even have voted 'aye' rather than abstain.[54] For the fact that this result was not realised, Midleton blamed Plunkett, 'a stickler for forms', who insisted that a vote on the subject was not yet in order and that a week must be devoted to consideration of the report of the Land Purchase Subcommittee.

On 14 January, the day before the Convention was to resume serious business, Redmond, whose health had kept him in seclusion for the ten days since his speech, returned to Dublin. His motion had technically violated a decision taken at his own suggestion by an informal Nationalist caucus of 2 January that no notices of amendment be tabled until the group had decided upon a course of action. He told Stephen Gwynn on the evening of 14 January that he was uncertain what would happen and asked him to find a leading local government representative to second his motion.[55] Word reached him of possible trouble, and he sent a note by hand to Bishop O'Donnell at the Minerva Hotel. Apologising for the fact that his illness had prevented him from writing earlier, he pointed out that his amendment did not 'commit anyone to giving up Customs unless the Government accepts the scheme and gives it legislative effect *forthwith*. If they did this,' he continued, 'I am quite convinced that we would be guilty of a great dereliction of duty if we did not accept the compromise, quite regardless of what Sinn Féiners might say outside.' Conceding that his amendment might receive some opposition—'certainly from Murphy, Lysaght, and Russell'—he said that he was moving it entirely on his own responsibility, and would allow all Nationalists freedom to vote as they liked.[56] From the tone and the brevity of his remarks, it is clear that he anticipated the sort of reply which the Bishop wrote late that night.

O'Donnell was unimpressed by Redmond's assertion that the motion did not commit its supporters to abandonment of the full fiscal claim if the government did not act, for the Bishop was not looking so much to the calm, reasoning forum of the Convention in which the subtleties of a conditional resolution would be appreciated by all parties, but to the realities of political life outside the Convention.

In my opinion [he wrote], should the Government not carry through the proposed agreement, the Nationalist, who votes for it, cannot stand where he stood before. To say that he could have a Parliament in Dublin two months hence without Customs but not two years later will not bear examination. The principle is given away. If Ulster had come in or had promised to come in, we could give something away. But with Ulster out we never agreed to give anything away and in my opinion it is fatal to do so. With Ulster out even a favourable Cabinet could not carry an agreement that excluded Customs. There would be no Irish public opinion at . . . the back of the measure to make itself heard. Ulster opposes; and elsewhere it would be said that the Convention failed in the main purpose of bringing in Ulster and now presented the public with an agreement that denied Ireland the little power it had over Customs in the 1914 Act and gave her a most undemocratic Parliament. The proposition would be drowned in scorn and ridicule before it was a week before the public.[57]

Perhaps when Redmond read the reference to an 'undemocratic Parliament' he felt a special twinge of anger, remembering who it was that originated undemocratic expedients to exclude more obvious 'safeguard' proposals of local autonomy for Ulster. The Bishop professed not to have given up hope of the Midleton plan being enacted, but in his view the only way to secure that end was for the Nationalist majority to hold out for fiscal autonomy. The government would then be offered three reports—Nationalist, Southern Unionist and Ulster Unionist—and would, he believed, legislate on the basis of the middle course advocated by the Southern Unionists. He had already expressed this view to Lord Midleton, who evidently had been trying to alter the Bishop's views. 'No man has influenced my views,' O'Donnell continued.

My views are my own. But I entertain them so strongly that at any sacrifice I must express them. When your notice of motion yesterday reached me I sent forward a notice from myself. I dare say it may not be reached. But it puts my position on record at once so that members of the Convention will have no doubt about where I stand in this matter. In my opinion the very worst service that can be done to the chances of settlement on the Midleton lines would be by our concurrence in the absence of a promise from Ulster to come in.[58]

'May God direct us,' he concluded. 'It is needless to say with what pain I write in this way.' With those words the Bishop severed the ties which for nearly eighteen years had bound him to the Irish leader.

Almost as disastrous as this letter was the news, which reached Redmond before the session opened on the following morning, that Devlin had decided to side with the Bishop. When Redmond entered the hall, Gwynn reported that he had fulfilled his mission. 'It's all right,' he said. 'Martin McDonagh will second your motion.' 'He needn't trouble,' Redmond replied brusquely. 'I'm not going to move it; Devlin and the Bishops are voting against me.'[59] O'Donnell, according to an Ulster account, strode past Redmond, 'casting to left and right swift, challenging glances', and Devlin 'slipped quietly into his seat beside the leader he had thrown over, without a word or gesture of greeting'.[60] When Plunkett had taken his place in the chair, Redmond rose to say without hesitation:

The amendment which I have on the paper embodies the deliberate advice I give to the Convention.

I consulted no one—and could not do so, being ill. It stands on record on my sole responsibility.

Since entering the building I have heard that some very important Nationalist representatives are against this course—the Catholic bishops, Mr. Devlin—and others. I must face the situation—at which I am surprised; and I regret it.

If I proceeded I should probably carry my point on a division, but the Nationalists would be divided. Such a division would not carry out the objects I have in view.

Therefore, I must avoid pressing my motion. But I leave it standing on the paper. The others will give their advice. I feel that I can be of no further service to the Convention and will therefore not move.[61]

When Redmond sat down Bishop MacRory rose and made what Plunkett regarded as 'an ignorant, demagoguist [*sic*], anti-English speech'[62] aligning himself with O'Donnell's position on customs. The one break in Catholic episcopal ranks became evident when a letter from Bishop Kelly, who remained seriously ill and confined to bed at the Gresham Hotel, was circulated. Kelly, though he expressed the hope that Southern Unionists would take the further step of conceding customs, pleaded with his fellow Nationalists to yield the point if the Southern Unionists would not move.[63] Throughout the rest of the Convention's proceedings, however, the Bishop of Ross was unable—or perhaps unwilling—to leave his sickbed and challenge his brother bishops.

Redmond took no further part in the Convention's deliberations, and, as if by natural succession, Bishop O'Donnell began to preside at the caucuses of Nationalist delegates.[64] Both Redmond and O'Donnell had acted rationally and realistically in view of the different sets of interests which they were charged with protecting. Redmond's role was to preserve the constitutional Nationalist Party, which, he fully realised, was in extremely serious trouble. There was one, and only one, way to preserve the party, viz. to produce an actual working settlement of the Irish question before the next general election. If no settlement was produced, the party would be annihilated at the polls no matter what proposals they had accepted or rejected. If, on the other hand, a Home Rule settlement should come into force before the dissolution of parliament, the party leaders would be hailed as the fathers of their country. They might not win their usual three-quarters of the Irish representation, but they would very probably win enough seats in the new parliament to form a government either alone or—as Redmond had seriously suggested to Midleton—in coalition with the Unionists.[65] What would constitute a settlement capable of saving the party? The answer is that almost any scheme which would set up a body clearly labelled 'Irish parliament', embracing representatives from all thirty-two counties, would suffice, provided that it were actually, visibly and undeniably *in operation*. The fine constitutional details and financial intricacies which were debated in the Convention only became real electoral issues in later years, under very different circumstances.

Redmond can therefore be defended as acting properly, under the circumstances, by staking all on Lord Midleton's plan, no matter how slim the chances of its being realised, for it was the last opportunity to save the party—indeed, in Redmond's view, the last chance to avert chaos. Moreover, there are reasons to suspect that, but for the O'Donnell-Devlin revolt, the chances for realisation of the scheme were not so slim as has been generally supposed. To be sure, even if, as Lord Southborough believed would be the case, the

Ulster Unionists had given at least tacit acquiescence to the scheme, the Prime Minister would undoubtedly have had to brave very strong Ulster opposition to enact it; and Lloyd George was, to say the least, not noted for his fidelity to the spirit of his promises or for any romantic attachment to Irish national aspirations. Nevertheless, it would certainly have been to his advantage to be rid of the Irish issue for the duration of the war, if a settlement could be achieved at minimal cost and if the first Irish government would be a Redmondite-Unionist coalition which could be expected to govern with a firm hand until after the war. More important, he was subject to political pressure from genuinely powerful quarters. Midleton himself, unlike most of the Southern Unionist spokesmen, had influential political connections in England. He had held the War Office and the India Office in the Salisbury and Balfour governments, and his activities in England during the critical period of the Convention had not been limited to his direct appeal to Lloyd George. North-cliffe, the press lord, who had just returned from his duties as chairman of the British War Mission to the United States, had spent an hour and a half with Lloyd George on 9 January, impressing upon the Prime Minister the urgency of an Irish settlement to avert dangerous Irish-American opposition to the war effort. Northcliffe assured Midleton that he was 'ready to use the whole organization of the newspaper world to back this settlement if arrived at, and will make it his personal concern'.[66] This would be no trivial gesture, for by just such action in 1916 Northcliffe had helped to topple Asquith and bring Lloyd George to the premiership. As recently as November 1917 Lloyd George had attempted unsuccessfully to persuade Northcliffe to join the ministry,[67] no doubt with the intention of protecting himself from Asquith's fate. (The best that Lloyd George could do was to persuade Northcliffe in February 1918 to become director of propaganda in enemy countries—a post which, Northcliffe was careful to insist, did not constitute membership in the government or fetter the freedom of his newspapers to criticise the government.)[68]

Clearly Northcliffe was in a position to transform a Nationalist-Southern Unionist agreement from a hypothetical arrangement in the Regent House, Trinity College, to a matter of urgent practical politics at 10 Downing Street. When Northcliffe began to give the matter his 'personal concern', he asked his *Daily Mail* not to offer any opinion on Ireland for the time being, stating: 'I have strong political reasons.' He complained about a leading article on the Irish question which would 'injure some negotiations I am making'.[69] On 20 January, apparently unaware of Redmond's humiliation five days earlier in Dublin, Northcliffe wrote the Prime Minister outlining the Midleton-Redmond arrangement, mentioning the danger that without an indication of government support to 'Mr. Devlin and his friends', Murphy might carry an amendment claiming customs and thereby render the Convention's work valueless, and stressing the importance of an Irish settlement for relations with the United States and Australia.

I desire to ascertain [he continued] what is the intention of the Government in the matter. Has it made up its mind? If not, I suggest with great respect that it should do so *now* and not to-morrow. If it is decided to act on the Redmond Amendment, if carried by roughly 70 percent of the Convention, it should now determine that fact, and we can probably arrange that the Government will receive such an amendment so carried.[70]

He went on to outline a programme for carrying such a decision into law, including 'proper press propaganda to explain to an entire world the immense advantages that will accrue to Ireland economically as the result of this measure'. A further indication of the pressure Northcliffe had begun to apply is provided in a letter from Carson, who had been a member of the war cabinet for the past several months, to him on 23 January:

I suppose the argument I am expected to use is something like this: 'You Ulster people are loyal and devoted to England. You have helped with men, money and ships. But the best way you can help us now is to agree to a Govt. that you loathe and hate. This is your reward.'
It is not easy.[71]

When he wrote those words, Carson had already resigned from the cabinet over a vaguely worded offer by the government to assist the Convention 'finally to reach a basis of agreement which would enable a new Irish Constitution to come into operation with the consent of all parties'.[72] Carson was genuinely fearful that a settlement would be imposed, and Lloyd George appears to have done nothing to allay his fears.[73] It does seem from Lloyd George's willingness to sacrifice a key minister in this way that he was keeping open the possibility of a confrontation with Ulster if the coalescence of all other Irish elements should materialise and if, for example, Northcliffe should apply the sort of pressure of which he was capable. Northcliffe, however, had only promised to back the compromise if it were 'arrived at'—a condition which was never fulfilled.

There is, then, some reason to believe that, if O'Donnell and Devlin had not revolted and Redmond had led the Nationalists, Southern Unionists, labour representatives and perhaps one or two independent-minded Ulstermen into the same division lobby, Lloyd George would have seen fit to enact the Midleton scheme. The risk that he would not was considerable, but, in view of the party's desperate situation, that risk from Redmond's standpoint was worth taking. From O'Donnell's standpoint, it was not worth taking. O'Donnell, after all, sat in the Convention as a representative not of the party, but of the Church, and the reasoning which made it desirable for the party to grasp this last chance for survival manifestly did not apply to the Church. It would, of course, be facile to suggest, as many Unionist observers did suggest, that O'Donnell's tactics on this occasion were part of a considered policy of the whole hierarchy. Nevertheless, his ecclesiastical position gave him a certain independence of the party, as an institution, which Redmond could not achieve. O'Donnell would still be a bishop after the next general election even if Redmond and his friends were no longer M.P.s, and he could, unlike Redmond, hope to exercise influence within some new political synthesis similar to that which, for the past eighteen years, he had exercised in the party's organisation. For O'Donnell, therefore, it made sense not to risk being politically discredited by accepting the compromise without a guarantee of legislation, but to wait for a new, more favourable situation in the unpredictable future.

Beyond the question of O'Donnell's tactics at the time of the crisis in January—a question in which O'Donnell the ecclesiastic and O'Donnell the politician are difficult to distinguish—there was a specifically ecclesiastical dimension to whatever responsibility he must bear for the failure of the Convention. The Ulster Unionists, though they were completely satisfied with the legislative Union, had come to the Convention prepared to listen to proposals for compromise between the 1914 act, which they rejected, and the concessions which they had already made in June 1916. They expected to be asked to state their objections to the Home Rule Act, 'and then to see whether Mr. Redmond could make any concessions which would persuade Ulster to accept something less than the permanent exclusion of six counties, which had been their *minimum* hitherto'.[74] The concession which they probably expected was some form of Home Rule within Home Rule, but this, with its implication of Protestant control over Ulster education, was precisely what the bishops would not contemplate. The bishops made plain their opposition to the Swiss federal system, under which Ulster would have been a sort of Protestant canton, and O'Donnell went to desperately undemocratic lengths to frame his draft scheme so as to exclude any suggestion of even limited provincial autonomy. The advisory committee in Ulster was acting quite reasonably when it rejected O'Donnell's scheme of representation. As Stephen Gwynn remarked, the concessions offered to the minority were 'quite inconsistent with the current democratic view of what a Constitution should be'.[75] An expedient so out of harmony with the spirit of the age could have had no permanence. Moreover, O'Donnell's scheme exposed a basic nationalist misunderstanding of Ulster. The ethos of Ulster Presbyterianism is really very democratic, though it would have been most difficult to convince the average Irish Catholic of that fact. Ulster's objection to Home Rule had always been that it would set up not a democratic, but a theocratic, state. Although this belief may have been bigoted and misguided, it was sincerely held. For Ulster to enter a Home Rule parliament with artificially swollen representation would be to negate what was most praiseworthy in Ulster tradition.

Early in February Archbishop Crozier had written a despairing letter to Walter Long lamenting the fact that discussion had focused on a much more advanced scheme than the 1914 Home Rule Act rather than the compromise for which he had vainly worked, a scheme analogous to the Canadian Constitution:

a Central Parliament to unify, and *Provincial* autonomy as in Quebec, Ontario, etc.

The safeguards in the proposed Home Rule Bill are *too absurd*. (1) An Upper House with a large Conservative majority and absolutely a power of veto—(2) A Lower House with 40 per cent of Conservatives for 15 years.

I really cannot imagine how anyone believes that democratic Ulster would accept such a scheme or how long the English Democracy would stand it. If this scheme were once out of the way I think a scheme based on the Canadian 'Compromise' of 1867 might be hammered out.[76]

O'Donnell, as author of the framework for discussion, must bear a large share of the responsibility for the unfortunate course which Crozier was lamenting. Though it is difficult to evaluate his role in the continued exclusion of provincial federalism from the discussion, he clearly was anxious to avoid such an expedient. 'Our people would yield not a little to Ulster for coming into an Irish Parliament,' he wrote to Redmond late in December, 'especially if there were no reservations to an Ulster body.'[77]

The pervasive episcopal aversion to any measure of Ulster autonomy became even more evident in the Convention's final phase. Within a few days after Redmond's fall, the Convention found itself in what the Lord Mayor of Dublin called 'an absolute quagmire'.[78] At Lloyd George's suggestion a deputation was sent to London to confer with the cabinet. After private conferences with the various groups in the deputation, the Prime Minister wrote a long letter to Plunkett. The government, he stressed, was determined to legislate upon receipt of the Convention's report, but he emphasised the urgent importance of a settlement by consent. Moreover, in the government's view, certain controversial questions would have to be deferred until after the war. Police must be, and postal service should be, reserved until after the emergency. Moreover, neither customs nor excise could be handed over during the war, and the government suggested that they might be reserved until two years after the end of the war, a Royal Commission being appointed to submit proposals on the best means of adjusting the financial relations of the two countries thereafter. On the question of safeguards for Ulster, the Prime Minister noted the schemes for additional Unionist representation and suggestions which had been made (apparently by the Unionists) for an Ulster Committee in the Irish parliament with special powers over the application of certain measures to Ulster. The government suggested that the Convention consider a plan for the Irish parliament to meet alternately in Dublin and Belfast and for location of 'the principal offices of an Irish Department of manufacturing industry and commerce' in Belfast.[79] The letter only served to harden episcopal resistance to compromise. Even Cardinal Logue, who devoutly hoped for some alternative to Sinn Féin, poured scorn on the letter when it was shown to him confidentially. He referred to the suggested safeguards as 'partition, real and effective, though disguised',[80] and though his criticisms of the fiscal proposals were, in Plunkett's phrase, 'normally ignorant', he had definitely associated himself with O'Donnell's view.[81] O'Donnell, of course, was indignant and pointed out to the Convention that their terms of reference 'had laid down but one limitation. The Prime Minister's letter laid down many.'[82] Let each section present its separate report. 'For his part he claimed for Ireland full powers of self-government in order to put down offences they all deplored and prevent their recurrence.'

In view of the new situation created by Lloyd George's letter, Midleton's scheme was dropped, and Lord MacDonnell put forward a series of resolutions essentially accepting the financial arrangements contemplated in Lloyd George's letter. Plunkett and Gwynn tried to work out a version of the postponement of the customs-excise issue which might bring Midleton and O'Donnell together on the principle of eventual (but not immediate) fiscal autonomy. Lloyd George wrecked this effort by indicating that he would only be embarrassed by a Nationalist-Southern Unionist coalition on such a basis. At this point O'Donnell and Murphy, in Plunkett's phrase, 'tried to rush the Convention on to the rocks'. The Bishop called a Nationalist caucus at lunch hour on 5 March and tried to obtain a final declaration against compromise and in favour of the full claim. 'He seems to have been too autocratic', Plunkett noted in his diary, '& some reaction set in.'[83] As Gwynn, more charitably, observed, 'Many men were drifting back to Redmond's view, and recoiled from the prospect of dividing the Convention once more into its original component parts—Nationalists on the one side, Unionists on the other.'[84] At this juncture Redmond died, and the Convention adjourned until after the funeral in Wexford.

When the Convention reassembled on 12 March, the first division in its eight-month existence was taken on the first of MacDonnell's resolutions, that 'the matters specified as unfitted for immediate legislation', i.e. Irish control of customs and excise, be postponed and be decided by the imperial parliament within seven years after the end of the war, special Irish representation being called to the imperial parliament for the purpose. The vote was 38 in favour, 34 against. A moderate group had been created, but its majority over the combined extremes was only four votes. The majority consisted of 21 Nationalists led by Stephen Gwynn, 10 Southern Unionists, 4 labour representatives and 3 independent men, two of whom (Granard and MacDonnell) decided in the end to call themselves Nationalists. The minority was composed of 17 Nationalists, led by the three bishops (Kelly being still bedridden), Devlin and Murphy, and 17 Ulster Unionists.[85] Once this crucial issue had been decided, the Convention proceeded to consider, clause by clause, O'Donnell's scheme as it had emerged from the Grand Committee. On most points, the ultra-nationalist group joined with the moderate majority while the Ulster Unionists sullenly opposed virtually everything.

During debate on the composition of the House of Commons, O'Donnell demonstrated once again that his only answer to Ulster demands for safeguards was more and more undemocratic expedients. 'Ulster wanted not nomination but election,' he conceded.

Let Ulster have it, he declared, as fully as she desired. For his part he wanted Ulster strongly represented in an Irish Parliament. Why not create special rural, as well as urban, areas and constituencies? These could provide for isolated groups such as Protestant farmers. They were estimable men, as he knew and respected them in his own diocese, but were at present wholly unrepresented. By this plan the desired overweight for Ulster might be attained; but might it not do more?[86]

'Might it not sweep away Exclusion, Provincial Councils, Grand Committee, and other devices for safeguarding Ulster which must', he rationalised, 'perpetuate mistrust?' The Bishop had carried his desire to avoid these 'devices' to an absurdity—the creation of a gigantic system of rotten boroughs. Although the Ulstermen politely declined his offer, they did not bother to vote on the issue, and the proposal was incorporated into the patchwork scheme which was emerging. When the entire scheme had been considered, Plunkett wrote a report which was endorsed by the moderate group and opposed by the Ulster group and the ultra-nationalist group. Both of the dissident parties presented lengthy minority reports, and five other notes were appended by various component groups of the moderate majority. The blue book in which all these reports were published early in April was scarcely more than a grim joke.

The Convention's chances for success had, admittedly, been very slim from the beginning. Nevertheless, the conversion of the Southern Unionists, the willingness of Northcliffe to press for a solution, and the apparent fear on the part of Carson and some of his followers that they might be obliged to make terms might have combined to bring about a settlement which, though it would not satisfy the Sinn Féin activists, would have deprived them of their greatest advantage—the failure of the Irish Parliamentary Party to secure a working settlement with Ulster included. Unionist commentators have tended to blame the Catholic Church, as represented by O'Donnell, for the failure of the Convention, and have regarded his action on 15 January as the decisive blow to hopes for success. The January crisis only arose, however, because of the Convention's failure to enter serious negotiations on safeguards for Ulster. The most remarkable feature of the January crisis is that Ulster Unionists were prepared to make even very tentative suggestions that they might silently acquiesce in the compromise. No serious attempt had been made to deal with the issue which they regarded as most vital—a fact for which the bishops must bear a large measure of responsibility. Whether the Ulstermen might have been more pliable on finance if their views on safeguards had been dealt with sympathetically no one can say. It was manifestly foolish, however, to ask them to agree on what powers the Irish parliament should have in such a sensitive specific area before they were satisfied that the constitutional framework within which that parliament would operate would adequately protect their interests in general. The financial issue was one on which both sides had strong feelings, but it was also very little understood in the country. From the standpoint of winning acceptance from their 'constituents', both sides could afford to make concessions on finance. Such concessions, however, could only be reasonably expected after the two sides had come to provisional agreement on the central issue—that there was to be an Irish state constituted in such-and-such a way. Therefore, O'Donnell's refusal to meet the Ulstermen on their own terms in the area of safeguards was an important factor in the Convention's failure. His action in the January crisis was important, but its importance lay less in its effect upon the proposed fiscal compromise than in the fact that it snuffed out, at one stroke, whatever good feeling had been fostered in the Ulster delegation. The Ulstermen had come to respect Redmond during the Convention and to regard him as not a bad alternative to de Valera. Then, suddenly, to all appearances, he was dramatically overthrown by bishops (in coalition with Devlin, the Nationalist politician most intensely disliked in Ulster) and all the old fears of clericalism in a future Irish state were instantly revived. From that moment, there was no further chance for meaningful discussions with Ulster.

Of course, the Church's direct interests in public finance, as discussed in Chapter XIII, quite apart from other considerations, would have impelled the prelates to *advocate* fiscal autonomy in the Convention. Their *insistence* upon customs powers, however, was motivated by other considerations than calculations of the Church's direct interests in government finance. Indeed, Kelly, who of all the bishops was most knowledgeable about the mundane questions of pounds, shillings and pence, was willing to surrender customs. During the war, taxation had, of course, increased enormously, and Irish local expenditure had remained virtually constant. Kelly no doubt realised that if an Irish government could begin its career after the war by yielding *only* customs as an imperial contribution, it would start on a much more favourable financial footing than had seemed possible in 1911, when he was studying the problem with the Primrose Committee. Before his illness had removed him from the Convention's deliberations, Kelly had, according to Plunkett, pronounced the financial details of Midleton's scheme 'quite workable',[87] and he probably recognised, as well, that those details were quite consonant with the Church's interests in the realm of public finance. He had thus hoped for substantial agreement among all parties other than the Ulster Unionists, who, he held, 'would never in words agree, but would silently *submit* with a greater or less degree of good grace'.[88] 'If I had been able to attend the Grand Committee in December and the Convention in January,' Kelly confided to Plunkett, 'I would have openly and vigorously advocated that view, even though the Bishop of Raphoe might have differed from me.'

O'Donnell's insistence upon the customs powers was not dictated so much by ecclesiastical interests in public finance as by pessimism over the Convention's prospects—pessimism which his own actions had done much to justify. If the Convention did not with certainty enable the Nation to supplant the State immediately, then the Church must make terms with a new generation of the Nation—and this task took precedence over that of making terms with Ulster. The task was already well under way in the country, and the refusal of three out of four of the Church's representatives to compromise on fiscal autonomy, while a basis for disagreement with the Unionists, was a point of likely agreement with Sinn Féin.

CHAPTER XVIII

Nihil Obstat Sinn Féin

AT the same meeting in June 1917 at which they selected delegates to the Irish Convention, the hierarchy attempted to reach at least a temporary consensus on the current political situation. Some seventy-nine priests from all parts of the country had subscribed to a fund to defray the election expenses incurred by the new movement in South Longford.[1] Moreover, Sinn Féin was beginning to establish a network of local branches on the pattern of earlier political and agrarian movements, and in many cases priests were presiding at organising meetings or being elected officers in the new branches.[2] It was therefore appropriate that the hierarchy's attempted consensus took the form of a letter of instruction to be sent to all the priests of Ireland. The only substantial feature of the letter was a reiteration of the long-standing statutes of the National Synod governing political activity by priests. Before attending a public meeting, a priest was required to obtain the express consent of the parish priest of the parish in which it was to be held (except for meetings in Dublin, in which case the permission of the priest's own Ordinary was sufficient unless the Archbishop of Dublin directed otherwise). Priests were also forbidden to speak of 'political or kindred affairs' in the churches. The instruction contained a long and very loosely worded admonition about the danger that the 'spirit of lawlessness' might, during the great crisis the country was experiencing, tempt men 'to indulge in pernicious excesses'.[3] The clergy 'should earnestly exhort their people to beware of all dangerous associations and sedulously shun all movements that are not in accord with the principles of Catholic teaching and doctrine'. The bishops, however, carefully abstained from specifying what associations and movements they had in mind, beyond noting that 'As is well known to students of theology, all organisations "that plot against the Church or lawfully constituted authority, whether openly or secretly", are condemned by the Church under the gravest penalties.' Without using the word 'republic' the statement referred to 'forms of government . . . that are popular at the moment' being associated with 'civil tyranny and religious persecution', but the conclusions drawn from this assertion amounted to little more than a counsel of prudence and moderation. Similarly, there was a reference to the divine source of the authority of temporal, as well as spiritual, governors, but the inference drawn from this principle was a masterpiece of platitudinous ambiguity: 'God and country are best served when pastors and their flocks are knit together in intimate fellowship with Christ by the strict observance of their common faith.' The entire statement was patently a desperate compromise between those members of the hierarchy who were terrified of the Sinn Féin movement and those who wished to turn the new movement to the Church's purposes.

Bishop Cohalan of Cork gave a revealing interpretation of the instruction when he remarked on 1 July that

The Sinn Fein Party . . . is, henceforth, on its trial. Its work has been the work of opposition, of pulling down. If it is to justify its existence it must have a practical, constructive policy. Sinn Fein, it is said, is divided. So far, there has been no authoritative statement of constructive Sinn Fein policy.[4]

The Bishop mentioned abstention from parliament and an appeal to the post-war Peace Conference as policies which might possibly be advocated, and though he thought both these policies futile, preferring to rely on the Convention for a settlement, he did not condemn either possibility. He deplored physical force and appealed 'to the young men of the diocese to have nothing to do with any policy or organisation that would put them in a position of hostility to their Church'.

The episcopal instruction was issued at a particularly critical point in the development of the post-Rising Sinn Féin movement. A parliamentary vacancy was created in East Clare by the death in action of Redmond's brother, Major

William Redmond. In the two previous by-elections, Sinn
Féin had offered political nonentities as candidates. Now for
the first time, the movement brought forward a man who
proved to have real political ability—Eamon de Valera. De
Valera, born in New York of an Irish mother and a Spanish
father, had been a rebel commandant during the Rising, but
he managed to escape execution. Together with all other interned rebels still in custody, he was released in June in a
gesture which was intended to create an atmosphere of conciliation for the Convention. Obviously, no adequate assessment of a man whose political career has spanned six decades
can be made in a study which touches upon only the first
few years of that career. It does seem, however, that this early
part of his public activity has been obfuscated by the fact
that during the 1920s de Valera led a military opposition to
the Free State government in defiance of the strictest ecclesiastical ban—a fact that has led to the misconception that
throughout his early career he was a doctrinaire anticlerical.
In the East Clare campaign of June-July 1917, the first electoral campaign of his career, he demonstrated an acute sense
of the difficulties he would face in leading a revolutionary
movement without alienating the all-important support of
the clergy. Answering charges that he was an anarchist and
an atheist, he told a crowd at Killaloe that 'all his life he had
been associated with priests, and the priests knew him and
were behind him in this election', which was 'the best guarantee to the people of Clare that the statements made by his
opponents were unfounded'. He did not attack the bishops'
instruction, but cleverly accused his opponents of misusing
the circular—which, he implied with some justice, had not
been intended for publication—to deceive ignorant people
who did not know that the rules cited were standing orders,
and to create the impression 'that the bishops were afraid that
his friends were starting a new campaign of immediate revolution'. Echoing the theology textbooks, he said that 'the only
case in which he considered revolution justifiable under
present circumstances would be when there would be good
chance of success', and then he carefully balanced this statement, which was for clerical consumption, with one for the
benefit of his more militant colleagues: 'The British Empire

was at a great crisis, and it would not be impossible that during that crisis a favourable opportunity would arise.'[5] When the *Freeman's Journal* accused him of shifting ground, he called the charge unfounded, and he produced another masterful piece of ambiguity in answer to the suggestion that he intended to 'lead the young men into an abortive rebellion'. The Easter Rising, he maintained, had saved 'the national soul of Ireland', and

Another Easter week would be a superfluity. He and his friends had been called wild red revolutionary Jacobites [*sic*], because they said that they would not altogether eliminate physical force from their programme. Why should they eliminate it? If they did it would mean that John Bull could kick as much as he liked.[6]

In part, this statement seems to have been a reply to a public letter by Father Slattery, P.P., Quin, urging support for Mr Lynch, the candidate endorsed (against Dillon's better judgement)[7] by the Irish Parliamentary Party, rather than 'red ruin and revolution'. Even Father Slattery, however, had felt obliged to attest to de Valera's personal merits and to dissociate himself from 'many things in its [the party's] policy of the last ten years'. He even conceded that 'there are many points of the Sinn Fein policy of which most Irishmen would approve', and that 'the events of the last fifteen months would make a natural appeal to every man with a drop of Irish blood in his veins'.[8] When one of the party's clerical supporters was so equivocal, it should not be surprising that most of the priests in the constituency enthusiastically backed de Valera. Although about ten clergymen, mainly canons and parish priests, endorsed Lynch, nearly twice as many—mainly curates, but including at least five parish priests—took the Sinn Féin side.[9] In the event, de Valera surprised even his own followers by accumulating 5,010 votes to Lynch's 2,035, and the Sinn Féiners loudly proclaimed that one of the votes for de Valera was that of Bishop Fogarty of Killaloe.[10]

The accession of Fogarty to the Sinn Féin cause was of critical importance, for on 19 August O'Dwyer, the only prelate who had hitherto given unequivocal support to Sinn Féin, died. As de Valera later revealed, the Bishop of Limerick had told him on the eve of the East Clare election: 'There will be no advance in Ireland until you sweep the rubbish out of the land,' to which de Valera replied that the party would die of its own accord. O'Dwyer rejoined: 'If you want to have a real Irish nation, such as you desire, you, first of all, must clean out the rubbish and build from a decent foundation.'[11] Such a colourful episcopal advocate as the late Bishop of Limerick was perhaps too much for the Sinn Féiners to hope for, but the Bishop of Killaloe, who delivered a panegyric upon O'Dwyer at the memorial service held one month after his death,[12] was perhaps a more valuable ally, for he did not have O'Dwyer's record of contentiousness within the hierarchy. Moreover, unlike O'Dwyer, he had hitherto been counted as one of the party's supporters, though Redmond had, no doubt, realised from Fogarty's despondent letter of June 1915 that he had lost confidence in the party. In the eyes of the general public, as Sir James O'Connor observed, Fogarty had been considered a member of the 'sensible bishop' class.[13] As recently as July, Fogarty had attempted, through O'Brien's old friend, Father James Clancy (who was soon to declare for Sinn Féin), to persuade O'Brien to enter the Convention.[14] He had apparently been moved to take this action by assurances from his colleague, Bishop Kelly, that the government were prepared to grant 'Grattan's Parliament' or dominion status. The Bishop of Killaloe threw off the restraint he had practised since early in the war when, in September, forcible feeding resulted in the death of a hunger-striker, Thomas Ashe, who was serving a sentence for successfully ambushing a party of police. 'The world sees already in these hideous atrocities', Fogarty wrote to the press, 'what the triumph of English culture means for small nationalities.'[15] Reading the letter at a Sinn Féin meeting in Navan, John Sweetman declared that Fogarty 'was evidently a worthy successor to the late Dr O'Dwyer of Limerick'.[16]

Fogarty's newly elected M.P. was already well on his way to establishing his primacy within the advanced nationalist movement. After his victory in East Clare, de Valera was co-opted to the Sinn Féin National Council and was placed upon a committee to draft a new constitution to be submitted to the forthcoming Árd-Fheis (Annual Convention) of Sinn Féin, which this year would be of far greater importance than it had ever been before. In this committee de Valera once again demonstrated his political skill by contriving a formula which could be accepted both by Griffith, who refused to commit himself to strive for a republic, and by the doctrinaire republicans who were prominent in advanced nationalist circles:

Sinn Féin aims at securing the International recognition of Ireland as an independent Irish Republic.

Having achieved that status the Irish people may by referendum freely choose their own form of Government.[17]

After stating this curious compromise, the new constitution endorsed, practically verbatim, the aims of the old Sinn Féin organisation, with the additional admonition that 'Sinn Féiners should make it their business to secure that workers are paid a living wage.'[18] When the Sinn Féin Árd-Fheis met on 25 October, it unanimously accepted the scissors-and-paste document. Although Griffith had held the presidency of the organisation for six years, he stood too far to the right among the anti-party forces to retain effective leadership. When his own name, along with those of Count Plunkett and de Valera, was placed in nomination, he and the Count wisely withdrew, and de Valera was elected President without opposition. Griffith and Father Michael O'Flanagan were elected Vice-Presidents, and two other priests, Father Matt Ryan of Co. Tipperary and Father Thomas Wall of Co. Limerick, were elected to the executive. When the name of Eóin Mac Néill was proposed for the executive, objections were raised because of his countermanding order at the time of the Rising, but de Valera spoke on his behalf, and he was easily elected.[19] Actions like these, by which de Valera retained the right wing of the movement he was now leading, were balanced by some rather inflammatory rhetoric in his presidential address. He spoke of drawing 'the naked sword' to make England 'bare her own naked sword, to drag the hypocritical mask off her face, and to show her to the world for what she is, the accursed oppressor of nations'. Again he stressed the theological point that the movement's 'final success' would be its moral justification. He uttered the words which were to haunt him in later years—'We are not doctrinaire Republicans,'[20] but he added 'that there is no contemplation . . . of having a Monarchy in which the Monarch would be of the House of Windsor'.[21] Although this statement appeared to exclude 'Hungarian' dual-monarchy theories, Griffith was not deterred from publishing a new edition of *The Resurrection of Hungary* a few months later. At a separate convention of the Irish Volunteers, de Valera secured the presidency of that organisation as well, with the backing of the I.R.B., despite the fact that he refused to join the I.R.B. (with which he had been associated briefly before the Rising) on the grounds that membership of a secret society would violate his religious principles.[22]

Sinn Féin was coming to be a more concrete phenomenon than it had been earlier in the year, but its nature remained highly ambiguous. It was not a secret society in the sense that would necessarily call down ecclesiastical condemnation, but many of its key posts were held by I.R.B. members and persons in close communication with the I.R.B. It sought to establish a republic, but it did not exclude the possibility of a monarchy. It did not eschew physical force, but it put forward a programme which had long been advocated as an alternative to physical force. Nevertheless, no matter what zealots or detractors might say, it was manifestly devoting its primary energies to the unexceptionably constitutional activity of winning elections. Austin Harrison, editor of the *English Review*, who visited Kilkenny in August during another by-election which Sinn Féin won easily, was impressed above all by the lack of violence. 'All the leaders of Sinn Féin', he wrote, 'are now preaching discipline, order, organization—constitutionalism.'[23] Apparently the Kilkenny clergy made a particular effort to forestall disturbance,[24] but in general an effort was being made to play up the nonviolent facet of the very paradoxical movement. The October Árd-Fheis called forth more extreme language from de Valera than he ordinarily used on the hustings and on the speaking circuit, for at the Árd-Fheis his task was not to persuade waverers, but to rally those already committed to advanced nationalism.

During the autumn a few prominent divines, including Bishops Foley and Gilmartin, addressed themselves to the question of Catholic teaching on the ethics of rebellion.

Gilmartin's summary of the theological requirements for a justifiable rebellion were as follows:

(1) The Government must be in the judgment of the large body of the peope tyrannical.

(2) That constitutional or legal means—that is, means in accordance with the civil law—are not available.

(3) That there is good hope of success so that resistance by armed force will not entail greater evils than it seeks to remedy.[25]

The bishop gave it as his opinion that these conditions did not exist in Ireland at that time. He apparently did not discuss the three conditions separately, and he disclaimed any intention 'to cast any aspersion on the motives of those who may have seemed to take a different view'.

This sort of approach on the part of the bishops only made it easier for the priests who were inclined toward Sinn Féin to emphasise the constitutional side of the movement. At a Sinn Féin meeting attended by 10,000 persons at Bailieborough, Co. Cavan, a letter was read from the Very Rev. B. Gaffney, P.P., V.F., exhorting Sinn Féiners to shun secret societies and persons who would wish to incite rebellion. 'The eyes of the world are upon you;' he wrote, 'show that you are Constitutional.'[26] The tendency for even priests who strongly distrusted the new movement to try to direct it into acceptable lines was illustrated by a public letter from the Rev. David Bolger, P.P., of Co. Wexford. Father Bolger quoted statements and documents associated with Sinn Féin leaders which implied that armed revolt was intended, but in warning against 'this coming disaster,' he wrote: 'Be Sinn Féiners if you like. Cherish your country, your love of liberty, your political opinions as much as you like. But be no party to any cause which must end as this rebellion—preached and taught and contemplated—must end.'[27]

The development of an ideological basis for the Church's organised support of Sinn Féin was temporarily impeded by a pastoral from Cardinal Logue read in the churches of his archdiocese on 25 November. The other conservative prelates who had spoken out had concentrated upon the possibility of armed rebellion and had left considerable room for accommodation between the Church and Sinn Féin. The Cardinal, who had a positive phobia about republics, left little doubt as to his intentions when he deplored 'an agitation' which

has sprung up and is spreading among our people which, ill-considered and Utopian, cannot fail, if persevered in, to entail present suffering, disorganisation and danger, and is sure to end in future disaster, defeat and collapse. And all this in pursuit of a dream which no man in his sober senses can hope to see realised: the establishment of an Irish Republic, either by an appeal to the Potentates of Europe seated at a Peace Conference, or an appeal to force by hurling an unarmed people against an Empire which has five millions of men under arms, furnished with the most terrible engines of destruction. . . . The thing would be ludicrous if it were not so mischievous and fraught with such danger.[28]

By thus simultaneously invoking the theological requirement for a reasonable prospect of success in armed revolt and ridiculing the idea of an appeal to the Peace Conference, the Cardinal left little doubt as to his hostility to Sinn Féin. During the week before the pastoral appeared, the leader-writer for the *Irish Catholic*, which had been giving prominent coverage to clerical criticism of the movement, had managed to detect a new tone in Sinn Féin's propaganda which, he hinted, might become the basis of an acceptable movement.[29] The Cardinal had now diminished, for a time, the chances for such an accommodation.

Though neither Fogarty nor Logue seems to have used the term 'Sinn Féin' in a public pronouncement, it was quite clear that Fogarty was encouraging the new movement and that Logue was terrified of it. The divergence was particularly significant because both these churchmen belonged to the segment of the hierarchy which was disenchanted with the Irish Parliamentary Party. Until the party's episcopal enemies could come to some understanding about the proper course to pursue, there could be no hope of the whole hierarchy arriving at a clear policy relevant to the rapidly changing situation in the country. The June instruction had been no more than a stopgap measure, and it had neither hindered the rise of Sinn Féin nor formed any basis for directing the efforts of the large number of priests who were now flocking to the new movement. One reason for this parlous state of affairs was that many churchmen were hoping against hope that the Irish Convention might produce a settlement which would eliminate the problem. Not only did it become clear inside the Convention early in the new year that such hopes were unfounded, but outside the Convention Cardinal Logue's pastoral manifestly was failing to curb the activities of young militants. Although violence was nowhere near the level it had attained during the agrarian struggle and would attain within two years, isolated outrages and raids for arms were becoming more frequent.[30] Bishop Fogarty felt obliged to denounce arms raids as 'an odious and most detestable form of crime'.[31] Even the clergy themselves were not immune from attack. At Curry, Co. Sligo, for example, Canon Mulligan, P.P., warned his parishioners on several occasions to beware of revolutionary propaganda and, at the instigation of his bishop, Dr Morrisroe, withdrew his permission for a Sinn Féin priest to address a meeting in his parish. On 2 March a party of men raided and commandeered part of Canon Mulligan's farm which was diocesan property attached to his residence.[32]

While the Cardinal's attitude did not seem to affect Sinn Féin excesses, it may have contributed somewhat to a revival of the Irish Parliamentary Party's electoral fortunes which was evident in three by-election victories early in the year. One of these, in Redmond's Waterford constituency, was no doubt simply a reflection of local respect for the late leader. The other two vacancies, South Armagh and East Tyrone, happened to fall in Logue's archdiocese. In South Armagh late in January, one of the party stalwarts, Canon Quinn of Camlough, campaigned with vigour against the Sinn Féin candidate, frequently citing Logue's opposition to the new movement, and on one occasion physically assaulting Laurence Ginnell, who had thrown in his lot with Sinn Féin. Only a few priests joined the party campaign, however, and it was clear that a large number of clergy favoured Dr McCartan, the Sinn Féin candidate, but were restrained from engaging in much open campaigning by the Cardinal's attitude. 'His Eminence', Healy wrote to his brother, 'is against Republics and Revolutions, but his priests are against the Party, and he is in a dilemma.'[33] Logue even received Mr Donnelly, the party candidate, when he visited Armagh—

one of the very few occasions on which the Cardinal ever gave public countenance to the party since its expulsion of Healy in 1900—but he also consented to receive Count Plunkett, though an audience was refused to de Valera.[34] In the East Tyrone contest during March and April, the Cardinal again tried to keep his priests out of the Sinn Féin campaign. Many defied his orders, however, and Devlin was prompted to attack them after the election as 'subtle gentlemen, who went around telling people that their sons would be taken by Conscription'. When a heckler asked a Sinn Féin speaker about the Cardinal's opinion, he retorted that 'there were greater and more intellectual bishops than the aged Cardinal on the side of Sinn Féin'.[35] Though the Irish Party won both contests by respectable majorities,[36] it is difficult to say how far they were helped by the Cardinal's attitude. Perhaps a more important factor was a more efficient local organisation in these Ulster districts where the party had always to be ready for a Unionist challenge—in contrast to divisions such as East Clare and North Roscommon which the party had previously been able to take for granted. Moreover, the most immediate problem facing the electors of South Armagh and East Tyrone was exclusion from Home Rule, and they may have realised that Sinn Féin, though it protested loudly against partition, offered little constructive policy to avert it. In any case, the Cardinal could take small comfort in the fact that the voters had agreed with him, for the elections had made plain that a significant section of his clergy was in revolt against his political opinions.

It was just at this point that the Irish Convention breathed its last. Cardinal Logue had lost hope that the Convention might produce a settlement without what he would regard as partition—i.e. any measure of provincial autonomy for Ulster.[37] If, then, there was no prospect of the Nation supplanting the State forthwith, it was incumbent upon the Church finally to come to terms with the Nation's emergent leadership. An opportunity soon presented itself. The government was preparing a new bill to raise the upper age-limit for conscription in Great Britain from fifty to fifty-five years, and as it was felt that English opinion would tolerate no further extension of the system as long as Ireland was exempted, a clause was inserted giving the government authority to apply conscription in Ireland. Although the Irish Party had been instrumental in preserving Ireland's exemption, a substantial segment of Irish public opinion translated its own hostility to the war effort and the party's support of it—perfunctory though it had become—into a belief that the party really favoured conscription. No informed person could doubt that an attempt to raise troops by force in Ireland would be met, at the very least, by widespread disorder, or even by actual armed resistance—for those men who had been active in seizing arms in the past few months would be the first called up. Thus the Church's abhorrence of disorder seemed about to be offended and her instinctive opposition to any measure which might further the depopulation of the country was called into play. The introduction of the new measure on 9 April virtually coincided with the submission to parliament of the Irish Convention's report, which, the Prime Minister stated, provided another opportunity 'of approaching the vexed question of Irish autonomy with more hope of success'. Though he stressed the independence of the two issues of Home Rule and conscription, it soon became clear that they were, in fact, very much interdependent.

On the same day that the conscription bill was introduced, the Episcopal Standing Committee met and declared that there would now be no need for 'forced levies' if the government had

in any reasonable time given Ireland the benefit of the principles which are declared to be at stake in the war. . . . What between mismanagement and mischief-making this country has already been deplorably upset, and it would be a fatal mistake, surpassing the worst blunders of the past four years, to furnish a telling plea now for desperate courses by an attempt to enforce conscription. With all the responsibility that attaches to our pastoral office, we feel bound to warn the Government against entering upon a policy so disasterous [sic] to the public interest, and to all order, public and private.[38]

During the following week several of the bishops spoke out against conscription. The zest with which they took up the issue varied according to their political attitudes—the cautious Bishop Brownrigg of Ossory appealing to the young men and young clergy not to be drawn 'into foolish courses', while Bishop Fogarty boldly proclaimed: 'The Irish people are not slaves.' In one significant case, however, the response was rather stronger than one might have predicted. The Very Rev. Joseph Brady, Adm., of Armagh Cathedral, 'following the eminent example set us a few years ago by Sir Edward Carson', organised a series of meetings of 'the priests and people of the Cathedral Parish' to found 'a Solemn League and Covenant against conscription'. It was stressed, however, that unlike Carson's movement, the new league would eschew arms and drilling and would rely upon 'the constitutional weapon of passive resistance' for which there was 'the highest theological authority'. Father Brady was authorised to tell his demonstration near the Cathedral on Sunday, 14 April, that Logue 'was heart and soul with the meeting', and the Cardinal himself told a congregation at Dungannon that the conscription proposals 'would lead to the utmost disorder and chaos in Ireland and would be met with the most strenuous passive resistance'. He had, he announced, convened a meeting of the hierarchy for 18 April to consider the problem.[39] After two years of indecision, the Cardinal had settled upon a course of action.

On 16 April the new Military Service Bill passed its third reading, the Irish section having been carried by more than two to one. The Irish Parliamentary Party filed out of the House in protest and followed the old tradition, associated with Coercion Acts, of returning to Ireland to organise resistance. The Dublin Corporation had already called for a united national opposition to conscription, and Lord Mayor O'Neill had invited representatives of Sinn Féin, the Irish Party, the All-for-Ireland League and the Irish Trade Union Congress to the Mansion House for a conference to carry out this proposal on the same day as the hierarchy's scheduled meeting at Maynooth. Dillon, who had succeeded Redmond as leader of the Irish Party, Devlin, de Valera, Griffith, Healy, O'Brien and three labour leaders, Thomas Johnson, Michael Egan and William O'Brien, accepted the invitation. Apparently the other delegates did not realise how efficient the lines of communication between the Sinn Féin leaders and the hierarchy were. As early as the spring of 1917 Walsh's secretary, Father Curran, was carrying on an active correspondence with moderate Sinn Féin leaders.[40] Several years later, when Walsh died, de Valera wrote: 'Although I had not met his Grace so very often, I felt for him something of the intimate personal affection of a son for a father. You can scarcely realise what confidence it gave to me, a novice, during the three or four years I have been in public life, to feel that there was always one at hand on whom I could rely for ripe counsel and wisdom in any hour of need.'[41] On the morning of the Mansion House Conference de Valera solicited some of that ripe counsel and gave the Archbishop a copy of a resolution he had drafted deeming passage of the Conscription Bill to be 'a declaration of war on the Irish nation' and calling for resistance to its enforcement.[42] The other delegates, apparently not suspecting that he had communicated with the Archbishop, were puzzled when he refused to alter a word of the resolution[43] and astonished when he proposed that they send a deputation to Maynooth to wait upon the hierarchy. Healy remarked—no doubt partly with tongue in cheek and more for Dillon's benefit than for de Valera's—that he was unaccustomed to meeting bishops and archbishops. 'Oh, there's nothing in that,' de Valera ingenuously replied. 'I have lived all my life among priests.' 'Have you lived all your life among bishops?' Healy retorted.[44]

After some banter over who would share a car with whom, a deputation consisting of Dillon, de Valera, Healy, O'Brien the labour leader, and the Lord Mayor set out for Maynooth where they received a cordial welcome from the bishops who had just adjourned for lunch. As Healy and de Valera alighted from their car, Healy remarked to one of the bishops: 'Here we are, my Lord, the lion and the lamb.' 'Oh, yes,' the bishop replied, 'but which is which.' The five were seated at a table with Logue and Walsh, and after some small talk over lunch the deputation presented its case. De Valera stressed that they should avoid any nuance which might be construed as condemning the Volunteer movement, because 'no matter who decided anything the Volunteers would fight if conscription was enforced and they had no use for passive resistance'. 'Well now, Mr. de Valera,' the Cardinal replied, 'when I talk about passive resistance, I don't mean we are to lie down and let people walk over us.'[45] The deputation suggested that the following pledge, drafted by de Valera, be taken by the people in every parish:

Denying the right of the British Government to enforce compulsory service in this country, we pledge ourselves solemnly to one another to resist Conscription by the most effective means at our disposal.[46]

After deliberating privately, the hierarchy recalled the deputation, and Logue asked O'Donnell to read the resolution they had adopted as no one else could read his handwriting.[47] It was, as O'Donnell had intimated to William O'Brien moments earlier, all they had asked for and more.[48] The bishops directed the clergy to announce public meetings of their respective parishes on the following Sunday for the purpose of administering the proposed pledge, to celebrate a public Mass of intercession 'to avert the scourge of conscription', and to announce that at an early date a collection would be made outside the church gates to finance resistance. Furthermore, they declared,

In view especially of the historic relations between the two countries from the very beginning up to this moment, we consider that conscription forced in this way upon Ireland is an oppressive and inhuman law, which the Irish people have a right to resist by every means that are consonant with the law of God. We wish to remind our people that there is a higher Power which controls the affairs of men. They have in their hands the means of conciliating that Power by strict adherence to the Divine law, by more earnest attention to their religious duties, and by fervent and persevering prayer.[49]

They had, the bishops noted, 'already sanctioned a National Novena in Honour of Our Lady of Lourdes', beginning on 3 May, 'to secure general and domestic peace', and they exhorted 'the heads of families to have the Rosary recited every evening with the intention of protecting the spiritual and temporal welfare of our beloved country, and bringing us safe through this crisis of unparalleled gravity'.

Although accounts of these events have made it appear that the initiative came from the lay leaders at the Mansion House Conference, clerical forces were at least as significant as lay forces in launching the new movement. Father Brady's demonstration at Armagh had been only one of over three hundred anticonscription meetings held during the week ending Saturday, 20 April, according to a report of the Inspector-General of the Royal Irish Constabulary. 'At very many of these', the I.-G. reported, 'the R.C. Clergy presided.' He expressed the hope that the Church, by supporting the movement, would be enabled 'to exercise a restraining influence', but he added that the pledge of passive resistance, which was being signed everywhere on 21 April, was being refused by some elements of the Volunteers, 'as restricting their right to use arms'.[50] Duke reported to the cabinet grave fears on the part of police officials that the bishops would induce young Catholic policemen not to assist in enforcing the act, and that their replacement by police from England would be useless.[51] Although the crisis became the occasion for replacing both Duke, the Chief Secretary, and Wimborne, the Lord Lieutenant, by Edward Shortt and Lord French, respectively, no advance was made upon either of the government's announced Irish policies. Lloyd George could tell Home Rulers that there could be no Home Rule until conscription could be applied and Unionists that there could be no conscription without Home Rule. The Irish question was thus effectively disposed of for the remaining months of the war. Balfour, the Foreign Secretary, did undertake to notify Count de Salis, British Minister to the Holy See, of 'any cases that might come to light of the improper interference of the Irish priesthood in secular affairs and more particularly the recent promise of absolution to persons engaged in resistance to the Military Service Act',[52] but the result of his efforts was more comical than effective. He dispatched a sheaf of police notes of highly colourful remarks by clergymen to the Count, who dutifully handed them over to the appropriate Vatican authorities.[53] The Holy See, of course, was not anxious to compromise its neutrality by intervening in a matter of this kind. The Cardinal Secretary of State, however, did forward the extracts to Cardinal Logue and give de Salis a copy of Logue's explanation—viz. that though there were no doubt a few priests who had exceeded the bounds of prudence and moderation, the extracts were unreliable because they were based 'simplement sur le souvenir

des agents de police . . . qui ignorient les principes element-
aires de la doctrine catholique'.[54] Balfour was, no doubt, less
than enthusiastic over this explanation.

John Henry Bernard, the Church of Ireland Archbishop
of Dublin, who had been a leading figure in the Southern
Unionist bloc in the Convention, had been in correspondence
with the Archbishop of Canterbury, Dr Davidson, during its
deliberations. During the April conscription crisis, Davidson
asked for Bernard's thoughts upon the Catholic bishops'
policy. His lengthy reply was informed by a calm, reasoned
judgement of which few Protestants were capable at this
juncture. There were, he observed, three explanations of
the bishops' motives in circulation. First, 'It is argued that
they do not really desire Home Rule, although they always
pretend that they do desire it, because they wish to be on the
popular side. They opposed the only line of settlement, during the last weeks of the Convention, and put forward extreme
demands, which they must have known the Government
could not concede.'[55] Though this explanation was plausible
and was believed by 'all Ulster'—and, he might have added,
by Lord Midleton—Bernard rejected it because

(a) All these prelates are peasants, bred in the Home Rule
tradition, surrounded in their homes, at Maynooth, and during
their ministerial life, by those who are all Home Rulers. It is
impossible for me to believe that, as soon as they became bishops,
they were all converted to the belief that British rule was best.
(b) However badly one may think of them, I cannot accept the
view that they are all, one and all, deliberate and consistent liars;
and that when they meet in conclave, they agree to tell the world
a lie. Yet so it must be, if they do not desire Home Rule, for they
repeat it in public and in private, with unvarying consistency.
Gossips are apt to say that 'Cardinal Logue has often admitted
that he does not want Home Rule'; but when one asks for chapter and verse, one is told that of course these things are only
said privately. That will not do.[56]

Some of the bishops, Bernard admitted, 'are far-seeing enough
to see the danger of their influence—especially in matters of
education—if Home Rule were granted'. One of them, he
revealed, had spoken to him quite candidly about this. 'But
he is a Home Ruler, none the less. This explanation, to me,'

14

he concluded, 'involves an impossible psychology.'

A second possible explanation was that the bishops were taking 'their marching orders' from the Vatican, which, it was alleged, desired and expected a German victory. Bernard dismissed this theory because (a) he doubted that the Vatican would order the Irish hierarchy to work to embarrass the British government in its hour of danger without giving a similar directive to the English Catholic hierarchy, and (b) earlier in the war two or three of the Irish Catholic bishops had spoken in favour of recruiting.

The third explanation, which Bernard himself accepted, was 'that the dominant motive governing the actions always of the Roman hierarchy is the desire to keep control over their people. They would have forfeited their influence years ago', he argued,

if they had not condoned the Plan of Campaign. They would have forfeited their influence with the Sinn Feiners (a growing body) if they had accepted the scheme of Home Rule which the constitutional Nationalists and the Southern Unionists accepted in the Convention; for in this scheme Imperial interests were safeguarded, and the Imperial control maintained. And they would forfeit their influence now, if they did not fall in with the popular dislike of conscription. That is one thing. And another is that I believe them honestly to desire to prevent bloodshed. Undoubtedly many lives would be lost, were any serious attempt made *now* to impose compulsory service on Ireland. It could have been done quite easily two years ago, and it could have been done—though with some trouble—one year ago. And you will observe that the Roman bishops, as a body, did *not* denounce it then, although it was being discussed in the press. They denounce it now, because they are afraid of losing control of their people. By the action they have taken, in putting themselves at the head of the anti-Conscription campaign, they have regained the confidence of all Roman Catholic Ireland.[57]

'They are', Bernard warned, 'intensely anti-British at heart, thoroughly disloyal to the King, to Great Britain, and to the Empire. That is in their blood. And they will always do what they can to injure England. That you may reckon upon as quite certain. But that they are positively pro-German, I don't believe—except in two or three instances.'

Bernard had correctly singled out most of the important

motivations of the Catholic bishops and clergy: their genuine nationalistic sentiments, their desire not to forfeit their influence over the people and their horror of violence and bloodshed. One can perhaps best understand these motivations by taking a particular example of clerical action, which, I believe, also illustrates another consideration which Bernard did not yet perceive. On 23 March, in connection with the celebration of the Irish Parliamentary Party's victory in Waterford City, an altercation had occurred in Cootehill, Co. Cavan, between local partisans of Sinn Féin and the Irish Parliamentary Party respectively. On the morning of 16 April, rather belatedly, the police arrested four members of each group in their beds and hauled them away to the police barracks for trial under the Crimes Act. The local parish priest, the Very Rev. P. O'Connell, V.G., had already associated himself with the anticonscription movement two days earlier—the Sunday on which Father Brady initiated his 'Solemn League and Covenant' at Armagh—by writing to assure an anticonscription meeting at Virginia, near Cootehill, that he would have been present but for a prior arrangement to accompany 'the whole people of this parish' to meet Count Plunkett in another neighbouring village. While the prisoners were being detained in the police barracks on 16 April, a crowd gathered at the barracks door, and Father O'Connell 'went amongst them . . . and counselled them not to interfere with the police in the discharge of their duty, and his advice was taken by all'. Messengers had gone out into the surrounding countryside, and during the trial crowds of people were arriving in the town. The brass bands of both the local Sinn Féin club and the local U.I.L. (as well as the fife and drum bands of Maudabawn, Middle Chapel and Kill) paraded the streets. 'The incident was made the occasion of a demonstration against conscription. Banners, improvised for the occasion, bearing the words: "No Conscription" and "We will not be conscripted", were displayed on all sides.' Inside the courtroom, both groups of prisoners were convicted, and it was evident that they were on rather more friendly terms with each other than they had been on the night of 23 March. Given the opportunity to put up bail, all the prisoners refused, and they were ordered to be removed to Belfast by train. When the time came for their removal, 'Father O'Connell directed the enormous crowd that congregated to make way for the police, which they did.' Cheers were raised for the prisoners, and the crowd followed in procession singing 'The Soldiers' Song'. When they arrived at the station 'the crowd did not go into the railway premises by Father O'Connell's direction, but returned to the Market Square, where Father O'Connell delivered a rousing speech against conscription, assuring his flock, whom he had shepherded safely through this potentially very explosive situation, that 'they would be more than a match for the British Army'.[58]

Apart from the remarkable skill of this priest in combining the roles of anti-British agitator and preserver of law and order, the incident illustrates a fundamentally new political situation which was coming about at the time of the conscription crisis. For the first time since the Rising there seemed to be some chance for a united nationalist front, embracing elements of both Sinn Féin and the Irish Parliamentary Party. Sinn Féiners had been trying to sound 'constitutional' to avoid ecclesiastical denunciation. Devlin and a number of other politicians associated with the Irish Party's organisation had signed the ultra-nationalist report at the Irish Convention. Now the Irish Party, which after three by-election victories was beginning to look a bit more formidable, seemed to be adopting the Sinn Féin strategy by withdrawing from parliament and by participating in the Mansion House Conference, which Sinn Féin dubbed the 'National Cabinet'.[59] The Mansion House Conference, moreover, continued in existence, meeting from time to time thereafter, though the Sinn Féin seats were taken by Eóin Mac Néill and an Alderman Thomas Kelly after de Valera and Griffith, along with a number of other Sinn Féiners, were arrested in May and lodged in English jails on questionable charges of participating in a 'German plot'. Arrangements were made to administer the funds collected in each parish, through local committees to be composed of representatives of the different parties 'roughly in proportion to the numerical strength of each party in the district who have taken the pledge',[60] and Archbishop Walsh consented to act as one of three national trustees of the fund.[61] There had been rumours during the East Tyrone election campaign that the Sinn Féin candidate, apparently at clerical urgings, was considering standing aside to allow the Irish Party a walkover.[62] The second day of the Mansion House Conference's initial meeting was nomination day for another vacancy in the Tullamore division of King's County, and the party refrained from nominating a candidate, thus conceding the seat to Sinn Féin. During the Conference, de Valera apparently spoke of not offering opposition to Dillon himself in East Mayo in the next general election.[63] The Cootehill incident, therefore, was not just an isolated instance of goodfeeling between the two parties, but was part of a larger pattern of events—a pattern which inspired in some ecclesiastics the hope of political unity among Catholics.

This hope was a motivation for the bishops' action which Bernard had failed to perceive, though perhaps it could have been deduced from the motivations which he did recognise. Of course, in areas of mixed Protestant and Catholic population, Catholic ecclesiastics, as well as thoughtful laymen, always deplored a split in the Nationalist vote which might allow a Unionist to be elected despite a Catholic majority. Clerical desires for unity, however, extended beyond such special cases and were founded upon more general considerations. In Ireland, contested elections, though rare in many districts, were frequently accompanied with violence when they did occur. Rival mobs had been a common feature of the contests between Parnellites and Anti-Parnellites in the 1890s and of the 1910 contests precipitated by O'Brien. Now, in 1918, the prospect of widespread electoral contests conjured up visions of similar violent clashes in which at least one side would have more formidable weapons than blackthorn sticks. The bloodshed of which clergy were apprehensive might not be confined to injuries inflicted by or upon police or military forces. Moreover, avoidance of election contests between rival nationalist candidates was a desideratum from the standpoint of maintaining clerical influence. In the mid-nineteenth century, the priests could march to the polling place at the head of the electors of his parish and virtually cast their votes *en bloc*, but those days had passed. The influence of clergy upon political affairs was now best safeguarded when there was an agreed national policy and a single national party so that the important *local* decision would be made not at the polling place, but in the selection of a candidate, where the clergy could expect to exercise influence far out of proportion to their numbers. The bishops realised that clerical influence had suffered in the 1890s despite the fact that the 'clerical' party captured most of the seats in the 1892 general election. If there were two parties who both commanded widespread national support the clergy could not but lose favour with the partisans of one side or the other—or, by remaining neutral, of both.

The episcopal desire for a new synthesis of political forces was soon demonstrated, for another Nationalist seat, East Cavan, had fallen vacant. From the beginning, the clergy of the division, under the leadership of Father O'Connell of Cootehill, seem to have sympathised with Sinn Féin, which nominated Arthur Griffith. When the Irish Party held a convention at Bailieborough on 26 April and nominated a Mr O'Hanlon, no clergy were present. The Bishop, Dr Finegan of Kilmore, tried to intervene with a public letter stating that a contest would 'seriously endanger, if not break up, the present national unity'. He appealed to Dillon and de Valera, 'that for the sake of the union so necessary in the face of the coming crisis, they make some compromise by which this deplorable contest may be avoided'. Furthermore he urged the nationalists of the constituency, 'both Sinn Féin and Parliamentarian', to hold parish meetings either together or separately on Sunday, 5 May, 'and from them to send messages to their leaders that for the sake of national unity a contest must be avoided'. The clergy were requested to convene the meetings outside the churches after Mass, 'and to earnestly exhort their people of both sections, with a view to having this suggestion carried out'.[64] The clergy obediently held the meetings and read the Bishop's letter, though not in every case with the sort of judicial impartiality Finegan had in mind. At Killann, for example, Father McEntee, C.C., said that 'the Bishop had requested the priests to call for unity, but his Lordship did not give the priests definite lines upon which to go'. He then proceeded to analyse the Sinn Féin and Irish Parliamentary Party policies:

On the one side, he remarked, was Mr. Griffith who wanted to go to the Peace Conference, and on the other Mr. O'Hanlon, who represented the National Imperialist Party, who were going to the House of Commons for £400 a year, and who recognised the right of England to legislate for Ireland.[65]

Lack of enthusiasm for compromise among the priests was, however, of little importance, for on the same day de Valera, appearing on the same platform with Dillon at an anti-conscription meeting in Ballaghaderreen, Co. Roscommon, killed the suggestion. 'We have the right unity,' he said, 'the unity of co-operation. The unity of amalgamation would be no unity and that we cannot have.'[66] Speaking at Shercock, Griffith proposed that in place of the Bishop's plan for compromise, the two sides should agree to have the people cast their ballots after Mass on the following Sunday, whereupon the loser would withdraw. After performances like that of Father McEntee on the preceding Sunday, it is small wonder that the Irish Party were not anxious to have the election decided at the chapel gates. Griffith and de Valera no doubt perceived that Finegan's initiative had placed them in a commanding position, for once he had proposed a compromise with Sinn Féin, he could scarcely turn around and denounce them with the sort of theological arguments which had been made several months earlier. The priests joined enthusiastically in the campaign, which lasted nearly two months, and an Irish Party spokesman was reduced to attacking the clergy directly[67]—always a sign that hope of clerical support has been abandoned. On 20 June Griffith, who by that time had been jailed in connection with the 'German plot', was elected by 3,795 votes to 2,581.[68]

The effects of Finegan's action were being repeated nationwide as a result of the bishops' sanction of the anti-conscription movement on an inclusive basis. When the hierarchy granted de Valera an audience at Maynooth and urged co-operation between all parties, they gave to Sinn Féin the moral sanction of a legitimate political party and removed it from the realm of theological and moral suspicion in which it had operated for the preceding year. But for its own internal differences, the hierarchy probably possessed the power, up until this point, if not to crush Sinn Féin, to forestall the overwhelming mandate which it received eight months later. The political power of the Irish Church in this period, however, could only be exercised in such a sweeping, nationwide fashion when the fundamental issue could be depicted as a religious, moral or theological one within the framework in which those terms were understood in Ireland. A generation earlier, Parnell's moral indiscretion had provided such an issue. During the period before the conscription crisis the flirtations of Sinn Féin with armed rebellion and secret societies had offered another such issue upon which the Church might have chosen to mobilise her political power. In April 1918 she deliberately forfeited that option.

From the East Cavan election in June until the closing days of the war, there was a disarming lull in Irish affairs. Most of the articulate spokesmen for Sinn Féin were in jail, conscription and Home Rule had been shelved by the government, and there were no more by-elections. A number of districts were proclaimed under the Crimes Act and the Defence of the Realm Act. Meetings of certain organisations, including Sinn Féin, Irish Volunteers and the Gaelic League, were declared illegal, and there were a number of scuffles between police and young nationalists. Nevertheless, no attempt was made to interfere with the Sinn Féin Ard-Fheis in October, at which Father O'Flanagan was re-elected a Vice-President and four more priests were added to the two other clerics already serving on the executive.[69] Father O'Flanagan himself, who had not refrained from occasional attacks on bishops, was suspended by his own bishop, Dr Coyne of Elphin, during the summer. Some of his parishioners in Crossna, Co. Roscommon, retaliated by bolting the church door against the priest appointed to succeed him, and the *Roscommon Herald*, a paper with Sinn Féin sympathies, noted that 'A rumour is afloat that the Sinn Féiners will try to close the other Roman Catholic churches in Roscommon and throughout Ireland until the Roman Catholic Hierarchy retreat from the course they have taken.'[70] In fact, no such revolt materialised, and the Bishop quickly put down the local resistance to his authority.[71] At the Sinn Féin Ard-Fheis a proposed resolution protesting against Father O'Flanagan's suspension was passed over at his own, very wise, request.[72] The fact that a bishop was now able to discipline severely such a popular figure as Father O'Flanagan without provoking serious popular reaction is evidence of the strengthening of the hierarchy's position which had resulted from their action on conscription.

Despite the disciplining of an occasional zealot such as O'Flanagan, the episcopal endorsement of the anticonscription movement had generally worked in favour of greater co-operation between clergy and Sinn Féin. Probably the increased co-operation was most marked in the West. In the East Riding of Co. Galway, for example, the police reported: 'The moment the anti-conscription movement amalgamated the clergy and Sinn Fein, the former appear to have thrown off all restraint and indulged in the most extreme Sinn Fein propaganda, utilising their position as priests to push their political opinions.'[73] In the West, Bishop Fogarty and Bishop Hallinan had already announced their support of Sinn Féin in very explicit terms—stressing, of course, the constitutional side of the Sinn Féin policy—and Sinn Féiners also claimed Dr O'Sullivan, the new Bishop of Kerry, as an advocate of their policy of abstention from parliament.[74] As the war drew to a close, however, and the long-delayed general election loomed ahead, many of the other bishops still hoped for a new synthesis of Sinn Féin and parliamentary forces. On 23 October Bishop Cohalan of Cork, who sixteen months earlier had scoffed at the idea of an Irish appeal to the Peace Conference, proposed that another gathering similar to the Mansion House Conference be assembled to prepare Ireland's case for self-government and to present it before the Peace Conference.[75]

Although the threat of conscription was rapidly fading away, both of the principal parties had been keeping the Mansion House Conference alive in hopes of turning it to their own purposes. In August Dillon had apparently contemplated a unity movement based on the Conference.[76] During the first week of November, Eóin Mac Néill made a public overture for unity on the basis of Ireland's claim to self-determination, and an effort was made by the Sinn Féin side to get the Mansion House Conference to assume the responsibilities which Cohalan had suggested and to request 'from the Irish people their full confidence and support upon the grave and far-reaching decision'. The possibilities for unity upon such a basis were not entirely illusory, for Dillon had come to adopt much of the Sinn Féin programme except for abstention from parliament and many of the Sinn Féin extremists likely to resist a union were in prison.[77]

On 10 November, at an early nominating convention in Longford, a letter was read from Bishop Hoare of Ardagh and Clonmacnoise, who began by endorsing the Irish Party as 'just now, the only rational and true Representative'.[78] 'But what about our claim before the coming International Peace Congress?' he asked. 'Who will present it?' They would be told, he argued, that self-determination implies agreement among the people themselves, and he asked:

Is there any Strong Man in Ireland to-day capable of uniting—I will not say Orange and Green; that I look upon as impossible, at least in our generation—but Irishmen that were of old united under O'Connell and Parnell? If there is, he would be the saviour of our country. . . . We should then, as a civilised, and patriotic nation, be capable of a successful appeal. If there is not such an union, what hope of success could we entertain?[79]

The only obstacle to a union, in the Bishop's view was 'the Revolutionary policy of our young men', which, 'in our present circumstances is both sinful, and foolish (*hear, hear*)'. 'All our other differences', he maintained, 'are open to debate. They could be easily settled by a score of capable and patriotic representatives.' Hoare invited the Longford convention to respond to his suggestion, and apparently a perfunctory resolution endorsing his idea was adopted, but the nominee, J. P. Farrell, made it clear that he 'would be no party to the unity which Sinn Fein seemed to want—unity by cutting off the heads of all their political opponents'.[80]

Nevertheless, Hoare's proposal was kept alive, for two days later Bishop Foley of Kildare and Leighlin, sent a similar letter to a meeting of the Co. Carlow executive of the U.I.L. which had been called to map a course of action in view of the retirement of the sitting member for Carlow.[81] Foley said he did not know if the meeting had been convened 'to prepare the way for another which shall be representative of the whole county' or was simply a gathering of 'those who believe in the principle of electing members of Parliament and requiring them to give a constant attendance therein'. If it was of the former kind, it had his 'heartiest approval', but if it had the latter character, he warned that unless some plan were devised to unite the 'warring factions' of nationalists he could see 'no hope whatever, so far as the time of the next Parliament is concerned'. He deplored in the strongest terms the contest which had occurred in East Cavan 'at a time when we were all supposed to be standing shoulder to shoulder in that great, and, as is now clear, successful fight against conscription'. Echoing Bishop Hoare, he hoped for the appearance of 'some man of acknowledged character and political sagacity . . . who would bring home to the Irish people the truth of the words used by that hard-headed commonsense Scotchman, the late Campbell-Bannerman, "Let us drop our fooling and on to business"'. In particular, he hoped for 'a conference of about a dozen men representative of the various elements that go to make up the Irish people which might devise a plan upon which 'all sound nationalists of every brand may agree to unite and to demand with one voice that effect be immediately given to our right to rule ourselves in the way we deem best and to take our place among the newly emancipated nations of Europe'. The meeting obligingly passed a resolution 'on the lines of that adopted at Longford on the basis of Most Rev. Dr. Hoare's suggestions', which were practically identical with Bishop Foley's ideas, and there was an indication of more zeal than had been shown in Longford to give actual effect to the resolution. M. Governey, Chairman of the Carlow Urban Council, who presided at the meeting, expressed optimism that some basis for unity would be found.[82]

Hopes of a united nationalist front, however, were rapidly fading, as both sides went ahead with separate plans for the election. Bishop Morrisroe of Achonry, in a sermon on the following Sunday, made a half-hearted plea for unity, but seemed resigned to widespread contests when he said:

Only when the people were united would the priests give a lead, and not when the people were wrangling and rending one another in the most abominable way. When the people were divided he hoped the priests would stand clear, but if they were united and asked him what policy was practicable and attainable the priests would help.[83]

If there were to be differences, he counselled charity and justice, stating that 'every man had a right to his opinion, and he should not be thought less of if he did his best in his own way and with moderation'. This *laissez-faire* attitude was, of course, of much greater benefit to Sinn Féin than to the Irish Parliamentary Party, for it recognised the new movement's title to be treated as a legitimate option, untainted by moral stigma. Moreover, Morrisroe, whose see was located in Dillon's own constituency of East Mayo, was not naïve about the probable consequences of widespread contests. A month earlier Morrisroe had told one of Healy's friends that Dillon had no chance of retaining his own seat, and, Healy recounted, 'My informant noted no chroniclers' sighs on the announcement.'[84]

As late as 20 November, a unity arrangement was mooted by Bishop O'Donnell. In a public letter read at the East Donegal Irish Party convention, the Bishop of Raphoe made plain his continued support for active attendance at Westminster by Nationalist M.P.s and lucidly explicated the futility of expecting the Peace Conference to provide a settlement and the inevitability of partition if Nationalists refused to sit in parliament. He himself would do anything in his power 'to help to compose the differences of Irish Nationalists in every part of the country. It is not yet too late', he maintained, 'for representatives on both sides to try what they can do.' He seemed, however, to have abandoned hope of unity outside the districts of Ulster in which a large Protestant minority might profit from a nationalist split.[85] A clerical movement to realise the more limited goal of unity in the 'safe' nationalist seats in Ulster which would be endangered by a split in the Catholic vote was already afoot under the leadership of Bishop McHugh.

For the Bishop of Derry, whose city was divided almost equally between Catholics and Protestants, nationalist politics was essentially a fight against Protestant bigotry in local affairs. He considered every issue in the light of whether it would strengthen or weaken the political power of Protestants in his own community and the rest of the province.

Thus, the exclusion proposals of March 1914, under which four counties would have remained under the direct jurisdiction of Westminster, were tolerable to McHugh, but the partition proposals of June 1916, under which six counties would have been granted certain elements of a local executive, inevitably dominated by Protestants, were absolutely intolerable. Whatever sympathy McHugh might have had for Sinn Féin in 1918 was founded not on its ideology, but upon despair over the Irish Party, which, in his view, had sold out his flock by acquiescing in the 1916 partition proposals. His attitude was illustrated in his reply in the middle of September 1918 to a Sinn Féiner who had suggested that Eóin Mac Néill be adopted forthwith as the nationalist candidate for Derry City in the forthcoming election—a proposal which was, to say the least, premature. McHugh wrote that he had no objection to Mac Néill, and, indeed, would 'hail his selection with delight', if he were assured that he had the support of the local nationalists. There were some nationalists in the city, however, the Bishop pointed out, who viewed matters differently from his correspondent, and it would require 'the combined effort of all to secure the seat against Orange ascendancy. You cannot force political principle & policy down the throat of those who differ from you,' McHugh observed pragmatically,

but you may win them over by showing the wreck of Catholic rights & interests that would follow from division in our ranks. Up to this in spite of the divided political opinions held by Catholics in Derry they always showed that they could combine as Catholics in opposition to their hereditary foes when election time came round. . . . It would seem to many a very high handed action to select a candidate without even consulting those who were mainly responsible for maintaining the fight for Catholic rights in the revision Courts during the past dozen years.[86]

To avert the danger of antagonising these Catholics, dividing nationalist forces, and handing the seat over to the Unionists, the Bishop recommended either the summoning of a public meeting, which, 'in all probability' would select Mac Néill, or the holding of 'a plebiscite of the national voters'. 'In Derry', he stressed, 'we cannot forget that we are Catholics.

To be a party to any action that would lose the seat would be very uncatholic.'

The extension of the franchise and redistribution of seats which had just taken place made exact calculation impossible, but as early as 10 October two Ulster bishops confided to Healy their fears that eight Catholic seats would be lost, unless, in Healy's colourful phrase, 'a composition was come to between Shins & Hibs'.[87] On 16 November, as hopes of a nationwide compromise between 'Shins and Hibs' were evaporating, McHugh wrote to the press suggesting that, if such a compromise could not be reached, 'Surely we in the North are not going to allow seven or eight safe Nationalist seats to pass into the hands of Sir Edward Carson and his followers through dissension in our ranks.' He proposed a conference at Dungannon, under the chairmanship of Bishop McKenna of Clogher, to be composed of two priests, and two representatives each from the Irish Party and Sinn Féin from each of the constituencies in question.[88] Several days later Dean Byrne of Dungannon wrote to the press outlining detailed plans for the conference, setting 27 November as the date, and, at McHugh's request, adding two labour spokesmen to the representation of each constituency.[89] Meanwhile, the Sinn Féin executive had met and issued a statment refusing to enter such a conference unless Dillon would accept the principle of abstention from parliament and the demand for sovereign independence. Recognising that he would not concede these points, they went on to outline a plan for deciding, by plebiscite of the nationalist voters, which party would oppose the Unionists in each of the constituencies in question—a plan which, in fact, Fermanagh Sinn Féin clergy were already actively promoting in that county.[90] The Bishop of Derry's plans were flexible, and his imagination was fertile in devising schemes to meet difficulties raised by Sinn Féin's statement. He immediately prepared a complicated and obviously unworkable plan to render the Sinn Féin proposal workable.[91] Before the Bishop's effort to deal with the problems raised on the Sinn Féin side got into print, however, more serious difficulties were raised by the other side. In a speech in Dublin on 21 November Dillon declared that Sinn Féin was obviously not interested in co-operation with the

Irish Parliamentary Party except by absorbing the party as it had apparently already absorbed the O'Brienites and the Irish Labour Party. 'When he was invited, as he had been from many quarters—some of them quarters that had pursued the Irish Party for 30 years with unsleeping hostility and hatred—to go into conference with their opponents, he noticed the peculiarity of the proposal that he should walk into a Conference outnumbered by three to one.' From this statement one may infer that Dillon now counted the Ulster clergy, as well as the Irish labour movement, among his 'opponents'. He would not enter a conference unless it fulfilled two conditions:

First, it must be fairly constituted, so that the representatives of the Irish Party should not be outnumbered, and that there must be an absolutely impartial chairman—not a partisan of Sinn Fein. *The next condition was that it should be called for the genuine purpose of preventing contests throughout, and not in one part of Ireland, and that no tests such as those in the Sinn Fein statement should be laid down.*[92]

Those tests—parliamentary abstention and 'absolute independence', which he interpreted to mean an Irish Republic—were totally unacceptable to Dillon, who thought it was now idle to persist in proposals for conferences. As to the proposal 'for a plebiscite at the chapel doors under the presidency of the local clergy and with, he had no doubt, an adequate bodyguard of Volunteers', he was 'too old a politician to be caught by those kind of traps'. He was determined to 'fight this thing out to the bitter end'.

Bishop McHugh was indignant at 'Dillon's wrecking speech'.[93] The Dungannon conference was dropped, and the Ulster bishops met on 26 November and called upon the Lord Mayor of Dublin to meet Dillon and de Valera (or, in his absence, Mac Néill) and divide the seats in question between them. Still giving lip-service to the ideal of nationwide unity, they added the remark, 'We earnestly trust that a like provision may be much more widely applied, especially where the need is similar.'[94] The plan, which seemed to promise an equal division of the seats, was eagerly accepted by Dillon. The Sinn Féiners were less eager, but they finally agreed as well, and on 3 and 4 December Dillon, Mac Néill and the

Lord Mayor met. They agreed that eight seats—South Fermanagh, South Down, Derry City, North West Tyrone, North East Tyrone, East Donegal, South Armagh and East Down—should be divided evenly between the two parties, but they referred to Logue the decision as to which seats would be allotted to the respective parties. The Cardinal promptly decided to assign South Down, North-East Tyrone, East Donegal and South Armagh to the Irish Party and the other four divisions to Sinn Féin.[95] (In North Fermanagh, it should be noted, a plebiscite had been agreed upon locally, and in the event went in favour of Sinn Féin.) The Cardinal's decision came too late to prevent filing of nominations in the eight seats. Except for East Down, however, where Irish Party supporters refused to accept the decision and thereby allowed a Unionist to win, the candidate against whom Logue had decided in each division received only a scattering of diehard votes.[96] 'No one, I think could suspect me of favouring the Sinn Féin policy,' Logue had written, with notable understatement, during the controversy. 'I have never concealed my views of its futility.'[97] Yet *The Leader* could observe:

When the Roman Catholic Church blessed the union of Mr. Dillon and Mr. de Valera to resist conscription it took a serious step, but it pronounced no judgment on the political merits of either Nationalist party. Now it has made a further and very significant advance. . . . The fate of these eight seats is less important than this disclosure of the mind of the Roman Catholic Hierarchy of Ireland. A cardinal and seven bishops not merely accept the fait accompli of a republican party; they accept its title to make political bargains with the 'constitutional' party.[98]

No one could any longer claim that the Cardinal regarded the new movement as unambiguously evil.

Once the hopes of nationwide unity were dead, a few bishops did express preference for the Irish Party's policy of attending parliament. Bishop Hoare, who had tried to initiate the unity movement, forwarded a subscription to the Longford U.I.L. election fund with the comment, 'Now that we are obliged to engage in another fraternal strife—Oh! how I loathe the thought of it—I appeal to the consciences of all, friend and foe, to abstain from violence in act and word.'[99]

Archbishop Gilmartin of Tuam in a letter to the North Galway U.I.L. convention, wrote that when the Catholic people were divided on 'questions of pure politics' the pastor should not take an active part on either side. There were 'good Irishmen and good Catholics' on each side. Speaking for himself, he preferred 'non-abstention from Parliament' because it seemed the safer policy.[100] Among the entire hierarchy, no stronger criticism of Sinn Féin than this was publicly uttered during the campaign. Bishops might speak of Sinn Féin's policy as unwise or impracticable, but no longer did they hint that it was tainted with immorality. Moreover, when the three other bishops of the province of Dublin— Codd of Ferns, Foley of Kildare and Leighlin and Brownrigg of Ossory—each expressed a lack of faith in the policy of abstention,[101] Archbishop Walsh wrote to the press that he felt 'that it might easily lead to a grave misconception if, in the circumstances, I were to continue to keep silence, and if, in fact, I were to abstain from stating in the same public manner, that my views on the matters thus publicly dealt with, in reference to the momentous issues before the country are altogether different from those expressed in the letters of those three venerated prelates'.[102]

Walsh was being a bit unfair to Foley, for the Bishop of Kildare and Leighlin was actually trying to nudge the Carlow Irish Party organisation toward withdrawing from the contest. A few days later he succeeded, the party's local election committee deciding, on the motion of Foley's administrator, 'in view of the lack of Nationalist organisation in the county to act upon the advice of the Most Rev. Dr. Foley and avoid the turmoil of a contested election until time and the pressure of events shall have made a fair trial of the issues feasible'.[103] Carlow was only one of twenty-five safe nationalist seats in which the party offered no opposition to Sinn Féin. Indeed, in the closing days of the campaign Bishop O'Donnell urged Dillon to arrange for all Irish Parliamentary Party candidates, except perhaps Dillon himself, to retire from the contest and allow Sinn Féin a clear field throughout the country. The Bishop tried to soften the blow of what he was saying to his old political friend by suggesting that the party could 'disappear to reappear', but Dillon, in a moving letter, rejected O'Donnell's advice.[104] In the four south-western counties of Clare, Limerick, Cork and Kerry, only three seats were contested. The Sinn Féin sympathies of the Bishops of Killaloe, Limerick and Kerry were well known, and Healy was apparently referring to Bishop Cohalan of Cork when he told O'Brien that his brother Maurice had written 'that Crosby [George Crosbie, publisher of the *Cork Examiner?*] is holding out against the Bp, who favours giving the Shins no opposition'.[105] (The Bishop's brother, Canon Cohalan, campaigned actively for Sinn Féin.)[106] Bishop Kelly and Bishop Browne of Cloyne seem to have avoided interfering, though Browne did receive the (unopposed) Sinn Féin candidate for East Cork when he visited Queenstown.[107] Had the Irish Party offered candidates in most of the south-western constituencies, it seems unquestionable that they would have been vigorously opposed by most of the clergy.

Only in a few eastern constituencies, such as East Wicklow, and in the Donegal constituencies lying in O'Donnell's diocese, did the Irish Party candidates receive concerted clerical support.[108] In many other areas a few clergy clung to their old allegiance to the party. In general, however, the party met substantial opposition from clergy, who the embittered Dillon believed were 'most dishonestly using S.F. to carry out a purpose they have long nursed—the destruction of our independent lay party and the recovery of their own [? direct] power over Irish politics, which the Parnellite movement had to a very large extent destroyed'.[109] In the diocese of Clonfert, whose bishopric was vacant, the administrator of the bishop's parish became an active campaigner for Sinn Féin.[110] Laurence Ginnell, who stood as a Sinn Féiner in Westmeath, received very substantial clerical support, perhaps a reflection of long-standing clerical distrust of the Irish Party in the diocese of Meath.[111] In the neighbouring constituency of South Roscommon, clerical grievances dating back to the 1890s against the Irish Party candidate, J. P. Hayden, owner of the allegedly anticlerical *Westmeath Examiner*, were resurrected for the occasion.[112] In the archdiocese of Tuam, Dr Gilmartin seems to have succeeded fairly well in restraining his clergy from active campaigning. Bishop Morrisroe of Achonry, however, had less success in enforcing his expressed desire for clerical neutrality in contested elections. De Valera was nominated against Dillon in East Mayo, and the issue was clearly drawn between the old leadership and the new. When a number of the senior Achonry clergy entered the campaign on the Irish Party side, many young priests enthusiastically championed de Valera.[113]

For the first time, polling took place on the same day (14 December) in every constituency in the three countries. In Dublin Walsh let it be known that he voted for the first time since he became Archbishop, and that his ballot was cast for Sinn Féin.[114] After a delay of two weeks, to allow for receipt of absentee ballots from the armed forces the results were announced. Apart from the four seats allotted to them by Logue, the Irish Parliamentary Party retained only two seats. One of these victories, in Waterford City, was a tribute to Redmond's memory. The other, in the Falls division of Belfast (a new division created by the Redistribution Act and inhabited almost entirely by Catholics), where Devlin defeated de Valera by a large margin, was a striking indication of the hold which Devlin still possessed over the Belfast Catholics. Both these contests were special cases. Sinn Féin won 73 seats and the Unionists 26. The mood of Ireland, outside the North-east, was symbolised by the results in East Mayo:

| E. de Valera (S.F.) | 8,975 |
| J. Dillon (Nat.) | 4,514. |

CHAPTER XIX

The Nation under New Management

THE general election had clearly produced a new departure in Irish history. During the next two and a half years the Church would have to deal with a revolutionary situation which was in many ways unprecedented. Still, there was a good deal of past experience to go on. At least since the 1880s the Church had clearly recognised the claims of the Nation to future legitimacy. On the basis of this recognition, Church and Nation had worked out conventions by which their relations were governed. The essential difference in 1919 was that the Nation's representatives proceeded to claim sovereignty, not for the indefinite future, but now. On 21 January twenty-seven Sinn Féin M.P.s who were not imprisoned, abroad, or otherwise prevented from attending answered an invitation which had been sent to all newly elected Irish M.P.s—even Carson—to the first Dáil Éireann (Assembly of Ireland). The Dáil promptly adopted a declaration of independence ratifying the proclamation of the Irish Republic at Easter 1916 and claiming the allegiance of the Irish people as the only parliament competent to legislate for Ireland. It was a curious revolution, for, far from throwing up barricades to fight the *ancien régime*, the Dáil actually enjoyed the protection of the metropolitan police against any possible disruption of its deliberations. The Dáil seemed close to meeting the Church's first condition for national leadership. Though they did not explicitly renounce physical force, the deputies passed up the opportunity to declare war upon England, contenting themselves with the assertion:

We solemnly declare foreign government in Ireland to be an invasion of our national right which we will never tolerate, and we demand the evacuation of our country by the English Garrison.[1]

If the Dáil avoided the rhetoric of physical-force national-ism, what of the Church's other condition, that national leaders respect the Church's vital interests, especially in edu-cation? At its first session, the Dáil adopted a statement of social policy, the 'Democratic Programme', which had been drafted by Thomas Johnson, a labour leader, and revised by Seán T. O'Kelly, one of the Sinn Féin leaders whose con-tacts with important churchmen were particularly close.[2] One of O'Kelly's revisions was the deletion of a sentence in the section on education: 'A condition precedent to such educa-tion is to encourage by every reasonable means, the most capable and sympathetic men and women to devote their talents to the education of the young.'[3] Probably even the bitterest clerical detractors of the organised teaching pro-fession would have objected to these words, but the Nation's new leaders were taking no chances.

There was a very concrete way in which the Church might have sanctioned the Dáil's claim to present legitimacy. Some £250,000 collected for the anticonscription campaign was still held by trustees in each parish, in most cases the parish clergy. The Dáil coveted this money as a national treasury. Three choices were open to the Church: (1) to hand the money over to the Dáil, (2) to apply it, as many clergy longed to do, to religious purposes, or (3) to return it to the sub-scribers. After some uncertainty, a pattern emerged by which the funds (less ten per cent for the expenses of the Mansion House Committee) were offered back to the subscribers but applied to ecclesiastical charities if unclaimed. Sinn Féin collectors were present in some cases when the refunds were made and managed to garner about £17,000[4] for the Dáil's purposes. Although Bishop Fogarty set the example of send-ing his refunded contribution to the Dáil,[5] in general the Church passed up this chance to endorse the present sover-eignty of the Nation.

It does not follow that the Church was failing to live up to her end of the tacit understanding with the Nation. Avoid-ance of physical force and respect for the Church's rights in education entitled the Nation to the Church's sanction not for its present legitimacy, but for its future legitimacy. These had been the rules in the past, and the Church was still playing by them. One of the Dáil's first acts had been to appoint delegates to the Peace Conference, two of whom, de Valera and Griffith, were still in prison. The logical way for the Church to fulfil her obligation to the Nation was to promote the effort to place Ireland's claims before the Versailles Conference. Early in February Michael Collins and his colleagues masterminded de Valera's escape from Lincoln Jail, and one of the hideaways used by the Sinn Féin leader during the next few weeks was the gate-lodge of Archbishop Walsh's residence in Drumcondra—a place where the Crown forces would hardly dare arrest him even if they had known he was there. This remarkable appropriation of the Church's resources for the Nation's purposes was arranged by Father Curran without the Archbishop's knowledge.[6] Walsh was a good enough lawyer never to know anything he did not need to know. De Valera spent most of his time in the gate-lodge revising a draft statement of Ireland's case for the Peace Conference, the historical section of which had been written by Father Curran and two Jesuits.

Late in March, an influenza outbreak which had killed one Irish internee prompted the new Chief Secretary, Ian Mac-Pherson to order a general release of political prisoners. This allowed de Valera to come out of hiding and the Dáil to hold a better-attended meeting than had been possible in January. De Valera was elected Priomh-Aire or President of the Dáil, and he formed a ministry which included, among others, Griffith (Home Affairs), Count Plunkett (Foreign Affairs), and Mac Néill (Industries) from the moderate section of Sinn Féin, and Cathal Brugha (Defence) and Michael Collins (Finance) from the more militant section. At a further session in May the Dáil welcomed a delegation of Irish-American politicians commissioned by the Irish Race Convention in Philadelphia to get a hearing for the Dáil delegates at the Paris Peace Conference.[7] In a week's tour of the country, these American 'Commissioners' had well-publicised interviews with Cardinal Logue, Archbishop Harty, and Bishops MacRory, Cohalan, Hallinan and Fogarty, the last of whom escorted them for part of their visit.[8] Ironically, this tour, in which the Commissioners indulged in some of the John Bull-baiting they had learned in American politics, produced

British protests to the American government which gave Wilson just the excuse he needed to shelve the issue of a particularly troublesome small nationality.[9] Hopes for the appeal to Paris faded rapidly, but it is unlikely that many bishops were ever sanguine of its success. Bishop Finegan of Kilmore was probably expressing a prevalent pessimism when he sent a £5 subscription to the fund for putting Irish claims before the Conference with the discouraged comment, 'It may be that something will come from the effort.'[10] The purpose of churchmen associating themselves with the appeal to the Peace Conference was to reaffirm in terms the new national leadership would understand that the Nation still enjoyed ecclesiastical sanction of its future legitimacy.

As the appeal to Paris had clearly failed, it was now necessary for the Church to find other ways of expressing her position. The next court of appeal was public opinion in the United States, where a bitter debate over the terms of the Versailles Treaty was beginning. To the dismay of his colleagues in the Dáil ministry, de Valera decided to go to America for the double purpose of drumming up support in that country for recognition of the Republic and soliciting contributions to the Dáil Éireann National Loan. The Dáil President was keeping his eye firmly fixed on the need for non-physical-force methods of achieving the Nation's goal. The National Loan was authorised to issue bonds payable from six months 'after the Irish Republic has received International Recognition, and the English have evacuated Ireland'.[11] Bishop Fogarty became one of the three trustees of the National Loan,[12] and while his episcopal colleagues did not yet go this far, they did take up the related appeal to American public opinion at their general meeting in June.

'At this fateful stage in the history of the human family,' they unanimously declared, 'Congress in the United States of America, where our people always received a warm welcome, and soon learned to appreciate the advantages of the liberty denied to them at home, finds an unredressed wrong in Ireland that calls to it to speak out in the hearing of the world.'[13] There followed a brief recital of grievances which, by echoing the tone of the American Declaration of Independence, might have stirred the blood of a patriotic congressman. He probably would, however, have been more puzzled than enraged by the bishops' further complaint of rumoured reform plans for education. They went on to claim that Ireland was 'a distinct and ancient Nation' and to assert that

It is vain to hope that things will go well for Ireland or for England until Ireland's rights are duly recognised. She is fully entitled to a government that will be the free choice of all her people. Her right is to be the mistress of her own destiny. With the deepest affection for all her inhabitants of every persuasion, and in pursuance of the duties of our high trust in the interests of peace and religion, we desire to state with all the earnestness we can command that now is the time for doing justice to Ireland as a Nation.[14]

In conclusion, the hierarchy expressed gratitude to 'the Senate, the House of Representatives, the Hierarchy, clergy, and people of every denomination in America' for 'so nobly espousing the cause of Ireland at this turning point in her history'.

This particular moment was indeed a turning point—perhaps more so than the bishops yet realised. Up until this time, there had been relatively little violence: a few policemen had been shot in isolated incidents which were normally followed by public denunciation of the attacks by the bishop and some of the clergy where each incident occurred. In their June statement the bishops blamed the 'rule of the sword' for provoking these acts of violence which they truthfully insisted were few. The Irish Volunteer organisation had remained in existence, recovering from the effects of the post-Rising arrests and drawing new strength from the fear of conscription in 1918. For most of 1919 its relationship to the Dáil remained hazily defined, though the fact that three members of the ministry—de Valera, Brugha and Collins— held important Volunteer posts did create a kind of interlocking directorate. Even after the Dáil decided in August to require all Volunteers to take an oath of allegiance to 'the Government of the Irish Republic, which is Dáil Éireann', the situation remained complicated by rivalries between Brugha, the Volunteer Chief of Staff, and Collins, whose nominal subordination to Brugha in the Volunteer organisation was counterbalanced by his leading position in the I.R.B.

(of which Brugha was not a member), his equality with Brugha in the ministry and his superior organising genius.

Formal chains of command notwithstanding, small groups of Volunteers were very difficult to control. Although de Valera's trip to America put the emphasis upon those aspects of the Republican programme—international recognition, diplomatic pressure and fund-raising—which did not necesarily involve violence, it deprived Ireland of the one man whose prestige among the Volunteers (now coming to be called the Irish Republican Army) was great enough that he might have checked the growth of violence. During the summer, acts of violence became more frequent, and in August attacks upon police barracks for the purpose of seizing arms began. The British authorities decided to proclaim Dáil Éireann an illegal organisation during the following month, and for nearly two years the Dáil was only able to meet surreptitiously and infrequently (no meeting at all being held between October 1919 and June 1920). Moreover, early in September, some two hundred British troops stationed at Fermoy, Co. Cork, enraged that a coroner's jury refused to return a verdict of wilful murder in the case of one of their comrades shot from ambush on his way to a service in the local Wesleyan Church, descended upon the town and wrecked the shops of jury members.[15] It was the first of a grim succession of 'unauthorised reprisals'. In the atmosphere of escalating violence it was becoming harder and harder to maintain the optimism Bishop Hallinan of Limerick, a Sinn Féin supporter, had voiced a few months earlier:

If we rely on the justice of our cause, and the guiding hand of the loving Providence of God, if we are patient, calm and confident, avoid those devious, dangerous, sinful ways into which inexperienced and enthusiastic youths are sometimes led in moments of exasperation and excitement, we may look forward with bright hope to the attainment of our long-cherished aspiration [—] the independence of our native land.[16]

The government proclamation of Dáil Éireann as an illegal organisation was quickly followed by the suppression of a number of nationalist journals which had carried advertisements for the National Loan. The Castle authorities had finally decided to make no distinction between the quasi-constitutional and the physical-force sides of the national movement, and thus made it increasingly difficult for the Church to sustain the distinction by which she sanctioned the future sovereignty of the Nation and, with waning enthusiasm, the present sovereignty of the State. The Church was clearly in a dilemma. Shortly before it was suppressed, one pro-Sinn Féin journal, *New Ireland*, compared the political situation to a chess game: 'We can't move our Bishops at all. And worse, they use our Bishops against us. That may lose us the game for a time. And if it does, who can respect pieces that will not move even diagonally.'[17]

In the wake of the Dáil's suppression, there seems to have been an awkward political silence in episcopal ranks which was broken after two months by a letter from Archbishop Walsh to Cardinal O'Connell of Boston. The Archbishop of Dublin asked the Cardinal 'to make known in America' the fact that he was contributing 100 guineas 'to the Irish National Fund inaugurated under the auspices of the elected body known as Dáil Éireann, our Irish Parliament'.[18] He was obliged to resort to this roundabout procedure, he explained, because

We are living under martial law, and amongst the numerous devices to which our present Government has had recourse in its foolish attempts to crush the national spirit of our people is the issuing of sundry military orders. In one of these, they have given notice to the editors or managers of our popular newspapers to the effect that the fate of any newspaper venturing to publish the names of contributors to the Fund, or the amounts contributed, will be immediate suppression.[19]

After enumerating the various civil liberties which were currently abrogated, Walsh lamented: 'All this has had its natural effect—the driving of disaffection underground—with the no less natural result that disaffection, driven underground, naturally finds an outlet in crime.' Although Walsh's dramatic gesture brought his own position into line with Bishop Fogarty, the most advanced member of the hierarchy, the letter proves on analysis to be a careful application of the Church's longstanding position which only Walsh and Fogarty among the hierarchy were at the moment willing to follow to its logical conclusion. The phrase 'Dáil Éireann, our Irish Parliament' is neatly balanced by a reference to the British authorities as 'our present Government', (not, as the Dáil leaders would have it, the 'occupying forces'). As Walsh had anticipated, the text of his letter was suppressed in the Irish press, but the *Morning Post* of London printed it on 9 December together with an interview with 'a high official who possesses his [Walsh's] complete confidence'—obviously Father Curran. The Archbishop's secretary was careful to avoid imputing his own views to Walsh, but he did seem to be condoning raids for arms and at one point stopped himself from saying 'murders' and referred instead to the 'shooters of these soldiers and police'.[20] A few days later, T. M. Healy heard that Father Curran had 'lost his post over recent interview',[21] though the latter's subsequent appointment as Vice-Rector of the Irish College, Rome,[22] seems as much reward as punishment. In any event, when an unsuccessful attempt was made on the life of Lord French, the Lord Lieutenant, on 19 December near Dublin, Walsh telegraphed congratulations on his escape[23] and sent the Dublin clergy a letter reiterating the moral law against 'the crime of murder, or attempted murder'.

Is there any rational man [he asked] capable of deluding himself into the belief that such a method of seeking redress for the misgovernment of this country is likely to help the efforts of the righteous men who are working earnestly for the purpose of re-establishing in our own country the reign of liberty and justice?[24]

Of course, any political action by the Archbishop of Dublin would have greater symbolic significance than the identical action by, say, Bishop Fogarty. Walsh was, however, unable because of advancing age to lead the hierarchy in the direction indicated by his subscription to the National Loan. Though he still made occasional public appearances,[25] he seems to have stopped attending meetings of the hierarchy,[26] and the *Morning Post* of London was able to insinuate, though probably falsely, that the letter to Cardinal O'Connell was the work of the 'high official', i.e., Father Curran. Moreover, Walsh's ablest colleagues in the hierarchy were either —like O'Donnell and Kelly—incapacitated from effective leadership by their previous association with the Irish Par-

liamentary Party, or—like McHugh and MacRory—too pre-
occupied with the problems of the Northern Catholics which
were becoming more and more a special case. Leadership
thus devolved mainly upon Logue, who was, as usual, inde-
cisive. A correspondent of the *Morning Post* tried to draw
him out in an interview in the middle of December:

We spoke of Archbishop Walsh's letter to America. Had he
anything to say about that, I asked. 'Nothing whatever,' was the
reply. 'It is the first time you have openly associated yourselves
with Sinn Fein,' I said. The Cardinal looked up quickly as if
he were about to give me full change for the declaration. Then
his lips closed tightly like those of a lady when she has said,
'I won't,' for the third and last time.[27]

The problem of a leadership vacuum was compounded by
two government moves at this time. Lloyd George had again
decided to attempt a legislative settlement of the Irish question. The 1914 Home Rule Act lay, a dead letter, on the
statute book. The majority of the coalition cabinet favoured
some grant of self-government to two separate geographic
entities, North and South. The prospect of a separate, Orange-
dominated government in the North, rather than simple exclusion of the northern counties from the Irish parliament's
jurisdiction, had been haunting the Northern bishops ever
since Lloyd George's attempted settlement in 1916 when a
candid Ulsterman had told him, contrary to the public professions of most Northern Protestant spokesmen: 'My belief
is that the rank and file in Ulster would like to have a little
legislature of their own.'[28] According to T. M. Healy, Lloyd
George now let it be known that he was considering dis-
regarding the cabinet's wishes to press instead a scheme which
would grant Dominion Home Rule to the twenty-six southern
counties, 'while leaving the 6 counties exactly as they are
today without any power to organize themselves as a separate
entity'. The Ulster bishops met in Dublin on 8 December,
and, Healy understood, 'agreed to acquiesce in this plan,
Dr. O'Donnell dissenting—the rest being persuaded that the
magnet of a tax-free state [i.e., one free from contributions
to the war debt], and soon attract Belfast &c.'.[29] Though I
have found no evidence of this episode except Healy's second-
or third-hand account, it has the ring of truth. At this

stage, the Northern bishops had no cause to hope for anything better than to deprive the Orangemen of 'a little legislature of their own'. Healy suspected that the entire overture was a trap since Lloyd George would not dare defy Unionist opinion in the cabinet and parliament to give the Orangemen what they only pretended to want, continued government from Westminster, while giving the Southern Irish what might at least placate them—Home Rule with fiscal autonomy. Archbishop Walsh, Healy had heard, agreed with his view.

Healy and the Archbishop turned out to be correct, for a few days later the government announced its Better Government of Ireland Bill, which provided for separate Home Rule governments in the northern six and southern twenty-six counties. The powers of the two new legislatures would be little greater than those contemplated for an all-Ireland parliament in the 1914 Home Rule Act. The bill did, however, contain a novel proposal for a Council of Ireland composed of an equal number of representatives from each parliament which might work to harmonise the actions of the two parliaments, and a provision for the two parliaments to establish, by joint action, an all-Ireland parliament to supersede the Council. This bill was, of course, a very different matter from the proposal that the Northern bishops had considered early in December, providing neither security against Orange persecution of the Church in the North nor any symbolic advance over the 1914 act to meet the demand of the Nation's younger generation for something more than their fathers had accepted. The bill was generally spurned by Catholics throughout the country, and the bishops did not even dignify it by commenting on it directly in their January pronouncement on the state of the country, declaring instead

that the one true way to terminate [our] historic troubles and establish friendly relations between England and Ireland to the advantage of both countries is to allow an undivided Ireland to choose her own form of government.[30]

The main significance of the bill for our purposes, therefore, is that the uncertainty over what its provisions might be probably kept the hierarchy off balance during the autumn of

1919. The eagerness with which the Northern bishops greeted even a hint of a more-or-less satisfactory settlement early in December suggests that at least part of the hierarchy would not have wanted any episcopal action to foreclose the chance of the Church's relations with the State bearing fruit, even at this late date.

Concerning the government's other move, the bishops could more easily agree. During the war the combination of rising costs and restricted government expenditure for domestic needs had placed the educational systems of Ireland, and particularly the teachers, in even more severe financial straits than the squeeze of 1903–07. After a good deal of badgering by the teachers, the government agreed during the last year of the war to appoint two viceregal committees, one, under the chairmanship of Lord Killanin, to inquire into the primary education system, and the other, under the chairmanship of Lord Chief Justice Maloney, to inquire into the intermediate system. Both included Catholic clerical representatives—in the case of the Killanin committee, Bishop O'Donnell—and their reports were published early in 1919. The Killanin Committee recommended improvements in the salary scale of teachers and the establishment of local school committees empowered to levy rates for school maintenance. O'Donnell, reasoning no doubt that, in view of the war debt, further opposition to school rates would be futile, did not dissent from this recommendation. The Maloney Report recommended, among other things, the establishment of an education department. Thus, the two proposals most bitterly opposed by the Church during the 1903–07 controversy were again up for consideration, and at a time when Catholic Ireland was virtually unrepresented in the Commons. Protestant Ireland was far from unrepresented; indeed, the coalition cabinet which included Bonar Law and Walter Long was especially sympathetic to Irish Protestant opinion. Immediately after the armistice, leading Belfast Protestants had begun agitating for a reform of Irish education at least insofar as it affected the northern metropolis where the war had exacerbated a severe shortage of school accommodation. The fault probably lay with the Belfast Protestant Churches,[31] which had none of the zeal for school-building of their Catholic counterparts, but many more children to provide for than their co-religionists in Southern rural communities. Belfast's proposal, not surprisingly, was a basically secular system, which was unreservedly condemned by Bishop MacRory and other Catholic spokesmen.[32]

The needs of the teachers and those of the Belfast Protestant children were undoubtedly urgent. The fact that the government was preparing a grant of self-government for both Northern and Southern Ireland, however, was a rather strong argument in favour of temporarily relieving these two problems with special grants and leaving larger questions of educational reform and finances to the Irish parliaments. Nevertheless, administrators in Dublin Castle and at the treasury could apparently not bear to pass up this opportunity to enact reforms which they had for so long deemed essential to efficiency in Irish education. Accordingly, a bill replacing the semi-independent boards with an education department and establishing county education committees responsible for school maintenance was introduced on 24 November. Perhaps MacPherson—the third Chief Secretary in as many years—was so little in touch with ecclesiastical opinion as to imagine that a clause in the bill guaranteeing continuation of 'the principles and practices which at the time of the passing of this Act govern religious instruction in national schools'[33] would allay any episcopal fears. If so, he was soon to be disabused of the notion.

The Standing Committee of the hierarchy met on 9 December (the day after the Ulster bishops had met and considered the short-lived scheme to keep the six counties under direct Westminster control) and issued a long and sometimes repetitious denunciation of the bill. The scheme, they charged with some justice, had been brought forward 'at the instigation of an intolerant minority in one angle of the country who demanded that others should be taxed with them to do what they, like their poorer neighbours, should long ago have done voluntarily for themselves'.[34] On the issue of rates and local school committees it was necessary to tread lightly, as one of the bishops' own number had endorsed such a proposal in the Killanin Report. The Standing Committee contented itself with a brief reference to 'the prospect of very heavy additional taxation throughout Ireland', and, on the remuneration of teachers, cited the findings of the Childers Commission in 1895 that Ireland had been overtaxed since the Union. The issue which the bishops recognised as having the greatest political potential for them was the composition of the proposed education department. The department was to consist of three men: the Chief Secretary as president, a vice-president who would also be the Vice-President of the existing Department of Agriculture and Technical Instruction, and a permanent member. Although the president and vice-president would, as members of the government, be the parliamentary spokesmen for the department, the actual conduct of its day-to-day affairs would fall to the permanent member. It was assumed that, Starkie being near retirement, the first permanent member would be A. N. Bonaparte Wyse, Principal Secretary to the National Board and a member of an old Catholic family,[35] but no nomination for the post was publicly announced. As the current Chief Secretary was a Scot and the current Vice-President of the Department of Agriculture and Technical Instruction, H. T. Barrie, was an Ulster Presbyterian, the bishops could depict the proposed department as having 'no particular educational strength, unless it be that its members, so far as they are known, are neither Catholic nor Irishmen'.[36] The permanent member, whoever he might be, could not 'make up for the glaring deficiencies of his colleagues', who would only defend his administration in parliament when they agreed with him and whom the bishops characterised as 'party hacks'. Summoning the Nation to its defence, then, the Standing Committee declared that the majority of Irishmen would tolerate no department but one set up by their own parliament, presided over by a Minister for Education 'acknowledged as the highest educational authority in the land'. Until then, 'The people of this country will set their faces against the appointment of any minister or combination of ministers who, as foreigners, are absolutely unfit to guide the intellectual destinies of Ireland.'

The leaders of the teachers' organisation, who were in London on the day the Standing Committee's statement was published, tried to get MacPherson to introduce their new salary scales without waiting for passage of the bill. The Chief Secretary made it plain, however, that more money would not be forthcoming until the government was 'assured that more effective measures would be taken to ensure that it would be expended to the best advantage'[37]—or, as the *Freeman* put it, 'No Bill, no money.'[38] Though the bishops professed sympathy with the teachers' plight, the teachers could take small comfort from such a statement as that of Bishop Hallinan: 'Unless he was greatly mistaken in them [the teachers], as a body they would rise up in their anger, refuse to touch this unholy thing, and say to their poor old Mother Erin, "Mother, death is better."'[39] The issue was temporarily postponed when on 15 December Joe Devlin and his little handful of Irish Party M.P.s engaged in five hours of parliamentary obstruction to prevent the bill from receiving a second reading as scheduled.[40] This action, in effect, killed the bill for the 1919 session, but Bonar Law indicated that it would be reintroduced early in the 1920 session and without the pressure of impending adjournment, the party remnant would be helpless to prevent its passage.

The leadership of the teachers' organisation bravely went ahead with support for the bill[41] despite furious denunciation of the measure by individual bishops and clergy,[42] endorsement of the Standing Committee's statement by the entire hierarchy in January,[43] and attempts by a few teachers to get the entire organisation to repudiate its leaders' policy.[44] The rhetoric of the bishops seems generally more unmeasured than any they had engaged in during earlier education disputes, though their attitude toward the teachers, while increasingly hostile,[45] was not translated into a ban on their organisation as it had been two decades earlier. These facts are symptoms of the situation in which the Church now found herself. One of the Church's most vital interests as churchmen perceived it—the prevention of popular control of education—was at stake. The Church could probably rely upon the Nation's representatives to defend this interest as soon as the Nation had achieved *de facto* sovereignty. It would be much more difficult to get rid of popular control, however, if it were already in operation when *de facto* sovereignty was attained. By early 1920 the Church had so far withdrawn her sanction from the State, and the relevant officers of State were so little in touch with the workings of the Irish political system, that nothing was to be gained by restraint of episcopal rhetoric. If, however, the Church was entirely dependent upon the Nation for her defence, and the Nation was in a very weak position to make that defence, then no element of the Nation—not even the much-despised teachers—should be too greatly abused. The Church must make her position crystal-clear, so the Nation would know where its duty lay, in the present and in future, but this was not the moment for harsh retribution.

The Church's most dramatic gesture was the proclamation of a solemn novena at the instance of Cardinal Logue to culminate on St Patrick's Day, asking divine aid against 'the threatened calamity'. Logue urged that in each parish the fathers of families be assembled after devotions on Passion Sunday to register their votes against the bill. 'Anything in the form of a petition to Parliament would be not only cumbrous, but,' he added, with unwonted understatement, 'would likely be thrown aside.'[46] Instead, the vote should be communicated to the press, though in the event the exercise was apparently not well enough organised to produce any clearly stated vote of opposition.

Bishop Foley, who still sat on the National Board, went so far as to suggest that the Church might withdraw all those Catholic schools which it legally could from the jurisdiction of the new department if the bill were enacted.[47] The intensity of the Church's opposition to the bill apparently persuaded the government that it would create an unnecessary addition to the already heavy burden of governing Ireland. Perhaps the fact that nearly all areas outside the Protestant North-east returned local government bodies with Sinn Féin majorities at the January 1920 municipal elections dampened MacPherson's zeal for creating a further set of local councils under an educational bill.

At the same time many of the newly elected councils were joining in the Church's protest against the Education Bill,[48] they were declaring their allegiance to Dáil Éireann[49] and declining to have dealings with the Local Government Board, sending official correspondence to its counterpart in the Dáil

ministry instead. It is interesting to inquire what was the
Dáil's education policy at this juncture. No Minister for Education had been included in the ministry formed after de
Valera's escape from prison. At the Dáil's October 1919 meeting, however, when a request was received from the Gaelic
League to appoint a Minister for the Irish Language, one
deputy suggested that a Minister for Education be appointed
instead. From the rather laconic *Minutes of Proceedings*, it
appears that several deputies found the idea attractive, but
J. J. O'Kelly, who was Deputy Speaker of the Dáil, President of
the Gaelic League and editor of the *Catholic Bulletin*, recognising, do doubt, the delicacy of the issues being raised, suggested that the entire matter be deferred until de Valera's
return. Cathal Brugha opposed deferring the more limited
issue of a Minister for Irish, but 'thought President de Valera
had some definite reason for not appointing a Minister of
Education when constituting his Ministry'. He, therefore,
suggested that the President of the Gaelic League be appointed Minister for Irish, pending the President's return,
and the ministry adopted his suggestion.[50] During the following few months, while the controversy over MacPherson's
Education Bill was raging, the Dáil was unable to assemble,
even in secret. From one of the reports of the Department of
Irish after the Dáil resumed secret meetings, however, it
emerges that the Department actually submitted its plans
to the old National and Intermediate Education Boards. As
the other Dáil departments were doing their best to create
the impression that they had supplanted their 'British'
counterparts in Ireland, this action is most remarkable, but
there is no indication that it prompted any criticism in the
Dáil.[51] Clearly then the Nation's new leaders understood the
meaning of the Education Bill controversy. The Church had
pronounced against attacks on the present Education Boards,
and even at the cost of possible embarrassment to the national
cause at a crucial moment, the Nation would honour that
pronouncement.

There is just a chance that the Sinn Féin party may have
been tempted to take the side of the teachers against the
Church—two members of the Sinn Féin executive privately
expressed sympathy with the teachers' position.[52] In the event,

however, Sinn Féin remained silent at the national level—in the same spirit that its leaders a year earlier had deleted from the Democratic Programme that sentence which would have committed the Nation 'to encourage by every reasonable means the most capable and sympathetic men and women to devote their talents to the education of the young'.[53] If the Nation's representatives were temporarily unable to defend the Church's vital interests, they would at least do nothing to hinder her own defence of those interests. The government quietly allowed the bill to die, and separate arrangements were made to meet the teachers' salary demands. At one stage, when officials seemed unwilling to concede an important claim of the teachers, T. J. O'Connell, the I.N.T.O. General Secretary won his point by playing upon fears that a strike would add education to the growing list of services over which the State's authority was now in question.[54]

In his letter proposing the novena and the parish meetings on the Education Bill, Cardinal Logue wrote: 'Though we have not yet, thank God, arrived at the stage dreamt of by the extreme Socialists, when the children of the people shall become the mere chattel of the State, the Bill in question seems to tend notably in that direction.'[55] Since the Cardinal here resurrected some of the misunderstanding which clouded the Church's relations with working-class movements just before the war, it is worthwhile to inquire into the current status of those relations, especially as they might affect the larger operations of the Irish political system. The Dáil, after all, claimed to be the direct successor to the Republic proclaimed in 1916 over the signature, among others, of James Connolly, one of the two main spokesmen for the socialist principles the Church had so roundly denounced.[56] During and after the 1918 election, Dean Innocent Ryan of Cashel objected vehemently to a Sinn Féin election handbill which advocated, in Connolly's words, 'the vesting of all property rights in the free Irish nation as against the claim of the individual'.[57] The Dean's namesake, the Rev. Matt Ryan, P.P., declared in reply that the Sinn Féin executive, of which he was a member 'condemned everything in the nature of Atheism, Bolshevism, and Socialism, which were condemned by the Pope'.[58]

Nevertheless, the Sinn Féin movement did contain a few idealistic admirers of socialism—it was hard to be a revolutionary, even a 'constitutional' one, in 1918 without feeling some sympathy with those who deposed the Czar—and it owed something to the Irish labour movement for agreeing to stand aside in the general election and allow Sinn Féin a clear field against the Irish Parliamentary Party. As noted early in this chapter, before the First Dáil convened, Thomas Johnson, one of the labour leaders, was asked to draft a statement of social policy, the 'Democratic Programme', for adoption at the Dáil's first meeting. Although I.R.B. leaders tried to have the Programme suppressed as potentially divisive on the day before the meeting, Sinn Féin leaders insisted on presenting it. Seán T. O'Kelly was commissioned to tone down the document, however, before its presentation.[59] Johnson's draft of the Programme began with assertions from the Republican Proclamation of 1916 and from an essay by Pearse similar to the quote from Connolly which had upset Dean Ryan. O'Kelly kept the 1916 declaration of 'the right of the people of Ireland to the ownership of Ireland' and Pearse's assertion that the Nation's sovereignty extends to material possessions, soil, wealth, and wealth-producing processes as well as persons. Pearse's conclusion that 'No private right to property is good against the public right of the Nation,' however, was toned down to 'All right to private property must be subordinated to the public right and welfare.' Johnson's further corollary that the Nation might resume possession of soil or wealth 'whenever the trust is abused or the trustee fails to give faithful service' was replaced by an innocuous guarantee of 'the principle of Liberty, Equality, and Justice for all'.[60]

One should not infer from this butchering of a robust socialist declaration that labour was getting unfair treatment in the new order of things. It is well to remember that in the years before the war, the urban working-class movement had occupied a very weak position, totally isolated from all three centres of power in the political system. In those days, as a writer in *The Leader* recalled, 'Beyond sending their banners and contingents to occasional political processions, the Trade Union movement in Ireland had little or no connection with the then Irish national politics.'[61] Connolly's participation in the Rising and labour's involvement in the anticonscription movement were steps toward the creation for labour of a definite niche within the Nation. The urban labourers' relatively small numbers did not call for the Nation's acceptance of their goals in an unadulterated form. Their willingness to subordinate those goals to the national goal, however, won them the protection afforded by the conventions of the political system. Whereas before the war, labourers had been practically defenceless against the reckless attacks of clerical conservatives, now there were clearly forces within the Church working to minimise conflict with the labour movement. Late in 1918, when the Irish Trade Union Congress and Labour Party adopted a new constitution, Father William Moran, a Maynooth theology professor, made discreet inquiries through an intermediary with a view to bringing that document into line with clerical thinking.

It would be a tremendous pity [he wrote] if the split which threatened between Sinn Fein & Irish Labour, & which is now happily averted, were to be replaced by a quarrel with the Church specially when, as far as I can guess, the demands of Irish labour are theologically right enough themselves, but are expressed in formulae which have got a bad meaning owing to the use of the same formulae by certain people on the continent. Now when the whole Irish movement is starting is the time to get all these things right.[62]

There were others besides himself at Maynooth he noted, who were 'very much interested in these questions', and there is evidence that consultations between theologians and labour leaders such as he envisaged did take place.[63]

Father Moran laid some theological groundwork for accommodation between the Church and socialism in an article entitled 'Some Causes of the Present Social Unrest', published in the early spring of 1919 in the *Irish Theological Quarterly*.[64] While arguing that the socialists went too far in calling for the total abolition of private property, he maintained that private property was not dictated by natural law, which, rather, gave men equal rights of access to the resources of the earth. The appropriation of particular tracts of land by individuals had been justified at the time when increasing population drove men from a nomadic to an agricultural life style. When, however, the available supply of land had been fully appropriated, the rights of the proprietors were not to be held absolute as against the natural rights of all men to livelihood. In the Middle Ages, the Church had placed restrictions upon the exercise of property rights, which only came to be regarded as absolute in the individualistic milieu of the Reformation. Father Moran suggested schemes of co-operation, co-partnership and profit-sharing as means of bringing 'our present industrial system into line with the more human conception of industry which obtained in [the Middle Ages]'. Rather than relying on voluntary Christian charity for the alleviation of distress, he advocated the active intervention of the State to prevent 'a grasping employer from exploiting the necessities of his workers to force them to consent to an unjust labour contract', and to provide or compel employers to provide suitable housing for workers.[65]

Various bishops began taking up some of the themes Father Moran had sketched. If they felt it necessary to continue condemning socialism, they tended to define the latter quite narrowly.[66] Some began to stress the points of agreement between socialism and Catholic teaching and to offer solutions to the social question such as arbitration boards and profit-sharing which, if not precisely the remedies favoured by the labour movement itself, at least evidenced conscious effort to come to terms with the problem.[67] When Father Peter Finlay, S.J., one of the leading pre-war clerical opponents of socialism, implied in a lecture that Irish trade unionists were excommunicated by virtue of vague ties to continental organisations under papal ban, he was promptly contradicted in the pages of the *Irish Theological Quarterly*.[68] It is, moreover, quite significant that when Cardinal Logue, who, despite all the arguments of theologians, was terrrified by recent events in eastern Europe,[69] linked the Education Bill with socialism, he was using the old bogey to attack not the Nation but the State.[70]

Insofar as the Nation can be said to have implemented any social policy, it was through the arbitration courts—Supreme, District (County) and Petty—established in 1919. Despite some opposition, it was provided 'that clergymen be *ex-*

officio Justices' in the Petty Courts.[71] In the growing territory where it was actually possible to set up the courts, there seems little reason to doubt the observation of the Unionist commentator W. Alison Phillips, that 'they usually consisted of a Roman Catholic curate and one or two prominent local Sinn Feiners'.[72] The Church was thus able to gain, through the lower clergy, a voice in the national movement (as it had in the U.I.L. and earlier national movements) without the risks of direct episcopal involvement. Of course, the same had been true, through the organisation of the Sinn Féin movement since 1917, but through the arbitration court scheme the Nation was granting churchmen the right to hold a kind of civil office. The denial of this right by the State, for example in the 1898 Local Government Act, had long been a sore point for some ecclesiastics.[73] Moreover, clerical participation in the arbitration courts, whose justices were required to pledge (though, interestingly, not to swear) allegiance to the Republic, obviously conferred at least a measure of legitimacy on the Republic.

The Republic soon found itself confronted by a serious problem of social policy. In large areas of the West, where the King's writ had practically ceased to run, the landless peasants, whose grievance Church and Nation had championed in 1898 and forgotten in 1903, began to take advantage of the power vacuum early in 1920 to achieve their economic goals. A wave of cattle-driving, fence-breaking, and improvised subdivision of grazing lands swept the western counties. Sentiment in the Dáil, as in the Church, favoured subdivision of grazing land to provide the tillage plots that would, it was hoped, stem emigration, but, like the Church, the Dáil respected the claims of existing owners to compensation. Some brave schemes were proposed in 1919 in the Dáil for financing land redistribution,[74] but the problem was too formidable to be solved by a bureaucracy 'on the run'. 'Had they a National Government,' declared Bishop O'Doherty of Clonfert in a sermon in Loughrea, 'this question of the distribution of grass lands would be among the very first to come up for solution. For the present, they had practically no Government in civil matters. The real representatives of the Nation were not allowed to act.' After this significant step toward full sanction of the Nation's present legitimacy, the Bishop added an admonition against violence and a reaffirmation of the right of compensation and noted that

Injustice had been attempted in the name of Sinn Fein, but he knew enough of the spirit of the men at the head of that movement, who were men of chivalry, honour, and with a noble sense of justice. They had given no sanction to acts such as those his lordship had condemned.[75]

If the Dáil was prevented from dealing with this problem at a national level, the arbitration court scheme offered an opportunity to intervene with some success on a local basis. Art O'Connor, Substitute Minister for Agriculture, was dispatched to the West to expedite arbitration court action.[76] At a meeting chaired by Mgr Considine, V.G., a number of leading Co. Galway clergy joined with O'Connor to work out details for implementing the arbitration court scheme. The chairman paid tribute to the arbitration courts already in existence, and this sentiment was echoed in a letter from Dean Macken of Dunmore, who declared that 'Christian Irishmen regarded it as desirable that the large grazing ranches should be equitably divided amongst the poor tenantry of Ireland,' but warned against abuses and the threat of 'anarchy and chaos'. O'Connor pointed out that the aim of British land legislation was 'to fix occupying tenants on the land', and declared that the Dáil's scheme was 'to fix non-occupying tenants on the land on a co-operative basis, so that they should not have to go to America'.[77] The Dáil ministry thus associated itself with a dominant social ideal of the clergy. Moreover, the Church's insistence upon fair compensation was so strictly adhered to in the arbitration proceedings that some Unionists willingly resorted to the arbitration courts because they tended to set higher prices upon land than had the British land-purchase machinery.[78] On balance, then, the Dáil's social policy was helping to build satisfactory relations between the Church and the Nation both through abstract agreement on means and ends and through practical involvement of clergy in the implementation of that policy.

The Vatican had scheduled ceremonies late in May for

the beatification of Oliver Plunket, the seventeenth-century martyr, and sixteen members of the Irish hierarchy went to Rome for the occasion. About a week earlier, Seán T. O'Kelly, who happened to be in Rome, had witnessed the ceremonies for the canonisation of Joan of Arc and observed that the French Ambassador gave a great reception for distinguished French visitors in Rome. Although he had not been accredited by the Dáil as Envoy to Rome, he wrote home for authority to act in that capacity and set up in the Grand Hotel where he proceeded to give a great reception for distinguished visitors gathered for the Plunket ceremonies.[79] Quite remarkably, Cardinal Logue and all but two of the other Irish prelates in Rome accepted the invitation. It was apparently quite a festive occasion, for by the time Logue arrived, one of the other bishops had been prevailed upon to sing 'Wrap the Green Flag Round Me, Boys' for the assembled 300 or 400 guests. The Cardinal was accompanied from the entrance of the hotel by a group of ecclesiastical students who insisted on waving the Republican flag over him, and, O'Kelly later recalled, he 'accepted these attentions with great good humour'. British authorities were less amused and Vatican officials let it be known that the Holy See had extended no recognition to O'Kelly and was not responsible for what Irish ecclesiastics and laymen may have done among themselves.[80] This action was consistent with the attitude Rome had recently been taking toward the Irish question. A few months earlier, Fogarty had managed to get a letter published denouncing a judge who had used the term 'moral degradation' in describing the state of Co. Clare, and Lord Curzon, the Foreign Secretary, directed the British mission at the Holy See to bring the matter to the Vatican's attention.[81] Officials at the Papal Secretariat of State replied with a very brief and vague note stating that the Holy See had considered the letter and 'made suitable dispositions in the matter'.[82] A few days later, however, when a Vatican official preaching at a requiem for Mgr O'Riordan at the Irish College used an 'intemperate' tone in referring to the Irish question, the Secretariat of State apologised to the British minister, Count de Salis, before he had even raised the issue. The offending papal official, de Salis was informed, had been duly admonished ('*dûment admonesté*') for speaking in terms which the Cardinal Secretary of State strongly deplored ('*vivement déplorer*').[83] De Salis, who was rather taken aback by this proceeding, was given to understand that the Pope himself had intervened, and that 'though it was of course open to the Irish clergy to hold such opinions as they liked with regard to political matters in their own country, it was by no means free to a Roman ecclesiastic to interfere in them'.[84]

The Plunket ceremonies provided an opportunity for the Pope to hear reports on the Irish situation from a number of Irish bishops.[85] Apparently the bishops reinforced the Vatican's resolution to keep hands off the Irish situation. In the 1880s the British government had twice obtained dramatic Vatican intervention against the national movement in Ireland. Indeed, throughout the nineteenth century, the Holy See had been surprisingly willing to deal with British emissaries behind the backs of Irish churchmen. The friendship of the world's strongest power—albeit a Protestant power—had counted for more than the desires of a small Catholic nationality. Now, however, conditions had changed. Memories of the temporal power had dimmed, the Pope's peace initiatives in the war had been politely ignored, and Vatican thinking was adjusting, ever so cautiously, to the realities of the modern world. Among those realities was that the Church's future would rest not on the machinations of *realpolitik* but on the devotion of Catholic peoples to the Church. In this context, the aspirations of a people whose very rebels joined in the rosary before going into battle were not to be trifled with. When he returned to Thurles, Archbishop Harty stated 'that after the recent visit of the Irish Bishops to Rome, the enemies of Ireland will no longer be able to malign the Irish people to the Vatican'. The Pope, he declared,

had the greatest possible sympathy for their national aspirations. When his Grace mentioned the subject, the Holy Father said the Irish people had a perfect right to independence—the same right as Poland or Belgium.[86]

Perhaps because the Irish bishops had impressed upon him their desire not to alienate moderate national leaders, the

Pope, despite the earlier denial of recognition to the Irish 'ambassador', agreed to receive Seán T. O'Kelly in private audience late in June. The Vatican let it be known that O'Kelly was being received 'as a private person and not as Irish Ambassador', a condition which was accepted by O'Kelly 'who, in his turn declared that he did not desire that his qualification should create any embarrassment to the Holy See'.[87] The audience, however, was no mere exchange of pleasantries. O'Kelly presented a statement of the Republic's position 'and was questioned closely by His Holiness as to the nature and activities indulged in by supporters of our Cause at home'.[88] A few days later a papal official suggested to a British representative that England should do 'something generous' in the matter of Ireland, and when the latter objected that 'the Irish would not take part in any scheme', the Vatican spokesman 'asked if it would not be possible to get someone to act as intermediary between the two nations, England to state the maximum that she was prepared to give and Ireland to state the minimum that she would accept —and try and strike some agreement'.[89] This formula, although proposed in quite an informal way, implied that Ireland, presumably as represented by its current national leaders, was a legitimate entity capable of entering into an international compact. If this did not go quite so far as many Irish bishops had gone in their public statements, it does seem to reflect their efforts during their visit to Rome. The papal official added, significantly, that 'it was impossible for the Holy See to move in the matter—as there might be danger of losing Ireland altogether'.[90]

By the summer of 1920, then, the Irish Church had fairly definitely confirmed for the present generation of national leadership the position she had taken vis-à-vis the Nation since the 1880s. The Nation was to be sovereign in the future if in the present it eschewed physical force and respected the Church's interests in education. The latter condition was clearly being met. As for the former condition, churchmen were extending to the farthest limit their long-standing ability to distinguish between avowed principles of leaders and regrettable excesses of followers. The shooting of Crown forces was frequently condemned from the pulpit, but almost

always treated as an aberration of the true national methods
of prayer and steadfast adherence to ideals. As the din of
pistol fire was rising in a steady crescendo, this rationalisation
might become harder and harder to sustain, but the further
clerical assertion that the excesses were merely the natural
response to British provocation was actually driving the
Church beyond her traditional position. Not only was the
Nation's sovereignty for the future affirmed, but the State's
sovereignty in the present was, by virtue of its growing reliance on naked force, virtually denied in some episcopal pronouncements. But why did the Church take nearly eighteen
months to confirm thus fully that the Irish political system
still stood and, indeed, to press on to the further tentative
but significant denial of the State's present legitimacy? Was
it because, as Sir James MacMahon, a 'Castle Catholic', told
the cabinet, 'The Roman Catholic Church had always been
opposed to a Republic'?[91] Perhaps this old bogy lingered on
in a few clerical minds, but a careful reading of episcopal
pronouncements early in 1919 indicates that even Cardinal
Logue was shedding his aversion to the notion of a Republic.
More to the point were fears about the kind of Republic to
be sought. Was it to be a Socialist Republic on the pattern
of Russia? The reason such fears were important was the
widespread clerical assumption that socialism (for reasons
discussed in Chapter XIII) would undermine the piety on
which the Irish political system was founded. This basic, if
scarcely tangible issue had to be settled, as indeed it was by
early 1920, before the Church could with confidence confirm
that, yes, the conventions of the political system still held—
and that she would bend every effort to make them operate
to the Nation's benefit.

CHAPTER XX

Killing No Murder?

AT their regular June meeting in 1920, the bishops issued no public statement. A story told by Griffith's publicity aide, Robert Brennan, apparently relating to this meeting, records how the latter drafted at Griffith's request a statement concerning British repression, in hopes that a certain 'friendly' bishop would present it to the hierarchy for adoption. When the two Sinn Féiners called upon the bishop at the Gresham Hotel,

He read the statement and said it was too strong and should be watered down. A. G. pointed out that it contained nothing but the facts, every one of which could be substantiated. His Lordship agreed, but said that the Bishops knew very well that we were losing the country, that the people were tired of the fight and that if they got a chance they would turn us down in favour of the Parliamentary Party.[1]

Brennan, who, with Griffith, was dumbfounded by the Bishop's reaction, probably misread whatever their episcopal friend actually said. Certainly only a highly coloured Sinn Féin imagination could have concocted the notion that the Irish Parliamentary Party was anything but dead and buried. A more plausible interpretation of the Bishop's response is that the hierarchy was wracked by divisions which he felt bound not to disclose to laymen and that he improvised an explanation as best he could. Perhaps the hierarchy's silence at this moment represents a mixture of fear and hope: fear that the British would take such stern measures that the Nation really would be crushed, leaving the Church out on a very long limb, and hope that in view of the strength of national resistance the British would offer some generous settlement, possibly through the bishops themselves.

Such seems to be the import of an interview which the Limerick County Inspector of the R.I.C., P. A. Marrinan, had at this time with Bishop Hallinan's administrator. This clergyman, who purported to be knowledgeable about the hierarchy's internal politics, depicted the bishops as 'sick of the extremists' and implied that Cardinal Logue had 're-gained control of the others'. He thought that the government might have a good prospect of success if it approached Logue with an offer of 'a pretty wide measure of Home Rule' by which he apparently meant 'some such dominion rule as Canada has with Ulster enjoying the same rights as Quebec'.[2] It would be interesting, in the light of Logue's long-standing aversion to the slightest hint of autonomy for the North, to know whether this last suggestion truly re-flected Armagh's view or was a mere Limerick gloss. Cer-tainly, the Canadian federalism which the Bishops worked so hard to avoid in the Convention would be less threatening to the Church's interests in the North than the measures proposed in the bill currently before parliament. It does seem that in the summer of 1920, with the Nation exercising a precarious *de facto* authority throughout much of Southern Ireland, and the Church (especially through the events in Rome) rather openly sanctioning that authority, the Church was waiting for the State to make a move.

Marrinan had suggested Sir James MacMahon (joint Under-Secretary with Sir John Anderson), as a possible inter-mediary with the Cardinal, and a few days after Marrinan's report circulated at cabinet level[3] MacMahon did indeed call on Logue. He brought, however, not an offer of a more gen-erous Irish settlement, but a query whether there was any means of stopping 'even temporarily . . . the present assassina-tions' without stating any *quid pro quo*. Although he found Logue weeping over the assassination in Cork of District Commissioner Smyth of the R.I.C., who had reportedly made a savage appeal to his men to shoot suspicious persons indis-criminately, the Cardinal replied to the Under-Secretary's query 'by asking what was the good of attempting the imposs-ible when the Government provided the excuse for these men to commit such outrages'.[4]

This remark reads like many of the episcopal pronouncements of the preceding year and a half: the I.R.A. excesses are deplorable but understandable in the light of government repression. Until recently, however, the repression had consisted chiefly of censorship, arrests of political leaders, searches of persons and houses and the outlawing of various national organisations. Such measures had clearly failed to prevent the extension of the Dáil's arbitration courts (now transformed into regular civil courts attended even by respectable members of the legal profession), the destruction of over three hundred previously evacuated police barracks, the paralysis of the British tax-gathering machinery and the adherence of many local authorities in the South to the Dáil. As late as the end of July there were rumours that Lloyd George was contemplating the 'great coup' of making an offer through the bishops 'and through them to induce Sinn Féin to come to breakfast at Downing Street'.[5] To have done at this time what he did a year later would have been a statesmanlike act. Unfortunately, the coalition government at Westminster gave small scope for statesmanship in Irish matters. Lloyd George presided over a cabinet which included three of the Conservatives most deeply implicated in the Ulster revolt of 1912–14—Bonar Law, Walter Long and Lord Birkenhead (formerly F. E. Smith)—and he relied heavily for advice upon the Chief of the Imperial General Staff, Sir Henry Wilson, whose meddling in politics on behalf of the Ulster Protestants since 1914 had been notorious.[6] Dependent upon a Conservative House of Commons and presiding over a cabinet of Conservatives and Liberal imperialists, the same Lloyd George, who two decades earlier had denounced the brutal measures taken against the Boers, now adopted similar measures against the Irish. The mere infringement of civil liberties which had counted for repression in episcopal reasoning hitherto, was now replaced by all the horrors of war, albeit undeclared, upon the Nation.

MacPherson had been replaced in April by Sir Hamar Greenwood, whose prior administrative experience had been, significantly, at the War Office. During the early months of his administration the Crown forces in Ireland were reinforced by three distinct groups, none of which was inhibited by any tender feelings toward Sinn Féin. In the North, Pro-

testant militants were organised into a part-time Special
Constabulary (the 'B Specials') to preserve 'order', despite
the fact that some of its members had been disturbers of
order in bitter sectarian rioting in July and August. For the
rest of Ireland, where a Dáil-sponsored boycott of the R.I.C.
had seriously thinned police ranks, full-time replacements
were enlisted in Great Britain. These police recruits, drawn
from the large pool of unemployed ex-servicemen, were soon
dubbed the 'Black and Tans'—an allusion both to the mixture of khaki uniforms with black belts and dark green
R.I.C. caps they were obliged to wear because of a shortage
of police uniforms and to the name of a famous pack of
hounds. The 'Tans', who began arriving in the early spring,
were in many cases quite brutalised by the war and demoral-
ised by the peace. They were augmented in July by a third
force, the Auxiliaries, recruited from among ex-officers as a
kind of elite corps.

General Sir Nevil Macready, who was placed in command
of all Crown forces in Ireland (some 40,000 military and
police) was armed with special powers to arrest without
charge, to try by court martial and to substitute military
inquiries for coroners' inquests. He was not given full martial
law powers for the entire country, which he would have
preferred, for the government resolutely refused to admit
that a state of war existed. Although the soldiers generally
stayed within strict military discipline, the police soon adopted the tactic of responding to attacks by I.R.A. gunmen by
wreaking vengeance on nearby towns. Having gained no
peace overtures by their silence in June, and faced with a
reign of counter-terror even greater than the terror the I.R.A.
had initiated, the hierarchy spoke out strongly at their
October meeting against

countless indiscriminate raids and arrests in the darkness of
night, prolonged imprisonments without trial, savage sentences
from tribunals that command and deserve no confidence, the
burning of houses, town halls, factories, creameries and crops, the
destruction of industries to pave the way for want and famine
by men maddened with plundered drink and bent on loot, the
flogging and massacre of civilians, all perpetrated by the forces
of the Crown who have estabilshed [*sic*] a reign of frightfulness

which, for murdering the innocent and destroying their property, has a parallel only in the horrors of Turkish atrocities, or in the outrages of the Red Army of Bolshevist Russia.[7]

Significantly, the bishops rejected the claims of the government that the reprisals were not official policy: 'Outrage has been connived at and encouraged, if not organized, not by obscure and irresponsible individuals but by the Government of a mighty Empire, professing the highest ideals of truth and justice.' In addition, they denounced 'the iniquity of furnishing a corner of Ulster with a separate government, or *its worst instrument, a special police force, to enable it all the more rapidly to trample underfoot the victims of its intolerants*'.[8] Reaffirming the 'indefeasible right of Ireland as of every other nation to choose the form of Government under which its people will live', the bishops gave even higher priority to a demand for 'a full inquiry into the atrocities now being perpetrated in Ireland, by such a tribunal as will inspire the confidence of all and with immunity to witnesses from the terrorism which makes it impossible to give evidence with safety to life or property'. The statement concluded by ordering a national novena 'in preparation for the feast of the Irish saints', and special devotions 'while this trial lasts'.

Like previous episcopal pronouncements, this statement did express opposition to 'crimes' committed on the Irish side, but this expression was so muted and perfunctory as to be easily overlooked in the outraged anti-British rhetoric. One might easily conclude that, after hesitation in June, the whole hierarchy had been pushed one step closer to full sanction for the Republic simply by the violence of the State. This reasoning is complicated somewhat by the fact, to be discussed below, that in December Bishop Cohalan of Cork declared in formal excommunication: 'Anyone who shall, within the diocese of Cork, organise or take part in an ambush or in kidnapping or otherwise, shall be guilty of murder or attempted murder.'[9] Cohalan's action contrasts sharply with the behaviour of Bishops O'Doherty of Clonfert and O'Dea of Galway and Archbishop Gilmartin of Tuam who during the latter half of 1920 began to take Greenwood and Macready to task publicly for instances of reprisals in their dioceses.[10] The tone of their remarks became, at times, almost mocking, as when Bishop O'Doherty predicted, with bitter irony, that Greenwood would regard evidence of R.I.C. rowdyism and vandalism which he offered 'as coming from a "tainted" source, since it does not come from the actual culprits.'[11]

The difference between the attitude of these prelates and that of Cohalan probably reflects the fact that prior to the coming of the 'Tans' actual violence against persons had been practically confined to north-east Ulster, Dublin and its environs and the south-western counties of Cork, Kerry, Limerick and Tipperary. In the remaining areas the Dáil's authority had been extended through the transfer by local authorities of their allegiance to the Dáil, the destruction of previously evacuated police barracks, the formation of Republican police and courts and the disruption of British tax-gathering functions. This extension had been largely devoid of bloodshed in this wide area—in other words it had gone according to the expressed hopes of ecclesiastics for the success of resolute and prayerful adherence to national ideals—and it had gone farthest in Counties Clare and Galway. Indeed, Archbishop Gilmartin, harking back to medieval precedent, called for a 'Truce of God' throughout his diocese on 25 July, and six months passed before this 'Truce' was violated by an I.R.A. ambush of police.[12] Throughout the dioceses of Gilmartin, O'Dea, and O'Doherty, as well as Fogarty, when Crown forces laid waste to a town or drove through a district firing randomly into houses in professed reprisals for I.R.A. attacks which truly were, in this area, isolated, these bishops understandably viewed them as the aggressors. More important, however, they were attacking not the perpetrators of crimes which the bishops had always denounced, but the mechanism of relatively peaceful extension of the Nation's authority, which the bishops had tried to sponsor.

Thus Fogarty, who seemed earlier to be virtually alone among the bishops in pressing their policy to its practical, if not its logical, conclusion, was no doubt provided with several colleagues who saw matters much as he did. Even quite cautious prelates who had gone along reluctantly with Sinn Féin were bitterly alienated by the Black and Tans. Early in

November Bishop Hoare of Ardagh and Clonmacnoise wrote to Devlin:

We had no murders here nearer than Ballinamuck, 8 miles from Longford. The Sinn Fein Leaders were very moderate men, did not like these murders of policemen at all, and gave no provocation to police or military.

Notwithstanding these so called Black and Tans, about ten days ago visited us, went to the house of Magenniss, who is Chairman of the Co. Council, took [him] out of his house into the public street, put a sandwich-like placard before him 'God save the King' and another behind him 'To Hell with De Valera' took off his hat, and walked him up and down the Town at the point of the revolver. That was an appalling indignity perpetrated on Longford's foremost citizen.[13]

A few days later, the Bishop recounted, someone ('it is convincingly believed it was done by the Police—home or foreign') succeeded in burning half of the parochial hall apparently because it had been used for Sinn Féin meetings. The police lent no assistance in extinguishing the fire.

I need not tell you [the Bishop wrote] I am no Sinn Feiner. I opposed this unhappy Society from the beginning, and I denounced any murder that took place; and pointed out to the people that Police were a necessity for every country, and it was better to have their own kith and kin as Police, than Scotchmen, Welshmen or Englishmen. They see it now; but are not converted.[14]

Yet in a sense, Hoare himself was 'converted', however reluctantly, for he concluded: 'Oh it is a horrible state of things and I have not a particle of doubt that this work of [arson] and murder happens according to plan, and is connived at, if not originated by, the Government.'

The crucial member of the hierarchy was, of course, Logue, who, like Hoare, was never predisposed in favour of Sinn Féin. The Cardinal also was outraged by Black and Tan reprisals in the town of Ardee, of which he told Bishop Amigo of Southwark: 'As far as I could ascertain there was not a murder in that whole district for a hundred years.'[15] A Black and Tan camp at Gormanstown, he told Amigo, seemed 'to be a nest of bandits and homicides'. He publicly complained of local Black and Tan excesses in a pastoral letter at the beginning of Advent,[16] which happened to fall one week after that apogee of terror and counter-terror known in Irish history as 'Bloody Sunday'. On that day, 21 November 1920, a squad of handpicked I.R.A. gunmen in Dublin systematically shot fourteen suspected army intelligence officers in their Dublin homes. Later the same day, a detachment of Black and Tans and a military party were sent to Croke Park to search the several thousand spectators of a football game for weapons in hope of discovering the gunmen. A lone shot was apparently fired at the Black and Tans who took the occasion to open fire on the crowd, killing twelve and wounding sixty. In his pastoral, Logue condemned the I.R.A. assassinations, but added: 'If a balance were struck between the deeds of the morning and those of the evening, I believe it should be given against the forces of the Crown.'[17]

Since the 1918 general election the bishops had tended to avoid careful theological explication of what was going on. It will be recalled that in the two years following the Easter Rising a few bishops had drawn attention to the conditions of a justifiable rebellion laid down by the Catholic textbooks on ethics, usually with the implication that one or more of these conditions had not been met. The conditions were formulated in various ways, but a fair summary is that: (1) The government must be habitually and intolerably oppressive. (2) Other means must have been tried and have failed before resorting to rebellion. (3) There must be a reasonable probability of success and of not making matters worse. (4) The resistance must be undertaken, or at least approved, by the majority of the people.[18]

After the initial wave of popular disapproval following the Easter Rising, there was no difficulty about the fourth condition, and the repeated postponement of Home Rule could easily be construed as fulfilling the second. The problem boiled down to conditions one and three. It had been a commonplace of nationalist rhetoric for generations that the government of Ireland was oppressive, but in an age in which agrarian grievances had been largely alleviated and civil disabilities against Catholics largely removed, how far did ecclesiastics really take that rhetoric seriously? Most churchmen, however deeply they may have sympathised with nationalist grievances, probably did not care to restrict their political flexibility either by enshrining platform oratory as a teaching of the Church or by denying its truth. Consequently, during the two years after the Easter Rising the prospect of success was the aspect of the ethics of rebellion which received the most attention.

By 1920, however, the prospects for 'success' in resistance to the British looked distinctly more favourable, if not certain.[19] In the meantime, the threat of conscription in 1918 provided an instance of what the bishops genuinely regarded as intolerable oppression. However much they may have been moved to sponsor the anticonscription agitation by pressing political considerations, one should not discount the bishops' deep disquiet over the depopulation of Ireland, of which conscription would be, in their view, the cruelest example. During the conscription crisis the *Irish Ecclesiastical Record* carried an article by the Rev. P. Coffey, Professor of Philosophy in Maynooth, entitled 'The Conscription Menace in Ireland and Some Issues Raised by It'.[20] Conscription, Father Coffey maintained, with the bishops, was 'an inhuman and oppressive measure' which justified resistance by any Irishman. He went further, however, to maintain that the imperial parliament's jurisdiction over Ireland was based on an unjust conquest and a fraudulently enacted Union. It was therefore a usurpation, none of whose laws commanded obedience except insofar as they were the only alternative to a worse evil, anarchy. Coffey did concede that if British rule had ever ceased to be oppressive, the right of resistance would have lapsed. He obliquely indicated that the resistance he envisaged would not be open physical-force rebellion,[21] but an appeal to the Peace Conference combined with 'patient, disciplined, ennobled' fidelity to 'Christian ideals'.

The article thus stayed within the bounds of the bishops' attitude toward violence, but it pressed somewhat beyond the hierarchy's position in two ways. Firstly, it generalised upon the specific 'oppression' of conscription to question the moral validity of British rule at any time in Ireland. Secondly, it anticipated the attitude by which, over the next two years, the hierarchy would come to sanction nonviolent resistance to the whole of British jurisdiction in Ireland rather than to a single measure—albeit that more general sanction was never given so explicitly and dramatically as the sanction for resistance to conscription. The *Record* carried an imprimatur of the Dublin archdiocese, and Father Coffey's argument represented an option the bishops no doubt wanted to keep open. With the armistice, conscription ceased to be a practical issue. During 1919 Father Walter McDonald brought out a little book entitled *Some Ethical Questions of Peace and War with Special Reference to Ireland,*[22] challenging Coffey's argument on a number of grounds such as whether there was any united Irish State whose jurisdiction had been usurped by the Anglo-Normans and whether Ireland had not lost its right to resist English jurisdiction by acquiescence. McDonald was playing his accustomed role of gadfly to the bishops, and his arguments were greeted mainly by silence. Throughout 1919 and most of 1920 the theological journals carried little of significance on the issues raised by Coffey. There was some theological discussion of the social question[23] and a continuing debate over the ethics of hunger-striking.[24] This latter issue had been raised following the death of Thomas Ashe, a political prisoner who was killed by forcible feeding while on hunger strike in Mountjoy Jail in 1917. Actually, the debate over whether death by hunger strike was morally suicide was temporarily rendered academic by British reliance on the 'Cat and Mouse Act' following Ashe's death,[25] but it took on grave significance in the autumn of 1920 when Terence MacSwiney, the Republican Lord Mayor of Cork, was convicted by court martial and sentenced to two years' imprisonment for possession of an R.I.C. cypher and documents whose publication might cause 'disaffection'. MacSwiney vowed to go on hunger strike, and as the authorities now refused to apply the Cat and Mouse Act, he died in Brixton Prison, after seventy-five tense days, and was given impressive funerals both in Southwark Cathedral through the courtesy of the sympathetic Bishop Amigo and in Cork.[26] As Bishops Cohalan of Cork, O'Sullivan of Kerry and Browne of Cloyne, as well as several other prelates of Irish extraction had visited him in prison[27] and as the Lord Mayor's exemplary piety and his adoption of the ultimate appeal to moral force made him a sort of model of the kind of resistance the hierarchy had been urging, it was crucial that he should not be deemed a suicide. The question was too important to be left to the theologians. As MacSwiney's health sank, Rome was being pressed secretly by English Catholic spokesmen to pronounce forthwith that death by hunger strike was suicide. Details of what happened are unclear, but MacSwiney's biographer relates how 'a prominent Irish ecclesiastic' in Rome (very likely Mgr O'Hagan or Father Curran of the Irish College—the Irish hierarchy's main listening post in Rome) got wind of the overtures and pulled the necessary strings to delay a decision 'until the views of the Irish Bishops, together with all the circumstances of the case, could be ascertained from Ireland'.[28] Several weeks after MacSwiney's death, Count de Salis was still hopeful that his English friends in the Curia would procure a decision unfavourable to MacSwiney,[29] but in fact no decision on the point was ever forthcoming. It is a striking example of the strength of the Irish Church in Rome, which was discussed at the close of Chapter XIX. Moreover, it illustrated the subordination of theological discussion to political considerations in the minds and actions of the Irish hierarchy. Father Walter McDonald's entire career had been wrecked upon the treacherous shoals of that episcopal predilection, which can be seen operating more subtly on a larger problem at the end of 1920.

It is clear that many Volunteers, with the concurrence of some clergymen close to their organisation, had persuaded themselves that the killing of a policeman or British soldier was not murder, but an act of war. In denouncing an attack on police during August 1920, Bishop O'Dea enunciated the Church's position as follows:

Apart from self-defence and the execution of a just sentence after a fair trial, God allows the taking of life only by public authority in a just war, and no legitimate authority in Ireland has declared or authorized war against the police.[30]

This statement could cut two ways, for indeed the Dáil had not declared war or formally accepted responsibility for the acts of the I.R.A.[31] Was the Bishop hinting that if the Dáil would declare war, the Church would cease to regard the I.R.A. shootings as sinful? Perhaps not, but the fact that he would let slip a statement from which that inference could

be drawn suggests that ecclesiastics were beginning to contemplate such a contingency. As Father Coffey had taken
advantage of the bishops' alarm over the conscription threat
in 1918 to point them toward a bolder stance which they
implicitly adopted during the succeeding two years, might
they not, in view of their similar alarm over Black and Tan
reprisals, be nudged toward the even bolder stance of deeming a state of war to exist?

In October the *Irish Theological Quarterly* carried an
article entitled 'Some Theology about Tyranny' by Alfred
O'Rahilly, a layman who held a lectureship in mathematics
in University College, Cork. O'Rahilly, who had been publishing frequent articles in the Jesuit quarterly, *Studies*,
arguing that Catholicism was fully compatible with democratic theories of popular sovereignty, now developed the
thesis that the schoolmen were much more willing to grant
the right of resistance to tyranny—whether of usurpation or
oppression—than were the theologians who had come to
dominate Catholic thinking since the French Revolution.
'Many of the older theologians', he wrote, 'and most of the
canonists and summists contented themselves with declaring
bluntly that the usurper's laws were no laws and need not
be obeyed except under compulsion as the lesser of two
evils.'[32] Unlike Father Coffey, O'Rahilly studiously avoided
any mention of contemporary Ireland throughout the article,
but few could have missed his meaning when he listed 'two
obvious cases (which may happen together)' in which the
hypothesis that the usurper's administration 'is a lesser evil
than its absence . . . fails to hold':

(1) The usurpation may abandon all pretence at social and civil
administration, except of course, its phraseology; a highly moral
vocabulary is too useful to be readily discarded. The invaders
may resolve themselves into an immoral military self-legalized
terrorism, supplemented by sundry apparatus for extracting the
people's wealth. Their room is then a decidedly lesser evil than
their presence. (2) The nation may have so perfected its own
organization as to be able to secure social order (apart from acts
of war on the enemy's side), to establish courts and raise loans
and contributions. In this case, too, the last vestige of obligation
to respect the invader's so-called laws or authority is swept away.[33]

Usurpation is 'an objective verifiable fact which is initiated by a hostile invasion or by a public repudiation on the part of the community or by both', and

The Scholastic view is that the subsequent relationship of usurper and nation is essentially a state of war. Furthermore, they are of the unanimous opinion that in these circumstances each individual is free to commit acts of war on the unjust invader of his country.[34]

Finally, O'Rahilly argued, there is in such a case no need for a declaration of war, as the usurper 'by his continued occupation has declared war on the nation'.[35]

The next issue of the *Quarterly* carried an apology to the archdiocesan censor. 'Through some accident or other', the editors rather lamely explained, the proofs of O'Rahilly's article never reached the censor, and they were unaware of this fact 'until the issue was published and in the hands of the subscribers'.[36] They carried a reply to O'Rahilly by Father John Fitzpatrick entitled 'Some More Theology about Tyranny'. Fitzpatrick maintained that the older Catholic theologians cited by O'Rahilly in favour of popular supremacy had been thoroughly repudiated by the nineteenth-century popes. Further, he argued that a government, once established through usurpation, may, over time, attain a rightful jurisdiction by prescription. Interestingly, however, he conceded that 'Whether the people may actively resist an oppressor, as a last resort, and under specified conditions, is a free question among theologians.'[37] Such a right of resistance would, in Fitzpatrick's opinion, be founded 'not on any radical sovereignty of the people, but on the principle of self-defence', and he cited the anticonscription movement as an instance of such self-defence, directed not toward the overthrow of the government but toward 'the elimination of the oppression'.[38]

It is not easy to take the story of those lost printer's proofs at face value, but we will probably never know what actually happened. Probably Walsh was displeased that he, by his imprimatur, should seem to be endorsing an argument which would make the 'state of war' theory not just a tenable, but an obligatory, position for Catholics. The Fitzpatrick reply had the effect of reiterating the obvious—that the bishops

would retain freedom of action in these matters and not be
bound by any such lay scholastics as Professor O'Rahilly. The
most notable exercise of that episcopal freedom of action was
Bishop Cohalan's excommunication decree of 12 December.[39]
The decree followed several weeks of particularly intense terror and counter-terror around Cork in which seventeen
Auxiliaries were killed in ambush at Kilmichael, an old
inoffensive priest, Canon Magner, was shot by a mentally
unbalanced constable, and, on 11 December, a large part of
Cork was destroyed by Black and Tan arsonists. Cohalan's
decree seems to have had no more than a momentary effect
on the violence. Indeed, on the morning of the Kilmichael
ambush a friendly parish priest had heard the confessions of
the ambushing party, and, being assured that 'the boys' were
'going to attack the Sassanach [Saxon]', he gave them his
blessing.[40] After the decree, according to one I.R.A. commandant, 'most priests continued to administer the Sacraments,
and the I.R.A. practised their religion as before.'[41] Father
Dominic, O.F.M. Cap., the chaplain of one I.R.A. brigade,
sent a message to the brigade adjutant explaining that if the
Volunteers were acting 'as private persons', then their kid-
nappings, ambushes and killings 'would fall under the Excommunication'. As, however, they were acting 'by and with
the authority of the State—the Republic of Ireland', their
actions were 'not only not sinful' but were 'good and meritor-
ious'. 'Let the boys keep going to Mass and Confession and
Communion as usual,' Father Dominic counselled. 'Just as
there is no necessity for telling a Priest in Confession that
you went to Mass on Sunday so there's no necessity to tell
him one is in the I.R.A. or that one took part in an ambush
or kidnapping, etc.'[42]

Clearly, then, Cohalan had embarked on a line of policy
which was ineffective and could only hurt the Church's
interests. In an explanation of his decree one week after it
was issued, the Bishop seemed to be suggesting that the
Republican forces should assume a defensive posture against
reprisals.[43] Obviously, such a strategy would have been tantamount to suicide for young men whose main advantage in
the struggle was their ability to disappear in the face of
paramount force. Bishop Finegan did join in contradicting

the 'state of war' theory a few days later, but to the rhetorical question, 'What am I to say to the actual murderers?' he replied: 'Nothing. I leave them to the justice of God: He will punish them. But I pray, and let us all pray, that it may not be by final impenitence and everlasting death.'[44] Neither Finegan nor any other prelate followed Cohalan's lead by issuing an excommunication. Perhaps Sir James O'Connor hoped for a general application of Cohalan's policy when he called Cardinal Logue's attention 'to the "war" theory as expounded in several quarters'. The Cardinal's reply on 23 January 1921 was disappointing:

I brought the matter referred to in your letter under the notice of the bishops. They all declared, without exception, that they brought that matter under the notice of their priests at the usual theological conferences and strictly warned them against the very unsound teaching [i.e., that the shootings were justifiable] to which some priests are said to give expression.[45]

If, as this extract suggests, the hierarchy met in January, they issued no public statement. It was again a time for silence, for the possibility that the bishops might be offered the role of intermediaries between the two sides was again looming up, more substantially than it had the previous summer. By the close of 1920 the competition in frightfulness had reached its zenith with two noteworthy effects. First, it had caused some bishops to fear that the Nation might actually be defeated. When not only Canon Magner, but a Co. Galway priest, Father Griffin, were murdered by Crown forces and when an abortive attempt was made to kidnap and murder Bishop Fogarty and throw his body in the Shannon in a weighted sack,[46] there seemed briefly to be no limit to the atrocities which the British government would permit. Bishop Cohalan, in his explanation of his decree, had alluded to the fact that Crown forces had re-established British jurisdiction in areas which a few months earlier had enjoyed *de facto* Republican rule.[47] Bishop Finegan had invoked the 'well-grounded hope of success' clause of the ethics of war, which had seen little service since 1918, in pronouncing the 'war' theory invalid.[48]

There is some ground for believing that defeat was close at hand for the Republican forces at this time, but for the other effect of the reign of frightfulness: the fact that the press, the churches, the opposition parties and other outlets of opinion in England would no longer tolerate the beastliness of the Crown forces. The government's wilful prevarication as to what its forces were up to no longer convinced the British public. Influential military and police spokesmen were also dissatisfied with the government's policy, but mainly because ministers refused to accept responsibility for the reprisals. 'If these men ought to be murdered,' the candid Sir Henry Wilson had told Lloyd George in the early autumn, 'then the government ought to murder them.'⁴⁹ At the end of the year the cabinet yielded to the increasing pressure of opinion so far as to adopt in part the military profession's view. Martial law was finally declared in four south-western counties (four more were added early in January) and a policy of 'authorised' reprisals was put into effect. This latter policy 'proved far less effective than the rough and ready measures of the special police', Churchill noted. 'On the morrow of an outrage the military sallied forth in a brigade to burn a cottage; in the night the Sinn Féiners padded out and burned a country house.'⁵⁰ Churchill and his colleagues were facing an early example of what was to become a classic dilemma of the strong power facing a popular insurgency in a weak country. Such insurrections can indeed be put down, as soldiers are wont to urge, by barbaric methods which border on the genocidal, but no civilised people possessed of information and the power of the ballot box will allow its government to practise such methods for long enough to do the job. The English are a civilised people.

Notwithstanding the monstrous acts perpetrated with his condonation—with his connivance, the bishops believed— David Lloyd George was not a monster. He was a master politician who so manipulated the British political system as to stay in power for several years after his own party slipped into a coma. That expertise in the ways of British politics, however, was not matched by any comparable familiarity with the Irish political system. No Prime Minister since Rosebery had had less practical, direct experience of Irish affairs before accepting the premiership.⁵¹ None, moreover, had been served by such a kaleidoscopic succession of Chief

Secretaries with neither prior knowledge of Ireland nor the opportunity to learn before being replaced. The fact that Lloyd George's first serious peace overtures were made in December 1920, just at the moment when the government had, through martial law and 'authorised reprisals', to acknowledge its responsibility for the awful business it was engaged in, is testimony to his recognition of English political realities. In the background and conduct of those and succeeding peace overtures, however, one can find little appreciation of the Irish political system.

Ignorance of Ireland was not confined to the government. In May 1920 Randall Davidson, the Archbishop of Canterbury, had written to the Prime Minister noting that the Irish Catholic hierarchy occupied a position in Ireland corresponding to his own in England.[52] Now this is a remarkable statement, acknowledging, in effect, that the Catholic Church was the established church in Ireland. Yet Davidson's conclusion from this observation betrays his failure to understand the true implication of what he has said. 'As I try to put myself in their place,' the Primate of All England wrote, 'the kind of appeal I should expect to receive from the Government is something like this——.' He then outlined a sort of formal query to be addressed to the Irish bishops which recognised their 'great and responsible position' and asked their 'counsel' as they were 'recognized by the people as leaders'. The specific counsel to be sought, however, was an answer to the blunt question 'Do you, or do you not, back the loudly proclaimed desire and intention to secure an independent Irish republic?' Davidson envisaged the publication of the correspondence, and he reflected that, if he were in the position of the Irish Catholic archbishops, 'I should expect to be thus formally brought into the open.' His suggestion, which Lloyd George apparently rejected, is of interest because he imagined the Irish bishops' position to be different from his own only in degree. He seemed to think that their moral authority was something like his own —only slightly less vacuous. The fact that, unlike his own, their institution had not a mere symbolic ascendancy, but real power in a political system, seems to have nearly escaped him. They would no more submit to the foreclosing of their options through such a device as he contemplated than would Lloyd George himself—a fact the Archbishop perhaps perceived when he concluded rather pathetically 'that to ask the question thus, whether the answer be given or evaded—and I presume it would be evaded—is in every sense right'.

At that very moment, indeed, the government had had a golden opportunity to strike a bargain with the Irish hierarchy. The MacPherson Education Bill, which posed such a distinct threat to ecclesiastical interests, was still hanging fire. A government more sensitive to what was really important in Irish politics might have opened negotiations with the bishops to gain episcopal influence in favour of an Irish settlement in return for quietly dropping the Education Bill. Although there were rumours of negotiations with the Church over that bill,[53] there seems to be no evidence that they went beyond the bill itself, if indeed they even took place. Without extracting any advantage from the hierarchy's terror of the contemplated reforms, the government dropped the bill, as noted in Chapter XIX. In official minds, the duty of ecclesiastics was to articulate moral precepts from a sort of ivory tower by strict reference to established ecclesiastical teaching and authority. The notion that ecclesiastics might be politicians like themselves with very real stakes in the game was abhorrent to the ministry. Symptomatic of this outlook was a telegram sent in July 1920 by Curzon, the Foreign Secretary, to Count de Salis directing him to 'point out to Vatican from British Government that mixture of politics and cold-blooded murder is undermining whole fabric of morality in Ireland and suggest to His Holiness that from point of view of Christian morality it would be right to send a special representative to Ireland to inquire into matter and report to him upon it'.[54] This was an unabashed attempt to prompt a replay of 1887 when Pope Leo XIII sent a Mgr Persico to Ireland to collect information on the Plan of Campaign. The Persico mission had been followed by a papal rescript condemning the Plan and the tactic of boycotting, and no doubt Curzon hoped for a similar result.[55] He was to be disappointed. The Cardinal Secretary of State received the message coolly, but took the matter under advisement. After a few days he replied 'that the despatch of a delegate to Ireland would not be opportune but might, on the contrary, help to create excitement and hinder any pacificatory action on the part of the Pope'.[56] He went on to recall that the Holy See had been working for peace on the occasion of Cardinal Logue's visit to Rome for the Plunket beatification and assured de Salis that there would be no difficulty in reminding the Cardinal that the offences being committed in Ireland 'merit every reprobation from the point of view of Christian morality'.

Once again the Holy See was demonstrating its unwillingness to undercut the Irish bishops for the sake of winning British approbation. The 1880s were not to be replayed. Rome several times did try to nudge the British toward negotiations in which they would accept the national movement's right to speak for Ireland. As noted in Chapter XIX, an unsigned memorandum in the archives of the British mission to the Vatican dated 30 June 1920 records a suggestion by a Mgr Tedeschini that someone be commissioned 'to act as intermediary between the two nations, England to state the maximum she was prepared to give and Ireland to state the minimum she would accept—and try and strike some agreement'.[57] Despite the rumour late in July that Lloyd George was contemplating an offer through the bishops which would 'induce Sinn Féin to come to breakfast at Downing Street',[58] nothing came of Tedeschini's suggestion. A few months later the Cardinal Secretary of State pressed de Salis for a reason why conversations between the two sides could not begin. The Count replied by listing the difficulties—Irish insistence upon a Republic for the whole of Ireland, the 'creation of a *corpus separatum* in the North' because of excessive Irish insistence upon racial differences, and 'the difficulty of finding someone to speak for Ireland' (a specious claim). Gasparri expressed the view 'that the bishops, even if they did not control the situation, would be followed by the people if they put forward a moderate solution'. De Salis replied 'that I could not say that I felt sure that this was the case. Were they prepared to try?'[59] No doubt it would have been difficult to get the Irish hierarchy as a whole to initiate negotiations— a fact perhaps reflected in a hint from Gasparri a few weeks later that the Holy See itself, contrary to an earlier statement he had made to de Salis,[60] would now be prepared to take some peace initiative.[61] De Salis gave a discouraging response, citing recent evidence of growing feeling in England against the Catholic Church (and omitting, no doubt, similar evidence of feeling against the government's Irish policy).

The most promising source of ecclesiastical mediation, in any event, was neither the Irish hierarchy, whose power in the coming new order could easily be weakened by being too ready to promote a compromise, nor the Holy See, which was scarcely equipped to take an initiative as opposed to making a well-intentioned pronouncement, but from the ranks of churchmen in the Irish diaspora. In particular, Irish ecclesiastics from Australia who regularly passed through the British Isles on their way to and from Rome, would be well suited to the role of intermediaries. An Australian Catholic prelate of Irish birth or extraction would combine a symbolic attachment to, and a practical detachment from, each of the three elements of the Irish political system: the Church, the State and the Nation. Two men exactly fitting this description presented themselves in the latter half of 1920, and the contrast between their visits is instructive.

Mgr Mannix, who a decade earlier had been a veritable *bête noire* of young nationalists for his role in the O'Hickey case as President of Maynooth, had been made coadjutor to the Archbishop of Melbourne in 1912 and had succeeded to the see in 1917. An overseas Irish community could provide a heady atmosphere for an ecclesiastic. Freed from the responsibility to steer the Church safely between State and Nation, he could follow his natural inclination and veer sharply over to the Nation's side in his safe haven in the antipodes. Mannix soon became an outspoken champion of Irish national claims, and when the war came he led a nationwide campaign in Australia against the imposition of conscription. The fact that a majority of the Australian electorate agreed with him in a referendum on the subject only embittered those elements in the Australian governing class who had become infected with the romance of Empire. In a private audience with the Pope in December 1919, Sir Gerald Strickland, an English Catholic who had served as Governor of Tasmania, Western Australia and New South Wales, urged

His Holiness find some means of removing Mannix from his see. When the Pope—probably to suggest obliquely the difficulties in what he was asking—inquired 'how it would answer if Mannix were sent to Ireland', Strickland responded that personally he 'thought the agitators in Ireland were so numerous and virulent that one more or less would be hardly noticeable'.[62]

A few months after this amusing episode Mannix set out from Australia for his regular *ad limina* visit to Rome. Breaking his journey in Honolulu, he refused to stand for the playing of 'God Save the King', and as he travelled across the United States he contributed his rather bellicose oratory to the American agitation for Irish independence.[63] A curious sense of panic seems to have gripped British officialdom, and when the King heard a rumour that Mannix might be translated to Dublin in the event of Walsh's death, he suggested that the Vatican be asked to prevent such an eventuality.[64] Curzon dashed off a telegram to de Salis instructing him to make a veiled threat of a break in relations if Mannix were appointed to Dublin.[65] De Salis was dismayed that he was being asked to play such a high trump card when Walsh was still very much alive and Vatican officials were well aware of the embarrassment with which de Salis had had to disavow the remarks Sir Gerald Strickland had made to the Pope while he himself was on vacation.[66] Curzon, who was apparently piqued at being reminded of the diplomatic silliness of his hasty instructions, did alter the instructions so that de Salis was to use the hint of a break in relations to prompt the Vatican to stop Mannix's political utterances.[67] The Foreign Office also hoped that the Vatican might prevent Mannix from going to Ireland, as he planned to do, on his way to Rome,[68] but Vatican officials made it plain that they would not accept such a responsibility which properly rested with the civil authorities.[69] In consequence, the cabinet decided late in July to prohibit Mannix from landing in Ireland, and, as if to add a further element of farce, directed the Archbishop's ship, the *Baltic*, from Queenstown to Liverpool and even dispatched a destroyer to remove Mannix before it landed. Mannix then spent several months in London under the watchful eyes of Scotland Yard detectives.

The most Rome would do was to send Mannix an exhortation to moderate his language. What the Pope himself hoped was that Mannix might be able to use the popularity he had won through his exploits to assume the role of mediator.[70] It is not unreasonable to speculate that this was Mannix's intention all along. When Rome communicated to Mannix 'through an indirect channel that it would be advisable for him to come to Rome', he declined, but let it be known 'that if he is allowed to leave England, he would proceed very quietly and without demonstrations to Ireland and would use his influence to pacify the country and bring the opposing elements to a Conference'.[71] At the end of September Mannix publicly declared 'that if he went to Ireland, he would speak out against contention and to promote peace'.[72] Lloyd George, however, insisted upon treating the Archbishop as a suspicious person and adamantly refused even to allow— let alone dispatch—him to go to Ireland without exacting guarantees which would compromise his credibility as a free agent. In one exchange in November, conducted through Shane Leslie, the Foreign Office agreed to allow him to go on condition that Sinn Féin 'cease its terror . . . for a fortnight'[73]—a stipulation which, under the circumstances of Black and Tan counter-terror, would amount to unconditional surrender even if Mannix could have fulfilled it. Cardinal Gasquet, a prominent English Benedictine from Rome, urged Lloyd George to seek a settlement through Mannix, but the Prime Minister insisted that the Archbishop must make the first move and 'offer some sort of guarantees'.[74] In other words, Lloyd George had no intention of treating Mannix as a responsible intermediary.

Within a month another Irish-Australian prelate, Archbishop Clune of Perth, arrived in the British Isles on the way to Rome. Having witnessed some British reprisals in Co. Clare, and having lost his own nephew to police gunfire in what was described as an escape attempt in Dublin Castle, the Archbishop approached Lloyd George on 1 December in the hope that he could do something to promote peace. The Prime Minister encouraged such efforts and granted him facilities to see Griffith and Mac Néill who, rather to Lloyd George's dismay,[75] had been arrested without cabinet authorisation a few days after Bloody Sunday. Lloyd George clearly distinguished Clune from Mannix. In writing to Greenwood he described Clune as 'an Australian Bishop who during the war was chaplain to the Catholics in the Australian Forces. He is thoroughly loyal. His real anxiety is to promote peace and I think he can be trusted.'[76] Griffith put the Archbishop in touch with Collins who, following Griffith's arrest, had assumed the role of acting President. Collins and the Archbishop met in secrecy on 4 December and hammered out a formula for a truce, apparently consistent with the latter's conversation with Lloyd George.[77] Under this formula, the British would cease all acts of violence (including arrests and courts martial) and the Irish would do the same 'with the object of creating an atmosphere favourable to the meeting together of the representatives of the Irish people, with a view to bringing about a permanent peace'.[78]

It soon became evident that even if Lloyd George was willing to bend a bit to gain an end to the bloodshed, his flexibility was greatly restricted by those around him. In his letter introducing Clune to Greenwood, the Prime Minister had tried to nudge the Chief Secretary into real enthusiasm for the peace effort: 'It would . . . undoubtedly be a great triumph for you if, as the result of your policy, the leaders of the Republican Army were to give an undertaking that no new murders would be committed.'[79] Clune was apparently shrewd enough not to divulge the truce formula immediately to Greenwood when he returned from seeing Collins and Richard Mulcahy. These two, he told Greenwood, 'were much more reasonable than he expected they would be'— no doubt hoping to elicit from Greenwood a similar display of reasonableness. 'They all wanted peace,' the Archbishop had continued, 'but didn't want to give up their ideals.' The Chief Secretary's cynical gloss upon this remark in his report to Lloyd George was a signal of how the diehards in the cabinet and the military would respond to the whole enterprise: 'In plain English, they want to save their faces and their skins.'[80] Greenwood concluded his report with a straightforward avowal of his feelings:

We are coming to grips, but I feel we must be firm as to terms or any settlement will not be permanent. We are on top, with the House, the Country, and I believe, most Irishmen—wishing us well. Our position and strength is [*sic*] rapidly improving. The S. F. cause and organization is breaking up. . . .

There is no need of hurry in settlement. We can in due course and on our own and fair terms settle this Irish question for good.[81]

Lloyd George was thus made aware that he could expect footdragging from some of his closest associates.

Clune was quite alert to the intricacies of the situation. Sir John Anderson, the joint Under-Secretary, had apparently mentioned surrender of rebel arms as a condition some Castle officials would demand for any truce. When Clune returned to London, he urged Lloyd George to resist pressures from the military to add this condition. The Prime Minister himself added the stipulation that Collins and Mulcahy would have to disappear and not attend Dáil meetings during a truce, but he did not commit himself on the surrender of arms until after a conference with Bonar Law, Greenwood, Churchill, Anderson and Macready, who persuaded him to call explicitly for a surrender of arms in a Commons speech two days later. The diehard element had been strengthened by several gestures which could be construed as a weakening of Irish resolve. Among these gestures was a series of public telegrams from Father Michael O'Flanagan, who was still Vice-President of Sinn Féin, though he was scarcely closer to the real leadership of the Nation than he was to that of the Church, appealing to Lloyd George for truce negotiations.[82]

The surrender of arms was unthinkable to the Irish leaders, and Clune doggedly refused to accept this condition as non-negotiable on the British side. He secured a tentative waiver from Sir John Anderson in the Castle, and even seemed close to persuading Bonar Law shortly before Christmas,[83] but at a cabinet meeting on Christmas Eve, this condition was upheld.[84] Lloyd George's secretary, Philip Kerr, held several further conversations with the Archbishop, in the first of which he suggested some direct intervention by the Irish hierarchy to bring about a settlement. Clune was, by this time, quite well apprised of the Irish hierarchy's stance, having conferred at least with Fogarty, who had accompanied him during one of his meetings with Griffith and Mac Néill. He replied astutely 'that while the bishops would be willing to discuss matters with representatives of Dail Eireann, they "could not think of usurping the functions of the National Assembly"'.[85] He had learned more about the Irish political system in a month than Lloyd George had learned in four years. He did take up the theme of Irish ecclesiastical support for a settlement on a more realistic basis, however, in a final proposal to Kerr on 29 December. This proposal embodied a cease-fire for one month, a full meeting of the Dáil, and, significantly, the removal of the ban on Archbishop Mannix 'in order that he and Dr. Mannix should be free to go to Ireland with a view to helping to bring about a settlement in concert with the Irish bishops when the Dail assembled'.[86] The government not only rejected the proposal but refused even a separate request from Clune that 'as a personal favour' the ban on Mannix be withdrawn 'so that he could proceed to Ireland with him, as he thought it would be a moderating influence'.[87]

For the insistence upon surrender of arms and exclusion of I.R.A. leaders from the Dáil—which prolonged the bloodshed until July, when a truce was arranged without such conditions—we may blame Greenwood and the military and police spokesmen, whose weight with the conservative forces in the cabinet overrode Lloyd George's initial conciliatory attitude. Lloyd George, however, was a prisoner not only of his diehard colleagues but of his own lack of sensitivity to the Irish political system. He discriminated between Catholic bishops in terms of 'loyalty' and 'disloyalty', choosing Clune over Mannix because he was 'loyal'. He could not grasp what Clune himself recognised when he co-opted Fogarty to his mission and attempted to obtain Mannix's freedom of movement: that it was precisely the appearance of 'disloyalty' which gave the Church whatever influence she might have to serve his purposes. Clune left for Rome, bitterly disappointed, early in January, and Mannix followed two months later.[88]

During the early part of January, Lloyd George held some discussions with Father O'Flanagan, who came to London in the company of James O'Connor. The latter was extremely anxious to use his contacts with Cardinal Logue and his official position to promote some sort of settlement, and it was at this time that he made the appeal to Logue for a clarification of the Church's position on the 'state of war' theory.[89] These efforts were condemned to failure for three reasons: (1) the Church was not prepared to go along with the prescriptions of this 'Castle Catholic', as evidenced by Logue's evasive reply quoted above, (2) the State was now determined to place in operation the Better Government of Ireland Act which had received the royal assent in December, and (3) the Nation now enjoyed, for the first time in eighteen months, the effective leadership of its President who had finally returned from America after the arrest of Griffith and Mac Néill. Lloyd George had expressed doubts to Judge O'Connor over Father O'Flanagan's authority to negotiate,[90] and de Valera soon confirmed those doubts.[91]

As the President grasped the reins of his 'government', he made two poorly calculated moves which might have cost him dearly if he had not been adroit enough to adapt rapidly to the situation. He attempted without success to ship Collins off to the United States on a mission to achieve the unity among Irish-Americans which had eluded him.[92] Moreover, in a statement to the Dáil on 25 January, he offered the assessment that the enemy possessed superior forces while 'all Ireland had was the power of moral resistance'. He advocated a quiet shift to a policy of delaying tactics which could lighten 'the burden on the people'. 'This policy,' he suggested, 'might necessitate a lightening off of their attacks on the enemy.'[93] Only two deputies supported the President's policy in the debate which followed, and a number denounced the idea of slackening off attacks upon the Crown forces. These denunciations, however, tended to be focused more upon one of the supporters of the policy—Roger Sweetman, who had written a public letter urging peace shortly after Bloody Sunday—than upon de Valera. The President, in reply, stated that he had been 'purposely indefinite in his statement about easing off' and construed the sense of the meeting not as a censure of his ministry, but as 'a complete endorsement of their action'.[94] Moreover, he raised, but did not press, the question of 'whether it was feasible for them to accept formally the state of war that was being thrust upon them, or not'.[95] The President's abortive shift in policy reflected a number of considerations, including his genuine, expressed concern over needless suffering and his need to assert his authority vis-à-vis Collins, who had emerged as his strongest rival for dominance in the Nation's leadership. It also reveals, however, his sensitivity to the dangers on the Nation's clerical flank. Slackening off of such actions as the Kilmichael ambush might remove the greatest danger of episcopal repudiation. Frustrated in this effort, he would try another approach in the coming months.

The bishops' Lenten pastorals, which made little advance upon the attitudes of several months earlier, were cause for concern. Ironically, the effectiveness of the Black and Tan terror in destroying the Republican courts and other nonviolent organs of the Nation in areas which had been quite peaceful in mid-1920 had called forth I.R.A. actions. This fact was making it difficult, for example, for Archbishop Gilmartin to sustain the rationalisation on which his attitude had until recently been based—that the national movement was basically constitutional, at least in his diocese—and this difficulty is reflected in his pastoral.[96] Bishop Cohalan took the opportunity to elaborate his refutation of the theological justifications of the rebellion, denying explicitly that 'the proclamation of an Irish Republic by the Sinn Fein members of Parliament after the last general election' was 'sufficient to constitute Ireland a republic according to our Church teaching'.[97] Though only Bishop Coyne of Elphin seems to have joined Cohalan in taking up the issue on theological grounds,[98] the pastorals as a whole indicated that the bishops were becoming, if anything, more uneasy about the I.R.A. methods.

At about this time de Valera wisely drafted an appeal to the Irish hierarchy 'setting forth the claims of the Irish Republic' and asking the prelates, in the words of a Castle summarist into whose hands the document fell 'not to denounce crimes until they had heard an explanation from the Republican Gov't'.[99] Unable to carry his colleagues with him in a policy of reducing violence, the President had resolved, in some sense, to explain it. Though this might seem an impossible task, there was one line of approach which might be worthwhile. As has been noted, one consideration in the theological dispute over the ethics of war was the fact that the Dáil had never formally declared war. Furthermore, a passage in Logue's Lenten pastoral could be read as specifically condemning the tactics of guerrilla warfare as opposed to the 'war' itself:

Even in regular warfare, private assassination would be reprobated, condemned and punished. . . . If we made a clean fight for freedom, a fight which would have the blessing of God upon it, and would maintain and increase the sympathy which now is so universal, we would finally succeed.[100]

Whatever Logue may have meant by these curious words—and precision of expression was not his *forte*—it was felt in various quarters that guerrilla tactics contravened the rules of war. Some weeks later Archbishop Gilmartin, prompted perhaps by a widely publicised ruling of the Court of King's Bench that a 'state of war' existed in the martial law areas, told a Co. Mayo congregation that a state of war was something 'they did not want' there.

At the same time, he (the Archbishop) believed in the distinct nationality of Ireland as much as anyone, and her right to independence, but towards these ends they must adopt just means. Guerilla war was no war, nor was it war to shoot a policeman from behind a wall and run away. . . .
 Killing was always [murder], except in self-defence, or when done by public authority or in open, just warfare.[101]

If de Valera was unable to lower the level of violence, then, perhaps he could improve relations with the Church by the bolder—and subtler—approach of clarifying the status of the conflict and bringing its tactics into line with conventional standards. At a session of the Dáil on 11 March de Valera asked for and received permission to announce formal acceptance of 'a state of war with England', and of responsibility for I.R.A. actions, and on 30 March he issued such an announcement in a press interview.[102] Though he refused to disclaim guerrilla tactics,[103] the I.R.A. was in fact beginning to plan and execute a few larger, more conventional engagements with the British army which were less subject to the charge of unfairness.[104]

More important, for the moment, than changes in Dáil policy and I.R.A. tactics in preventing any awkward declaration by the bishops, was the fact that they once again—more tangibly than in the summer of 1920—found themselves in a position to promote negotiation. Lord Derby, who had recently ended a tour as British Ambassador in Paris but who at the moment held no official position, was persuaded by two English Catholic M.P.s to undertake private efforts for a settlement. He decided that the best way to establish his credentials on the Irish side as an intermediary was through Logue.[105] A Liverpool Catholic priest, Father James Hughes, was therefore dispatched to Armagh, where he found the Cardinal willing 'to do anything I can to assist in bringing about peace'.[106] When the hierarchy gathered for a general meeting during the first week of April, de Valera received (through Collins) a message from Fogarty, his principal contact in the hierarchy now that Walsh was near death. The Bishop of Killaloe asked the President to meet Derby, and he agreed.[107] The preoccupation of the bishops with the prospects for peace is reflected in the fact that on the following day Gilmartin met separately with both Greenwood and de Valera, though without any immediate result.[108]

Father Hughes came to Ireland again a few days later to arrange secret interviews for Derby with both Logue and de Valera.[109] De Valera, fearing that Logue might compromise Republican goals, made contact, through Father O'Flanagan, with Bishop Mulhern of Dromore, who was both geographically and ideologically closer to Logue than was, say, Fogarty. The President asked Bishop Mulhern to suggest two alternatives to Logue. He should either 'say flatly that the Irish people were fighting for a republic and, on the principle of self-determination, were entitled to what they had voted for', or, if he would not take this line, 'he should simply say that it was a matter for the temporal authorities—the Republican Government—and that discussions should be with them'.[110] Mulhern conveyed the Cardinal's response to Father O'Flanagan in a cryptic letter:

It may interest that Dr. friend of yours [de Valera] whom I met on Tuesday last to hear how his prescriptions have been carried out. His Eminence boasts that occasionally Doctors have given him medicines to take but he always preserves the bottles and boxes unopened! Before your friend's remedies reached, another dabbler in remedies had arrived. The patient says that this doctor came unsent by anyone, was anxious to prescribe, etc., that he is thoroughly convinced of the doctor's singleness of purpose, etc. He, however, gave him to understand that he would carry out your friend's recommendations, except that he would give up *yachting* and *rifle practice*! You know, I suppose that he is crazed on the former, whilst the latter is now out of the question. Beyond these two points no doctor can move him. And as he has been so healthy on his own way of going, he is likely to go on living in that way to the end, and to live longer.[111]

Apparently this letter was written after Derby had visited Logue,[112] and if Derby was the other 'dabbler in remedies' Mulhern must have been trying to assure de Valera that Logue had not suggested a willingness to agree behind the Nation's back to Dominion Home Rule or some other compromise, perhaps based on fiscal autonomy, between the Better Government of Ireland Act and the Republic. De Valera was convinced from his conversation with Derby, which took place in a house in Fitzwilliam Place in Dublin, that Logue had in fact exposed a line of division to the intermediary. He wrote to Collins: 'The old man up North has given them his views. I would like to use bad language, but I won't.'[113] In a letter to Harry Boland, one of the Dáil's representatives in America, he predicted 'a definite move . . . by the British to split the country on the basis of fiscal autonomy; they are intriguing to make this an issue between ourselves and the Church—that is the real meaning of the Derby affair.'[114] It was, of course, absolutely true that financial autonomy was one of the few points of the Republican programme which the Church had a direct interest in obtaining, apart from her interest in maintaining good relations with the Nation. The President, however, was overreacting when, in a letter to Bishop Fogarty, he described Derby as 'the scout' who

has been able to go back and report just that cleavage which Lloyd George should never have been shown. He will scarcely fail to take advantage of it. The anti-conscription attitude and combination alone can secure for Ireland any real peace. I would implore Your Lordship to work for it night and day.[115]

Lloyd George did use Derby's lines of communication with de Valera to pose the tricky question of whether the Irish leaders would refuse to enter negotiations 'unless the principle of complete independence is first conceded', to which the President gave an equally clever reply.[116] The fear, however, that Derby was a 'scout' for a government campaign to split the Church from the Nation by concessions on financial relations was unfounded. Indeed, at this very time Judge O'Connor was in London trying unsuccessfully to persuade the cabinet to make precisely such concessions—even attempting to enlist the help of the Archbishop of Canterbury in his efforts.[117]

There was certainly some sentiment in the cabinet for an unconditional truce and negotiation with a view to expanding 'Southern Ireland's' fiscal autonomy.[118] The most powerful elements in the coalition, however, still refused to consider truce except upon terms which would amount to rebel surrender. High priority was being given to getting the 1920 act into operation. Elections under the act were held, North and South, in the latter half of May. As Churchill reflected several years later, the effect in the North was to create

a separate entity clothed with constitutional form, possessing all the organs of government and administration, including police and the capacity of self-defence for the purposes of internal order. From that moment the position of Ulster became unassailable.[119]

Indeed, the anticipation of this result no doubt contributed to the intransigence of Ulster sympathisers in the cabinet toward negotiations between enactment in December and implementation in May. Predictably, 40 of the 52 seats in the Northern Ireland parliament were won by Unionists. In the South, only Sinn Féin candidates, pledged to boycott the new parliament of 'Southern Ireland', were nominated, except in the four Dublin University seats. The appointment of a Catholic Lord Lieutenant, Lord Fitzalan (formerly Lord Edmund Talbot)—a legal possibility now for the first time since the enactment of the penal code—was treated with contempt, and the 'Southern Ireland' parliament was rendered a nullity.

As the June meeting of the hierarchy approached, de

Valera began intensive efforts to persuade them 'to give straight-out recognition to the Republic'.[120] He wrote to Fogarty urging, in the words of a Castle summary,

that the Bishops should make a 'straightforward recognition' of the facts concerning Ireland's cause in order to startle the world into a consciousness of the real issue, to hearten the people to continue the struggle, and to nullify the propaganda 'which is almost as much Britain's right arm against us as her military forces'. He goes on to say that such pronouncement, if the present struggle goes on, will prevent it from degenerating to a squalid civil riot, and maintain it at its proper level in the eyes of the world in its true character as a 'national war of liberation'.[121]

Anxious to capitalise on the victory, if he was successful, the President instructed his Publicity Department to 'be ready on Tuesday to see that the Newspaper headlines are: THE IRISH BISHOPS RECOGNIZE THE REPUBLIC'.[122] De Valera went personally to Maynooth on 21 June to present his case to the hierarchy.[123] There is an oral tradition among the Irish clergy that after the President had retired from the room, Bishop Kelly, who had never reconciled himself to the eclipse of the Irish Parliamentary Party, threatened to violate the rule of unanimity on resolutions of the hierarchy and publicly declare his dissent if the recognition were granted. In any event, the recognition de Valera sought was not forthcoming. The bishops did, however, pass a resolution which, after thanking the Pope for a recent pronouncement calling for reconciliation, declared: 'Until repression ceases, and the right of Ireland to choose her own form of government is recognized, there is no prospect that peace will reign amongst us, or that the reconciliation which his Holiness so ardently desires will be accomplished.'[124] While this statement made little advance upon earlier episcopal pronouncements, its issuance at this critical juncture is evidence that the bishops wanted at least to appear responsive to the Nation's leader.

On the following day, the King opened the Northern Ireland parliament with a speech appealing for peace, and, ironically, de Valera was arrested, apparently by accident. Within twenty-four hours, the President was released, to his own astonishment, and two days later Bishop Mulhern handed him a letter from Lloyd George making 'a final ap-

peal, in the spirit of the King's words' for a conference between himself, de Valera and Sir James Craig, the new Prime
Minister of Northern Ireland.[125] This time there were no
conditions about surrender of arms or restrictions upon the
Dáil. Indeed, according to Judge O'Connor, the new initiative was facilitated by Sir Alfred Cope getting into touch
'through the Under Secretary, an Irish Catholic, Mr. Mac-
Mahon, who is a friend of every Catholic ecclesiastic in
Ireland . . . with clerics who were in touch with the men
who pulled the strings—Richard Mulcahy and Michael
Collins'[126]—i.e. the very men who six months earlier were
told they would have to 'disappear' before the Dáil could
meet openly. The way was now open to a settlement in which
the Nation would supplant the State. The Church had picked
her way through the treacherous passage leading to this point
with skill and determination. She would be amply rewarded.

Epilogue and Conclusion

WITHIN two weeks arrangements for a cease-fire were concluded, and on 14 July 1921 the President of the Republic of Ireland sat down at 10 Downing Street in conference with the Prime Minister of the United Kingdom of Great Britain and Ireland. An elaborate minuet would be danced around that contradiction in the next five months. After a week of conversations, Lloyd George made an offer of dominion self-government subject to free trade between the two islands, Irish assumption of a share of responsibility for the war debt, and certain reservations on military and naval matters. It would be up to 'Irishmen themselves to determine by negotiations between themselves' whether this arrangement would be established for the whole of Ireland or separately for North and South.[1] De Valera rejected the offer but, at Lloyd George's insistence, took it back to Dublin and presented it to the Dáil ministry, who confirmed his action, as did the full Dáil, unanimously, on 23 August. There ensued a month-long correspondence between de Valera and Lloyd George, treating mainly the status each government would accord the other in negotiations which were finally commenced in the middle of October.

Throughout this preliminary shadow-boxing and the serious bargaining which followed, the Church kept an extremely low profile. In mid-August the Catholic Lord Lieutenant, Fitzalan, wrote to the Prime Minister that he had heard that Logue and Fogarty had conferred in Dublin and agreed 'that things should move slowly with a view to the weight of evidence in favour of acceptance sinking into the minds of the people'.[2] However, not all ecclesiastics were quite so patient. After the publication of one of the Prime Minister's letters, Bishop Cohalan, according to T. M. Healy, 'was innocent enough to . . . wire Armagh *in Latin* asking for meeting of Bishops to instantly accept George's offer. I dont know if you ever heard,' Healy chortled,

that Latin is a dead language alleged to have been spoken in Rome (I dont believe this) but strange to say the Shins got the telegram & actually were able to decipher it (marvellous chaps). Fancy the tongue of Caezar [*sic*] & Cicero & Pontius Pilate translated at the Mansion House.[3]

Healy had also heard that de Valera was in communication with Logue 'about Ulster',[4] but the Cardinal assured Lord Derby, who had written to ask that he urge acceptance of the British offer,[5] that he was 'pretty much excluded from the counsels of Mr. de Valera and his party'.[6] From what he could gather, however, de Valera's insistence upon recognition of Ireland as an independent entity in the correspondence with Lloyd George was not intended 'to close the door against negotiations'. The Cardinal believed that 'the majority of the people' would be satisfied by the 'general terms' of Lloyd George's offer and that 'Any further action on the part of de Valera's following will not be a holding out for a Republic or separation, but mere manoeuvring to secure favourable terms on the details of the Prime Minister's proposals. It cannot be denied that there are many details which require very careful handling, especially the financial arrangement between the two countries.' Any such intervention on his own part as Derby was suggesting would be 'imprudent', for 'If any miscarriage took place, unfavourable to Ireland, in arranging those details the responsibility would be laid upon my shoulders.' Moreover, 'in such an important matter' he could only act in concert with the other bishops. There was 'likely to be a clearer view of things' at the time of the hierarchy's regular October meeting, so Logue deemed it 'inexpedient for them to strike in at present'. His personal view was that Lloyd George had made 'an offer which in its general terms is fair and satisfactory, and which, if details were fairly and satisfactorily arranged would bring lasting peace'. He hastened, however, to add that the chief obstacle to peace was 'Belfast and the miserable Parliament which the Ministry in an evil moment have set up there'. He went on to lament a new anti-Catholic pogrom which had broken out in the North and the inflammatory speeches of members of the Northern Ireland parliament 'urging the Orange Lodges to be more aggressive, threatening to make an end of "Romanis", threatening to seize and secularise our Catholic schools.'

When negotiations opened in London on 11 October, the Irish delegation—Griffith, Collins, Robert Barton and two lawyers, Eamon Duggan and George Gavan Duffy—faced a formidable array of British political talent including Lloyd George, Austen Chamberlain, Birkenhead, Churchill and Greenwood. De Valera remained in Ireland where he busied himself selling to doctrinaire Republicans a scheme by which Ireland would remain a Republic, outside the Empire but 'externally associated' with it. Thus was created an unfortunate division of labour by which the President sought to achieve agreement within the Nation at the very time his principal subordinates were trying to forge an agreement between the Nation and the State. Discussions in London soon focused upon the symbolic issues—allegiance and relationship to the Empire—and the Ulster question, all other matters being relatively easy to agree upon. Accounts of the negotiations generally depict the Irish side as deliberately trying to avoid hostile confrontation over the symbolic issues in hopes that if discussions had to be broken off the occasion for this action might be Ulster's refusal to join in a united Ireland rather than British refusal to recognise the Republic. A break over the latter issue, it was reasoned, might lead to a resumption of the war, whereas lack of agreement because of Ulster's obstinacy would not. The failure of this strategy is attributed in large measure to the undoubted political wiliness of Lloyd George. In early sessions of the conference the Irish delegates repeatedly called for guarantees of the 'essential unity' of Ireland, brushing aside a pragmatic proposal from Lloyd George for a plebiscite over the entire nine counties of Ulster.[7] At one point they thought they had a commitment from Birkenhead and Lloyd George to resign if the North could not be brought into an all-Ireland settlement on some basis. When Craig proved recalcitrant, however, Lloyd George put forward the idea of a Boundary

Commission which would readjust the border to reflect the wishes of the inhabitants. Griffith's mind, steeped as it was in the economics of Friedrich List, was easily persuaded that the four Protestant counties which would be left after such readjustment would not be an economically viable unit and would hence throw in their lot with the rest of Ireland. The Prime Minister then depicted himself as fighting the diehard elements of the coalition and allowed Griffith to view the Boundary Commission idea as a tactical manoeuvre in that fight.[8] He thus wooed Griffith into making unguarded remarks which were later used to torpedo the 'break on Ulster' strategy.

Yet in a longer perspective, the subordination of Ulster to the symbolic issues—indeed the erection of Ulster itself into a symbolic issue through precipitate rejection of the early plebiscite offer—reflects more than a negotiating strategy. As early as 10 August de Valera had explicitly renounced force as a means of achieving Irish unity in his correspondence with Lloyd George and repeated the naïve nationalist dogma, which surely he did not believe, that if only the British government would stand aside 'we can effect a complete reconciliation'.[9] The simple truth was that Ulster's actual inclusion in a self-governing Ireland (as opposed to some theoretical recognition that it was part of Ireland) occupied a low position in the priorities of the current generation of national leaders. They had come to power precisely on the implicit principle of subordinating the Ulster difficulty to the symbolic issues. They were the beneficiaries of a political system which operated only outside the Protestant North-east. Within the conventions of that system they had achieved the Church's sanction for their impending political legitimacy—her requirement of constitutional methods having been bent to the limit, but her requirement of protection of her vital interests being maintained intact. There were only two ways of attempting to woo the North into the settlement: (1) to abandon the symbols of separate nationhood, or (2) to give some indication of abandoning the defence of the Church's interests. The former of these alternatives would have meant denial of the very *raison d'être* of the present national leadership. They were prepared to take only tiny, halting steps in that direction, totally inadequate to the task. The second alternative, given their questionable fulfilment of the Church's requirement for constitutional action, would have undercut the only secure basis for their legitimacy within the Irish political system. Indeed, not the slightest step in this direction seems to have been so much as contemplated, though the Irish leaders would have been willing to accept a locally autonomous Northern parliament within a self-governing Ireland—Northern autonomy, much to the detriment of the Church's vital interests there, being already an accomplished fact.

The symbolic issues—allegiance and the Republic—thus occupied most of the conference's attention, their importance underscored shortly after it opened by an indignant reaction from de Valera to an exchange of telegrams between Pope Benedict and King George. The Pope's expression of joy over the negotiations had been inoffensive in content, though its being sent only to the King and not to de Valera emphasised that the Vatican did not recognise the Republic. The King replied that he prayed that the conference 'may achieve a permanent settlement of the troubles in Ireland and may initiate a new era of peace and happiness for my people'. When the telegrams were published, de Valera dashed off one of his own to the Pope voicing confidence 'that the ambiguities in the reply sent in the name of King George V will not mislead you, as they may the uninformed, into believing that the troubles are "in" Ireland or that the people of Ireland owe allegiance to the British King'.[10] During November the two delegations produced a draft agreement containing an oath of allegiance and a form of association with the Empire which seem to the outsider only a shade away from de Valera's 'external association' idea. The North would be permitted to opt out, but in that event the Boundary Commission plan would come into effect. Free trade between the two countries was provided for, as were some contribution to be determined later to the war debt and British use of certain defence facilities. In consultations with the Dáil cabinet early in December the delegates found de Valera and several of his colleagues gravely disturbed by the proposals under discussion, and a breakdown of the negotiations seemed imminent when the delegates returned to London. Then on 5 December Lloyd George presented an ultimatum: the draft agreement must be signed immediately or war would be resumed within seventy-two hours. Though the Irish delegates were formally plenipotentiaries, they had secretly agreed to check with the Dáil cabinet before signing anything, and in their anxiety they apparently never thought of using the telephone. After much soul-searching, they signed.

In Ireland the agreement was greeted with relief and joy by the Church. Six prelates—Logue, Gilmartin, McKenna (Clogher), Hackett (Waterford), Gaughran (Meath) and Hallinan (Limerick)—immediately made public statements welcoming it.[11] On the following day Fogarty joined the chorus with an effusive statement:

This Treaty is worth the bitter price paid for it. Ireland is now free to live her own life without interference from outsiders.

The men who made it will be immortal.

Its moral effect throughout the world will be worth half a navy to England.

I have confidence that the Irish Free State will soon have the cordial allegiance of every Irishman. Belfast will find Dublin not an enemy, but a warm-hearted friend.

This peace is God's gift.[12]

On the very same day, however, Fogarty's friend de Valera publicly repudiated the agreement and summoned the Dáil for 14 December to consider it.

The hierarchy met on 13 December in a more cautious mood than some of its individual members had exhibited before they realised the deep division the Treaty would precipitate in the national leadership. The resolution they published praised 'the patriotism, ability and honesty of purpose with which the Irish representatives have conducted the struggle for national freedom', and expressed confidence that the Dáil would 'be sure to have before their minds the best interests of the country and the wishes of the people to whom they and we happily belong'.[13] No judgement on the merits of the Treaty was given, though several bishops did individually endorse it during the Dáil deliberations. The Dáil was soon embroiled in an acrimonious debate over the Treaty and de Valera's 'external association' alternative known as

'Document No. 2'. On 7 January 1922 the Treaty was ratified by 64 to 57, and de Valera resigned the presidency. Griffith and Collins took over the reins of government for the transitional period, with Griffith as President under the 1919 Dáil constitution and Collins as chairman of a parallel 'Provisional Government' specified in the Treaty.

De Valera formed a new Republican Party and was soon drawn into alliance with a significant fraction of the I.R.A. officers who repudiated both the Treaty and the Provisional Government at a convention held, in defiance of a ban by the Dáil cabinet, in late March and early April. There were hopes for peace, based upon an agreement between de Valera and Collins to have their two factions nominate an agreed panel of Sinn Féin candidates, reflecting the existing proportions of Pro- and Anti-Treaty sentiment in the Dáil, for the new elections in June. Sporadic violence had been occuring since early in the year, however, and late in June civil war began in earnest when the Provisional Government decided to bombard a garrison of Anti-Treaty troops in the Four Courts. In ferocity and bitterness the new war surpassed even the one terminated a year earlier. Collins himself was fatally shot from ambush in August, ten days after Griffith had died of a cerebral haemorrhage, and leadership of both the Dáil cabinet and the Provisional Government (which formally became the Irish Free State government in December 1922) fell to William Cosgrave. The Dáil elected in June assembled in September, but without the thirty-six Anti-Treaty members of the panel who had been elected but were now 'on the run', and voted confidence in Cosgrave's government. De Valera formed an irregular Republican government to which the Anti-Treaty guerrillas gave their allegiance. The Provisional Government prosecuted the war ruthlessly, executing seventy-seven of the 12,000 prisoners they took. Finally, in May 1923, de Valera called upon his harried supporters to cease fire.

In the early months of 1922 a number of bishops made clear their support for the Treaty, but in general they relied upon the voters to elect candidates who favoured it in the coming election. At this stage de Valera still seemed committed to constitutional opposition, a kind of behaviour the bishops were most anxious to see restored to Irish politics. Some of them pointedly urged that the elections be free from intimidation, and several warned against political violence which was already beginning to reappear at the time of their Lenten pastorals.[14] By the time the hierarchy met in April the army had repudiated the Provisional Government and civil war was imminent. The bishops issued a statement expressing their own view that acceptance of the Treaty was best for Ireland's welfare, but recognising it as 'a legitimate question for national discussion and debate' on which 'every Irishman is entitled to his own opinion, subject, of course, to truth and responsibility to God'.[15] They pronounced a 'solemn censure and reprobation', however, upon 'the claim that the army, or a part of it, can, without any authority from the nation as a whole, declare itself independent of all civil authority in the country'. There could be no doubt, in practice, what the 'organ of supreme authority in the country' was, 'as long as the Dáil and the Provisional Government act in unison'. Unless 'the young men connected with this military revolt' heeded 'this fundamental maxim of social morality', they would 'involve themselves and their followers in conscientious defects of the gravest character', for

When in the prosecution of these principles they proceed to make shameful war upon their own country they are parricides and not patriots. When they shoot their brothers on the opposite side they are murderers. When they injure public and private property they are robbers and brigands, bound to restitution—all sins and crimes of the most heinous guilt.[16]

Nevertheless, the bishops hoped for a constitutional resolution of the crisis. Not until all such hope was exhausted and the Civil War was well under way, did the hierarchy, at their October meeting, pronounce a general excommunication on the Anti-Treaty forces for as long as they persisted in making war on the government.[17] There were, no doubt, a few priests who continued to administer the sacraments to the Irregulars.[18] Significantly, some of the Anti-Treatyites actually organised an appeal to Rome against the bishops' action.[19] De Valera was no doubt writing with deep sincerity when at the low ebb of his fortunes, in April 1923, he told Mgr Luzio, an envoy from the Vatican studying conditions in Ireland:

Please give to the Holy Father my dutiful homage. Though nominally cut away from the body of Holy Church we are still spiritually and mystically of it, and we refuse to regard ourselves except as his children.[20]

Although a few of the Anti-Treatyites nurtured grudges against the Church for decades, de Valera, with the end of hostilities in 1923 and his return to constitutional politics in 1927, did not become the focus for any anticlerical party. Indeed, by 1929 the Fianna Fáil Party which he founded had begun to promote itself as a more truly Catholic party than Cosgrave's Cumann na nGaedheal.[21]

The Irish political system, as I have used that term, came to an end in 1921 during the interval between the Truce and the Treaty. As far as the Church was concerned, the Nation had supplanted the State, details to be settled in due course. When some of the national leaders tried to erect certain of those details as matters of principle they imagined that the system was still in operation: the Provisional Government was but a tool of the British State and they the true representatives of the Irish Nation. The Church would have none of it. In her eyes the game was up: there were no longer any ambiguities over political legitimacy in Ireland. For several months she tried gently to coax the Anti-Treatyites into regarding their grievances as the internal politics of the Nation-State. When they persisted in considering them an extension of the old quarrel between State and Nation, she visited upon them her most extreme penalties.

In the years covered by this study the Church so played out her role in the Irish political system that she achieved, for a half-century at any rate, a position in the new political order that might be the envy of churchmen throughout the world. The Republic of Ireland, like its predecessor, the Irish Free State, has not been a theocracy, but it is a State in which the Church has had considerably more influence than any ordinary interest group.[22] A significant element in the Church's favourable position consists of interests which she built up under the Irish political system before 1921, particularly in education. These interests had been achieved and maintained because she had never veered completely over to the side of the Nation in that system, but they survived in the new order because she had steered clear of whole-hearted alignment with the State as well. She had respected and exploited the conventions established during Parnell's ascendancy, which Emmet Larkin has described as 'an informal but effective concordat'.[23] Successive Ministers for Education since 1922 have—like the National Board before them—seen their task as primarily to cater to ecclesiastical wishes within the funds at their disposal. Although the old National Board was abolished in 1922,[24] none of the basic reforms which the bishops feared might accompany such a move—diminution of managerial authority, rate-aid, popular control, amalgamation —made any substantial headway until at least the mid-1960s. Moreover, during its early years the new State responded to clerical ideals by enacting certain features of the Catholic moral code into law, particularly in the area of sexual morality and family relations.

Although the source of the Church's influence since 1921 is the same as it was before—the extremely strong religious devotion of the people—the reasons for its political effectiveness have changed. As far as the southern twenty-six counties are concerned, the Church is no longer an arbiter between two primary political institutions both claiming sovereignty (though in the North the words and actions of Catholic churchmen are sometimes read in that light). There is, moreover, no serious question of her using the ultimate sanction of excommunication upon any of the principals of politics in the Republic, though, of course, the I.R.A. and similar organisations are still subjected to such penalties. The primary means by which the Church exercises influence in the Republic must surely be the expectation any politician has that the active disapproval of his actions by the Church will cost him votes—more votes than would the disapproval of any other agency. It may be that this fact has given the Church more influence since 1921 than she exercised before independence because of a convention that perished at that time. No longer did the politics of Nation *versus* State dictate the convention that unity behind a single national party was essential. Throughout the period of this study most of the constituencies outside the North-east were usually uncontested. Where 'no contest' was the norm, the Church, or any other agency that wanted to influence the policy of the Irish Parliamentary Party or of a particular M.P. through electoral politics, had to produce not only an alternative candidate (a 'factionist') but also a credible threat of capturing fifty per cent of the vote *de novo*. It was not a game frequently played after Healy's 1900 disgrace. When the Nation became the State, however, the politics of consensus gave way to a well-functioning democracy in which there would normally be two or more candidates, and a swing of only a few percentage points in the vote could be decisive. As Professor Larkin has pointed out, it might have been otherwise: the politics of consensus might have become the tyranny of the general will. That it did not is due in large measure to the Church's long-standing insistence that the Nation's representatives play the game of politics according to rules.[25]

The change from consensus politics to well-functioning democracy could redound to the Church's benefit, however, only by virtue of the fact that her actions had created no anticlerical elite substantial enough to lead a major political party. Both Fianna Fáil and Cumann na nGaedheal (or Fine Gael after the mid-1930s) have, for at least part of the time been willing to play the game of trying to appear more solicitous of Catholic interests than their opponents.[26] In part this is because there have been no English Liberals—or, more to the point, no Ulster Protestants—looking over their shoulders with more than an academic interest.[27] Perhaps equally important, however, is the fact that the Church so defined the conventions of the Irish political system that the generation which assumed power in the Nation-State in 1921 envisaged the Nation as fundamentally Catholic.[28] Among its earliest 'political' experiences was the process by which Protestants were made uncomfortable in the Gaelic League around 1900, and its rise to power in the latter years of the First World War was based in part on relegating the Ulster question to a secondary priority.

The Church paid a significant price for the happy situation she gained in the South. Predictably, Northern Ireland opted out of the Free State, and the Boundary Commission, which Catholics hoped would award most predominantly Catholic territory to the Free State, miscarried. The Northern

Ireland government has not, to say the least, been animated by tender solicitude for Catholic interests. In particular, Catholic schools in the North were soon placed at a substantial financial disadvantage vis-à-vis the secular schools which the Northern government established and to which most Protestants have sent their children. At no time, presumably, did the bishops consciously decide to write off their interests in the North for the sake of gaining a predominantly Catholic State in the South. Yet the fact that little account need be taken of Protestant interests and prejudices in the Republic's politics[29] has undeniably smoothed the way to achievement of the Church's ends there. Within the 'given territory' in which the Nation could successfully supplant the State, the Church, in the period of this study, made the Irish political system serve her interests with consummate skill and determination.

Notes

Introduction

1. Louis Paul-Dubois, *Contemporary Ireland*, ed. T. M. Kettle, Dublin 1908, 492.
2. Diary of Sir Horace Plunkett, 17 Jun. 1907 (Sir Horace Plunkett Foundation for Co-operative Studies, London, hereafter cited Plunkett Diaries).
3. Max Weber, *From Max Weber: Essays in Sociology*, trans. and ed. H. H. Gerth and C. Wright Mills, New York 1946, 78. The phrase 'monopoly of the legitimate use of physical force' is italicised in this translation.
4. A. V. Dicey, *Introduction of the Study of the Law of the Constitution*, 5th ed., London 1897, 347ff.
5. F. W. Maitland, *The Constitutional History of England*, paperback ed., Cambridge 1961, 398.
6. Conor Cruise O'Brien, *Parnell and His Party, 1880–90*, 2nd impression, Oxford 1964, 184. My italics.
7. *Ibid.*, 89-90.
8. There was, however, some restriction of the clergy's role in the selection of candidates with the decay of the nominating convention system between 1885 and 1890 (*ibid.*, 260-1).
9. The fullest account of these events is F. S. L. Lyons, *The Fall of Parnell, 1890–91*, London 1960. For the Church's role in the affair see three articles by Emmet Larkin, 'The Roman Catholic Hierarchy and the Fall of Parnell', *Victorian Studies* IV (Jun. 1961); 'Mounting the Counter-Attack: The Roman Catholic Hierarchy and the Destruction of Parnellism', *Review of Politics* XXV (Apr. 1963); 'Launching the Counter-attack: Part II of the Roman Catholic Hierarchy and the Destruction of Parnellism', *ibid.* XXVIII (Jul. 1966).
10. Cruise O'Brien, *Parnell*, 85-6; L. P. Curtis, Jr, *Coercion and Conciliation in Ireland, 1880–1892, A Study in Conservative Unionism*, Princeton 1963, 270-7.

11. At the present time the tiny diocese of Ross is 'in the charge' of the Bishop of Cork, though it was administered by its own bishop in the period of this study. This reform, for all practical purposes, has reduced the number of independent dioceses to twenty-six. On the other hand, the hierarchy's numbers are almost always augmented by one or more auxiliary or coadjutor bishops. On the details of Irish Catholic ecclesiastical polity see Jean Blanchard, *The Church in Contemporary Ireland*, Dublin 1963. See also John H. Whyte, 'The Appointment of Catholic Bishops in Nineteenth-Century Ireland', *Catholic Historical Review* XLVIII (Apr. 1962).

12. There is a fairly good biography of Walsh, though it concentrates on the years before the period of this study: Patrick J. Walsh, *William J. Walsh, Archbishop of Dublin*, Dublin 1928. See also T. Joyce, 'Walsh, William Joseph', in *New Catholic Encyclopedia* XIV.

13. Shane Leslie, 'Logue, Michael', *Dictionary of National Biography* (1922–30).

14. Richard Burdon Haldane (1st Viscount Haldane), *Richard Burdon Haldane: An Autobiography*, Garden City, New York 1929, 142.

15. Cf. Larkin in *Review of Politics* XXV, 181-2.

16. David James O'Donoghue, 'Croke, Thomas William', *D.N.B.* (1901–11).

17. Curtis, *Coercion and Conciliation*, 234-35, 274-75.

18. *Ibid.*, 256, 276.

19. Larkin in *Victorian Studies* IV, 332.

I: Two Leagues

1. Maud Gonne MacBride, *A Servant of the Queen: Her Own Story*, Dublin 1950, 216-36.

2. On the C.D.B., see William L. Micks, *An Account of the Constitution, Administration and Dissolution of the Congested Districts Board for Ireland, from 1891 to 1921*, Dublin 1925, A useful survey of the Irish economy at this time is Department of Agriculture and Technical Instruction for Ireland, *Ireland: Industrial and Agricultural, Handbook for the Irish Pavilion, Glasgow International Exhibition, 1901*, Dublin, n.d.

3. Michael MacDonagh, *The Life of William O'Brien*, London 1928, 148; see also *Fourth Report of the Congested Districts Board for Ireland . . . 1895*, p. 11 [C. 7791], H.C. 1895, lxxxix.

4. [Intelligence Notes, United Irish League] (P.R.O., C.O. 903/8/12-13). This very useful volume of 'Confidential Print' covers the activities of the U.I.L. from its foundation until the end of 1901. Like all police reports it must be used with caution. In recording the activities of clergy it is not absolutely thorough. Many U.I.L. meetings were reported with no mention of the presence or absence of clergy. I have tried, therefore, to generalise only where there appears to be a fair sample of reports in which clerical activity or inactivity is mentioned.

5. *Ibid.*, 903/8/14.   6. *Ibid.*   7. *Ibid.*, 903/8/17.
8. *Ibid.*, 903/8/23.   9. *Ibid.*, 903/8/20.   10. *Ibid.*
11. *Ibid.*, 903/8/18, 22-3, 25-6, 28, 29-30.
12. *Ibid.*, 903/8/20.   13. *Ibid.*, 903/8/28.   14. *Ibid.*
15. *Ibid.*, 903/8/35, 37, 40.
16. *Ibid.*, 903/8/35, citing *Freeman's Journal and National Press* (Dublin) (hereafter cited *FJ*), 17 Nov. 1898.
17. *Ibid.*, 903/8/24-5.   18. *Ibid.*, 903/8/29-30, 33.
19. *Ibid.*, 903/8/31.   20. *Ibid.*
21. *Ibid.*, 903/8/35, 36, 39, 40, 42, 44. Early clerical resistance at Straide seems to have later been abandoned (*ibid.*, 903/8/32, 69).
22. *Ibid.*, 903/8/39.   23. *Ibid.*, 903/8/42-3.
24. Larkin in *Review of Politics* XXVIII, 360-5. For evidence of continuing Parnellite sentiment in at least one priest see C.O. 903/8/22.
25. William O'Brien, *An Olive Branch in Ireland and Its History*, London 1910, 84-5.
26. C.O. 903/8/23, 24, 25, 33, 35, 39, 47, 62.
27. *Ibid.*, 903/8/132-3, 144.
28. *Ibid.*, 903/8/161.   29. *Ibid.*, 903/8/143-4.
30. Between November 1898 and April 1900 clerical participation in U.I.L. activities was reported from fourteen places in Elphin diocese (*ibid.*, 903/8/40, 44, 54, 58, 69, 77, 130, 139, 146, 147, 151, 159, 161, 162-3). The only reported case of a negative clerical response in the diocese in this period, at Ballygar, was complicated by a dispute over whether division of a local grazing farm should be carried out under the auspices of the U.I.L. or of the Co-operative Society (*ibid.*, 903/8/55-6), and the priest later became an active League supporter (*ibid.*, 903/8/162-3).
31. *Ibid.*, 903/8/54.   32. *Ibid.*, 903/8/162-3.
33. *Ibid.*, 903/8/174.

34. *Ibid.*, 903/8/84-5, 138, 139, 169. In one incident at Cooneal, on 22 October 1899 (*ibid.*, 903/8/89), the clerical position was ambiguous, but the significance of the incident seems to be that it illustrates the powerlessness of the clergy to come to terms with the movement within the limitations of diocesan policy.

35. A priest had presided at a meeting in Ballinasloe on 18 December 1898, but from the description of the proceedings the meeting seems to have been less a part of the League's agrarian agitation than a straight political gathering concerned with party unity and the forthcoming county council elections (*ibid.*, 903/8/41). On 29 June 1899 an indoor convention was held in Loughrea to form a U.I.L. executive for East Galway. Only one priest was present, which seems to indicate that most of the diocesan clergy were still holding aloof from the movement (*ibid.*, 903/8/63).

36. *Ibid.*, 903/8/138, 146, 168, 170 (actions of Revs Coghlan, Pelly and Meagher).

37. *Ibid.*, 903/8/189-90.

38. *Ibid.*, 903/8/194. Cf. *Irish Catholic Directory*, 1902, 449.

39. On the history of the system, see Donald H. Akenson, *The Irish Education Experiment: The National System of Education in the Nineteenth Century*, London 1970.

40. Emmet Larkin, 'The Quarrel among the Roman Catholic Hierarchy over the National System of Education in Ireland, 1838-41' in Ray Broadus Browne, William John Roscelli and Richard Loftus, ed., *The Celtic Cross: Studies in Irish Culture and Literature*, West Lafayette, Indiana 1964.

41. Speech at Roman Catholic Reunion in the Birmingham Town Hall, 14 Jan. 1900, reported in *Irish Catholic Directory*, 1902, 428.

42. Thomas Fitzpatrick, 'A Peaceful Revolution', *Westminster Review* CLVI (Oct. 1901), 402.

43. T. J. MacNamara, 'The Problem of Irish Education', *Contemporary Review* LXXXVI (Oct. 1904), 478.

44. T. J. O'Connell, *History of the Irish National Teachers' Organisation, 1868–1968*, Dublin [1968], 42-4.

45. *Ibid.*, 45-52.

46. *Weekly Freeman* (Dublin), 28 May 1898 (hereafter cited *WF*).

47. O'Connell, *Hist. of I.N.T.O.*, 56.

48. *Ibid.*, 55.   49. *Ibid.*, 57-8.

50. *Ibid.*, 58-9; *WF*, 15 Apr. 1899.

51. O'Connell, *Hist. of I.N.T.O.*, 60-1. Most Protestant teachers retained their membership in the I.N.T.O. as well, but agreed to drop efforts to discuss issues prejudicial to the Catholic teachers' relationship with their managers within it.

52. *Irish Times* (Dublin), 19 Apr. 1900; *FJ*, 18 Apr. 1900; *Daily Nation* (Dublin), 7 May 1900.

53. Quoted in P. S. O'Hegarty, *A History of Ireland under the Union, 1801 to 1922*, London 1952, 618; see also Donal McCartney, 'Hyde, D. P. Moran, and Irish Ireland' in F. X. Martin, O.S.A., ed., *Leaders and Men of the Easter Rising*, Ithaca, New York 1967, 43-6.

54. Eamonn Ó Tuathail to Eóin Mac Néill, n.d. ('Monday') (Eóin Mac Néill Papers, 'Aran' folder. This collection, hereafter cited McNP, is the property of Mrs Eibhlín MacNeill Tierney and was consulted, by her kind permission, in the National Library of Ireland.)

55. S. S. Mac a' Bhaird to Mac Néill, 25 Nov. 1899 (McNP).

56. John Hogan to Mac Néill, 7 Oct. 1899 (McNP).

57. *Ibid.*

58. Copies of Walsh to [?], 16 Aug. 1897, 10 Oct. 1897, in hand of Charles MacNeill (McNP).

59. Copy of Walsh to [?], 10 Oct. 1897, (McNP).

60. *An Claidheamh Soluis*, 18 Mar. 1899.

61. *Ibid.*, 9 Sep. 1899.

62 John Hogan to Mac Néill, 7 Oct. 1899 (McNP).

63. Walsh to Mac Néill, 30 Nov. 1894 (McNP).

64. Quoted in William J. Walsh, *Bilingual Education* (Gaelic League Pamphlet no. 8), n.p. [1900], 6.

65. *Irish Daily Independent* (Dublin), 8 Mar. 1900. This paper absorbed the *Daily Nation* in 1900 and used the title *Daily Independent and Nation* until 1904 when it became the *Irish Independent*. Hereafter it will be cited simply as *Independent*.

66. *An Claidheamh Soluis*, 17 Mar. 1900; *Independent*, 18 Jul. 1900.

67. *Daily Express* (Dublin), 23 Jul. 1900.

68. Walsh to Mac Néill, 4 Dec. 1897 (McNP).

69. Walsh to John Redmond, 21 Jul. 1900 (N.L.I., Redmond Papers, hereafter cited RP).

70. *FJ*, 8 Nov. 1901.

71. D. D. Sheehan, *Ireland since Parnell*, London 1921, 61.

72. McCartney in Martin, ed., *Leaders and Men*, 45.

73. *Ibid.*

74. R. Farmer to Mac Néill, 11 May 1899 (McNP).
75. John Hogan to Mac Néill, 3 August 1899 (McNP).
76. *Ibid.*
77. *Ibid.*; McCartney in Martin, ed., *Leaders and Men*, 47.
78. McCartney in Martin, ed., *Leaders and Men*, 47.
79. *The Leader*, 1, 15 Sep. 1900.
80. Rev. John M. O'Reilly, Adm., *The Threatening Metempsychosis of a Nation* (Gaelic League Pamphlet no. 24), n.p., n.d., 1, 5.
81. McCartney in Martin, ed., *Leaders and Men*, 51; cf. Desmond Ryan, *The Sword of Light from the Four Masters to Douglas Hyde, 1636–1938*, London 1939, 216: 'He [Hyde] had a natural sympathy and kindliness that made him welcome everywhere, and he was so much one of the people that they were not surprised that he, a Protestant rector's son, prized the old heritage and shared in a round of the Rosary round the peat-fires just as he would play a game of cards and drink a glass of whisky with his friend Johny Lavin, old Fenian and his Gaelic tutor unofficial-in-chief.'
82. *The Leader*, 27 Jul. 1901.
83. See controversies with Standish O'Grady (*ibid.*, 11 May 1901) and T. W. Rolleston (*ibid.*, 5 Jan. 1901).
84. T. W. Rolleston to Mac Néill, 16 Aug. 1901 (McNP).
85. Arthur E. Clery, 'The Gaelic League, 1893-1919', *Studies* VIII (Sep. 1919), 401-3.
86. *Daily Nation*, 26, 27 Jul. 1900.

II: 'Two United Irish Parties'

1. F. S. L. Lyons, *The Irish Parliamentary Party, 1890–1910*, London 1951, 42 and 38ff.
2. *Ibid.*, 78.
3. *Ibid.*, 78-9.
4. Denis Gwynn, *The Life of John Redmond*, London 1932, 93.
5. For clerical reaction in Ardagh see esp. reports on John O'Donnell's activities in South Leitrim and Co. Longford in C.O. 903/8/80, as well as scattered reports in C.O. 903/8/44, 87, 128, 140, 199. For Kilmore see C.O. 903/8/81, 82-3, 128, 138, 171. For Killaloe see C.O. 903/8/26, 45, 78, 129. Though a curate did preside at a U.I.L. meeting at Tulla in January 1899 (C.O. 903/8/45), the clergy 'held aloof' from a meeting held in the same town five months later to form a U.I.L. executive for East Clare. East Clare was a Parnellite stronghold, being represented by John Redmond's brother,

William. The clergy may have avoided the meeting because it was addressed by two Parnellites, J. J. O'Kelly and E. Haviland Burke, but, ironically, it was reported that the leading local Parnellites, as well as the clergy, 'held aloof' (C.O. 903/8/63).

6. C.O. 903/8/146.   7. C.O. 903/8/72-3, 84.
8. *Irish Catholic* (Dublin), 28 Apr. 1900.   9. *Ibid.*
10. The number of branches known to police was as follows: 30 Nov. 1898, 94; 30 Nov. 1899, 396; 31 Mar. 1900, 440; 1 Nov. 1900, 758 (C.O. 903/8/39, 134, 169, 244).
11. Harrington to Redmond, 11 May 1900 (RP).
12. Lyons, *Party*, 51-3, esp. 52, n. 2.
13. D. Gwynn, *Redmond*, 87n.
14. *Dundalk Examiner*, 6 Oct. 1900.
15. *Westmeath Examiner* (Mullingar), 22, 29 Sep., 6 Oct. 1900.
16. *FJ*, 28, 29 Sep., 1, 8 Oct. 1900.
17. *Westmeath Examiner*, 6 Oct. 1900; C.O. 903/8/175, 199, 200, 202, 203.
18. *Drogheda Independent*, 29 Sep., 6, 13 Oct. 1900. In one other division in this region, South Louth, there was a contest, but it seems to have been provoked mainly by local issues.
19. *The People* (Wexford), 19 Sep. 1900.
20. *Leinster Leader* (Naas), 6 Oct. 1900.
21. *Ibid.*, 29 Sep. 1900.   22. *Ibid.*, 6 Oct. 1900.
23. *The People*, 19 Sep. 1900.
24. *Ibid.*, 19 Sep., 3, 6 Oct. 1900.
25. As late as August 1900, a U.I.L. organiser touring the west coast of Donegal was unable to enlist clerical support in at least seven villages, while from only one place, Dungloe, was there a report of a priest participating in one of his meetings (C.O. 903/8/187, 191). Despite O'Donnell's early involvement in the League, there is curiously little evidence of participation by his clergy in the movement before the election campaign.
26. Two priests refused to be bound by a resolution of the East Donegal convention pledging unity behind the nominee. *FJ*, 29 Sep. 1900.
27. *Ibid.*
28. *Westmeath Examiner*, 13 Oct. 1900.
29. C.O. 903/8/200; *FJ*, 2, 3, 8 Oct. 1900. Though the U.I.L. candidate tried to claim clerical support in the part of the division in Derry diocese, the only clerical signatory of his

17

nomination papers whose name appeared in the brief *FJ* report (3 Oct. 1900) was from the part of the constituency in Raphoe diocese.

Unless explicitly noted otherwise, all election returns quoted in this work are from the tabulations in *The Constitutional Year Book*, 1919, 194-378.

30. *Connaught Telegraph* (Castlebar), 6, 13 Oct. 1900.
31. *Cork Examiner*, 24, 26, 27, 28, 29, Sep. 1900.
32. O'Brien, *Olive Branch*, 83.
33. *Leinster Leader*, 6, 13 Oct. 1900.
34. *Midland Tribune and King's County Vindicator* (Birr), 29 Sep. 1900; *FJ*, 12 Oct. 1900.
35. T. M. Healy, *Letters and Leaders of My Day*, II, London 1928, 449.
36. *Ibid.*, 451.
37. *The Times* (London), 3 Nov. 1900; *Irish Catholic*, 1 Dec. 1900.
38. Margaret Banks, *Edward Blake, Irish Nationalist*, Toronto 1957, 242.
39. *The Times*, 15 Dec. 1900.
40. *Ibid.*
41. Rev. Patrick Keown, Adm., to Redmond, 4 Dec. 1900 (RP).
42. Redmond apparently did not preserve a copy of this letter, and this quotation is from Father Keown's reply, 12 Dec. 1900 (RP).
43. *Ibid.*
44. Father Keown to Redmond, 14 Dec. 1900 (RP).
45. *FJ*, 15 Dec. 1900.
46. *The Times*, 18 Dec. 1900.
47. *Ibid.*
48. Rev. P. Callan, P.P., to Redmond, 18 Dec. 1900 (RP).
49. *The Times*, 18 Dec. 1900.
50. *Ibid.*, 20 Dec. 1900.
51. *Ibid.*
52. Rev. J. J. MacCartan to Redmond, 5 Oct. 1900 (RP).
53. *The Times*, 20 Dec. 1900.
54. Donal Sullivan to Redmond, 23 Jan. 1901, with enclosure (RP).
55. Copy of Redmond to Father Keown, undated (RP).
56. Father Keown to Redmond, 19 Jan. 1901 (RP).
57. Copy of Redmond to Father Keown, undated (RP).
58. Father Keown to Redmond, 26 Jan. 1901 (RP).
59. Copy of Redmond to Father Keown, 29 Jan. 1901 (RP).

60. *FJ*, 25 Sep. 1900.
61. Lyons, *Party*, 98.
62. I.-G.'s Monthly Rep., Sep. 1903 (S.P.O.I., C.S.O., P. & C. Division, C.B.S. 29006/S). Oliver MacDonagh briefly suggests a pattern of the recurrent 'supersession of one generation by another' in Irish history, similar to the one I have sketched, and adds 1959 as a similar 'watershed'. (*Ireland*, Englewood Cliffs, N.J. 1968, 12.)

III : Ideals and Interests

1. Statement of Episcopal Standing Committee, Mar. 1889, quoted in Royal Commission on University Education in Ireland, *Appendix to First Report*, p. 385 [Cd 826], H.C. 1902, xxxi. (Hereafter cited as R.C.U.Ed., *App. to 1st Rep.*)
2. Curtis, *Coercion and Conciliation*, 276.
3. Haldane, *Autobiography*, 137-44.
4. R.C.U.Ed., *Final Report*, p. iv [Cd 1483], H.C. 1903, xxxii.
5. *FJ*, 17 Nov. 1900.
6. R.C.U.Ed., *App. to 1st Rep.*, 29-30.
7. Starkie to James Bryce, 5 Mar. 1906 (N.L.I., Bryce Papers (hereafter cited BrP), MS 11,012).
8. E.g. *FJ*, 7, 13 Dec. 1901.
9. *Ibid.*, 17, 18, 20, 21 Dec. 1901.
10. *Independent*, 23 Dec. 1901; see also leading article in *FJ*, 21 Dec. 1901.
11. This letter, together with the *I.E.R.* articles, was reprinted as a pamphlet, which was, in turn reprinted in R.C.U.Ed., *Appendix to Final Report*, pp. 28-54 [Cd 1484], H.C. 1903, xxxii.
12. Article republished in *Irish Catholic*, 22 Feb. 1902.
13. R.C.U.Ed., *Appendix to Third Report*, pp. 581-5 [Cd 1229], H.C. 1902, xxxii.
14. *FJ*, 20 Mar. 1902.
15. R.C.U.Ed., *App. 3rd Rep.*, 571.
16. J. W. Mackail and Guy Wyndham, *Life and Letters of George Wyndham*, II, London [1925], 434.
17. *FJ*, 11 Feb. 1902.   18. *Ibid.*, 29 Oct. 1902.
19. Rev. Joseph Canon Guinan, *The Soggarth Aroon*, Dublin 1905, 201. Although fictitious names of persons and places are used in this book, the author described it as 'a bundle of reminiscences' (*The Tablet*, 13 Jan. 1906).
20. Guinan, *Soggarth*, 201-2.
21. *Ibid.*, 15-16.

22. *Ibid.*, 180.   23. *The Tablet*, 26 Apr. 1902.
24. *Irish Catholic*, 4 Nov. 1905.
25. Rev. James McCaffrey, 'A Plea for the Young', *New Ireland Review* XIV (Feb. 1901), 347.
26. *FJ*, 6 Jan. 1902.   27. *The Tablet*, 14 Mar. 1903.
28. *Ibid.*, 6 Jul. 1907.
29. *Record of the Maynooth Union*, 1902–03, 73-5.
30. *Ibid.*, 77-8 (Rev. T. B. Byrne, C.C.).
31. *Ibid.*, 76-8 (Father Fenelon, Dr O'Hickey and Dean Lynch of Manchester).
32. *Ibid.*, 1901–02, 49.   33. *Ibid.*, 1898–99, 31-2.
34. *FJ*, 1 Oct. 1900.   35. *The Tablet*, 5 Jul. 1902.
36. *Record of the Maynooth Union*, 1901–02, 49-50.

IV: Land for the People

1. *The Tablet*, 18 Oct. 1902. The text of Shawe-Taylor's letter is given in D. Gwynn, *Redmond*, 99.
2. *Irish Catholic Directory*, 1903, 436.
3. See *Annual Register*, 1902, [217-8].
4. George Wyndham to A. J. Balfour, 24 Sep. 1902 (B.M., Balfour Papers, Add. MS 49804, f. 68).
5. *Ibid.*
6. See Healy, *Letters and Leaders*, II, 459, Wyndham to Healy, 4 Aug. 1902: 'I will do more for Louth than for any other county.'
7. Mackail and Wyndham, *George Wyndham*, II, 448-9.
8. *Irish Catholic Directory*, 1903, 451.
9. *FJ*, 7 Oct. 1902; John C. Rooney to Redmond, 7 Oct. 1902, with telegram from Cardinal Vaughan to *FJ*, 7 Oct. 1902, and copy of *FJ*'s reply to Vaughan on back of telegram (RP).
10. *FJ*, 28 Nov. 1902.   11. *Ibid.*
12. *Irish Catholic Directory*, 1903, 453.
13. See *Extracts from Minutes of the Proceedings of the Commissioners of National Education (Ireland), and Other Documents, in Relation to Recent Action Taken by the Most Reverend W. J. Walsh, D.D., Archbishop of Dublin, Respecting Alleged Irregularities in the Transaction of Business in the Office of the Commissioners, and to the Withdrawal or Amendment of Letters Alleged To Have Been Incorrect*, H.C. 1901 (261), lvii. See also *Copy of 'the Second Memorandum . . .'*, *ibid.* (366) lvii.
14. *FJ*, 1 Mar. 1900; Robert H. Murray, *Archbishop Bernard, Professor, Prelate and Provost*, London 1931, 153; Walsh

to Redmond, 14 May 1901 (second of two letters of this date) (RP).

15. *FJ*, 12 Sep. 1902.
16. *Irish Catholic*, 11, 18, 25 Oct., 1, 8, 15, 22, 29 Nov. 1902.
17. *FJ*, 20 Sep. 1902.
18. See, e.g., Rev. M. O'Riordan, *A Reply to Dr. Starkie's Attack on the Managers of National Schools*, Dublin, n.d.
19. *FJ*, 12 Sep. 1902.
20. Average daily attendance in Ireland was 65 per cent, compared with 84 per cent in England and 85 per cent in Scotland (MacNamara in *Contemporary Review* LXXXVI, 476).
21. *Irish Catholic*, 11 Oct. 1902.
22. *Ibid.*, 25 Oct. 1902.
23. *FJ*, 1, 17 Nov. 1902; C.O. 903/9, p. 679.
24. Bishop Patrick O'Donnell to Redmond, 26 Nov. 1903 (RP): 'Though he [O'Brien] resisted my urgent advice about . . . the English Education Act (when you were in America) I have on every ground public and private the greatest admiration for him.'
25. *Irish Catholic*, 29 Nov. 1902 (letter dated 24 Nov. 1902).
26. *FJ*, 28 Nov. 1902.   27. *Annual Register*, 1902, [224-5].
28. *FJ*, 25 Nov. 1902.   29. *Ibid.*, 28 Nov. 1902.
30. *Ibid.*, 1 Dec. 1902.   31. *Ibid.*, 4, 8, 15, 17, 18 Dec. 1902.
32. *Irish Catholic*, 20 Dec. 1902, gives a list of the 'abstentionists' who returned for the divisions, together with another list of ten Nationalists, including Healy, who had 'declined to accept the abstention ordinance'.
33. *Return of the Resolutions and Statement Adopted by the Irish Landowners' Convention on the 10th day of October, 1902; and Report of the Irish Land Conference, Dated 3rd day of January, 1903; and Minute on the Land Conference Report, Adopted on the 7th day of January, 1903, by the Executive Committee of the Irish Landowners' Convention*, H.C. 1903 (89), lvii.
34. 'Income' being recognised to be as much as 10 per cent less than the rent itself on account of costs of collection.
35. *Irish Catholic*, 31 Jan. 1903.
36. *FJ*, 27 Jan. 1903.   37. *Ibid.*, 12 Feb. 1903.
38. *Ibid.*, 16 Feb. 1903 (letter dated 13 Feb. 1903).
39. *Ibid.*, 14, 16, 19, 28 Feb., 3, 5, 7, Mar. 1903.
40. *Ibid.*, 17 Feb. 1903.   41. *Ibid.*, 18 Feb. 1903.
42. *Ibid.*, 19 Feb. 1903.   43. *Hansard* 4, cxviii (1903), 822-3.
44. *FJ*, 28 Feb. 1903.

45. Leon Ó Broin, *The Chief Secretary: Augustine Birrell in Ireland*, London 1969, 11.
46. Walsh to Redmond, 23 Mar. 1903 (RP).
47. *Irish Catholic*, 4 Apr. 1903; *FJ*, 4 Apr. 1903.
48. Wilfrid Scawen Blunt, *My Diaries* (London 1919–20; repr. London [1922]), New York 1921, II, 48.
49. *FJ*, 2, 15 Apr. 1903.
50. *Ibid.*, 23, 28 Apr., 2 Jun. 1903.
51. Blunt, *My Diaries*, II, 48.
52. *Ibid.*, II, 50-52. Davitt is not mentioned on the second occasion but is probably implied.
53. *Irish Catholic*, 18 Apr. 1903.
54. *Record of the Maynooth Union*, 1902–03, 79.
55. Bernard Shaw, *John Bull's Other Island* . . . London 1907, 60.
56. A parish priest in a district of Co. Cavan which had been 'in a state of turbulence' before land purchase had been effected under the less generous provisions of previous land acts, told a government official: 'Purchase has brought peace. The people are more industrious, more sober, and more hopeful as to their future prospects.' (*Report by Mr. W. F. Bailey, Legal Assistant Commissioner, of an Inquiry into the Present Condition of Tenant Purchasers under the Land Purchase Acts*, p. 13, H.C. 1903 (92), lvii.)

V: High Hopes

1. In 1901, 23.2 per cent of the population of Ireland lived in towns of over 10,000 inhabitants, whereas the comparable figure in 1841 was 7.6 per cent. T. W. Freeman, *Pre-Famine Ireland*, London 1957, 27; Augustus D. Webb, *The New Dictionary of Statistics*, London 1911, 479.
2. In later years language enthusiasts came to recognise the need to redistribute land to make Gaeltacht districts economically viable. At the height of the U.I.L. agitation for redistribution of the grazing lands, ironically, I have found little evidence of Gaelic League involvement in the agitation.
3. Copies of P. J. Magee to William Field and William O'Doherty, 26 Jun. 1901; copy of Field to Magee, 27 Jun. 1901; copy of Magee to Field, 16 Jul. 1901; Magee to Redmond, 14 Aug. 1901; copy of Redmond to Magee, 16 Aug. 1901; Magee to Redmond, 23 Sep. 1901; copy of Redmond to Magee, 26 Sep. 1901; Magee to Redmond, 2 Oct. 1901; copy of Redmond to Magee, 7 Oct. 1901; Magee to Redmond, 5

Nov. 1901; copy of Redmond to Magee, 23 Dec. 1901 (RP).

4. Clipping from *Ulster Echo*, 26 Apr. 1902, attached to John Rooney to Alfred Webb, 28 Apr. 1902 (RP).

5. P. Finlay, 'Religion and Civil Life', *New Ireland Review* XIV (Feb. 1901), 332.

6. Michael J. F. McCarthy, *Rome in Ireland*, London 1904, 305.

7. Sergeant F. Waters (R.I.C., Detective Dept, Belfast) to D.I., D.D., 8 Apr. 1903 (S.P.O.I., C.S.O., Crime Branch Special, 29372/S).

8. *Record of the Maynooth Union*, 1902–03, 66.

9. *FJ*, 26, 28 Nov. 1902; *Irish Catholic*, 1 Nov., 13 Dec. 1902.

10. *Irish Catholic Directory*, 1903, 460-1.

11. *FJ*, 27 Mar. 1903.

12. Quoted in the *Northern Star*, 28 Feb. 1903. The *Star* prints this sentence in capitals.

13. *The Leader*, 7 Feb. 1903.   14. *FJ*, 27 Mar. 1903.

15. Sergeant F. Waters to D.I., D.D., 8 Apr. 1903 (S.P.O.I., C.S.O., Crime Branch Special, 29372/S).

16. Copy of Redmond to Dillon, 30 Sep. 1903 (RP).

17. *Record of the Maynooth Union*, 1902–03, 62.

18. *Ibid.*, 66.   19. *Ibid.*, 66-7.

20. *Handbook of the Catholic Association, Being an Account of the Origin of It, an Argument of the Need for It, and an Exposition of Its Objects and Proposed Methods of Working,* Dublin [*c.* Sep. 1903].

21. *Irish Catholic*, 3 Oct. 1903.

22. Mackail and Wyndham, *George Wyndham*, II, 468.

23. Memo from Chief Secretary's Office, 28 Sep. 1903, 'A General Sketch of Irish Policy' (B.M., Balfour Papers, Add. MS 49804, f. 191).

24. Copy of Redmond to Dillon, 30 Sep. 1903 (RP).

25. Outline of a university scheme drafted by MacDonnell, dated 10 Oct. 1903 (Bodl., MacDonnell Papers (hereafter cited McDP), MS Eng. hist. c. 367, ff. 8-14).

26. Walsh to Sir Antony MacDonnell, 28 Oct. 1903 (McDP, c. 351, f. 144).

27. Lisle March-Phillipps and Bertram Christian, ed., *Some Hawarden Letters, 1878–1913*, New York 1918, 318.

28. Dr Healy had appended a reservation to the Robertson Commission's report on these same points. R.C.U.Ed., *Final Rep.*, 62. Dr O'Dea was particularly sensitive on the May-nooth question and during the summer of 1903 had pub-

lished his own testimony before the Commission in pamphlet form as an 'appeal' from the Commission's decision on Maynooth 'to the wider tribunal of public opinion, and especially of Irish Catholic opinion'. Thomas O'Dea, *Maynooth and the University Question*, Dublin 1903, iii.

29. Walsh to MacDonnell, 28 Oct. 1903 (McDP, c. 351, ff. 144-5).
30. *The Times*, 22 Oct. 1903.
31. *Ibid.*, 28 Oct. 1903, citing the *Daily Express*.
32. Walsh to MacDonnell, 28 Oct. 1903 (McDP, c. 351, ff. 144-5).
33. *The Times*, 6 Nov. 1903; *Irish Catholic*, 7 Nov. 1903.
34. *Irish Catholic*, 21 Nov. 1903.
35. Walsh to MacDonnell, 28 Oct. 1903 (McDP, c. 351, ff. 144-5).
36. Walsh to MacDonnell, 20 Nov. 1903 (McDP, c. 351, ff. 146-7).
37. Walsh, *Walsh*, 555.
38. *Independent*, 4 Jan. 1904. There is a draft of the letter on official stationery in McDP, c. 367, ff. 15-19.
39. *FJ*, 7 Jan. 1904.
40. Bishop O'Dwyer of Limerick to MacDonnell, 6 Jan. 1904 (McDP, c. 350, ff. 11-14). The author of this letter is incorrectly identified as Thomas Bunbury, the C. of I. Bishop of Limerick, in the Bodleian's index of these papers.
41. Walsh to MacDonnell, 7 Jan. 1904 (McDP, c. 351, ff. 149-50).
42. See Larkin in Browne, Roscelli and Loftus, ed., *Celtic Cross*.
43. Apparently, however, O'Dwyer would not have been in violation of the legislation if he had acted as Walsh and MacDonnell feared in this instance. The relevant statutes of the 1900 Maynooth Synod, *Acta et Decreta Synodi Plenariae Episcoporum Hiberniae Habitae apud Maynutiam An. MDCCCC*, Dublin 1906, 119-20 (sections 390-1), prevented a bishop from *accepting* a bill (within certain broadly defined categories) proposed or enacted by the government before the hierarchy had met and declared it to be accepted. However, the Dunraven scheme emanated technically from a private individual rather than the government, and O'Dwyer was threatening not to accept it but to reject it. For an instance of how the legislation affected a prelate who agreed with a government proposal, see Walsh's comments to MacDonnell in February, 1907, pp. 179-80.
44. *Irish Catholic Directory*, 1905, 434.
45. Walsh apparently intimated to MacDonnell that O'Dwyer did not concur. Though there is no indication of O'Dwyer's abstention (or of unanimity) in the resolution itself, MacDonnell wrote to James Bryce in August 1906 that he was

forwarding to him 'two copies of the Resolution passed by all the Archbishops and Bishops (except O'Dwyer) assembled at Maynooth in January 1904' (MacDonnell to Bryce, 16 Aug. 1906 (BrP, MS 11,013)).

46. 'Memorandum by MacDonnell of negotiations between the archbishop of Dublin and George Wyndham on the scheme outlined in Dunraven's letter' (McDP, c. 367, f. 24 [cf. ff. 22-3]).

47. *Ibid.*

48. MacDonnell to Bryce, 27 Jun. 1906 (BrP, MS 11,011).

49. *FJ*, 14 Jan. 1904.

50. *Ibid.*   51. *Annual Register*, 1903, [240].

52. *Irish Catholic*, 2, 16 Jan. 1904.

53. *The Times*, 11 Jan. 1904; *Irish Catholic*, 16 Jan. 1904.

54. *The Times*, 11 Jan. 1904.   55. *Ibid.*, 18 Jan. 1904.

56. *Irish Catholic*, 16 Jan. 1904.

57. Wyndham to Balfour, 18 Jan. 1904 (B.M., Balfour Papers, Add. MS 49804, ff. 207-8).

58. *Annual Register*, 1904, [241].

59. Dillon to Redmond, 24 Jan. 1904 (RP).

VI: The Flowing Tide

1. *The Times*, 22 Feb. 1904.

2. *Irish News and Belfast Morning News* (hereafter cited *Irish News*), 14, 19 Oct. 1903.

3. See speech by John Rooney (*ibid.*, 21 Dec. 1903).

4. *Constitutional Year Book*, 1919, erroneously shows this election as an uncontested victory for Arnold-Forster. For the B.C.A.'s version of the entire affair see *Irish News*, 1 Dec. 1903.

5. *Northern Star* (Belfast), 8 Apr. 1905. John Rooney to Redmond, 10 Nov. 1903 (RP). Head Constable A. Donohoe to D.I., D.D., 1 Dec. 1905 (apparently an error), and attached clipping from *Northern Star*, 5 Dec. 1905 (S.P.O.I., C.S.O., Crime Branch Special, 29372/S).

6. Sergeant F. Waters to D.I., D.D., 21 Jan. 1904 (S.P.O.I., C.S.O., Crime Branch Special, 29372/S). A minute by MacDonnell dated 10 February 1904 in this file suggests doubt about this information, but does not go into detail.

7. *Irish News*, 1 Feb. 1904.

8. *Northern Star*, 23 Apr. 1904.

9. *Irish News*, 7 Mar. 1904.

10. *FJ*, 16 Oct. 1903.

11. Memorandum from the Chief Secretary's Office, 'A General Sketch of Irish Policy', 28 Sep. 1903 (B.M., Balfour Papers, Add. MS 49804, ff. 186-94).

12. *Report of Mr. F. H. Dale, His Majesty's Inspector of Schools, Board of Education, on Primary Education in Ireland,* 89-90 [Cd 1981], H.C. 1904, xx.

13. *Ibid.,* 44.   14. *Ibid.,* 86.   15. *Ibid.*

16. *Ibid.,* 12.   17. *Ibid.*   18. *Ibid.,* 86.

19. *Ibid.,* 90.   20. *Hansard* 4, cxxxi (1904), 1283.

21. Bishop O'Donnell to Redmond, 3 Apr. 1904 (RP).

22. Although no copy of this letter appears to have survived in the Redmond Papers, its general character can be inferred from Bishop O'Donnell to Redmond, 6 Apr. 1904 (RP), in which the Bishop describes a minor editorial change he is making in the copies he is sending out.

23. *FJ,* 18 Apr. 1904.   24. *Independent,* 14 Apr. 1904.

25. *FJ,* 11 Apr. 1904.   26. *Hansard* 4, cxxxiii (1904), 420.

27. *Ibid.,* 429-39.   28. *FJ,* 19 Apr. 1904.

29. Letter from Rev. David Humphrys, P.P., Killenaule, *FJ,* 31 May 1904.

30. O'Connell, *Hist. of I.N.T.O.,* 59.   31. *FJ,* 2 Jun. 1904.

32. *Ibid.,* 20 Jun. 1904.

33. O'Connell, *Hist. of I.N.T.O.,* 59.

34. *FJ,* 23 Jun. 1904.   35. *Ibid.,* 28 Jun. 1904.

36. *Independent,* 21 Jul. 1904.   37. *FJ,* 30 Aug. 1904.

38. *Ibid.,* 12 Aug. 1904.   39. *Independent,* 3 Oct. 1904.

40. E.g. *FJ,* 17, 27 Aug., 24, 31 Oct. 1904.

41. *Ibid.,* 10 Oct. 1904.   42. *Independent,* 13 Oct. 1904.

43. *Irish News,* 25 Jul. 1904.   44. *FJ,* 18 Jan. 1905.

45. Dillon to Redmond, 30 Jan. 1905 (RP).

46. *The Tablet,* 11 Feb. 1905.

47. *Irish News,* 14 Feb. 1905.   48. *FJ,* 13 Feb. 1905.

49. *Ibid.*   50. M. Joyce to Redmond, 14 Feb. 1905 (RP).

51. Thomas Maguire *et al.* to Standing Committee of the U.I.L., 13 Feb. 1905 (RP).

52. D. MacCartan to Redmond, 17 Feb. 1905; Denis Johnston to Redmond, 21 Feb. 1905 (RP).

53. Father Crolly to Redmond, 12 Feb. 1905 (RP).

54. Clipping from *Belfast News-Letter,* 13 Feb. 1905 (RP).

55. *Northern Star,* 18 Feb. 1905.

56. Bishop O'Donnell to Redmond, 17 Feb. 1905 (RP).

57. Copy of Redmond to Alfred Webb, 27 Feb. 1905, in *Northern Star,* 11 Mar. 1905.

58. Bishop O'Donnell to Redmond, 23 Feb. 1905 (RP).

59. Bishop Henry to Bishop O'Donnell, 22 Feb. 1905, in *Northern Star*, 11 Mar. 1905.

60. *Northern Star*, 11 Mar. 1905.   61. *Ibid.*

62. *Ibid.*, 6 May 1905.   63. D. Gwynn, *Redmond*, 112-13.

64. *Irish News*, 12, 17, 18 May 1905.

65. *Ibid.*, 6 Jun. 1905.   66. *FJ*, 17 Mar. 1905.

67. *Irish Catholic Directory*, 1906, 439-40.

68. *Copy of Minutes of the Proceedings of the Commissioners of National Education Relating to Rule 127(b) of Their Code of Regulations*, p. 5, H.C. 1905 (184), lx.

69. *FJ*, 21 Mar. 1905.

70. *Copy of Minutes . . . Rule 127(b) . . .*, 7.

71. There are indications of support from twenty-two of the twenty-seven prelates for the agitation in *FJ* and *Independent* during the period from 18 March to 3 May 1905. For equivocal responses from Bishops Browne of Ferns and Brownrigg of Ossory see *FJ*, 14 Apr. 1905 and *Independent*, 1, 10 Apr. 1905, but cf. *Independent*, 21 Apr. 1905.

72. *Copy of Minutes . . . Rule 127(b) . . .*, 9.

73. *Ibid.*, 10.   74. *Irish Catholic*, 28 Nov. 1903.

75. Letter of Rev. David Humphrys, P.P., Killenaule, *FJ*, 21 Sep. 1905.

76. *Hansard* 4, cl (1905), 253.   77. *FJ*, 18 Aug. 1905.

78. Pádraig Ó Dálaigh to Mac Néill, 5 Sep. 1905 (McNP).

79. *FJ*, 22 Sep. 1905.   80. *Ibid.*, 20 Nov. 1905.

81. *Autobiography of the Ruairi O'More Branch of the Gaelic League, Portarlington*, Dublin 1906, 11 (and *passim*).

82. *FJ*, 12 Oct. 1905.

83. Seóirse Ó Muanáin to Mac Néill, 18 Nov. 1905 (McNP); *FJ*, 24 Nov. 1905.

84. *FJ*, 13 Dec. 1905.   85. *Ibid.*, 26 Feb. 1906.

86. MacDonnell did, however, try in 1906 to break down the rule of denominational balance on the Boards. He approached Archbishop Walsh and inquired if it 'was . . . necessary to adhere to the Rule (merely of practice) of appointing a Catholic to succeed a Catholic'. He mentioned Douglas Hyde and [Stephen?] Gwynn, both Protestants, for a 'Catholic' vacancy on the Intermediate Education Board. Though Walsh ruled out Gwynn, he evidenced some enthusiasm for Hyde, but indicated that he would have to consult Logue before consenting to a breach of the rule. I have not found Logue's reaction, but Hyde was in fact offered the

appointment, and he declined. (MacDonnell to James Bryce, 6 Jul. 1906; Douglas Hyde to Bryce, 16 Jul. 1906 (BrP, MS 11,013).)

87. Seóirse Ó Muanáin to Mac Néill, 22 Nov. 1905; cf. Ó Muanáin to Mac Néill, 18 Nov. 1905 (McNP).
88. Bishop O'Dea to Mac Néill, 21 Jul., 10 Aug. 1905; but cf. O'Dea to Mac Néill, 21 Apr. 1905 (McNP).
89. Bishop Lyster to Mac Néill, 13 Jan. 1906 (McNP).
90. Bishop Lyster to Mac Néill, 20 Jan. 1906 (McNP).
91. O'Hegarty, *Ireland under the Union*, 650-1; Robert Mitchell Henry, *The Evolution of Sinn Fein*, Dublin [1920], 69-70.
92. Seán Ó Lúing, 'Arthur Griffith and Sinn Fein' in Martin, ed., *Leaders and Men*, 57.
93. O'Hegarty, *Ireland under the Union*, 636.

VII: The State under New Management

1. *Irish Catholic*, 28 Oct. 1905.
2. D. Gwynn, *Redmond*, 115.
3. Lyons, *Party*, 103-11.
4. On this subject, see R. T. McKenzie, *British Political Parties: The Distribution of Power within the Conservative and Labour Parties* (London 1955), 2nd ed., New York 1963, esp. 419-20, 485-6.
5. *The Times*, 4 Nov. 1905.   6. *Ibid.*, 1 Dec. 1905.
7. Walsh to Redmond, 3 Dec. 1905 (RP).
8. Copy of Redmond to Walsh, 5 Dec. 1905 (RP).
9. *The Times*, 12 Jan. 1906.   10. C.O. 904/117, Jan. 1906.
11. C.O. 904/118, May 1908.   12. *The Times*, 2 Jan. 1906.
13. *Ibid.*, 5 Jan. 1906.   14. *Ibid.*, 8 Jan. 1906.
15. *Ibid.*, 6 Jan. 1906.   16. *Ibid.*, 8 Jan. 1906.
17. *Ibid.*, 9 Jan. 1906.
18. *Irish Catholic*, 13 Jan. 1906. Healy's assertion that the party could find no suitable candidate (*Letters and Leaders*, II, 476) can be dismissed as mere rationalising.
19. MacDonnell to Bryce, 12 Jan. 1906 (BrP, MS 11,012).
20. Dillon to Redmond, 6 Feb. 1906 (RP).
21. O'Connor to Redmond, 26 Oct. 1905 (RP).
22. Bryce to Campbell-Bannerman, 31 Dec. 1905 (BM., Campbell-Bannerman Papers, Add. MS 41,211/334).
23. Quoted in Michael Davitt's reply, *FJ*, 22 Jan. 1906.
24. Logue to T. F. Molony, 5 Dec. 1905, enclosed in MacDonnell to Bryce, 11 Dec. 1905 (BrP, MS 11,011).
25. Walsh to Molony, 4 Dec. 1905, enclosed in MacDonnell

to Bryce, 11 Dec. 1905 (BrP, MS 11,011).

26. Copy of Sheehan and Henry to Redmond, 25 Jan. 1906, enclosed in Redmond to Bryce, 29 Jan. 1906 (BrP, MS 11,012).
27. Redmond to Bryce, 29 Jan. 1906 (BrP, MS 11,012).
28. Copy of Redmond to Bishops Sheehan and Henry, 29 Jan. 1906, enclosed in *ibid.*
29. O'Connor to Redmond, 28 Jan. 1906 (RP).
30. Bourne to Redmond, 14 Feb. 1906 (RP).
31. Redmond's memorandum of 'interview with Archb. Bourne', 16 Feb. 1906 (RP).
32. MacDonnell to Bryce, 3 Feb. 1906 (BrP, MS 11,012).
33. *Ibid.*
34. MacDonnell to Bryce, 8 Feb. [1906] (BrP, MS 11,012).
35. MacDonnell to Bryce, 1 Mar. 1906 (BrP, MS 11,012).
36. MacDonnell to Bryce, 8 Mar. 1906 (BrP, MS 11,012).
37. MacDonnell to Bryce, 'Saturday' [14 Apr. 1906?] (BrP, MS 11,012).
38. MacDonnell to Bryce, 29 Apr. 1906 (BrP, MS 11,012).
39. MacDonnell to Bryce, 8 Mar., 27 Jun. 1906 (BrP, MSS 11,012, 11,011).
40. Royal Commission on Trinity College, Dublin, and the University of Dublin, *Final Report*, pp. v–vi [Cd 3311], H.C. 1907, xli. (Hereafter cited R.C.T.C.D., *Final Rep.*)
41. *FJ*, 23 Mar. 1906.
42. *Irish Catholic Directory*, 1907, 455.
43. Copy of Redmond to Dillon, 3 Apr. 1906 (RP).
44. Copy of Redmond to Dillon, 5 Apr. 1906 (RP).
45. *Hansard* 4, clv (1906), 1031.
46. *Ibid.*, 1033-4; Augustine Birrell, *Things Past Redress*, London 1937, 189-90.
47. Telegram from Bourne to Redmond, 26 Apr. 1906 (RP).
48. Memorandum in Bourne-Redmond correspondence marked '26 April 1906' in Redmond's handwriting (RP).
49. *The Times*, 27 Apr. 1906.
50. *Ibid.*, 28 Apr. 1906.
51. *Irish Catholic Directory*, 1907, 456.
52. *Ibid.*, 456-7.
53. *Irish Catholic*, 5 May 1906.
54. *Ibid.*, quoting *Evening Herald*, 2 May 1906.
55. *Hansard* 4, clviii (1906), 848.
56. Copy of Redmond to Devlin, 18 Jun. 1906 (RP).
57. The instructions are contained in a series of numbered slips, most of which are preserved in the Redmond Papers. Slip no.

8 is marked 'With the Archbishop's compliments' in Bourne's handwriting. Evidence as to the source of the slips is provided by a statement of Lord Edmund Talbot (*Hansard* 4, clix (1906), 679), in which he read resolutions of the 'Watching Committee of the Catholic Educational Councils' which, but for very slight verbal differences on one or two points, are identical with Slips nos 30, 31 and 32.

58. Bourne to Redmond, 15 Jun. 1906 (RP).
59. *Hansard* 4, clix (1906), 1437-1514; *Irish Catholic*, 7 Jul. 1906.
60. Slips nos 3, 4, 5, 6, 9 (with subsequent correction) 10, 11, 12, 13, 14, 15, 16, 17, 23 (RP).
61. Slip no. 25 (RP).
62. Memorandum marked 'Handed to me by the Archbishop 19 June 1906' in Redmond's handwriting; cf. Bourne to Redmond, 16 Jun. 1906 (RP).
63. Undated note in Bourne's handwriting (RP).
64. *Hansard* 4, clix (1906), 1041-8.
65. *Ibid.*, 1067-74.
66. Bourne to Redmond, 29 Jun. 1906 (RP).
67. Bourne to Redmond, 15 Jul. 1906 (RP).
68. Copy of Redmond to Bourne, 16 Jul. 1906 (RP).
69. Bourne to Redmond, 9 Jul. 1906 (RP).
70. *Hansard* 4, clxi (1906), 240.
71. *Ibid.*, 1074.
72. Copy of Redmond to Dillon, 24 Jul. 1906 (RP).
73. A. W. Mountain to Bourne, 26 May 1906 (Archives of the Archdiocese of Westminster, Bourne Papers).
74. *Irish Catholic*, 7 Jul. 1906.
75. *Ibid.*, 20 Jun. 1906.
76. Duke of Norfolk to Redmond, 12 Jul. 1906 (RP).
77. Bourne to Redmond, 1 Aug. 1906 (RP).
78. *Irish Catholic*, 21 Jul. 1906.
79. *Ibid.*, 11 Aug. 1906.

VIII: The Art of the Improbable

1. R.C.T.C.D., *App. to 1st Rep.*, pp. 22-3 [Cd 3176], H.C. 1906, lvi.
2. *Ibid.*, 110-15.
3. See correspondence between Walsh and George Fottrell in *FJ*, 31 Jul. 1906.
4. *Irish Times*, 2 Aug. 1906.   5. *FJ*, 30 Jul. 1906.
6. *Irish Times*, 1 Aug. 1906.   7. *Ibid.*, 2 Aug. 1906.
8. R.C.T.C.D., *App. to 1st Rep.*, 116-17.

9. MacDonnell to Bryce, 18 Aug. 1906 (BrP, MS 11,013).
10. R.C.T.C.D., *App. to Final Rep.*, pp. 478-80 [Cd 3312], H.C. 1907, xli. (repr. from *Independent*, 15 Sep. 1906).
11. *Ibid.*, 421.
12. *Ibid.*, 421-2. There are copies of this letter in the MacDonnell Papers (c. 351, ff. 151-3) and the Bryce Papers (MS 11,014).
13. *Independent*, 26 Oct. 1906.
14. Fathers of the Society of Jesus, *A Page of Irish History: Story of University College, Dublin, 1883–1909*, Dublin 1930, 534-6; R.C.T.C.D., *App. to Final Rep.*, 438-9.
15. R.C.T.C.D., *App. to Final Rep.*, 271.
16. *FJ*, 14 Nov. 1906.
17. *FJ*, 11 Oct. 1906.
18. Bourne to Redmond, 23 Nov. 1906; Dillon to Redmond, 25 Nov. 1906 (RP).
19. In his own narrative of the events of this period in a letter to the Duke of Norfolk dated 6 January 1907, Bourne writes: 'At length on November 26th I learned that the Government was prepared to consider some of the amendments which we had consistently urged.' (Bourne Papers, item 12 in a pink folder marked 'II Duke of Norfolk on Education almost all 1907', hereafter cited Norfolk Ed. folder.)
20. Copy of Redmond to Bourne, 30 Nov. 1906 (two-page letter) (RP).
21. *Ibid.*
22. Dillon to Birrell, 29 Nov. 1906 (P.R.O., Ed. 24/111, file B.11).
23. *FJ*, 30 Nov. 1906.
24. Copy of Redmond to Bourne, 30 Nov. 1906 (single-page letter) (RP).
25. Bourne to Redmond, 1 Dec. 1906 (RP).
26. Copy of Bourne to Norfolk, 6 Jan. 1907 (Bourne Papers, Norfolk Ed. folder, item 12).
27. Redmond to Bourne, 2 Dec. 1906 (RP).
28. Redmond to Birrell, 2 Dec. 1906 (P.R.O., Ed. 24/111, file B.11).
29. Statement accompanying Bourne to Redmond, 4 Dec. 1906 (RP).
30. Copy of Redmond to Dillon, 17 Dec. 1906 (RP).
31. Bishop Burton of Clifton to Norfolk, 3 Jan. 1907 (Bourne Papers, Norfolk Ed. folder, item 8).
32. Redmond to Bourne, 4 Dec. 1906 (Bourne Papers); Redmond's copy is in RP.

33. Bourne to Redmond, 8 Dec. 1906 (RP).
34. Ripon to Birrell, 10 Dec. 1906, enclosing extract from Bourne to Ripon, 8 Dec. 1906 (P.R.O., Ed. 24/111, file B.11). Bourne's version of the amendments was:
    1. Extended facilities to be granted everywhere except in *single school* areas.
    2. Proportion to be not higher than three-fourths in a ballot where only the voters actually voting would be considered: non-voters to be treated as neutral.
    3. Alternative school to be required as a condition only, if a *reasonable* number of children need it.
    4. Teachers to be appointed with at least concurrence of Parents' Committee.
    He also mentioned the anxiety of the bishops over the question of new schools to be provided in the future.
35. Redmond to Bourne, 12 Dec. 1906 (RP).
36. *Hansard* 4, clxvii (1906), 467-72. T. M. Healy and William O'Brien voted against the government.
37. Copy of Bourne to Norfolk, 6 Jan. 1907 (Bourne Papers, Norfolk Ed. folder, item 12).
38. *Hansard* 4, clxvii (1906), 215-19.
39. *Ibid.*, 386-93.   40. *FJ*, 15 Dec. 1906.
41. See G. K. A. Bell, *Randall Davidson, Archbishop of Canterbury*, I (London 1935), New York 1935, 510-30.
42. *Ibid.*, 527.   43. *FJ*, 15 Dec. 1906.
44. *Ibid.*, 17 Dec. 1906.   45. *Ibid.*, 3 Dec. 1906.
46. *Ibid.*, 15 Dec. 1906.   47. *Ibid.*   48. *Ibid.*
49. *Ibid.*
50. Dillon to Redmond, 15 Dec. 1906 (RP).
51. Dillon to Redmond, 19 Dec. 1906 (RP).
52. Dillon to Redmond, 15 Dec. 1906 (RP).
53. Copy of Redmond to Dillon, 17 Dec. 1906 (RP).
54. Bishop O'Donnell to Redmond, 19 Dec. 1906: 'It would be difficult to exaggerate the importance of the correspondence of which you have kindly sent me a copy.' (RP).
55. *Hansard* 4, clxvii (1906), 1382-91.
56. Quoted by Redmond, *ibid.*, 1748-9.
57. *Irish Catholic*, 29 Dec. 1906.
58. *Hansard* 4, clxvii (1906), 1750.
59. Norfolk to Bourne, 2 Jan. 1907 (Bourne Papers, Norfolk Ed. folder, item 1).
60. Copy of Bourne to Norfolk, 6 Jan. 1907 (Bourne Papers, Norfolk Ed. folder, item 12).

61. Bishop Casartelli to Bourne, 6 Jan. 1907 (Bourne Papers, Norfolk Ed. folder, item 7).

62. 'Memorandum sent to Bps of Birmingham, Clifton and Salford' (undated) (Bourne Papers, Norfolk Ed. folder, item 11).

63. Devlin to Redmond, 1 Jan. 1907 (RP).

64. *Irish Catholic Directory*, 1908, 465-6.

65. D. Gwynn, *Redmond*, 141-2; Lyons, *Dillon*, 291-2.

66. R.C.T.C.D., *Final Rep.*, 8, 37-41.

67. *Ibid.*, 8, 72-3.   68. *Ibid.*, 8, 32-6.

69. Draft of MacDonnell to [Walsh], 11 Jan. 1907 (McDP, c. 354, f. 162).

70. Bryce to Campbell-Bannerman, 23 Jan. 1907 (B.M., Campbell-Bannerman Papers, Add. MS 41,211/364-5).

71. *FJ*, 26 Jan. 1907.

72. Bryce to Campbell-Bannerman, 27 Jan. 1907 (B.M. Campbell-Bannerman Papers, Add. MS 41,211/366-7).

73. MacDonnell to Bryce, 28 Jan. [1907] (BrP, MS 11,012).

74. Walsh to MacDonnell, 4 Feb. 1907 (McDP, c. 351, ff. 154-7).

75. Bryce to Campbell-Bannerman, 27 Jan. 1907 (B.M., Campbell-Bannerman Papers, Add. MS 41,211/366-7).

76. Walsh to MacDonnell, 4 Feb. 1907 (McDP, c. 351, ff. 154-7).

77. Walsh to MacDonnell, 13 Feb. 1907 (McDP, c. 351, ff. 158-9).

78. *Independent*, 22 Feb. 1907.

79. *FJ*, 26 Feb. 1907.

80. Ó Broin, *Chief Secretary*, 22.

81. *Hansard* 4, clxix (1907), 3.   82. *Irish Times*, 17 Apr. 1907.

83. *Hansard* 4, clxxiv (1907), 113.

84. See D. Gwynn, *Redmond*, 142-9, which attempts to minimise Redmond's leanings toward the bill, and Lyons, *Dillon*, 294-7.

85. See reports of meetings on education in various parts of the country in *FJ*, Oct. 1906-Feb. 1907, *passim*.

86. *Ibid.*, 25 Mar. 1907.

87. *Irish Catholic Directory*, 1908, 467-8; *Irish Catholic*, 11 May 1907.

88. *Ibid.*   89. *Irish Catholic*, 18 May 1907.

90. *FJ*, 13 May 1907.   91. *Ibid.*

92. *Ibid.*, 17 May 1907.   93. *Ibid.*, 13 May 1907.

94. *Irish Catholic*, 18 May 1907.   95. *Ibid.*, 25 May 1907.

96. *FJ*, 13 May 1907.   97. *Ibid.*, 17 May 1907.

98. M. Joyce to Redmond, 14 May 1907 (RP).

99. *FJ*, 22 May 1907.   100. Birrell to Campbell-Bannerman, 24 May 1907 (B.M., Campbell-Bannerman Papers, Add. MS 41,239/250-251); Ó Broin, *Chief Secretary*, 15-16.

IX: Leaving Sir Antony in the Lurch

1. Birrell, *Things Past Redress*, 200-1.
2. Birrell to MacDonnell, 25 Aug. 1907 (McDP, c. 350, ff. 15-16).
3. Copy of MacDonnell to Birrell, Sep. 1907 (McDP, c. 354, ff. 7-11).
4. *Ibid.*　　5. *FJ*, 5 Apr. 1907.
6. *Ibid.*, 23 Nov. 1907.　　7. *Ibid.*
8. *Ibid.*, 24 Jun. 1908.　　9. *Ibid.*, 3 Jul., 28 Jul. 1908.
10. *Report of the Vice-regal Committee of Inquiry into Primary Education in Ireland*, I [Cmd 60], 37, H.C. 1919, xxi.
11. Haldane, *Autobiography*, 137-44.
12. Walsh, *Walsh*, 560-1.
13. Birrell, *Things Past Redress*, 203.
14. *Irish Times*, 4 Apr. 1908, quoting *Catholic Times*.
15. *Irish Universities Bill (as amended by Standing Committee C)* [Bill 306], p. 16, H.C. 1908, ii. In the original bill the registrar was omitted, the Crown was to nominate six, the Convocation was to elect five, six were to be co-opted and there was no restriction on whom the college governing bodies might elect.
16. This account is based on a synopsis of the article in the *Irish Times*, 5 May 1908.
17. *FJ*, 13 Jun. 1908.　　18. *Ibid.*, 15 Jun. 1908.
19. National University of Ireland, *Calendar for the Year 1961*, 270-83; . . . *1964*, 55-7; . . . *1969*, 44-6, 329-47.
20. *Irish Catholic Directory*, 1971, 865, 870-1, 873.
21. Birrell, *Things Past Redress*, 202.
22. *The Tablet*, 20 Jun. 1908.
23. *Irish Times*, 20 May 1908.　　24. *FJ*, 2 Jun. 1908.
25. *The Times*, 3 Jun. 1908.
26. R.C.U.Ed., *App. to 1st Rep.*, 49.
27. *Ibid.*, 303.
28. *The Tablet*, 20 Jun. 1908.
29. *FJ*, 18 Jun. 1908; *Report from Standing Committee C on the Irish Universities Bill*, p. 23, H.C. 1908 (219), ix.
30. *FJ*, 18 Jun. 1908. The covering letter from Bishop Sheehan is dated 17 June and carefully states that the resolutions are 'for insertion in your issue of to-morrow'.
31. *Ibid.*, 1 Jul. 1908.　　32. Walsh, *Walsh*, 561.
33. *Irish Catholic*, 18 Jul. 1908.
34. *Hansard* 4, cxciii (1908), 773-4.
35. *Irish Times*, 3 Aug. 1908.
36. *Hansard* 4, cxciii (1908), 416, 418.

X: The Ebbing Tide

1. D. Gwynn, *Redmond*, 151. Gwynn is in error, however, in implying that Esmonde resigned his seat and was defeated in a by-election. Cf. Lyons, *Dillon*, 299-301.
2. *Irish Catholic*, 17 Aug. 1907.
3. *Ibid.*, 21 Sep. 1907.   4. Lyons, *Party*, 117-24.
5. Dillon to Redmond, 11 Dec. 1907 (RP).
6. O'Brien, *Olive Branch*, 431.
7. Copy of Redmond to Bishop O'Donnell, 9 Dec. 1907 (RP).
8. Bishop O'Donnell to Redmond, 10 Dec. 1907 (RP): 'What you say of the Convention is essential in my opinion. Then if we were referring anything to a convention, we could only "recommend". I suppose "to report" is the function of *persons* having a [commission?].'
9. O'Brien, *Olive Branch*, 431.   10. Lyons, *Party*, 121-3.
11. This account is based mainly on Fergus MacDonald, *The Catholic Church and the Secret Societies in the United States*, New York 1946; Emmet Larkin, *James Larkin, Irish Labour Leader, 1876–1947*, London 1965, 313-14; and H. B. C. Pollard, *The Secret Societies of Ireland*, London 1922, 110-32.
12. T. F. McGrath, *History of the Ancient Order of Hibernians . . .* , Cleveland 1898, 207.
13. C.O. 904/11, Mar. 1905.   14. *Ibid.*   15. *Ibid.*
16. C.O. 904/117, Jul. 1905.   17. C.O. 904/117, Mar. 1905.
18. C.O. 904/117, Jul. 1905.
19. C.O. 904/119, Jun. 1909: 'Local people [in Donegal] too would not give houses for the holding of meetings of this [Scottish] Section owing to the clergy's opposition.'
20. C.O. 904/117, Oct., Nov. 1905.   21. *Ibid.*, Mar. 1906.
22. *Ibid.*, Jun. 1906.   23. *Ibid.*, Oct. 1907.
24. *Ibid.*   25. C.O. 904/118, Mar. 1908.   26. *Ibid.*
27. *Ibid.*, Jun. 1908.   28. C.O. 904/117, Sep., Dec. 1905.
29. *Ibid.*, Jan. 1906.   30. *Ibid.*   31. *Ibid.*
32. C.O. 904/118, Jun. 1908.   33. *Ibid.*, May 1908.
34. C.O. 904/119, Mar. 1909.   35. C.O. 904/118, Jul. 1908.
36. *Ibid.*
37. William O'Brien and Desmond Ryan, ed., *Devoy's Post Bag, 1871-1928*, Dublin 1948 and 1953, II, 358.
38. Dan O'Donnell of Sligo. C.O. 904/117, Jun. 1906.
39. *Ibid.*
40. Pollard, *Secret Societies*, 113; C.O. 904/117, Oct. 1907, 904/118, Feb. 1908.

41. C.O. 904/118, Feb. 1908.
42. According to Father McKinley. Apparently the Bishop of Edinburgh did not sign the memorial. C.O. 904/118, Sep. 1908.
43. *Ibid.*, Dec. 1908.
44. Ian Malcolm, ed., *Irish Facts for British Platforms* (Union Defence League) III (1909), 233, quoting *Independent*, 14 May 1909.
45. *Ibid.*, I (1907), 262.
46. Dillon to Redmond, 11 May 1907 (RP).
47. *Irish Catholic*, 22 Jun. 1907.
48. C.O. 904/118, Nov. 1908.
49. *History of Ireland, 1798–1924*, II, London 1926, 158.
50. E.g. C.O. 903/13, p. 48.
51. C.O. 903/13, 20-21; 903/14, pp. 6-7.
52. C.O. 903/14, pp. 11-13, 49-51.
53. *Irish Catholic*, 7 Dec. 1907.
54. Malcolm, ed., *Irish Facts* I, 317, quoting *FJ*, 26 Nov. 1907; C.O. 903/14, pp. 205-6; 903/15, p. 18.
55. Malcolm, ed., *Irish Facts* II (1908), 271, 414, 494.
56. *Sligo Independent*, 29 Feb. 1908.
57. Malcolm, ed., *Irish Facts*, I, 317, quoting *FJ*, 26 Nov. 1907.
58. *Ibid.*, I, 317-18; II, 49, quoting *Daily Express* (Dublin), 23 Nov. 1907.
59. *Ibid.*, I, 317-18.
60. *Ibid.*, II, 414, citing *Roscommon Herald*, 8 Aug. 1908; C.O. 904/118 Aug. 1908.
61. Henry, *Evolution of Sinn Fein*, 79.
62. Lyons, *Dillon*, 289.
63. See above (Chapter VIII).
64. *An Claidheamh Soluis*, 11, 18, 25 May 1907; N. I. Mac Cuináill to [Eóin Mac Néill?], 20 May 1907 (McNP).
65. *Leitrim Advertiser* (Mohill), 27 Feb. 1908.
66. *Impartial Reporter and Farmers Journal* (Enniskillen), 4 Jul. 1901: 'Manorhamilton[.] Mr. Charles Dolan, son of Mr. John Dolan, J.P., received the degree of Licentiate Philosophy at Maynooth College last week.'
67. Denis Johnston to Redmond, 27 Jun. 1907 (RP).
68. *Sligo Champion*, 29 Jun. 1907.   69. *Ibid.*, 6 Jul. 1907.
70. *Ibid.*
71. P. A. McHugh to Redmond, 1 Jul. 1907 (RP).
72. Redmond to T. C. Harrington, 19 Aug. 1907 (RP).
73. Harrington to Redmond, 20 Aug. 1907 (RP).

74. C.O. 904/117, Dec. 1907. 75. *Ibid.*

76. *Sligo Champion*, 15 Feb. 1908. 77. *Ibid.*, 22 Feb. 1908.

78. *Ibid.*, 15 Feb. 1908.

79. *Leitrim Advertiser*, 27 Feb. 1908.

80. *Ibid.*, 20 Feb. 1908.

81. Denis Johnston to Redmond, 27 Jun. 1907 (RP).

82. *Leitrim Advertiser*, 27 Feb. 1908.

83. O'Hegarty, *Ireland under the Union*, 656.

84. Brian Inglis, 'Moran of the *Leader* and Ryan of the *Irish Peasant*' in Conor Cruise O'Brien, ed., *The Shaping of Modern Ireland*, London 1960; repr. New York 1970, 115-23.

85. P. H. Pearse to Eóin Mac Néill, 24, 27 Feb. 1908 (McNP).

86. Copy of Mac Néill to Pearse, 4 Mar. 1908 (McNP).

87. Father Curran to Mac Néill, 15 June 1908 (McNP, Walsh folder).

88. Randolph S. Churchill, *Winston S. Churchill*, II, Boston 1967, 252, 430.

89. *Manchester Guardian*, 13 Apr. 1908.

90. Statement by Canon Richardson to District Committee of Manchester Catholic Federation, *Irish Catholic*, 9 May 1908.

91. *Ibid.*, and *Manchester Guardian*, 17 Apr. 1908.

92. *Irish Catholic*, 9 May 1908; *Manchester Guardian*, 20 Apr. 1908.

93. *Manchester Guardian*, 18 Apr. 1908.

94. Churchill to Asquith, 18, 19 Apr. 1908 (Bodl. MS Asquith, 19/285-90).

95. *Irish Catholic*, 9 May 1908.

96. Churchill to Asquith, 18 Apr. 1908 (Bodl. MS Asquith, 19/286).

97. *Manchester Guardian*, 21 Apr. 1908.

98. *Ibid.*, 22 Apr. 1908. 99. *Ibid.*, 23, 24 Apr. 1908.

100. Churchill to Asquith, 22 Apr. 1908 (Bodl. MS Asquith 19/297).

101. *Irish Catholic*, 9 May 1908.

102. Churchill, *Churchill*, II, 430-1.

103. Dillon to Redmond, 29 May 1907 (RP).

104. H. Boardman, 'The Leeds Convention and the Catholic Religion', *New Ireland Review* XXIX (Jul. 1908), 304.

105. *Irish Catholic*, 13 Jun. 1908.

106. *The Times*, 29 Jun. 1908.

107. *Annual Register*, 1908, 195-7.

108. *Irish Catholic*, 26 Sep. 1908.

109. *Annual Register*, 1908, 197. The Liberal vote was very far

below that of both the preceding and following general elections, and it seems likely that the procession incident did have a substantial influence, if only to cause large-scale Catholic abstention.

110. *Irish Catholic*, 3 Oct. 1908.
111. *Ibid.*, 10 Oct. 1908. The Limerick Guardians had also sent a copy of their resolution to Logue, but 'The Cardinal's letter, sent through his secretary Fr. Quinn, consisted of a simple acknowledgement of the resolution.'
112. *Ibid.*, 24 Oct. 1908.
113. *Ibid.* 114. *Ibid.*, 31 Oct. 1908.

XI: The Strange Ailments of Nationalist Ireland

1. Similar messages were received and read during the Convention from three other Irish prelates and Cardinal Moran, Archbishop of Sydney (*FJ*, 10, 11 Feb. 1909). The members of the Irish hierarchy who made the gesture were Logue (Armagh), Healy (Tuam), Fennelly (Cashel and Emly), McHugh (Derry), Hoare (Ardagh and Clonmacnoise), Brownrigg (Ossory), Clancy (Elphin), O'Neill (Dromore), O'Donnell (Raphoe), Fogarty (Killaloe), Browne (Cloyne), Mangan (Kerry), O'Dea (Clonfert), Tohill (Down and Connor) and Foley (Kildare and Leighlin). Archbishop Healy limited his message to perfunctory acknowledgement of the invitation, and several prelates, notably Logue, avoided specific endorsement of the party.
2. *The Times*, 10 Feb. 1909.
3. *Page of Irish History*, 492-3.
4. *The Times*, 10 Feb. 1909.
5. *FJ*, 9 Feb. 1909; *Page of Irish History*, 498-9.
6. *The Times*, 11 February 1909.
7. *Page of Irish History*, 494-6.
8. Walsh to Mac Néill, 16 Dec. 1908 (McNP).
9. *Irish Catholic*, 2 Jan. 1909.
10. *Ibid.* He also offered the less practical suggestion that the League bring its influence to bear on Trinity to adopt a similar requirement.
11. John Sweetman to Mac Néill, 28 Dec. 1908; cf. Liam Ó Doighnéain to [?], 17 Dec. 1908 (McNP).
12. Printed letter from Thomas Roche to members of N.U.I. Senate, 5 Dec. 1908; Thomas McGrath to [?], 20 Dec. 1908, with enclosure; C. Tierney and P. MacGeough to Mac Néill, 7 Jan. 1909; Tomás de Bhál [Rev. Thomas Wall] to

[?], n.d. [probably early Jan. 1909] (McNP). *The Times*, 31 Dec. 1908, 6 Jan. 1909.

13. Liam Ó Doighnéain to [?], 11 Jan. 1909, quoting Fionan [Mac Coluim?] (McNP).
14. *The Tablet*, 23 Jan. 1909.
15. Walsh to a Dr Henry, 20 Feb. 1909. (McNP).
16. *The Times*, 11 Feb. 1909.
17. *An Claidheamh Soluis*, 6 Mar. 1909.   18. *Ibid.*
19. Copy of Col. Maurice Moore to Canon Arthur Ryan, n.d. [c. 1 May 1909] (N.L.I., Col. Maurice Moore Papers, MS 10,567). *An Claidheamh Soluis*, 13 Feb. 1909, charged that priests had been 'suppressed' in Elphin and Raphoe dioceses, but noted with pleasure the speeches of clergymen at Wexford, Ennis and Nenagh (in Ferns and Killaloe dioceses) in support of the League's position during the preceding week. On Raphoe policy cf. letter from E. Mag Uidhir, O.D. (*ibid.,* 20 Feb. 1909).
20. *An Claidheamh Soluis*, 13 Feb. 1909.
21. *Ibid.,* 1 May 1909, quoting *Catholic Press* (Sydney).
22. Copy of Col. Maurice Moore to Canon Arthur Ryan, n.d. [c. 1 May 1909] (N.L.I., Moore Papers).
23. Canon Ryan to Moore, 5 May 1909 (N.L.I., Moore Papers).
24. Mac Néill to Moore, 14 May 1909; O'Hickey to Moore, 8 May 1909 (a letter followed by a postcard) (N.L.I., Moore Papers).
25. Copy of Moore to Ryan, 17 May 1909 (N.L.I., Moore Papers).
26. Ryan to Moore, 29 May 1909 (N.L.I., Moore Papers).
27. O'Hickey to Moore, 15 Jun. 1909 (N.L.I., Moore Papers).
28. Rev. Michael P. O'Hickey, *An Irish University, or Else—*, Dublin 1909, 31-2.
29. Walter McDonald, *Reminiscences of a Maynooth Professor*, ed. Denis Gwynn, London 1925, 243.
30. 'An Irish Priest', *The Irish Bishops and an Irish University*, Dublin 1909.
31. O'Hickey to Moore, 3 May 1909 (N.L.I., Moore Papers).
32. O'Hickey to Moore, 15 Jun. 1909 (N.L.I., Moore Papers).
33. Regrettably, the 1967 paperback abridgement of this work butchers the account of the O'Hickey case so that a general reader can probably make no sense of it.
34. *Irish Ecclesiastical Record*, ser. 4, XXXVI (Sep. 1909), 304.
35. John Sweetman to Mac Néill, 25 Jun. 1909 (McNP, Pearse folder).
36. On the politics of the General Council of County Councils

in this affair see Joseph Dolan to [?], 13, 15 Jul, 23 Aug. 1909, 24 Apr., 2 May, 30 Jun. 1910 (McNP).

37. *Page of Irish History*, 500-1.
38. D. Gwynn, *Redmond*, 165.
39. John Horgan, *Parnell to Pearse: Some Recollections and Reflections*, Dublin 1948, 190-1.
40. *Cork Examiner*, 26 Apr. 1909.   41. *Ibid.*, 20 Apr. 1909.
42. *Ibid.*, 21, 29 Apr. 1909.
43. Healy, *Letters and Leaders*, II, 486.
44. Rev. Michael Curran, 'The Late Archbishop of Dublin: 1841–1921', *Dublin Review* CLXIX (Jul.-Sep. 1921), 104-5.
45. C.O. 904/119, Mar. 1909.   46. *Ibid.*, Apr. 1909.
47. *Irish Catholic*, 22 May 1909; C.O. 904/119, May 1909.
48. C.O. 904/119, Jun. 1909.   49. *Ibid.*, Aug. 1909.
50. See O'Brien, *Olive Branch*, 420-1n.
51. *Irish Catholic*, 27 Feb. 1909.
52. See his references to Sinn Féin in his letter published on 15 December 1906 denouncing the party's action on the English Education Bill, above (Chapter VIII).
53. Birrell, *Things Past Redress*, 209.
54. Dillon to Redmond, 9 Jul. 1906 (RP).
55. Rev. E. Maguire to Eóin Mac Néill, 14 Apr. 1906 (McNP).
56. *Irish Catholic Directory*, 1906, 465.
57. See report in *FJ*, 16 Jul. 1906.
58. S. S. Mac a' Bháird to Mac Néill, 15 Mar. 1909 (McNP).
59. *Ibid.*; *An Claidheamh Soluis*, 13 Mar. 1909.
60. Joseph J. Dolan to Mac Néill(?), 5 Jun. 1909 (McNP).
61. *The Tablet*, 21 Aug. 1909; also information kindly supplied by the Rev. Kevin O'Doherty in a letter to the author, December 1970.
62. O'Hickey to Moore, 15 Jun. 1909 (N.L.I., Moore Papers).
63. Bishop Kelly to Redmond, 13 Dec. 1905 (RP).
64. Churchill, *Churchill*, II, 270.
65. Sir Henry Robinson, Vice-President of the Local Government Board for Ireland. The Irish report was signed by all the members of the majority group except one who was honest enough to confess his ignorance of Irish affairs. (Another commissioner appended a note indicating her agreement only insofar as the Irish report coincided with the majority English report.) Nevertheless, it was Robinson and Bishop Kelly who undertook the responsibility of defending the peculiarities of the Irish report against criticisms from Mrs Webb's group. In doing so they styled themselves 'the

members appointed on the Commission specially to represent Ireland, and to apply to the Irish problems our lifelong knowledge and experience of that country' (Royal Commission on the Poor Law and Relief of Distress, *Report on Ireland*, p. 87 [Cd 4630], H.C. 1909, xxxviii). It seems likely that for the sake of harmony most of the commissioners simply went along with whatever Robinson and Bishop Kelly wanted with respect to Ireland.

66. The minority preferred government subsidy of existing trade union insurance schemes to a nationwide insurance programme.

67. *Report on Ireland*, 53.   68. *Ibid.*, 85-6.

69. Churchill, *Churchill*, II, 291; Companion Volume II, 831-2, 867.

70. See above (Chapter III).   71. *Independent*, 3 Jun. 1909.

72. *Cork Accent*, 1 Jan. 1910.

73. *Independent*, 31 May 1909.

74. As a better use for the proposed State contribution to land purchase, *FJ*, 27 Jan. 1903.

75. D. Gwynn, *Redmond*, 162-5.

76. *Irish Catholic*, 27 Nov. 1909; Healy, *Letters and Leaders*, II, 489.

XII: Redmond Imperator

1. D. Gwynn, *Redmond*, 169.

2. *Cork Accent*, 11 Jan. 1910.

3. See reports of West Waterford and Ossory conventions, *ibid.*, 3 Jan. 1910.

4. *Ibid.*, 4 Jan. 1910.

5. *Ibid.*, 7 Jan. 1910.

6. *Cork Examiner*, 3 Jan. 1910.

7. E.g. *ibid.*, 7 Jan. 1910.

8. Based on examination of *Cork Examiner, Cork Accent, Waterford Star* and *Kerry Sentinel* for Jan. 1910.

9. *Kerry Sentinel* (Tralee), 1, 5, 8, 19, 22 Jan. 1910. A Mgr O'Leary did sign the nomination paper of Mr Murphy, the Irish Parliamentary Party candidate, however (*Cork Examiner*, 19 Jan. 1910).

10. *Cork Examiner* and *Cork Accent*, Jan. 1910, *passim*.

11. *Cork Accent*, 3 Jan. 1910.

12. *Cork Examiner*, 18 Jan. 1910.

13. *Cork Accent*, 8 Jan. 1910: 'In East Limerick almost every priest of Limerick Diocese is supporting Mr Bennett against

Mr Lundon.' If any significant number of Cashel priests had supported Bennett, the O'Brienite, presumably the *Accent* would not have qualified its statement in this way.

14. London 1912, 116-21.
15. *Connaught Telegraph*, Dec. 1909, Jan. 1910, *passim*; C.O. 903/16, 78-9.
16. Rev. James Stephens to Redmond, 10 Mar. 1910 (RP).
17. Copy of letter from secretaries of South Mayo clergy to Redmond, n.d. (RP).
18. Rev. James Stephens to Redmond, 11 Feb. 1910 (RP).
19. *Dundalk Democrat*, 18 Dec. 1909-22 Jan. 1910.
20. *Westmeath Examiner* (Mullingar), 15 Jan. 1910.
21. This account is based on *Westmeath Examiner*, 1, 15 Jan. 1910, *Midland Reporter* (Mullingar), 20 Jan. 1910.
22. He had supported Healy in the 'seats deal' controversy of 1895 (Lyons, *Party*, 52n.).
23. *Ulster Herald* (Omagh), 1, 15 Jan. 1910.
24. G. F. Brunskill (Con.), 2,475; J. Valentine (Nat.), 2,070; G. Murnaghan (Ind. Nat.), 1,244.
25. *Weekly Freeman* (Dublin), 1 Jan. 1910; *Cork Examiner*, 3 Jan. 1910; *Frontier Sentinel* (Newry), 29 Jan. 1910.
26. *Weekly Freeman*, 8 Jan. 1910.
27. *Ibid.*, 15 Jan. 1910.
28. Healy, *Letters and Leaders*, II, 491.
29. *Cork Accent*, 18, 19 Jan. 1910.
30. *Ibid.*, 24 Jan. 1910.
31. *Weekly Freeman*, 5, 19 Mar., 2, 16 Apr. 1910.
32. Healy to O'Brien, 13 May 1910 (N.L.I., O'Brien Papers (hereafter cited O'BP), MS 8556/3).
33. Copy of O'Brien to Healy, 19 Mar. 1910 (O'BP, MS 8556/3).
34. Healy, *Letters and Leaders*, II, 498.
35. Healy to O'Brien, 13 May 1910 (O'BP, MS 8556/3).
36. *Dundalk Democrat*, 21 May 1910; *Dundalk Examiner*, 21 May 1910.
37. Healy, *Letters and Leaders*, II, 498, 502.
38. *Dundalk Democrat*, 26 Nov. 1910; *Cork Free Press*, 24 Nov. 1910.
39. *Independent*, 1, 8 Dec. 1910.
40. Healy, *Letters and Leaders*, II, 502-4.
41. *Cork Free Press*, 3 Dec. 1910; cf. letter from Dean Shinkwin in *Irish Catholic*, 10 Dec. 1910.
42. *Cork Free Press*, 22 Dec. 1910.
43. See esp. *Kerry Sentinel*, 10-17 Dec. 1910, for South Kerry

election; *Limerick Leader,* 5 Dec. 1910, for East Limerick election; *Kilkenny People,* 24 Dec. 1910, and *Independent,* 19 Dec. 1910, for South Kilkenny election; *Waterford Star,* 10 Dec. 1910, for West Waterford election; *The People* (Wexford), 30 Nov., 10 Dec. 1910, for South Wexford election.

44. *Independent,* 29 Nov. 1910.
45. *Cork Free Press,* 22 Dec. 1910.

XIII: Home Rule Politics

1. Quoted in George Dangerfield, *The Strange Death of Liberal England* (London 1936), New York 1961, 1.
2. *Irish Catholic,* 23 Sep. 1911.
3. See remarks of Cardinal Logue, speaking at a new church in Glenties, Co. Donegal: 'The other day in England, one of their PROMINENT POLITICIANS assured his audience that the Irish people are prepared to give up their religion for Home Rule.' *Irish Catholic,* 7 Oct. 1911.
4. *Weekly Freeman* (Dublin), 22 Apr. 1911.
5. Emmet Larkin, 'Socialism and Catholicism in Ireland', *Church History* XXXIII (Dec. 1964).
6. *Ibid.,* 462.
7. Walter McDonald, *Some Ethical Aspects of the Social Question: Suggestions for Priests,* London 1920, 4.
8. Of course, the agricultural society was intricately stratified. I do not mean to suggest that Dublin labourers tended to come from the same strata as did priests. Probably a high proportion of priests came from the 'strong farmer' class while a majority of the Dublin labourers came from the landless agricultural labouring class. It is not clear, however, that in the rural setting Irish priests consistently extended their sympathy more to one agricultural class than to another. All these points deserve further exploration than has been undertaken in this study.
9. But see statement by the Rev. R. Fitzhenry, Adm., preaching in Enniscorthy Cathedral: 'Socialism . . . aimed at destroying the purity of the home and the sacredness of marriage.' *Independent,* 15 Jan. 1912.
10. *Irish Catholic,* 5 Oct. 1907.
11. J. Dunsmore Clarkson, *Labour and Nationalism in Ireland* ('Studies in History, Economics and Public Law', Vol. CXX, whole number 266, New York, 1925), 200.
12. Larkin, *Larkin,* 51.
13. *Weekly Freeman,* 1 Oct. 1910.

14. Sermon by Father O'Donovan at Birr, *Irish Catholic*, 30 Sep. 1911.
15. *Ibid*   16. *Ibid*.
17. *Irish Ecclesiastical Record*, ser. 4, XXX (Nov. 1911), 543-4.
18. *Irish Catholic*, 27 Sep. 1913.
19. Larkin, *Larkin*, 138, quoting *FJ*, 21 Oct. 1913.
20. Larkin, *Larkin*, 138-40. In fairness it should be noted that the operations of several Protestant-dominated adoption agencies in Ireland created the impression, probably partly justified, that one motive of Protestant families in taking Catholic children into their homes was to make converts. Interestingly, an organisation to combat these agencies, the Catholic Protection and Rescue Society, was formed in this very year (John Whyte, *Church and State in Modern Ireland, 1923–1970*, Dublin 1971, 191).
21. *Irish Catholic*, 22 Nov. 1913.
22. Larkin in *Church History* XXXIII, 480.
23. *The Tablet*, 1 Jul. 1911.   24. *Ibid*.
25. *Hansard* 5, xxxi (1911), 208-332.
26. This figure involves certain adjustments made necessary by the disruption in public accounts because of the 1909–10 budget controversy. *Report by the Committee on Irish Finance*, pp. 3-4 [Cd 6153], H.C. 1912-13, xxxiv.
27. *Ibid.*, 5. One important service, the Congested Districts Board was financed largely out of money from the Irish Church Fund (created by the disestablishment of the Church of Ireland), which was not included in annual parliamentary votes. The Ireland Development Grant was being consumed, almost in its entirety, by the Land Purchase Guarantee Fund.
28. Birrell, *Things Past Redress*, 210-11.
29. This is clear from Bishop Kelly to Redmond, 16 Sep. 1911 (RP): 'I have just now heard from him [Primrose] that all have applauded the Draft except one. However, he is the least important. The Chairman, the City men, Gladstone, Pirrie—these are the big names before the English public.'
30. These remarks are, necessarily, very simplified. For a more complete summary of the various schemes, see *Rep. Comm. Irish Finance*, 9-16.
31. *Ibid.*, 25.
32. Kelly to Redmond, 16 Sep. 1911 (RP).
33. *Cork Accent*, 1 Jan. 1910.
34. Horgan, *Parnell to Pearse*, 251.
35. *FJ*, 5 Feb. 1912.

36. Dillon to Redmond, 14 Jan. 1912 (RP).
37. Kelly to Redmond, 21, 28 Dec. 1911, Dillon to Redmond, 14 Jan. 1912, Kelly to Dillon, 17 Jan. 1912, and memorandum by Bishop Kelly, 'Home Rule v. Devolution', 17 Jan. 1912 (RP).
38. *Irish Weekly Independent* (Dublin), 27 Apr. 1912.
39. *FJ*, 15 May 1912.
40. RP. The original of this letter appears to have been lost. Before arrangement of the Redmond Papers, which was done by my wife and myself in 1965–66, there was a small folder in the unsorted collection marked 'Archbishop Walsh and Bishop O'Dwyer—Home Rule Fund 1912'. The folder, however, contained only one letter, that from O'Dwyer to Redmond quoted below. During the sorting operation, the only trace which was found of correspondence with Walsh in 1912 was a typed extract headed 'Archbp Walsh to R Dublin March 20 '12', among what appear to have been Denis Gwynn's notes for his biography of Redmond. It is not clear whether the extract includes the entire letter.
41. O'Dwyer to Redmond, 10 Mar. 1912 (RP).
42. *Hansard* 5, xxxv (1912), 722-8.
43. O'Dwyer to Redmond, 10 Mar. 1912 (RP).
44. *The Tablet*, 16 Mar. 1912.
45. Telegram from Bishop O'Donnell to Redmond, 18 Mar. 1912 (RP).
46. Copy of confidential memorandum to Bishop O'Donnell, 21 Mar. 1912 (RP).
47. Bishop O'Donnell to Redmond, 24 Mar. 1912; see also Bishop O'Donnell to Redmond, 18 Mar. 1912 (RP).
48. *Irish Times*, 11 Sep. 1912.
49. *Ibid.*, 9 Oct. 1912.
50. *Correspondence between the Chief Secretary for Ireland and the Catholic Healmasters' Association in Reference to the Proposed Grant of £40,000 Per Annum for the Improvement of the Position of Secondary Teachers in Ireland*, [Cd 6924], H.C. 1913, l.
51. *Hansard* 5, xlii (1912), 2271.
52. This information, together with much of what follows, is from a calendar of material in the Armagh diocesan archives. Though the material itself is not open to inspection, I was allowed, by kind permission of His Eminence Cardinal Conway, Archbishop of Armagh, to inspect the calendar, which is in the possession of the Rev. Professor Tomás Ó Fiaich of

St Patrick's College, Maynooth. Material from the calendar will be cited *Armagh dio. cal.* with the heading and item number under which it is entered. This document is *Armagh dio. cal.*, Government of Ireland Bill—1912, 1, Logue to O'Donnell, 5 Nov. 1912.

53. *Ibid.*, 2, James Murnaghan to O'Donnell, 7 Nov. 1912.

54. *Ibid.*, 3, Birrell to Redmond, 7 Nov. 1912.

55. Bishop O'Donnell to Redmond, 7 Dec. 1912 (RP).

56. *Government of Ireland Bill*, p. 3 [Bill 136], *Government of Ireland Bill [as amended in Committee and on Report]*, pp. 3-4 [Bill 347], H.C. 1912–13, ii. See also *Hansard* 5, xlii (1912), 2035-91, 2215-2331.

57. This discussion is based upon the copy of Murnaghan's memorandum enclosed in Bishop O'Donnell to Redmond, 7 Dec. 1912 (RP). Though the memorandum was submitted to the bishops in five parts between 9 November and 30 November 1912, I have not attempted to distinguish here among the various parts by separate footnotes.

58. Bishop O'Donnell to Redmond 7 Dec. 1912.

59. *Armagh dio. cal.*, Government of Ireland Bill—1912, 11, Logue to O'Donnell, 3 Dec. 1912.

60. Bishop O'Donnell to Redmond, 7 Dec. 1912 (RP).

61. Murnaghan memorandum, enclosed in *ibid.*

62. *Armagh dio. cal.*, Government of Ireland Bill—1912, 9, Logue to O'Donnell, 20 Nov. 1912.

63. *Ibid.*, 10, Logue to O'Donnell, 22 Nov. 1912.

64. *Ibid.*, 11, Logue to O'Donnell, 3 Dec. 1912.

65. *Ibid.*, 12, Logue to O'Donnell, 6 Dec. 1912.

66. O'Donnell to Redmond, 7 Dec. 1912 (RP).

67. Copy of Redmond to O'Donnell, 12 Dec. 1912 (RP).

68. *Armagh dio. cal.*, Government of Ireland Bill—1912, 16, Logue to O'Donnell, 14 Dec. 1912.

69. *Ibid.*, O'Donnell Archives, 190, Logue to O'Donnell, 20 Dec. 1912.

70. O'Donnell to Redmond, 15 Dec. 1912 (RP).

71. *Irish Times*, 20 Dec. 1912.

XIV: The Protestant Rebellion

1. A. T. Q. Stewart, *The Ulster Crisis*, London 1967, 47-8.

2. *Ibid.*, 69.   3. *Ibid.*, 61-2.

4. *Irish Catholic*, 2 Aug. 1913.

5. *The Times*, 11 Sep. 1913.

6. Synopsis of the speech in *Annual Register*, 1913, [209], in-

correctly dated as 9 Oct. Actually 8 Oct. 1913.

7. D. Gwynn, *Redmond*, 231-2.
8. Roy Jenkins, *Asquith: Portrait of a Man and an Era*, New York 1966, 294; D. Gwynn, *Redmond*, 234-7.
9. O'Donnell to Redmond, 9 Oct. 1913 (RP).
10. O'Donnell to Redmond, 5 Jan. 1914 (RP).
11. Jenkins, *Asquith*, 301; D. Gwynn, *Redmond*, 250-4.
12. In the Redmond Papers, a letter from O'Donnell to Redmond, which seems to be dated 18 February 1914, is written on Charing Cross Hotel stationery and appears to contain O'Donnell's reflections on a conference he had just had with the party leaders. Another letter dated 25 February 1914, from O'Donnell to Redmond, in RP, refers to a decision which had been made 'by you and your colleagues . . . when I was with you'.
13. O'Donnell to Redmond, 18 Feb. 1914 (RP).
14. Reprinted in F. X. Martin, ed., *The Irish Volunteers, 1913–1915, Recollections and Documents*, Dublin 1963, 57-61.
15. Kevin B. Nowlan, 'Tom Clarke, MacDermott, and the I.R.B.' in Martin, ed., *Leaders and Men*, 109-10.
16. Diarmuid Lynch, *The I.R.B. and the 1916 Insurrection*, ed. F. O'Donoghue, Cork 1957, 22-3.
17. Bishop McHugh to Redmond, 28 Feb. 1914 (RP); D. Gwynn, *Redmond*, 264-7.
18. O'Donnell to Redmond, 25 Feb. 1914 (RP). I believe Denis Gwynn's transcription of Bishop O'Donnell's scarcely legible handwriting to be faulty in this case (*Redmond*, 262-3).
19. McHugh to Redmond, 28 Feb. 1914 (RP).
20. D. Gwynn, *Redmond*, 265-6.
21. *Ibid.*, 266.
22. O'Donnell to Redmond, 5 Jan. 1914 (RP).
23. O'Donnell to Redmond, 25 Feb. 1914 (RP).
24. D. Gwynn, *Redmond*, 258-60.
25. Devlin to Redmond, 5, 6 Mar. 1914 (RP).
26. Devlin to Redmond, 6 Mar. 1914 (RP).
27. Devlin to Redmond, 'Saturday' [7 Mar. 1914] (RP).
28. D. Gwynn, *Redmond*, 270.
29. Copy of telegram from Redmond to Bishop McHugh, n.d. [20 Mar. 1914?] (RP).
30. McHugh to Redmond, 21 Mar. 1914 (RP).
31. C.O. 904/93, Jun. 1914, Report of I.-G. On Archbishop Healy's action see *Irish Catholic*, 13, 20 Jun. 1914.
32. *Irish Catholic*, 20 Jun. 1914.

33. C.O. 904/93, Jun. 1914, County Inspectors' reports for Armagh, Clare, Co. Dublin, Fermanagh, Galway (E.R.), Galway (W.R.), Kilkenny, Leitrim, Limerick, Longford, Louth, Meath, Roscommon, Tipperary (N.R.), Tipperary (S.R.), Tyrone, Waterford and Wexford.
34. *Irish Catholic*, 8 Aug. 1914 (repr. from the city edition of *ibid.*, 1 Aug. 1914).
35. Stephen Gwynn, *John Redmond's Last Years*, London 1919, 131.

XV: The Catholic Rebellion

1. D. Gwynn, *Redmond*, 354, quoting *The Autobiography of Margot Asquith*, II, 163.
2. D. Gwynn, *Redmond*, 355-7.
3. *Ibid.*, 380-1.   4. *Ibid.*, 391-4.
5. *Irish Catholic*, 15 Aug. 1914.
6. C.O. 904/14, Aug. 1914.
7. Redmond to Asquith, 22 Aug. 1914 (Bodl. MS Asquith, 36/79).
8. *Irish Catholic*, 3 Oct. 1914.
9. *Independent*, 29 Sep. 1914.
10. Healy to O'Brien, 2 Jan. 1915 (O'BP, MS 8556/9).
11. C.O. 903/18, 63.
12. *Irish Catholic*, 6 Nov. 1915. The main features of the controversy can be followed in the *Irish Catholic* from shortly after the outbreak of the war to late 1915. Early in 1916, Mgr Amigo, Bishop of Southwark, admitted to Sir Henry Howard, British Minister to the Holy See, 'a want of cordial co-operation between the Archbishop of Westminster and the Irish Bishops' (Howard to Eric [Drummond, private secretary to the Foreign Secretary], 5 Feb. 1916 (P.R.O., Archives of British Ministry to the Holy See, F.O. 380/8/16).)
13. *Irish Catholic*, 24 Apr. 1915.
14. D. Gwynn, *Redmond*, 449.
15. Royal Commission on the Rebellion in Ireland, *Minutes of Evidence and Appendix of Documents*, p. 58 [Cd 8311], H.C. 1916, xi.
16. Healy to O'Brien, 24 Dec. 1914 (O'BP, MS 8556/8).
17. C.O. 903/18, p. 63.
18. *Irish Catholic*, 17 Oct. 1914. •
19. *Ibid.*, 31 Jul. 1915.   20. *Ibid.*, 6 Nov. 1915.
21. Healy to O'Brien, 21 May 1915 (O'BP, MS 8556/9).
22. After Irish Parliamentary Party protests, Campbell was given

the lesser post of Irish Attorney-General instead. Ironically, Campbell later became (as Lord Glenavy) more moderate in his views and served in the Irish Free State Senate.

23. Copy of Fogarty to Redmond, 3 Jun. 1915 (Bodl., MS Asquith, 36/98-9).
24. Redmond to Asquith, 7 Jun. 1915 (Bodl., MS Asquith, 36/94).
25. *Irish Catholic*, 21 Aug. 1915. The Bishop of Limerick published the correspondence with Redmond's permission.
26. *Ibid.*   27. *Ibid.*, 9 Oct. 1915.
28. Dorothy Macardle, *The Irish Republic*, New York 1965, 138.
29. Cavan, Clare, Cork, Donegal, Down, Galway, Kerry, Kildare, Kilkenny, King's, Leitrim, Louth, Mayo, Sligo, Tipperary, Tyrone and Wexford, as well as the city of Belfast; C.O. 904/120/2, Nov., Dec. 1915.
30. Attributed to Rev. M. Hogan, P.P., Silvermines, 21 Nov. 1915, C.O. 903/19/1, p. 48.
31. *Irish Catholic*, 21 Aug. 1915.   32. *Ibid.*
33. *Ibid.*, 14 Aug. 1915.   34. *Ibid.*
35. *Ibid.*, 28 Aug., 27 Nov. 1915.   36. *Ibid.*, 14 Aug. 1915.
37. *Ibid.*, 27 Nov. 1915. The full text of the letter, however, is not printed.
38. *Ibid.*, 11 Dec. 1915.
39. Seán Ó Lúing, *I Die in a Good Cause*, Tralee 1970, 48-59.
40. *Ibid.*, 58, quoting P. Béaslaí in *Independent*, 16 May 1957.
41. F. X. Martin, 'Eoin MacNeill on the 1916 Rising', *Irish Historical Studies* XII (Mar. 1961).
42. *Ibid.*, 239.
43. Statement by Bulmer Hobson, quoted *ibid.*, 229-30.
44. A summary of the arguments for and against the document's authenticity may be found in Desmond Ryan, *The Rising: The Complete Story of Easter Week*, 3rd ed., Dublin 1957, 64-75.
45. Martin in *I.H.S.* XII, 248, 257.
46. 'M' [Rev. Michael Curran] to 'Con' [C. P. Curran], 22 Apr. 1949. Letter in possession of C. P. Hyland, 82 Ranelagh, Dublin, and containing an extract from Father Curran's diary for 21 April 1916.
47. 'Proceedings of a General Court-Martial held at Dublin on the 22nd day of May 1916. . . . Trial of John alias Eoin Mac-Neill a Civilian' (typescript in possession of Mrs Eibhlín MacNeill Tierney, used by her kind permission).
48. Martin in *I.H.S.* XII, 267. Father Martin's reference to the

court martial proceedings should read 'pp. 97-100' instead of 'pp. 77-80'.

49. 'Extracts from the Papers of the Late Dr. Patrick McCartan,' Part Two, *Clogher Record* V (No. 2, 1964), 199; Mainchín Seoighe, 'Limerick and the Easter Week Rising', in *Cuimhnionn Luimneach*, Limerick [1966], 35-6.

50. Moirín Chavasse, *Terence MacSwiney*, Dublin 1961, 56-90, 207-12; Florence O'Donoghue, *Tomás MacCurtain*, Tralee 1958, 94-103, 210-14.

51. Father Aloysius, O.F.M.Cap., 'Easter Week 1916—Personal Recollections', *Capuchin Annual* (1942), 211-16.

52. O'Connor, *History of Ireland*, II, 278.

53. Ryan, *Rising*, 68; John Whyte, '1916—Revolution and Religion' in Martin, ed., *Leaders and Men*, 223.

54. Walsh, *Walsh*, 592-3.

55. From the text of Vatican communiqué forwarded to Foreign Office by Sir Henry Howard, telegram from Howard to F.O., 3 May 1916, F.O. 380/8/52. That the original Vatican telegram was sent during Easter week is clear from a cutting from *Corriere della Sera* (Milan), 29 Apr. 1916 in F.O. 380/8/53. This press report indicated that the papal telegram went to the 'cardinale arcivescovo di Dublino', an error which was repeated in the English press, but upon enquiry Cardinal Gasparri quickly corrected the obvious mistake and assured Howard that the telegram was in fact sent to Logue (Howard to Drummond, 3 May 1916 (F.O. 380/8/53)).

56. *Irish Weekly Independent*, 29 Apr.-13 May 1916, quoting telegram from Rome correspondent of *Daily Mail* dated 2 May 1916.

57. Telegram from Foreign Office to Howard, 2 May 1916 (F.O. 380/9/34), citing press telegrams and repeating the error that the Archbishop of Dublin was the recipient of the papal message. This passage is almost a literal translation from the *Corriere della Sera* report noted above: '. . . raccomandare ai cattolici di cooperare a restabilire l'ordine e di non far nulla che possa intralciare l'opera della autorità inglesi.' (F.O. 380/8/53).

58. Howard to Drummond, 3 May 1916 (F.O. 380/8/53).

59. Vesey Knox to Lloyd George, 26 May 1916 (Beaverbrook Library, Lloyd George Papers (hereafter cited LGP), D/14/1/16).

XVI: The Terrible Beauty

1. *Irish Catholic*, 13 May 1916.   2. *Ibid.*

3. *Irish Weekly Independent*, 29 Apr., 6, 13 May 1916.
4. *Irish Catholic*, 13 May 1916.　　5. *Ibid.*
6. *Ibid.*, 20 May 1916.
7. Whyte, '1916—Revolution and Religion' in Martin, ed., *Leaders and Men*, 221.
8. Seoighe, 'Limerick and the Easter Week Rising' in *Cuimhnionn Luimneach*, 43.
9. *Ibid.*, 45.
10. Cf. the efforts of the police to persuade Archbishop McEvilly to curb the actions of one of his priests in 1898 (Chapter I). If, as seems likely, Maxwell's famous letter to O'Dwyer was only one of several such letters to bishops of priests on the Castle's list of 'disloyal' clergy, the General covered his tracks well. The police intelligence notes for 1916 do contain a reference to an action by Bishop Hackett of Waterford and Lismore similar to that requested of O'Dwyer, but there is no indication that it was officially requested (Chief Secretary's Office, Dublin Castle, *Intelligence Notes, 1913–16*, ed. Breandán Mac Giolla Choille, Dublin 1966, 216).
11. D. Gwynn, Redmond, 502-23; Ian Colvin, *The Life of Lord Carson*, 1936, III, 162-79.
12. Devlin to Redmond, 'Sunday night 3/6/16' (RP). 3 June was a Saturday. From internal evidence the correct date seems to be 4 June 1916.
13. *Ibid.*　　14. *Ibid.*
15. *Ibid.*, and MacVeagh to Redmond, 'Tuesday Midnight' [6 Jun. 1916] (RP).
16. MacVeagh to Redmond, 'Tuesday Midnight' [6 Jun. 1916] (RP).
17. Telegram from Logue to Redmond, 7 Jun. 1916 and Redmond's copy of his reply (RP).
18. Logue to Redmond, 11 Jun. 1916 (RP).
19. Copy of Redmond to Logue, 12 Jun. 1916 (RP).
20. D. Gwynn, *Redmond*, 508-9.
21. Devlin to Redmond, 4 Jun. 1916 (RP). See also Dillon to Redmond, 5 Jun. 1916 (RP): 'Devlin called me up from Belfast just now—He said that *everywhere* outside Belfast the proposed terms were rejected with contempt—Everybody absolutely refused to discuss or consider them.'
22. In Devlin to Redmond, 4 Jun. 1916 (RP), Devlin says that Bishop McHugh showed him the letter, signed by these men, soliciting an expression of support from him. McHugh indicated that he would reply 'that he feels sure the Irish

Party will take no action with regard to Ulster without consulting the Nationalists of Ulster'. If he did make any such suggestion of confidence in the party, the *Weekly Independent* did not include it in its report of McHugh's letter in the issue of 17 June 1916.

23. *Irish Weekly Independent*, 17 Jun. 1916.
24. Dillon to Lloyd George, 11 Jun. 1916, 10 a.m. (LGP, D/14/2/25).
25. *Irish Weekly Independent*, 17 Jun. 1916.
26. *Irish News*, 17 Jun. 1916.
27. *Irish Weekly Independent*, 24 Jun. 1916.
28. *Ibid.*, 17 Jun. 1916.
29. *Ibid.*, 24 Jun. 1916.
30. Telegram from Devlin to Redmond, 19 Jun. 1916 (RP).
31. S. Gwynn, *Redmond's Last Years*, 235.
32. *Irish News*, 17 Jun. 1916.
33. Dillon to Lloyd George, 16 Jun. 1916, 7 p.m. (LGP, D/14/3/2).
34. *Irish Weekly Independent*, 24 Jun. 1916.
35. Cf. D. Gwynn, *Redmond*, 372.
36. *Return Showing Government Proposals in Connection with the Government of Ireland Bill*, H.C. 1914 (143), lxvii.
37. *Headings of a Settlement as to the Government of Ireland* [Cd 8310], H.C. 1916, xxii.
38. *Irish Weekly Independent*, 24 Jun. 1916.
39. *Irish Catholic*, 24 Jun. 1916.
40. *Ibid.*
41. *Record of the Maynooth Union*, 1915-16, 48.
42. D. Gwynn, *Redmond*, 511; S. Gwynn, *Redmond's Last Years*, 235.
43. *Irish News*, 24 Jun. 1916.
44. *Ibid.*, 17 Jun. 1916.
45. *Hansard* 5, lxxxiv (1916), 1427-34.
46. Timothy Patrick Coogan, *Ireland Since the Rising*, London 1966; New York 1966, 20.
47. F. X. Martin, '1916—Myth, Fact, and Mystery', *Studia Hibernica* 9 (1967), 115.
48. T. P. O'Connor to Lloyd George, 13 Jun. 1916 (LGP, D/14/2/35).
49. See statement attributed to M. P. Colivet released by Irish executive in July 1918 (*Notes from Ireland* XXVII (1918), 82; Martin in *Studia Hibernica* 9 (1967), 112).
50. *Ibid.*, 116.

51. T. P. O'Connor to Lloyd George, 13 Jun. 1916 (LGP, D/ 14/2/35).

52. *Ibid.*

53. Michael O'Connell, Sergeant, D.M.P., to Superintendent, E Division, D.M.P., 4 Jun. 1916 (S.P.O.I., C.S.O., Registered Papers, 1916/11840); Dillon to Lloyd George, 11 Jun. 1916, 10 a.m. (LGP, D/14/2/25).

54. It is possible that the discontinuance of the imprimatur had something to do with another series of articles, 'Ritual Murder among the Jews', which the *Catholic Bulletin* had been publishing, and which had understandably disturbed the Dublin Jewish community. See C.O. 904/161/8.

55. *Irish Weekly Independent*, 22 Jul. 1916.

56. *The Times*, 26 Jul. 1916, citing *Derry People and Donegal News*, 22 Jul. 1916.

57. *Irish Weekly Independent*, 29 Jul. 1916; *New Ireland*, 19 Aug. 1916.

58. *The Times*, 14 Aug. 1916.

59. *Irish Weekly Independent*, 16 Sep. 1916, and *passim*; O'Connor, *History of Ireland*, II, 283; *The Times*, 2 Oct. 1916.

60. *Irish Weekly Independent*, 29 Jul. 1916.

61. *Ibid.*

62. Richard Canon O'Kennedy, 'The Most Rev. E. T. O'Dwyer', *Irish Monthly* XLVI (Jan. 1918), 29-30.

63. *Ibid.*, 30.

64. *Letters of the Late Bishop O'Dwyer*, n.p., n.d.

65. *Ibid.* The statement 'Sinn Fein is, in my judgement, the true principle' was apparently censored out of the Dublin press reports. It appeared, however, in the report published here and in the *Limerick Leader*.

66. *Irish Weekly Independent*, 28 Oct. 1916.

67. Healy to O'Brien, 17 Oct. 1916 (O'BP, MS 8556/11): 'One of Redmonds friends—I presume Dr O'D—proposed or suggested a resolution of confidence in the Party & its Leader. This audacity was at once eloquently attacked by Dr McHugh who was strongly backed by the Cardinal Dr Walsh & Dr O'Dwyer. The proposal was therefore either withdrawn or defeated.' Healy adds that he has given the information to William Martin Murphy, who presumably obtained more refined information before publishing the account in the *Weekly Independent* quoted above.

68. Ó Broin, *Chief Secretary*, 204.

69. *Cork Examiner*, 13 Nov. 1916.

70. This account is based on *Cork Examiner*, 30 Oct.-16 Nov. 1916, and Cork Free Press, 11 Nov. 1916. The votes were O'Leary, 1,866; Healy, 1,750; Shipsey, 370.

71. Redmond to Asquith, 30 Nov. 1916 (Bodl., MS Asquith, 37/134-137).

72. *The Leader*, 10 Feb. 1917.

73. C.O. 903/19/1, p. 47; O'Connor, *History of Ireland*, II, 256-7.

74. *Roscommon Herald*, 10 Feb. 1917.

75. *Ibid.*

76. *Ibid.*, 31 Mar. 1917, quoting *New Ireland*.

77. *Ibid.*, 3 Feb. 1917.   78. *Ibid.*, 10 Feb. 1917.

79. *The Times*, 6 Feb. 1917.

80. Henry Dixon to George Gavan Duffy, 11 Feb. 1917. (N.L.I., George Gavan Duffy Papers, MS 5581).

81. F. J. O'Connor to George Gavan Duffy, 7 Mar. 1917 (N.L.I., Duffy Papers).

82. Dixon to Duffy, 11 Feb. 1917 (N.L.I., Duffy Papers).

83. O'Connor to Duffy, 6 Apr. 1917 (N.L.I., Duffy Papers).

84. *Ibid.*

85. J. J. O'Kelly to Duffy, 30 Mar. 1917 (N.L.I., Duffy Papers).

86. *Independent*, 20 Apr. 1917. The figure 127 seems to be a fair estimate. The *Irish Times*, 20 Apr. 1917, quoted in *Notes from Ireland* XXVI (1917), 17, reported it as 'about a hundred', and Griffith placed it at 'nearly 150' (*Nationality*, 28 Apr. 1917).

87. *Irish Weekly Independent*, 20 Apr. 1917.

88. Warre B. Wells and N. Marlowe, *The Irish Convention and Sinn Fein*, New York [1918?], 34.

89. A. Nicholls to George Gavan Duffy, 4 Apr. 1917 (N.L.I., Duffy Papers): 'Several local men are spoken of. *McKenna* is the man the "Party" favour. *Garraghan has* many Sinn Fein relatives, personally he inclines to the "Party" [.] *Flood* is being "run" by the Bishop (Dr Hoare) and he was introduced to the Constituency a couple of weeks ago. He is a clerk in the Natl Edn office, & is a great pet with Dr Starkie! ! !'

90. This resolution is mentioned by Dillon, but omitted by other sources. Dillon to Redmond, 12 Apr. 1917 (RP).

91. *Roscommon Herald*, 14 Apr. 1917.

92. D. [Canon] Reynolds to Mr Farrell, 'Thursday' [12 Apr. 1917] (RP).

93. Dillon to Redmond, 12 Apr. 1917 (RP).

94. *Roscommon Herald,* 21 Apr. 1917.
95. Dillon to Redmond, 13 Apr. 1917 (RP).
96. Quoted in *Roscommon Herald,* 21 Apr. 1917.
97. *Ibid.,* 28 Apr. 1917.
98. Dillon to Redmond, 12 Apr. 1917 (RP).
99. *Roscommon Herald,* 28 Apr. 1917.
100. Dillon to Redmond, 14 Apr. 1917 (RP).
101. Telegram from Father Confrey to Redmond, 23 Apr. 1917 (RP).
102. Copy of Redmond to Bishop Hoare, 25 Apr. 1917 (RP).
103. Hoare to Redmond, 26 Apr. 1917 (RP).
104. *Roscommon Herald,* 28 Apr. 1917.
105. *Ibid.,* 14 Apr. 1917.
106. *Ibid.,* 21 Apr. 1917.
107. A point used against Flood by a Sinn Féin speaker at Clondra, *ibid.,* 28 Apr. 1917.
108. See note 89, above.
109. *Roscommon Herald,* 12 May 1917.
110. *Ibid.,* 5 May 1917.
111. Quoted in *Notes from Ireland* XXVI (1917), 37-8.
112. *Roscommon Herald,* 12 May 1917.
113. *Independent,* 8 May 1917.
114. Copy of Rev. M. J. Curran to 'Seag[h]an', 25 Mar. 1917, enclosed in Seán T. O'Kelly to George Gavan Duffy, 27 Mar. 1917 (N.L.I., Duffy Papers).
115. *Irish Catholic,* 12 May 1917.
116. *Notes from Ireland* XXVI (1917), 38, quoting *Irish Times,* 10 May 1917.
117. *Ibid.,* quoting *FJ,* 10 May 1917.
118. *Roscommon Herald,* 12 May 1917.
119. *Nationality,* 21 Apr. 1917; letter from Rev. M. O'Mullin, P.P., Fahan, to Count Plunkett's convention, *Independent,* 20 May 1917.
120. Editor's note to John MacNeill, 'War and Reconstruction —Irish Settlement', *English Review* XXV (Sept. 1917), 253.

XVII: The Irish Convention

1. See above, p. 337. Perhaps Cardinal Logue in using these words meant 'English rule' over the six north-eastern counties, not the whole country, and was really expressing fear of local Orange domination. Even if he had articulated this subtlety it would probably have had little impact on public debate.

2. R. B. McDowell, *The Irish Convention, 1917–18*, London 1970, 73-6.

3. Kelly to Redmond, 25 May 1917 (RP).

4. McDowell, *Irish Conv.*, 79; T. P. O'Connor to Redmond, 24 May 1917; Kelly to Redmond, 25 May 1917 (RP).

5. John Quinn, ed., *The Irish Home-Rule Convention*, New York 1917, 157-9.

6. Telegram from H. E. Duke to Lloyd George, 3 Jun. 1917 (LGP, F/37/4/26); T. M. Healy to William O'Brien, 13 Jun. 1917 (O'BP, MS 8556/12).

7. Copy of O'Brien to Healy, 9 Jun. 1917 (O'BP, MS 8556/12).

8. It was to be composed as follows: chairmen of county councils (33), lords mayor and mayors (6), representatives of urban councils (8), chairman of chambers of commerce (3), labour spokesmen (5), Irish Parliamentary Party (5), Ulster Unionist Party (5), Irish Unionist Alliance (Southern Unionists) (5), Sinn Féin (5), All-for-Ireland League (2), Irish representative peers (2), Roman Catholic hierarchy (4), Church of Ireland Archbishops of Armagh and Dublin (2), Moderator of Presbyterian General Assembly (1), government nominees (15). Wells and Marlowe, *Conv. & S. F.*, 45-6.

9. Copy of Sir Horace Plunkett to Bishop O'Donnell, 18 Jun. 1917 (Horace Plunkett Foundation for Co-operative Studies, Plunkett Papers).

10. Plunkett Diaries, 14 Jun. 1917 (Plunkett Papers).

11. *Notes from Ireland* XXVI (1917), 54.

12. McHugh to O'Brien, 16 Dec. 1917 (O'BP, MS 7998).

13. Healy to O'Brien, 1 Aug. 1917 (O'BP, MS 8556/14), citing a statement attributed to Father Curran.

14. Healy to O'Brien, 4 Jun. 1917 (O'BP, MS 8556/12).

15. Healy to O'Brien, 13 Jun. 1917 (O'BP, MS 8556/12).

16. [Sir Horace Plunkett] *The Irish Convention: Confidential Report to His Majesty the King by the Chairman*, 6. This unpublished report was composed in sections, copies of which were distributed to some of Plunkett's friends during the Convention. Therefore parts of the report are available in the papers of various delegates. The pagination by which it will be cited here is that of the final version, a copy of which is in the Horace Plunkett Foundation for Co-operative Studies. Hereafter it will be cited *Confidential Report*.

17. Earl of Midleton, *Records and Reactions, 1856–1939*, London 1939, 237-8.

18. Dillon had declined nomination, recommending the selec-

tion of an Ulster Nationalist in view of McHugh's attack (Dillon to Redmond, 21 Jun. 1917 (RP)). Harbison, who was from Tyrone, was not an M.P. at this time, though he was elected for East Tyrone in April 1918.

19. Earl of Midleton, *Ireland—Dupe or Heroine*, London 1932, 116.
20. Plunkett Diaries, 22 Aug. 1917; *Confidential Report*, 16.
21. *Confidential Report*, 31-2; S. Gwynn, *Redmond's Last Years*, 299-300.
22. *Confidential Report*, 22-4; S. Gwynn, *Redmond's Last Years*, 286.
23. *Confidential Report*, 24.
24. Late in the proceedings, Plunkett, analysing the respective attitudes of the four Catholic prelates toward financial issues, remarked: 'The Archbishop [of Cashel], alone among the Roman Catholic prelates, had stated the views of his Church upon education—a subject the subordination of which to economics in the episcopal contributions to our discussions provoked some comment.' (*Confidential Report*, 68.)
25. MacDonnell oscillated between Southern Unionism and Nationalism.
26. Plunkett Diaries, 30 Sep. 1917.
27. Telegram from O'Donnell to Plunkett, 1 Oct. 1917 (Plunkett Papers).
28. Healy to O'Brien, 1 Aug. 1917 (O'BP, MS 8556/14).
29. Apparently Kelly and Harty, however, had given some indication that they might consider provincial federalism before the Convention opened. O'Brien, who disliked Kelly intensely, and whose version may therefore be distorted, wrote as follows to Father Clancy when the latter (Clancy to O'Brien, 18 Jul. 1917 (O'BP, MS 7998)) conveyed a message to him from Bishop Fogarty urging that he reconsider his decision not to attend the Convention: 'I am aware that Dr Kelly has been circulating all over the country stories about the wondrous concessions we are to have at the Convention. But his versions of the Government's intentions do not always agree. The version he and Dr Harty gave at Killarney lately was that the Government's plan is Four Provincial Parliaments, with a sort of a Senate in Dublin—otherwise Partition, not only into two but into four Irelands.' (O'Brien to Clancy, 19 Jul. 1917 (O'BP, MS 8506/4).)
30. Horgan, *Parnell to Pearse*, 309. Windle noted that 'other leading members' also opposed the scheme, but the fact that

he singled out the bishops suggests that he regarded their opposition as the most determined.

31. Printed in *Report of the Proceedings of the Irish Convention*, pp. 11-16 [Cd 9019], H.C. 1918, x, hereafter cited *Rep. Proc. Ir. Conv.*

32. O'Donnell to Redmond, 6 Jan. 1914 (RP).

33. *Rep. Proc. Ir. Conv.*, 59.

34. *Ibid.*, 70.   35. *Ibid.*

36. Healy to O'Brien, 3 Dec. 1917 (O'BP, MS 8556/16).

37. Plunkett Diaries, 11 Dec. 1917.

38. S. Gwynn, *Redmond's Last Years*, 311-13.

39. *Ibid.*, 312-15.   40. D. Gwynn, *Redmond*, 575.

41. Most Rev. Patrick O'Donnell, *Some Reasons for Giving an Irish Parliament Full Control of Taxation* (Trinity College Library, Irish Convention Papers, Box I). See also *Confidential Report*, 59, and Healy to O'Brien, 28 Dec. 1917: 'Dr O'Donnell signed a Circular drafted by AE explaining the vital importance of Customs.' (O'BP, MS 8556/16.)

42. D. Gwynn, *Redmond*, 574.

43. Apparently some Southern Unionists had, in fact, intimated their preference for fiscal autonomy. George Russell wrote to Lloyd George on 5 February 1918: 'I know in spite of the fact that Lord Midleton has induced the representatives of Southern Unionism to adhere to his proposals that nine-tenths of them believe that fiscal autonomy ought to be the basis of a settlement and they have said this openly in the Convention and privately also.' (Alan Denson, ed., *Letters from AE*, London 1961, 138-40.)

44. O'Donnell to Redmond, 22, 23 Dec. 1917 (RP). The transscription of these letters in D. Gwynn, *Redmond*, 575-6, is imperfect.

45. Copy of Redmond to O'Donnell, 26 Dec. 1917 (RP); D. Gwynn, *Redmond*, 569-77.

46. O'Donnell to Redmond, 27 Dec. 1917 (RP).

47. D. Gwynn, *Redmond*, 578-9. The almost cynical attitude of one of the P.M.'s colleagues is revealed by a note from Curzon to Lloyd George: 'I handed the pencil note to Midleton. He was more than satisfied with it, and said that he could not possibly have expected more.' (Curzon to Lloyd George, 31 Dec. [1917] (LGP, F/11/8/4).)

48. *Confidential Report*, 61-2.

49. D. Gwynn, *Redmond*, 580-2.

50. S. Gwynn, *Redmond's Last Years*, 321.

51. Midleton, *Records and Reactions*, 241-2.
52. S. Gwynn, *Redmond's Last Years*, 321.
53. Midleton, *Records and Reactions*, 242.
54. *Ibid.*, 242, 245; D. Gwynn, *Redmond*, 568-9n.
55. S. Gwynn, *Redmond's Last Years*, 322.
56. Copy of Redmond to O'Donnell, 14 Jan. 1918 (RP).
57. O'Donnell to Redmond, 14 Jan. 1918, 'Late at Night' (RP);
D. Gwynn, *Redmond*, 584-5.
58. *Ibid.*
59. S. Gwynn, *Redmond's Last Years*, 322.
60. Ronald McNeill, *Ulster's Stand for Union*, London 1922, 261.
61. S. Gwynn, *Redmond's Last Years*, 322-3.
62. Margaret Digby, *Horace Plunkett, An Anglo-American Irishman*, Oxford 1949, 230.
63. *Confidential Report*, 69.
64. McNeill, *Ulster's Stand*, 262; *Confidential Report*, 75.
65. Midleton, *Records and Reactions*, 243-4: 'Redmond ... came to me and said that ... if the scheme was passed, and the Unionists were willing to join the Nationalists in governing Ireland and preserving it from Sinn Fein, which I assured him they would, he would be prepared to serve under Carson. There would thus have been a National Government, as in England a few years later.'
66. D. Gwynn, *Redmond*, 583.
67. Reginald Pound and Geoffrey Harmsworth, *Northcliffe*, London 1959, 592-3.
68. *Ibid.*, 612-13.   69. *Ibid.*, 614.
70. Lord Northcliffe to Lloyd George, 20 Jan. 1918 (LGP, F/41/8/4).
71. Pound and Harmsworth, *Northcliffe*, 614.
72. Colvin, *Carson*, III, 308-11.
73. Indeed, a few days later, W. G. S. Adams, a member of the cabinet secretariat, tried to nudge Carson towards acceptance of an Irish parliament with suggestions of an Ulster committee with power to initiate and veto legislation affecting Ulster and of alternate sittings in Belfast and Dublin. (McDowell, *Irish Conv.*, 156-7.)
74. McNeill, *Ulster's Stand*, 258. Cf. para. 10 of 'Report of Ulster Unionist Delegates to Irish Convention', *Rep. Proc. Ir. Conv.*, 31.
75. S. Gwynn, *Redmond's Last Years*, 284.
76. Extract from Archbishop Crozier to Long, 4 Feb. 1918, enclosed in Walter Long to Lloyd George, 5 Feb. 1918 (LGP,

F/32/5/4).
77. O'Donnell to Redmond, 23 Dec. 1917 (RP).
78. *Confidential Report*, 77.
79. *Rep. Proc. Ir. Conv.*, 20-2.
80. Copy of Logue to James O'Connor, 1 Mar. 1918, enclosed in A. W. Samuels to Lloyd George, 10 May 1918 (LGP, F/44/9/3).
81. Plunkett Diaries, 3 Mar. 1918; *Confidential Report*, 91.
82. *Ibid.*, 90-1.
83. Plunkett Diaries, 5 Mar. 1918. See also *Confidential Report*, 92-3; copies of Plunkett to O'Donnell, 2, 3 Mar. 1918, O'Donnell to Plunkett, 3, 4 Mar. 1918 (Plunkett Papers).
84. S. Gwynn, *Redmond's Last Years*, 328.
85. *Ibid.*, 331-3; *Rep. Proc. Ir. Conv.*, 108, 140. McDowell, *Irish Conv.*, 174, classifies Granard and MacDonnell as Liberals. I have preferred, however, to treat them as independents because within the Convention they did not try to act as a specifically Liberal bloc.
86. *Confidential Report*, 112-13.
87. *Ibid.*, 69.
88. Kelly to Plunkett, 19 Jun. 1918 (Plunkett Papers).

XVIII: *Nihil Obstat* Sinn Féin

1. *Nationality*, 5, 12, 19, 26 May, 2, 9, 23 Jun. 1917.
2. See *ibid.*, Jun., Jul. 1917, *passim*.
3. *Irish Catholic*, 7 Jul. 1917.   4. *Ibid.*
5. *Notes from Ireland* XXVI (1917), 50, quoting *Irish Times*, 6 Jul. 1917.
6. *Ibid.* XXVI, 51, quoting *Irish Times*, 9 Jul. 1917.
7. Dillon to Redmond, 21, 26 Jun., 3 Aug. 1917 (RP).
8. *Saturday Record* (Ennis), 7 Jul. 1917.
9. *Ibid.*, 23, 30 Jun., 7, 14 Jul. 1917.
10. *Ibid.*, 14 Jul. 1917.
11. Speech at Crossmaglen, *Armagh Guardian*, 1 Feb. 1918.
12. Most Rev. Michael Fogarty, Bishop of Killaloe, *The Great Bishop of Limerick*, Dublin 1917.
13. O'Connor, *History of Ireland*, II, 289.
14. Clancy to O'Brien, 18 Jul. 1917 (O'BP, MS 7998).
15. O'Connor, *History of Ireland*, II, 288-9; *The Times*, 8 Oct. 1917.
16. *Notes from Ireland* XXVI (1917), 69-70, 77 quoting *FJ*, 3 Oct. 1917.
17. Macardle, *Irish Republic*, 232.

18. *Ibid.*, 916. 19. *Ibid.*, 231-5.

20. Piaras Béaslaí, *Michael Collins and the Making of a New Ireland*, I, 174. The words are omitted from Miss Macardle's version of the speech.

21. Macardle, *Irish Republic*, 917-18.

22. *Ibid.*, 235; Béaslaí, *Collins*, I, 177.

23. 'Ireland', *English Review* XXV (Sep. 1917).

24. In the *Kilkenny Journal*'s reports of election meetings there seem to be no references to clerical participation. The Rev. Father O'Keeffe, Adm., of the Cathedral, laid stress on the importance of judging the issue 'dispassionately and without heat' (*Kilkenny Journal*, 25 Jul. 1917; cf. *ibid.*, 15 Aug. 1917). At a time when the tide was running in favour of the more radical party, of course, this sort of studied clerical neutrality had the effect of support for that party.

25. *Irish Catholic*, 10 Nov. 1917. For Bishop Foley's remarks see *ibid.*, 13 Oct. 1917.

26. *Ibid.*, 3 Nov. 1917. 27. *Ibid.*, 1 Dec. 1917.

28. *Ibid.* 29. *Ibid.*, 24 Nov. 1917.

30. See *ibid.*, 12, 19 Jan., 2 Mar., 6 Apr. 1918; *Notes from Ireland* XXVII (1918), 28, 29. The official crime reports do not give a monthly breakdown, but in 1918 there were 256 cases of 'Demand or Robbery of Arms' known to police, compared with 21 in 1917 (*Judicial Statistics (Ireland), 1917*, p. 42 [Cmd 43], and *Judicial Statistics (Ireland), 1918*, p. 42 [Cmd 438], H.C. 1919, lii).

31. *Notes from Ireland* XXVII (1918), 36, quoting *Cork Examiner*, 11 Mar. 1918.

32. *Roscommon Herald*, 2 Feb. 1918; *Notes from Ireland*, XXVII (1918), 31.

33. Healy, *Letters and Leaders*, II, 591.

34. *Ibid.*; Macardle, *Irish Republic*, 244; *Irish News*, 21 Jan.-4 Feb. 1918, *passim.*; *Armagh Guardian*, 25 Jan., 1 Feb. 1918.

35. *Irish News*, 26 Mar.-5 Apr. 1918, *passim*; *Roscommon Herald*, 6 Apr. 1918.

36. South Armagh: Donnelly (I.P.P.), 2,324; McCartan (S.F.), 1,305. East Tyrone: Harbison (I.P.P.), 1,802; Milroy (S.F.), 1,222.

37. Copy of Logue to James O'Connor, 1 Mar. 1918, enclosed in A. W. Samuels to Lloyd George, 10 May 1918 (LGP, F/44/9/3).

38. *Irish Catholic*, 13 Apr. 1918.

39. *Ibid.*, 20 Apr. 1918; Wells and Marlowe, *Conv. & S. F.*, 147-8.

40. See above, pp. 355.   41. *FJ*, 14 Apr. 1921.

42. The Earl of Longford and Thomas P. O'Neill, *Eamon de Valera*, Dublin 1970, 72; Macardle, *Irish Republic*, 250.

43. William O'Brien, *Forth the Banners Go* (as told to Edward MacLysaght), Dublin 1969, 164-5.

44. Healy, *Letters and Leaders*, II, 595.

45. O'Brien, *Banners*, 165-6.

46. Macardle, *Irish Republic*, 250.

47. Rough notes on the Mansion House Conference by O'Brien (N.L.I., William O'Brien [labour leader] Papers, MS 15,653 [2]). The author wishes to record his sympathy with the Cardinal on this point.

48. *Ibid.*

49. Wells and Marlowe, *Conv. & S. F.*, 148-51; Healy, *Letters and Leaders*, II, 595-6, Macardle, *Irish Republic*, 249-51; *Notes from Ireland* XXVII (1918), 22-3.

50. 'Public Feeling in Ireland. Weekly Report of Inspector General R.I.C.' (P.R.O., Cabinet Papers, Cab. 24/49/4326).

51. Minute 6 of cabinet, 23 Apr. 1918, W.C. 397 (Cab. 23/6/53).

52. Minute 14 of cabinet, 6 May 1918, W.C. 405 (Cab. 23/6/85).

53. Balfour to de Salis, 20 May 1918, with MS note by de Salis dated 1 Jun. (F.O. 380/17/201).

54. Cardinal Gasparri to de Salis, 9 Jul. 1918 (F.O. 380/18/272).

55. Rev. Robert H. Murray, *Archbishop Bernard, Professor, Prelate and Provost*, London 1931, 323.

56. *Ibid.*, 323-4.   57. *Ibid.*, 324-5.

58. *Anglo-Celt* (Cavan), 20 Apr. 1918.

59. Macardle, *Irish Republic*, 250.

60. *Irish Catholic*, 18 May 1918.

61. *Notes from Ireland* XXVII (1918), 23.

62. *Irish News*, 30 Mar. 1918.

63. Healy, *Letters and Leaders*, II, 607-8.

64. *Anglo-Celt*, 4 May 1918.

65. *Ibid.*, 11 May 1918.

66. Wells and Marlowe, *Conv. & S. F.*, 154.

67. *Anglo Celt*, 8 Jun. 1918.

68. This account based on *Anglo-Celt*, 27 Apr.-29 Jun. 1918.

69. *Independent*, 30 Oct. 1918.

70. *Roscommon Herald*, 27 Jul. 1918.

71. Edgar Holt, *Protest in Arms: The Irish Troubles, 1916–1923*, New York 1961, 161; *Irish Catholic*, 3, 17 Aug. 1918.

72. *Ibid.,* 2 Nov. 1918.
73. 'I.O.' (pseud. C.J.C. Street), *The Administration of Ireland, 1920* (London 1921), New York, n.d., 57.
74. See Sinn Féin advertisement in *Free Press* (Wexford), 14 Dec. 1918.
75. *Independent,* 23 Oct. 1918.
76. Healy, *Letters and Leaders,* II, 605.
77. *Ibid.,* 608; *The Times,* 11 Nov. 1918.
78. *Longford Leader,* 16 Nov. 1918.
79. *Ibid.*
80. *Ibid.; Independent,* 11, 18 Nov. 1918.
81. *Independent,* 11 Nov. 1918.
82. *Ibid.,* 18 Nov. 1918; *Cork Examiner,* 16 Nov. 1918.
83. *Sligo Champion,* 23 Nov. 1918.
84. Healy to O'Brien, 12 Oct. 1918 (O'BP, MS 8556/21).
85. *Derry Journal,* 22 Nov. 1918.
86. McHugh to Murrin, 15 Sep. 1918 (McNP).
87. Healy to O'Brien, 12 Oct. 1918 (O'BP, MS 8556/21). Healy and O'Brien apparently had hopes that that their faction might be called upon to serve as compromise candidates in some of these seats. See Healy to O'Brien, 11 Nov. 1918, copy of O'Brien to Healy, 13 Nov. 1918 (O'BP, MS 8556/22).
88. *Independent,* 16 Nov. 1918.
89. *Ibid.,* 21 Nov. 1918.   90. *Ibid.,* 18, 20 Nov. 1918.
91. *Ibid.,* 22 Nov. 1918.   92. *Ibid.*
93. McHugh to O'Brien, 23 Nov. 1918 (O'BP, MS 8557/10).
94. *Cork Examiner,* 28 Nov. 1918.
95. *Ibid.,* 4 Dec. 1918.
96. *Catholic Bulletin* IX (Jan. 1919), 6; C.O. 903/19, part 4, 8.
97. *Independent,* 2 Dec. 1918.
98. *The Leader,* 7 Dec. 1918.
99. *Independent,* 30 Nov. 1918.
100. *Ibid.,* 28 Nov. 1918.   101. *Ibid.,* 21, 27 Nov. 1918.
102. *Ibid.,* 28 Nov. 1918.
103. *Ibid.,* 6 Dec. 1918.   104. Lyons, *Dillon,* 449-51.
105. Healy to O'Brien, 29 Nov. 1918 (O'BP, MS 8556/22).
106. *Kilkenny People,* 30 Nov. 1918.
107. *Independent,* 27 Nov. 1918.
108. Account of general election based primarily on election reports in the *Independent,* supplemented by a number of provincial papers, for the period of the campaign.
109. Lyons, *Dillon,* 455.
110. See reports of activity of the Rev. T. Dunne, Adm., in South

Galway, *Independent*, 26, 28 Nov. 1918.
111. *Tullamore and King's County Independent*, 7 Dec. 1918.
112. *Roscommon Herald*, 21 Dec. 1918.
113. *Independent*, 27 Nov., 5 Dec. 1918.
114. *FJ*, 16 Dec. 1918.

XIX: The Nation under New Management

1. Dáil Éireann, *Miontuarisc an Chead Dála, 1919–21; Minutes of Proceedings of the First Parliament of the Republic of Ireland, 1919–21, Official Record*, 16. Hereafter cited *Dáil Éireann Proc. 1919–21*.
2. See, e.g., copy of George Gavan Duffy to Rev. M. J. Curran, 26 May 1917 (N.L.I., Duffy Papers, MS 5581) in which Duffy urges Curran to try to persuade Griffith to take a particular course of action 'either by your own intervention or through J. T. O'Kelly'.
3. A copy of Johnson's draft is in the N.L.I., Thomas Johnson Papers; the final text is in *Dáil Éireann Proc. 1919–21*, 22-3; see also O'Hegarty, *Ireland under the Union*, 727.
4. C.O. 904/109, May 1919. Cf. Collins's statement in the Dáil that the amount received from the Anti-Conscription Fund 'was not more than £18,000, and probably much less' (*Dáil Éireann Proc. 1919–21*, 151). See also C.O. 904/108, Feb. 1919.
5. *FJ*, 12 Mar. 1919.
6. Longford and O'Neill, *De Valera*, 89.
7. *Dáil Éireann Proc. 1919–21*, 79-109.
8. *FJ*, 6, 8, 9, 14 May 1919.
9. Alan J. Ward, *Ireland and Anglo-American Relations, 1899–1921*, Toronto 1969, 179-80.
10. He added: 'I wish it to be distinctly understood that my subscribing carries with it no commitment to any political party.' (*FJ*, 14 May 1919.) Perhaps this disclaimer accounts for the fact that this is the only such subscription from a bishop I have found recorded in *FJ*. The *Freeman's* editorial policy at this time was still rather unfriendly to Sinn Féin.
11. *Dáil Éireann Proc. 1919–21*, 133.
12. De Valera and James O'Mara were the other two trustees (*ibid.*, 132-4). The *future* payability of the bonds constitutes an intriguing parallel to the Church's sanction, as I have described it, for the Nation's *future* sovereignty.
13. *FJ*, 25 Jun. 1919.
14. *Ibid.*
15. Macardle, *Irish Republic*, 307-8; W. A. Phillips, *The Revo-*

lution in Ireland, 1906–1923, London 1926, 168-9.
16. *FJ*, 10 Mar. 1919.
17. C.O. 904/110, Sep. 1919.
18. *Morning Post* (London), 9 Dec. 1919, quoting *New Ireland.*
19. *Ibid.*
20. *FJ*, 10 Dec. 1919, which carried a fairly complete report of the interview but was apparently prevented from printing more than a brief account of the letter itself. By this time the *Freeman* was becoming sympathetic to Sinn Féin.
21. Healy to O'Brien, 18 Dec. 1919 (O'BP, MS 8556/24).
22. *Catholic Bulletin* IX (Mar. 1920), 143.
23. O'Connor, *History of Ireland,* II, 325.
24. Walsh, *Walsh,* 575-6.
25. See, e.g., *FJ,* 6 Feb. 1920.
26. *Irish Catholic,* 28 Jun., 25 Oct. 1919.
27. *Morning Post,* 18 Dec. 1919.
28. Vesey Knox to Lloyd George, 25 May 1916 (LGP, D/14/1/11).
29. Healy to O'Brien, 10 Dec. 1919 (O'BP, MS 8556/24). Cf. Healy, *Letters and Leaders,* II, 616-17.
30. *FJ*, 28 Jan. 1919.
31. See speech by Starkie in *Belfast Newsletter,* 29 Mar. 1919.
32. *Daily Express* (Dublin), 3 Dec. 1918; *FJ,* 3 Mar. 1919.
33. O'Connell, *Hist. of I.N.T.O.,* 293.
34. *Ibid.,* 297-300.   35. *Ibid.,* 293.
36. *Ibid.,* 297-300.   37. *Ibid.,* 297.
38. *FJ*, 15 Dec. 1919.   39. *Ibid.,* 22 Dec. 1919.
40. O'Connell, *Hist. of I.N.T.O.,* 302-3.
41. Though they did promise to work for alteration of the Department's 'objectionable' composition (*ibid.,* 309).
42. *Evening Telegraph* (Dublin), 8, 13, 24 Jan. 1920; *Independent,* 20 Dec. 1919, 22 Jan., 13 Feb. 1920; *FJ,* 23 Feb., 2 Mar., 1920.
43. *FJ*, 28 Jan. 1920.
44. O'Connell, *Hist. of I.N.T.O.,* 311-30.
45. With the notable exception of O'Donnell, who wrote in June 1920: 'The representatives of the teachers, who are as good men as we have in the country, are under great stress these times trying to obtain just remuneration for the teaching profession in circumstances of great difficulty. I shall cross their path as little as I can help it.' (O'Connell, *Hist. of I.N.T.O.,* 310-11.)
46. *Ibid.,* 319-20.   47. *Independent,* 13 Mar. 1920.

48. *Evening Telegraph*, 12 Jan. 1920; *Independent*, 16 Jan., 7, 11, 14, 16, 19, 20 Feb., 1 Mar. 1920; *FJ*, 10, 14, 19, 21 Feb. 1920.

49. Macardle, *Irish Republic*, 325-8.

50. *Dáil Éireann Proc. 1919–21*, 162-3, 172. Although O'Kelly apparently later described his role in this period as 'Minister for Education' (*Who Was Who, 1951–60*, 831; O'Connell *Hist. of I.N.T.O.*, 491), the Dáil's *Proceedings* make it plain that he was not entitled to this title.

51. *Dáil Éireann Proc. 1919–21*, 227. The Intermediate Board did not reply, but the National Board asked for an interview with the Dáil's Department of Irish. This response was probably unexpected, and the Department did not accede to the request.

52. O'Connell, *Hist. of I.N.T.O.*, 330.

53. See above p. 427.

54. O'Connell, *Hist. of I.N.T.O.*, 189.

55. *Ibid.*, 320.

56. The other spokesman, Jim Larkin, had gone to America early in the war, and only returned in 1923.

57. *FJ*, 4 Dec. 1918.

58. *Ibid.*, 10 Dec. 1918.

59. O'Hegarty, *Ireland Under the Union*, 727.

60. See note 3 above.

61. *The Leader*, 1 Feb. 1919.

62. William Moran to Mrs O'D., 3 Nov. 1918 (N.L.I., William O'Brien [labour leader] Papers, MS 15,654 (folder containing papers of Thomas Farren)).

63. See J. Kelleher, 'Are Irish Trade Unionists Excommunicated or Condemned by the Church', *Irish Theological Quarterly* XV (Jul. 1920), 213.

64. *Ibid.* XIV (Apr. 1919).

65. Moran elaborated his ideas in a series of articles entitled 'Social Reconstruction in an Irish State', *ibid.* XV (1920), 1-10, 101-12, 251-60.

66. See sermon by Archbishop Harty at Fethard, *FJ*, 7 May 1919.

67. See, e.g., pastoral of Bishop O'Dea of Galway and Kilmacduagh (*FJ*, 3 Mar. 1919), and statements by Bishop Hoare of Ardagh and Clonmacnoise (*ibid.*, 8 May 1919) and Archbishop Gilmartin of Tuam (*ibid.*, 13 Oct. 1919). Even Cardinal Logue endorsed the idea of profit-sharing (*ibid.*, 3 Mar. 1919).

68. Kelleher in *I.T.Q.* XV.

69. See his Lenten pastoral, *FJ*, 3 Mar. 1919.
70. O'Connell, *Hist. of I.N.T.O.*, 320.
71. *Dáil Éireann Proc. 1919–21*, 140 (19 August 1919). A brief decree formally establishing the courts was passed on 18 Jun. 1919 (*ibid.*, 122). Apparently there were already some Republican courts spontaneously organised in certain areas, and the provision for *ex officio* clerical membership may have simply ratified a practice already under way. Wilfrid Ewart, *A Journey in Ireland, 1921*, London 1922, 108, refers to a 'Sinn Féin court' operating as early as September 1918 in Co. Limerick under the presidency of a Catholic clergyman.
72. Phillips, *Revolution in Ireland*, 181.
73. See above, pp. 186, 288-9.
74. *Dáil Éireann Proc. 1919–21*, 159, 165.
75. *FJ*, 29 Apr. 1920.
76. J. L. McCracken, *Representative Government in Ireland: A Study of Dáil Éireann, 1919–48*, London 1958, 41.
77. *FJ*, 22 May 1920.
78. Phillips, *Revolution in Ireland*, 181.
79. *The Nation* (Dublin), 8 Mar. 1930. Cf. *Dáil Éireann Proc. 1919–21*, 172: 'The Speaker . . . was at present in Rome as an Envoy.'
80. Draft of Reuter's telegram in F.O. 380/27/325.
81. *Morning Post* (London), 18 Dec. 1919; Curzon to H. W. Gaisford, 30 Dec. 1919 (F.O. 380/26/10).
82. 'Le Saint Siége l'a prise en considération en donnant des dispositions opportunes à ce sujet.' (Cardinal Gasparri to Count de Salis, 21 Jan. 1920 (F.O. 380/26/29).)
83. Cardinal Gasparri to Count de Salis, 4 Feb. 1920 (F.O. 380/26/54).
84. De Salis to Curzon, 14 Feb. 1920 (F.O. 380/30/45).
85. *FJ*, 27 May 1920, reports nine Irish bishops having private audience on a single day.
86. *Catholic Bulletin* X (Aug. 1920), 449-50.
87. De Salis to Curzon, 3 Jul. 1920 (F.O. 380/30/231), quoting communiqué to Reuter, 28 Jun. 1920.
88. *The Nation* (Dublin), 8 Mar. 1930.
89. Unsigned memorandum, 30 Jun. 1920 (F.O. 380/27/350).
90. *Ibid.*
91. Report of a conference on 23 Jul. 1920, C.P. 1963 (Cab. 24/109/463).

XX: Killing No Murder?

1. Robert Brennan, *Allegiance*, Dublin 1950, 284.

2. P. A. Marrinan to Mr Wylie, 2 Jul. 1920 (LGP, F/17/1/5).
3. *Ibid.* A minute on the letter indicates that a copy was sent to Bonar Law on 15 July 1920.
4. Report of conference on 23 Jul. 1920, C.P. 1693 (Cab. 24/109/462-3).
5. *FJ*, 27 Jul. 1920, quoting Dublin correspondent of *Morning Post*.
6. Charles Loch Mowat, *Britain between the Wars, 1918–1940*, London and Chicago 1955, 65-6.
7. *FJ*, 20 Oct. 1920.
8. *Ibid.*   9. *Ibid.*, 13 Dec. 1920.
10. *Ibid.*, 21, 29 July, 25 Sep., 2, 26 Nov., 2 Dec. 1920.
11. *Ibid.*, 2 Nov. 1920.
12. *Ibid.*, 25 Jan. 1921.
13. Copy of Hoare to Devlin, 5 Nov. 1920, enclosed in Devlin to Lloyd George, 8 Nov. 1920 (LGP, F/15/1/2).
14. *Ibid.*
15. Copy of Logue to Amigo, 15 Feb. 1921 (Lambeth Palace Library, Davidson Papers, Box marked 'Ireland 1920–1'). The letter refers to events over several months previous to February, 1921.
16. *FJ*, 29 Nov. 1920.   17. *Ibid.*
18. See, e.g., A. O'Rahilly, 'Some Theology about Tyranny', *Irish Theological Quarterly* XV (Oct. 1920), 310.
19. What would count as 'success', of course, remained problematical.
20. 5th ser., XI (Jun. 1918).
21. 'It may be that she [England] will venture to add yet another to her long list of iniquities by forcing the Conscription issue on an unwilling nation, or finding some pretext for engineering another 'Ninety-eight.' (*Ibid.*, 498.)
22. 3rd ed., London 1920.
23. See above (Chapter XIX).
24. The debate is summarised in Chavasse, *MacSwiney*, 152-7.
25. The 'Cat and Mouse Act', devised in 1913 to deal with suffragette hunger-strikers, allowed the authorities to release a hunger-striking prisoner and then rearrest him or her after he or she had eaten and regained health.
26. Chavasse, *MacSwiney*, 141-90.
27. *Ibid.*, 174-5; copies of [Art Ó Briain?] to Under-Secretary of State, Home Office, 15, 16 Oct. 1920 (N.L.I., Ó Briain Papers, MS 8427/707, 713), requesting permits for Bishop of Kerry (O'Sullivan) to visit MacSwiney.

28. Chavasse, *MacSwiney*, 159.
29. De Salis to Curzon, 13, 28 Nov. 1920 (F.O. 380/31/433, 458).
30. *FJ*, 23 Aug. 1920.
31. Although Volunteers were supposed to have taken an oath of allegiance to 'the Irish Republic, which is Dáil Éireann', the situation is confused. There was no way of assuring that all Volunteers took the oath, and those who also belonged to the Irish Republican Brotherhood might argue that the legitimate government of the Republic was, and had for decades been, the Brotherhood's Supreme Council, which had always been at war with England. Whatever Bishop O'Dea meant by 'legitimate authority', however, he certainly did not mean the I.R.B. Supreme Council.
32. *I.T.Q.* XV (Oct. 1920), 317.   33. *Ibid.*, 318.
34. *Ibid.*, 319.   35. *Ibid.*, 320.
36. *Ibid.* XVI (Jan. 1921), 1n.
37. *Ibid.*, 15.   38. *Ibid.*, 10-11.
39. *FJ*, 13 Dec. 1920.
40. Tom Barry, *Guerilla Days in Ireland*, 3rd paperback impression, Tralee 1969, 40.
41. *Ibid.*, 57.
42. *Two Patriot Priests of Ireland, 1916–25*, New York 1960, 20-1.
43. *FJ*, 20 Dec. 1920.   44. *Ibid.*, 27 Dec. 1920.
45. O'Connor, *History of Ireland*, II, 311.
46. Richard Bennett, *The Black and Tans* (New English Library edition), London 1970, 111.
47. *FJ*, 20 Dec. 1920.   48. *Ibid.*, 27 Dec. 1920.
49. Bennett, *Black and Tans*, 79.
50. Winston S. Churchill, *The Aftermath*, New York 1929, 302.
51. Both Arthur Balfour and Campbell-Bannerman had served as Chief Secretary. Asquith had defended Parnell before the famous Special Commission. Salisbury had at least the advantage of two nephews, Arthur and Gerald Balfour, who served as Chief Secretary.
52. Davidson to Lloyd George, 9 May 1920 (LGP, F/14/2/4).
53. *Independent*, 28 Jun. 1920.
54. Telegram from Curzon to de Salis, 23 Jul. 1920 (F.O. 380/28/418).
55. Ironically, the Persico mission apparently was not specifically suggested by the British government, though it was no doubt greeted with satisfaction by the authorities. See C. Cruise O'Brien, *Parnell and His Party*, 214, n. 3.

56. De Salis to Curzon, 5 Aug. 1920 (F.O. 380/30/300). The actual note from Cardinal Gasparri to de Salis, 4 Aug. 1920, in French, is F.O. 380/28/440.
57. Unsigned memorandum, 30 Jun. 1920 (F.O. 380/27/350).
58. See above, p. 454.
59. De Salis to Curzon, 28 Nov. 1920 (F.O. 380/31/458).
60. De Salis to Curzon, 13 Nov. 1920 (F.O. 380/31/433).
61. Telegram from de Salis to Curzon, 12 Dec. 1920 (F.O. 380/31/477).
62. Copy of Sir Gerald Strickland to Col. Amery, 4 Dec. 1919, to be enclosed with Mr Gaisford to Mr Oliphant, 6 Dec. 1919 (F.O. 380/25/513).
63. See Thomas E. Hachey, 'The Quarantine of Archbishop Mannix: A British Preventive Policy during the Anglo-Irish Troubles', *Irish University Review* I (No. 1, Autumn 1970).
64. Lord Stamfordham to Lloyd George, 23 Jun. 1920, enclosing John H. Bernard (Provost of T.C.D., formerly Protestant Archbishop of Dublin) to Stamfordham, 22 Jun. 1920 (LGP, F/29/4/17).
65. Telegram from Curzon to de Salis, 25 Jun. 1920 (F.O. 380/27/334).
66. Draft of telegram from de Salis to Curzon, 30 Jun. 1920 (F.O. 380/30/226).
67. Telegram from Curzon to de Salis, 25 Jul. 1920; draft of telegram from de Salis to Curzon, 28 Jul. 1920; draft of de Salis to Eric Phipps, 30 Jul. 1920; Phipps to de Salis, 12 Aug. 1920 (F.O. 380/28/420; 380/30/283, 290; 380/28/484).
68. Telegram from Curzon to de Salis, 25 Jun. 1920 (F.O. 380/27/334).
69. Draft of telegram from de Salis to Curzon, 30 Jun. 1920 (F.O. 380/30/226).
70. Draft of telegram from de Salis to Curzon, 17 Aug. 1920 (F.O. 380/30/324).
71. Draft of telegram from de Salis to Curzon, 6 Sep. 1920 (F.O. 380/31/366).
72. *New York Times*, 24 Sep. 1920.
73. Hachey in *I.U.R.* I, 128. 74. *Ibid.*
75. See minutes of cabinet 79A (20), 29 Dec. 1920 (Cab. 23/23/339-40).
76. Copy of Lloyd George to Greenwood, 2 Dec. 1920 (LGP, F/19/2/26).
77. A letter of introduction for Clune from Griffith to

Diarmuid O'Hegarty, Secretary of the Dáil Ministry (Béaslaí, *Collins*, II, 110-11), refers to 'the proposals for a Truce the Archbishop conveys' as involving 'no surrender of principle on our part, I believe'. It is not clear from the letter, however, that he was conveying them in written form. I have found no draft of explicit truce proposals before the 4 December meeting of Clune and Collins.

78. Thomas P. O'Neill, Introduction to Frank Gallagher, *The Anglo Irish Treaty*, London 1965, 22.
79. Copy of Lloyd George to Greenwood, 2 Dec. 1920 (LGP, F/19/2/26).
80. Memorandum, n.d., by Greenwood, headed 'Archbishop Clune' (LGP, F/19/2/31).
81. *Ibid.*
82. Béaslaí, *Collins*, II, 109-37; O'Neill, Introduction to Gallagher, *Treaty*, 21-5.
83. Béaslaí, *Collins*, II, 137.
84. Minutes of cabinet 77(20)(6), 24 Dec. 1920 (Cab. 23/23/319-20).
85. O'Neill, Introduction to Gallagher, *Treaty*, 25.
86. Memorandum by Philip Kerr, 'Interview with Archbishop Clune', 29 Dec. 1920 (LGP, F/90/1/29).
87. Memorandum by Phillip Kerr, 'Interview with Dr. Clune', 31 Dec. 1920 (LGP, F/90/1/29).
88. O'Neill, Introduction to Gallagher, *Treaty*, 25; *FJ*, 24 Jan. 1921; Hachey in *I.U.R.* I, 130.
89. See above, p. 466. Greenwood to Lloyd George, 26 Jan. 1921 (LGP, F/19/3/2).
90. James O'Connor to Lloyd George, 16 Jan. 1921 (LGP, F/42/1/5).
91. Document sent by de Valera to 'a friend', 15 Jan. 1921, enclosed in B. H. Thomson to J. T. Davies, 24 Jan. 1921 (LGP, F/46/9/22).
92. Béaslaí, *Collins*, II, 141ff.
93. *Dáil Éireann Proc. 1919–21*, 241.
94. *Ibid.*, 249.   95. *Ibid.*
96. *FJ*, 7 Feb. 1921.   97. *Ibid.*   98. *Ibid.*
99. 'Epitome of Documents seized at Glenvar, Mount Merrion, Blackrock, on 22.6.'21 (Eamon de Valera)' (C.O. 904/23[7]/65), hereafter cited as 'de Valera Epitome'. See also Bennett, *Black and Tans*, 146.
100. *FJ*, 7 Feb. 1921.
101. *FJ*, 28 Apr. 1921.

102. *Dáil Éireann Proc. 1919-21*, 278-9; Macardle, *Irish Republic* 438.
103. Macardle, *Irish Republic*, 438.
104. Holt, *Protest in Arms*, 242-3.
105. Randolph S. Churchill, *Lord Derby, 'King of Lancashire'*, London 1959, 405.
106. *Ibid.*, 407.
107. O'Neill, Introduction to Gallagher, *Treaty*, 29.
108. Greenwood to Lloyd George, 6 Apr. 1921 (LGP, F/19/3/8).
109. Churchill, *Derby*, 407-9.
110. O'Neill, Introduction to Gallagher, *Treaty*, 29.
111. *Ibid.*, 30.
112. The date is not given by O'Neill, if in fact it was dated, but he says de Valera had already met Derby on 22 April. Derby's biographer gives the date of the Derby-de Valera meeting as 21 April (Churchill, *Derby*, 409).
113. O'Neill, Introduction to Gallagher, *Treaty*, 30.
114. Longford and O'Neill, *De Valera*, 122.
115. O'Neill, Introduction to Gallagher, *Treaty*, 31.
116. Churchill, *Derby*, 410-11.
117. 'Memo of a visit from Ld. J. O'Connor on evening of 23 April 1921' (Lambeth Palace Library, Davidson Papers, Box marked 'Ireland 1920-1').
118. Calton Younger, *Ireland's Civil War, 1922–1923*, London 1968, 133-4. Cf. Churchill, *The Aftermath*, 304-6.
119. Churchill, *The Aftermath*, 299.
120. Extract from de Valera to Staff Attaché, Publicity Department, 19 Jun. 1921, in de Valera Epitome (C.O. 904/23[7]/19).
121. Summary of de Valera to Fogarty, 19 Jun. 1921, *ibid.* (C.O. 904/23[7]/78).
122. Extract from de Valera to Staff Attaché, Publicity Department, 19 Jun. 1921, *ibid.* (C.O. 904/23[7]/19).
123. Macardle, *Irish Republic*, 465.
124. *FJ*, 22 Jun. 1921.
125. Longford and O'Neill, *De Valera*, 128-9.
126. O'Connor, *History of Ireland*, II, 337.

Epilogue and Conclusion

1. Dáil Éireann, *Official Correspondence Relating to the Peace Negotiations, June-September, 1921*, 8.
2. Fitzalan to Lloyd George, 20 Aug. 1921 (LGP, F/17/2/9).
3. Healy to O'Brien, 30 Aug. 1921 (O'BP, MS 8556/27).
4. *Ibid.*

5. Copy of Derby to Logue, 29 Aug. 1921, enclosed in Derby to Lloyd George, 29 Aug. 1921 (LGP, F/14/5/31).
6. Copy of Logue to Derby, 1 Sep. 1921, enclosed in Derby to Lloyd George, 5 Sep. 1921 (LGP, F/14/5/32).
7. Younger, *Civil War*, 162.   8. *Ibid.*, 172.
9. Dáil Éireann, *Official Correspondence . . .*, 11.
10. Longford and O'Neill, *De Valera*, 151.
11. *FJ*, 8 Dec. 1921.
12. *Ibid.*, 9 Dec. 1921.
13. *Ibid.*, 14 Dec. 1921.
14. *Ibid.*, 27 Feb., 1, 6, 7 Mar. 1922.
15. *Ibid.*, 27 Apr. 1922.   16. *Ibid.*
17. *Ibid.*, 11 Oct. 1922.
18. The bishops had tried to guard against this eventuality with an instruction to their clergy in the joint pastoral containing the excommunication (*ibid.*).
19. Eoin Neeson, *The Civil War in Ireland, 1922–1923*, Cork 1966, 328-30.
20. Longford and O'Neill, *De Valera*, 220.
21. J. H. Whyte, *Church and State in Modern Ireland, 1923–1970*, Dublin 1971, 41-3.
22. *Ibid.*, 362-76.
23. 'Church and Nation in Modern Ireland', an address delivered at a joint session of the American Historical Association and the American Committee for Irish Studies, 30 December 1972 (mimeographed), 20. In this provocative essay Professor Larkin uses the categories 'State' and 'Nation' in different senses than I have. In his analysis, an Irish State was a reality—though not a legal one—from the 1880s, when it was born as the 'offspring of a marriage between the Irish Church and the Irish Nation, which was celebrated by Daniel O'Connell . . . in the late 1820s' (p. 1). Although I withhold the designation 'State' from the Irish secular component of the political system until its *de jure* legitimacy in the present is recognised by the British State and the Irish Church, Professor Larkin and I are in broad agreement on the rules within which Irish politics proceeded up to 1921 and the significance of that process for Irish history since that date.
24. See *FJ*, 1 Feb. 1922. Given partition, there could be no further rationale for maintaining a board with a fifty-per-cent Protestant representation, and therefore its replacement by a department responsible to an overwhelmingly Catholic parliament was a rather different matter from the 'Department'

proposals of 1904–07 and 1920, to which the bishops had objected so strenuously. I have found no evidence that the hierarchy's prior consent for the move was solicited (I assume it was), but neither have I found a whisper of public disapproval from any Catholic ecclesiastic.

25. Larkin, 'Church and Nation', 20-1. I am here using the term 'Nation' where Larkin would prefer 'State'.

26. See Whyte, *Church and State*, 34-61 and *passim*.

27. At the time of this writing, however, the fluid situation in Northern Ireland is making Southern politicians more sensitive to the opinions of Ulster Protestants. The most concrete evidence thus far of this change is the recent government decision to submit to a referendum the provision of the 1937 Constitution recognising the 'special position' of the Catholic Church. The deletion of this provision was not actively opposed by the Church and was approved by a substantial majority of the voters.

28. On this point Professor Larkin's views in 'Church and Nation', 15-16, may be at variance with mine, partly because he chooses to group under the label 'Irish Ireland' a broader spectrum of organisations than do I.

29. The author hastens to add that the State has leaned over backwards to be scrupulously fair to the small Protestant minority in the South.

Select Bibliography

This bibliography lists all manuscript sources used in the preparation of this work. In general, however, I have listed published works only when they provided more than a few isolated bits of information germane to my subject or when they provided background of such a general character that they were nowhere cited in the notes. The bibliography and the notes together constitute a virtually exhaustive guide to my sources; the bibliography alone is intended to highlight the main lines of my research. Section V contains a very few recent items which became available to me only when the manuscript was virtually complete.

I. UNPUBLISHED MATERIALS

Ireland

National Library of Ireland
Bryce Papers, MSS 11,011-14.
George Gavan Duffy Papers, MS 5581.
Thomas Johnson Papers.
Mac Néill Papers.
Col. Maurice Moore Papers, MS 10,567.
William O'Brien [M.P.] Papers, MSS 7998, 8506, 8556, 8557.
William O'Brien [labour leader] Papers, MS 15,653.
Art Ó Briain Papers, MS 8427.
Redmond Papers.

Trinity College, Dublin, Library
Irish Convention Papers.

State Paper Office, Dublin Castle
Crime Branch Special Papers.
Registered Papers.

Miscellaneous
Transcript of Eóin Mac Néill's court-martial, 22 May 1916, in possession of Mrs Eibhlín MacNeill Tierney.

Letter from Rev. Michael Curran to C. P. Curran, 22 Apr. 1949, in possession of C. P. Hyland, bookseller, Dublin.
Calendar of materials in the archives of the Archdiocese of Armagh, in possession of Rev. Professor Tomás Ó Fiaich, St Patrick's College, Maynooth.

England

British Museum
Balfour Papers, Add. MSS 49804, 49805.
Campbell-Bannerman Papers, Add. MSS 41211, 41239.

Public Record Office
Cabinet Papers.
Colonial Office files, C.O. 903, 904 (transferred from the old Irish Office).
Education Office, 'private office papers', Ed. 24/211, file B.11.
Foreign Office, archives of British Mission to the Holy See, F.O. 380.

Archbishop's Residence, Westminster
Bourne Papers.

Lambeth Palace Library
Davidson Papers.

Beaverbrook Library
Lloyd George Papers.

Plunkett Foundation for Co-operative Studies, London
Plunkett Papers and Diaries.
[Sir Horace Plunkett] *The Irish Convention: Confidential Report to His Majesty the King by the Chairman* (printed but unpublished).

Bodleian Library, Oxford
Asquith Papers.
MacDonnell Papers, MS Eng. hist., c. 350, 351, 354, 367.

II. PUBLIC DOCUMENTS

United Kingdom
Parliamentary Debates (4th series, 5th series).
Parliamentary Papers:
> *Extracts from Minutes of the Proceedings of the Commissioners of National Education (Ireland), and Other Documents, in Relation to Recent Action Taken by the Most Reverend W. J. Walsh, D.D. . . .* H.C. 1901 (261), lvii.

Royal Commission on University Education in Ireland, *Appendix to First Report*, 1902 [Cd 826], xxxi.

───── *Appendix to Second Report*, H.C. 1902 [Cd 900], xxxi.

───── *Appendix to Third Report*, H.C. 1902 [Cd 1229], xxxii.

───── *Final Report of the Commissioners*, H.C. 1903 [Cd 1483], xxxii.

───── *Appendix to Final Report*, H.C. 1903 [Cd 1484], xxxii.

Report of Mr. F. H. Dale, His Majesty's Inspector of Schools, Board of Education, on Primary Education in Ireland, H.C. 1904 [Cd 1981], xx.

Copy of Minutes of the Proceedings of the Commissioners of National Education Relating to Rule 127(b) of Their Code of Regulations, H.C. 1905 (184), lx.

Royal Commission on Trinity College, Dublin, and the University of Dublin, *Appendix to the First Report*, H.C. 1906 [Cd 3176], lvi.

───── *Final Report of the Commissioners*, H.C. 1907 [Cd 3311], xli.

───── *Appendix to the Final Report*, H.C. 1907 [Cd 3312], xli.

Royal Commission on the Poor Laws and Relief of Distress, *Report on Ireland*, H.C. 1909 [Cd 4630], xxxviii.

Report by the Committee on Irish Finance, H.C. 1912–13 [Cd 6153], xxxiv.

Correspondence between the Chief Secretary for Ireland and the Catholic Headmasters' Association in Reference to the Proposed Grant of £40,000 Per Annum for the Improvement of the Position of Secondary Teachers in Ireland, H.C. 1913 [Cd 6924], i.

Return Showing Government Proposals in Connection with the Government of Ireland Bill, H.C. 1914 (143), lxvii.

Royal Commission on the Rebellion in Ireland. *Minutes of Evidence and Appendix of Documents*, H.C. 1916 [Cd 8311], xi.

Headings of a Settlement as to the Government of Ireland, H.C. 1916 [Cd 8310], xxii.

Report of the Proceedings of the Irish Convention, H.C. 1918 [Cd 9019], x.

Report of the Vice-regal Committee of Inquiry into Primary Education in Ireland, Vol. I, H.C. 1919 [Cmd 60], xxi.

Ireland

Dáil Éireann, *Miontuarisc an Chead Dála, 1919–1921; Minutes of Proceedings of the First Parliament of the Republic of Ireland, 1919–1921, Official Record.*

───── *Official Correspondence Relating to the Peace Negotia-*

tions, June-September, 1921.
State Paper Office, *Intelligence Notes, 1913–16, preserved in the State Paper Office,* ed. Breandán Mac Giolla Choille, Dublin 1966.

III. CONTEMPORARY NEWSPAPERS AND PERIODICALS

Newspapers constitute the most important single category of sources for this study. The *Irish Catholic* (Dublin) was examined systematically for most of the period up to 1918, as was the *Freeman's Journal* (Dublin) for 1919–21. A number of other papers such as *The Tablet* (London), *The Times* (London), the *Irish Weekly Independent* (Dublin) and the *Weekly Freeman* (Dublin) were consulted for specific periods or events. Some thirty-five provincial papers were used, mainly for election campaigns. Much of the information on education matters, especially from the Dublin dailies—*Freeman's Journal, Daily Nation, Irish Daily Independent (Daily Independent and Nation,* 1900–04; *Irish Independent,* 1904–), *Irish Times*—was derived from a very careful collection of newspaper cuttings maintained by the Irish Education Office and now available in the Public Record Office of Ireland (shelf-mark: 2C-64).

Periodicals, other than general newspapers, which were particularly useful include *The Leader, Irish Catholic Directory, An Claidheamh Soluis, Irish Theological Quarterly, Irish Ecclesiastical Record, Catholic Bulletin, Irish Facts for British Platforms, Notes from Ireland, Record of the Maynooth Union.*

IV. BOOKS AND ARTICLES BY CONTEMPORARIES

Tom Barry, *Guerilla Days in Ireland,* 3rd paperback impression, Tralee 1969.
Piaras Béaslaí, *Michael Collins and the Making of a New Ireland,* 2 vols, London, 1926.
Augustine Birrell, *Things Past Redress,* London 1937.
Robert Brennan, *Allegiance,* Dublin 1950.
Arthur E. Clery, 'The Gaelic League, 1893–1919', *Studies* VIII (Sep. 1919), 398-408.
Rev. Michael Curran, 'The Late Archbishop of Dublin: 1841–1921', *Dublin Review* CLXIX (Jul.-Sep. 1921), 93-107.
Frank Gallagher, *The Anglo-Irish Treaty* (with introduction by T. P. O'Neill), London 1965.
Rev. Joseph Guinan, *The Soggarth Aroon,* Dublin 1905; 9th impression, Dublin 1946.
Stephen Gwynn, *John Redmond's Last Years,* London 1919.
Richard Burdon Haldane, *Richard Burdon Haldane: An Auto-*

biography, London 1929; New York 1929.

T. M. Healy, *Letters and Leaders of My Day*, 2 vols, London 1928.

R. M. Henry, *The Evolution of Sinn Fein*, Dublin [1920].

John Horgan, *Parnell to Pearse: Some Recollections and Reflections*, Dublin 1948.

Rev. P. J. Joyce, *John Healy, Archbishop of Tuam*, Dublin 1931.

Rev. Walter McDonald, *Reminiscences of a Maynooth Professor*, ed. Denis Gwynn, London 1925.

—— *Some Ethical Aspects of the Social Question: Suggestions for Priests*, London 1920.

—— *Some Ethical Questions of Peace and War with Special Reference to Ireland*, 3rd ed., London 1920.

J. W. Mackail, and Guy Wyndham, *Life and Letters of George Wyndham*, 2 vols, London [1925].

Ronald McNeill, *Ulster's Stand for Union*, London 1922.

William St John Brodrick, 1st Earl of Midleton, *Records and Reactions, 1856–1939*, London 1939.

William O'Brien, *The Irish Revolution and How It Came About*, Dublin 1923.

—— *An Olive Branch in Ireland and Its History*, London 1910.

Sir James O'Connor, *History of Ireland, 1798–1924*, 2 vols, London 1925.

Most Rev. Edward Thomas O'Dwyer, *Letters of the Late Bishop O'Dwyer*, n.p., n.d.

Rev. Michael P. O'Hickey, *An Irish University, or Else—*, Dublin 1909.

'An Irish Priest' [Rev. Michael P. O'Hickey], *The Irish Bishops and an Irish University*, Dublin 1909.

Rev. M. O'Riordan, *Catholicity and Progress in Ireland*, London 1905.

Sir Horace Plunkett, *Ireland in the New Century*, popular ed., London 1905.

W. P. Ryan, *The Pope's Green Island*, London 1912.

D. D. Sheehan, *Ireland since Parnell*, London 1921.

Warre B. Wells, and N. Marlowe, *The Irish Convention and Sinn Fein*, Dublin 1918; New York [1918?].

V. LATER WORKS

Donald H. Akenson, *The Irish Education Experiment: The National System of Education in the Nineteenth Century*, London 1970.

D. G. Boyce, 'British Conservative Opinion, the Ulster Question, and the Partition of Ireland, 1912–21', *Irish Historical Studies*

XVII (Mar. 1970), 89-112.

Moirín Chavasse, *Terence MacSwiney*, Dublin 1961.

J. Dunsmore Clarkson, *Labour and Nationalism in Ireland*, New York 1925.

Padraic Colum, *Arthur Griffith*, Dublin 1959.

Ian Colvin, *The Life of Lord Carson*, Vols II and III, London 1934–36. (In continuation of Vol. I. By Edward Marjoribanks.)

Conor Cruise O'Brien, ed., *The Shaping of Modern Ireland*, London 1960; New York 1970.

Margaret Digby, *Horace Plunkett, An Anglo-American Irishman*, Oxford 1949.

Denis Gwynn, *The Life of John Redmond*, London 1932.

A. C. Hepburn, 'The Irish Council Bill and the Fall of Sir Antony MacDonnell, 1906–7', *Irish Historical Studies* XVII (Sep. 1971), 470-98.

Edgar Holt, *Protest in Arms: The Irish Troubles, 1916–23*, London 1960; New York 1961.

Roy Jenkins, *Asquith: Portrait of a Man and an Era*, London 1964; New York 1966.

Michael Laffan, 'The Unification of Sinn Fein in 1917', *Irish Historical Studies* XVII (Mar. 1971), 353-79.

Emmet Larkin, *James Larkin, 1876–1947, Irish Labour Leader*, London 1965.

———— 'Economic Growth, Capital Investment, and the Roman Catholic Church in Nineteenth-Century Ireland', *American Historical Review* LXXII (Apr. 1970), 852-84.

———— 'The Roman Catholic Hierarchy and the Fall of Parnell', *Victorian Studies* IV (Jun. 1961), 315-36.

———— 'Mounting the Counter-Attack: The Roman Catholic Hierarchy and the Destruction of Parnellism', *Review of Politics* XXV (Apr. 1963), 157-82.

———— 'Launching the Counterattack: Part II of the Roman Catholic Hierarchy and the Destruction of Parnellism', *Review of Politics* XXVIII (Jul. 1966), 359-83.

———— 'Socialism and Catholicism in Ireland', *Church History*, XXXIII (Dec. 1964), 462-83.

Earl of Longford and Thomas P. O'Neill, *Eamon de Valera*, Dublin 1970.

F. S. L. Lyons, *The Irish Parliamentary Party, 1890–1910*, London 1951.

———— *John Dillon: A Biography*, London 1968; Chicago 1968.

———— *Ireland since the Famine*, London 1971.

Dorothy Macardle, *The Irish Republic*, London 1937; repr. 1968;

1st American ed., New York 1965.

R. B. McDowell, *The Irish Convention, 1917–18.* London 1970.

F. X. Martin, O.S.A., 'Eoin MacNeill on the 1916 Rising', *Irish Historical Studies* XII (Mar. 1961), 226-71.

——— ed., *Leaders and Men of the Easter Rising: Dublin 1916,* London 1967; Ithaca, New York 1967.

——— '1916—Myth, Fact, and Mystery', *Studia Hibernica* 7 (1967), 7-126.

T. W. Moody, and J. C. Beckett, *Queen's Belfast, 1845–1949, The History of a University,* 2 vols, London 1959.

Leon Ó Broin, *The Chief Secretary: Augustine Birrell in Ireland,* London 1969.

——— *Dublin Castle and the 1916 Rising: The Story of Sir Matthew Nathan,* Dublin 1966.

T. J. O'Connell, *History of the Irish National Teachers' Organisation, 1868–1968,* Dublin [1968].

Florence O'Donoghue, *Tomás MacCurtain,* Tralee 1958.

Patrick O'Farrell, *Ireland's English Question, Anglo-Irish Relations, 1534–1970,* New York 1971.

Seán Ó Lúing, *I Die in a Good Cause: A Study of Thomas Ashe, Idealist and Revolutionary,* Tralee 1970.

John E. Pomfret, *The Struggle for Land in Ireland, 1800–1923,* Princeton 1930.

Desmond Ryan, *The Rising: The Complete Story of Easter Week,* 3rd ed., Dublin 1957.

——— *The Sword of Light from the Four Masters to Douglas Hyde, 1636–1938,* London 1939.

Fathers of the Society of Jesus, *A Page of Irish History: Story of University College, Dublin 1883–1909,* Dublin 1930.

Patrick J. Walsh, *William J. Walsh, Archbishop of Dublin,* Dublin 1928.

Alan J. Ward, *Ireland and Anglo-American Relations, 1899–1921,* London 1969; Toronto 1969.

F. J. Whitford, 'Joseph Devlin and the Catholic Representation Association of Belfast, 1895–1905', *Bulletin of the Irish Committee of Historical Sciences* 78 (Mar. 1957), 2-4.

John Whyte, 'The Appointment of Catholic Bishops in Nineteenth-Century Ireland', *Catholic Historical Review* XLVIII (Apr. 1962), 12-32.

———*Church and State in Modern Ireland, 1923–1970,* Dublin 1971.

Calton Younger, *Ireland's Civil War, 1922–1923,* London 1968.

19

Index